THE AMERICAN POLITICAL PROCESS

THE AMERICAN POLITICAL PROCESS

CHARLES R. ADRIAN
and
CHARLES PRESS

Department of Political Science
Michigan State University

MC GRAW-HILL
BOOK COMPANY

New York, St. Louis
San Francisco, Toronto
London, Sydney

The Thomas Nast cartoons on
pages 1, 2, 3, 235, 236, 237,
569, 570, 681, and 682 are
from the collection of The Bettmann Archive
and are used with their permission.

THE AMERICAN POLITICAL PROCESS

Library of Congress Catalog Card Number 64-25164

00430

PREFACE

The writing of a new textbook introducing American government would seem to require some justification. We rest the case for our attempt on a belief that available empirical data from all the social sciences should be used in seeking to explain the political aspects of the social process. In our admittedly ambitious undertaking, we make no claim to having found time- or thought-saving shortcuts to an understanding or to a new and improved general theory of politics. We are not confident that we have used every major piece of relevant research, but we have tried to utilize available relevant resources, many not previously used in introductory books, without neglecting conventional materials. We have not endorsed any of the general theories of politics currently in vogue among the *avant garde,* for none has adequate empirical support or professional acceptance. Instead, we have concentrated on analyzing the social functions of political institutions and the social roles of participants in the political process, emphasizing the conceptual framework on which these functions and roles are based.

In writing this book, we have begun with the assumption that the reader can comprehend materials at the freshman or sophomore level in college. Any person who can understand the processes of elementary college algebra, or follow an explanation of a conditioned response in a beginning psychology course, or keep reasonably well sorted the legion of characters in a Russian novel, can also understand that courts make public policy as well as adjudicate claims, that democratic elections can function with a relatively small cadre of informed voters, that Congress is a vital stabilizer for the political system rather than a center for innovation, and that the Presidency can be simultaneously a powerful and a weak institution. The reader is probably capable of understanding as much as political science currently has to offer, provided he is given some guide to the significance of the data.

In presenting data or in analyzing them, a clear, interesting style of writing is essential, and we have striven to achieve this. We believe that American English is an effective medium of communication and that most jargon should be left for the professional journals (and perhaps some of it for the rubbish collector). On the other hand, we believe that political science, although not a discipline in a technical sense, is moving toward becoming one.

As such, it needs a set of terms carefully defined and exactly used. With this goal in mind, we have defined technical terms in the text and included an amplified list of terms in the glossary.

Instructors in American government courses have various backgrounds of training and interests; the student may have nothing more than a high school course in social studies as formal background training; some adults may not read this as a textbook, but may want to use it to improve their perspective on political events as reported by the news media or to prepare themselves for effective participation in politics. With this variety in mind, we have assumed that the reader brings only a minimal knowledge with him as he begins the book. We do not expect the reader to know about empirical research methods or statistics. We do assume him to be intelligent, willing to learn, and capable of following a discussion in readable, reasonably precise prose, and to understand the approach of the scientific method.

The book is divided into four parts. The first deals with the methodological and conceptual tools used in political science. It emphasizes the techniques and problems of the scientific method and describes the "four I's" of political science. Part II articulates and analyzes the processes of government. Part III deals with the products of these processes: civil rights and liberties, and domestic and foreign policy, with emphasis on why the process produces the kinds of policy it does rather than on the details of myriad substantive activities. The last section offers projections of current demographic, social, economic, and political trends into the future and discusses implications of these for a viable, satisfaction-promoting democracy.

It is impossible for us to give full credit to all those to whom we owe intellectual debts. Our own teachers made contributions that cannot easily be separated from the results of our own efforts. We both benefited from undergraduate and graduate instructors who offered us inspiration, insight, and perspective. We both did graduate work at the University of Minnesota shortly after World War II, and it was there that our professional perspectives took shape. Of the many contributors to our education and training, special mention is probably due William Anderson, whose wise counsel—back in the 1940s—that the training of a political scientist necessarily included a working knowledge of statistics, had a tremendous influence on both of us. Earl Latham, now of Amherst College, opened up the intriguing vistas of the philosophy of logical positivism, and of interest-group and small-group behavior. Mulford Q. Sibley, whose perspectives on political science were very different from ours, convinced us that a political scientist cannot exaggerate the importance of superior teaching.

In addition, one or both of us studied with, among others, the late Asher N. Christensen, beloved by two generations of Minnesota students, Alfred de Grazia (now of New York University), Walter Heller, an economist with a keen knowledge of the political process, Evron M. Kirkpatrick (now Executive Director of the American Political Science Association),

Herbert McClosky (now of the University of California at Berkeley) who shared with his students an enthusiasm for the psychological and ideological aspects of politics, Lloyd M. Short, who helped us distinguish between opinion-mongering and disinterested study, the sociologist Arnold Rose, and the practitioner-scholar Arthur Naftalin.

Credits for direct assistance in the preparation of this study are due many persons. A book of this kind is based upon the research findings of generations of scholars. We have tried to give proper credits in footnotes and bibliography, but we cannot claim to have done justice to all deserving contemporaries and predecessors. Nor can we name all who aided us, but among those we believe to be especially deserving of mention for their constructive suggestions and assistance, we mention Gary P. Brazier of Boston College, Theodore B. Fleming, Jr., of Wayne State University, Joseph P. Harris of the University of California at Berkeley, Samuel Krislov of the University of Minnesota, Richard H. McCleery of Antioch College, Donald Urquidi of Los Angeles State College, and Stephen L. Wasby of Moorhead State College. Benjamin Hourani of Queens College, a former student, assisted in important ways. Others who were helpful by letting us make use of previously unpublished material or who checked specific data for us include Maurice Klain of Western Reserve University, Joseph LaPalombara of Yale University, Warren Miller of the University of Michigan, and Samuel C. Patterson of the State University of Iowa. In addition, there were unidentified individuals who helped enormously through their critical readings of two manuscript drafts, our undergraduate students at Michigan State University, who served as alert, if captive, guinea pigs for try-outs of much of the material, and to our colleagues who answered many questions involving their own special fields of political science. Shirley Decker and LuVerne Johnson, typists of great skill, provided us with clean, accurate copy—an aid of the highest importance to any author. All interpretations, errors, and controversial conclusions are, as they must always be, the responsibility of the authors alone.

Charles R. Adrian
Charles Press

CONTENTS

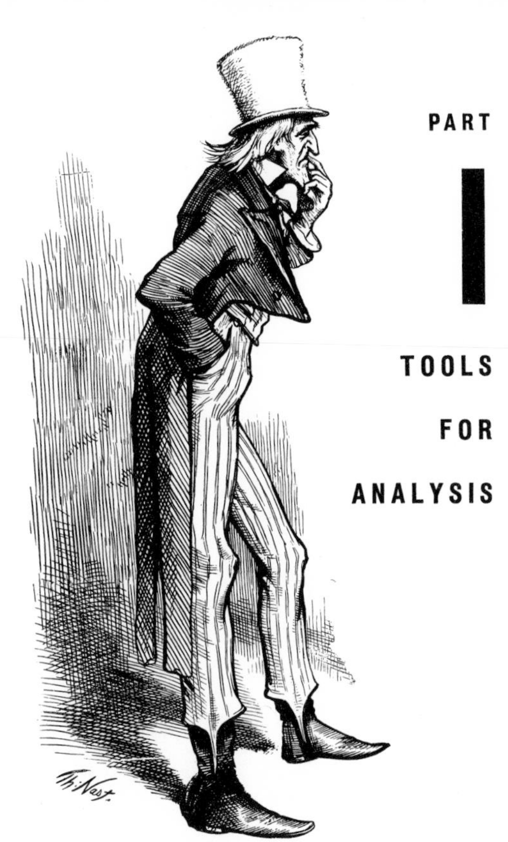

PART I

TOOLS FOR ANALYSIS

What does

a citizen

need to know

in order to analyze

American government

meaningfully?

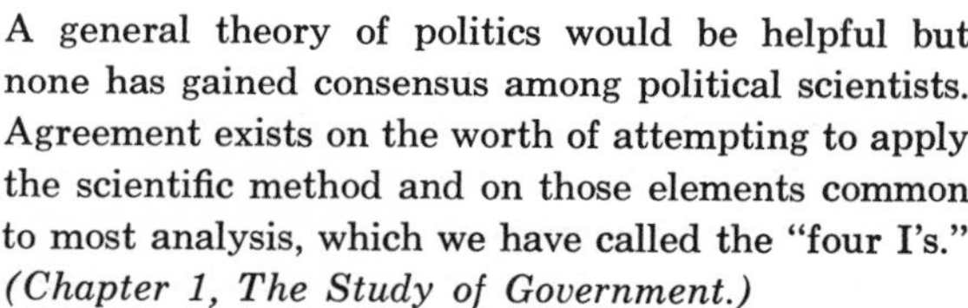

A general theory of politics would be helpful but none has gained consensus among political scientists. Agreement exists on the worth of attempting to apply the scientific method and on those elements common to most analysis, which we have called the "four I's." *(Chapter 1, The Study of Government.)*

The setting for the study of American government is the culture. American conditions have developed a unique American life style. American geography, class system, and economy help shape the nation's political style. But all of these, while of some value, are blunt tools for analysis. *(Chapter 2, The Cultural Setting for Politics.)*

The findings of empirical research have modified the traditional views of how democratic systems operate. A systematic study of the American political process requires a realistic view. Certain conditions—social, economic, ideological, and legal—appear essential to democracy, but these are not necessarily those drawn from classic theory or supported by popular belief. *(Chapter 3, The American Idea of Democracy.)*

The Constitution establishes the rules for the distribution of power and sets the limits on the use of power. The American constitutional system is unique in important respects that produce a pluralistic system of decision making with many competitive centers of power. *(Chapter 4, Constitutions: Ground Rules for Government.)*

One of the major institutional techniques for fractionalizing power is a division of political and governmental powers between state and national governments. The result is a complex system of shared decision making characterized by both competition and cooperation. *(Chapter 5, Federalism: Shared Decision Making.)*

Unique historical experience leads each generation to manufacture a set of ideas with which it can explain and manipulate the environment. The frontier was especially important for the impact of its interpretation of democracy on American governmental functions. *(Chapter 6, Ideology: The Frontier Foundation.)*

Subsequently Americans have modified the frontier interpretation as their life experiences and life styles have changed. New concepts of American democracy and new functions for American institutions have evolved as the nation has industrialized, urbanized, and suburbanized. *(Chapter 7, Ideology: Conflicts in an Industrial Age.)*

In a pluralistic society, some means must be developed to articulate particularistic interests before government. In modern American society the interest group is the principal mechanism for performing this function, although the unorganized are not powerless. *(Chapter 8, Interests and Interest Groups.)*

CHAPTER

1

THE STUDY OF GOVERNMENT

Americans have supreme confidence in themselves. Until the Soviet Union won the first few rounds in the battle to control space, almost no significant event in our history had given us any reason to doubt the image we have held of ourselves. That image includes the idea of progress, of man's life as not being static, but as moving ahead to ever-higher plateaus of achievement. It reflects the idea that government should be controlled by all citizens; that nearly every citizen is capable of sharing rationally in the decisions that determine the policy of the government; that government is limited and yet has obligations to protect the citizen from the great insecurities that frighten him; and that no social, economic, or political system is equal to—much less superior to—the American.

A book written about American government must recognize this feeling of self-confidence, this notion of the essential rationality of all citizens and the political implications it creates. Given the basic values of the American culture, it is not surprising that nearly all textbooks about American government at the high school level have emphasized a vast collection of facts and detailed descriptions of governmental programs; they have paid little attention to the process that ties the pieces together. A different approach is taken here. Without passing judgment on the basic beliefs that seem to have given courage and incentive to Americans for three centuries, the authors would suggest that effective citizenship is dependent not upon the temporary hoarding of encyclopedic facts, but rather upon an understanding of the process by which public offices are filled and decisions about public policy are made.

The function of all governments is, of course, the making and carrying out of public policy. We will, therefore, seek to explain how government works, using the American form of democratic government as a particular variant or case.[1] The process of public

[1] This book deals only with American national government. For the function of state and local governments, see Charles R. Adrian, *State and Local Governments,* McGraw-Hill Book Company, New York, 1960 (2d ed., 1966), or Charles R. Adrian, *Governing Our Fifty States and Their Communities,* McGraw-Hill Book Company, New York, 1963 (paperback).

policy making will be examined in some detail in later chapters, as will the relevant factors underlying the process. An attempt will be made to show both the parts and the whole. In seeking to do this, we will examine in each case the evidence from historians and from the social and behavioral sciences. We will try to avoid using folklore or what John

Figure 1-1

Laws Are Rules for the Organization of Society

"We'll never get anywhere by creating law. If people are going to eat each other, they'll eat each other, that's all."

We introduce J. Wesley Smith, ordinary citizen. His creator, Burr Shafer, sees him as a person totally lacking in historical perspective or imagination. Here Smith argues, as many others have, that man cannot influence moral values or effect social change through law. As usual, he is wrong. (By permission of Burr Shafer. The J. Wesley Smith cartoons used in this book appeared originally in The Saturday Review.)

Kenneth Galbraith has called "conventional wisdom"[2]—the beliefs that most citizens take for granted as correct, but that do not always survive close and systematic examination. Perhaps the appropriate place to begin is with government itself—its nature and its role in society.

GOVERNMENT'S FUNCTION AS AN INSTITUTION FOR SOCIAL CONTROL

Government is but one of the institutions of social control. It is not necessarily the most important; indeed, it cannot always be identified separately from other institutions. Generally speaking, the more complex the society, the more important the role of government, but this is by no means universally true. In very primitive societies, the family and the family group or clan is nearly always the central institution; the concept of government existing independently of the family group may be absent, or nearly so. In more sophisticated societies, government is always a separately identifiable institution, but its boundaries cannot easily be drawn. In the United States, for example, the Federal Reserve Board and the state bar associations straddle the line between governmental and private social institutions.

As society becomes more complex, governments compete with other institutions for the control of social behavior. Religion and magic are particularly important competing institutions, and the medicine man, priest, or other person who represents these institutions may be the most powerful leader in the community. As society reaches the complexity that it did in much of the world during the nineteenth century, still more institutions may become important instruments for conditioning man's behavior: the school, the trade union, and the business or professional organization.

The pattern for the development of government is not completely predictable, but an anthropologist has described the usual pattern as follows:[3]

> Simple societies have little need of law, and on the earliest levels of human culture there were probably no legal institutions. . . . Almost all relations in the tribe are face-to-face and intimate. The demands imposed by culture are relatively few. . . . Ridicule is keenly felt, for there is no escape in anonymity. . . . Special interests are few, for there is little accumulated wealth. Conflict arises mostly in interpersonal relations.

As society grows more complicated, however, "conflict of interest grows and the need for legal devices for settlement and control of the internal clash of interests begins to be felt." Then increasingly, "private law is replaced by public law. The state and its agencies corrode away the family

[2] John Kenneth Galbraith, *The Affluent Society,* Houghton Mifflin Company, Boston, 1958.

[3] E. Adamson Hoebel, *Man in the Primitive World,* 2d ed., McGraw-Hill Book Company, New York, 1958, pp. 482–483.

and its legal powers." Even with the relatively complex system that follows from these developments, government need not become a pervasive influence upon policy making. In the United States and the democracies of Western Europe, for example, government remained fairly modest in scope until the full effects of an industrial society were felt. What followed will be discussed in Chapters 6 and 7.

Private Governments. The importance of governmental institutions in respect to others varies with time, place, and the individual. In some cases, the individual necessarily chooses among social institutions, for these may compete for loyalty rather than reinforcing one another. The relative importance of the church in relation to the government, say, or of educational institutions versus the family in child rearing, is to a considerable extent a function of the culture—the sum total of the learned behavior patterns that are characteristic of members of a particular society. But except in very simple societies, the order of importance of various social institutions may be to some extent a matter of personal selection. Thus, in a number

Figure 1-2

Government Helps to Order Interpersonal Relationships

"I'm sorry Mr. Thoreau, but Mr. Walden says you can't fish in his pond."

Henry Thoreau dreamed, in Walden, *of a society without law. Here is what probably would have happened to him. (By permission of Burr Shafer.)*

of countries that came under the control of Communist governments after World War II, individuals had to decide whether they were going to obey the teachings of their church or the new government. Occasionally an American citizen will feel so strongly about a matter—for example, a religious teaching, or a belief learned as a child in the family about the behavior of members of one race toward those of another—that he will defy the law. These conflicts of loyalty are not unusual. Should a Christian Scientist, who opposes medical treatment, be required to submit to vaccination in the event that the law requires it during an outbreak of smallpox? Can a Roman Catholic be sterilized to prevent his having children if the law requires it as a condition of release from a mental institution, even though his agreement would be a violation of Church law?

The conflicts may involve any type of institution. In the 1930s, a labor union organizer who believed that what he was doing was to the benefit of the workingman sometimes found that he could not be effective because of the interpretation of existing laws. The workingman sometimes preferred to give his loyalty to a trade union rather than to a conservative government. Was he bound to obey the law? Did he always do so?

A different situation has arisen in more recent years. A worker who does not wish to allow a trade union to be one of the institutions making rules about his behavior has nevertheless found that often he must do so because of the union shop, which requires an employee of a firm having such a contract to join a union within a certain period of time. Furthermore, this type of compulsory acceptance of a union has been reinforced by the rules of government.

The occupational association. The citizen is told by television pitchmen that he should "think for himself"—because he likes to believe he does. But in fact, he lets leaders of groups to which he belongs do much of his thinking for him. Throughout his life he associates with many groups that exercise some control over his behavior; the most important are those of the home, work, and religion.

The behavior of the individual is thus not controlled alone by government. If he is a businessman, the conditions of competition that are considered fair may be determined by a trade association to which he belongs; if he is a physician, his medical association establishes rules concerning ethical behavior and even seeks to guide him toward the beliefs he "should" hold toward some social issues. The same is true of the trade union. In the case of both the professional association and the trade union, the organization may be able to control the conditions under which a member can pursue his trade or profession. The medical society reinforces its rules with the help of government, for it normally dominates state boards of medical examiners and public health agencies at all levels of government. Similar powers rest with many other professional groups.

These groups control individual action because the individual accepts such control to achieve his goals. His motivation is a feeling of need to meet the expectations of his coworkers, family, and neighbors. He accommodates to their expectations and to the groups of which they are also members and thereby hopes to advance himself in the social world with which he identifies.

Schools and churches. Other institutions are also powerful in socialization, that is, in molding our individual behavior. The schools, which are often controlled by a local unit of government but are commonly relatively independent of other government, exist at the subcollegiate level primarily to transmit knowledge to the next generation. But they also have a second vital responsibility—to inculcate in students the values of the culture in which they live. In doing so, they go far toward maintaining—and subty changing—the beliefs that citizens use in developing attitudes toward the policies of government and other social institutions. Churches also serve as institutions for social control, though institutional influence over the individual varies by denomination. They use a number of techniques for affecting individual behavior, including sometimes the operation of separate school systems.

Businesses. The business firm is another vital instrument for social control. If it is not extremely small, it tends to be operated—as do all American social institutions today—by a bureaucracy (an organization of persons with specialized skills) that is likely to be quite impersonal in character. Decisions to promote or not to promote, to hire or fire, to transfer an individual from Seattle to Cincinnati, or to change work assignments may all be made with little or no consultation with that individual. Yet these decisions may be of the greatest significance to the employee and his family. Furthermore, the longer an individual works for a particular firm, the more dependent he tends to become upon it. Legally he can quit his job at any time. In practice, many factors serve to discourage interjob mobility—the provisions of retirement systems, the importance of seniority in claiming preferred jobs, and the desirability of having favorable references from a former employer, for example. The employer hence becomes an important maker of the rules by which the individual lives.

Trade unions. Trade unions now commonly have union shop contracts, by which persons being hired by a firm must join a particular union. The union controls the conditions under which an individual may be a member and therefore virtually determines whether a person is to be permitted to earn a living in a particular trade.

Community Chest organizations. Voluntary organizations of the Community Chest or United Fund type make many decisions about public policy, particularly in regard to welfare matters. These organizations are not directly subject to popular control (except through the power of the strong minded to resist social pressures to contribute at fund-raising time). Yet the life style and income level of many citizens may be dependent upon what these groups choose to do or not to do.

Organized crime. Because Americans, a moralizing people, tend to make illegal the things they believe to be bad or believe they should consider to be bad, an underworld provides many services that people demand—particularly gambling, narcotics, and prostitution. Organized crime has long provided a ladder permitting persons of low status to seek power and wealth. It also serves as an institution for social control. The ability of its hierarchy to apply sanctions, especially those of force, is a standard source of material for television programs.

Social groups. Social organizations are also important as rule makers for the individual. Whether a particular lodge, country club, or other organization will accept and retain an individual has much to do with his status in the community and his self-esteem. In such a group, even if its purpose is only recreation, the values and behavior patterns of the leading members tend to be imitated by the others. And because Americans belong to large numbers of social groups of all types, a conformity to certain values, a prescribed way of behaving, becomes a part of American culture. One's

Figure 1-3

Behavior Is Not Controlled by Government Alone

"Two gentlemen from the American Medical Association to see you, Doctor."

Each profession has its own definition of "ethical behavior" that is enforced by the rules and sanctions of the union or professional association. (Drawing by Richard Decker; © 1961, The New Yorker Magazine, Inc.)

group memberships are likely to be determined not at random, but through a felt need to meet the expectations of one's coworkers and neighbors.

GOVERNMENT AS THE DOMINANT INSTITUTION

The Uniqueness of the Political System.* Although the rules that establish the permissible limits of behavior of an individual are made by many different social institutions, and although nongovernmental institutions may be of enormous consequence (determining such things as the way in which a man may earn a living or the probable fate of his soul), government in modern societies has a place of special importance. Indeed, it is not just "another institution," whose functions might well be performed by some other agency of society. (Of course, the church or the family cannot wholly be replaced by any other arrangement either, even though one institution can, to some degree, be substituted for another.)

***A POLITICAL SYSTEM involves all of the interrelated institutions and processes by which the decisions of government are made. More specifically, a political system involves "actions" of persons in many patterned, interrelated "roles." Thus the study of politics involves the analysis of what, why, and how persons do things in carrying out their political activities and how their actions affect other persons. By "patterned roles," we mean that actions can, to a considerable extent, be anticipated in advance and that both the political actor and his observers share, to a considerable degree, an understanding of what the particular role should be.**

Although government is not necessarily the most important means of social control, it does set the general boundaries of social action. Other institutions exert their influence over individuals within these governmentally sanctioned limits.

Government, in other words, is unique. It is the machinery or institution through which the political system operates. Within its territory, it is superior to any other agency. It has a formal monopoly over the legitimate use of force. To the social scientist Max Weber, this was the unique characteristic of government. Government has the power to establish a system of compulsory punishment. Most private organizations also have systems of sanctions. They may levy fines or deprive one of privileges or opportunities, or they may invoke the intercession of the deity. But only government can incarcerate an individual, and only government can deprive him of his life. (Even in the case of the great inquisitions of the thirteenth century, carrying out a death sentence was in the hands of government, not the Church, and the violation of law was deemed to be not that of the Church alone, but of government as well.)

If you violate a fundamental rule of the group, ordinary organizations may throw you out of the club. Government may do more. It may send you to prison or the death house. And in practice, the sanctions of other social institutions are used at the sufferance of government. What it permits other institutions to do, however, may be of utmost importance to the individual. American society permits private associations to exercise a great deal of social control. Loss of membership in a trade union or professional organization may deprive a person of an opportunity to earn a living by use of his best skills. Defiance of a trade association may cause a businessman to be driven to bankruptcy. Being dropped from the rolls of the Bubbling Brooke Country Club may spell disaster for the social ambitions of a young industrial executive and his wife. Deliberate withdrawal from membership in a church or excommunication by its leadership may carry with it extremely serious sanctions, including the threat of eternal damnation.

Why Obey Government? The great power of modern government over our social, political, and economic lives makes it worthwhile to note briefly the reasons why individuals accept its authority and abide by its decisions. The reasons are several:

First, we immediately think of the fact that government has many ways by which to punish the individual and that the results of these possible punishments may range from inconvenience through unpleasantness and unhappiness to loss of life. Fear of punishment is no doubt often an inhibiting factor in behavior, but it is by no means the only one or necessarily the most important one. Psychologists tell us, for example, that a murderer rarely calculates possible punishment costs in determining whether or not he will kill. Similarly, the potential costs of law violation may seem inconsequential. A $50 fine for a traffic violation is not much of a threat to a millionaire, and some persons who violate the Internal Revenue Code seem to regard the rather small threat of fines and even smaller threat of imprisonment as minor considerations.

Second, probably more incentive for obedience comes from the social and economic costs of defiance. The individual who is arrested, fined, or imprisoned will lose status in the eyes of friends and persons with whom he has business and social relationships. His social standing may suffer as a result; so may his business. Even if there is no permanent damage to his way of life, he can expect to suffer some degree of embarrassment. Occasionally a person who violates the law is honored by his friends and he may even become a folk hero—perhaps by defying the crop-control regulations of the U.S. Department of Agriculture or by refusing to pay his income tax on the grounds that it is to be used, in part, for the purchase of hydrogen bombs. The professional criminal, of course, lives in a subculture in which high status can be achieved by skillful defiance of the law. But in most cases of violation of the law, a man's friends and associates will think him misguided, confused, or a fool, and he will lose status if he is caught.

Finally, and perhaps of greatest importance, people obey governments because they believe that they *ought* to. In a complex society, human beings seem to feel the need for order, safety, and predictability. They see obedience as proper and desirable and the rules of government as legitimate. The sense of legitimacy does not always cause us to obey the law, but it does tend to make us feel guilty if we violate it. Even those who disobey are likely to share in this reaction. Most individuals believe that change should be accomplished according to the established rules—in the American democratic system, through the "consent of the governed," achieved by voting or lobbying, for example. They also believe that disobedience of government is generally in and of itself wrong, even without considering the social costs and punishments that may result from illegal acts.

The importance of this sense of legitimacy of the law as an inhibiting force among Americans, particularly of the middle classes, has been dramatized by the comments of an eminent Negro leader, the Rev. Martin Luther King. He has noted that one of the great obstacles to the accomplishment of his action program for the social and economic equality of persons of all races in America has been the unwillingness of citizens who are essentially sympathetic to the goals he has expressed to support the means he believes necessary to achieve them—not the overt opposition of groups such as the Ku Klux Klan or white citizens' councils. Middle-class white citizens, he has found, often refuse to join in demonstrations, sit-ins, protest marches, or other activities disapproved of by persons in formal positions of authority who can quote from the law to support their opposition.[4]

One's Conscience: The Ultimate Sovereign. Despite the presumption in favor of obeying government, Americans and most philosophers of Western Civilization assume that government could someday fall into what they would regard as evil hands. Judeo-Christian teachings hold that the individual must be able to live with his conscience and that ultimately he must decide himself if government is acting legitimately and morally.

William Shakespeare faced this particular problem, as he faced many political problems, and resolved it much as many political philosophers would today. In *Henry V,* the English king in disguise observes his troops on the eve of the battle of Agincourt (1415) and talks with them. One soldier wonders what would happen to him should he die—if the King's cause "be not good." (Henry claimed to be the legal heir to the crown of France and was pressing his claim in the war.)

"If the king's cause is wrong," says another, "our obedience to the King wipes the crime of it out of us."

But Henry disagrees: "Every subject's duty is the King's. But every subject's soul is his own."

This was precisely the assumption upon which many of the cases at the

[4] Martin Luther King, Jr., "Letter from Birmingham Jail," *The Christian Century,* June 12, 1963, pp. 767–773.

Nuremberg trials following World War II were based. Could the Nazi leaders excuse themselves for behavior that much of the world considered beastly by arguing that "orders are orders"? The trial court sided with King Henry—or rather, with Shakespeare—and many Americans did too; perhaps most of them did. Yet the man who willfully chooses to disobey the orders of established authority—and especially if he challenges the concepts of legitimacy—takes a grave risk. Society does not expect him to challenge governments often and assumes that he will do so only out of a sense of great moral urgency. Even then, he can seldom expect sympathetic understanding from his fellow citizens.

THE STUDY OF POLITICAL SCIENCE

Political scientists have never agreed on the exact content of their field of study. Outside the United States, political science has had little recognition as a separate field. Within this country, it has developed somewhat, but probably lags behind the other social sciences, particularly in theory building.*

***Throughout this book, THEORY refers not to models of an ideal as seen by some individual, but to an explanation for the functions performed by the various parts of an interrelated system and to the way in which these parts relate to one another. In this sense, theory does not differ from practice; rather, the former explains the latter.**

Political science began to emerge in the late nineteenth century, stemming from developments in philosophy (normative ideas concerning what *ought* to be the purpose, functions, and process of government), law (formal statements of the rules and procedures of governments), and history (the chronology of salient events). Early political scientists tended to interpret the field broadly: anything that in the past, present, or future touched or might touch upon government was a possible field for study. But there was usually little concern with what actually happened (informal rules and facts), with why it happened (the motivations of those involved), or with a disinterested analysis (the scientific approach). The concern was primarily with a description of formal rules and institutions and an evaluation of whether an event was good or bad (the hortatory approach), or whether it was compatible with some normative ideal of government.

Early political philosophers tended to build theories, but they had in mind contributions to *ideal models* rather than *process models*. That is, they concentrated on describing the various parts of the model in terms of what it ought to be like, rather than contenting themselves with trying to diagram what actually happened in the development, modification, and carrying out of public policy. The ideal models were often built on systems of logic and were little constrained by existing observable factors. But at no time has political science been totally unconcerned with observable facts or "empirical evidence," to use the customary term. The early empiricists had no interest in theory building, but concentrated on collecting extensive and detailed facts about the legal and institutional* arrangements of government.

***An INSTITUTION is a component part of a system. In politics, it is a part of the mechanism through which government carries out its tasks. It is established on a formal legal basis in most cases and is usually intended by its builders to be permanent, though not necessarily unchanging. Congress, the Presidency, and the Department of Health, Education, and Welfare are political institutions, for example.**

The standard textbook in American government in the 1920s was a veritable encyclopedia of facts, but it contained almost nothing in the way of analysis. From it, one might learn the size of membership of the Supreme Court for any given year in the nation's history, the legal title for the act creating the first Federal grant-in-aid for highways, or the age of the youngest and oldest men to be elected President. But the reader or his instructor had to try to figure out for himself what to do with such information and why it should be learned.

Empirical Political Science: The Theory Builders. Despite the pattern so far described, political science has had its innovators in empirical theory building from ancient times, beginning in recorded history with Plato and his student Aristotle. In recent decades, a number of men—described in courses in political thought—have made important contributions. We mention here only recent American theorists. Around the beginning of the twentieth century, Arthur F. Bentley suggested that politics as a process might best be studied in terms of the interactions of various political interests; out of this came an interest or group theory of politics.[5] Harold Lasswell, beginning around 1930, sought to explain politics in terms of individual motivations and personality characteristics. A tentative theory of voter behavior began to emerge in the 1920s with the works of two political scientists, Charles E. Merriam and Harold F. Gosnell. Further contributions were later made by social psychologists, including Paul F. Lazarsfeld and Bernard Berelson. After World War II, Herbert Simon and others sought to describe much of the political process, particularly administration, through a theory of decision making. Recently, a more general "choice" theory has been a subject of increasing consideration.

[5] Arthur F. Bentley, *The Process of Government,* 4th ed., Principia Press of Illinois, Evanston, Ill., 1955. See especially chap. 7. The book was first published in 1908. Bentley's theory is polished and developed in David B. Truman, *The Governmental Process,* Alfred A. Knopf, Inc., New York, 1951.

Post-World War II: Behavioralism. We ought, at this point, to mention a term that came into vogue in political science after World War II: "behavioralism." To be associated with the term has become, to some persons, a badge of accomplishment to be worn conspicuously. To others, the term is an epithet to be used against those who are viewed as misguided, confused, naïve, or even intellectually dishonest.

What is behavioralism? It is not a theory of the political process. Essentially, it is a point of view and an approach to the study of politics. It involves a research method that is strongly empirical, making use particularly of recently developed techniques and perspectives of research such as survey sampling, scalogram analysis, systems analysis, simulation techniques, and other devices for controlling the number of variables in a study and relating them to one another. The principal unit of analysis is not the political *institution*, but the *individual* as he behaves in politics.[6] For behavioralists—and in the 1960s they are a definite but growing minority—the essence of study is the political process and, more particularly, power relationships among individuals involved in the process. Thus, Harold D. Lasswell has said that politics is the study of influence and the influential and involves questions of who gets what, when, how.[7]

But in turning to the individual and his motivations, political behavioralism by no means breaks new ground. For while the "barefoot," or theory-less, empiricists of the fact-gathering years were institution-oriented, most political philosophers from Aristotle's day to the present have been concerned with the individual in politics as well as with the state as an institution. Perhaps the principal difference between traditional political philosophy and contemporary behavioralism is that the latter places greater emphasis upon *systematic* analysis and description; most of the former concentrated on *prescriptive* statements concerning the "good society." Behavioralists generally concede that the image of a set of preferred social goals is important in a political system. Most deny that one set of values is necessarily equal to any other, but they disclaim any scientific (and hence, for themselves, justifiable) basis for selecting the goals a society "ought" to seek.

Political philosophers generally disagree with the behavioralist view that

[6] We acknowledge here the ideas presented in Joseph LaPalombara, "Graduate Education in the Social Sciences: A Glimpse at the Future," *Proceedings of the Midwest Conference for Graduate Study and Research,* Chicago, April, 1963, pp. 11–22.

[7] Harold D. Lasswell and Abraham Kaplan, *Power and Society,* Yale University Press, New Haven, Conn., 1950; and Harold D. Lasswell, *Politics: Who Gets What, When, How,* McGraw-Hill Book Company, New York, 1936, and also available in paperback through Meridian Books, Inc. For more background on the history, theories, and conflicts of political science, see Arnold Brecht, *Political Theory: The Foundations of Twentieth Century Political Thought,* Princeton University Press, Princeton, N.J., 1959; David Easton, *The Political System,* Alfred A. Knopf, Inc., New York, 1953; and Robert A. Dahl, *Modern Political Analysis,* Prentice-Hall, Inc., Englewood Cliffs, N.J., 1963.

the "oughts" can never be discovered. They are not, however, so arrogant as to believe that they have a right to decide arbitrarily the meaning of the "good life" for all of society, and they do not claim that the meaning of the good life is a matter of opinion. Rather, they tend to see it as stemming from God's will, from immutable natural laws, from man's intuitive sensing of what is right, or from logical derivations stemming from such will, law, or intuition.[8]

Behavioralism in political science is interdisciplinary in approach. That is, it tends to bring together the concepts, empirical findings, and research techniques developed in all of the social sciences. Sociology, anthropology, economics, and psychology have each had their impact on political science. In the past, the findings of other social sciences were often applied in crude ways, sometimes so as to distort their meanings. Sometimes the political scientist became so much a devotee of a sister field that he lost sight of the central focus of his own.

Political Science Today. The effect of the ferment of the last two decades or so has been to make political science somewhat anarchic, but also to encourage a desire to reach consensus on a central purpose. Those who have become convinced of the importance of theory tend to believe that the political segment of life should be fitted into the framework of a general theory undergirding all of the social sciences.

What emerges as the central feature of political science study? Probably the most widely accepted statement to date is that of David Easton,[9] who sees political science as the study of "the authoritative allocation of values for a society."* Harold Lasswell, as we noted above, sees politics in a somewhat broader, but essentially similar, framework.

***A definition of terms used in Easton's phrase may be in order. A policy has AUTHORITY when "the people to whom it is intended to apply or who are affected by it consider that they must or ought to obey it." In this book the authors apply this definition to LEGITIMACY, a term from sociology that we consider less ambiguous than Easton's. By VALUES, Easton means "benefits or rewards." Since the authors of this book use "value" in the sociologists' sense of "an enduring awareness and feeling about any object, idea, or person," we do not use Easton's term. Easton seems to use SOCIETY to refer to persons and institutions within the authority of a single unit of government.**

Using the concepts of Easton and Lasswell as basic, then, and translating their terms into those used in this book, our definition is this: *Political science is the study of the legitimate allocation of benefits and rewards for a society*. In saying this, however, we recognize that a study of legitimate allocations in practice must also include cases where legitimacy is lacking (power is wrongly used). Similarly, benefits and rewards

[8] See Brecht or Dahl, *op. cit.*, for development of this point.

[9] Easton, *op. cit.*, pp. 129–134.

also have their negative aspects, for deprivations and punishments as well as benefits and rewards are allocated by governments.

THE POLITICAL SYSTEM IN OPERATION

Government sets the boundaries of action for other social groups and for government itself. It is the final means of enforcing controls. The decision makers in government, therefore, decide which groups and ideas will be favored and which will not. They do this even when they generally permit groups in society to decide the relative places that each will occupy in society, for at any point government may intercede in the process and make rules that help or handicap a particular group or idea. They have done so, for example, in holding that relations among races will no longer be determined without formal governmental regulations being involved in the process. Similarly, governmental policy has imposed a rule against plural marriages of the type once practiced within the Mormon church.

In a democracy, government exercises controls or gives rewards that are favored by the effective social forces in the society, subject, however, to certain procedures and to certain rights of minorities. Totalitarian nations, communistic or fascistic nations, for example, operate on another principle. It holds that government will remold social institutions and relationships to suit a central purpose wanted by a favored segment of the society. And even in a democracy, actions of government remold social forces. But as society is modified, it in turn modifies government. For example, action by government outlawed slavery. This action, in turn, shifted the balance of social forces in America and has gradually resulted in the reshaping of many other governmental policies in respect to descendants of freed slaves, and to other minority groups as well.

The Parts of the Governmental Process. Government, then, allocates the resources of society among its members. How does it do this? Does a democratic government always represent an accurate reflection of social forces? What, in fact, are the social forces that shape governmental policy?

These questions have frequently been discussed by political scientists in recent years. There is, as yet, no consensus. We cannot, therefore, present a neat theoretical model of how the American policy-making process operates. To the extent that there is agreement, it is reflected in a quite imprecise formula stemming from a phrase coined by Pendleton Herring. Political decisions, he concluded, stem from "a working union of interests, ideas, institutions, and individuals."[10] These are the "four I's" of political science.

One group of political scientists has attempted to combine these variables under the one heading of the organized interest group. In the shared

[10] Pendleton Herring, *The Politics of Democracy,* Holt, Rinehart and Winston, Inc., New York, 1940, p. 421.

attitudes and interactions of individuals forming an organized group, they see the root of all ideas, individual action, and institutional arrangements. In *The Governmental Process,* David Truman presents an extensive statement of the group approach. Empirical study has failed to establish the validity of this view to the satisfaction of all political scientists.

Political scientists have achieved a new sophistication in respect to institutional arrangements as a result of the work of group theorists, however. Governmental structure and rules are now recognized as being not neutral, but as a means of access or advantage to selected groups and ideas. For example, most state legislatures are apportioned in ways that give rural and small-town groups and ideas an advantage in policy making. Complicated registration procedures discourage political participation by the low-income, less-educated groups.

Some political scientists have moved from an examination of legal institutions to a study of the roles established by both the legal and informal processes, because every institution of government provides for certain roles that lead to expectations concerning the proper activities of role performers. The stimulation of the other sciences—notably sociology and psychology—has increased emphasis on the study of interpersonal relations among decision makers and the formal and informal communications networks among them. What, for example, is the effect on policy making if the President and the Attorney General are brothers? What happens when this condition is changed? What is the effect on legislation when a club or clique feeling arises among members of Congress? What is the relevance of the personality characteristics of decision makers to actual policy decisions?

Some political scientists have emphasized the importance of the social backgrounds of decision makers, including voters, on the decisions that are made. Others have assumed that the political ambitions of decision makers offer explanations of their behavior.

A number of studies have centered on what sociologists call "institutional values," that is, the ideology developed by organized groups such as business firms or professional associations. Others have considered the ideologies of collectivities that are not formally organized groups, but are, in fact, subcultures within a larger society—a particular class, race, or ethnic group. Finally, there has been an examination of what Gabriel A. Almond has called the "political culture"—the grouping of political ideas associated with a particular nation-state.[11] The Swedish sociologist Gunnar Myrdal once concluded that America has possessed such a mystique from its beginning.[12] He called it "the American Dream" and saw it as a vague grouping of ideals that derived mainly from the British liberal tradition and from rationalist thinkers such as Thomas Jefferson, who

[11] Gabriel A. Almond, "Systematic Theory," in Heinz Eulau and others, *Political Behavior,* The Free Press of Glencoe, New York, 1956, p. 34.

[12] Gunnar Myrdal, *An American Dilemma,* Harper & Row, Publishers, New York, 1944.

Probably no social scientist denies that a structure of economic power may exist. Certainly large corporations in America do commonly work together in seeking to influence policy, and they exercise influence and probably dominate decision making of some types. But this type of power is only a part of the total system. For one thing, the resources of influence are more than simply economic—though these resources, of course, can be used to purchase others, such as skills and publicity. But the market of total resources is too great to corner. The sit-in is a political resource, and for a group with the few economic resources Negroes collectively possess, it has proved to be effective. Votes, of course, are also resources. Family prestige is a resource, as is organization into solidary groups (i.e., the Catholic Church, the United Steel Workers, or the American Legion).

In a democracy, money, numbers, and group cohesiveness are perhaps the most important resources. The combination of these and other resources in efforts to influence a specific issue is often of great importance, and the leaders who control such resources are often of dominant importance in policy making *in a specific area of public policy*. If this is the normal pattern, as it seems to be, the designation of certain individuals as being part of "the power structure" is not meaningful. The only justifiable conclusion is that the individuals who have the highest positions in economic, social, and governmental spheres probably, on the average, have considerable influence and therefore can be designated as an elite. This does not, however, imply that they are united, for they may actively oppose one other.

Time and effort are political resources. The individual who makes a nuisance of himself long enough may eventually influence a particular policy in the way he desires. The assassin of Huey Long decisively influenced policy. He was willing to make the effort—and pay the costs—involved in killing a political leader. In this sense, no one is without some political resource. One cannot know, of course, whether a political resource will be spent skillfully or whether it will be used at all. One wealthy American may prefer to spend his money on chorus girls, another to further the election of Senator Zilch. Most persons do not care to spend their time in politics—many do not even vote. Lack of political activity by the individual is, however, not necessarily irrational or irresponsible behavior. It was perhaps as well for the Western world that Mozart and Beethoven did not divert their energies toward becoming precinct captains.

The resources distributed among individuals and groups to some extent cancel one another out. Labor's strength in numbers is countered by the financial resources of business. Individuals seldom identify completely with a single influential group or community subsystem. No group can expect to mobilize all of its membership in support of any one issue. The Catholic businessman and the Catholic laborer do not oppose each other on every issue, nor do their Methodist counterparts.

The Classification of Political Systems. Aristotle, noting the unequal distribution of society's resources, concluded that it resulted in different kinds of political systems: the rule of one, the rule of a few (less than a majority), and the rule of the many. He called the resulting systems "monarchy," "aristocracy," and "polity" (democracy). He also identified corrupted versions of each form. Further observation led him to conclude that a mixed system was both possible and preferable. The social basis, or "social constitution," for a mixed system was, he said, a large middle class that encouraged a widespread distribution of political resources.

Modern political scientists have revised and refined Aristotle's typology. Max Weber classified governments according to the basis on which an elite held its political power—the basis of its legitimacy. Another classification might be made according to the number of political subsystems that possess some degree of autonomy. Combining these elements, one political scientist has devised a classification system providing for sixteen different types.[13]

An alternative classification system has been devised by students of comparative government. Gabriel A. Almond and James S. Coleman, building on the sociological theories of Talcott Parsons, have offered a "functional" model for political analysis.[14] It assumes that in every viable political system, certain functions must be performed—whether or not the system is a democracy. Some institutional means must exist, they conclude, for rule making, rule application, and rule adjudication, as well as for social methods of interest articulation, interest aggregation, and political recruitment. These functions may or may not be handled by separate institutions. In American government, both administrative boards and the courts are concerned with rule adjudication, for example. The courts, in turn, are concerned with both rule adjudication and rule making. Almond and Coleman see political institutions as typically performing more than one function. Their method of analysis is logical and has attracted much interest, but it is not widely accepted by political scientists—at least at the present time.

In the chapters describing the political process, we have followed the customary approach of examining each of the major governmental institutions in turn—Congress, the Presidency, the courts, the bureaucracy. We do, however, borrow in part from the systems method by asking in each case what function the institution performs in the decision-making process of American democracy.

There is as yet no consensus on classifications in the field of political science. Classification is, of course, always determined in part by the purposes of the classifier. But rough consensus does exist about the American

[13] Robert A. Dahl, *Modern Political Analysis,* Prentice-Hall, Inc., Englewood Cliffs, N.J., 1963, pp. 25–38.

[14] Gabriel A. Almond and James S. Coleman (eds.), *The Politics of Developing Areas,* Princeton University Press, Princeton, N.J., 1960, chap. 1.

political system of today. The effective social forces in America result in a system that is pluralistic rather than one ruled by a small group from the top. Many social components are politically effective. The allocation of benefits and rewards is accomplished through a complex process in which the many exert influence, though most of the time minorities with resources to spend join in compromises among themselves that produce policies not too different from present ones. The result offers only partial fulfillment for the goals of any group. The legitimacy of ruling elites is achieved by regularized procedures and is accepted by most citizens. Political subsystems (states, counties, cities) are many and have a relatively high degree of autonomy. Most political scientists are content to classify such a system of allocation as one form of democracy. Even though the classification is gross and crude, it will serve as the basis for the definition we accept and use in this book.

STRUCTURE AND PROCESS IN POLITICS

The process of public policy making is modified by the structure of government, just as the path of a turbulent river is modified by natural and artificial barriers. Structure helps shape the process, but the process influences the character of the structure. In other words, it is not accurate to say that only the beliefs of a people and the interests of groups determine what policies a government will follow. The institutional arrangements themselves modify the outcome of the policy-making process.

The structure of American government includes an independently elected President. This allows the chief executive to behave differently from the way he would behave if he were chosen by Congress. The seniority system in Congress, which usually determines who will head a committee, produces a different pattern of legislative leadership and a different set of leaders with different values and policy goals from what would be the case if congressional leaders were chosen by a political party committee, for example. The seniority system most frequently produces committee heads who are conservatives from "safe" or noncompetitive districts, that is, congressmen and senators who face little competition in staying in office and who, therefore, have little incentive to be concerned about the most recent political demands. A party committee would probably represent primarily the more populous states and, in particular, the larger cities in those states. Its concerns would be principally matters of current controversy, particularly those of an urban character. The differences in policy would be considerable if changes of the kind mentioned here were to be made.

If the United States were (to use a most improbable example) to adopt the British parliamentary system, we could expect not only that the patterns of party leadership recruitment would change, but that the relative influence of various interest groups would also change. The Southern cotton and tobacco interests and the Southwestern oil interests would decline in power, for example, and Northern liberal demands for expanded social service programs and strengthened civil rights legislation would increase. Many other changes would also take place, and the reader might find it an interesting exercise to try to determine what they would be and the reasons for them.

The point is, then, that the structure of government is only one of the influences upon policy and hence only one of the things to be studied in an examination of the workings of American government. Structure, on the other hand, is not to be dismissed lightly. It too affects the pattern of decision making.

THE PURPOSE OF THE BOOK

There are many possible approaches to the study of government. In this book, the *political process* by which public policy is made is used as a reference point. The objective is to provide the reader with *tools for the analysis of political events* that affect him and his society. Encyclopedic detail is not supplied. It is available in the nearest library; much of it will, in any case, have been learned in high school courses, and the bibliographical essay at the close of this chapter lists ample citations. We are much less concerned with details that are quickly forgotten by the typical reader than we are with describing how the system works—a description that will, we hope, make a lasting impression and give the citizen some useful insights into the political combat that shares the front pages of local newspapers with stories of automobile accidents, felonies, and sentimental events in the lives of children and animals.

Considerable attention will be paid to ideology,* to folk beliefs about the process and substance of politics, and to public policy (see Chapters 6 and 7). The authors do not claim ideology to be the most important ingredient in the political stew. It would be impossible, given the current state of the social sciences, to test such a claim. There are no doubt millions of factors—past and present—that affect political decisions. These range from thousands of traditions (frequently in conflict), material interests of small and large groups, and the formal structure of government to a great variety of personality patterns and psychological motivations. Millions of different combinations of personal experiences and countless

***IDEOLOGY may be described as "folk philosophy" concerning the good life. It is not as systematic or as sophisticated as philosophy; it evolves gradually, not as the product of any single thinker. In this sense, it resembles folk songs more than the works of serious composers. Ideology consists of a network of interrelated normative values that emerge from a particular life-style and environment. It serves a double role: it helps to direct action toward the satisfaction of existing wants and to establish new goals for an individual or group.**

miscellaneous items are involved—down to such minute items as the state of the decision maker's home life or the disconcerting influence of street noises upon him.

The authors use ideology, then, not as the principal consideration, but as a reference point from which we can depart—and to which we can occasionally return—as we study the various ramifications of the political process. Knowledge of ideology does not allow us to predict what policies will be or how much power a President will be given, for example; it does help us to gain an idea of what the *probabilities* are relative to possible decisions, and it sets the general limits within which effective, socially acceptable decisions must be made. It is likely that ideology both influences politics and is itself influenced by it. That is to say, ideology is constantly changing. It is affected by changes in the environment, but it also influences the environment. Ideology is not known to *cause* particular economic, political, or social systems to be created; nor is it known to be merely the rationalization or rhetorical explanation of these systems, as Karl Marx and others have believed. Thus we do not raise the old philosophical question of determinism versus free will as a basis for man's activities. From a scientific standpoint there is almost no proof regarding cause-and-effect relationships in social phenomena. In the absence of proof, it seems most reasonable to assume that in a particular economic environment, a number of social and political systems are possible and that different individuals may make different decisions within a given political system.

Hence the possible variety of political patterns and decisions is enormous, and neither ideology, nor interest, nor political structure, nor personality should be assumed to be the cause of an individual decision. Each factor influences without determining; each tends to point in a particular direction and hence to shape the decisions that are made in the political world and to change the environment and the ideology of the next generation. We will discuss all of these phenomena as influences upon the political process and particularly upon the democratic process as it exists in the United States.

We make no effort to outline a set of ethical norms for the reader's guidance—to tell the reader what government ought to do or how it ought to be organized—for analysis requires an objective, or amoral, examination of relevant data if understanding of politics is the goal. We have tried here to be as objective as social scientists can be in reporting research findings. Scientists do not succeed in divorcing themselves completely from their personal beliefs and values; we cannot hope to have been completely successful in doing so. A word of warning, however: Although the authors have sought to avoid as much as possible introducing their own preferences into this book, values are an essential ingredient in the decision-making process of politics. When one votes, or joins a group that seeks to influence governmental policy, or runs for office, or otherwise takes political action, he relies heavily on his concept of what is right or wrong, good or bad, in deciding what to do. At such times, personal values are of critical importance. They are the yardstick. However, to introduce one's personal preferences into an analysis of the political process is to blur the image. This the authors have tried to avoid. But no reader should assume that one choice is as good as another, or that no matter what one does, things will turn out the same anyway. The analysis given in this book does not imply or justify such conclusions.

A Note on Method in Political Science. No one method of research produces the findings of political science. Historically, the field grew primarily out of philosophy, law, and history. It continues to rely heavily on the methods of those disciplines. From philosophy, it derives the methods of logical reasoning. Law has its own traditions of research, centering on case analysis. History relies principally on a detailed examination of the available written evidence, usually after the emotional content of an event has been partly drained by the passage of time. As one social scientist has noted, "The task of the historian is . . . to make what he believes are correct images of the past from an extremely imperfect sample of recorded data."[15] Yet his interpretations may be all that is available to the political scientist, who needs to use events of the past in his analysis of the present.

Political science borrows from other long-established fields, too. It secures data from the journalist, whose approach differs from that of the historian in that he must try to be as disinterested as possible even when writing about contemporary, emotion-laden subjects. And he must write against a deadline, while the historian and social scientist can usually pursue research for as long as is necessary in order to trace an inquiry to a satisfactory stopping point. Social scientists are often critical of journalists, saying they are superficial, careless, and imprecise. Many of them no doubt are. But the most competent journalists add greatly—if unsystematically—to political science data through effective empirical research. Working journalists who have expense accounts and many points of entrance into the political system are frequently more effective at data gathering than are political scientists.

Behavioralism in political science has introduced a number of new techniques to the research methods available. Most of these are borrowed from the other social sciences. Some are empirical, such as depth study, participant observation, and open-end interviews from anthropology and psychology, or closed-schedule interviewing from sociology. Other techniques are largely mathematical, particularly those relying on the science of statistics. Today, increasing use is being made of high-speed computers that can, in a few minutes, perform calculations that would take an individual years if he worked alone. In all cases, the intent is to become more precise in measurements and in stating relationships. Because be-

[15] Kenneth E. Boulding, *The Image,* The University of Michigan Press, Ann Arbor, Mich., 1956, p. 69.

havioralism is so new, political scientists have tended to strike out in all directions, hoping to hit pay dirt, often without having much of an idea of where it is or how to reach it. Sometimes they have only documented the obvious; sometimes they have reached seriously erroneous conclusions through inexperience with methods (as in the 1948 election) or have learned only trivial things after lengthy and expensive research. Still, there is some merit in documentation, even when it seems to be documentation of the obvious. What conventional wisdom holds to be common sense may not make sense at all; it may be seriously in error. When President Kennedy was assassinated in 1963, 52 per cent of the respondents to a Gallup poll indicated they believed that some group or "element" was involved, in addition to the actual killer.[16] This view was held even though members of the Secret Service, the FBI, and other knowledgeable people had suggested from the beginning of their studies that the killing was probably a one-man psychopathic act rather than a group political act. Other "common sense" beliefs that have been tested by empirical study include the following:[17]

1. In the Armed Forces, men from rural backgrounds have higher morale than those from cities—because they are more accustomed to hardships.
2. Southern Negro soldiers prefer Southern to Northern white officers—because they understand one another better.
3. White privates in the Army are more eager for promotion than are Negro privates—Negroes lack ambition (upward mobility).
4. Well-educated soldiers show more neurotic symptoms under combat conditions than do less well-educated soldiers.

The fact that all four of these beliefs were found to be incorrect tells us something about the importance of checking every detail in a social science study. We can take little for granted.

Techniques are constantly being refined, and this gives us cause to hope that in future years the observational aspect of the social sciences will become much more exact than it now is. As an example of this change, only a generation ago, students of public opinion had to rely on a statistical method known as quota sampling. It was often found to be an inaccurate method for reaching a cross section of the public and sometimes led to wildly incorrect estimates of prevailing opinion. Not until about 1940 was the much more accurate technique of area sampling developed (in the U.S. Bureau of Agricultural Economics and the U.S. Bureau of the Census). Further refinements in sampling, in model construction to control the number of variables to be studied, in multivariate analysis to

[16] Gallup poll, published Dec. 6, 1963.

[17] Samuel A. Stouffer and others, *The American Soldier*, Princeton University Press, Princeton, N.J., 1949.

permit the simultaneous study of the effects of more than two variables upon one another, and in other techniques are constantly being made.

The greatest limitation upon political science lies in its restricted opportunity to use the most important tool for the earlier periods of development in a scientific field: the controlled experiment. In this sense, political science is in much the same situation as is one of the natural sciences: astronomy. In that field, the advancement of knowledge has been relatively slow, but advances have been made. For example, the hypothesis that the heavens contain not a single system, but a great many systems, with each nebula a separate galaxy, was first offered by the philosopher Immanuel Kant in 1755; but it could not be empirically verified until 1917. Adequate refinement of telescopic equipment and techniques required over a century and a half. The rate of accumulation of knowledge has increased since Kant's day, but theory building and testing remains a difficult problem for all the sciences. The astronomer is concerned with the geometry of space, for example. Is it infinite or not? Is it linear? Is it curvilinear? Albert Einstein and others have proposed various models. In the absence of either mathematical or empirical proof, astronomers argue about these problems as political scientists argue about various models of a political system:[18]

> As of the present no one model can lay exclusive claim to being the best representation of the actual universe. The choice sways from one to another as we choose to emphasize now one, now another set of partial observations, or as new horizons bring new knowledge. But the faith of science in the rule of law and the uniformity of nature bids us continue the search, confident that if we ask the right questions, and as we produce the means to answer them, all the parts of the puzzle will fall together into a consistent picture of the universe which portrays truth in the only sense in which science can sanction the word.

Exactly the same statement could be made concerning present-day political science.

SELECTED BIBLIOGRAPHY

In an evolutionary sense, the study of government must begin with the writings of anthropologists, the social scientists who are especially concerned with primitive man. An introductory text in cultural anthropology can provide useful bibliography on the development of government as an instrument for social control. See, for example, the suggestions in Hoebel [15]. An early classic study of primitive government was done by Linton [18]. In more recent years, Pye [20] and Almond and Coleman [1] have looked at the political institutions

[18] Howard P. Robertson, "The Universe," in Dennis Flanagan (ed.), *The Universe,* Simon and Schuster, Inc., New York, 1956, p. 13. Reprinted by permission.

of the economically underdeveloped nations and have tried to construct a general theory. Anthropologists are helpful in finding similarities between primitive and sophisticated cultures; they also explain how similar functions are handled in different types of cultures.

People who act in concert tend to join groups. This type of behavior is extensively discussed by both anthropologists and political scientists. The latter have depended heavily on Bentley [2], a pioneer political scientist, and Truman [25]. More on the subject, including criticism of the notion that all politics can be studied as group interaction, may be found in other writings [7, 10, 12, 16, 23].

A recent trend has been toward the development of political choice theory. This has centered around the study of politics as a set of problems in collective choice making (or consensus building or conflict resolution). Concentration has been on studying the objectives of individuals and groups in terms of their efforts to maximize opportunities and to minimize costs. For this purpose, scholars have borrowed heavily from the methods and concepts of economics (especially welfare economics) and game theory. Conflicts may exist between or among groups or individuals or within the individual, who must often choose among alternative uses for his own resources or among a variety of unrelated, often contradictory, personal goals. Important contributors to choice theory include political scientists and others. See the writings of Black [3], Buchanan and Tullock [4], Dahl and Lindblom [6], Downs [8], Riker [22], and Schelling [24], for example.

Much has been written about nongovernmental institutions for social control. The textbooks on introductory sociology deal with the subject, as do some specific studies of business associations [14], organized crime [19], the mob [5], and other institutions.

A Note on Contemporary Sources. Political science is not the study of current events, although current political events are relevant to political science and may be used effectively to find illustrations of phenomena described in this book. The most obvious source of current events information is the local newspaper, but it must be used with care, and may be seriously inadequate for the citizen who would be well informed. Editorials can be understood only if the values and policy preferences of the editor or his editorial staff are known. Reporting of nonlocal news is often sketchy and superficial. The local newspaper probably depends heavily upon the Associated Press or United Press International, both of which have competent staffs. But their reporting is circumscribed by the traditions of journalism, which tend to emphasize the sentimental, dramatic, spectacular, and controversial. The significant is given extensive coverage only if it fits one of these categories. Newsmen frequently assume that conflict is news—irrespective of whether or not the antagonists are disagreeing on principle or "grandstanding," and whether or not they are informed on the subject they are discussing. They avoid explanatory passages—even though explanation is needed to give sense to a story—on the grounds that to do so is to editorialize. Even more important, perhaps, is the fact that reporters tend to reinforce conventional wisdom—reporting the views of the man on the street instead of emphasizing comments by specialists—and talks or discussions that challenge conventional wisdom may only be reported as eccentric oddities. Furthermore, editors generally will not permit analysis of important issues in depth because they assume that the typical reader has only a superficial interest and cannot distinguish between mediocre and excellent reporting in any case. Similarly, an editor will seldom seek to explain theoretical concepts from the social sciences, in part perhaps because he does not understand them himself, but also because these theories often challenge conventional wisdom.

There are some important exceptions, of course. For example, many newspapers print the observations of informed columnists who attempt to discuss business-cycle developments in terms of a theoretical framework, and many print the informed, insightful words of Walter Lippmann—although many more prefer the spectacular "inside-dope" approach of Drew Pearson. In general, radio and television follow the same approach, as few programs attempt to *analyze* news events, although spectacular events, such as nominating conventions and presidential inaugurations, are given saturation coverage.

Newspapers, radio, and television, then, make little effort to educate the citizen in the sense that a college or university faculty attempts to. They are generally superficial and sometimes woefully irresponsible and inaccurate, as A. J. Liebling delighted in telling readers in the *New Yorker* and in one of his books [17]. But there are exceptions among newspapers, and scholars regard the *New York Times,* the *Christian Science Monitor,* and the *National Observer,* which is the Sunday edition of the *Wall Street Journal,* as being among the principal newspapers devoted to in-depth, careful reporting of significant events.

In general, the weekly news magazines feature good reporting and do an interpretive job far superior to that of the newspapers. Like the newspapers named above, however, they do not reach the typical citizen, but have a select clientele. The *New York Times* is read primarily by such persons as business executives and college professors. In 1963, *Newsweek* reported that its typical reader had a college education and earned $14,144 annually, while the typical American had a high school education and earned $5,660. *Newsweek* makes an effort to be disinterested rather than partisan in its regular news columns. *Time* and *Life* have highly competent staffs, but they are often much more opinionated than *Newsweek. Time* is written in a style many enjoy, but some critics say is "smart alecky." *Look* effectively combines news reporting and interpretation with pictures. *U.S. News and World Report* has a pronounced conservative outlook, but it has frequent and very good articles on American ecological and political trends. The *Reporter* has a liberal tone, especially on international politics, and is perhaps the periodical closest to being a widely read liberal newsmagazine in the United States (though its circulation is far below those of the journals above). Both the *Nation* and the *New Republic* are long-established liberal magazines of news and opinion that feature a New Deal slant. The *Progressive* carries on in the tradition of a movement of a few generations ago. All three of these magazines seem to be less influential and less read today than in the past. The *National Review,* also of relatively small circulation, reflects views of extreme conservatism. *Harper's* and the *Atlantic Monthly* often have interesting—if occasionally somewhat superficial—articles on politics and politicians. The *New Yorker* has a superior Washington events analyst in Richard Rovere.

There are other major sources of information for the citizen who wishes to be well informed. Every major library contains copies of the *Congressional Record,* the detailed record of the debates and actions of Congress—it is undigested source material that runs to thousands of pages a month when Congress is in session. The *Congressional Quarterly,* published by a private organization, issues what scholars consider to be very able weekly, quarterly, and special reports on the activities of Congress, as well as analyses of major national issues. Libraries also shelve such useful summaries as *Facts on File* and *Vital Speeches* and a reprint series of important political science studies [21]. Perhaps the best of all resources for the citizen who wants to learn is his public or college library, where the librarian can help anyone from the most naïve citizen to the professional scholar in locating materials that will be of the greatest possible use for his particular needs.

Numbers cited above refer to the corresponding numbers in the alphabetical list below.

1. Almond, Gabriel A., and James S. Coleman (eds.): *The Politics of Developing Areas,* Princeton University Press, Princeton, N.J., 1960.
2. Bentley, Arthur F.: *The Process of Government,* The Principia Press, San Antonio, Tex., 1908, reissued, 1949.
3. Black, Duncan: *The Theory of Committees and Elections,* Cambridge University Press, London, 1962.
4. Buchanan, James M., and Gordon Tullock: *The Calculus of Consent,* The University of Michigan Press, Ann Arbor, Mich., 1962.
5. Caughey, John W. (ed.): *Their Majesties, the Mob,* The University of Chicago Press, Chicago, 1960.
6. Dahl, Robert A., and Charles E. Lindblom: *Politics, Economics, and Welfare,* Harper & Row, Publishers, New York, 1953.
7. Dowling, R. E.: "Pressure Group Theory: Its Methodological Range," *American Political Science Review,* 59:944–954, December, 1960.
8. Downs, Anthony: *An Economic Theory of Democracy,* Harper & Row, Publishers, New York, 1957.
9. Easton, David: *The Political System,* Alfred A. Knopf, Inc., New York, 1953.
10. Eldersveld, Samuel J.: "American Interest Groups: A Survey of Research and Some Implications for Theory and Method," in Henry W. Ehrmann (ed.), *Interest Groups on Four Continents,* The University of Pittsburgh Press, Pittsburgh, Pa., 1958, pp. 173–196.
11. Galbraith, John Kenneth: *The Affluent Society,* Houghton Mifflin Company, Boston, 1958.
12. Golembiewski, Robert T.: "The Group Basis of Politics," *American Political Science Review,* 54:962–971, December, 1960.
13. Hagan, Charles B.: "The Group in Political Science," in Roland Young (ed.), *Approaches to the Study of Politics,* Northwestern University Press, Evanston, Ill., 1958.
14. Handlin, Oscar, and Mary Handlin: *The Dimensions of Liberty,* Harvard University Press, Cambridge, Mass., 1961.
15. Hoebel, E. Adamson: *Man in the Primitive World,* 2d ed., McGraw-Hill Book Company, New York, 1958.
16. Kariel, Henry S.: *The Decline of American Pluralism,* Stanford University Press, Stanford, Calif., 1961.
17. Liebling, A. J.: *The Press,* Ballantine Books, Inc., New York, 1961.
18. Linton, Ralph: *The Study of Man,* D. Appleton-Century Company, Inc., New York, 1936.
19. Moynihan, Daniel P.: "The Private Government of Crime," *The Reporter,* 25:14–20, July 6, 1961.
20. Pye, Lucian W.: "The Non-Western Political Process," *Journal of Politics,* 20:468–486, August, 1958.
21. Reprint Series in the Social Sciences, The Bobbs-Merrill Company, Inc., Indianapolis. (Continuing.)
22. Riker, William H.: *The Theory of Coalitions,* Yale University Press, New Haven, Conn., 1962.
23. Rothman, Stanley: "Systematic Political Theory," *American Political Science Review,* 54:15–33, March, 1960.
24. Schelling, Thomas C.: *The Strategy of Conflict,* Harvard University Press, Cambridge, Mass., 1960.
25. Truman, David: *The Governmental Process,* Alfred A. Knopf, Inc., New York, 1951.

CHAPTER

2

THE CULTURAL SETTING FOR POLITICS

In examining this chapter, the reader should bear in mind that understanding the political system is difficult for the specialist as well as for the typical citizen. It is difficult for the sophisticated student and for the professional political scientist, because all of us read through glasses that are ground to a prescription written by the culture in which we grew up and the one in which we now live (the two are not the same, and each affects the prescription). In addition, our personal values and individual personalities are consonant or dissonant factors that affect our interaction with the culture. Often, then, we see what we want to see and believe what we want to believe. We can hope to minimize these factors in our reading, writing, and thinking. We cannot reasonably expect to eliminate them.

American political man, in varying degrees, participates in the decision-making processes of government. The values to which he subscribes and the associations to which he belongs are often primary factors in the political choices he makes. But neither his ideology nor his group interests—which are interrelated—can be understood in a vacuum. They are a function of and, in turn, creators of his psychological, regional, social, and economic environments. In other words, they influence and are influenced by his life experiences. Before we can begin to understand American politics, we must isolate and take note of some of the effects of these features of environment.

POLITICAL CULTURE AND NATIONAL CHARACTER

The views held by Americans on most social and political matters are widely divergent. We have a few extremists on the left who follow the line of international communism and a handful who are members of the Communist party. On the far right, we have a few who call themselves American Nazis and frankly spread hate for Jews or Negroes. We also have a few who, in their hate and fear of communism, believe that democracy should be sacrificed if necessary in order to destroy communism. The vast bulk of Americans, however, reject these extremes, and members of this large majority share many beliefs and predispositions. Because this is the case, there is a tendency for some historians and social scientists to talk in terms of a "national character" in the United States as well as in other countries. For example, here is the testimony of an eminent historian:[1]

> Of all problems that challenge the student, that of the national character is, as Henry Adams observes, the most difficult and the most important. That character itself all but eludes definition, yet those who met Americans abroad [during World War II] had no difficulty in distinguishing them from men of other countries, nor did Americans themselves doubt for a minute that they were different. Clearly neither the heterogeneity of our racial background nor the immense diversity of our environments has frustrated the creation of a character that is unmistakably American.
>
> Perhaps the best personification is William Allen White of Emporia, Kansas. Born and brought up in the geographical center of the country, he remained, for all his cosmopolitanism, a man of the Middle Border and a small-townsman. For him, as for most Americans, life had been good, and he was incurably, even romantically, optimistic. He was a sturdy individualist—he neither smoked nor drank nor played cards nor fished—but he was hopelessly gregarious, never really happy away from a crowd of men, preferably from his own county. He was reflective rather than philosophical, distrusted theories and abstractions, and was saved from complacency by his abounding humor. He was restless and energetic, conscious of change and sure that that change spelled progress. As a newspaper editor he was close to his people, understood why they considered church socials more important than international relations, was democratic by instinct and habit rather than by philosophical conviction, regarded politics largely as a game but played the game with passionate sincerity. All this might also be a portrait of Benjamin Franklin; that it applies to William Allen White suggests that the American character formed early and did not change in fundamentals.

The collective "character," the respected personal values, described above may well serve as a frame of reference, setting the boundaries within which most citizens will expect decisions in government to be made. In this sense, the dominant belief system of a nation has relevance for the study of politics, but some social scientists consider the values reflected in a national character—so-called—to be too general and too inconsistent to serve, in themselves, as a basis for political analysis.[2]

At best, the notion of a general American character can be applied only to the predominant set of values; it is most meaningful when the content of the beliefs is not made specific—just as an overall enduring American ideology must be kept general in order to secure broad acceptance. Within this overall belief system, however, a number of social types act as symbols, major role models that guide people positively, by imitation, or

[1] Henry Steele Commager, "Portrait of a Progressive," *Tomorrow,* 5:65–67, June, 1946; a book review of *The Autobiography of William Allen White.*

[2] See Nathan Leites, "Psycho-cultural Hypotheses about Political Acts," *World Politics,* 1:102–119, October, 1948.

negatively, by avoidance. One sociologist has classified any culture's stereotypes as including one each for the hero, the villain, and the fool.[3]

In our heterogeneous American culture, there are many different subcultures, and they do not encourage equally the development of the same character types. Yet, out of the egalitarianism of the frontier arose a set of values and an ideal (hero) type that became the dominant yardstick against which behavior was measured and political acts evaluated. From the frontier, it moved into the small towns and then into contemporary suburbia, where it continues to help people make judgments about right and wrong, good and bad. It does not serve equally well for all American subcultures, and some reject much of it, but for many Americans it represents an ideal toward which behavior patterns are directed.

THE AMERICAN CHARACTER

The basic characteristics of the American culture may perhaps most briefly and effectively be suggested (we can do no more) by using the analytical framework of the anthropologist. Some years ago, Clyde Kluckhohn took a look at Americans and attempted to see them in the same light in which he might view the primitive cultures that are usually the subject of his profession. The following section draws extensively, though not exclusively, from his summary.[4]

What are some of the major traits of Americans? And what relevance do they have to the uniqueness of the American political system?

Material generosity. The most bitter critics of America concede that its citizens show material generosity; "most Americans are outgoing and genuinely benevolent." We have given billions of dollars to other nations since World War II with only vague ideas as to how this might help mankind, win us friends, or defeat communism. To be sure, we often expect that other countries should, in turn, remake their culture along American lines, but this form of ethnocentrism differs only in detail from similar attitudes of the British, French, or Russians.

Humor. Perhaps no huge society has ever had such generalized patterns for laughter.

No man becomes too prestigeful for us to make fun of him. There are

[3] Orrin E. Klapp, *Heroes, Villains, and Fools: The Changing American Character,* Prentice-Hall, Inc., Englewood Cliffs, N.J., 1962.

[4] Clyde Kluckhohn, *Mirror for Man: The Relation of Anthropology to Modern Life,* McGraw-Hill Book Company, New York, 1949. For a similar analysis by another anthropologist, see Margaret Mead, *And Keep Your Powder Dry: An Anthropologist Looks at America,* William Morrow and Company, Inc., New York, 1942. Mead was writing in the context of the great effort to win World War II; Kluckhohn was concerned with an America that was attempting to adjust in the new role of world leader in the late 1940s.

Unidentified quotes in the following section are from Kluckhohn's chap. 9.

some limits on what is considered good taste, of course, but President Truman was made human by jokes about his piano playing, Eisenhower about his golf, Kennedy about his vast fortune and large family.

Yet politics and humor do not mix too readily, even in America. We ridiculed Hitler, a technique which helped to destroy him in the eyes of Americans although many were fully aware of the unacceptability of his ideology. Adlai Stevenson probably did not enhance himself in the eyes of any but the intellectuals in the use of his brilliant sense of humor. Americans will react unfavorably to any politician who seems to be making light of something they believe to be a serious matter.

Equality for women? Although an American folk saying has it that the frontier was "hell on horses and women," the expression itself was something of an apology for a necessary but unwanted circumstance. The American man has sought to put an idealized woman on a pedestal, as European critics note with disapproval. Today, few except the wealthiest of Americans have servants who live in, but labor-saving devices have helped to free the American woman from the drudgery that has characterized the task of the housewife in most societies throughout history. As a result, women spend a great deal of their time working in voluntary organizations of many types—women's clubs, little theaters, community activities, and the like. We interest women in careers, but do not really encourage them to follow career patterns as do such labor-short nations as the Soviet Union and Sweden.

Many American women are active in politics, but to a considerable extent politics remains one of the few areas still considered a man's world in this country. Women are becoming influential in the politics of suburbia, however, and their greater leisure as compared with men, especially men in professional and executive positions, seems to be bringing them into increasingly important positions in political organizations at the state and national levels. Much of the routine work (doorbell ringing, envelope stuffing) is done by women today, and this brings them into party headquarters buildings and provides access to party leaders. Furthermore, sustained international tensions appear to have caused women to take a greater interest in politics. For the first time in the history of the Presidency, women voted in a significantly different pattern from men in the Eisenhower elections. (Women favored him more strongly, seeing him as the better bet for ending the Korean conflict and for preserving peace.)

Nonverbalized ideology. An educated Russian can give a coherent statement of his beliefs and can argue ideology effectively with persons from other nations; so can an educated Englishman. Even many who have not had university training can do quite well. But most Americans have difficulty explaining to foreigners what their fellow citizens believe in. This is one of the paradoxes that, as Kluckhohn has stated, characterizes the American culture. We talk much of "the American way of life," but we are almost incapable of telling others about it. Much of the political ideology we do have stems from an intellectual movement of the late eighteenth century, a development discussed in later chapters. It was beautifully expressed by the most "egghead" of American Presidents, Thomas Jefferson, but since his time we have had difficulty in organizing our changing thoughts about beliefs. The Jacksonian movement of a generation later, for example, never had a philosopher who could systematically state its beliefs. The credo of the American businessman, dating from the post-Civil War days, is also a haphazard set of ideas. Furthermore, America had little in the way of a systematic foreign policy until the time of World War II, and hence until recently we learned a political rhetoric that concentrated on domestic issues rather than on foreign policy. In contrast, the Englishman's basic ideology concerning relationships with other nations has been relatively clear and has not changed fundamentally in 400 years. For that reason alone, he is far more likely to be able to state his nation's position in international affairs.

Faith in reason and reasoning ability. "The dominant American political philosophy has been that the common man would think and act rationally."*

***RATIONALITY. For a man to be "rational" has not meant the same thing throughout history or to each writer on the subject, for the term has been used by philosophers as well as psychologists. Here we used the word to mean consistent with reason, that is, having deductions logically inferred from known data.**

Figure 2-1

The Average Man Wants to "See the Evidence"

"SHOW me some of these atoms, Lucretius, and maybe I'll accept your theory."

The American cult of the average man emphasizes the "practical"—but the "practical" is not always what it seems to be. (By permission of Burr Shafer.)

This view from eighteenth-century radical philosophy seemed admirably suited to the essential classlessness of the American frontier. It still characterizes politics in this country. Indeed, it seems to many Americans slightly immoral to suggest that man reaches his political attitudes and opinions through any means other than reason. Yet the conflicting thought persists that there are things the common people ought not to know or, if they do know, ought not to talk about. Thus we are often told that we should "think positively" about the economy. To say that times are bad, we are told, may help to deepen a recession. (Americans generally do not like to face up to unpleasant realities such as threats of depression or of war, but this is probably not unique to our culture.) John F. Kennedy was strongly criticized during the 1960 presidential contest for saying that American prestige abroad had been on the decline. This criticism was certainly only in part a routine countermove by the political opposition. It was also a reflection of a common belief that such frank talk would be damaging to the nation.

Most Americans seem to believe in rationality, but oppose intellectualism, which is the full application of rationality. If it is assumed that the ordinary citizen is rational and possesses common-sense wisdom, it follows that there is probably no need for an elite that specializes in rational approaches to problem solving. Consistently with this, Americans accord less status to intellectuals than do the people of practically any other nation.

Moralizing. "No people moralize as much as we do." The pursuit of power, prestige, and pleasure for their own sakes must be disguised, if public approval is to be obtained, so that it may be explained as action taken for a moral purpose. At the same time, a contemplative life is often considered idleness.

Some commentators on American life have traced the moralizing tendency to the teachings of John Calvin and the Protestant groups that followed him. They were important in colonial America and later, and their emphasis upon just material rewards for hard work and thrift seemed to fit a frontier society. So did the idea that the accumulation of wealth is a sign of heavenly favor. Even though they may not be the complete explanation for American moralizing, both ideas are still important in American ideology. And certainly it is only one short step from saying that success (in terms of the values of the culture) is a sign of God's favor to saying that all efforts to increase one's wealth and status must be explained in moralistic terms.

Action orientation. Americans are extreme pragmatists; they believe that every activity should have some practical purpose. Consequently, Americans admire technology, but are confused by science, for the former applies knowledge in ways that the culture considers useful, while the latter pursues knowledge for its own sake. College students sometimes find it difficult to believe that political scientists want to study government merely to find out how it works. And when a National Aeronautics and Space

Administration scientist said that his organization wanted to put a man on the moon "because it's there," reporters seemed to think he was making an attempt at humor. As Kluckhohn pointed out, Americans regarded Albert Einstein as a symbol of intellectual dilettantism and political naïveté until it became known that his mathematical theories made atomic bombs possible. Americans believe that man can understand the world around him *and hence can control it.* They believe that everyone should join in the effort to do so. It is incomprehensible to the average American that vast numbers of people in other parts of the world not only do not accept this view, but that some cannot even conceive of it. As a foremost economist has noted:[5]

> The century after 1815 saw the elaboration of an American style distinctive in its balancing of universal dilemmas. The evocation of moral and idealistic goals helped give a sense of nationhood to a sprawling continent full of diverse peoples; but this active commitment was, as it was bound to be, partial. It was linked to social and political practice which incessantly hammered out compromise solutions . . . to conflicts of interest and value, solutions by no means wholly consonant with the nation's articulated standards.
>
> The challenge of exciting material problems yielded a philosophic style empirical in method and narrowly pragmatic in its solutions. At the same time, this approach to reality was joined to the habit of spacious generalization which universalized without great reflection or refinement what could be perceived on the American scene.

Individualism. American individualism remains powerful even today, when most economic, social, and political organization is collective in character, centering around highly professionalized bureaucracies—the corporation, the Boy Scouts of America, the California Fruit Growers' Association, or the U.S. Department of Commerce.

This individualism is a product of the agrarian frontier, of the yeoman farmer, who worked his own land and whose profits were in large measure directly proportional to his own sweat. (In England and other European countries, the traditions of individualism are largely a product of capitalistic-industrial views.) So we dislike taking orders from anyone; we dislike strong government and accept it reluctantly. (In other nations, strong central governments have generally been the product of demands from business leaders; in this country, these same people usually oppose it.)

Americans, taken collectively, offer less support to officers of the law than do Englishmen, but the degree of support varies with presumed violation. There is no consensus that all laws should be supported equally (see Table 2-1). Americans distrust government and those who hold public office, but they revere the Constitution, which has symbolized the rights of the individual rather than the powers of government through much of our history.

[5] W. W. Rostow, *The United States in the World Arena,* Harper & Row, Publishers, New York, 1960, p. 62.

Equality. "Americans are characteristically more interested in equality than in liberty." Alexis de Tocqueville pointed this out in the nineteenth century, and we have never settled the dilemma between liberty and equality (see Chapter 18). To most Americans, liberty or freedom seems to be more a means than an end. It is a means for the chance to get ahead, the chance to achieve success. Americans place emphasis upon achievement for themselves or their children. Class or caste distinctions diminish the opportunities for social mobility, so they are opposed.

"In a phrase, the American creed is equality of opportunity, not equality of man." Perhaps it is even less than this, for as one study has concluded:[6]

> People tend to care less about *equality* of opportunity than about the availability of *some* opportunity. Men do not need the same life chances as everyone else; indeed, they usually care very little about that. . . . Popular satisfaction with one's own status is related less to equality of opportunity than to the breadth of distribution of some opportunity for all, however unequal this distribution may be.

Ambivalent feelings about leaders. Americans are ambivalent—torn between conflicting feelings—in their attitudes toward leaders. We engage in much poking of fun at them, seeking to cut them down to size. Politicians recognize this, and a regular part of the campaign ritual is to show that the candidate is actually a "good Joe," who thinks and acts as a typical citizen. As such, of course, he would not be a boss, but a friend in a position of power or perhaps service.[7] But we also admire the successful man—success being the ultimate American goal—and accord him deference even while we are somewhat jealous of him and suspicious of his potential power, especially if his success has been in politics. We also distinguish between our folk heroes (the Mercury astronauts, Charles A. Lindbergh, Daniel Boone, Davy Crockett), who became famous for things that almost all Americans favor, and administrators and other leaders who make difficult decisions in cases where there is no consensus (Abraham Lincoln, Franklin D. Roosevelt, Robert A. Taft, and most congressional leaders). Of course, a controversial leader may, in time, become a folk hero. Abraham Lincoln is an example.

Americans distrust the potential "man on horseback"—the leader who becomes a dictator—but they want strong leadership in the areas that concern them the most. So "the public has rather ambivalent attitudes towards power and power-holders. In the case of the President, it wants to endow him with very full powers while he is in office. In fact, the grant of power—at least in the realm of foreign affairs—amounts almost to an abdication of popular and Congressional decision making." On the other

[6] Robert E. Lane, *Political Ideology: Why the American Common Man Believes What He Does,* The Free Press of Glencoe, New York, 1962, p. 79. For ideas on liberty, see Lane's chap. 27. By permission.

[7] *Ibid.,* p. 195.

TABLE 2-1
HIGH SCHOOL AND COLLEGE STUDENTS WHO WOULD REPORT OBSERVED LAW VIOLATIONS

Violation	Per cent who would report
Illegal hunting or fishing	14
Under-age drinking in a bar	18
Carrying a concealed weapon	49*
Wife beating	53†
Stealing a coat	75
Stealing a car	92
Dope peddling	94
Hit-run driving	97

* More girls would report.
† Slightly more girls would report.
NOTE: The question was: Which of the following acts would you report to authorities if you saw someone else doing them?
SOURCE: George Gallup and Evan Hill, "Youth, the Cool Generation," *Saturday Evening Post,* Dec. 30, 1961, pp. 63ff.

hand, these same citizens are "generally concerned over a possible abuse of power," so they want power holders restricted to a definite time limit of formal office holding.[8] In a study by Roberta S. Sigel, 75 per cent of the respondents in a sample agreed that the President should send troops abroad if he thought it necessary, even if most Americans were opposed to sending them. And 66 per cent of the same sample approved of the Twenty-second Amendment, which limits the President to two terms in most cases. ("Eight years is long enough for any man," is a typical comment.)

Conformity. The cult of the average man means conformity to the standards of the current majority. Conformity and its meaning for a culture is often misunderstood.

Erich Fromm, writing from the perspective of the European intellectual, has suggested that contemporary Americans (the great bulk of them urbanites, of course) seek to avoid the isolation of modern life in "automaton conformity."[9] Man fears freedom and individuality, he says, using a psychoanalytical approach. In an interdependent world, he is afraid to go it alone. He does not desire to emphasize creativity or opportunity for individual action. The person who deviates from the norm, even very slightly, is subject to immediate criticism from a mediocre,

[8] Roberta S. Sigel, "Presidential Leadership Images," a paper read at the 1962 meetings of the American Political Science Association, Washington, D.C.

[9] Erich Fromm, *Escape from Freedom,* Holt, Rinehart and Winston, Inc., New York, 1941; see also Margaret Mary Wood, *Paths of Loneliness: The Individual Isolated in Modern Society,* Columbia University Press, New York, 1953.

unimaginative, fearful society. It is safer—more conducive to security—if he conforms. No one will attack him; no one will have a reason to exclude him from the children's play group, the country club, the Kiwanians, or a deaconship in the church if he loses his individuality in entire, uncritical conformity. He becomes *accepted,* and it is a deep-seated need for social acceptance that he feels.

Building on the concepts presented by Fromm, David Riesman has shown that until recent decades, Americans derived their security from conformity to parental, and particularly paternal, authority.[10] The middle-class American of today, however, seeks social approval not from his family and close personal friends, but from his associates—for the most part, associates in secondary relationships. And this process begins before he enters school as a child and extends through his funeral.

In the postwar years, orthodoxy and conformity became matters of concern to social psychologists and others. It must not be assumed, however, that conformity to prevailing value patterns is a product of mass communication or mass education. It is not a modern phenomenon. The American frontiersman, the vaunted "rugged individualist," was probably at least as much of a conformist as is today's urbanite. The pressures on him to conform to the values and expectations of society were even greater than they are today. Indeed, in every society, conformity to prevailing value patterns is a device for maintaining social control. Most persons everywhere are content to follow the leadership of those in whom they have established confidence. And criticism of conformity is not a postwar phenomenon. Before the Great Depression, the folk humorist Will Rogers commenting on a University of California football player who had run 75 yards in the wrong direction in the Rose Bowl, giving his opponents a safety and the margin of victory, said:[11]

> All I want is ten per cent of Sunday's collection to get this boy a medal for at least doing something different from one million other college boys. Even if it was wrong, his mind wasn't standardized.

It is easy to exaggerate the sameness of American culture. In the case of food alone, differences by regions in the United States are great. The shrimp gumbo of Louisiana, the *mahimahi* of Hawaii, the taco of Arizona, the pasties of Michigan's Upper Peninsula, the blintzes of New York—each is familiar to citizens of the area and often unknown to those coming from elsewhere. The differences in economic and social patterns are also great. The urban, industrial life of New Jersey is vastly different from the pastoral ways of North Dakota. The lumber economy of Washington produces a way of life different from that of the tourist economy of

[10] See two works by David Riesman: *The Lonely Crowd* (1950); and *Faces in the Crowd* (1952). Both books are published by the Yale University Press, New Haven, Conn.

[11] Will Rogers's syndicated column of Jan. 4, 1929.

Nevada. The South never knew the yeoman farmer and his life-style, but this American hero was long the dominant figure of the Midwest. Hawaii, Mississippi, and South Carolina all once centered on a plantation economy, and in all of them, the white man is in the minority. But there are few nonwhites in Maine or Montana. A childhood in a Boston tenement is not much like one on a Wyoming ranch. Yet the motto of the land, *e pluribus unum,* is fitting, for out of this great diversity does come a single nation with a number of dominant, shared cultural characteristics.

Ours is a nation of conformity, but it is also one of great diversity. Furthermore, conformity has itself often been misunderstood. Kluckhohn, more perceptive than many scholars because, as an anthropologist, he was a professional observer of nonintellectuals, has noted:

> The American voluntarily and consciously seeks to be like others of his own age and sex—without in any way becoming an anonymous atom in the social molecule. On the contrary, all the devices of the society are mobilized to glamorize the individual woman and to dramatize every achievement of men and women that is unusual—but still within the range of approved aspirations of the conforming majority.

Europeans tend to emphasize conformity to traditional values and behavior; Americans tend to emphasize conformity to the demands of their "reference group"—those with whom they identify and whose acceptance they seek. In Riesman's terms, they are "other-directed," that is, directed toward other persons. He notes that they are not "inner-directed" toward their own personal resources, their own thoughts and reasoning. And Robert E. Lane has concluded that "democracy as a popular concept centers in the freedom of the nondeviant individual [the conformist] to do what the majority thinks right."[12]

Complaining. Griping is regarded by Americans as a fundamental aspect of free speech, and it is used for a variety of purposes—to cut the public figure down to size by revealing his human frailties, to excuse one's own lack of success by engaging in envy of others in a socially acceptable way, and so on. In the political realm, we disparage politicians, grumble about the red tape of bureaucracy, gripe about the level of governmental services (it is too high or too low), and complain about taxes. Especially, we complain about taxes. Undoubtedly, many of these complaints are meant seriously, but others are ritualistic—we are *expected* to gripe about taxes. It is regarded as a safe topic of light conversation, in about the same category as the weather. Elected officeholders fear retribution of voters if they raise taxes, yet there seem to be few instances above the local level of government where those in power have been turned out for doing so. The politician, however, cannot become accustomed to the fact that practically no one speaks in favor of increasing taxes. The person who says, "I think a tax increase at this time is necessary and justified," is either

[12] Lane, *op. cit.,* p. 83.

the President, especially well informed concerning the need for more dollars to meet some national emergency, or a social deviant whose views will not be taken seriously.

The simple solution. The American believes that every citizen has a right to an explanation of every issue or a solution to every problem that arises. But because he has many interests clamoring for his attention, he wants the answers to be simple enough for him to understand with ease. This, again, is a result of the cult of the average man: If one man is as good as another, an explanation should be such that every man can understand it. As the philosopher John Dewey once pointed out, Americans "lust after absolutes." They want to see things as being black or white, good or bad, useful or useless, American or un-American. But the social, economic, diplomatic, and military matters that are the grist of politics nearly always come in shades of gray rather than in black or white.

The political scene is strongly affected by the desire for the simple solution. Seekers after public office are pressured by campaign managers and public-relations specialists to offer easy answers to fantastically complicated questions (the "desirable" growth rate of the American economy, say, or whether to recognize Communist China). The demagogue, a familiar figure in American politics, is characterized by his willingness to exploit the anxieties* of citizens by offering unworkable, irresponsible, simple solutions to complex issues of public policy. The citizen himself expects the wide-angle-screen, technicolor picture that is the reality to be reduced to the small-screen, black-and-white picture he can comprehend. And, as Kluckhohn pointed out, because the citizen can pose the question simply, he believes the answer can be equally simply stated. He customarily does so in his own political discussions. ("All we have to do to put the Russians in their place. . . .")

***ANXIETY. A vague, unfocused, and highly persistent fear. It produces a compulsion toward some type of behavior, which may be a political action.**

Universal education. "During the last generation, education has supplanted the frontier as a favorite means of social mobility, for we have continued to define success in terms of mobility rather than in terms of stability." The parents of American children have always wanted their offspring to be well educated; usually they have wanted them to have more education than they themselves have had. In an open-class, socially mobile culture, education and status advancement have been closely linked. Frontier egalitarianism produced the public school system and gave it its character as a locally controlled and locally financed institution. Coupled with this desire for educational opportunity has been, however, the strong belief that an educated person should not be a highbrow and that his learning should be pragmatic and put to use for the benefit of society. Out of frontier life came a powerful tradition in support of learning and in opposition to intellectualism.

The issues surrounding public education today are complicated by the dual role performed by contemporary schools. They serve both as educational and custodial institutions. There is a great deal of confusion and inconsistency in public education resulting from a variety of factors:

1. Parental anxieties about the best way for their children to get ahead lead to curriculums that emphasize a vocational orientation.
2. The need to find a place to keep children until they can be permitted to enter the job market tends to leave children in school, whether or not they are able or willing to learn, to discourage intellectual interest on the part of the bright minority, to prevent effective ranking of students by ability, and to put an end to flunking out.
3. Doubts about the wisdom of abandoning traditional educational curriculums has led us to retain some traditional learning. Often we teach French to students who cannot or will not learn it, but do not give the college-bound student sufficient command of English to meet the expectations of his professors.
4. Some of the functions that have traditionally belonged to the family have been transferred to the schools.

The issues themselves are evidence that Americans regard education as important and hence worthy of attention and debate. And the school systems have undoubtedly improved in each generation in terms of the amount of knowledge and sophistication the student takes with him when he leaves.

Formal religiosity. Because of the tradition of moralizing and because most of America's immigrants were genuinely and often deeply religious, we pay deference to religion. Some groups in our society remain strongly religious, of course, and it is believed that there has been some sincere revival of interest in the teachings of our churches in the postwar years. However, most Americans today probably regard their churches as social institutions rather than instruments for the redemption of souls, and "very few of our leaders are still religious in the sense that they are convinced that prayer or the observance of church codes will affect the course of human events." American attitudes appear to have changed a great deal in the last generation or so. In 1960, some Democrats quietly used the argument that non-Catholics could safely vote for John F. Kennedy because he "is not a *serious* Catholic." It cannot be checked, but it is not likely that such an argument would have been effective in 1928, when the Democrats ran another Catholic, Alfred E. Smith.

Voting figures indicate that religion was still a factor in the 1960 election. It seems likely, however, that Catholics who were prejudiced in Kennedy's favor were expressing the ethnic solidarity that is characteristic of minority groups in America rather than a theological preference in the strictest sense. Similarly, those who were prejudiced against him on "religious grounds" probably would describe their objection in terms of organized power, or anxieties about ethnic strivings, or in other than theological terms[13] (see Table 2-2).

In Kansas, Kennedy's religion benefited him among Catholics—Democratic, Republican, and Independent—but cost him votes among all non-Catholic voters. The result has been estimated to have been a net loss of 3 per cent of what he would have had as a Protestant.[14] In Detroit, 81 per cent of Catholic Democrats who had voted for Eisenhower in 1956 said they would vote for Kennedy in 1960, while only 56 per cent of Protestant Democrats for Eisenhower said they would change back to support Kennedy.[15]

Religion and psychology. Americans often talk of *guilt* feelings, which is a psychological concept, but rarely of *sinfulness*, a theological concept. We pay homage to theologians such as Reinhold Niebuhr, but his teachings deviate too far from the American cultural norm to be followed seriously by the typical citizen, for his highly sophisticated teachings seem to be rooted in the Thirty-ninth Psalm:[16]

> Verily every man at his best state is altogether vanity. Surely every man walketh in a vain show; Surely they are disquieted in vain: He heapeth up riches, and knoweth not who shall gather them. And now, Lord, what wait I for? My hope is in thee.

We seem unwilling or unable to apply religious teachings to everyday life. Paul Tillich, another noted theologian, has commented that Americans would be shocked if anyone were to denounce the Sermon on the Mount, but they would be horrified if someone tried to put its teachings into effect. And Bishop Fulton J. Sheen has noted that the world, and perhaps especially America, "has sought Divinity in Power, in Popularity, in Progress, in Science; it has ignored the possibility of ever finding it in simplicity, in the unexpected, in defeat, and in frailty."[17]

The American Culture: Summing Up. The American culture is infinitely complex. We have been able only to suggest some of the principal factors in our

[13] See John F. Fenton, *The Catholic Vote,* The Hauser Press, New Orleans, La., 1960. See also forthcoming publications of the Survey Research Center, University of Michigan, Ann Arbor, Mich., and Chap. 13 of this book.

[14] John G. Grumm, "A Profile of the Kansas Voter," *Your Government,* 17:5, May 15, 1962.

[15] Roberta S. Sigel, "Race and Religion as Factors in the Kennedy Victory in Detroit, 1960," a paper read at the 1962 meetings of the Michigan Academy of Science, Arts, and Letters, Detroit.

[16] King James version. Niebuhr equates vanity and sin.

[17] Fulton J. Sheen, *The Moral Universe,* The Bruce Publishing Company, Milwaukee, 1936, p. 8.

TABLE 2-2
EVALUATIONS OF CANDIDATES' PERSONAL QUALITIES BY CATHOLIC AND PROTESTANT INDEPENDENTS, 1960 (Per cent)

	Catholics		Protestants, regular churchgoers	
Evaluation	Nixon	Kennedy	Nixon	Kennedy
Favorable	31	75	70	36
Neutral	49	24	27	37
Unfavorable	20	1	3	27
Total	100	100	100	100

SOURCE: Survey Research Center, University of Michigan, Ann Arbor, Mich.

culture that help shape the environment in which political decisions are made. Much that is characteristic of American culture has been passed over here, though some excluded items will come up for consideration in later chapters. We might have discussed our preference for physical comfort, for bodily cleanliness, for the discussion of personalities rather than issues; our notion that the bigger something is the better it is; our emphasis on the rights of property; or our tendency to give hair-trigger reactions when confronted with a challenge of any kind.

The political implications of the ideas presented so far are many. They provide a framework or target within which political decisions will be found acceptable and they give us indications of the kinds of decisions that will be greeted with skepticism or even hostility. The life-styles of citizens, furthermore, are largely shaped by the culture or subculture (that is, variants of the mainstream, such as particular ethnic or minority groups). People value the life-style to which they are devoted and customarily use political means to preserve it when it is threatened. But do these cultural traits, when tied together, have a broader, more central, political implication? Some observers have concluded that they do. The anthropologist Clyde Kluckhohn pointed out the keystone in the arch of our culture in these terms:

> American social institutions are the most distinctive contributions made by the United States to world culture. The cult of the average man is an even more characteristically American invention than the assembly line. Philosophers of many nations had dreamed of a state guided by a skillfully trained but small group of the good and wise. The United States, however, was the first country to dedicate itself to the conception of a society where the lot of the common man would be made easier, where the same opportunities would be available to all, where the lives of all men and women would be enriched and ennobled. This was something new under the sun.

Putting the average man at the center has given American politics its distinctive tone and style—a characteristic that has often alienated European observers. The behavior of the typical citizen as a participant in the political process will be expanded upon in later chapters. The way that democracy, designed to fit his values and wants, operates in America will be the subject of Chapter 4.

If there is something unique about American democracy—the placing of the typical citizen, rather than the extraordinary man or a leadership class, at the center—what style of politics is implied by this? It would seem to emphasize conventional wisdom, symbolism, and emotional appeals in political communication; to tend to give equal weightings to all political opinions, regardless of the competence of the speaker; to give pragmatic considerations, rather than broad philosophical considerations, predominance. Such a politics glorifies the public-opinion poll and the simple solution to complex problems. Such a politics is ambivalent as to its substantive goals, emphasizing simultaneously personal self-reliance and sentimentality toward the socially unfortunate, for example. It is one in which the individual citizen seeks to find a reference group* upon which he can rely for guidance in making political decisions and to whose leaders he can turn for guidance in the interpretation of political events and issues.

***REFERENCE GROUP.** **The individuals or groups (real or imagined) whose values as standards an individual takes into consideration in the making of his self-evaluation and in forming attitudes.**

THE LAND AND ITS PEOPLE

Regional Variations and Politics. Modern patterns of migration and communication have blurred traditional boundaries of American regionalism, but a variety of factors in different geographic regions produce differences in life-styles and political patterns. Long-established life-styles in various regions influence politics: Southern traditions affect attitudes toward civil rights; those of New England encourage many people in that area to consider themselves the last of the rugged individualists, and the rural or small-town New Englander is likely to be very conservative in his political views; the Westerner still has much of the frontier spirit and is therefore likely to view politics as an instrument for economic growth, for he is highly conscious of change and views it as being desirable—if government can help produce it, he is likely to approve. The Middle West was settled largely by Germans, Dutch, Scandinavians, and Irish, many of whom sought to avoid militarism and poverty in Europe; they are likely to view America as an island of safety and plenty and hence to be skeptical of internationalism in politics.

Some economic interests, and corresponding political attitudes, coincide generally with regional boundaries (the boundaries themselves are not easily drawn). The South has for years sought to attract industry, using its low wage rates as a particular incentive for corporations to locate there.

This has encouraged Southern congressmen to oppose legislation (such as an increase in the national minimum wage) that would increase labor costs. Eastern congressmen for years opposed the St. Lawrence Seaway project, fearing that it would encourage industrial development in the Midwest at the expense of the East. Most of the West is short on water and power. Its spokesmen have long favored governmental assistance through public dams and hydroelectric plants that will divert tax dollars into capital development in the West and raise the standard of living by improving the area's economic base. New England, faced with industry's movement away toward the nation's population centers and lower-labor-cost areas, seeks government support to shore up its slumping economic base and government policies designed to equalize the economic positions of various regions and thus reduce competitive advantages.

There are some regional differences in campaign styles too. The South is popularly supposed to be the home of the flamboyant campaigner and to produce more than its share of demagogues. To the extent that this is true, it is perhaps a matter of tradition and life-style, but it is probably also related to the fact that educational levels are lower in the South than in any other part of the nation. Members of the upper class or aristocracy are more likely to run for office in New England and New York than in other parts of the country. Civil rights policies color almost every campaign in the South, just as public power policies do in the West and agricultural policy in the Middle West.

The Rural-to-Urban Trek and Politics. The most characteristic thing about American population trends throughout history has been the inexorable move toward the city. The rapid urbanization of the United States has been responsible in great part for the high standard of living we enjoy, but it has also been accompanied by many conflicts over social and political issues.

We were once a nation of rural and small-town dwellers who enjoyed stable values. Ethnic groups of differing values and life-styles were separated by physical distance. Today we are an overwhelmingly nonagricultural society. About 10 per cent of the American population now earns its living from the land; another 17 per cent lives in small towns outside urban areas. The rest is made up of city and suburban dwellers (see Figure 2-2). Urban society is characterized by close physical proximity, which makes conflict between social groups more likely; by an interdependent and impersonal economic system, which produces many insecurities; and by demands for complex and expensive governmental services in health, education, welfare, highways, and other areas. Urbanization has somewhat blurred regional differences and helped to establish a set of widely shared life experiences. Hence urbanization has produced vast changes in the functions of government and in the style and content of political campaigns.

The population of American cities doubled between 1860 and 1900. In

Figure 2-2

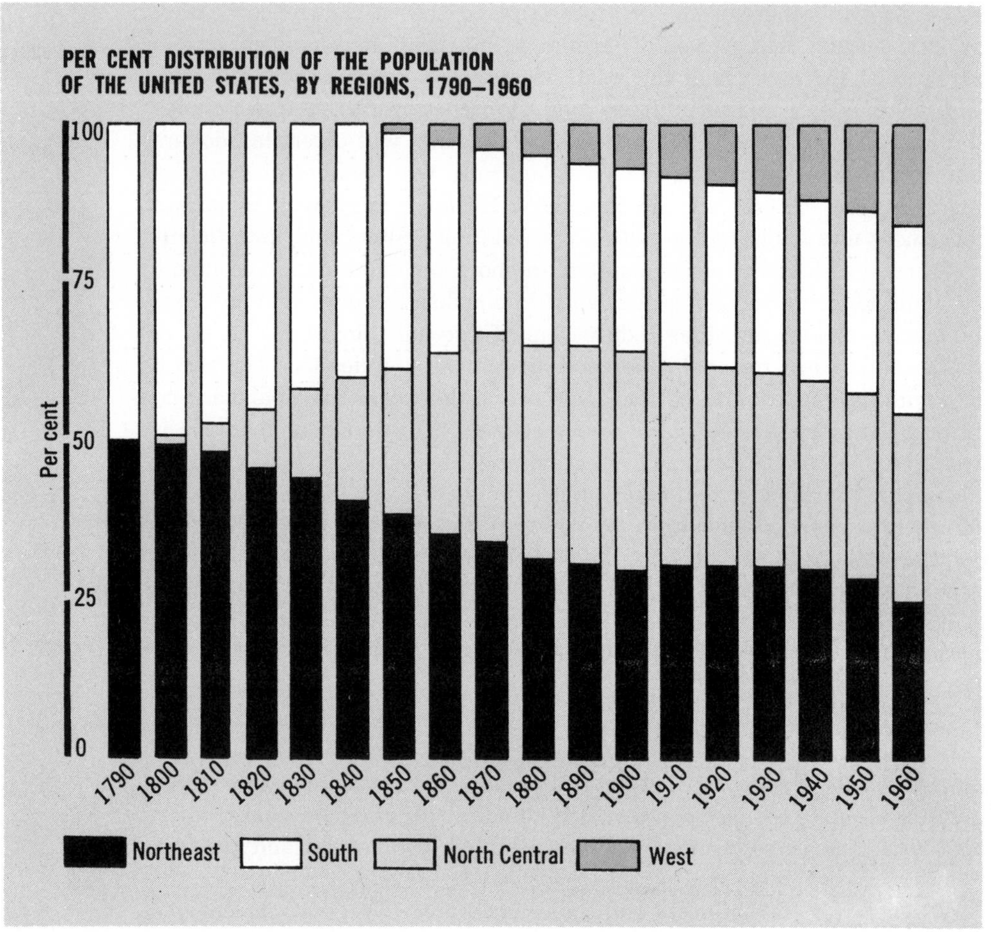

Bureau of the Census, U.S. Department of Commerce.

the next quarter of a century, it doubled again. By 1920, over one-half (51.2 per cent) of the American people were living in cities.[18] The percentage in 1960—with a somewhat modified definition—was 70.2, and it continues to climb. And at the time of the last decennial census, nearly two-thirds of the American population lived not merely in urban, but in *metropolitan* communities, that is, in population concentrations having a central city of at least 50,000 people. Approximately one-fourth of the total was located in the twelve largest metropolitan areas.

[18] The Census Bureau definitions of urban, nonrural (urban plus rural nonfarm), and metropolitan areas may be found in the introduction to the 1960 census reports.

Figure 2-3

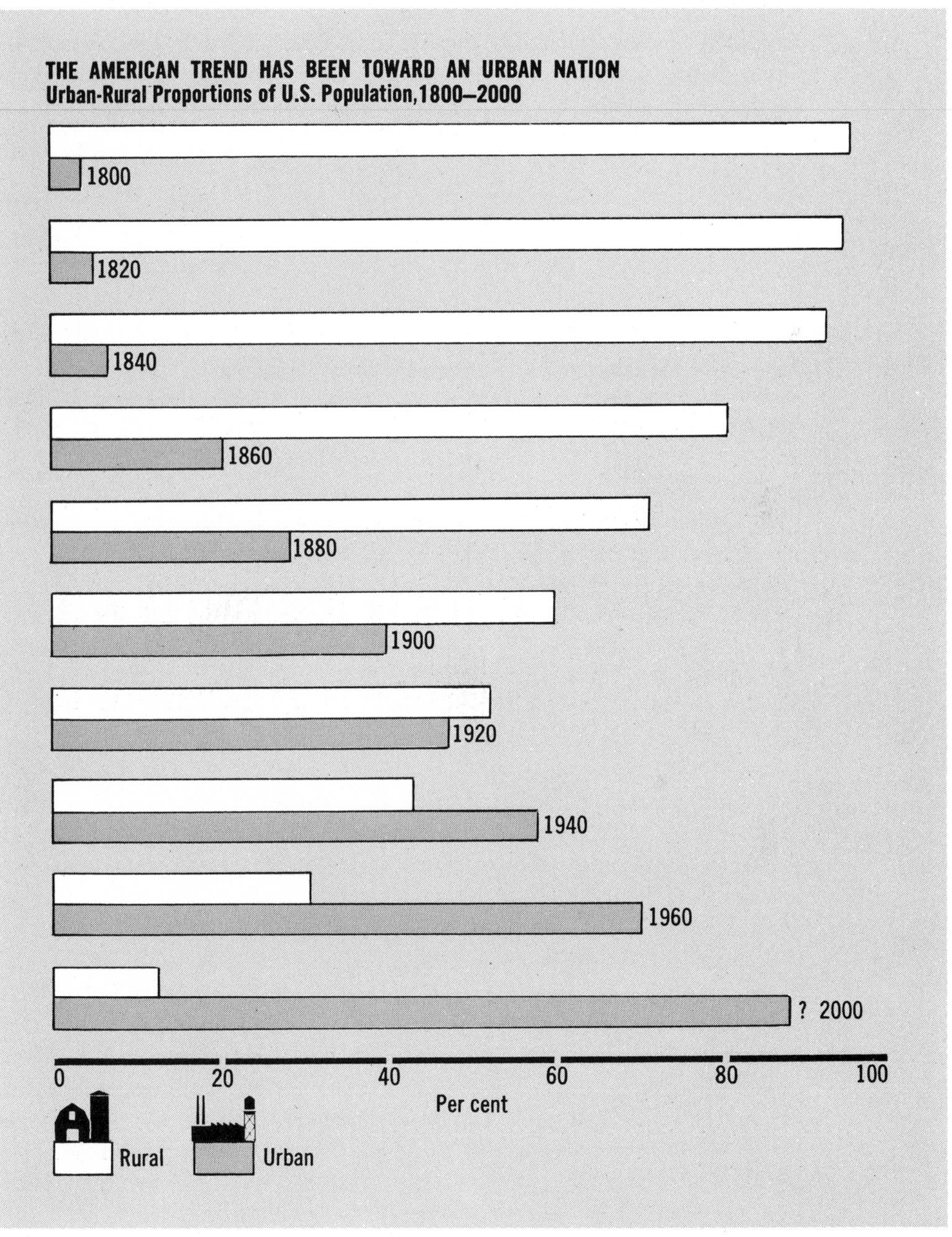

Bureau of the Census, U.S. Department of Commerce.

The Contemporary Pattern. The population of the United States reached 170 million in the census of 1960 and was increasing at a rate of about 3 million a year. All of the postwar increase was urban, for the population that earns its livelihood from working the soil declines each year, as it has since shortly after the beginning of this century; only the years of the Great Depression are an exception. The 1950–1960 gain was high (about 24 per cent) in the 192 metropolitan areas, but it was highest of all in the suburbs.

Figure 2-4

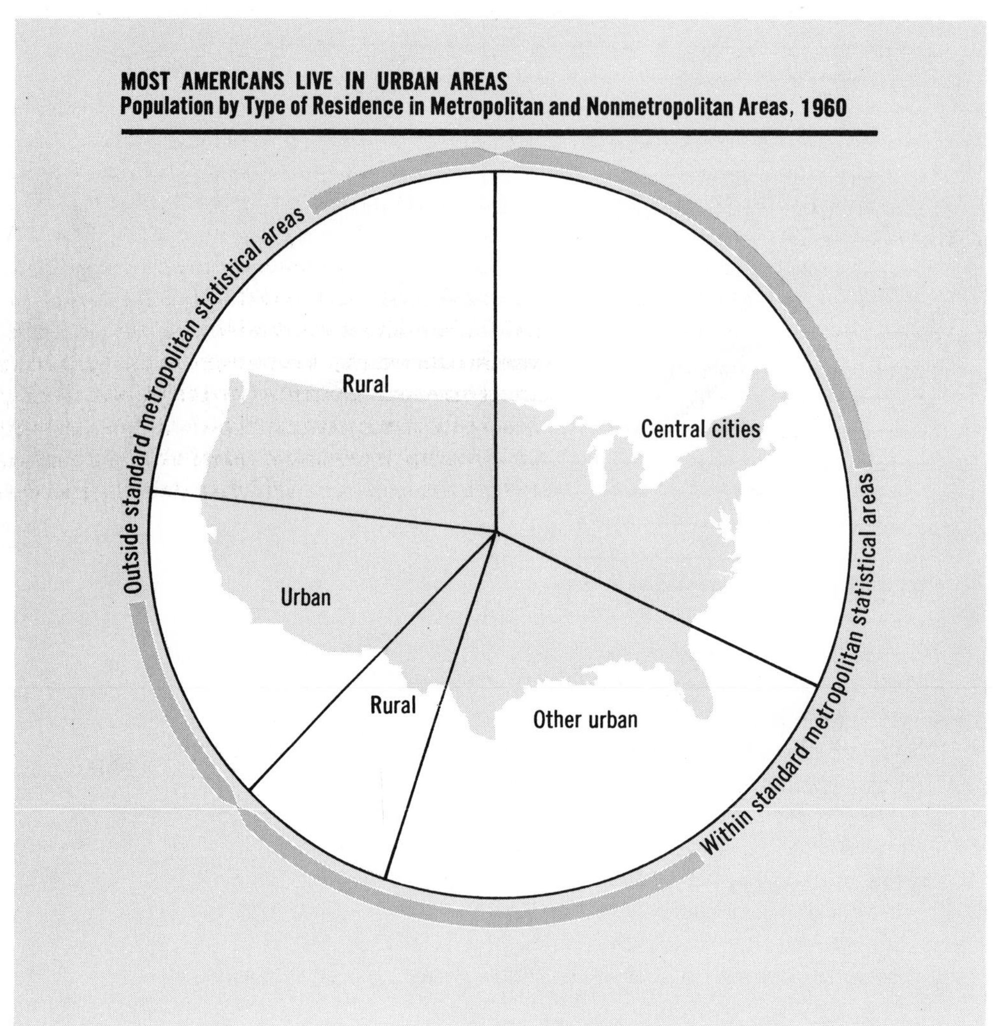

Bureau of the Census, U.S. Department of Commerce.

The huge cities (except for Los Angeles, which gained 24 per cent) generally lost population as people showed a preference for suburban living. The suburbs of Detroit gained 79 per cent, in contrast to the core city, which lost 10 per cent; in Los Angeles, the suburbs gained 83 per cent.

The nation, with nearly 70 per cent of its population crowded into only about 6 per cent of the area of the fifty states, had become urban, if indeed not metropolitan. Americans had moved from rural to urban areas, from the core city into the suburbs, from the inner ring of suburbs to the outer ring, often creating strip cities two lots to two blocks wide and dozens of miles long (some of them potentially hundreds of miles long) stretching out into the countryside. The number of nonschool local units of government had mushroomed along with the population, and the problems of supplying governmental services had grown with them—especially in metropolitan areas, where people were concentrating and where the number of units of government might run into the hundreds. The Federal government was increasingly being asked to assist in supplying highways, water supply, sewage disposal, and other services to the urban areas and to help educate the growing number of children. Greater Federal action in these areas had been retarded by ideological conflicts—some believing that services must be provided by any unit that is in a position to act, and others believing that decisions about services traditionally provided at the local level should continue to be made at that level.[19] Another factor had been the suburbanites' fear that they might lose their independent local governments and be forced into the core city. But there is no question that the 1960s and 1970s will produce further demands from an increasing variety of interest groups for Federal action to meet the (culturally defined) needs and wants of an urban and largely metropolitan people.

SOCIAL CLASSES AND POLITICS

America is the stronghold of the average man, but is it made up of a society that consists only of average men? To what extent does the stratified society of much of Europe, Asia, and Africa play a part in America? And if we do have classes, in what ways do their behavior patterns affect the political process?

A Classless Society? It has always been popular among tellers of the great American myth to say that this nation is lacking in classes, that all are equal, and that anyone can do anything that his ability and determination dictate. Less romantic sociologists point out that while we have a good deal of mobility between classes, classes do indeed exist. Some sociologists

[19] See Robert H. Connery and Richard H. Leach, *The Federal Government and Metropolitan Areas,* Harvard University Press, Cambridge, Mass., 1960.

Figure 2-5

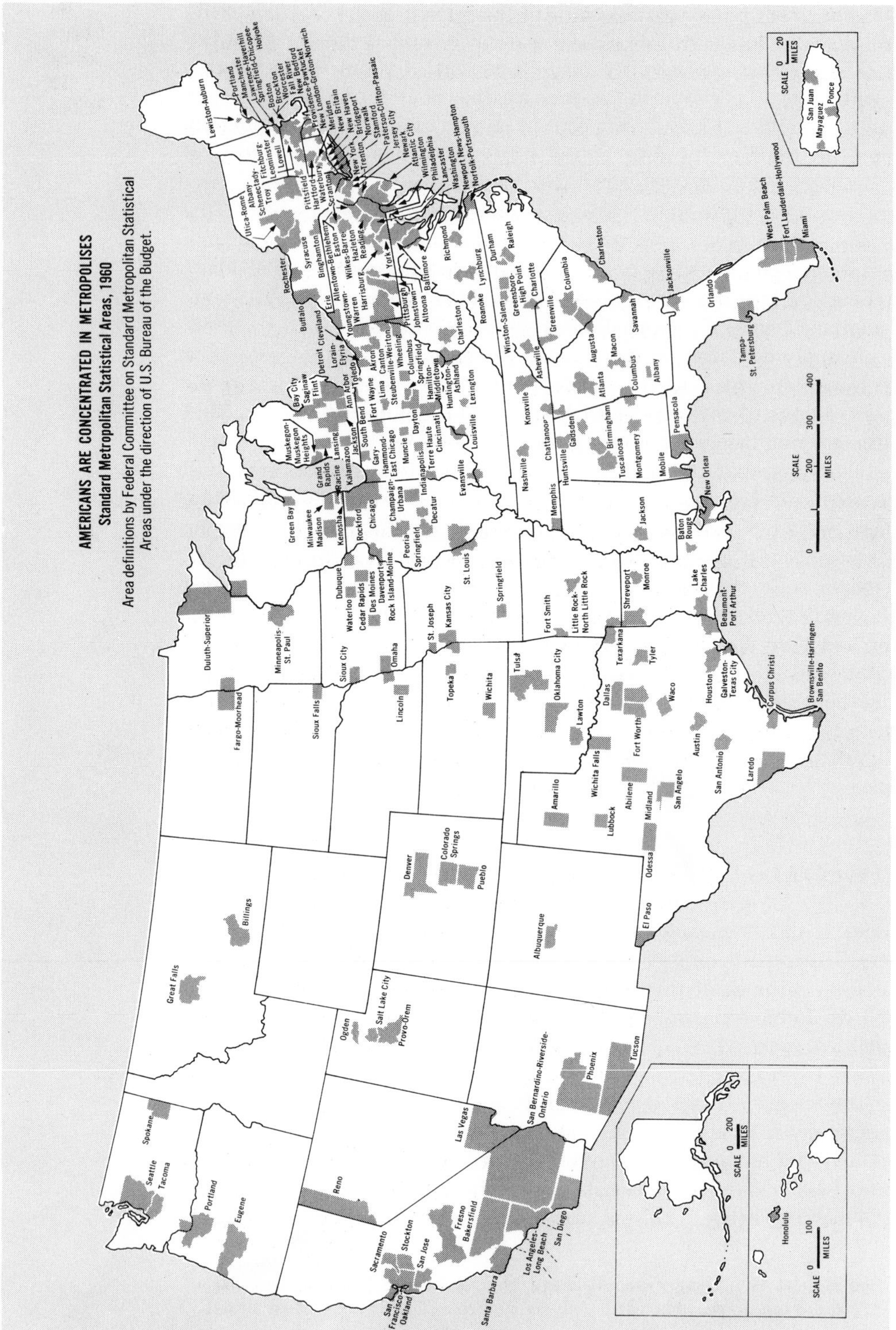

AMERICANS ARE CONCENTRATED IN METROPOLISES

Standard Metropolitan Statistical Areas, 1960

Area definitions by Federal Committee on Standard Metropolitan Statistical Areas under the direction of U.S. Bureau of the Budget.

Bureau of the Census, U.S. Department of Commerce.

would go further and say that, because of the inferior social position of the Negro, America has both a class and a caste system, although the rapid postwar changes in the status of Negroes has discouraged use of a caste concept.

A social class is a division of society in which individuals are recognized as belonging to a certain social-status group. Subjectively, a class derives its identification from its members, who have a sense of belonging to one another and of being separate from nonmembers: Nonmembers of a class view its members as being different from themselves in terms of behavior patterns and values. Objectively, class membership can be measured in terms of occupation, education, and income. A social caste exists when the status position of the individual is determined by birth and cannot be changed by individual effort. A class thus exists only in a small- or middle-sized community. On a nationwide basis, the upper, middle, and working classes are statistical abstractions rather than self-conscious classes.[20]

Differences in life-styles continue to exist, however, even though they are not perfectly related to class. These differences are important and influence the political process. Differences in life-styles result in differences in interests, which are reflected in differences in political demands. Yet in terms of our cultural values Americans are expected to avoid recognizing class differences. Classlessness is the asserted goal of many a suburbanite, for example, but he seeks to achieve it, not by accepting as his neighbor anyone who can afford to buy the house next door, but rather by retreating into a particular suburb in which the life-style and ethnic membership are in accord with his own tastes. He achieves the appearance of consensus by excluding from his community and its decision-making process those who are "different"—in beliefs, in income, or in physiognomy. This is not classlessness, but an attempt to avoid the consequences of the lack of classlessness in America.

The Vanishing Adamses. There remains some semblance of an aristocracy or upper class in America. Its members live their own life-styles, aloof from the more typical American behavior patterns. They serve democracy by assuming important positions in the government and occasionally are condemned for their disdain of "togetherness." For example, Henry Cabot Lodge earned the resentment of reporters when he ran for the vice-presidency in 1960. Although he came from a family that had long honored government service as a class responsibility, his personality did not lend itself to the behavior patterns of conventional politicians. Because it was his habit to be "correct" and a bit aloof rather than a backslapping "good Joe," he received what his supporters considered a bad press.

The famous Adams family of Massachusetts suffered far more from unpopularity. The family stemmed from a line of New England farmers

[20] See Arnold W. Green, *Sociology,* 4th ed., McGraw-Hill Book Company, New York, 1964, pp. 194–196.

(American aristocracy has had modest beginnings and rarely has been descended from European aristocracy). The Adamses furnished the nation two able Presidents, a Minister to England (Charles Francis ably carried out President Lincoln's instructions to keep the British from allying themselves directly with the Confederacy during the Civil War), a leading railroad builder, another cabinet member, a philosopher and historian, and a novelist. But the family was aloof, conservative, and unwilling to accept the cult of the average man. It has had no public officeholders in major positions since the Great Depression; the last was another Charles Francis Adams, who served as Secretary of the Navy under Herbert Hoover.

The Harrisons of Virginia were a comparable family of aristocrats with a sense of public service. Benjamin (1726–1792) was a leading Virginia landowner and political leader, a signer of the Declaration of Independence. His son, William Henry (1773–1841), became President of the United States. One of his sons, John Scott (1804–1878), was a congressman from Ohio—the family moved westward with the nation. And a son of his, Benjamin (1833–1901), served as a Senator from Indiana and became President. A number of Roosevelts, members of a family descended from the early Dutch immigration to New York, have held high government positions, and two served as President.

The early American Presidents came from aristocratic families. The first to be generally regarded as a self-made man was the seventh President, Andrew Jackson. His father was an Irish linen weaver who came to this country and became a Carolina farmer.

The Function of the Aristocracy. Many governmental leaders have come from aristocratic families since Jackson's time, but most of America's best-known men have come from families of humble people. The upper class is small, difficult to define, and so atypical in its life-style that it has not found it easy to be a major influence in either major political party. The Republican party, which has been dominated by middle-class—especially lower-middle-class—businessmen, and the Democratic party, which has been dominated by spokesmen for Southern agrarians, immigrants, and the working class, have neither one been comfortable or logical centers for the upper class. Many aristocrats tend to deviate from social expectations and become leaders of liberal movements and of the liberal wing of the Democratic party. They may do this for many reasons: to find careers for themselves; to protest against family expectations and domination; because their high status and perhaps their wealth provide an insulation against the insecurities that cause middle-class persons to want to separate themselves from less prestigeful working people; or for other reasons.

Men such as Franklin D. Roosevelt and Adlai Stevenson in the Democratic party and Theodore Roosevelt and Nelson Rockefeller in the Republican party have supported social change. Actually, these aristocrats are not traitors to their class, as some have alleged, but agents of one of its traditional roles. We must distinguish them from the self-made men, who have become rich through business success (the *nouveaux riches*), but come from working- or middle-class backgrounds and lack the traditional upper-class emphasis upon honor, status, freedom, and dignity. Aristocrats have, from colonial times, sought to ally themselves with ordinary citizens to give them leadership, to ensure social stability, and to prevent the *nouveaux riches* from undermining that stability. They have viewed this as an obligation of their class, or *noblesse oblige*. They have not sought to change the economic system very much, though they have opposed certain changes proposed by others; for example, aristocrats led the opposition to the trusts during the time that one of them, Theodore Roosevelt, was President.

Members of the upper class have provided much of the leadership for reform movements that have been concerned with personal freedom (civil rights) and have been highly influential in the periodic modernizing of American foreign policy. Thus, aristocrats were the leaders—in the abolitionist movement before the Civil War, in the Progressive movement in the late nineteenth century, in the development of a professional civil service, in the elimination of governmental corruption, and in the move toward internationalism in foreign policy.[21]

There is an American *noblesse oblige* tradition. The dying words of the delirious William Henry Harrison, in the Presidency only a month, were spoken not to members of his family, but to the Vice President: "Sir, I wish you to understand the true principles of government. I wish them carried out. I ask nothing more." This tradition is not dead, but it does not carry the weight that it does in, say, Great Britain.

The odd mixture of the acceptance of and near indifference to upper-class leaders is symbolized by two Senators from Massachusetts. In the early 1950s, that state was represented in the Senate by two members of old aristocratic families, Henry Cabot Lodge and Leverett Saltonstall, both Republicans. In 1952, Lodge was soundly defeated (despite the Eisenhower landslide) by John F. Kennedy, the son of a rich Boston Irishman and the great-grandson of an immigrant who lived his life in the low status of the Irish of that city. Yet in 1960, when Kennedy brought to final climax the saga of a simple immigrant family in the perfect reflection of the American Dream and carried his home state by a landslide, Leverett Saltonstall, the dignified great-great-grandson of Massachusetts aristocrats, was reelected to the United States Senate—against an Irishman.

The Upper Middle Class. The concept of an upper middle class cannot be specifically defined, and the term is used somewhat differently by different

[21] This section borrows from Seymour Martin Lipset, *Political Man,* Doubleday & Company, Inc., Garden City, N.Y., 1960, pp. 298–301. See Lipset's citations.

social scientists. To some extent, it applies to higher-income members of the middle class, but that distinction is not in itself adequate.

In this book, some differences in life-style are also involved. In particular, members of this category are likely to be quite well educated—graduates of colleges of some status; they are likely to have had middle-class, rather than working-class, parents, and they are likely to feel secure in their status. Today, members of this class are likely to be professional people or members of the bureaucracy of large corporations (organization men) who have positions of considerable responsibility. Their secure position in society permits some of them to be moderate or even quite liberal in political views. They are likely to be called upon for important public service of either an appointive or elective character at some time. They are a stable influence in society: they are not haunted by fears of being confused with working-class people (as are members of the lower middle class), of being rejected as nonconformists (as are some members of the aristocracy), and they do not fear that civil rights legislation will encourage an invasion of lower-status persons into their neighborhoods. They are the people who serve on presidential study commissions or head their political party's Citizens-for-Torkelson Committee, who contribute to the party coffers, and who vote in almost every election. They are the civic leaders of the community who devote many hours to voluntary associations like the Community Chest, and whose names appear frequently on the front, local news, and society pages of the newspaper.

The General Middle Class. If we except the members of the aristocracy, farmers, and working-class people, the remainder can be classified as the middle class. The most prestigeful and highest-income sector of this class was mentioned above, as a special case; the marginal members at the lower end are also a special case. The others, the bulk of the middle class, are the less prestigeful or less prosperous members of the professions, the less-than-executive organization men of corporations, the rather successful small-business men. This group of citizens, taken in very general terms, is likely to have gone to college, expects its children to do so, was near the lead in the suburban exodus from the core cities, and is noted for conformity to social expectations, current fashions, and fads. Middle-class citizens are likely to go to the polls and vote, to consider the Republican party (except in the Deep South) the party of middle-class respectability, to have moderately conservative views. As a group, members of this class are fairly well informed about politics and current events.

The Lower Middle Class. The persons who just escape membership in the working class by job classification pursue a different political style from that of the rest of the middle class—or from that of any other group in America, for that matter. Many members have lower incomes than do some working-class people. They are not likely to have gone to college. A great many of them are small-business men. Many are small-town dwellers.

Considered as a voting bloc, they are the most conservative group in politics. Except in the Deep South, they tend to be fiercely Republican and to follow a life-style that is intended to identify them as closely as possible with the rest of the middle class and to separate them from the working class. They are white collar rather than blue collar.

The lower middle class is the most insecure group in our society and in the societies of many other countries. Its members view the increasing importance and power of trade unions with alarm and they see the trend toward unionization as a threat to their status. They are especially likely to be bitter about the success of unions in raising workers' wages. They are frequently low-tax advocates, for they see little chance for much increase in their own salaries or business profits. To them, every tax increase means a loss in their standard of living. They also see the benefits of governmental domestic programs as going principally to urban working people, so they have a twofold reason for opposing the trend toward the social service state. The small-town merchant, in particular, is likely to feel bewildered and outnumbered—it may seem to him that he is living in a world that has passed him by, one that he does not understand.

Members of the lower middle class in Germany and Italy were the first and most loyal supporters of Nazism and fascism in the 1920s and 1930s; these movements provided them with a chance for greater security and an opportunity to "be somebody" by identifying with the organizations. Hitler and Mussolini also gave them something else they needed—a scapegoat. That is, they could blame their psychological and economic insecurities on some general class or type of people upon whom they could then project their hatred and fears. Their victims were the Jews and the Communists.

The lower middle class has generally behaved differently in the United States, however. In this country, Nazi and fascist groups have always been regarded by the great bulk of the citizenry as the lunatic fringe. They have not had broad appeal. But members of the lower middle class, in the frustration that results from a feeling that they are a permanent minority unable to have much effect upon political decisions, are the most common source of membership for extremist groups. In postwar America, they have tended to establish the Communists as their scapegoat, blaming all the problems of the world upon Communists—the many problems that do in fact result from Communist policies, as well as the many that do not. The lower middle class, then, is likely to include many who feel that they are isolated, that no one wants to hear about their views or concerns, that no public policies reflect their wants. It is just one step from this feeling to a paranoid reaction to perceived threats to one's life-style or standard of living. (To psychologists, a paranoid is a person who suffers anything from mild to severe systematic delusions of persecution.) Alienation and paranoia are, however, individual rather than group or class reactions to stimuli. Their effect upon politics will be examined further in Chapter 9.

The Small-town Dweller. Some extra attention is due the small-town member of the lower middle class, for the popular image of his life-style continues to be romanticized, and the image has influenced middle-class suburbanites. Furthermore, small-towners are disproportionately powerful in politics because they have been overrepresented, in terms of population, in state legislatures, where they support conservative policies. In turn, this has tended to encourage urbanites, blocked in their efforts at legislation at the state level, to turn to the Federal government for help. Thus, the small-town dweller's low-tax ideology and opposition to the social service state has probably done much to encourage the growth of Federal domestic programs in the last generation.

The small-town-dominated state legislatures also affect national public policy because they can determine the pattern of districting a state for purposes of electing congressmen. As we shall see in Chapter 14, these districts have generally been designed to benefit the rural and small-town areas at the expense of the metropolises. This has, in turn, tended to cause the House of Representatives to be more conservative than a cross section of the public would seem to want. In other words, the views of the small-town merchant have tended to be quite strong in the House—more so than in the Senate, and much more so than in the White House.

The small town, dominated by its Main Street merchants, was once regarded by Americans as "the climax of civilization." But by the end of World War I, it had passed its peak of popular support and soon became a major target of social criticism.[22] It has since been changing in character, and its economy is becoming ever more unstable. Its leaders must strive, not for growth, as do their counterparts in the nearby city, but to prevent economic decay and population loss.

Governmental programs seldom seem to offer assistance; instead, they are seen as threatening to undermine the small-town merchant's self-reliance and to raise his costs by increasing taxes. The Main Street merchant is likely to see unemployment compensation or social security as programs to benefit only the urban worker; he sees them as expenses for which he receives in return little, if any, benefit. The new limited-access highway, again, seems to be a service for urbanites; by making it easy for small-towners and farmers to get to the nearby city to do business, the highway spells potential disaster for the local economy. Federal aid to education, he is told, will provide better education, but in his relatively simple economy, he wonders what "practical" use the better education has. It will only increase his costs and encourage still more of the abler local youngsters to go away to college and thence to the suburbs as organization men or wives of organization men. Federal funds for urban renewal make little sense to him either. Nearly all such work is done in the slums of large cities. Again, he sees himself as helping to pay for something that

[22] See the preface to Sinclair Lewis, *Main Street,* Harcourt, Brace and Company, Inc., New York, 1920.

will benefit him only in the most obscure way, if at all. Indeed, he has probably been taught from childhood that large cities are evil places anyway and that their problems are the result of their own wrongdoing. He does not understand that slums are the result of complex economic factors, and he only dimly sees that the social problems that emerge from them are a burden on all citizens and affect him more directly than he realizes: Juvenile delinquency in slums may affect his grandchildren, who live in the city; his taxes help to pay for the prisons that house the serious deviants from society, many of whom grew up in slums.

Public welfare programs, all of them expensive, make little sense to the small-towner. The problems of the urban worker, who is totally dependent upon someone else for an income, are foreign to him. Furthermore, the small-town dweller is better able to take care of family disasters and emergencies through his own resources than is the urban dweller in the economically interdependent and socially impersonal city. The great bulk of governmental domestic programs today are thus not designed to meet the concerns of the lower-middle-class member of small-town society. And he is likely to see costly foreign-aid programs as a threat to his income to such an extent that he may be encouraged to lean toward isolationism (see Chapters 6 and 7), or at least to listen to those who argue that these programs can be cut substantially without hurting anything.

The Farmer: Where Does He Belong? Except in the South, the rural life that dominated America until the time of World War I was organized around the yeoman farmer, who worked with his own hands the land that he owned, was buying, or hoped to buy. It is likely that there have always been differences in life-styles and political objectives among farmers, despite the appearance—which was probably never a reality—that all

TABLE 2–3
FARM OWNERSHIP, SELECTED STATES AND THE UNITED STATES, 1959 (Per cent)

	Ownership			
Location	Individual	Corporate	Public	Other
Iowa	96.4	1.9	0.2	1.5
North Dakota	89.0	4.1	6.6	0.3
Wisconsin	97.7	1.5	0.5	0.3
United States	85.4	5.6	7.9	1.1

SOURCE: U.S. Bureau of the Census.

NOTE: Iowa is the wealthiest general farming state. Wisconsin is a major dairying state. North Dakota is the most rural of the states. Individual owners do not necessarily farm the land they own. Many commercial farmers today prefer to own a "home base" but find it more profitable to put any other funds they have into machinery and to rent additional land, so that land ownership is no longer a measure of success in farming.

farmers joined in the various agricultural political-action movements. In the years since the Great Depression in particular, there have been growing distinctions among subsistence farmers, part-time farmers who also hold city jobs, and commercial farmers. It would be difficult to fit them into an overall class structure, although the more well-to-do commercial farmer today tends to live by the values and much of the life-style of the urban middle class.

The farmer has, however, been important in American politics since colonial days. He has often reflected politically the traditional conservatism of those who work the land and has wanted to be able to forget the problems of his European ancestors. So he has often been isolationist in his views toward foreign policy. On the domestic scene, however, he has periodically joined in programs of agrarian radicalism; he gave strong support to the Progressive and Populist movements, which were important strains in the American political song from the 1870s until the 1920s. The yeoman farmer was, in fact, the first (reluctant) American collectivist of political importance. (The urban industrial employee began to join working-class political parties as early as the 1820s—even earlier than European workers—but these efforts had little payoff until the coming of the great labor unions of the 1930s, because the workingman has always faced the threat of being displaced by immigrants from abroad or migrants from rural areas.) The powerful agrarian reform movements that began in the 1870s are discussed in Chapters 5 and 6.

The Working Class. Below the middle class is a category that logically should be the lower class. Some sociologists use the term. But opinion samples have indicated that members of this class reject it. They are willing to be identified with the working class, however, and we bow to this cultural expectation.

Most rural Americans apparently could vote even in colonial times, according to the findings of recent research. Robert E. Brown[23] has estimated that nearly 90 per cent of the adult white males could vote in Massachusetts at the time of the Revolution. Those excluded were largely urban workers. It was on their behalf (and on behalf of some landless farmers and farmhands) that the Democratic party of the 1830s, during Jackson's period, supported the total elimination of voting conditions for adult males.

For many decades—during which the nation was urbanizing rapidly—the principal manifestation of universal manhood suffrage (for whites) existed in the urban political machines; this represented a response to the insecurities and poverty of the urban slums with their low wages and insecure employment. The workingman was, however, strongly disadvantaged in the political arena until after the restriction of immigration fol-

[23] Robert E. Brown, *Middle-class Democracy and the Revolution in Massachusetts,* Cornell University Press, Ithaca, N.Y., 1955, chaps. 1–5 in particular.

lowing World War I. Early union activities were often punished by the use of strikebreakers or by summary dismissal. In an age when the development of America depended upon capital accumulation and the American ideology held that the most important social institution was business, neither the workingman nor his union could expect sympathy. Even the aristocracy restricted its concern for the workingman's welfare to private social welfare agencies. While the unions were struggling for their existence—and with little support from the workingman himself—they could not become effective political instrumentalities.

After the restriction of immigration in the early 1920s, the urban worker still faced competition from the rural-to-urban migrant. It was not until the Great Depression, which began in the fall of 1929, that the workingman became disillusioned enough with industrial individualism to demand effective governmental action and to join labor unions for unskilled workers. The Congress of Industrial Organizations (CIO) was organized in 1935. (It was at first known as the Committee for Industrial Organization.)

From the days of the Great Depression and the New Deal that followed Franklin D. Roosevelt's election in 1932, union members have been well represented in the political arena by the highly professional bureaucracies of organized labor. Working people, at least those who belong to unions, have recognized that they can use the machinery of government to their social and economic advantage. As a result, they have developed a confidence in political action that is lacking in the life-style of the lower middle class. They do not vote as consistently as middle-class citizens do, but their lack of knowledge of candidates and specific issues (see Chapter 8) does not reflect their relatively high level of support for government as an institution for social change.[24]

Perhaps the most significant thing about non-Communist European—as well as American—members of the working class is that they see democracy primarily as a means of economic advancement. Even social reforms are seen in pocketbook terms. A fair employment practices law may be viewed by members of the upper class and intellectuals as a device for greater social justice; it is likely to be seen by minority-group workers as a means for them or their children to achieve better-paying jobs. So we find:[25]

> The poorer strata everywhere are more liberal or leftist on economic issues; they favor more welfare state measures, higher wages, graduated income taxes, support of trade-unions, and so forth. But when liberalism is defined in noneconomic terms—as support of civil liberties, internationalism, etc.—the correlation is reversed. The more well-to-do are more liberal, the poorer are more intolerant.

[24] Robert E. Lane, *Political Ideology: Why the American Common Man Believes What He Does,* The Free Press of Glencoe, New York, 1962, p. 474. By permission.

[25] Lipset, *op. cit.,* pp. 101–102.

The workingman's insecurities—the fact that he lives close to the margin in our society—is reflected in his views on such matters as tolerance of others and concern for his fellow man. Union leaders often argue in favor of civil liberties and tolerance, but unless they can show that these provide an economic advantage to their membership, they are not likely to make much of an impression. White workers are often prejudiced against Negro workers, for the two are intensely competitive economically. Similarly, workers of one ethnic group show prejudice against workers of another group, even while their union leaders are supporting the Fair Employment Practices Commission (FEPC) ordinances. Karl Marx thought that workers had more to unite them than to divide them in their relations with other classes; American workers have found many areas in which they could present a united front, but their agreement is far less solid than Karl Marx—or even Walter Reuther—has claimed. For example, working-class members have usually followed the middle-class pattern of segregation in suburbia—where the working class was a slight majority by 1964. Despite the lack of class unity and despite the rapid postwar growth of the middle classes in America, organized labor has become an enormously effective force in political decision making.

Ethnic Groups: A Special Case. As in all pioneer societies, a social division exists in America between the older settlers and the newer immigrant groups. The earliest arrivals, whose background was largely Anglo-Saxon and Protestant, firmly stamped their heritage on American society and their characteristics were given special deference in the class structure. Members of later immigrant groups, especially those of southeastern Europe, were short of occupational skills, had to overcome barriers of language, and were often Catholic or Jewish—hence outside the mainstream. This placed them at a status disadvantage. The resulting social discrimination became manifest as an organized political expression in the American, or Know-Nothing, party of pre-Civil War days and the Ku Klux Klan of the 1920s.

Socially, the later immigrants were, as a group, separated from what was regarded as "genteel society." Within the new immigrant groups themselves, a separate social ladder developed, but with each rung lower than the corresponding one in the main cultural pattern. A Polish lawyer had higher status than a Polish mechanic, but lower status than a Yankee lawyer. The lower rungs were constantly replenished until 1924, when the national government sharply reduced immigration and set up a quota system for eligibility to enter the country.

In the 1960s, there were still more persons of Polish background in Chicago than in Warsaw. They, like other ethnic groups, have continued to maintain foreign-language radio stations and newspapers. But in most ethnic communities, the strength of ties has been weakened. Second- and third-generation Americans who have earned college degrees and achieved business success have been accepted into the broader society and accorded a higher place in the status hierarchy.

The achievement of middle-class status, intermarriage with older immigrant groups, and the movement to the suburbs have been accompanied by Americanization of names, the decline in foreign-language church services and newspapers, and the general loosening of ethnic ties. Social acceptance has been accompanied by rapid political acceptance. The rags-to-riches saga of the Kennedy family and the election of John F. Kennedy, third-generation descendant of an Irish-Catholic immigrant peddler, to the Presidency symbolizes the diminution of the social and political gap. Ethnic politics is still important as a device for status striving, particularly in heavily industrialized areas, but voter support of ethnic candidates now more commonly comes voluntarily and out of pride than as the result of social discrimination. Generally, a common religious heritage is the major adhesive for such ties. Balancing political tickets with foreign-sounding names (called "League of Nations politics") will still catch votes, but it is becoming less fashionable—particularly in the suburbs, where ethnicity is often denied rather than encouraged.

The Negro: Another Piece in the Class Puzzle. The Negro does not fit into a neat pattern of class structure any more than does the farmer. The Negro is born into an inferior-status position. Within each occupational category, his is the lowest-status position. Because his physical characteristics are difficult to disguise, he usually cannot disappear into the melting pot, as most ethnic-group members have. Changes in the social status of the Negro have been rapid in the period since the end of World War II, however; although Negroes are still, in practice, excluded from most higher-status jobs and living areas, they are experiencing rapid changes in their status positions. Even so, it will probably be some time before a Negro with the same job and same income as a white man will enjoy the same social standing and privileges.

Many behavior patterns of the Negro have their roots in his early menial position as a slave—literally as the property of another. Because, as slaves, Negroes could not vote, and because they were effectively disfranchised after Federal troops were withdrawn from the South following the Civil War (1877), Negroes have traditionally been apolitical. Furthermore, until recent years, they have always viewed government as a white man's institution, designed to keep them subjugated. Because even Negro leaders have not seen politics as an instrument for economic or social advancement, it is understandable that the ordinary Negro has been apathetic. Negroes who did vote prior to the Great Depression continued to say "thank you" to Abraham Lincoln; they were overwhelmingly Republican. The Great Depression and the New Deal changed their political behavior, however. Franklin D. Roosevelt made a deliberate appeal for their support, and many New Deal programs were of enormous help to unemployed and marginal Negroes.

After World War II, Negro leaders found the courts effective and sympathetic decision-making centers and increasingly used them as a means for achievement of their goals. At the same time, they sought to encourage effective political organization among the rapidly growing Negro populations of northern cities, as well as among those in the South (see Chapter 10). The increasingly clear evidence of the effectiveness of political action brought about a great change in the political style of Negroes. From almost total apathy, they moved to intense activity, and in several northern industrial states (especially Illinois, Michigan, New York, and Pennsylvania), they became the balance of political power,

Figure 2-6

NEGRO POLITICAL ATTITUDES AND BEHAVIOR*

Boycotts: weapon of the future?

	Total	Non-South	South	100 Leaders
HAVE YOU STOPPED BUYING IN CERTAIN STORES IN TOWN BECAUSE THEY WON'T HIRE NEGROS?				
Yes	29	24	30	55
No	71	76	70	45
HAVE YOU STOPPED BUYING CERTAIN COMPANIES' PRODUCTS BECAUSE YOU HAVE HEARD THEY DISCRIMINATE AGAINST NEGROES?				
Yes	19	14	18	52
No	81	86	82	48
IF ASKED, WOULD YOU DO THE FOLLOWING? (PERCENTAGE AFFIRMATIVE)				
Picket a store?	47	54	40	57
Stop buying at a store?	63	66	59	66

Dislikes: targets of the present

	Total	Non-South	South	100 Leaders
WHAT TWO OR THREE WHITE LEADERS AND ORGANIZATIONS DO YOU DISLIKE THE MOST AND TRUST THE LEAST?				
Ku Klux Klan	31	32	28	42
(White) Citizens'Council	26	20	27	52
Ross Barnett	8	8	8	11
George C. Wallace	8	10	6	10
Barry Goldwater	3	5	1	8
Orvai Faubus	2	2	1	5
American Nazi Party	2	2	1	10
John Birch Society	3	3	1	15

*Figures are in per cent.

even though many remained apathetic and still required vigorous prodding before they would vote.

Classes and Interests: A Recapitulation. Despite the cult of the average man, classes do exist in America, and they provide categories that have some value for political analysis. Classes are often so used in studying European democracies. There will be numerous references to classes throughout this book because they are significantly related to differences in life-style and subcultural values, hence, to political behavior patterns.

Interest groups and ideological commitments, rather than classes, will

Figure 2-7

THE AMERICAN ECONOMY IS AN EXPANDING ONE
Growth of Federal Expenditures, Gross National Product, and Other National Aggregates, 1955–1964, Percentage Change*

National aggregate	Per cent change: Seven years to 1962	Average annual growth rate	Nine years to 1964 (estimate)†
Gross national product	+ 39	+ 4.9	+ 54
Personal income	+ 42	+ 5.1	+ 57
Population (as of July 1)	+ 12	+ 1.7	+ 16
Personal consumption expenditures	+ 39	+ 4.8	+ 53
Business spending for new plant and equipment	+ 30	+ 3.8	+ 40
Consumer price index	+ 13	+ 1.8	+ 17
Federal expenditures, other than defense, space, and interest:			
Administrative budget	+ 52	+ 6.4	+ 69
Trust funds	+ 195	+ 16.7	+ 231
Federal expenditures, total, including defense, space, interest, and trust funds	+ 55	+ 6.5	+ 74
State and local expenditures‡	+ 72	+ 8.0	+ 100

* Federal expenditures are on a fiscal year basis; other series are on a calendar basis except as noted.
† On assumption of same growth rate as during first seven years.
‡ Minus Federal grants-in-aid.

Financing America's Future, *Committee on Federal Tax Policy, New York, 1963, table 2.*

generally be used throughout this book as an analytical tool, for these reasons:

1. Not all Americans can be fitted into a class analysis. Negroes, farmers, and self-conscious ethnic groups are examples. In contrast, probably all Americans belong in some, often many, interest groups, and all have some kind of ideological-belief system.

2. There are too few classes and subclasses to break down the total population for useful analysis in connection with many kinds of public issues and decisions.

3. Issues often cut across class lines, making class irrelevant for analysis. For example, there is no single working-class interest in the matter of civil rights. Members of one working-class ethnic group may clash with another, and each group may have its own position on the meaning and purpose of civil rights legislation. The lower middle class is divided on questions involving differences of interests between small-town dwellers and white-collar urbanites within the same class. Of course, there is often considerable overlap between classes and interest groups. For example, the aristocratic (upper-class) concern with honor and liberty is a collective interest. There is much overlap between members of the working class and union members or factory workers as groups, but the correlation is imperfect. Similarly, an ideology may be viewed as an interest, but advocates of a particular ideology are not necessarily organized as an interest group.

4. Finally, interest-group activity is frequently a consciously planned and organized effort; thus it provides a convenient basis for the analysis of decision making in a way that class does not. Thus, the American Dairy Association is deliberately organized to further the interests of dairymen. It takes quite specific stands on certain public issues, say the tariff on cheeses, in furthering the goals implied by the interest. Such overt activity aids us in making political analysis.

POLITICS AND LIVELIHOOD WITHIN THE AMERICAN ECONOMIC STRUCTURE

In our society, which strongly emphasizes the importance of material goods, the means of production is central to the social organization, and the economic system is interrelated with the political system. President Calvin Coolidge, who coined a number of phrases that soon became hackneyed popular quotations, once said that "the business of America is business." In his world—that of most Americans in the 1920s—this statement probably was not far wrong. Today Americans no longer believe as strongly as they once did that business is the most important social institution. But business remains highly significant, and its various component parts are of political significance. Not all the interests of business and industry are allied; sometimes they are in serious conflict with one another, yet this does not negate their importance in affecting public policy.

The business firms of our nation range from tiny one-man proprietorships to enormous multibillion-dollar corporations. The one is operated by the small-business man, who has been romanticized in American folklore; the other is operated by the organization man, whose roots in American traditions are far more shallow, and who is hence more often the subject of skepticism, criticism, and even ridicule. The two have vastly different political outlooks, as will be seen in Chapter 6.

Small Business. The small-business man operates on the outer margin of our economic system. There are well over 4 million business units in the United States. The vast bulk of them are organized as individual proprietorships, partnerships, or small corporations. They are intensely competitive, facing not only one another, but big business as well. (Thus the corner grocer must try to stay in business against the combined efforts of the grocer on the next corner and of the far more efficient chain supermarket.) Some small-business men are very successful, earning a fairly high income. Some businesses remain in the same family for many generations. But as one authority on the American economy has put it, "most do not earn for their owners much more than they could get with less effort and risk by working for somebody else."[26]

The average life expectancy of a business is only six years. Under the circumstances, the small-business man finds economic life a matter of deadly earnest. With no guaranteed weekly income, he is not likely to demonstrate the sense of humor of one of his kind a few years ago when, satirizing television advertising, he put a sign in his show window saying, "We feature Brand X."

The number of new businesses in America continues to grow, although the small-business sector of the economy each year enjoys a less-than-proportionate share in the total increase of the nation's wealth. Faced with keen competition, the increasing power of big business, increasing government regulation (much of it adding to his costs by establishing minimum wages, retirement plans, and workman's compensation insurance, for example), the small-business man feels afraid, beset, and frustrated.

The Main Street shopkeeper has remained ideologically close to the traditional American views of hard work and long hours, self-reliance, and thrift; the economic system of the small-town merchant in particular demands this kind of devotion for success. His way of earning a living is vastly different from that of the factory worker or the white-collar organization man, who handles only some highly specialized part of the work of a large corporation. His income is not predictable, and he cannot assume

[26] Paul A. Samuelson, *Economics,* 6th ed., McGraw-Hill Book Company, New York, 1964, p. 78. Samuelson's chap. 5 summarizes business organization in America.

that it will tend to rise at no less than the rate of monetary inflation, as the factory worker and the organization man can. But the self-employed businessman is becoming increasingly uncommon in our society. Department stores, supermarkets, branch-banking systems, motel chains, and other forms of centralized service activities are displacing him. He can still do some things on a par with or better than big business—shoe repair or automobile maintenance, for instance. Yet even in repair services—his traditional stronghold—he is losing out to shops maintained by department stores and large agencies that perform these functions as a convenience to customers.

The Giants and Near-giants. The large corporations are far fewer in number than proprietorships, but they possess almost every competitive advantage over small business. They have superior brainpower, superior administrative talent, superior information-gathering arrangements, superior levels of training among their decision makers, better business sense, better-educated bureaucrats, and leaders with a better understanding of the forces that are affecting their businesses, the nation, and themselves personally. They, of course, also possess vastly superior resources for financing their operations and for competing with the small-business man. We cannot examine the reasons for this competitive advantage here; they are many and seem to be becoming more persuasive each year.

A few hundred huge corporations "occupy a strategically dominant position" in the modern American economy.[27] These huge organizations own 40 per cent of the total assets of all nonfinancial corporations, over one-third of all banking assets, and 85 per cent of all life insurance assets. The largest 200 corporations own between 20 and 25 per cent of the income-producing national wealth, and they employ one out of every eight workers in the nation. They are continuing to grow, but despite popular belief, the very largest corporations have stopped swallowing up portions of the economy: They actually control somewhat less of the economy than they did half a century ago. The fastest rate of growth in the last two generations has been among the middle-sized corporations, which occupy an important economic area between small business and the 200 giants.

The industries making aluminum, telephone equipment, electric light bulbs and electrical equipment, breakfast foods, cigarettes, automobiles, and steel all have over one-half of their production controlled by a handful of companies—less than ten in each case. Such huge companies have great political as well as economic power—so much so that they may sometimes risk defiance of the law (though the executives who make their decisions doubtless consider themselves law-abiding citizens, if not civic leaders). In 1961, a number of high officers from the electrical-appliance industry were convicted and jailed for violation of the Federal antitrust laws. They

[27] *Ibid.*, pp. 77, 89–92.

Figure 2-8

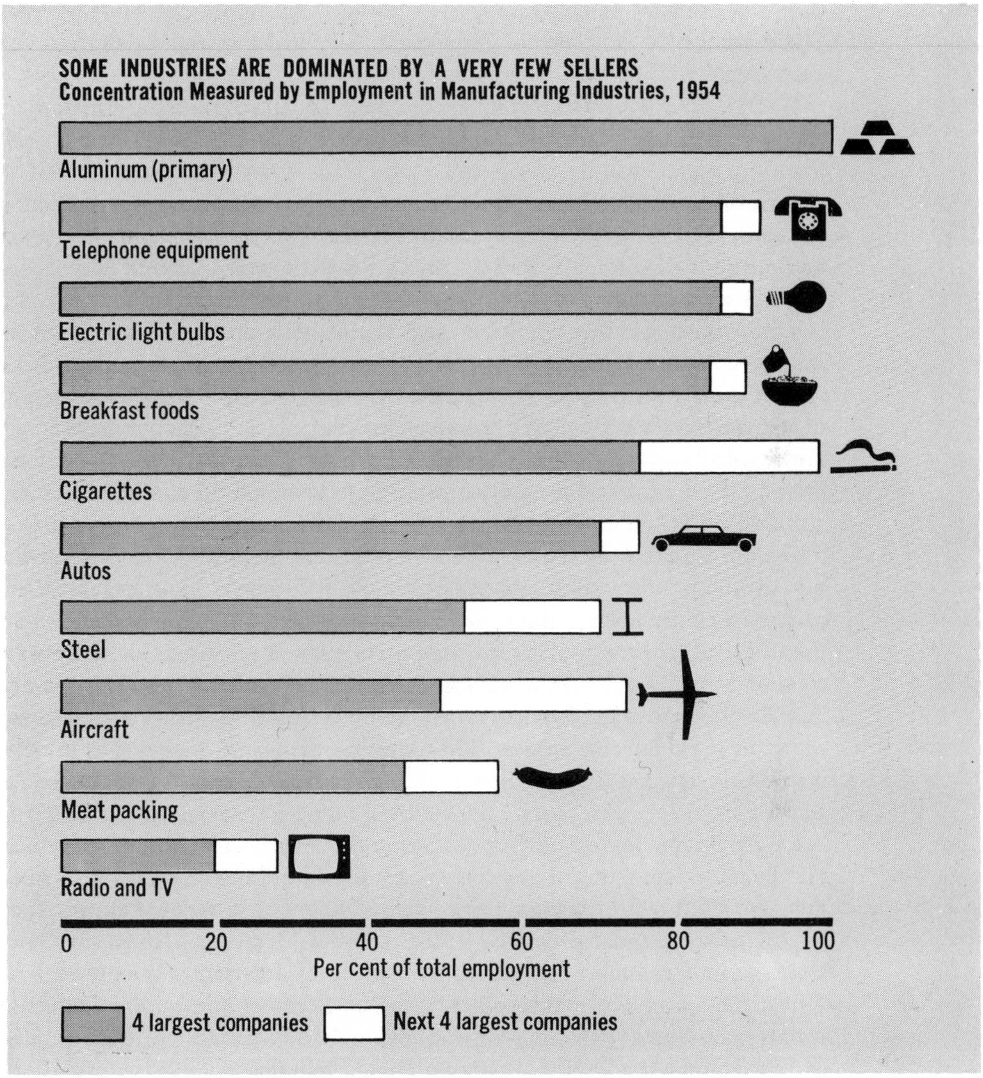

SOME INDUSTRIES ARE DOMINATED BY A VERY FEW SELLERS
Concentration Measured by Employment in Manufacturing Industries, 1954

In the aluminum, automobile, steel, and many other industries, a few firms get most of the business. This is in contrast to the notion of perfect competition among innumerable small sellers (e.g., farmers), each too small to affect the market price. But some qualified economists think concentration was probably even greater in 1900. (Federal Trade Commission.)

were found guilty of conspiring to fix bidding on contracts for the sale of the equipment that they manufactured; they had even rigged bids for contracts with the Federal government itself. Testimony at the Senate hearings seemed to indicate that those responsible regarded the Federal law as more of a nuisance to be circumvented than a statement of public policy or of social morality.

How bad are the "bad guys"? Two points should be made about the giant corporations.

1. They have probably done more to raise the American standard of living than to depress it (as the critics of monopoly, using classic economic theory, argued would be the case). In some instances, such as that of automobile manufacturing, the product could probably not have become the property of the common man without the existence of the giant corporation. (In some other countries, the companies would have been made government corporations, of course.)

The farmer and the small-business men—both of whom encounter intensely competitive conditions—have always been hostile to big business, and in American folklore the giants are regarded as evil. The opponents of big business also fear big government, but at times in our history—if not at all times—they have feared big business more, and hence they have pressured government to control monopolistic trends. Although the giant corporation is not as much of a villain as it once was (organized labor, for example, is not as hostile to the corporation as one might expect—the big company also generally pays the best wages), political pressure against it continues in subtle ways. Thus there are unending demands that the Federal government grant more Defense Department contracts to smaller companies, and the government tries to accede to these demands. But technological knowledge is available in the large corporations, and sometimes expediting a new technique for national defense is almost necessarily placed in the hands of, say, General Electric or General Motors.

2. All but a few of the large corporations and a great many of the middle-sized ones are characterized by a separation of ownership from management. While the number of shareholders is very large, most stock is still in the hands of relatively few people. Most Americans who hold stock cannot influence corporate policy. The American Telephone and Telegraph Company makes an advertising point of the large number of people who "own" the company—they totaled over 2.2 million in 1964, and the number had approximately doubled in a decade. Similar situations prevailed in other corporations. In the typical case of a large number of stockholders, however, the holdings were very unevenly divided. The great majority of stock is normally held by relatively few people. Obviously, when the "owners" come by battalion, they cannot also manage. Therefore, we have developed trained, professional bureaucracies that not only manage these companies, but, since successful outside challenges to their control are rare, serve as self-perpetuating leadership groups. Although in a giant corporation, 3 per cent of the stock is all that is typically held by the executives and directors,[28] these managers have become "the dominant members of our society. . . . it is from their ranks that are coming most of the first and second echelons of our leadership, and it is their values which will set the American temper."[29] They are called upon to assume Cabinet posts and other positions in the Federal government; they advise on governmental policy; they serve as lobbyists; they assume many of the responsibilities of action and leadership that other citizens expect of persons in their important positions; and in general, they are important in their influence upon the corporations to which they belong and upon government at all of its levels.

Government in the Economy: Shared Decision Making. The decision makers of government affect and delimit the decisions of the decision makers of private enterprise. And because congressmen and government bureaucrats thus "cramp their style," corporate bureaucrats try to influence governmental policy. They seek to have as much influence as possible over the agencies that control their businesses and to get persons who sympathize with them appointed to the various independent Federal regulatory commissions and administrative agencies and are often successful.

The pattern of governmental influence on business decision making has varied through time. The economist Paul Samuelson has summarized the development in this fashion:[30]

> Perhaps nineteenth-century America came as close as any economy ever has to that state of *laissez faire* that [Thomas] Carlyle called "anarchy plus the constable." The result was a century of rapid material progress and an environment of individual freedom. Also there resulted periodic business crises, wasteful exhaustion of irreplaceable natural resources, extremes of poverty and wealth, corruption of government by vested interest groups, and at times the supplanting of self-regulating competition by monopoly.
>
> Gradually, and in the face of continuing opposition, the methods of Alexander Hamilton began to be applied toward the objectives of Thomas Jefferson: the constitutional power of central and local government were interpreted broadly and were used to "secure the public interest" and to "police" the economic system. Utilities and railroads were brought under state regulation; after 1887, the federal ICC (Interstate Commerce Commission) was set up to regulate rail traffic across state boundaries. The Sherman Antitrust Act and other laws were invoked after 1890 against monopolistic combinations in "restraint of trade." Regulation of banking became thoroughgoing; after 1913, the federal reserve system was set up to serve as a central bank, aiding and controlling member commercial banks; and since 1933 most bank deposits have been insured by the Federal Deposit Insurance Corportion.
>
> Pure food and drug acts were passed following the revelations of the

[28] *Ibid.*, p. 91 and citations.

[29] William H. Whyte, Jr., *The Organization Man*, Anchor Books, Doubleday & Company, Inc., Garden City, N.Y., 1957, p. 3.

[30] Samuelson, *op. cit.*, pp. 146–147.

> "muckraking era" of the early 1900's. . . . The abuses of high finance, before and after 1929, gave rise to ever more stringent regulation of the financial markets by the SEC and other bodies.
>
> Humanitarian legislation to better factory conditions for children and women won at first only a grudging acceptance by the courts. But with the passage of time, the radical doctrines of one era became the accepted and even reactionary beliefs of a later era: state and federal legislation was expanded to include minimum-wage legislation, compulsory workmen's accident compensation insurance, compulsory unemployment insurance and old-age pensions, maximum-hour laws for children, women, and men, regulation of factory conditions of work, compulsory collective bargaining, fair labor relations acts, and so forth.

Big Labor as Countervailing Power. An open society, in which individuals are free to form voluntary associations of all kinds, provides conditions under which organized power is likely to be balanced against organized power. The existence of countervailing power helps to prevent any single group or interest from dominating our society.

With the coming of "big business" in the 1870s, it was thus probably only a matter of time before those who worked on an hourly basis for big business would form into groups to protect and further their interests. Working people were rather slow in doing this in America for a number of reasons (see Chapter 6), but for the last generation, much of the behavior of the business world has been modified by the desires of "big labor." The older skilled-trades unions, organized into the American Federation of Labor (AFL), had not been interested in unskilled workers for they saw in them no way to create unions involving a monopoly of labor. The AFL did not join together with any single political party, but sought to reward its friends and punish its enemies. It had no sweeping social programs, but sought to further the welfare of its members and to make it possible for them to live in emulation of the white-collar middle class. For the most part, it favored "business unionism"—the highest possible wages for the shortest possible hours with the best possible working conditions.

In 1935, the CIO was formed, with the objective of organizing the unskilled factory workers of the nation into a single union. Encouraged by a favorable national administration, by the decline in immigration and (temporarily) cityward migration, and by fresh memories of the Great Depression, the CIO was able to find the favorable environment for its goals that had earlier been missing in America. The union early showed itself, through its highly professional leaders, to be keenly interested in social problems, and it became a strong supporter of the ideology of the social service state.

After years of conflict and attempted compromise, the two great federations of national unions were merged as the AFL-CIO in 1955. A political arm, the Committee on Political Education (COPE), was established. The new organization, in general, began to follow the social action philosophy of the CIO. The unions grew to great size. In 1965, membership in all of them, including the independents, was about 18 million, but the ratio between union members and total number of hour-rated employees was no longer increasing.

With the coming of big labor, then, came such things as industry-wide bargaining, nationwide strikes (on occasion), and lobbying for legislation in the interests of the members of the working class. With the adoption of the National Labor Relations (Wagner) Act in 1935, big business and big labor opposed one another in a battle to dominate the labor-management-relations policies of what was increasingly another "big"—big government. That battle, which has been fought before all three branches of government, together with other interests of organized labor, will be noted in Chapter 8.

A Closing Note. It is possible to view politics from the perspective of national character, class, geography, or the economic system—all of these have been used by social scientists. Each one taken alone, however, offers only a gross measuring device by which to test political phenomena. All are too vague for precise measurement and offer even less in the way of analytical concepts than do the four I's—institutions, interests, ideas, and individuals—introduced in the previous chapter. A description of national character has only a restricted meaning when we consider the characteristics of, say, the Negro or Polish-American subculture. Class concepts do not allow for consideration of parallel Negro and white class systems or significant clashes of interests within a particular class. Regional geography bears a relationship to politics, as was demonstrated in a classic study by V. O. Key, Jr.,[31] but anyone who wishes to deal with New England, Eastern, Western, or Midwestern politics finds the task enormously difficult if he seeks to do more than simple description and wants to develop analytical concepts and use comparative techniques. Economic analysis does not explain as much as some theorists, such as Karl Marx or Charles A. Beard, hoped. Much political motivation seems to be related to psychological phenomena and to ideological commitments for which there is no direct economic explanation. Certainly we cannot talk simply of labor against business. There is a vast difference in attitude and interests of the Teamsters as compared with the United Steel Workers. The General Dynamics Corporation wants a missile contract from the government as badly as does the Boeing Corporation. The Hawaiian missionaries and their descendants, who came to control the economy of the islands, refused to permit the potentially profitable manufacture of rum from sugar cane because they believed the use of intoxicants to be wrong—ideology was more important than economics.

[31] V. O. Key, Jr., with Alexander Heard, *Southern Politics,* Alfred A. Knopf, Inc., New York, 1949.

The various factors discussed in this chapter are, however, important in setting the tone, style, and general limits within which American politics operates. They are significant variables in the political process. The fact that they do not—taken individually or even collectively—explain any more of the American political process is an indication of the enormous complexity of politics in a pluralistic democracy that is lacking in disciplined political parties and has a strong tradition of individualism.

SELECTED BIBLIOGRAPHY

The American life-style and character are the subject of countless books and articles. See especially those by historians Lerner [16] and Perkins [21]. Kluckhohn [14] and Mead [18] offer anthropological views. Hyman [13], a sociologist, sees American political behavior as a product of learning and socialization. Rosenburg, a psychologist, and White, a journalism professor, are concerned with our "mass culture" [25]. Americans are described from the perspective of foreign observers in a collection edited by Commager [4].

The characteristic lack of a well-articulated American ideology is described in Chapters 5 and 6. Nineteen men whose ideas have particularly influenced American thought have their say in Padover's collection [20].

A great deal has been written about conformity in America, Fromm [9] and Riesman [23, 24] have discussed conformity in relation to the responsibilities demanded by democracy. The tendency of mass society to produce anxieties and inhibit self-expression is the subject of Stein and others [29]. Whyte [31] examines the large corporation and the executive personality it produces.

The tradition of egalitarianism is one of long standing in America [2], as is the idea of the individual as a reasoning person who makes decisions based on facts. But social psychologists tell us that the individual psyche is more complex than that [15], and we know that many citizens are hypnotized by the dramatic leader using nonrational appeals [8, 22].

Ecological trends are discussed in a great many population surveys and analyses. The Bureau of the Census publishes analyses, in addition to its regular reports [30]. The most significant trend in population change is in the development of metropolitan areas. This will have important implications for future Federal government policy [5, 34].

Every introductory textbook in sociology discusses social classes. In this book, we have relied especially on the ideas of Lipset [17] and Centers [3]. Eulau [7] and Lipset [17] have discussed the relationship of class to voting; Hutchinson to immigration patterns [12], and Murphy and Morris to employment patterns and party affiliation [19].

The interaction between politics and economics is developed by Samuelson [27], who also provides ample citations to other works. A classic study by Rostow [26], shows how the United States developed into a great industrial nation and indicates its standing, relative to other nations. The economic areas of the United States—which are also to a degree politically differing areas—are described by Bogue and Beale [1]. The most enigmatic and most rapidly developing area, the South, gets attention from Dunn [6].

For further material on the subject matter of this chapter, see the bibliographies of introductory textbooks in cultural anthropology, sociology, social psychology, and economics.

1. Bogue, Donald J., and Calvin L. Beale: *Economic Areas of the United States,* The Free Press of Glencoe, New York, 1961.
2. Brown, Robert E., *Middle-class Democracy and the Revolution in Massachusetts,* Cornell University Press, Ithaca, N.Y., 1955.
3. Centers, Richard: *The Psychology of Social Classes: A Study of Class Consciousness,* Princeton University Press, Princeton, N.J., 1949.
4. Commager, Henry Steele (ed.): *America in Perspective,* Random House, Inc., New York, 1947. (Also available in Mentor Books paperback.)
5. Connery, Robert H., and Richard H. Leach: *The Federal Government and Metropolitan Areas,* Harvard University Press, Cambridge, Mass., 1960.
6. Dunn, Edgar S., Jr.: *Recent Southern Economic Development, as Revealed by the Changing Structure of Employment,* University of Florida Press, Gainesville, Fla., 1962.
7. Eulau, Heinz: *Class and Party in the Eisenhower Years,* The Free Press of Glencoe, New York, 1962.
8. Friedrich, Carl J.: "Political Leadership and the Problem of Charismatic Power," *Journal of Politics,* 23:3–24, February, 1961.
9. Fromm, Erich: *Escape from Freedom,* Holt, Rinehart and Winston, Inc., New York, 1941.
10. Fuchs, Lawrence H.: *The Political Behavior of American Jews,* The Free Press of Glencoe, New York, 1956.
11. Handlin, Oscar (ed.): *American Principles and Issues: The National Purpose,* Holt, Rinehart and Winston, Inc., New York, 1961.
12. Hutchinson, E. P.: *Immigrants and Their Children, 1850–1950,* John Wiley & Sons, Inc., New York, 1956.
13. Hyman, Herbert: *Political Socialization,* The Free Press of Glencoe, New York, 1959.
14. Kluckhohn, Clyde: *Mirror for Man: The Relation of Anthropology to Modern Life,* McGraw-Hill Book Company, New York, 1949.
15. Krech, David, and others: *Individual in Society,* McGraw-Hill Book Company, New York, 1962.
16. Lerner, Max: *America as a Civilization,* Simon and Schuster, Inc., New York, 1957.
17. Lipset, Seymour Martin: *Political Man,* Doubleday & Company, Inc., Garden City, N.Y., 1960.
18. Mead, Margaret, *And Keep Your Powder Dry: An Anthropologist Looks at America,* William Morrow and Company, Inc., New York, 1942.
19. Murphy, Raymond J., and Richard T. Morris: "Occupational Situs, Subjective Class Identification, and Political Affiliation," *American Sociological Review,* 26:383–391, June, 1961.
20. Padover, Saul K.: *The Genius of America,* McGraw-Hill Book Company, New York, 1960.
21. Perkins, Dexter: *The American Way,* Cornell University Press, Ithaca, N.Y., 1957.
22. Polsby, Nelson W.: "Towards an Explanation of McCarthyism," *Political Studies,* 8:250–271, October, 1960.
23. Riesman, David: *Faces in the Crowd,* Yale University Press, New Haven, Conn., 1952.
24. Riesman, David: *The Lonely Crowd,* Yale University Press, New Haven, Conn., 1950.
25. Rosenburg, Bernard, and David M. White (eds.): *Mass Culture,* The Free Press of Glencoe, New York, 1957.
26. Rostow, Walt W.: *The Stages of Economic Growth,* Cambridge University Press, New York, 1960.

27. Samuelson, Paul A.: *Economics,* 6th ed., McGraw-Hill Book Company, New York, 1964.
28. Sklare, Marshall (ed.): *The Jews: Social Patterns of an American Group,* The Free Press of Glencoe, New York, 1958.
29. Stein, Maurice, and others (ed.): *Identity and Anxiety,* The Free Press of Glencoe, New York, 1960.
30. U.S. Bureau of the Census: *Census of Population* and special reports. (Recurring publications.)
31. Whyte, William H., Jr.: *The Organization Man,* Anchor Books, Doubleday & Company, Inc., Garden City, N.Y., 1957.
32. Wilson, James Q.: *Negro Politics,* The Free Press of Glencoe, New York, 1960.
33. Wood, Margaret Mary: *Paths of Loneliness: The Individual Isolated in Modern Society,* Columbia University Press, New York, 1953.
34. Wood, Robert E.: *1400 Governments,* Harvard University Press, Cambridge, Mass., 1961.
35. Wriston, Henry M. (ed.): *Goals for Americans: The Report of the President's Commission on National Goals,* Prentice-Hall, Inc., Englewood Cliffs, N.J., 1961.

CHAPTER 3

THE AMERICAN IDEA OF DEMOCRACY

Democracy is a word variously used. It is the kind of word that has, as Thorstein Veblen would have said, an "honorific connotation." As a result, to switch to Jimmy Durante, "Everyone wants to get into the act." The word is commonly used for propaganda purposes by those who lift the pen or sit down at the typewriter on behalf of a cause. Only the Fascists and quasi fascists hold democracy openly in contempt. Even the Communists—using it in a very special way, to be sure—have made extensive use of the term since the mid-1920s.[1] Many Communist nations of today include the word in their official names.

DEMOCRACY IN HISTORICAL PHILOSOPHY AND POPULAR IMAGE

Democracy has not always been loved. The Greek philosophers generally took a dim view of democracy (government by the people). Aristotle viewed it as a degenerate form of government. To him, it represented rabble-rousing, government by the emotions, the exploitation of the middle classes by the propertyless. The term was not popular in the United States at the time of the War for Independence. Even Thomas Jefferson avoided it. He preferred to speak of "our experiment," or to say that we lived under a republic. He was correct in this usage in that the United States has a government of what he called a "second grade of purity." That is, the people do not rule directly, but choose those who do.

The accepted term for a representative democracy is "republic." Jefferson's party was known as the Republican party. Later, in the 1820s, the rather daring term "Democratic-Republican" was advanced, but it was not until the full tide of Jacksonianism in the 1830s that "democracy" became a respectable word. Today, only the most conservative politicians in America hesitate to use it and continue to prefer "republic." Technically, of course, ours is a republic and not a democracy, but the cult of the average man

[1] Ithiel de Sola Pool, *Symbols of Democracy,* Stanford University Press, Stanford, Calif., 1952.

Figure 3-1

A Fable: What If Complete Candor Characterized Politics?

the

Once, a little while from now, there was a presidential election. First one party held its convention -

where everyone balled around, made speeches, picked a candidate, got drunk, and went home -

Then the other party held **its** convention where everyone balled around, made speeches -

By the second week in October the convention was still convening. Television had quit its coverage. The first party's nominee was already practicing to say "MY FELLOW AMERICANS!"

Then, toward the end of the month, the convention announced -

WE THE DELEGATES HAVE DECIDED THAT CONSIDERING THE INCREASED IMPORTANCE OF THE PRESIDENCY IN THIS TROUBLED TIME, WE DON'T HAVE ANYBODY WHO'S QUALIFIED.

And everyone packed up and went home.

The first party got very worried. Scathing attacks were made on it for its pomposity in naming a candidate

"IF THE ELECTION WERE HELD TOMORROW," said the pollsters, "THE PARTY WITHOUT A CANDIDATE WOULD WIN IN A LANDSLIDE."

The first party did the only thing possible under the circumstances. Its candidate resigned.

The publicity machines of both parties worked furiously to establish their own inadequacy. Humility trains were sent whistle-stopping across the land. Local candidates resigned by the hundreds. Confessions of guilt virtually **overwhelmed** the air waves.

Election day dawned.

Nobody came to the polls.

"WHAT DO **I** KNOW ABOUT PICKING A PRESIDENT?" asked the guilt-oriented American public.

And they all stayed home.

VOTER

BY JULES FEIFFER

but could **not** pick a candidate.

The convention dragged on for weeks - into September - into October -

"WHAT A MOCKERY OF THE DEMOCRATIC PROCESS," said the first party's **nominee**.

"WHAT A NATIONAL DISGRACE," said the nation's press.

"WHAT A SHOO-IN," said politicians in the know.

The country's reaction was instantaneous. Millions of congratulatory wires flooded in.

"WHAT ADMIRABLE HONESTY," wired Mr. P.R. of Port Jervis.

"ITS ABOUT TIME SOMEBODY AROUND HERE ADMITTED HE WAS INCAPABLE," wired Mrs. G.L. of Baton Rouge.

Editorials across the land praised the forthrightness of at least **one** of the major parties.

"IS AMERICA AT LAST ENTERING ITS MATURITY?" queried Walter Lippmann. Max Lerner explained the whole thing in terms of sex and the rejection of the father figure.

Then in a moving emotional bid, he went on nationwide TV and confessed to a life of intellectual sham and dishonesty -

"WHAT COMPELLING CANDOR," cried the press. Instantly public opinion swung back in his party's favor.

immediately the original candidateless party demanded equal time to reveal **its** intellectual dishonesties. They were enormous!

Torn between rival outbreaks of morality the electorate fell into confusion

Political scientists were growing alarmed. "A TWO-PARTY SYSTEM CAN NOT FUNCTION IN AN ATMOSPHERE OF ULTIMATE MORALITY," they warned.

But nevertheless morality **was** the issue! Each party battling down to the wire, attempting to prove its good faith by denying it had any.

On election eve both parties went on TV announcing that though there weren't any candidates it was every American's duty to vote.

Then at two minutes to seven, just before the polls closed, a Miss Gladys Flamm -

(just turned 35) of Mineola, Long Island, who never particularly kept up with things, entered the polling booth.

And seeing there were no names printed anywhere -

she entered her **own** on the first line.

By permission of Jules Feiffer.

has made the term so firmly accepted that we will use it in this book in referring to the American form of government.

Classical Theory and Its Faults. The philosophers who first formulated the ideas upon which democratic writings were later based lived in the seventeenth and eighteenth centuries. There is no need to develop their detailed arguments here, but they have been summarized in this fashion:[2] Democracy "is that institutional arrangement for arriving at political decisions which realizes the common good by making the people itself decide issues through the election of individuals who are to assemble in order to carry out its will."

This description of democracy has been and still is widely accepted in America. It is based on the assumption that man is an informed political participant. It accords with the deeply held beliefs of our people. Yet as we shall see, it is not an operational description. That is, it does not serve to describe the actual phenomena that we can—and every day do—observe in the real political world. There are many reasons why the informed- or rational-man theory is not a satisfactory explanation of actual political behavior.

In the first place, it assumes that people are quite fully informed concerning political events and issues. In fact, however, the attentive public is small. The rational-man theory implicitly assumes that information is free. But the costs of securing information may be high, particularly in the case of a low-status person for whom education is an economic impossibility. Even a specialist in political science is not likely to know the attitudes toward organized crime of candidates for county prosecutor prior to election day—yet this public officer makes important policy decisions that potentially affect every citizen.

Second, the theory assumes that citizens make their choices on the basis of rational conclusions drawn from the evidence. But people often do not make use even of information that is easily available. As we shall see in Chapter 6, people conceive of political controversy on three levels: the philosophical, the ideological, and the symbolic. The last of these, which is the furthest removed from the rational, is the most, rather than the least, common.

Third, the classic theory assumes a "common good" or, as it is often expressed, a "public interest" that exists separately from individual or group interests and that can somehow be ascertained by decision makers. As we shall see in Chapter 8, the existence of agreement on such an

[2] Joseph A. Schumpeter, *Capitalism, Socialism, and Democracy,* 2d ed., Harper & Row, Publishers, New York, 1947, p. 250. The major philosophers concerned were John Locke, Charles de Montesquieu, and Jean Jacques Rousseau. The ideas of these men and others are presented in George H. Sabine, *History of Political Theory,* rev. ed., Holt, Rinehart and Winston, Inc., New York, 1950.

interest or good is the exception (mostly in relation to foreign affairs) rather than the rule.

Nineteenth Century Developments of Classical Theory. The ideas of the Glorious Revolution in seventeenth-century England and the eighteenth-century French and American revolutions were modified somewhat in the nineteenth century, but the basic assumptions remained the same. Thomas Jefferson, who bridged both eighteenth and nineteenth centuries, held to the conventional liberal views of his day. After Shays' Rebellion in Massachusetts (1786), which had unnerved some conservatives, Jefferson commented:[3]

> God forbid we should ever be twenty years without such a rebellion. The people cannot be all, and always, well informed. The part which is wrong will be discontented, in proportion to the importance of the facts they misconceive. If they remain quiet under such misconceptions, it is a lethargy, a forerunner of death to the public liberty. . . . The remedy is to set them right as to facts, pardon and pacify them.

The idea of this early American philosopher, then, was that people were not always informed, but they were educable. Even if lacking in the facts, they should be permitted the right to protest. The assumption was that there was a correct public policy and that citizens could come to understand it if they were properly informed.

At about the time of Jefferson and shortly after him, some other philosophers—Jeremy Bentham and John Stuart Mill, in particular—discussed democracy as the government offering the "greatest good for the greatest number." This was a basic tenent of the utilitarian school of thought which believed that man's decisions were essentially rational and that they were based on a "calculus of pleasures and pains." The utilitarians seemed to believe in politics, as Adam Smith had believed in economics, that the sum total of individual wills added up to some kind of balance that was the public interest—the greatest good for the greatest number. The notion was that millions of individuals pursuing their individual goals, using government as one of the means toward these goals, would end up with something that represented the best interests of all.

The arguments for democracy were based on *assumptions*. In most cases, the writers were either discussing a system of government that had existed for such a short time that they could have had no opportunity to make empirical observations, or they were engaged in building philosophical systems based on logical derivations rather than systematic observations of what actually happened under given conditions.

A Definition of Democracy Today. For our purposes, then, we will treat the concepts of democracy mentioned above as part of the philosophical

[3] In a letter to William S. Smith (1787).

rationale that helps to hold our people together. That rationale becomes the background for a variety of ideological beliefs that have been held through the ages. Whether or not man's political actions are derived from rational thought, and whether or not there is a public interest represented in one best public policy that would be the correct one (if only the legislators and congressmen could find or follow it), the American people act *as if* both propositions were true. So the beliefs become a part of the political process and assume a certain reality that cannot simply be dismissed as not fitting the actual facts.

How can we describe democracy *as it actually works?* The task is not an easy one, and empirical studies are still far from complete enough for us to proceed without a caution to the effect that future findings may require some modification of what follows. But let us start with a definition by a contemporary political sociologist:[4]

> Democracy in a complex society may be defined as a political system which supplies regular constitutional opportunities for changing the governing officials, and a social mechanism which permits the largest possible part of the population to influence major decisions by choosing among contenders for political office.

Another social scientist, seeking a definition that fitted his observations of the process, defined democracy as "that institutional arrangement for arriving at political decisions in which individuals acquire the power to decide by means of a competitive struggle for the people's vote."[5]

Neither of these seems adequate. Neither appears to recognize the fact that Americans, and to some extent members of other democracies, do not choose policies when they elect public officials; that they influence such policies principally through interest-group action rather than through voting; and that they may prefer to have many rules for social control made by self-perpetuating, largely self-governing voluntary groups,* not by formal government.

***VOLUNTARY GROUPS are formed without government coercion and gain their membership from persons who join of their own volition.**

Without being sure that we can be more successful, let us try a definition that may be more complete and may serve as the definition for this text. *Democracy in a complex society is a political system that affords frequent opportunities for changing the governing officials and a social mechanism that permits nearly all of the adult population to influence major public-*

[4] Seymour Martin Lipset, *Political Man,* Doubleday & Company, Inc., Garden City, N.Y., 1960, p. 45.

[5] Schumpeter, *op. cit.,* p. 269.

policy decisions by choosing from among genuine competitors for public office and through other procedures viewed by most citizens as legitimate. Obviously, many of the expressions used in this definition require development. What is meant by "adult population"? Who are the "governing officials"? Does the definition exclude the use, for example, of a permanent civil service?

We have noted the inability of Americans to agree on goals except in terms of glittering generalities (see Chapter 2). Our definition of democratic government reflects this trait. American consensus is on procedures—a faith that democratic procedures will, most of the time, result in policy that approximately satisfies the wants and desires of a substantial number of citizens. A similar faith holds that judicial procedures will attain that indefinable quality we call "justice," or that scientific procedures will aid in the discovery of "truth." The democracy we have been discussing has been called "liberal democracy" by many writers.

Totalitarian democracy: End over means. A radically different method for achieving ideal ends dates back to Plato's search for civic justice in *The Republic*. His concepts were restated in terms of the community interest or general will by the French philosopher Jean Jacques Rousseau, who wrote at the time of the American Revolution. Such systems begin by defining a goal that is often seen in idealistic terms and attempt to mold society into a pattern designed to lead to that goal.

Communists claim they have a plan that will benefit all of humanity and make the world bloom with roses and turnips by bringing about a society that is dominated by the working class, thus ending the exploitation of this group by the owners of the means of production. This goal of a good life for the proletariat is the basis for Communist claims to the word "democracy" and the term "people's democracies."

Totalitarian democracies, as distinguished from liberal democracies, are more interested in the ends (goals) than in the means (procedures by which rules are made). In practice, they tend to become tyrannical—given habit and human frailty, utopia can be established only by force. Peaceful change in liberal democracies is a gradual process that tends to be pragmatic rather than logically consistent, whereas the quick transformation to a "heaven on earth" requires a concentration camp for the misfits. As a society becomes totalitarian, information channels, with their feedbacks from the citizens, dry up. Even a government genuinely seeking humanitarian goals loses contact with reality in trying to learn where the shoe pinches. Without self-correcting democratic mechanisms, leaders may make serious errors. And, as Madison suggested, all men are prone to folly or worse. In Lord Acton's famous and often-quoted phrase, based on his observation that Nero gave no sign of aberration prior to becoming Roman Emperor; "All power tends to corrupt, absolute power corrupts absolutely." The memoirs of ex-Communists liberally document the process by which the quest for the ideal decays.

Totalitarian forms of "democracy" have not been chosen by Communist nations alone. In underdeveloped countries some of the new nations have also adopted this form of government. Most advocates of liberal democracy do not accept these forms as democratic.

Questioning Some Assumptions. Can democracy be discussed in polite society? Before developing the assumptions upon which our democracy operates, we must mention one especially important and deeply embedded American attitude: that the unarticulated assumptions upon which some fundamental institution of our society is based should not be openly questioned. The culture seems to tell us that it is best not to look behind the façade. Many Americans still think it is in doubtful taste, if indeed not downright subversive, to suggest that people do not always make decisions on a rational basis or that democracy does not require the common man to hold rational and informed opinions. We may know secretly that it does not make much sense, in light of our actual observations, to say that democracy is based upon an informed public. But the folkways of American democracy discourage mention of these observations. Rejecting this cultural impediment, the authors of this book believe that empirical observation should be the basis for the study of political science.

The assumption that democracy cannot work unless it is based upon an informed electorate leads to two possible conclusions: first, that democracy cannot survive; or secondly, that democracy, in order to survive, must be based on something less than universal suffrage. Doubts about the former assumption are raised when we note that democracy, as it has been defined by changing cultures, has been in existence for about three centuries and still thrives. As to the second assumption, there is a flaw in all plans to devise a system of democracy based upon a restricted suffrage: There is no way to determine objectively criteria for a suffrage that is less than universal; therefore, we are not likely to gain consensus on where to draw the line between the qualified and the unqualified. Shall it be on the basis of education, race, religion, or property? Some intellectual critics are not content with a simple test of ability to read, but hold that prospective voters prove that they read beyond the comics and the pulp magazines. But this reasoning leads ultimately to the nondemocratic conclusion that no one should vote "save thee and me, and I am not sure about thee."

Is rationality necessary? We are then left with universal suffrage as a basis for democracy because of a failure to find a criterion for limited suffrage. This is not to be taken as an unhappy lesser of two evils. It is a mistake to think that a system permitting nearly all individuals to vote can be successful and justifiable *only* if each voter makes a rational choice. Democracy does not require so much. The voter is not asked to decide political issues in an American election; rather, he is asked to make a choice between candidates, each of whom desires to hold the reins of government. The voter's decision need not be based on a general consideration of policies; he needs only to decide whether he is satisfied with the *status quo* or wishes to register a protest. Indeed, he need not be even this purposive. Some voters opposed Thomas E. Dewey because he wore a mustache and John F. Kennedy because of his Harvard accent. Many citizens vote a straight party ticket and would not change, regardless of the candidate. A seemingly irrational system may serve rational ends by being responsive to the wants and concerns of a wide variety of citizens.

If a voter is not satisfied, he may have only the vaguest idea of what is wrong, why the cold war does not end, why he is ineligible for unemployment compensation, or why those in office are talking of a tax increase. But it is not necessary that he have more than the conviction that something is wrong. A man need not be a baker to know whether his bread is tasty, or a mechanic to know that is car does not start. And if the bakery or garage he is patronizing cannot improve its service, he will try another. So it is with democratic government. If the voter is relatively content, he will vote to continue the party, faction, or individual currently in office rather than take a chance on the opposition, which is likely to be an unknown quantity to him. If he is genuinely discontented or feels threatened somehow, he will vote for the opposition. In either case, the issues are usually framed and developed for him by leaders who are also likely to have great influence over his perception of how issues and policies will affect him personally.

If all that is expected of the voter is an indication of his contentment, or lack of it, only the broadest limitations on suffrage are necessary. Outside of denying the ballot to the dependent child and the legally insane, no restrictions would appear to be tenable. Of course, there must be some minimum age for eligibility. The prevailing age of twenty-one does not assure a man's rationality. It is a result of the medieval practice of settling upon multiples of magic numbers—in this case, seven—whenever possible. In lieu of this legerdemain, the criterion that is implicitly used today is this: An individual should be permitted to vote at approximately the age when he develops some concept of what *he believes* to be his own economic and social interests. Whether this age should be twenty-one or earlier, as it is in four states, cannot be determined by objective measurement. The evidence available would seem to indicate that the exact age settled upon is not too important, but it should be at approximately the time when young people leave the parental home and develop economic and social interests somewhat independent from those of their family.

Must empirical practice make neat theory? A politics based upon references to voter satisfaction may not fit an ideal model, but it works in practice. Inasmuch as the primary aim of all politicians is to hold office, those in power will seek to carry out a program aimed at keeping voters satisfied; those in opposition will appeal to the voters' dissatisfactions and promise to overcome them. The problem for the politician is that he can never perfectly calculate voter response. He cannot be sure of what his optimum strategy should be, and hence, he tends to promise more than may be necessary and may expend efforts in areas that have little payoff. But the end result is a governmental program that is constantly adjusting itself toward making the maximum contribution to the sense of well-being of most of the voters. The uncertainty of the politician is heightened, however, by the fact that small shifts within some constituencies may spell defeat or victory.

Self-interest and long-range national or social interests may not be identical, of course. In fact, the individual's short-range and long-range self-interests may be quite antithetical. To use a medical analogy, a compulsive eater may, in the short run, want little more than to eat his fill five times a day. In the long run, this preference may put him—despite a strong wish to the contrary—in his grave years earlier than would otherwise be the case. It is also likely that the voter will sometimes react violently to transitory emotion-laden matters, that he cannot always know his own interests in a given situation, and that he is subject to being made the prey of quacks who cynically exploit his gullibility and anxieties.

Undoubtedly, the voter makes frequent mistakes. But in the long run, who can know his state of satisfaction better than he himself? Reacting largely to habit and social pressure, he votes for what *he believes* will aid him and his interests. And he knows, at least vaguely, that his mistakes may be costly. That they may be fatal to his way of life is at least theoretically possible, but this danger must perhaps be written off as one of the calculated risks of democracy. Fatal errors, in fact, have been made by citizens and leaders under every type of government.

Democracy has failed to match the great expectations of the eighteenth-century philosophers who assumed that it would be operated by knowledgeable men. Yet as Winston Churchill has said, "Democracy is the worst form of government except for any other that has ever been tried."

CONDITIONS ESSENTIAL FOR DEMOCRACY

In order to have an effective mechanism for democracy, there are prerequisites in addition to universal suffrage.

Competition. A choice by the voter from among candidates who are genuinely competing for office is essential to democracy. This choice may take place in either a primary or general election, but choice must be available. It might be mentioned in passing that democracy of the modern kind (representative rather than direct) does not ask the people to rule themselves, but merely gives them the right to choose those who will rule. (The initiative and referendum at the state and local levels, and the New England town meetings are exceptions to the usual practice.)

Changes in power. There must be a regular system of elections, with limited terms for officials and a general understanding that those who win elections will, if found legally eligible, be allowed to assume office. This may seem obvious to Americans. It is unthinkable to us that on some January 20, the President should announce the suspension of the Constitution, call out the Armed Forces and direct them to occupy all government establishments, order the FBI to arrest all members of Congress, have the Secret Service shoot the "disloyal" President-elect as he drives up to the White House on his way to his inauguration, and declare himself President for life. Without considering it the least bit unusual, we expect one of the most powerful public officials in the world willingly and graciously to give up all of his authority and to step off the daily front page into relative obscurity. Yet, in many nations, no such expectation exists, and the supposedly outgoing Chief Executive pulls a *coup d'état* on the order of that just described. The point is that citizens must have a sense of the legitimacy of the rules, particularly of the rules that are most fundamental to a democratic system.

Freedom of expression. Freedom of expression must exist, for it is the only way by which those out of office or those in the minority on a political issue can seek to persuade others to join with them. The minority must be given the opportunity to become a majority. Persons who wish to hold public office must be given a chance to compete for it.

Protection of minorities. Minority rights must be protected in some fashion. (Because of the complexity of this particular problem, it will be discussed separately in Chapter 19.) Of course, there is no clear concept of majority and minority in our society. Almost every majority is a coalition of minorities (Chapter 10). And almost any segment of society, taken separately, constitutes a minority—businessmen, factory workers, Negroes, the wealthy, farmers, Catholics, Jehovah's Witnesses, for example. The interests of minorities that are not dominant in making policy must somehow be protected if the democratic system is to endure. There are a number of ways in which this may be done. In some countries, heavy emphasis is placed upon society's commitment to the principle of minority rights. It is also possible to leave the matter to the legislative body, trusting it to preserve the interests of minorities, since any majority in the legislative body may become a minority at the next election, and all parties contain minority groups. Some have argued that the minority must not have a veto power over majority will, for if it did, the minority would rule, and there would be no democracy.

Americans accept the theoretical principle of majority rule. The tendency is to say "Let the majority decide." But we always insist upon modifications of the rule in practice. For example, we allow the courts to review both legislation and administrative procedures in order to determine if civil rights—the rights of the individual as against society at large—have been violated. We have not encouraged the development of disciplined political parties, parties that run on stated platforms to which candidates are committed and to which parties are held after election by the majority. Instead, we encourage political activity by a wide range of persons who are committed to various ideologies within each party. We tend to allow public policy to be made through the interaction of interest groups, thus creating a pluralistic system of government in which it is most difficult even to ascertain the meaning of "majority" at any given moment on any given issue of public policy. Furthermore, Americans have long made much of the prerogatives of the courts to protect property rights, freedom of speech, and other civil rights, for example, regardless of what legislatures and voters may desire.

The philosophy of government presented by James Madison in *The Federalist* (1789) represented a major attempt to achieve a compromise between the powers of majorities and minorities, between the political equality of all adult citizens on one side and the desire to limit their sovereignty on the other. Out of the United States Constitution and the philosophy of Madison and others came a plan that placed heavy reliance upon judicial administration of constitutional restraints upon the people and their elected representatives.

The consciences and values of most citizens safeguard the rights of the minority and the individual and forestall tendencies that might otherwise lead to the degeneration of democracy into oligarchy or dictatorship. But the Madisonians struck a responsive chord in Americans when they refused to put complete faith in a process of social restraints and insisted upon adding external controls, such as staggered terms in office for public officials, the executive veto, and judicial review.

These constitutional restraints have become widely accepted in America. They are important social stabilizers, since all proposed changes in the basic rules of government—if revolution is not resorted to—must follow elaborate procedural processes that guard against impulsive actions. Under this system, the *status quo* is entrenched. It assumes the protective coloration of institutionalization—the Constitution—which possesses great prestige and to which every political leader must pay homage.

Some persons have incorrectly concluded that constitutional restraints are unimportant, that only social values inhibit behavior. Actually, constitutional provisions often force reconsideration of a decision upon a hasty legislative body or public. On the other hand, even a constitutional provision cannot long withstand the onslaughts of determined and widespread opposition among citizens. Judicial review has been criticized by reforming liberals (as when the United States Supreme Court, over a period of about two years, 1935–1937, rejected much New Deal legislation, and when Thomas Jefferson saw the Court as a conservative device to protect property rights as against human rights) and by those who would preserve the *status quo* (as when the Supreme Court ordered racial desegregation in the public schools, and when it handed down a series of decisions in favor of individuals who had run afoul of congressional investigating committees). On balance, the system has not held up serious demands for social change, except very temporarily. Yet the controversy remains and, in fact, the problem of the right of the majority to rule despite the desire of the minority for protection continues to be "a paradox as yet unresolved in our political philosophy or constitutional system."[6]

Commitment to principle. The culture of the nation must provide a shared commitment to a set of ideas supporting all of the above points. No government, democratic or otherwise, can survive the strains and stresses that are inevitably placed upon it unless the bulk of the people believe in its *right* to rule and in the rightness of the principal institutions of the state. The political process must have legitimacy, as Aristotle long ago pointed out. Legitimacy "involves the capacity of a system to engender and maintain the belief that the existing political institutions are the most appropriate for society."[7] If most Americans believed that the people cannot be trusted or that the President is a tool of the Communists or that the best form of government is an absolute monarchy, our system of government as we know it would collapse. On the other hand, given a set of procedures regarded as legitimate, social change can take place peaceably.

Social and Economic Democracy. So long as democracy is viewed as a political mechanism, as it is above, certain objective criteria may be used for measuring its existence. But in addition, there are characteristics that many Americans would view as basic to their concepts of democracy—or what democracy should be. These additions to the recipe can perhaps best be classified as characteristics of social and economic democracy; they are *subjective,* and their importance depends upon personal values rather than any objective measurements.

Many would argue that freedom of religion is necessary to the existence of true democracy. This freedom is, however, quite different from freedom of expression, which was listed above as absolutely essential to any democracy. Whether democracy and a state church are incompatible or not is basically a question of philosophy.

Social equality is likewise often seen as a necessary aspect of democracy. Man is widely regarded as a creature with special dignity, with the similarities between any two members of the species being greater than their differences. On the other hand, many Americans do not accept the notion of complete social equality of all individuals, and some strongly reject it.

The concept of economic democracy also varies considerably with individuals. Nearly all Americans agree that no person should be allowed to starve or freeze to death. Some would indeed hold that there should be a floor placed under the standard of living, protecting all against utter poverty. Some would argue for positive steps to prevent anyone from becoming "overly" rich. Old-time socialists would want the narrowest possible gap between the wealthiest and poorest. Extreme individualists,

[6] See Henry Steele Commager, *Majority Rule and Minority Rights,* Oxford University Press, Fair Lawn, N.J., 1943, which argues against judicial review.

[7] Lipset, *op. cit.,* p. 77.

on the other hand, believe that democracy requires that there be almost no governmental activity to inhibit the free operation of the system of private business. The hypothesis of a number of social scientists (but difficult to prove or disprove) is that political democracy cannot survive where there are great extremes of wealth and poverty. A related hypothesis holds that democracy requires the existence of a large and politically effective middle class for success. The dominant view in America relative to economic democracy, though vague, undoubtedly includes the general idea of the social service state, with government performing certain equalizing and protective functions.

THE STATE OF DEMOCRACY IN AMERICA

How democratic is American government? From one point of view, the United States can be defended as one of the world's oldest democracies, since it was the first nation to grant universal manhood suffrage. At least such an argument can be made, but to take this position, the disfranchisement of the Negro must be explained away. It can also be argued that America is not yet a democracy for a variety of reasons: Negro voting is still overtly and covertly discouraged in some parts of the nation; an actual choice at the polls between genuinely competing candidates does not exist in every election; the minority rights to which we verbally pay allegiance are not always safeguarded; and the pattern of control over the mass mediums of communication inhibits freedom of expression, as do occasional Red scares, such as those of 1920–1921 and 1950–1953. Furthermore, not all Americans are fully committed to democracy. A great many seem to feel that, under certain circumstances, nondemocratic methods of procedure may properly be followed by government. Thus some individuals would favor the maintenance of educational segregation by force and in defiance of the courts, if necessary. During the post-World War II Red scare, some seemed to feel that due process of law need not be applied when persons were suspected of cooperating with Communists; and probably many feel that if normal judicial procedures cannot imprison professional criminals of the organized underworld, harsher methods should be used.

One study concluded that due processes of law—the elements of a fair trial—were seen by the American common man as *"primarily for people accused of crimes against property; not for those accused of violence, sexual crimes, or disloyalty."*[8] Another found a considerable amount of antidemocratic feeling among urban Americans, with authoritarian attitudes more widespread among working-class than middle-class persons.[9] Still another study reported "a disturbing amount of undemocratic spirit

[8] Robert E. Lane, *Political Ideology: Why the Common Man Believes What He Does,* The Free Press of Glencoe, New York, 1962, p. 194. Italics in original. By permission.

[9] W. J. MacKinnon and Richard Centers, "Authoritarianism and Urban Stratification," *American Journal of Sociology,* 61:610–620, May, 1956.

and authoritarian-type thinking" among members of the United Automobile Workers (UAW), especially among the lesser educated and workers past forty. (These same persons were found to have strong feelings of political futility.) It was found that 45 per cent of white UAW members had reservations about residential and social equality for Negroes, and 5 per cent opposed equal opportunities for employment.[10] Yet even when Americans are not fully committed to equality and tolerance, they feel guilty about the conflict between their personal values and the social ideal.[11]

As to contemporary political awareness and activity, "the more strongly a person feels a sense of obligation to discharge his civic duties, the more likely he is to be politically active";[12] and "citizens who feel that public

[10] Arthur Kornhauser and others, *When Labor Votes,* University Books, Inc., New York, 1956, p. 199. The results of a great many public opinion polls, some used in this chapter, may be found in Hadley Cantril (ed.), *Public Opinion: 1935–1946,* Princeton University Press, Princeton, N.J., 1951.

[11] Gunnar Myrdal, *An American Dilemma,* Harper & Row, Publishers, New York, 1944.

[12] Angus Campbell and others, *The Voter Decides,* Harper & Row, Publishers, New York, 1954, appendix B.

Figure 3-2

The Typical Citizen Is Sometimes More Interested in Personal Advantage than in Democratic Principles

"It isn't the lack of representation that upsets me—it's the taxation."

By permission of Burr Shafer.

officials are responsive and responsible to the electorate, who think individual political activity is worthwhile and capable of influencing public policy," and who think they can reach governmental decision makers by means in addition to the ballot box are also more likely to be politically active than citizens who feel overwhelmed or confused by the process.[13] It is significant that persons who are identified as community and political leaders have strong commitments to democracy and a clear understanding of its requirements.[14]

Popular Belief in Democracy. Does the typical citizen respect the essential ingredients of democracy? Does he have an idealized image of democracy as being based on the informed citizen, or does his concept of how democracy works coincide reasonably well with empirical findings? The evidence is, at present, conflicting.

Herbert McClosky, comparing the reactions of 300 delegates to the 1960 national conventions with those of 1,500 typical voters selected at random, found that 60 per cent of the latter had doubts about the integrity of elected officeholders; they believed that government was run from below their level of visibility by "people who do not even get known to the voters," and that issues are "beyond the understanding of most voters." A majority of them would not give the ballot to people who were unable to vote "intelligently," and they favored suppression of books with subversive viewpoints.[15] They would deny free speech to anyone who did not know "what he's talking about," and were pessimistic concerning the future of freedom. In contrast, the political elite—the convention-delegate sample—was more tolerant of freedom of expression (fewer than 20 per cent favored suppression). More than two-thirds of the respondents also believed that officeholders were honest. This study concluded that the American political system does not face serious internal danger because the elite members, rather than the followers, truly believe in democracy, and, because they make most of the important decisions, the system will not be likely to collapse.

In contrast to some of the above findings, a depth study by Robert E. Lane of fifteen white Eastern urban voters—ten of them in blue-collar occupations—found that all but three did have a general basic knowledge of what it takes for democracy to succeed. Some of the major findings of this study included the following:[16]

1. The interviewees accepted "with equanimity the confusion and dis-

[13] *Ibid.,* appendix A.

[14] Herbert McClosky, "Consensus and Ideology in American Politics," *American Political Science Review,* 58:361–382, June, 1964.

[15] Herbert McClosky and others, "Issue Conflict and Consensus among Party Leaders and Followers," *American Political Science Review,* 54:406–427, June, 1960.

[16] Lane, *op. cit.,* chap. 5. The small sample was chosen to permit the depth-interview technique of psychiatry; it is not large enough to have statistical validity for the general population. See pp. 84–85, 86, 83.

orderly processes of democracy (with reservations on 'bickering' in the Administration) in an age when democracy is challenged to be 'efficient.' "

2. "They know that ignorant and careless men, by voting, are helping to direct their own destinies; they acknowledge and accept the confusions and delays of parliamentary procedure; they are concerned over the need for swift, centralized power in emergencies, but they would want such power protected from abuse; they are not cynical about the uses of democratic procedures in their own local organizations; they believe democracy has a future on this continent and perhaps more broadly around the world."

3. Freedom, however, had a limited meaning for the common man, as was also indicated in the McClosky study. Lane found that democracy is regarded as "the right of the majority to do what is conventionally approved." In general, the interviewees believed in conformity to dominant norms, and their weakest commitment to democracy related to their views on freedom of expression. The notion that democracy requires an open society in which nonorthodox views may be expressed without penalty was not accepted. To them, "democracy as a popular concept centers in the freedom of the nondeviant individual to do what the majority thinks is right."

In sum, we can probably say that, despite some dark spots and blind spots, America has moved a long way toward democracy as defined in this chapter and that the trend continues in the direction supporting it.

SOME BASIC QUESTIONS

Is Democracy the Best Form of Government? This question has been debated since the days of the Greeks. It has been considered in fascist countries, where the answer for those who wanted to continue living in them was "No." It is debated in Communist countries, where the answer is "Yes"—if democracy is defined in terms of goals rather than procedures. It is debated in countries such as France, which has long had large groups of Fascists, Communists, and monarchists in addition to those supporting liberal democracy. And although Americans, along with the British and most of the people in the British Commonwealth countries, are among the most strongly committed supporters of democracy, the question is occasionally debated here. Some (a minority) of our intellectuals argue that "the masses are asses" and should not be permitted to choose the rulers. Others fear that democracy is too clumsy, too inflexible to meet the hard challenge of the highly flexible leaders of communism. The news analyst Walter Lippmann has argued that in foreign policy in particular, American leaders have too frequently responded to public pressures and momentary expediency, thus making more difficult the battle against communism. Issues of great importance for national survival, he has argued, are decided on the basis of immediate domestic political advantage. And there are other arguments. Most Americans, however, believe democracy based on popular opinion to be the best form of government. Can we prove that it is?

The answer to the question must be "No."[17] Whether it is the best or not depends upon the dominant values of the individual and the particular culture. The peasant of thirteenth-century Europe would not have understood what one was talking about if one mentioned the basic concepts of democracy to him. His loyalty was to his lord and the king and to a system that had no elections. In his society, the majority was made up of illiterate workers of the land, who thought that a better life in heaven, not "progress" on earth, was the goal to be striven for; that the proper institutions of society were those that had existed—for him, at least—from time immemorial; and that "justice" or "a man's rights" consisted of traditions as administered through the rulings of the lord of the manor. As far as he was concerned, that was the way it had always been and *ought to be.*

No doubt many of the goals of Americans could be achieved under other forms of government. In the 1920s, American tourists found in Italy many of the things they admired—the trains, for example, ran on time, as they wanted them to in America—but the head of the Italian government, Benito Mussolini, was no contributor to the democratic way of life. The Soviet Union has added to its industrial capacity at an enormous rate since the Communists took power in 1917. It put the first satellite and the first human being in orbit—achievements Americans admire and respect. Yet nearly all Americans despise the Communist form of government.

Even though some of our goals could be achieved under other forms of government, the great bulk of Americans regard democracy as the best form of government, and therefore, *so far as we are concerned, it is.* And we believe that it gives us the best chance to achieve the goals that we regard as most important. This book, indeed, is based on the assumption that this is the case, and it is frankly prejudiced in favor of democracy.

Does Democracy Work? Obviously from what has been said, this is a rhetorical question. Of course it works. But why? And how? Two relevant tests, by which most Americans would give it a high ranking are these:

Survival. It survives and, for several centuries, has survived in a form we consider to be acceptable. Our ideas about what constitutes democracy have changed over a period of time, but with each changing definition, democracy continues to remain a viable system of government.

Permits goal achievement. It helps to further—or at least does not unduly hinder the achievement of—the goals we most highly value. As far as we know, it does this as well or better than any other system could.

[17] But an attempt to present "a rational justification for democracy," using the methods of the logical positivistic philosophers is made in Thomas L. Thorson, *The Logic of Democracy,* Holt, Rinehart and Winston, Inc., New York, 1962.

It is sometimes argued that the best evidence that democracy works is that "the people are usually right in the long run." A superficial reading of American or British history might seem to substantiate this conclusion. It is, however, a conclusion that is reached by circular reasoning, and it is based on an implicit belief in Rousseau's romantic notion of a general will that exists independently of the summation of individual wills and is the true public interest.

Democracy is, in fact, a device for creating social consensus. It encourages people to believe in the decisions made because they believe they participated in making them. There are a number of reasons why, in reading history, we tend to marvel that the public—often after considerable struggle and doubt, to be sure—so often sided with democratic principle or did what was in their long-term rather than their short-term interest. It is easy to be lured by Rousseau's comforting but mistaken notion, and hence conclude that we need not worry, for the ultimate good sense of the people will bail us out of our troubles. There are reasons why the history of our nation *seems* to be relatively free of monumental blunders and relatively full of things we feel proud of. Without listing them all, we should especially keep in mind the following:

1. *We tend to rationalize decisions or actions that have been forced upon us,* to borrow a concept from Sigmund Freud rather than John Locke. Once we have acted, we tend to tell others, and what is perhaps more important, ourselves, that what happened was what *ought* to have happened, that it was for the national good. A great many Americans doubted the wisdom of our entering World War I; somewhat fewer doubted the wisdom of entering World War II. Their views are now usually given short shrift by most Americans, however. It is essential for us to believe that the large number of persons who died in those wars, as the result of our decisions, died for a worthwhile cause. It would be difficult for us to live with ourselves if we did not think so. So the history books tend to reflect this belief, and we see ourselves as a people who did what we had to do in order to preserve democracy and stamp out tyranny.

We also rationalize decisions in regard to civil rights and domestic policy, of course. During World War II, thousands of American citizens of Japanese descent were placed in concentration camps on order of military authorities and with the permission of President Franklin D. Roosevelt. The latter acted in response to his mandate to protect the safety of the nation. But what could easily be viewed as a flagrant violation of civil rights of the individuals concerned (there was no test of *individual* loyalty—there was no time for that) was argued by a majority of the Supreme Court to have been a necessary wartime emergency.[18] (No American of Japanese descent actually was involved in espionage or sabotage, but that could not have been known at the time, of course.) At the time, relatively few heeded the words of Justice Frank Murphy,

[18] The case was *Korematsu v. United States,* 323 U.S. 214 (1944).

dissenting, who argued that the military authorities had acted, not on reasonable legal grounds, but in response to pleas based upon "an accumulation of much of the misinformation, half-truths and insinuations that for years have been directed against Japanese Americans by people with racial and economic prejudices."

2. *We become accustomed to one way of doing things and tend to assume that it is the best way, if indeed not the only way.* The person who approves generally of the present system of public welfare programs is likely to conclude that it represents the correct way to approach the insecurities of an urban, industrial nation. He may see opponents of the program as stubborn, narrow-minded persons who do not understand the problems of the contemporary urban working-class citizen. He may be right; but it may also be true that there are several other ways in which the problems could be met to the basic satisfaction of the persons involved. Similarly, we are accustomed to coming out on top—to having the world's highest standard of living, to winning wars in which we become involved, for example. It is easy to assume that we have done so because of a superior system of government and economics. Yet scholars who spend their lifetimes studying history have great difficulty finding cause-and-effect relationships. The typical citizen is likely to take the short cut of defining the cause in terms of the effects.

3. *In serious crises, our most treasured beliefs sustain us; because these beliefs are so deeply held, acts taken in accord with them are, of course, later interpreted as having been "right."* In other words, we engage in circular reasoning. It is difficult for us today to picture the conditions that existed during the Great Depression, which began in 1929, but during that time there was so much despair, so little apparent reason for hope, so much to be angry and frustrated about that a revolution might well have occurred. There was some consideration of revolution, of course, but the great bulk of the American citizenry never supported the idea. They believed in the nation, in its way of doing things, and in the ultimate solvability of all problems. They did accept a new concept of the function of government in the economy, but did not seriously consider a radical change in either the governmental or the economic system.

Even given our store of fundamental beliefs, however, we do not necessarily reach the decisions that historians will later applaud without leadership. At the time of World War II, for example, we might have left all of Europe to fall to the forces of antidemocracy. It was the easier path, and a great many Americans wanted to choose it, but we ultimately decided not to do so. We acted, however, only after very considerable effort on the part of a President who prodded us along, and as a result of some serious miscalculations by leaders of the Empire of Japan. In similar fashion, it is because of our deepest beliefs that the most aggressive of demagogues usually last but a short time, although they often cause much confusion and conflict while they are on the political stage.

4. *Our fundamental values are often ambivalent in character.* Because they conflict or are not consistent with one another, it is possible to exercise a choice from among our values in explaining an action. At the time of the Civil War, each side borrowed from different parts of the cultural heritage and came to opposite conclusions concerning what was right. In nearly any circumstance, a decision can hence be called "the right one" by using the appropriate references.

We must not assume, however, that any event in our national life can be made to "look good" in the history books. There are limits to the kinds of things that can be justified within the cultural heritage. When those limits are exceeded in connection with important events, a nation is in danger of collapse. During the eighteenth century, the French middle class could not find justification for the existing political and economic system, and the aristocracy did not try to defend it. The revolution followed.

What Is Fertile Soil for Democracy? Can American democracy be exported? Many Americans believe that it can. Our postwar foreign policy has contained this implicit assumption. Many citizens probably believe that "common sense" would cause people to want to emulate our system of government or one quite like it, if they could. They see oppression as the reason they do not do so. Of course, oppression may be an important short-run factor, but social institutions, including governmental systems, must be examined in a fuller, longer-range context.

In what kinds of nations is democracy most likely to appear and to thrive? It is widespread in primitive societies, though not universal. But as societies become more complex, nondemocratic systems emerge and are the general rule. Beginning in the late seventeenth century, modern representative democracy began to appear. It is now a stable characteristic of a small minority of nations. What do they have in common? In a summary of the available evidence, Seymour Martin Lipset has listed (although not in rank order) the following as being of greatest importance.[19]

1. **An open class system rather than a closed class system.** In other words, one in which an individual has a relatively good chance of moving up to a higher class level than that of his parents, and at least partly as a result of his own efforts.

2. **Economic wealth.** The more prosperous a country, the better the chances for the survival of democracy (other things being equal).

[19] Seymour Martin Lipset, *Political Man*, Doubleday & Company, Inc., Garden City, N.Y., 1960, chap. 2. Another important empirical study is Lyle W. Shannon, "Is Level of Development Related to Capacity for Self-government?" *American Journal of Economics and Sociology* 17:367–382, September, 1958. The pioneer study of the factors related to democracy and industrialization was Max Weber, *The Protestant Ethic and the Spirit of Capitalism*, George Allen & Unwin, Ltd., London, 1930; English translation by Talcott Parsons. Weber's theory is no longer accepted in its entirety by social scientists because he fell into the fallacy of seeking the One Great Cause (in his case, it was Protestantism). Social scientists now believe that social phenomena are usually the result of a combination of several—normally, a great many—factors.

3. An equalitarian value system. If large numbers of people are considered inferior to others and *they themselves believe it,* democracy is likely to have difficulties. The medieval idea of a place for everyone and everyone in his place did not provide the soil in which democracies grow. The people of Britain do not fully accept the American belief in the common man, but they do generally agree that all classes should be permitted to take part in the political process.

4. A capitalist economy. This does not mean that *laissez faire* (extreme individualism and minimal government) is necessary for the survival of democracy, as is sometimes argued. It does mean that nations that had systems of private enterprise capitalism during the period of their industrial development are more likely to spawn democracy of a virile form than are other nations. In particular, the middle class that flourishes under capitalism seems to be helpful to democracy, as Max Weber and Karl Marx both concluded.

5. Literacy. Although we have noted that rationality is not a prerequisite for democracy, there is evidence to indicate that the more informed the typical citizen is, the more likely is the nation to be or become a democratic one. Of course, literacy, like any of the items listed here, is not in itself a guarantee of democracy. Germany is an outstanding example of a highly literate nation that has been slow to commit itself to democratic principles.

6. High participation in voluntary organizations. Any society in which people are free to join or refuse to join various organizations is likely to have a climate favorable to democracy. A society in which everyone is required, at least formally, to belong to a specified church or trade union or other social organization is organized to encourage some system of government other than democracy. Studies in the United States have demonstrated that persons who are most active in voluntary associations—the Community Chest, civic leagues, friends of the library—are also most tolerant of other people's opinions and of the process of shared decision making.

THE FUTURE

Democracy appears to develop, survive, and grow in nations with high levels of wealth, industrialization, urbanization, and education.[20] The evidence is strong that the conditions are not accidental.

What do we know, then, about the future of democracy in the United States and in the infant nations of Asia and Africa? The conditions for the growth and continued good health of democracy apparently are to be found in the United States. As to other nations, we can be fairly sure that few, if any, of the Communist states will move toward democracy as we know it in the near future. There are several factors in Communist states

[20] Lipset, *op. cit.*

that threaten the existing system and offer the possibility for democratic growth in the future, particularly increasing wealth and education levels. However, the absence of a capitalistic-democratic tradition and the existence of a value system that concedes to a leadership class (Communist party membership) the right to rule—as compared to the equalitarianism in our cult of the common man—supplies these states with soil of doubtful fertility. Also on the doubtful list are most of the newly independent nations. Some of them may be appropriate for democracy, providing they are carefully encouraged; but most will need both the cultural tradition that will permit democracy to exist (see points 1, 3, and 6 above) and in addition, will need rapid increases in national wealth, literacy, and the size of the middle class (see 2, 4, and 5 above). These countries will not, of course, necessarily turn to communism—most will probably be characterized by some kind of personalism* or elite leadership—but it is significant that communism seems to sprout and flourish in countries relatively *lacking* in wealth, a middle class, and a literate population (see points 2, 4, and 5 above).

***PERSONALISM* is a form of politics in which support or opposition is directed toward a specific individual, rather than toward policies, ideologies, or parties.**

In the postwar years, it has been a part of American government policy to aid these countries in overcoming the obstacles to democracy, but cultural and economic factors do not usually change in a day, a year, or even a decade. The process of stopping communism and of spreading democracy—the two are not the same—is a long-term one. An understanding that this is the case and why it is the case should be of help to the citizen who wonders what we are getting in return for our billions.

A Closing Note on the Educated Man and Democracy. In this chapter, some attention has been paid to the fact that we do not need to have all (or even any) individuals voting on the basis of a rational evaluation of facts in order for democracy to work effectively. The careless reader may conclude that the authors are arguing that an informed public plays no useful role in democracy. Such is not the case. We have already noted that democracy flourishes best in nations that have a high level of literacy.

Why should there be a relationship between educational levels and the health of democracy?[21] Studies show that the greater the level of education, the more leisure time an individual (and a nation) is likely to have—time to devote to politics, so that the management of political affairs is not left entirely to a special class of leaders. The more his education, the more tolerant is the individual of ideas and life-styles different from his own, the more he favors the climate in which democracy flourishes. And

[21] *Ibid.*, pp. 55–57 and citations of studies in footnote 19, p. 99.

the more his education, the more he tends to avoid extremes of action or belief in times of stress and to reject authoritarian ideologies.

Furthermore, education does more than simply encourage the tolerance of diversity and shared power that democracy requires. It also is almost certain that the more an individual's decisions are based upon accurate data, a knowledge of current and historical facts, and the logical development of ideas, the more they are likely to further his own long-range goals and those of the culture and the nation. It would be implausible to argue the opposite case, or to say that rationality plays no part in decision making.

If knowledge does aid one in reaching decisions that further his goals, knowledge should certainly be disseminated as widely as possible throughout all strata of the population. It is also important, and somewhat easier, to disseminate knowledge among the leaders and the future leaders of society. One of the implicit assumptions of this book is that its readers will tend to fall into the category of current or future community leaders and that such leaders can benefit from a maximum amount of knowledge concerning the process by which American democracy operates.

SELECTED BIBLIOGRAPHY

The historical development of democratic ideas dates, in written form, from the days of ancient Greece. These ideas have remained alive ever since, even in extremely hostile environments [28, 33]. The classic statement of the theory upon which the Anglo-American tradition is based is that of Locke [24, 34]. His ideas were challenged by Burke [6] and Hamilton [27], among others. Marx and Engels once issued a now-famous paean to democracy—and at the same time predicted its doom [25].

The several meanings of democracy to Americans are spelled out by Dahl [8]. Bryce [2, 3], offers an earlier classic study by an Englishman, while Baldwin [1] shows the way in which the American theory is one of limited democracy. Commager, reflecting the views of a Great Depression liberal, protests the use of one limiting device, judicial review [7]. Kendall [17], once an advocate of absolute majoritarianism, discusses the two majorities that produce congressmen and Presidents. The problems of defining democracy are more fully explained in Mayo [26]; the conflicts between ideal and practice are outlined by Myrdal [29].

Democracy has been reevaluated in the years since World War II on the basis of empirical data. Doubts about the classical theory were raised early and date back at least a generation to such men as Wallas [37]. Empirical evidence concerning the assumption of an informed public was presented beginning in the mid-1930s by public-opinion surveyors (see Cantril [5], Kornhauser [18], Lippmann [21,] and Verney [36]). Some writers have shown that there is an important, if imperfect, analogy between political and economic decision making [4, 9, 10] and another important one between what citizens believe is right and proper and the kinds of persons they will accept as leaders [22, 23]. Although early writers on democracy seemed to see the system as one that ordinary citizens would eagerly grasp in their desire for freedom, Fromm (see Chapter 2) and Lane [19] have shown this to be an oversimplified and not entirely correct interpretation.

The problems of democracy are discussed by the many textbooks on the subject, in a series edited by Carl Friedrich [11–16], and by Neumann [30], who is concerned about the relationship between freedom and political power.

1. Baldwin, Leland: *The Meaning of America,* The University of Pittsburgh Press, Pittsburgh, Pa., 1955.
2. Bryce, James: *The American Commonwealth,* Capricorn Books, G. P. Putnam's Sons, New York, 2 vols., 1960. Introduction by Louis Hacker; edited by Louis Hacker.
3. Bryce, James: *Modern Democracies,* The Macmillan Company, New York, 2 vols., 1921.
4. Buchanan, James M., and Gordon Tullock: *The Calculus of Consent,* The University of Michigan Press, Ann Arbor, Mich., 1962.
5. Cantril, Henry (ed.): *Public Opinion: 1935–1946,* Princeton University Press, Princeton, N.J., 1951.
6. Cobban, Alfred: *Edmund Burke and the Revolt against the Eighteenth Century,* Barnes & Noble, Inc., New York, 1960.
7. Commager, Henry Steele: *Majority Rule and Minority Rights,* Oxford University Press, Fair Lawn, N.J., 1943.
8. Dahl, Robert A.: *A Preface to Democratic Theory,* The University of Chicago Press, Chicago, 1956.
9. Dahl, Robert A., and Charles E. Lindblom: *Politics, Economics, and Welfare,* Harper & Row, Publishers, New York, 1953.
10. Downs, Anthony: *An Economic Theory of Democracy,* Harper & Row, Publishers, New York, 1957.
11. Friedrich, Carl J. (ed.): *Authority,* Nomos I, Atherton Press, New York, 1958.
12. Friedrich, Carl J. (ed.): *Community,* Nomos II, Atherton Press, New York, 1959.
13. Friedrich, Carl J. (ed.): *Responsibility,* Nomos III, Atherton Press, New York, 1960.
14. Friedrich, Carl J. (ed.): *Liberty,* Nomos IV, Atherton Press, New York, 1962.
15. Friedrich, Carl J. (ed.): *The Public Interest,* Nomos V, Atherton Press, New York, 1962.
16. Friedrich, Carl J. (ed.): *Rational Decisions,* Nomos VII, Atherton Press, New York, 1964.
17. Kendall, Willmoore: "The Two Majorities," *Midwest Journal of Political Science,* 4:317–345, November, 1960.
18. Kornhauser, Arthur, and others: *When Labor Votes,* University Books, Inc., New York, 1956.
19. Lane, Robert: "The Fear of Equality," *American Political Science Review,* 53:35–51, March, 1959.
20. Lindeman, E. C., and T. V. Smith: *The Democratic Way of Life,* New American Library of World Literature, Inc., New York, 1960.
21. Lippmann, Walter: *Essays in the Public Philosophy,* Little, Brown and Company, Boston, 1955.
22. Lipset, Seymour Martin: *Political Man,* Doubleday & Company, Inc., Garden City, N.Y., 1960.
23. Lipset, Seymour Martin: "Some Special Requisites of Democracy: Economic Development and Political Legitimacy," *American Political Science Review,* 53:69–105, March, 1959.
24. Locke, John: *Two Treatises of Government.* (Originally published in 1689 and 1690; many editions, including paperbacks.)

25. Marx, Karl, and Frederich Engels: *The Communist Manifesto.* (Originally published 1848; many editions.)
26. Mayo, Henry: *An Introduction to Democratic Theory,* Oxford University Press, Fair Lawn, N.J., 1960.
27. Morris, Richard B. (ed.): *Basic Ideas of Alexander Hamilton,* Pocket Books, Inc., New York, 1961.
28. Muller, Herbert J.: *Freedom in the Ancient World,* Harper & Row, Publishers, New York, 1961.
29. Myrdal, Gunnar: *An American Dilemma,* Harper & Row, Publishers, New York, 1944. (Also available in McGraw-Hill paperback, 1964.)
30. Neumann, Franz: *The Democratic and the Authoritarian State,* The Free Press of Glencoe, New York, 1957.
31. Prothro, James W., and Charles M. Grigg: "Fundamental Principles of Democracy: Bases of Agreement and Disagreement," *The Journal of Politics,* 22:276–294, May, 1960.
32. Rourke, Francis E.: *Secrecy and Publicity: Dilemmas of Democracy,* The Johns Hopkins Press, Baltimore, 1961.
33. Sabine, George H.: *History of Political Theory,* rev. ed., Holt, Rinehart and Winston, Inc., New York, 1950.
34. Schumpeter, Joseph A.: *Capitalism, Socialism, and Democracy,* 2d ed., Harper & Row, Publishers, New York, 1947.
35. Shannon, Lyle W.: "Is Level of Development Related to Capacity for Self-government?" *American Journal of Economics and Sociology.* 17:367–382, September, 1958.
36. Verney, Douglas V.: *The Analysis of Political Systems,* The Free Press of Glencoe, New York, 1960.
37. Wallas, Graham: *Human Nature in Politics,* University of Nebraska Press, Lincoln, Nebr., 1962. (Originally published in 1909.)

Case Cited in Chapter 3.

Korematsu v. United States, 323 U.S. 214 (1944).

CHAPTER

4

CONSTITUTIONS: GROUND RULES FOR GOVERNMENT

Every nation has a set of fundamental laws—rules about rule making—that deal with the distribution of political power and, indirectly, all power. These fundamentals are known collectively as a *constitution*. A constitution not only distributes power, it also sets the limits on the use of power. It determines the general process by which governmental decisions are to be made by establishing a pattern of power relationships between the governors and the governed; it provides a procedure for keeping the fundamental laws current by establishing an amending process.

In lending a sense of propriety to the arrangements for the delineation and distribution of power, it also creates *authority*, which is power made legitimate. A constitution is ineffective unless it receives acceptance by the dominant political forces of a nation, and unless those forces believe that the constitution rightly determines how political decisions are to be made.

Constitutions may be written or unwritten, detailed or general, transitory or enduring over centuries. The basic rules of society are by no means stated only in written form. The mores, or fundamental beliefs and values of a society, are basic rules, at least in part unwritten, that may sometimes be more important to citizens than are the formal rules of a constitution. And the unwritten parts of a constitution may be as important as the formal and written parts.

Every society has a constitution, no matter how primitive or complex its social organization may be. It exists because the established power relationships are accepted by consensus as legitimate. Some rules, it is felt, can be changed from time to time to adjust to changing circumstances; others are so central to the belief system of society that they are rarely and most reluctantly changed. The constitution of a primitive society exists in the mores of the people; it does not distinguish clearly between government as an instrument of social control and other means of controlling behavior.

The constitution of Great Britain is similarly a real thing: the British talk of their constitution and what is constitutionally possible much as we do, but their constitution is essentially unwritten, or at least, it consists of unwritten rules and a series of documents written at various times over many centuries. The origins of some parts of it are obscured in the mists of antiquity. Other parts date from the Middle Ages. When the British constitution first reflected a commitment to limited democracy (in the late seventeenth century), it was structured to permit middle-class control of government. Democracy based on universal manhood suffrage was established in the United Kingdom in the middle of the nineteenth century.

The American Constitution is more definitely a written document than is that of Britain, though it is by no means all written. More of it is to be found in the opinions of the United States Supreme Court than in the document called the Constitution of the United States, even if we include the amendments. There is thus an *informal* constitution as well as the formal document.

THE DISTRIBUTION OF POWER

Does Structure Make a Difference? Over the centuries, observers of politics have often wondered whether the formal structural arrangements of government made any real difference in the way that political decisions are made. Their question is whether it is possible to institutionalize the distribution of power.* Skeptics have used various arguments: they range from the crude assertion that the only thing that matters is what the rulers want to do, that is, the ruler's philosophy, not the rules, is important, to the argument that it is the *informal,* rather than the *formal,* rules of government that matter. In other words, the argument is that it is not constitutions or other rule books that determine what governments do or how they do it. Rather, the crucial variable is to be found in the interpersonal relationships of those in positions of power. These relationships, in turn, depend upon the personalities and personal drives of the rulers, as well as upon the values that they have absorbed in the process of becoming mature human beings.

***INSTITUTIONALIZED POWER exists whenever there is a regularly established set of relationships among participants in the policy-making process and this set of relationships is consciously understood by the participants.**

The various aspects of this debate cannot be examined in any detail here. It appears, however, that both the formal rules and the informal relationships are important in the policy-making processes of governments. Neither one is the answer alone. A Federal judge who is old and in ill health may be expected to act differently from a young, vigorous judge, even though both possess the same formal powers. It seems likely that two Presidents—Eisenhower and Johnson, say—would not act in the same way, even if they were confronted with identical situations. Whether a bill is reported out of a congressional committee or not may depend in part upon the ideological or political commitments of the man who is chairman at the time the decision is made.

Joseph Stalin for many years held only a minor post in the Soviet government. Yet he was a dictator. His power stemmed from his position as secretary-general of the Communist party, a nongovernmental post. This might lead one to say that obviously formal arrangements are not important, for the formal head of the Soviet government during this period was a figurehead with no real power. But in fact, it depends. When "summit" conferences were proposed during World War II, formal and informal leadership coincided in the United States and Great Britain, but not in the Soviet Union. To avoid possible confusion and embarrassment, Stalin had himself made Premier and met with Churchill and Roosevelt as chief of government. Formal structure did make a difference.

A switch in the United States to the parliamentary form of government would have a great effect upon the informal processes of decision making. Similarly, if congressional districts are reorganized so that they consist of equal populations, as the Supreme Court ordered in 1964, rural and small-town influence in the House of Representatives will be weakened, and the policies adopted by Congress will be different from what they were. And a slightly different formula for the selection of members of the Electoral College would have caused the election of Richard M. Nixon rather than John F. Kennedy in 1960. In all these examples, it is the formal structural arrangement that is the vital variable. The policy-making process is thus affected by the way in which the Secretary of State gets along with the chairman of the Senate Foreign Relations Committee, but it is also affected by the formal rules that establish the relationships between the two, assuming that other things remain unchanged.

The Decisions to Be Made. What are the questions concerning the rules about rule making that confront the writers of constitutions? What choices are available to them? What structural types exist for the government of nations? We cannot exhaust the possibilities, perhaps, but we can consider the questions that have most commonly concerned political philosophers and builders of model constitutions.

Where Are the Decisions Made? One means of classifying constitutions is according to *the way in which they establish formal centers for decision making.* This involves the problem of the geographic division of powers. The choices are these: centralizing power in a single national government, decentralizing power by spreading it among many regional governments within the nation, or compromising between the two possibilities.

Unitary government. A unitary government exists when all the power of the state is legally concentrated in one national government. Under this plan, there may be regional governments—provinces, counties, or districts—but they possess no legal powers. They can do only what the central government permits, and grants of authority can at any time be removed—there is no *right* to govern, only *permission* to do so. Great Britain, France, Czechoslovakia, and most of the nations of the world fit into this category.

Confederacy. Occasionally, independent countries join on a voluntary basis to form a single state, but without giving up any powers to the new enveloping nation. Such arrangements are usually made for purposes of aggression or defense. They are found among primitive peoples as well as in Western Civilization. The central government has no powers of its own—the opposite of a unitary state—and it can do only what the constituent members permit. Usually its powers are limited to matters of war, defense, and foreign relations.

The first constitution of the United States, the Articles of Confederation, provided for this type of government. At the time the United States declared its independence (1776), leaders in the various states considered their governments free and independent. They did not wish to have a central government with strong powers. Such a government had been the source of the troubles leading to the Revolution. So they agreed to establish a government with limited powers—except in the areas of defense and foreign relations. They specifically agreed that "each state retains its sovereignty, freedom, and independence"; and that all powers not specifically given to the central government should be retained by the states. The Articles were not considered to have established a new nation, but only "a firm league of friendship."

Figure 4-1

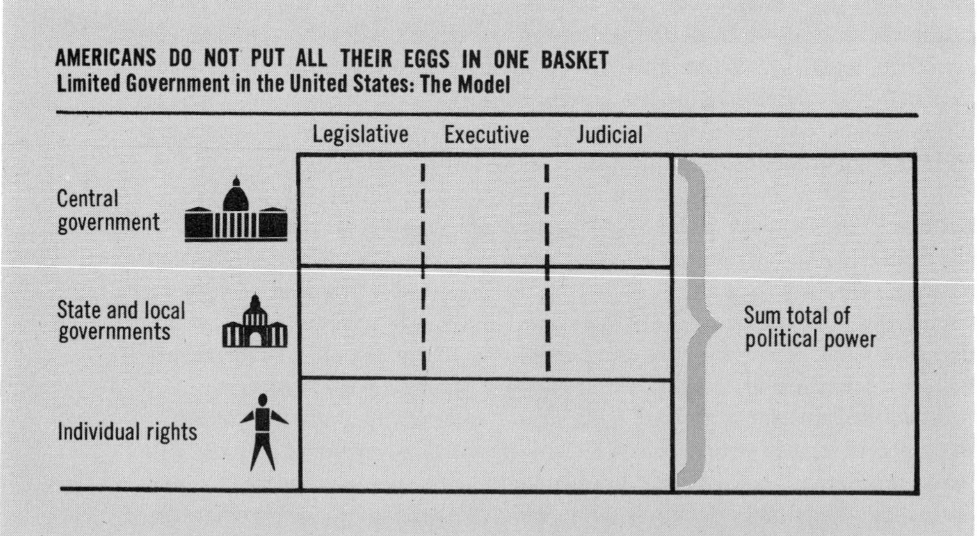

At the time of the Civil War, the Southern states, after declaring that they were seceding from the Union, also established a confederacy. Their leaders believed that the war had been caused by the undue possession of power by the Federal government, and they wanted to prevent the establishment of such a government in the future. We cannot know whether the Confederate States of America, with its highly decentralized system for decision making, could have survived for any longer than did the government under the Articles of Confederation (eight years). Appomattox and what went before it ended the experiment.

In more recent times, the African state of Mali has experimented with confederation, and some of the leaders of the Congo in its early years of independence insisted that this approach be used, although central government leaders successfully resisted the idea.

The federal system. A federal system of government offers a middle ground between the unitary and confederate approaches. In theory, it provides for a system in which the powers of government are divided between a central government and regional governments, each of which is legally supreme in its own area of jurisdiction. The regional governments are not subordinate to the central government; they share powers and responsibility for decision making. Of course, dividing authority in this way is certain to lead to some conflict, and a means for resolving such differences must be provided in every federation. Indeed, the lack of a single locus of final authority has led some critics to say that every federation exists in a state of unstable equilibrium, and that it will eventually either disintegrate or become a unitary state.

Some have suggested that the United States has outlived the necessity for a federal plan and *should* become a unitary state. Others complain that we *ought* to remain a federation, but that certain forces are at work destroying this arrangement and making us, alas, into a unitary state. Whatever we should or ought to do, the fact is that the federal system in America appears to be healthy, as we shall see, and the nation does not appear to be drifting into the unitary arrangement.

The federal plan has been used chiefly in areas where military and economic factors encourage the creation of a central government with some effective powers, but where strong divisive influences discourage the creation of a unitary state. These influences may be based upon cultural, religious, or geographic considerations, or a combination of them. Switzerland is a small nation, but it is divided by religion, language, and steep mountains. Canada is a land of vast spaces, with one culture and language descended from old France, another from Great Britain. Australia has cultural and language unity, but its original settlement was around the edges of a large continent; the interior was for a long time sparsely populated, with great distances making regional identifications more important than national identifications. The Soviet Union is an enormous nation, with dozens of subcultures and many languages.

All of the nations mentioned above seem to have found the federal plan a useful one, offering the advantages of both unity and diversity. Other nations have also made use of the plan to one degree or another, including Mexico and Brazil. Of course, the formal arrangements are not always honored in practice, but they can be important even in an authoritarian state such as the Soviet Union. There the centralizing influence of the Communist party far outweighs the centrifugal force of federalism, but it does not make the latter meaningless.

Who Makes the Decisions? A second way of classifying constitutions is according to *how many share in the decision-making process.* In theory, the number may range from one to all of the citizens of a nation, from *monarchy* to *democracy*. Or it may be somewhere in between, an *oligarchy*. For purposes of this analysis, we borrow from a typology used by Aristotle.[1]

Monarchy or dictatorship. "Monarchy" simply means government by a single person. We usually think of it applying to a king, that is, to a hereditary ruler, but this need not be the case. Indeed, most kingships that still exist, such as those in Norway or Thailand, are not monarchies in the literal sense because the king does not have absolute power, and he may have virtually no power at all. He may simply be the living symbol of the state. On the other hand, men of modest family backgrounds, men such as Adolf Hitler or Joseph Stalin, have served as authoritarian leaders or dictators of huge nations.

The king or dictator, in theory, holds all power, and no one else shares in the most important decision making except by his permission. In practice, of course, a monarch probably cannot rule alone except in the smallest of tribes. He must delegate a great deal of power in order to get the job of government done. More importantly, to retain his dictatorial position, he is probably highly dependent upon various factors: a working relationship with the nation's most powerful businessmen (Hitler in Germany or leaders in some of the Central American "banana republics" of the past); the support of an effective, well-organized party or bureaucracy (Stalin in the Soviet Union or Louis XIV in France); or mass popular support by keeping citizens entranced (some of the most successful South American dictators, and, again, Hitler).

Dictatorships are essentially products of a particular application of the art of administration. They require a high degree of organization of a sort not usually found among primitive peoples. A system of secret political police who can detect and obliterate serious challenges to the established leader is essential in a dictatorship. So is an effective means of communication, for without it there can be no central control over decision making.

Oligarchy. This term means government by the few—by an elite. Some political scientists have argued that all governments are, in practice, oligarchies because neither one nor all persons can actually do the decision making. They hold that one man cannot keep himself in power except

[1] See the *Politics* of Aristotle. Many editions are available.

with the assistance of a considerable support group, making concessions to and sharing decision making with this group in order to keep it on his side. The general public, on the other hand, is too unwieldy and too unknowledgeable to make policy decisions as a group. Hence, basic decisions are made by a minority of the people, but by some number greater than one. This argument has some validity, but it is probably based more

Figure 4-2

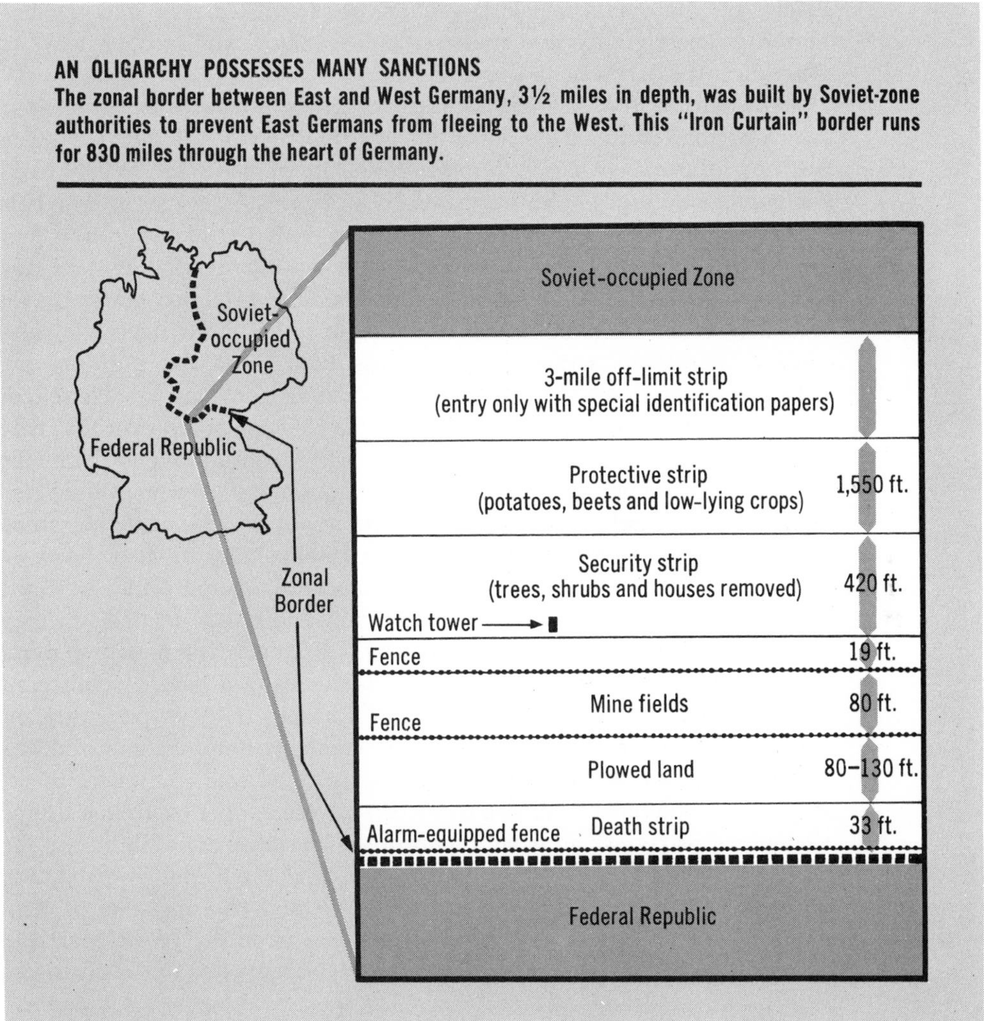

East Germany, a police state, is literally a prison.
(Berlin: Crisis and Challenge, *German Information Center, New York, 1962, p. 29.*)

on semantics than upon actual differences of opinion about the process of governmental policy making. It depends on what we mean by ruling or decision making. In every society, without doubt, there are gradations in the amount of influence over decisions that is possessed by various individuals. Stalin needed the Communist party apparatus in order to rule, but in the nearly thirty years of his dictatorship, no one person or group of persons was able to dislodge him. He was in a position of greater power than any of the other party leaders or any combination of them, apparently.[2] In contrast, while the common man does little actual ruling of the nation under a democracy, he does participate meaningfully in decision making, for he chooses among competing candidates for public offices that are decision-making centers; he is quite free to take membership in interest groups that influence public policy; and in other ways he does affect the decisions that are made.

If we narrow the meaning of oligarchy, then, to mean government in which a group of more than one, but less than a majority, of the citizens has *institutionalized power* to make decisions, we can more clearly make distinctions by types of governments. The oligarchs of a nation may hold their positions as a result of membership in some particular group. They may hold temporary power through coercion—by a reign of fear and terror—but this is not a firm base upon which to establish power that is intended to survive for long periods. It is much more likely that the elitists (oligarchs) are powerful because their particular positions are accorded great deference by the society; their positions are viewed as *legitimate*. In other words, most people think it fitting and proper that they *should* rule, and thus, they are always *indirectly* accountable to the public at large, even though this may be the case only in a narrow and ill-defined sense. If people believe that age and wisdom are related, or if they think that experience is more important than intelligence, we may have an oligarchy made up of the old men of the tribe (gerontocracy). If the dominant belief is that wealth, success, and ability are related, we may have government by the rich (plutocracy). If land is the most important basis of wealth, government may be in the hands of a landed nobility, as it was in the feudal period in medieval Europe. If the supernatural or mystical is more important than the observable matters of this world, the government may be turned over to the priests or medicine men (theocracy). In Communist countries today, the government is controlled by the Communist party, which is not a part of the government at all, but, in the ideology, the vanguard of the proletariat. The party holds power because its members are supposed to possess the full and true meaning of communism and the stateless, classless society that is, in theory, its goal. The typical citizen in a Communist state probably accepts this role of the party

[2] It is possible, of course, that a combination of party members did exist that could have overthrown Stalin, but because the group did not realize this or did not wish to challenge him, the effective power remained with the leader.

member and hence, in anthropological terms, such a state should probably be viewed as a theocracy. It is a state that is—in theory—led by a priestly class with utopian goals, a class that has a monopoly on the interpretation of the sacred writings of Communist prophets and makes the decisions that will bring about the utopia. The only difficulty with the analysis is that the utopia is to be located on earth, but this probably does not make the concept of the communist state as a theocracy invalid.

In all cases, we must be careful about the use of terms. The famed "democracy" of ancient Athens was actually an oligarchy. Only about one adult male in ten and no women could vote. (However, many practices we would today consider democratic were followed by the Athenian elite.) Democracy in John Locke's England at the end of the eighteenth century was actually an upper-middle-class oligarchy, although it was experiencing some changes and developing a philosophy that, after several more generations, would lead to what we consider to be democracy.

Democracy. This Greek word means government by the people (*demos*). A literal application of this form of government was greatly feared by most of the ancient Greek philosophers. They regarded democracy as a form of radicalism and feared that it would degenerate into tyranny led by a handful of demagogues. Greeks thought of democracy as essentially alien to their culture. This was true of the lovers of art, literature, and the good life in Athens, as well as of the warriors of Sparta.

The conditions necessary for democracy have been discussed (see Chapter 3). Democracies may be *direct,* as they often are in primitive societies, so that citizens make the major decisions in a popular assembly in which they hold membership. Some remnants of direct democracy remain in America in the New England town meeting and the use of the initiative and referendum. The last two are, in effect, nonassembled meetings of the citizenry in which actual issues of policy (whether to go into debt for a new school building or change the pension system for firemen, for example) are decided by direct vote. For the most part, however, modern democracy is representative democracy—"a mixed polity," Aristotle would say—in which the voters choose those who are to rule.

Who Is Responsible to Whom? A third way of classifying constitutions is according to *the relationship of the chief executive to the popular assembly.* In brief, the chief executive may be formally selected by the popular assembly or he may come to power independently. Political scientists usually say that in the former case, a parliamentary form of government exists, in the latter case, a presidential form.

The parliamentary form was developed in European democracies. They, plus the British Commonwealth countries and some of the newer nations that have been influenced by European colonialism, all generally depend on one variation or another of this plan.

The presidential form, on the other hand, has become identified as the American plan of government. Some other countries, especially in South

America, have sought to imitate it. The French Fifth Republic, established under the leadership of Charles de Gaulle in 1958, is also essentially a presidential plan. (De Gaulle was convinced that the numerous ideologically rigid parties of France could not develop strong leadership under the parliamentary system, so he deliberately borrowed from the American.)

Although the name "presidential system" reflects the title of the American chief executive, the plan is not necessarily limited to democratic systems. The chief executive is usually designated formally by some apparatus that purports to give power to the head of the government from some ultimate source. The Soviet Union preserves the form of the parliamentary system. On the other hand, the kings in Europe, who were real rulers, owed their office to the accident of birth or, as some of them viewed it, the favor of God. If there was a parliament, it was independent of or subordinate to the chief executive, the king.

The parliamentary system. The key to the parliamentary system, according to the model, is that members of the popular assembly choose an executive committee, which in turn chooses a chairman. We generally call the committee the cabinet, while its chairman is known as the prime minister, or premier. In practice, the selection of the committee by parliament is often strictly a matter of form, because the persons selected are always the leading members of the majority party or a group of parties that have formed a coalition in order to rule. Where the parliamentary system is combined with a two-party system, as is virtually the case in England (there is a small third party, the Liberals), a cabinet is rarely overthrown by a parliamentary vote of no confidence. On the other hand, in nations with a multiple-party system, the cabinet may represent an uneasy, precarious arrangement that is dependent upon the whims of a majority of members of the popular assembly, as is the case in Italy and Israel.

The presidential system. The best-known characteristic of the presidential system is the *separation of powers*. The three principal functions of government—the formal promulgation of the law, its administration, and its adjudication—are established in separate and coordinate branches. We call them the legislative, the executive, and the judicial; they are independent of one another, but are at the same time made interdependent. (The judicial branch enjoys a considerable degree of independence in all nations subscribing to the Anglo-American tradition of jurisprudence, regardless of whether they have adopted the presidential system.)

In the American states, members of all three branches are commonly elected directly by the voters. The Federal government does not have an elected judiciary; judges are appointed and can be removed only under most unusual circumstances.

The interdependence of the three branches is secured by what is the obverse of the separation of powers, namely, the *checks-and-balances* system. A variety of both formal and informal arrangements preserve the concept of independent branches, but actually make one branch dependent for effective operation upon the other branches, and make each branch an overseer of the other two. These checks and balances will be noted in the chapters that follow. A few examples may be mentioned here, however: Congress can pass a bill, but the President can prevent it from becoming law by vetoing it. On the other hand, by a check on the check, Congress can override the veto by a two-thirds vote in each house. If the bill does become law, it is subject to interpretation by the courts, which decide its actual application to specific cases. The courts may even declare the law to be unconstitutional, thus setting it aside. However, the judicial interpretation may, in turn, be overruled if Congress enacts legislation that overcomes the courts' objections to the earlier law.

The President can appoint a judge to a Federal court, but the appointment is subject to the approval of the Senate, and a judge, like the President himself, may be impeached and, if convicted, removed from office by a procedure involving the two houses of Congress.

If a member of the executive branch fails to perform some act that a citizen feels is his legal duty, the citizen may ask a court to issue an order requiring the official to perform his duty.

If congressional leaders are dissatisfied with the way in which an executive agency is administered, they may conduct an investigation that may cause the policies of the agency to be altered, either because of resulting new legislation, or because of the glaring headlines concerning the agency. An investigation may also be conducted by a Federal grand jury or, in certain circumstances, by a Federal judge.

The checks-and-balances system is based on the idea that in a democracy no one person or institution should ever be able to gain absolute control and that the best way to prevent this from happening is to have each officeholder hold some power over other officeholders. We have deliberately created a degree of inefficiency in order to achieve the higher goal of *limited government*. The plan has been used in the United States since 1789, when Washington was first inaugurated. It is not a perfectly self-correcting system, but it does tend to work because each person in high office is concerned with being elected, with the gratification of his own ego, with his self-esteem, or with meeting the obligations of his office as befits the image he has of it. In other words, his own life goals, including his political goals, are often furthered by taking action to block the proposed action of a member or agency of another branch. A judge is highly aware of the traditions of the legal profession, of his obligation to preserve individual interests and rights and the Constitution as he understands its meaning. A senator may see the use of the investigative powers of Congress as a means to personal publicity, power, or even to the Presidency. A President may be jealous of the powers and prerogatives of his office as he sees them and engage in a struggle with either Congress or the courts to keep them. Not every power is shared, but many of the most important are.

What Rights Does the Citizen Have? A fourth way of classifying constitutions is according to *the amount of power that is legitimately possessed by government and the amount that is reserved for the individual.*

All governments make such distinctions. In addition, they distinguish between citizens, who are full members of the body politic, and non-citizens, who have fewer rights and privileges. In most cases, citizenship is a matter of law rather than right. The original United States Constitution was vague as to the basis and meaning of citizenship, but the Fourteenth Amendment established the principle that citizenship by natural birth is a *right* and the Supreme Court has since tended to broaden the concept of citizenship as a right. Whether citizenship is a matter of law or right, the benefits and rights, if any, that accompany it vary from one nation to another. Under communism, fascism, and all dictatorships, power belongs in the ideal model and in practice exclusively to government, and freedoms—the right to the protection of legal procedures that constitute the elements of a fair trial, the rights of expression and belief, and equality before the law—if they exist at all, exist by permission of the rulers. Under communism, all power rightly belongs to the proletariat as a class. In Nazi Germany, all power was inherent in the state. To Louis XIV of France (1638–1715), all power was vested in the king, who received it directly from God.

In some other constitutions, particularly those of democratic nations and the constitutional kingships of nineteenth-century Europe, some power, or freedom from government, remains with the ordinary citizen. These rights may, in theory, stem from the natural law, as was the view of Thomas Jefferson and many writers before and after him. Or they may stem from a contract (see the next section of this chapter), a theory supported by both John Locke in England and Jean Jacques Rousseau in France. Or limitations on the actions of both ruler and ruled may be considered *logically necessary* in order to have democratic institutions.[3] But whatever the explanation of the origin of civil rights and liberties, the important thing for the purposes of this book is that they do exist in some societies and not in others. And the important question is whether or not they can effectively be guaranteed by procedures provided in a constitution (see Chapter 19).

DECISIONS FOR THE CENTURIES: THE UNITED STATES

The circumstances surrounding the writing of the United States Constitution in Philadelphia during the summer of 1787 were dramatic. They are extensively detailed in American history books and will be treated quite briefly here. It is appropriate, however, for us to recall some of them

[3] See the discussion in Giovanni Sartori, "Constitutionalism: A Preliminary Discussion," *American Political Science Review,* 56:853–864, December, 1962.

because the decisions made through complex compromises—often arrived at with great difficulty—shaped the institutions that we still rely upon.[4]

Factors of Influence. Men of outstanding ability wrote the Constitution. This was considered to be the case by observers at the time, and it has remained the consensus of historians. More than one-half were college graduates in a day when few men went to college. They were practical men, youthful on the average, and many of them on the threshold of promising careers. They understood why the existing Articles of Confederation were causing difficulties, and they had a sense of what the young United States required in order to develop its great resources.

What did they bring with them in the way of cultural and economic considerations? The following are the important ones:

Philosophies of the day. Many of the delegates were aware of the writings of John Locke, which had been designed to justify the Glorious Revolution of 1689 in England. Locke argued that each human being possessed natural rights of life, liberty, and property. Sometime in the distant past, he said, people had reached an agreement on a contract to create government in order to protect these rights. He also argued that if the government so created failed to perform its tasks properly, citizens could legitimately overthrow that government and establish a new one. The citizen should obey the state as long as its leaders act responsibly—that is, within the terms of the contract—but, because all individuals enjoy equal rights under the doctrine, Locke concluded that political decisions should rest on the base of majority rule. His ideas strongly affected the writers of the Declaration of Independence, the Articles of Confederation, and the Constitution. They had been so useful in the rhetoric designed to justify the War for Independence that the writers of these documents not unexpectedly thought his writings also had great significance for their work.

The members of the convention did not rely upon Locke entirely, however. Charles de Montesquieu, a Frenchman who had written in the days of Louis XIV, had also been concerned about the rights of the individual. Having lived under one of the great autocrats of all time, he had not placed much trust in a contract among the people for their government or in the idea of allowing the majority to make the rules. He feared governmental intrusion upon the rights of individuals and, rather than relying on a theoretical right of revolution or a mystical notion of a rational and responsible majority as Locke did, Montesquieu believed that government should rest upon the principle of a separation of powers, so that one branch of government could check another. Writers of his day were fond of searching for systems that remained in a state of stable equilibrium

[4] For details, see Alfred H. Kelly and Winfred A. Harbison, *The American Constitution: Its Origin and Development,* rev. ed., W. W. Norton & Company, Inc., New York, 1955, chaps. 4–6; or C. Herman Pritchett, *The American Constitution,* McGraw-Hill Book Company, New York, 1959, chaps. 1–2.

automatically, as do the stars. De Montesquieu, who erroneously believed he was describing the distinguishing characteristics of the British constitution, argued that dividing government into independent legislative, executive, and judicial branches would preserve liberty and discourage tyranny. The Founding Fathers, being in favor of doing both, were impressed by his arguments. Like him, they believed that all men are prone to make mistakes, to be uncritical of their own whims, and to be sometimes misled by advisers. So they wanted to safeguard procedures that would minimize irrational decisions and maximize responsible action by decision makers.

Postwar economic developments. The delegates were very much concerned about certain problems that had arisen after the end of the War for Independence. Some were generally fearful of the possibility of a revolution or the establishment of a king or a dictator. It was once common for historians to see the period covered by the Articles as one in which the lack of a uniform currency hampered trade among thirteen essentially independent nations; when the country gradually slipped deeper into a postwar depression; when the credit of the United States was almost worthless; when debtors, especially farmers, put pressure on legislators to prevent foreclosures of mortgages; when the states erected so many trade barriers against one another that businessmen had no confidence in the existing way of doing things and were reluctant to take the risks that would encourage the growth of the national economy. There is a considerable degree of doubt today as to whether these interpretations are correct. Some of them were certainly exaggerated by the conservatives and advocates of hard currency, enforcement of debt collection, and a stronger central government—exaggerations for the sake of effective propaganda. American leaders have always engaged in such battles for the support of the general public.[5]

The depression appears to have been ending before the Philadelphia Convention began; the Confederacy had been able to establish diplomatic relations with European nations, even though it had little luck in borrowing money from their creditors; and it had established a plan for the Western territories. But Congress was undoubtedly at a disadvantage in its inability to regulate either interstate or foreign commerce. The lack of a single currency and the inability to establish nationwide confidence in the integrity of contracts must have discouraged the development of commerce. Shays' Rebellion in Massachusetts (1786) undoubtedly frightened creditors, persons who considered property rights important, and people who feared extending too much power to the common people. (The rebellion, like some later efforts by farmers to prevent foreclosures of mortgages against their land, centered on the obstruction of the courts of law by preventing judges from holding sessions.)

[5] Compare Charles A. Beard and Mary R. Beard, *The Rise of American Civilization,* The Macmillan Company, New York, 4 vols., 1942, with Merrill Jensen, *The New Nation: A History of the United States during the Confederation,* Alfred A. Knopf, Inc., New York, 1950.

A swing from radicalism. A conservative reaction had set in by the time the Convention met. Some of the fervor with which the Revolution had been fought had subsided. The "life, liberty, and the pursuit of happiness" theme of Jefferson's Declaration had been partially replaced by Locke's original phrase, "life, liberty, and property." The men who came to Philadelphia were, for the most part, men of property, creditors, and members of the most prestigeful families in their communities. Charles A. Beard, a noted historian, once argued that the Constitution was in considerable measure an upper-class document, written by men who could personally gain from the changes in the rules that they were proposing. But once again, historians are not in agreement, and more recent research indicates that Beard probably exaggerated the situation.[6] In any case, regional interests and the concerns of the small states in relation to the large states were important considerations in the writing of the Constitution, and they must be added to the interests of the creditors and commercial groups.

The effects of familiarity. The Founding Fathers, like most persons who are called upon to make rules for society, considered not only the existing social and economic climate and the political ideologies they had been taught; they also tended to accept that with which they were familiar. Two-house legislatures had been the rule in the Colonies. So had an independent judiciary and a chief executive who did not have to depend upon the legislature for his power. Government had been limited and had operated on the basis of enumerated powers, for the colonial governments could do only what had been authorized by Parliament. A division of powers had always existed between the government of the Mother Country and that of each colony, a division that was not unlike federalism in its effect. The Founding Fathers were not mere creatures of habit, but as conservatives they did not reject any institution or process that seemed to them to work adequately on the basis of past performance.

Conflict and Compromise. The delegates in Philadelphia shared some interests, then, but they were also faced with some serious conflicts. Among the questions they had to answer were the following:

E pluribus unum? There was the problem of establishing a nation that was to be literally a single nation for commercial purposes. Consensus existed among the delegates on the need for economic stability, for a sound system of credit and currency, and for the protection of the institution of private property. So they were able with relatively little difficulty to provide that "full faith and credit shall be given in each state," and that "the citizens of each state shall be entitled to all privileges and immunities of citizens in the several states." They also agreed that no state should be permitted to enact legislation "impairing the obligations of contract," and that the

[6] Compare Charles A. Beard, *An Economic Interpretation of the Constitution of the United States,* The Macmillan Company, New York, 1913, with Robert E. Brown, *Charles Beard and the Constitution,* Princeton University Press, Princeon, N.J., 1956.

national-government debt should be assumed by the new government under the Constitution. All of these provisions helped to meet the demands and overcome the fears of the creditors and the well-to-do. More importantly, perhaps, they had the effect of establishing conditions for rapid commercial development, for the eventual establishment of the United States as the leading manufacturing nation of the world, and for the high levels of production that gave us eventually a very high standard of living.

What scope of action? It was necessary to decide early in the proceedings of the Convention whether or not the delegates should restrict themselves to their seemingly narrow instructions. The congressional resolution authorizing the meeting had said that it was for "the sole and express purpose of revising the Articles of Confederation." But delegate sentiment was predominantly in favor of writing a new document that differed radically from the Articles, and this they undertook to do.

We, the people—or the several states? The question of the degree of popular participation in the new government had to be decided. This involved the problem of whether the national government was to represent the states, as it had under the Articles, or the people directly. If it was to be the

Figure 4-3

To Turn Over Some Power to a Central Government Took Courage and Vision

"It is unthinkable that the citizens of Rhode Island should ever surrender their sovereignty to some central authority located way off in Philadelphia."

By permission of Burr Shafer.

latter, who should have a right to vote? In either case, the question was how to overcome the fears of the delegates from less populous states that they might be participating in a plan that would vastly increase the powers of the central government, while allowing it to be dominated by the large states.

The compromises were extremely difficult to arrive at, and the delegates at times were nearly ready to give up, but the final results represented the basis for a permanent foundation of our system of government. Ultimately, the delegates agreed that:

1. The national government should represent the *people,* not the states. The opening words of the Constitution, "We, the people of the United States. . . ," sound innocent enough to us today, but they were actually Federalist propaganda and produced strong negative reactions among Antifederalists, who wanted to preserve the principle of a confederation in which the central government is only an instrumentality of the component parts. In fact, the balance was tipped toward centralized federalism.

2. There would be two houses in Congress instead of the one that then existed. The Senate would represent the states on a basis of equality, and the members would be elected by the state legislatures. The House of Representatives would represent the people. Membership was to be determined on a basis of relative population, but no state should have less than one representative.

3. The question of who should vote—a few delegates favored the elimination of the property requirements that were then common, but most thought that a man would not vote responsibly unless he had a property interest to protect—was settled by leaving eligibility to be determined by the states and applying the rules to Federal elective offices.

4. The fears of the delegates from small states were further allayed by the provision that no state could ever be deprived of its equal representation in the Senate except by its own consent. No one expected a state ever to give such consent.

Shall we trust the people? Although most Americans would argue that ours is a democracy, even though an imperfect one, the Founding Fathers were well aware of another concept of constitution writing, one that fitted in well with the spirit of compromise that prevailed in Philadelphia. A strong body of opinion that went back to the Greek Polybius and had been emphasized by Aristotle had long influenced Western political thought. It held that a mixed constitution, or a combination of pure types, was the best. As the question was finally settled, (1) the executive, (2) the Senate and the courts, and (3) the House of Representatives, could be thought of as combining, in order, the features of (1) monarchy, (2) oligarchy, and (3) democracy in a single constitution. The conflict between the advocates of democracy as we know it and the more conservative persons who viewed with apprehension the granting of power to broad segments of the public was settled largely in favor of the latter, who were in a strong majority. Many of the leaders at the Convention thought that even a property requirement for voting was not an adequate guarantee for an informed electorate. The great majority of Americans of the day, especially those outside the cities (and over 95 per cent of the people lived outside the cities), owned some property and could vote.[7] The delegates agreed that only the House of Representatives should represent the citizenry in general, and its members were to be the only persons in the Federal government to be directly elected. Senators would be chosen by state legislatures. The President and Vice President were to be chosen by the Electoral College, which would act as a buffer between the people and the enormously powerful Chief Executive (see Chapter 10). All other Federal government officials were to be appointed to office.

Agreement between North and South? The conflicts of interest between the Southern slave states with their plantation economies and the Northern states with their yeoman farmers and emerging urban economies were resolved in a series of additional compromises. The planters feared that broad powers over interstate and foreign commerce might lead to policies that would increase the costs of the things they bought on the market without improving their profits from sales of their products. (Significantly, the South later became a center of opposition to the protective tariff, which planters saw as producing exactly these unwanted effects. The tariff raised the price of manufactured goods, while making it more difficult to trade extensively and profitably abroad, as the Southern economy required.) But the Southern representatives agreed to giving the national government these broad powers in return for provisions that (1) prohibited taxes on exports; (2) permitted the slave trade to continue for another twenty years; (3) required a two-thirds vote in the Senate for the approval of treaties, thus giving the South a veto power whenever it had a collective interest to protect; and (4) called for the counting of three-fifths of all slaves in determining the number of representatives for a Southern state and in apportioning direct taxes that might be levied by the Federal government.

A bill of rights? Some decisions had to be made about one of John Locke's major concerns: civil rights and liberties. During the subsequent debate on adoption, it was argued that the Constitution did not require a bill of rights because of Locke's theory that civil rights are always reserved to the people and hence lie outside the purview of government. It was also argued that the Federal government was to be, for the most part, one of delegated powers specifically enumerated in the document—although there was a significant "elastic" clause. ("The Congress shall have power . . . to make all laws which shall be necessary and proper for carrying into execution the foregoing powers, and all other powers vested by this Constitution in the government of the United States, or in any department or officer thereof.")

[7] See Robert E. Brown, *Middle-class Democracy and the Revolution in Massachusetts,* Cornell University Press, Ithaca, N.Y., 1955, chaps. 1–5 in particular.

But the delegates were practical politicians, for the most part. They wrote into the document what were intended to be safeguards against the kinds of abuses of liberty that most concerned them. They sought to preserve the right to the writ of habeas corpus. The writ is one of the most basic of civil liberties, for its use by a judge requires a jailer to bring a prisoner before the bench so that the judge may decide if he is being legally held. The holding of prisoners without charge or trial had been a sore point with the colonists in the skirmishing that led to the Revolution.

The delegates also prohibited bills of attainder (legislative acts declaring specific persons guilty of crimes and prescribing the punishment for them) and ex post facto laws (laws describing acts as crimes after the acts have taken place). They also agreed to outlaw the granting of titles of nobility, for most delegates were committed to the principle of a republic and were concerned that some members of the aristocracy favored a monarchy. All of these restrictions were also applied to the states.

In the judicial article, delegates guaranteed a jury trial in all Federal criminal cases. They also defined treason, limited the conditions under which a conviction for it could be obtained, and prohibited punishment for it from extending to the family of the accused. These limitations, again, grew out of the experiences of the colonists during the period of the Revolution. And, coming from states in which various religions were dominant, they provided that "no religious test shall ever be required as a qualification to any office or public trust under the United States."

Probably the property-oriented citizens who dominated the Convention did not see civil rights as the central concern of the nation at the time, but failure to include a separate article on the subject proved to have been a strategic and almost fatal error for their plans. The Antifederalists, who opposed the adoption of the Constitution when it was submitted to the conventions in the states, made this a major target of their criticism. Men such as Patrick Henry were outraged. Thomas Jefferson, who had praised the men selected as delegates (they had been chosen by state governors or legislatures, not by popular election), might have been concerned too, but he was in Paris at the time and relatively isolated from the ratification process. In any case, it became necessary for some of the leading proponents of adoption—they were called Federalists—to agree that one of the first orders of business for Congress under the new government should be the submission of amendments dealing with the unmentioned rights.[8] (See Chapter 19 on civil rights.)

A second revolution? The delegates had to face still another difficult decision. They had to decide whether to attempt to secure the adoption of the new Constitution by the proper legal procedures or to propose another easier method. Some of the delegates wished to use caution—three refused to sign the final document because it did not call for a second convention

[8] See Robert A. Rutland, *The Birth of the Bill of Rights,* The University of North Carolina Press, Chapel Hill, N.C., 1955.

that could consider the objections that were raised in debates once the document was released.

One difficulty with the amending procedure under the Articles was that it required submission to the state legislatures for approval. It was at this point that opposition to the proposed constitution could expect to be centered, for the legislators would be asked to vote a reduction in their own powers. Even more importantly, the Articles called for unanimous approval by the member states before an amendment could be adopted. This provision was logical, given the theory of a confederation, but it produced enormous obstacles to change. On two earlier occasions, a single state had vetoed proposed amendments.

The members of the Convention had great respect for the law, but they were practicing the art of politics. They recognized that there was little hope for change if they abided by the existing rules. So they settled for what was technically a revolution—a change in the basic system of government by a method other than the legally prescribed one. It was to be a bloodless revolution, of course, and the thought of revolution probably seemed less ominous to them than it would to us, for they had recently gone through a far more dangerous one. Furthermore, they offered many opportunities for their proposals to be blocked in case the revolution should not have considerable support.

Their amending procedure required that the Constitution first be approved by Congress and then be passed along to the state legislatures, which had to provide for calling state ratifying conventions and electing delegates to them. Failure of Congress or the state legislatures to act would have prevented adoption of the Constitution. But they both did act.

The delegates at Philadelphia had proposed that the new government should go into operation when nine of the thirteen states approved the Constitution, and the state conventions could only accept or reject it as a whole. Once nine agreed, the others would have little choice—except that the two largest states, New York and Virginia, could have made it ineffective by holding out. And these were the critical states, indeed. The New York convention finally accepted the document by three votes; the Virginia convention, by ten. The Federalists, who had been astute in handling the campaign for ratification, promptly organized torchlight parades in celebration. The Founding Fathers had worked out their compromises well; they could scarcely have come up with a more optimum set of strategies had they relied on high-speed computers.[9]

THE NEW PACKAGE

What was it that the people of the United States had agreed to buy by the end of 1788? By and large, it was a package with familiar contents,

[9] For details on the convention and the campaign for ratification, see a standard American history textbook and the bibliography.

though the balance of ingredients differed from that existing under British rule or the Confederation.

Limited Government. The new Constitution, we could say in summary, provided for a much stronger government at the national level, but a limited government of the republican, or representative democracy, type. Government was limited chiefly through deliberate decentralization of the powers of decision making:

A federal system. The federal system divided up the powers of government much more than had been the case under the Articles, which had left the great bulk of power in the states. A central government that could act directly upon the general population, rather than having to go through the states, could check the regional governments; but in turn, it was severely restricted as to its powers.

A presidential system. The capstone of the presidential system of government, as we have seen, is a system of checks and balances. By dividing up power among the legislative, executive, and judicial branches and by permitting each to countercheck the other, Montesquieu's plan for limited government was put into effect.

Figure 4-4

Few Americans Would Want the Military Equal to Civilian Power

"Oh, Jefferson is a good man–but I'm not sure I like the idea of a civilian being President."

By permission of Burr Shafer.

Civil rights. John Locke's theory, holding that the people had never given certain powers to governments at any level but had reserved to the individual certain rights, was accepted by the Founding Fathers and included in the Constitution. The fact that the writers did not place as much emphasis upon this as many of their critics demanded at the time of ratification does not mean that they did not accept the principle.

Subordinate position of the military. Throughout history some governments have had difficulty in retaining power in troubled times because of pressures from the professional military establishment. Military leaders, in such times, have sometimes enjoyed support from a fearful populace. At other times, these leaders have taken power in order to prevent political developments they have disapproved of. The Founding Fathers recognized that in a democracy the military must, in peace or war, be subordinate to the civilian officers of government. In order to help ensure that this would be the case, they limited military appropriations to a two-year time span and provided that the President should be Commander in Chief of the Armed Forces.[10]

THE LONG-LIVED CONSTITUTION

The United States Constitution has become the oldest written constitution in the world (remembering that only part of it is actually written and that much of it does not appear in the formal document called the Constitution, or in its amendments). This is probably so because of the soundness of its original conception and because of the relative stability of American society.

In addition, there are two other specific reasons that particularly account for its longevity. The first is the almost completely successful restriction of amendments to *constitutional law* as distinguished from *statute law* (see below). The second is the rarity of formal amendment and the availability of more informal means of alteration: this leaves interpretation largely in the hands of contemporary decision makers, so that our leaders have been able to fit the rules of the game to the conditions of their own times beneath the umbrella of our legal heritage. Thus, we get the seeming anomaly of a formally rigid Constitution surviving longer than has any other written constitution. The anomaly is not real, however, because the fundamental law is relatively flexible rather than rigid.

A Constitution of Fundamentals. The typical state constitution is a lengthy document, filled with detail. Since the states have wide powers, a public that has never been sure how much it trusted its legislators has gradually

[10] The outstanding defense of the Constitution appeared originally as a newspaper series in 1787. *The Federalist* was written by Alexander Hamilton, James Madison, and John Jay, who favored adoption. Many editions are available in book form. For other sources, see the bibliography.

added to the number of words in efforts to restrict these state powers. And when new functions have been demanded of state governments, the citizenry has found it necessary to amend the constitutions still further in order to free those governments to take action. Even more significantly, interest groups have found these constitutions—most of them easier to amend than the United States Constitution—a relatively secure place in which to protect their most valuable interests against the vagaries of legislators. It is easier to add provisions to constitutions than it is to remove them. Most state constitutions, therefore, contain a great deal of statute law—ordinary written legislation—in addition to the fundamental law described at the beginning of this chapter.

The United States Constitution, in contrast, has been restricted almost exclusively to basic law. There were some of the "thou shall nots" in the original document, just as there are in state constitutions, but they are an ordinary part of constitutions, involving the distribution of powers. For example, "No tax or duty shall be laid on articles exported from any state." There was some statute law in the original document, however. Congress, for example, was prohibited from regulating the importation of those who were delicately referred to as "such persons as any of the states now existing shall think proper to admit," i.e., slaves. But this provision had a twenty-year time limit. Treason was defined and limits placed on punishment for it. But there were few such provisions. Furthermore, the Constitution's writers did not even attempt to define most of the terms they used: "Congress shall have power . . . to regulate commerce . . . among the several states." What is commerce? When is it interstate? Such questions have been left to the courts to answer—and this is the key to the flexibility of the document. Judges under different social and economic conditions have interpreted terms differently.

An Exception: The "Noble Experiment." Amendments to the Constitution have largely followed the original pattern and have dealt with broad restrictive or enabling terms. There was, however, one major deviation from this pattern, one in which interest groups used the same strategy at the national level that they were accustomed to using at the state level. This was the Eighteenth Amendment, which—with the possible exception of the Fifth—is the only one that has been popularly referred to by its number.

For many years, persons who saw both social and moral evils in intoxicating beverages had campaigned for the prohibition of their manufacture and sale. The Woman's Christian Temperance Union and the Anti-Saloon League, in particular, and other groups as well, made a massive effort to influence congressmen and state legislators. They entered into campaigns, labeled the candidates as "wets" or "drys," and kept up unremitting pressure, effectively making use of the cultural values of the day—the early twentieth century. Finally they succeeded in getting Congress to submit to the states for ratification a proposed amendment on the subject. But it was an unusual amendment, modeled on what the drys had succeeded in placing in several state constitutions. Its most significant provision was that "the manufacture, sale, or transportation of intoxicating liquors . . . *is hereby prohibited.*"[11] It did not say, "Congress shall have the power to control or prohibit."

This was statutory law, deliberately planned to prevent Congress from backsliding should the pressures on it be changed. It was accepted by the required number of state legislatures and went into effect on January 29, 1919. It differed in form from the income tax amendment (the Sixteenth), which had been proclaimed six years earlier. The latter had said simply: "The Congress shall have power to lay and collect taxes on incomes. . . ." It was a broad grant of power indeed—as many a taxpayer may note each April 15.

And how did the experiment in legislation by constitution work at the Federal level? Historians tell us that the amendment—through no fault of its advocates—went into effect at the very time that American life-styles were changing radically. The proper, innocent years were giving way to the "roaring twenties." The census reports of a year later showed that the nation was more than 50 per cent urban. The automobile and the radio were about to give the nation mobility and a nationwide network for instantaneous communication. The American culture had become urban. Drinking within limits had always been accepted as part of the American way of life throughout the nation and in many of the nation's subcultures. Even the code of the West included the rule that a man never turn down a drink. With large numbers of Americans demanding beer, wine, and liquor, what of the Eighteenth Amendment? It was ridiculed, defied, and ignored. "Prohibition has found a new line of endeavor for the underworld," Alfred E. Smith complained during the 1928 presidential campaign. "It brought life to the bootleggers, and the bootleggers begat the hijackers, and the hijackers begat the racketeers." Bootleggers delivered liquor directly to the offices of congressmen and senators. President Warren Harding regularly served whiskey at White House poker parties.

Never before or since has a part of the Constitution been so deliberately flouted by so many. But efforts to remove constitutional provisions must be made in opposition to organized interests that want to preserve them and in opposition to the psychological right of possession. The typical citizen tends to believe that if something is in a constitution, it must belong there. So the burden of proof is on those working for its removal. It was difficult to argue for repeal of the Eighteenth simply on the basis of the fact that it was not enforceable. People might drink, but they were not sure they *ought* to, or that it was proper to admit that one considered drinking proper. The prohibitionists, in other words, enjoyed the advantage of having social sanctions on their side; the American habit of moralizing was a strategic asset to them.

The balance of forces changed with the coming of the Great Depression.

[11] Italics added.

The government could well use tax revenues from the sale of liquor; "temperance" as a social movement lost its appeal for reformers, who turned to the concerns of cyclical unemployment and the fate of the common man in urban society. But there was no way, legally, to end the "noble experiment" except through the time, effort, and cost of formal amendment. National prohibition died on December 5, 1933 when the Secretary of State proclaimed the Twenty-first Amendment to be in force. Law and social behavior came closer to accord. The Constitution had lost its most embarrassing provision.

Informal Amendment. A noted law school professor is said to have introduced the topic of constitutional law to his students with this comment: "Don't try to read the Constitution, it will just confuse you in trying to understand what American government is all about." He meant that much of the actual Constitution is based on interpretation of what those crisp, often tantalizingly ambiguous phrases of the Constitution really mean. And Charles Evans Hughes, Chief Justice of the United States, once said with only slight exaggeration that "the Constitution is what the judges say it is, and the judiciary [not the Constitution itself] is the safeguard of our liberties and of our property."

Much of what is popularly believed to be in the Constitution is not there. Important aspects of American government and politics—the committee system in Congress, the number of justices and most of the powers of the Supreme Court, the President's Cabinet, the merit system of civil service, the national party conventions—lack a formal position in the document.

The Supreme Court is commonly regarded as the master interpreter of the Constitution, but it is not the only one. Congress, Presidents, bureaucrats, political party leaders, and even ordinary voters have made significant changes in the Constitution's meaning. For example, the justices spend years refining their interpretation of constitutional phrases and sometimes, a generation or two later, change their minds, as they did with respect to "separate but equal" facilities for Negroes. (Compare *Plessy v. Ferguson,* 1896, with *Brown v. Board of Education of Topeka,* 1954.)

At the death of President Harrison in 1841, Vice President John Tyler was clearly the constitutional successor, but his powers were vague. Was he Acting President? Or did he assume the full status of his predecessor? He decided that he was, in fact, the President, and his interpretation has since been followed.

Political party leaders—independent of constitutional requirements—developed the presidential nominating convention; and Congress established the rule that the presidential candidate with a plurality of the vote in a state gets all of its electoral votes (by providing that electors are to be chosen at large). Voters generally will not elect anyone to Congress who does not live in their district, though the Constitution requires only that a representative be a resident of the state from which he is elected.

An extreme case in stretching interpretation came when convicted gangster Roger (The Terrible) Touhy and his partner, Basil (The Owl) Banghart, broke out of the Illinois state prison at Joliet during World War II, succeeded in evading a road block, and reached Chicago. Police believed that the pair could most quickly be apprehended with aid from Federal authorities. But the two had not been convicted of a Federal crime. FBI agents joined the hunt, however, and helped to capture the criminals. If the escapees, back in their cells, had any interest in the legal niceties, they may have been surprised to learn that their captors intervened on the authority of the Federal government's war powers (which, by the way, are not described in the Constitution either). It was argued that the criminals had violated Federal law when, having escaped from state prison, they failed to notify their draft boards of a change of address.

Thus the broad phrasing of the Constitution and its omissions permit majorities of each generation to fashion government so that it will respond to the political needs of the time, to make changes that, though informal, are given the stamp of legitimacy. These are based on interpretations made through accepted procedures. Even those who disagree are willing to grant them the status of constitutional law, properly binding on all citizens. The general, if reluctant, compliance of Southern whites to Supreme Court decisions on segregation indicates the strength of this feeling. Yet no changes, formal or informal, are lightly made. The Constitution is held in such reverence that it is difficult to make even minor alterations.

In later chapters, we will point to many informal additions and interpretations to the basic constitutional document. Sometimes, however, it has been politically necessary to add formal amendments to the Constitution.

The Formal Amendments. Almost the only time the Constitution is formally amended is when there would otherwise be doubt about the legitimacy of a change made by informal means.

The Constitution has been amended, on the average, less than once every seven years. If we count the Bill of Rights as one amendment instead of ten, and the three Civil War amendments as one, changes have been made only about once in fifteen years. Of course, a great number of amendments have been suggested; quite a few have been discussed by congressional committees or on the floor of one house or the other; and five have been proposed by Congress, but not ratified by the states.[12] Four of these proposed changes were subsequently achieved by informal means or were made moot by the Civil War.

Thus we see that Congress is the focal point for the important decisions about formal amendment. Political forces must convince a two-thirds majority in each house (which often cannot be achieved without the sup-

[12] *Proposed Amendments to the Constitution,* Sen. Doc. 93, 69th Cong., 1st Sess., 1926; and *Proposed Amendments to the Constitution,* Sen. Doc. 163, 87th Cong., 2d Sess., 1962.

port of the President) if a proposed change is to be submitted. Getting the necessary number of state legislatures to ratify has generally been a relatively easy task.

What kinds of issues require such an expenditure of political resources? The amendments actually adopted may be classified as follows:

To meet objections and concessions made at the time of the adoption of the Constitution. These are the first ten amendments (1791), which are known collectively as the Bill of Rights. In effect, the Federalists agreed to support these amendments in the first session of Congress in return for the votes of doubtful persons in the ratifying conventions, especially in New York and Virginia. The significance of the amendments was to give eventual legitimacy to the document in the eyes of the Antifederalists, who otherwise viewed the document with distrust.

To overrule the United States Supreme Court. These amendments were not, strictly speaking, necessary, for a small change of position on the Supreme Court could have produced the same result. The Eleventh Amendment (1798) was adopted specifically to overrule the case of *Chisholm v. Georgia*[13] and had the effect of restoring the traditional rule that a state cannot be sued without its own consent. The Supreme Court had, to the surprise of many, ruled that Chisholm had the right to sue the state of Georgia in Federal court without seeking permission to do so. The Court. was divided in its opinion, and judicial authorities still find the opinion rather implausible. The case had symbolic importance, as did the amendment, in that it involved the touchy question of whether the states retained at least some of the mantle of sovereignty after the Constitution was adopted.

The Sixteenth Amendment specifically reversed a 5 to 4 decision of the Supreme Court that involved the power of the Federal government to levy an income tax.[14] Congress had adopted an income tax for the first time during the Civil War. It was allowed to lapse later, but in 1894 Congress again adopted such a tax. It was challenged in the courts. The Supreme Court ruled it unconstitutional, but to do so, it had to reverse the rule of the century-old Hylton case, which dealt with the meaning of a "direct" tax in the Constitution. The spokesman for the bare majority indicated that the five feared the consequences of the tax—in other words, they disagreed with the implications of the social policy involved. As has been the case before and since, the Court's decision substituted the views of its majority for those of the congressional majority.

Later, as Federal revenues from the previously adequate tariff were threatened with decline, Congress debated whether to pass another income tax and depend on the Court of the day to reverse the earlier decision. But one view in Congress held this to be imposing an unnecessarily embarrassing burden upon the Court. This argument prevailed, and congressional

[13] *Chisholm v. Georgia,* 2 Dallas 419 (1793).

[14] *Pollock v. Farmers' Loan and Trust Co.,* 157 U.S. 429 (1895).

leaders decided to submit to the state legislatures a proposed amendment to permit levying taxes on incomes "from whatever source derived."

The argument concerning embarrassment of the Court may have been essentially a stalling tactic—the hope may have been that the state legislatures would not approve a formal amendment. Certainly, the Court had often previously reversed itself. But the Sixteenth Amendment was ratified by the state legislatures. In both of these cases, the important position of the Court as legitimate interpreter of the Constitution was preserved, while the desired changes were also achieved.

To legitimatize the results of salient events. In an effort to make the Constitution conform to the results of the Civil War, the Thirteenth Amendment (1865), the Fourteenth (1868), and the Fifteenth (1870) were adopted. The first prohibited slavery; the other two sought to give the freed slaves the same legal rights as other citizens. They were written in such broad language, however, that they have been of great importance to all citizens in the matters of civil rights (see Chapter 19). Reconstruction governments in states that had joined the Confederacy during the Civil War were required to accept the last two amendments while their territory was occupied by Federal troops. Their adoption signified that the Northern position, which had prevailed on the battlefield, would be accepted in law as well as in fact. The South was forced to recognize policies it had long opposed.

To make changes where specific provisions could not be altered by interpretation. A number of amendments have been absolutely necessary to accomplish the end desired. These involve changes in prescribed structure that could not take place as a result of Supreme Court or any other action—except by deliberately ignoring the written words of the Constitution. The Twelfth Amendment (1804) changed the means by which the Electoral College selects the President and Vice President. It was designed to permit the two officials to come from the same political party, thus recognizing the role of parties in the process of election, a provision neither made nor intended by the Founding Fathers (see Chapter 10).

The Seventeenth Amendment (1913) provided for the direct election of senators. Previously, senators had been chosen by legislatures, in recognition of the idea that the states, as such, should be represented in Congress. In practice, the state governments rarely had an interest that could be separated from that of the people who lived in them. Furthermore, through time, the Senate came under increasing criticism as being a "rich man's club" and undemocratic. There were charges, some of them well founded, that men got into the Senate by outright bribery of legislators and by making huge contributions to the appropriate political party—in other words, that they had purchased their offices. One of the Populist-Progessive reforms called for the election of senators by the people. We would consider nothing else acceptable today.

The Twentieth (Lame Duck) Amendment (1933) brought a recognition of modern means of transportation and communication to Federal elections. The original Constitution, written in the day of the buggy and stagecoach, had provided that the President would not take office until four months after his election and that members of Congress would not meet in regular session until thirteen months after election. A painful and confused waiting period in the depth of the worst depression in our history followed the election of Franklin D. Roosevelt in 1932. President Hoover had received a vote of no confidence and the President-elect refused to state his views on policy until he came into power. This situation helped to encourage the adoption of an amendment that cut the waiting period for congressmen to 2 months and for the President to 2½. (Time had to be allowed for Congress to meet and certify the vote or to choose a President or Vice President, should circumstances require it.)

The Twenty-third Amendment (1961) was designed to allow residents of the District of Columbia to vote for President. It gives the District three votes in the Electoral College. The disfranchisement of the District had long been a matter of discussion—it seemed ironic to many that residents of the capital city should have no vote—but efforts to change the Constitution were held up by Southern congressmen, who believed that their constituents would not approve of extending the vote to an area with a large Negro population. (Since the end of World War II, the District population has been more than 50 per cent Negro.) Once the proposal was made, it was adopted by the necessary number of state legislatures in a matter of only eight months.

To make certain specific and restrictive provisions. The Twenty-second Amendment (1951) limited the President to not more than two terms in office. (He may serve up to two full terms in addition to completing the term of his successor if he has served in that capacity for less than two years.) This article was proposed because most members of Congress in 1947 disapproved of Franklin D. Roosevelt's four elections to the office. Although several Presidents have considered running for a third term, and Theodore Roosevelt actually did so, at least within the terms of this amendment, F.D.R.'s success in defying a long-standing tradition annoyed some and alarmed others. While Republican-controlled state legislatures approved the proposal rather quickly, many Democratic states, even in the South where Roosevelt had been viewed with ambivalence, were reluctant. But after Harry Truman annoyed many Southerners by making civil rights a major issue in the 1948 campaign and afterwards, Southern states acted to ratify. The amendment was proclaimed in 1951. (Technically, the amendment did not apply to President Truman, but it would have been a great liability had he chosen to run in 1952.)

As was noted above, the Eighteenth Amendment (1919) not only took away Federal power, but wrote legislation into the Constitution. It was repealed by the Twenty-first (1933), which also provided for some state control over the importation of alcoholic beverages.

The Constitutional Convention did not attempt to define a Federal suffrage, and no subsequent effort to secure one has been successful. A number of amendments have dealt with the suffrage, however. The Fifteenth, one of the Civil War amendments (1870), sought to prevent anyone from being denied the vote in state or national elections "on account of race, color, or previous condition of servitude." The Nineteenth (1920) established the same kind of rule to prevent denial of suffrage "on account of sex." The Twenty-fourth (1964) prohibited use of the payment of a poll tax as a prerequisite for voter eligibility.

Future Formal Amendments. What amendments will be adopted in the future, there is no way of predicting. There have been long periods in the past when the Constitution has gone unamended. During the sixty-one years between 1804 and 1865 and the forty-three years between 1870 and 1913, no changes took place. In these periods, an occasional Fourth of July speech would praise the Constitution as a document inspired of God that had achieved something so near to perfection that it needed no further change and might never need it. But, as we have seen, there have been changes. They have generally come about as the result of some fairly specific want that could not be met in any other way and still be accepted as legitimate. Furthermore, we have seen that adoption of both the original document and the amendments have involved practical political decisions designed to meet the demands of the time and to accomplish the political goals of the leaders of the time.

TODAY'S RULES FOR TODAY'S WORLD

"Can one generation bind another, and all others, in succession forever?" Thomas Jefferson once asked. And he gave what is probably an obvious answer to a loaded question: "I think not." He believed that each generation "has a right to choose for itself the form of government it believes the most promotive of its own happiness." And he warned us not to confuse respect for traditions and institutions with uncritical acceptance of things from a world that is no longer with us:[15]

> Some men look at constitutions with sanctimonious reverence and deem them like the ark of the covenant, too sacred to be touched. They ascribe to the men of the preceding age a wisdom more than human, and suppose what they did to be beyond amendment. I am certainly not an advocate for frequent and untried changes in laws and constitutions. . . . [But] as new discoveries are made, new truths disclosed, and manners and opinions change with the change of circumstances, institutions must advance also, and keep pace with the times.

Generally, Americans have agreed with this sentiment. The Constitution is held in great respect, but a number of formal and informal means have

[15] The quotation is from a letter to Samuel Kercheval (1816). There are many editions of the letters and other writings of Jefferson.

been devised to modify it from time to time. The writers of the Constitution recognized the need for change, as did Jefferson. The plan they devised probably proved to be more difficult than they expected, but their Constitution was so general that a number of informal arrangements have permitted adequate flexibility. On only a few occasions in history has the conflict between public demands and the prevailing interpretation been stretched anywhere near the breaking point; except for the Civil War crisis, any disjuncture between the two has been corrected in a relatively few years.

The Formal Process of Change. Article V of the original Constitution provided for amending procedures. They were divided into two parts: proposal and ratification. Proposals for change were to come from the national government. Two alternatives were offered: (1) An amendment could be proposed by a two-thirds vote in each house of Congress (the President is not formally involved); (2) a national constitutional convention could be called by Congress "on the application" of two-thirds of the state legislatures.

The first method, to date, is the only one that has been used; the second has not been seriously considered, probably for a number of reasons. First

Figure 4-5

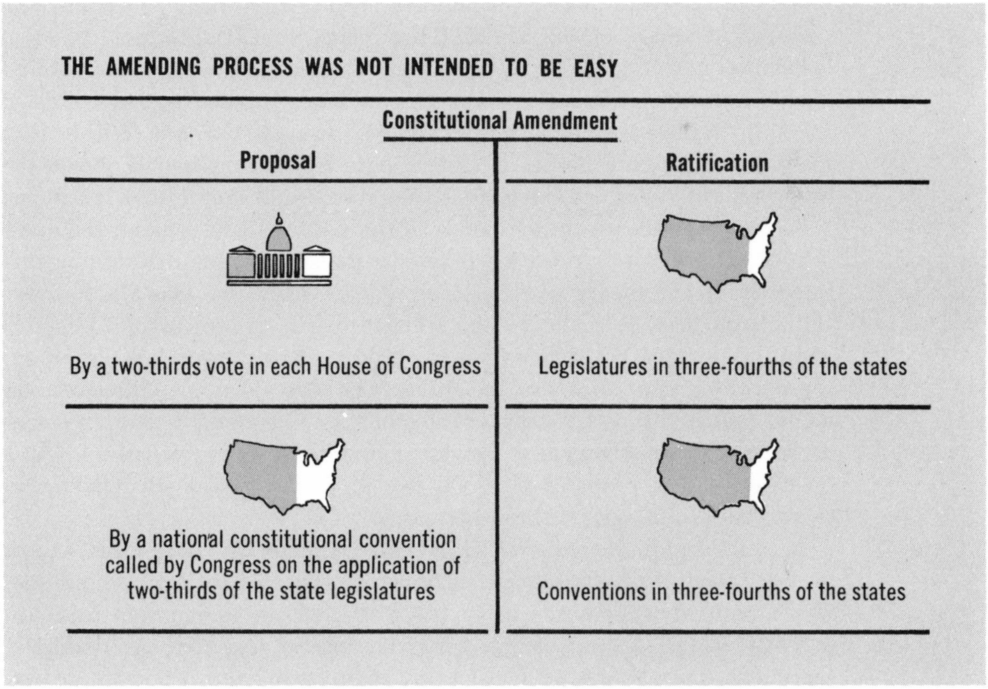

THE AMENDING PROCESS WAS NOT INTENDED TO BE EASY

Constitutional Amendment	
Proposal	Ratification
By a two-thirds vote in each House of Congress	Legislatures in three-fourths of the states
By a national constitutional convention called by Congress on the application of two-thirds of the state legislatures	Conventions in three-fourths of the states

of all, there has never been a situation in which a dominant portion of the population has felt that a major revision was needed, and a national constitutional convention would imply extensive reevaluation, rather than accommodation to some specific problem. Second, Congress would not likely give up its virtual monopoly over proposing amendments—even if two-thirds of the states petitioned, it could not be forced to act—unless there were a national crisis greater even than that which led to the Civil War. Finally, the convention method would be a clumsy and time-consuming operation in any case.

Thus the second alternative, proposal by a national constitutional convention, is a last-act safety valve to be used only in the gravest of circumstances. A few years after World War II, an effort was made to have a convention called. A number of conservative groups urged a constitutional amendment to limit the Federal income tax to a maximum of 25 per cent of gross income. When Congress, hard pressed for defense and other funds, ignored the demands, these groups began asking state legislatures to petition Congress to call a convention for the purpose of proposing such an amendment. A number of legislatures did so. Had the number reached two-thirds, congressional leaders would have been faced with a difficult decision, one that would have caused them some political embarrassment at the least.

The exclusive control over proposals for amendment possessed by Congress has been an occasional source of discontent, especially among States' righters. The protest of these groups has been manifested in proposals for constitutional amendment such as that made in 1962 by the General Assembly of the States. This group, consisting largely of state legislators and affiliated with the Council of State Governments, offered a procedure by which an amendment could be proposed by two-thirds of the state legislatures, with ratification in the usual fashion. Within four months, one or both houses of fifteen state legislatures had endorsed the proposal, but it seemed likely that Congress would ignore their petitions.

While proposals are in the hands of the national government, the question of ratification or rejection is left to the states, thus maintaining the integrity of the theory of federalism. Again, there are two alternatives: ratification may be made by the legislatures in two-thirds of the states (approval by the governor is not required), or by conventions called for the purpose in two-thirds of the states. The states can use either method unless Congress prescribes one or the other, as it has tended to do in recent decades. (Congress may also provide a time limit within which the states must act or the proposal dies. On five of the proposed amendments, a seven-year deadline was established.)

In practice, all amendments have been approved by legislatures, except for the Twenty-first. This amendment, which repealed national prohibition, was submitted to conventions in the states. Congress required this, apparently in the interest of speed and because of fear that prohibitionist sentiment was stronger in legislatures than among the people generally.

The public was in a mood to approve, and the Federal government needed the potential tax revenues. It was ratified within nine months. (The Twenty-third was approved by *legislatures* in even less time.)

Strategy for Ratification. The choice of amendment ratification offers a problem in strategies that must be decided by congressional leaders. Legislatures are ordinarily used for a number of reasons: (1) Congress does not always prescribe the procedure and the legislators prefer to keep the decision in their own hands. (2) The first time that the amendment procedure was used, action was taken by legislatures, which established a precedent. (3) Congressmen often have working relationships with legislators in their home states, and many of them are former legislators. As such, they are likely to view with favor the legislative route. (4) The procedure is cheaper and simpler.

But the balance of forces may be quite different in a convention from that in a legislature. Depending on how the legislatures establish the conventions, they may have a small-town–big-city balance different from that in the legislature. Or members may be citizens who are not politicians and they may have viewpoints far different from those of the legislators. In any case, they are called to vote on one issue alone and need not be concerned about subsequent political retribution. Most importantly, perhaps, a convention would produce pro and con candidates so that, except for any malapportionment of convention districts, the vote would become practically a referendum on the issue. The convention can act speedily, providing the legislature permits one to be called. It need only meet and in one day cast votes either in favor or against a proposal.

If the legislature is to decide, leaders may choose to avoid the issue—the legislature will not even consider it if the leaders bottle up the resolution of ratification in committee. A legislature, with many other items on its agenda, may ignore the proposal. It may, on the other hand, consider the proposal a number of times. But the Supreme Court has ruled that once the legislature approves of an amendment, it cannot withdraw its approval.[16]

There is currently only one moot amendment technically before the states, an amendment that would authorize Congress to regulate child labor. It was submitted in 1924, but never received the necessary approval; today it is dead, for practical purposes, because the Supreme Court long ago reversed its earlier position and now permits Congress to do without amendment everything the amendment would permit.[17] The Court's action has been accepted as providing sufficient legitimation. (To eliminate future chances for such constitutional flotsam cluttering the scene, Congress now

[16] *Hawke v. Smith,* 253 U.S. 221 (1920).

[17] The cases that made the amendment unnecessary were *National Labor Relations Board v. Jones and Laughlin Steel Corp.,* 301 U.S. 1 (1937), and *United States v. Darby,* 312 U.S. 100 (1941).

usually stipulates that a proposal loses its vitality unless ratified by the requisite number of states within seven years of submission.)

A Closing Note. The United States Constitution has demonstrated impressive resiliency since it went into effect in 1789. It has fitted the needs of a tiny rural frontier nation and a nation of huge cities and vast industrial production. It has survived in times when little was expected of government and when people have depended heavily upon government. It has functioned in peace and in war. It has sometimes been stretched and distorted. Its assurances of man's rights have been sorely tried at times, and its provisions for these rights have not been extended fully in a literal sense. Yet the Constitution has met challenges; no more than a few years have been needed in which to adjust the legal interpretation of the Constitution to meet the demands of the dominant groups in society at any given time. Even the celebrated conflict between Franklin D. Roosevelt and a Supreme Court dominated by conservatives who took a narrow view of Federal government powers lasted only two years (1935–1937). And it was settled without revolution, without "packing" the Court, without amendments—indeed, without even changing the membership of the Court. One or two justices simply changed their way of voting on critical issues.

The Constitution has had its critics. Some say that the power it gives the courts is not democratic; that it provides for planned inefficiency in slow, clumsy procedures; that it perpetuates an uncoordinated system of government. However true these charges may be, the Constitution has proved to be healthy, long-lived, workable, and it has almost continuously enjoyed unquestioned legitimacy.

SELECTED BIBLIOGRAPHY

A constitution is for the living. It changes in meaning with each generation, as does the historical interpretation of its past meaning. A fine example of history being rewritten to fit the mood of the times may be found in the post-World War II response to the writings of the historian Charles A. Beard. Beard, a product of the age of populism and "progressive" politics, reinterpreted the Constitution, seeing it not as a work of selfless statesmanship, but as a weapon of the influential classes in keeping control over society [2, 3]. His interpretation of the economic situation under the Articles of Confederation has been challenged in recent years by Jensen [11], and his work concerning the motivations of the Founding Fathers has been challenged by Brown [5, 6] and McDonald [13]. Yet the Beardian thesis should not be lightly dismissed, for he was certainly right in part and he has been given support by some contemporary historians, such as Main [15]. Whatever the explanation; the Constitution is always a political document, as Schubert [20] demonstrates.

Social stability and predictable behavior are products of a constitution, and few political leaders overtly advocate ignoring the established constitution or achieving change outside its context—though Kornhauser [12] and Nomad [17] show that the exceptional cases make history.

The American political, economic, and social environments as they existed near the end of the eighteenth century have interested many writers. The ideology of the day is discussed by Adams [1], Becker [4], Hamilton and his colleagues [10], and Mayer [16].

The period immediately preceding the Constitutional Convention of 1787 has been described by the Beards [3], Jensen [11], and Friedrich and McCloskey [9]. Portraits of the delegates are offered by Beard [2] and Umbreit [24]. Reports on the actual convention proceedings and efforts to secure adoption, including Madison's notes as a delegate, may be found in Solberg [21] and Tansill [22]. The historian Farrand has left us a classic portrait of the task [7, 8].

Amendments to the Constitution, including those proposed but never adopted, are discussed in the context of history by Rutland [19] and Tansill [23]. Padover [18] offers an overall view of the process of constitutional change.

1. Adams, Randolph G.: *The Political Ideas of the American Revolution,* Facsimile Library, New York, 1939. (Available in paperback.)
2. Beard, Charles A.: *An Economic Interpretation of the Constitution of the United States,* The Macmillan Company, New York, 1913.
3. Beard, Charles A., and Mary R. Beard: *The Rise of American Civilization,* The Macmillan Company, New York, 4 vols., 1942.
4. Becker, Carl: *The Declaration of Independence,* Harcourt, Brace & World, Inc., New York, 1922. (Available in paperback.)
5. Brown, Robert E.: *Charles Beard and the Constitution,* Princeton University Press, Princeton, N.J., 1956.
6. Brown, Robert E.: *Middle-class Democracy and the Revolution in Massachusetts,* Cornell University Press, Ithaca, N.Y., 1955.
7. Farrand, Max: *The Framing of the Constitution of the United States,* Yale University Press, New Haven, Conn., reprinted in 1940. (Also available in paperback.)
8. Farrand, Max: *The Records of the Federal Convention,* Yale University Press, New Haven, Conn., 3 vols., 1911.
9. Friedrich, Carl J., and Robert G. McCloskey (eds.): *From the Declaration of Independence to the Constitution,* The Liberal Arts Press, Inc., New York, 1960.
10. Hamilton, Alexander, James Madison, and John Jay: *The Federalist.* (Many editions, complete and abridged; originally published as newspaper articles, 1787–1788.)
11. Jensen, Merrill: *The New Nation: A History of the United States during the Confederation,* Alfred A. Knopf, Inc., New York, 1950.
12. Kornhauser, William: *The Politics of Mass Society,* The Free Press of Glencoe, New York, 1959.
13. McDonald, Forrest: *We the People, the Economic Origins of the Constitution,* The University of Chicago Press, Chicago, 1958.
14. McIlwain, Charles H.: *The American Revolution: A Constitutional Interpretation,* Cornell University Press, Ithaca, N.Y., 1961.
15. Main, Jackson T.: *The Antifederalists,* University of North Carolina Press, Chapel Hill, N.C., 1961.
16. Mayer, Milton (ed.): *John Locke, Adam Smith and The Federalist,* abr., Oceana Publications, New York, 1960.
17. Nomad, Max: *Aspects of Revolt: A Study of Revolutionary Theories and Techniques,* Noonday Press, New York, 1961.
18. Padover, Saul K.: *The Living U.S. Constitution,* New American Library of World Literature, Inc., New York, 1960.
19. Rutland, Robert A.: *The Birth of the Bill of Rights,* University of North Carolina Press, Chapel Hill, N.C., 1955.

20. Schubert, Glendon: *Constitutional Politics,* Holt, Rinehart and Winston, Inc., New York, 1960.
21. Solberg, Winton U. (ed.): *The Federal Convention and the Formation of the Union of the American States,* The Liberal Arts Press, Inc., New York, 1960.
22. Tansill, Charles C. (ed.): *Documents Illustrative of the Formation of the Union of American States,* H. Doc. 398, 69th Cong., 1st Sess., 1927.
23. Tansill, Charles C. (ed.): *Proposed Amendments to the Constitution,* Sen. Doc. 93, 69th Cong., 1st Sess., 1926.
24. Umbreit, Kenneth B.: *The Founding Fathers,* Harper & Row, Publishers, New York, 1941.

Law Cases. In this and other chapters, the authors will refer to formal decisions of the United States Supreme Court. These case reports are available in all law and college libraries, and in many public libraries. The means of locating them can perhaps best be described through an illustration. Suppose we take the case of *Brown v. Board of Education of Topeka,* 347 U.S. 483 (1954). This cryptic message is translated as follows: First is given the name of the person who technically brought the case before the Court (Brown). He may actually be representing a large group, an organization, or a unit of government, and he may have been either the plaintiff (complainer) or the defendant (the person allegedly in the wrong) in the original action. He is the person asking that the case be reviewed by a higher court. After the *v.* (*versus,* against) is the name of the defendant before the Court (the Board of Education). Next follows a reference to the *United States Reports* (U.S.), the official *verbatim* report on the decision. Until after the Civil War, these reports were listed under the name of the Supreme Court reporter, e.g., Dallas (or Dall.) at the end of the eighteenth century, or Wallace (Wall.) in the 1870s. There are other records of the Supreme Court as well as of the Courts of Appeals. A librarian can help the reader with these. Preceding the volume name (U.S.) appears the volume number (347), after it the page (483) on which the report of the case begins, and finally the year (1954) of the decision. Case titles are sometimes quite esoteric, as in those involving maritime law (the Laura), seizure of allegedly illegal property (*United States v. One Obscene Book Entitled "Married Love"*), and in the use of such terms as *ex rel.* (on relation or behalf of), or *ex parte* (on the part of—as when an individual petitions for a writ of habeas corpus, *Ex parte McCardle*). "United States" in the title of the case, incidentally, means that the United States government, through the Department of Justice, is a party, but in other cases a government agency is listed as a party in its own name (Subversive Activities Control Board, National Labor Relations Board, etc.).

Cases Cited in Chapter 4.

Brown v. Board of Education of Topeka, 347 U.S. 483 (1954).
Chisholm v. Georgia, 2 Dallas 419 (1793).
Hawke v. Smith, 253 U.S. 221 (1920).
Hylton v. United States, 3 Dallas 171 (1796).
National Labor Relations Board v. Jones and Laughlin Steel Corp., 301 U.S. 1 (1937).
Plessy v. Ferguson, 163 U.S. 537 (1896).
Pollock v. Farmers' Loan and Trust Co., 157 U.S. 429 (1895).
United States v. Darby, 312 U.S. 100 (1941).

CHAPTER 5

FEDERALISM: SHARED DECISION MAKING

"The United States," a British observer has noted,[1] "is a federal country in spirit, in its way of life, and in its Constitution. To write about American federalism, therefore, is to look at the whole of the American political system from a particular point of view, and to consider the working of government and politics, at *all* levels, as forming a single system."

In the preceding chapter, we noted the meaning of federalism and the reasons why it was made a part of the Constitution. We emphasized that in a federal system the regional (state) governments are, in theory, not subordinate to the central government in their own areas of jurisdiction. They share sovereignty,* power, and responsibility for decision making in a great many areas.

***SOVEREIGNTY. The supreme power of the state; the locus of ultimate decision making from which there is no appeal. It is a legal concept introduced by Jean Bodin in 1576. In modern political science, the term generally is not used, except in international relations theory. When applied to political relationships within a nation, the concept is often vague and ambiguous.**

The meaning of federalism in the United States has changed through time. The Founding Fathers were not themselves in complete agreement as to the kind of government they were establishing.[2] Over the years, the meaning of federalism has reflected the pragmatic American idea that government at any given level should perform whatever functions the dominant groups believe can be performed by that level of government better than by some other level or by private institutions. Cooperation among governmental levels on specific projects likewise has been arrived at pragmatically.

The question of what is the most logical function of a government generally or at any particular level may be treated as a

[1] M. J. C. Vile, *The Structure of American Federalism,* Oxford University Press, Fair Lawn, N.J., 1961, p. 1.

[2] Martin Diamond, "What the Framers Meant by Federalism," in Robert A. Goldwin (ed.), *A Nation of States: Essays on the American Federal System,* Rand McNally & Company, Chicago, 1963, pp. 24–41.

problem in ideal model building. But in a behavioral sense, it is a question of ideology, that is, of what people *believe* to be the proper function of government.[3] In this chapter, we will view American federalism from that perspective.

FEDERALISM IN A FRONTIER NATION

In early America, an age of slow means of transportation and communication, people came to think of themselves as Virginians and New Yorkers rather than Americans. Considering that even the state capital, much less the nation's capital, was in those days about as far away from his home town (in time) as Karachi is from Richmond or Albany today, it is little wonder that the frontiersman called on the Federal government rather seldom, except in regard to matters of protection from foreign threats. But the typical American citizen of the first half of the nineteenth century also almost certainly was not committed to the idea of *laissez faire*—why should a frontier farmer or the only general storekeeper in an isolated village care about a sophisticated economic theory that affected, primarily, manufacturers? He probably did not.

Early Federalism. The national government was weak in its early years—so weak, in fact, that neither President Washington nor many of the newly elected members of Congress hurried to New York (the temporary capital) to get the new government under way in 1789. But the national government did expand its powers in the years preceding the Civil War, and the evidence indicates that it did so in response to the demands of voters—and a gradually changing ideology—rather than out of acts of perversity. Furthermore, the national government did so despite vigorous support of the doctrine of States' rights and dual federalism* by a minority.

***DUAL FEDERALISM. The legal theory that the two levels of government in a federal system are coequal sovereignties, each supreme in its own sphere, and each performing functions separate and distinct from the other.**

Nineteenth-century Federalism. The Federal government played important early roles, not only in establishing systems of public education, but also in relieving the states of their war debts. It also worked closely with the states in the concerns of "the militia, law enforcement, court practices, the administration of elections, public health measures, pilot laws, and many other matters."[4]

[3] The characteristics of ideology and the principal American ideologies will be developed in the next two chapters.

[4] Morton Grodzins, "The Federal System," in the President's Commission on National Goals, *Goals for Americans*, Prentice-Hall, Inc., Englewood Cliffs, N.J., 1960, p. 269.

As Morton Grodzins, a specialist in American federalism, has noted:[5]

> Political behavior and administrative action of the nineteenth century provide positive evidence that, throughout the entire era of so-called dual federalism, the many governments in the American federal system continued the close administrative and fiscal collaboration of the earlier period. Governmental activities were not extensive. But relative to what governments did, intergovernmental cooperation during the last century was comparable with that existing today.

Indeed, Federal aids may have been more important during the nineteenth century than they have been since the end of World War II. Nineteenth-century Minnesota, for example, benefited from Federal *land-grant programs* for education (including common school, university, and agricultural college grants), grants for railroad construction, river and harbor improvements, public building construction, general internal improvements, welfare, reclamation, and conservation. The state also received *cash grants* in the nineteenth century—for internal improvements, veterans' welfare, defense, and education, as well as *goods and materials* for programs in science and technology, agriculture, conservation, education, and welfare. Cooperative state and Federal activities during the nineteenth century involved the fields of education, scientific research, law enforcement, conservation, land settlement, and agriculture.[6] Also the state received what was in effect *grants of service*—the loan of professional personnel, particularly engineers from the military, to aid in solving specific problems.

The importance of these grants in the two generations following 1840 was enormous:[7]

> The financial impact of these programs on the state of Minnesota was generally greater than that of the mid-twentieth-century grant-in-aid. In the last third of the nineteenth century, a greater portion of the state's revenues came from federal sources than in any subsequent period. At times, Federal sources comprised over 50 per cent of the total state revenues, and after 1865, never fell below 20 per cent. [In the 1960s, the figure averaged around 10 per cent.]

Thus, we see that:[8]

> The history of the American governments is a history of shared functions. All nostalgic references to the days of state and local independence are based upon mythical views of the past. There has in fact never been a time when federal, state, and local functions were separate and distinct.

[5] *Ibid.*, p. 270.

[6] Daniel J. Elazar, *The American Partnership,* The University of Chicago Press, Chicago, 1962, chap. 17.

[7] *Ibid.*, p. 279.

[8] Morton Grodzins, "Centralization and Decentralization in the American Federal System," in Goldwin, *op. cit.*, pp. 5–6.

The Marble Cake Pattern. The federal system, therefore, is not one of three levels—national, state, and local—that were once separate and distinct, but have in recent decades become corrupted. Instead it is "a marble cake":[9]

> Wherever you slice through it you reveal an inseparable mixture of differently colored ingredients, there is no neat horizontal stratification. Vertical and diagonal lines almost obliterate the horizontal ones, and in some places there are unexpected whirls and an imperceptible merging of colors, so that it is difficult to tell where one ends and the other begins. So it is with federal, state, and local responsibilities in the chaotic marble cake of American government.

So it has been from the beginning.

Federalism and States' Rights. A heterogeneous nation with widely varying cultural traditions and economic patterns could not be expected to become closely knit overnight or over several decades—even assuming that to be an American goal. In opposition to the nationalism of the Federalists, a strong belief in States' rights appeared early in the history of the Republic and has never since disappeared. This doctrine has regularly done service as a device for rationalizing a variety of protests against the establishment of a single policy for the nation as a whole.

As early as 1798, the Kentucky and Virginia Resolutions restated the Antifederalist position that the nation was formed by a compact among sovereign states (as had been the case under the Articles of Confederation), not established by the people directly. The resolutions (those from Kentucky drafted by Thomas Jefferson, those from Virginia by James Madison) held that states might take steps to veto any legislation they held to be unconstitutional. In this particular case, the objection was to the alien and sedition laws of the Federalists. (These laws attempted, among other things, to restrict severely criticism of the administration in power. As such, they were similar to laws not uncommonly found in nondemocratic states today; had they stood, they might have profoundly modified the pattern of American government. The story of these laws is developed in American history texts.)

In 1828, the South Carolina legislature passed a resolution of "exposition and protest" against the protective tariff adopted that year—the agricultural South opposed a high tariff that would encourage the development of industry in the North but would raise the cost of finished products to the consumer. The legislature attempted to nullify the tariff, ran into the strong opposition of President Jackson, was forced to retreat when the rest of the South did not give it full support, and finally achieved some measure of success by winning a downward revision. The principle expressed in the Constitution held, however; neither South Carolina (in this instance) nor any state at any later time has succeeded in nullifying a Federal law.

[9] *Ibid.*, pp. 3–4.

Calhoun's view. The doctrine of States' rights found an eloquent spokesman in John C. Calhoun of South Carolina. According to Robert J. Harris, States' rights became to Calhoun "an instrumentality primarily for the protection of property rights, with the protection of slavery foremost in his consideration."[10] Calhoun continued the classic struggle of the agrarian against the vested financial interests, but his agrarians were the Bourbon aristocracy of the Deep South. His arguments for the preservation of the Southern way of life as he knew it centered around the view that the Constitution was a compact among the states and that the Federal government, through its Supreme Court or otherwise, could not be the judge of its own powers. Rather, he argued, the states should properly resolve for themselves all conflicts.

The tidelands issue. The Civil War did not settle the issue of States' rights, although it made clear the fact that the national government would not tolerate secession any more than it would tolerate nullification. The doctrine was used later by the great financial, business, and industrial combines of the last half of the nineteenth century to protect themselves from control by any government, national or state. It was used again by oil companies interested in controlling the tidelands oil, that is, the offshore oil deposits under the oceans. Both the states and the Federal government claimed the right to control the use of the deposits. The Supreme Court awarded them to the latter, although it was within the power of Congress to turn them over to the states. The oil companies insisted that the deposits did belong to the states. However:[11]

> The solicitude of the oil companies for states' rights is hardly based on convictions derived from political theory but rather on fears that Federal ownership may result in the cancellation or modification of state leases favorable to their interests, their knowledge that they can successfully cope with state oil regulatory agencies, and uncertainty concerning their ability to control a Federal agency. The position of the oil companies [is reflected in statements which] . . . depicted the actions of the Federal government as the "Tidelands grab" by an oppressive central government from sovereign states.

Calhoun had used the symbolic term "States' rights" to defend both an economic interest (that of the slaveowners) and a life-style (that of the Bourbon aristocracy). The tidelands controversy, incidentally, ended differently from earlier contests: those wearing the States' rights mantle were this time successful. Republican leaders with one eye on votes in California, Texas, and Louisiana and another on campaign contributions from oilmen, promised in 1952 to vacate Federal title to the tidelands if elected. The party won the Presidency and Congress and delivered on the campaign commitment, assisted by the votes of many Democratic congressmen.

[10] Robert J. Harris, "States' Rights and Vested Interests," *Journal of Politics,* 15:457–471, November, 1954.

[11] *Ibid.,* p. 467.

The desegregation issue. States' rights once again became a weapon of those in the South who opposed the integration of schools before and after the United States Supreme Court decided in favor of a single national policy on this delicate but basic question. The decisions in relation to it are being made basically in the judicial arena and will be discussed further in Chapter 19. Here we will merely note that the States' rights argument has been used by the proponents of the *status quo*. States' rights is a doctrine that can be particularly effective as an argument in support of regional attitudes and policies against a contrary and dominant national view.

An attack on the Supreme Court. In the 1960s, States' righters became even more vigorous in their activities than they previously had been. Segregationists, conservatives calling for fewer national government programs, businessmen seeking less effective government regulation of their activities, and others joined in efforts to curb the powers of the United States Supreme Court. This institution had once guarded the *status quo*. Now they saw it as an instrument for unwanted social change.

In 1962, a proposal was submitted to create a "Court of the Union" (see Chapter 4) that would consist of the chief justices of all the states and would have power to review Supreme Court decisions in cases where five state legislatures resolved that the question involved rights or powers reserved to the states or to the people by the Tenth Amendment. Such a court would destroy the Supreme Court as an effective interpreter of the Constitution, which is the objective of the supporters of the amendment. By 1964, four state legislatures had called on Congress to have the proposal submitted. Their memorials were not likely to be seriously considered in Congress, but the movement to curb the Court shows some of the intensity of feeling that exists regarding the concept of States' rights.

Federalism and Freedom. A traditional argument for a federal system is that it establishes a countervailing power to strong central government and thus serves as an additional check on such power. At the same time, it has been argued that a federal system encourages local participation and thus promotes grass-roots democracy. At least one student of the subject disagrees with both propositions and argues that evidence for neither has been established. Unitary systems, he claims, have a record that is as good or better than that of federal systems for protecting political freedoms. He concludes that "there is no necessary connection between democracy and federalism. One may go even beyond it and say that many of the major advocates of federalism are critics, doubters and even enemies of democracy."[12]

The illustrations above reveal that federalism has indeed been utilized to preserve slavery and permit discrimination against minority groups by

[12] Franz Neumann, "Federalism and Freedom: A Critique" in Arthur W. Macmahon (ed.), *Federalism, Mature and Emergent,* Doubleday & Company, Inc., Garden City, N.Y., 1955.

local majorities. In 1964, the Supreme Court took a major step in requiring state legislatures to be apportioned by population. As we will discuss later (see Chapter 19), the United States Supreme Court has also been increasingly critical of lapses in criminal procedures at the state level. But the illustrations also suggest a positive relationship between federalism and freedom. Diversity has been sustained. Under the federal system, change—even when strongly supported by large majorities—has been gradual enough to allow for its absorption. Not only has federalism permitted diversity and experimentation at the state and local levels and provided a check on national government power; it has also permitted *national* government institutions occasionally to reorient particular states and localities toward the broad ideals of democracy. The President, the Supreme Court and, less often, Congress have acted to prevent undemocratic procedures and values from becoming entrenched at the regional and local levels. It is not always the same states or localities that may wander away from the long-term goals. Any of them, as well as the national government, may, at some point in history, become disoriented. Federalism provides machinery by which to bring the deviant back to the main path and, in this manner, serves to defend democracy. For example, President Eisenhower acted toward this end in the Little Rock Central High School integration crisis. The Supreme Court has sought to protect the right to a jury trial by one's peers in state courts. Congress has sought to maintain a balance of power between labor and management while some states have not.

FEDERALISM IN THE MODERN ERA

The period after the beginning of the Great Depression saw increasing demands by many different groups for greater governmental involvement in social and economic affairs as we will see in Chapter 7, where the ideology of the social service state is discussed. As new functions were assumed by government and old ones were expanded, the pattern of cooperative federalism was continued, with national, state, and local governments sharing the responsibilities.

The Effects of Grants-in-aid. National grants guided some state policies. From the viewpoint of conservatives, they misguided them and became dictatorial usurpations of state and local rights of decision making. The policy of President Franklin Roosevelt was seen as one in which the objective "was the centralization of power in the executive arm of the national government."[13]

The evidence does not support so simple a conclusion, however. Grodzins and others have documented the fact that the principal characteristic of

[13] Felix Morley, *Freedom and Federalism,* Henry Regnery Company, Chicago, 1959, p. 134.

federalism after 1930 was that the functions and expenditures of government at *all* levels increased. Certainly, the Federal government did offer grants with strings attached—grants that were difficult for states to reject. But often they were difficult to reject precisely because there was much demand for the services the grants made available. There had been such demand in the nineteenth century too—to help establish programs for agricultural research, for schools for the deaf and dumb, for swamp drainage, and for flood control, for example.

In the period of the Great Depression and afterward, there was demand for health, education, welfare, highway, and other programs in which the Federal government was asked to assist. Sometimes there were strings attached to set up standards—technical engineering standards for highways and professional-competence standards for welfare workers, for example. These requirements reflected more than just the desire of Federal bureaucrats to force the states and localities to professionalize their bureaucracies. They also reflected the congressman's desire to protect the taxpayers' money from being wasted on nonproductive patronage—patronage that he was, incidentally, not likely to benefit from if it were available.

The Grant-in-aid Pattern. The pattern of grants changed somewhat through time. When the Federal government had a great deal of land in its possession and was anxious to dispose of it for settlement purposes, the land grant was common. Later, when the Federal government's capacity to raise money became considerably greater than that of the states, and the most desirable parts of the public domain had been used up, a switch was made to cash grants. Significantly, just three years before the frontier was formally closed (by a statement in the introductory essay to the census of 1890), the first continuing cash grant was established. Of symbolic importance, given the future commitment of the Federal government to the development of science and technology, that first grant was to establish the experiment stations for scientific research at the state agricultural colleges.

There was another change in the pattern too. The early land grants had been nonrecurring. The states were expected to spend only the income produced by the use of the granted land, or the need was thought to be temporary or one that could be met on a one-shot basis. Later needs—the annual operating costs of the experiment stations or the support of persons receiving old-age assistance, for example—were considered to have a permanent nature; the grants came to be annual claims against the Federal budget, claims which Congress found difficult to disallow once they were established.

The States' Role. The grants did not, as is sometimes said by their critics, cause state and local governments to vacate their decision-making responsibilities. In fact, the Federal pattern was often more one of following the states than of leading them, and "whatever was the focus of state attention became the recipient of national grants."[14] Furthermore, contrary to conventional wisdom, the state and national governments did not come to pursue fundamentally antagonistic economic policies.[15] In recent years, state and local government debt has been increasing rapidly, and these governments have had more problems in raising funds than has the Federal government. Not only does the Federal government have the flexible and sharply graduated income tax as a better resource than the tax bases of other governments within the country; it also virtually controls its own credit, which makes deficit financing easier for the Federal government than it is for states or localities. The Federal government has, therefore, been appealed to by groups seeking expanded government programs because the marginal cost or sacrifice required to raise the necessary funds is generally less there than at other levels. It is also probable that Congress, although generally cautious if not outrightly conservative, may be less conservative than state legislatures, and it contains more persons who have first-hand experience with contemporary urban problems than does the typical state legislature.

On the other hand, efforts to secure greater Federal funds to assist state and local governments with domestic programs is countered by the more inelastic, highly expensive demands of the national defense program. While we cannot know for certain, it seems very likely that Federal participation in domestic programs would today be at a considerably higher level than it is if defense demands had not remained at a continuously high level since the end of World War II.

Federal Government Locally. While grants-in-aid have brought opposition, this kind of program follows essentially the system approved of by De Tocqueville, a French visitor to America during the time of Andrew Jackson; administration of programs is still in the hands of state and local authorities.

But in the twentieth century there has been a growth of what one scholar has called "Federal government locally": administration of Federal programs by Federal officials.[16] One need only consult the "United States" listings of a telephone book in any medium-sized American city to find the large number of Federal offices that deal directly with citizens rather than through state intermediaries—the FBI, the Veterans Administration, agencies for soil conservation and many other programs. In a study of a rural Minnesota county, Ylvisaker concludes that it has been the growth of Federal government locally, not cooperative federalism, that has spurred

[14] Morton Grodzins, "The Federal System," *op. cit.*, 270–271.

[15] Jacob Cohen and Morton Grodzins, "How Much Economic Sharing in American Federalism?" *American Political Science Review*, 57:5–23, March, 1963.

[16] Paul N. Ylvisaker, *Intergovernmental Relations at the Grass Roots: A Study of Blue Earth County, Minnesota to 1946*, Intergovernmental Relations in the United States Research Monograph, No. 7, The University of Minnesota Press, Minneapolis, 1956.

local resistance. Nevertheless, it is unlikely that the older system of dependence on local officials, with all its uncertainty, will be returned to. Federal officials seek to cooperate with local officials, but complete local control over the administration of an important activity has become rare.

THE BALANCE OF FEDERALISM

Although there has been a gradual and continuing expansion of government in the United States during the twentieth century, powerful ideological sentiments have slowed down the rate and discouraged assumption of policy domination by the Federal government. In terms of political strategy, there are many reasons why the Federal government has not taken over.

One of the most important reasons is the decentralization of the American party system (see Chapter 10 for discussion in greater detail). Nominations are controlled locally.[17] Most congressmen, for example, see their job as that of defending parochial rather than national interests. Many senators are former governors with a state-interest point of view. And our political parties are undisciplined and organized on a state rather than national basis; thus the state politician often sees his political advantage maximized if he can get the money from the Federal government (so that most people will feel it is costing them nothing) and have policy made at the state or local level (where many people feel they can gain influence more easily than they can before Congress or the Federal bureaucracy).

These considerations are all based on the traditional American opposition to great central power and a preference for grass-roots government close to the people as opposed to highly professional but essentially impersonal administration from a distant center of power.

Trends in Budgeting. To put developments in perspective, we might summarize some of the trends in the balance of federalism since the end of World War II:[18]

1. Expanding Federal budgets have not represented as substantial a burden upon society's earnings as is popularly supposed. In the postwar years, Federal domestic programs have consumed only about 2 per cent of our annual gross national product (GNP).* State and local governments

---

***GROSS NATIONAL PRODUCT. As calculated by the U.S. Department of Commerce, this figure is equal to the total amount paid for the production of goods and services, plus indirect business taxes paid, plus allowances for the depreciation of capital investments.**

---

[17] David B. Truman, "Federalism and the Party System," in Macmahon, *op. cit.*

[18] These points are developed in more detail in Charles R. Adrian, *State and Local Governments,* McGraw-Hill Book Company, New York, 1960. (Second edition to appear in 1966.)

spend about five times as much as the Federal government on domestic programs. The great bulk of Federal expenses are a result of World Wars I and II and efforts to prevent a third world war.

2. Federal spending for domestic purposes has been increasing, but the same trend may be seen at the state and local levels and to a greater degree. Between 1949 and 1957, while Federal domestic expenditures were increasing by 48 per cent on a per capita, constant-dollar basis, state and local expenditures increased by 59 per cent.

3. Federal grants-in-aid to state and local governments have been increasing in number and as a percentage of GNP almost every year. Furthermore, they have become a rather inflexible part of the Federal budget, for once such funds are incorporated into state and local budgets, these units come to expect the money, and it is politically difficult for Congress to deprive them of it.

4. There is no evidence to show whether the increasing number of Federal grants and domestic policy activity generally is depriving the states and communities of their policy-making powers. Indications are that it is not; rather, the trend seems to be toward professional administrators at all three levels of government sharing in policy making, using the established values and standards of their particular professions. That is, professional social workers, no matter the level of government at which they are employed, tend to take the same general view as to what is sound policy. If they are highway engineers, they see Federal standards generally as sound professional practice and therefore good. So to them, Federal regulations and standards may sometimes be a nuisance, but they represent neither a burden nor a substitution of the will of the Federal bureaucrat for their own.[19]

Both in terms of fund raising and, so far as can be seen, policy making, the states and their communities are therefore involved in a partnership with the Federal government that has old roots. Some differences in attitude and patterns of influence continue to exist, however. Activity at the state level "usually reflects the ascendency of private over public government."[20] That is, the state government is an arena in which the balance of pressures tends to be more on the side of the conservative business community than is the case in Washington. Of course, with Federal defense expenditures making up a large part of the economy, with Federal grants expanding into new areas with almost every session of Congress, and with the superior fiscal powers of the Federal government, it would be unrealistic to suggest that the states or local governments will in the future increase in relative importance to the Federal government. But there is no reason, on the evidence, to believe that they will be swallowed up either.

[19] See Edward W. Weidner, "Decision-making in a Federal System," in Macmahon, *op. cit.*

[20] John R. Schmidhauser, "Federalism in the United States," *Parliamentary Affairs,* 14:39–54, Winter, 1960–1961. Quotation from p. 54.

As Officials View Federalism Today. Most state and local officials apparently do not fear that their policy-making powers will be destroyed by the present system, although they are somewhat concerned (see Table 5-1).

In a 1963 study of attitudes of state governors, attorneys general, and budget officers, and of county officials, mayors, city managers, and school board members, the Subcommittee on Intergovernmental Relations of the United States Senate found only 11 per cent of their respondents to be committed to the traditional concept of dual federalism, favoring national-state competition rather than cooperation. The largest single category, 43 per cent, expressed many anticentralist and separatist views. These "Neo-Traditionalists," however, accepted the grant-in-aid device and at least a limited Federal role in dealing with the complex problems of metropolitan-area services. But the conventional wisdom of the layer-cake concept continued to affect their views strongly, and they believed the top layer to be too thick and to contain too much frosting.

Another large group, 33 per cent of the sample, were pragmatists. They "eschewed general ideological considerations in their . . . responses and generally permitted their respective official positions and/or sheer force of circumstances to condition their answers." They accepted the Grodzins marble-cake analogy. Their criticisms of the present system dealt with specific problems as they saw them, not with the system itself. Finally, 13 per cent indicated a belief that the nation needs an expanded national government that has more involvement in domestic policy, particularly in matters related to metropolitan areas. Many of these respondents felt that state and local governments were "unable to cope with the more pressing domestic problems confronting America in the 1960's." But a disproportionate number of these persons were school board members and academicians, so they may not be typical of public officeholders.[21] The States'

TABLE 5-1

ATTITUDE OF STATE AND LOCAL OFFICIALS TOWARD THE FEDERAL SYSTEM

Attitude	Per cent of sample
Orthodox States' Rights	13
Neo-Traditionalism	43
Pragmatic Cooperation	33
New Nationalism	11

SOURCE: Senate Subcommittee on Intergovernmental Relations, *The Federal System as Seen by State and Local Officials,* U.S. Government Printing Office, Washington, 1963, pp. 203–205. The sample totaled 460; of these, 56 were academicians and other nonpractitioners. The sample was not actually representative, *ibid.,* Table 1, but it probably offers a reasonable approximation.

[21] Data from Senate Subcommittee on Intergovernmental Relations, *The Federal System as Seen by State and Local Officials,* U.S. Government Printing Office, Washington, 1963, pp. 203–210.

righters are not typical either, however. The vast majority of respondents fell into the categories of Neo-Traditionalists and Pragmatic Cooperators. They shared many beliefs about American federalism. They saw national, state, and local governments as "loosely related parts of an overall system" in which domestic functions are not neatly parceled out and decision making is shared "fairly equally." To them, grant-in-aid programs were inescapable and important, and most of them believed that the state, rather than the national or local government, was the one most in need of improvement if an equal partnership were to be maintained. They saw intergovernmental relations as "primarily a maze of functional, financial, and administrative relationships, and not basically a strict matter of formal, institutional, juridical, or legal arrangements." They expected the system to remain that way.

SELECTED BIBLIOGRAPHY

The relationships of the states to the national government were first examined by three of the original advocates of the new Constitution [10]. Their analysis has been evaluated and criticized by many historians and legal scholars. For example, see the comments of Dietze [6].

Elazar [7], Goldwin [8], and Grodzins [9] have examined nineteenth-century relationships between Federal and state governments. Developments in the present century are emphasized in Anderson [1, 2], the *Report* of the President's Commission [4], and the Subcommittee on Intergovernmental Relations [18]. Rockefeller [17], a liberal, offers an opinion on the nature of federalism that contrasts with that of contemporary conservatives [13, 20].

1. Anderson, William: *Intergovernmental Relations in Review,* The University of Minnesota Press, Minneapolis, 1960.
2. Anderson, William: *The Nation and the States: Rivals or Partners?* The University of Minnesota Press, Minneapolis, 1955.
3. Benson, George C. S. (ed.): *Essays in Federalism,* The Institute for Studies in Federalism, Claremont, Calif., 1961.
4. Commission on Intergovernmental Relations: *A Report to the President for Transmittal to the Congress,* 1955.
5. Corwin, Edward S.: "The Passing of Dual Federalism," *Virginia Law Review,* 36:1–24, February, 1950.
6. Dietze, Gottfried: *The Federalist: A Classic on Federalism and Free Government,* The Johns Hopkins Press, Baltimore, 1960.
7. Elazar, Daniel J.: *The American Partnership,* The University of Chicago Press, Chicago, 1962.
8. Goldwin, Robert A. (ed.): *A Nation of States: Essays on the American Federal System,* Rand McNally & Company, Chicago, 1963.
9. Grodzins, Morton: "The Federal System," in the President's Commission on National Goals, *Goals for Americans,* Prentice-Hall, Inc., Englewood Cliffs, N.J., 1960.
10. Hamilton, Alexander, John Jay, and James Madison: *The Federalist.* (Many editions; first published, 1787–1788.)
11. Harris, Robert J.: "States' Rights and Vested Interests," *Journal of Politics,* 15:457–471, November, 1954.
12. Hutchins, Robert M.: *Two Faces of Federalism,* Center for the Study of Democratic Institutions, Santa Barbara, Calif., 1961.

13. Morley, Felix: *Freedom and Federalism,* Henry Regnery Company, Chicago, 1959.
14. Macmahon, Arthur W. (ed.): *Federalism, Mature and Emergent,* Doubleday & Company, Inc., Garden City, N.Y., 1955. See especially selections by Neumann, Truman, and Weidner.
15. Ostrom, Vincent: "State Administration of Natural Resources in the West," *American Political Science Review,* 47:478–493, June, 1953.
16. Riker, William H.: *Federalism: Origin, Operation, Significance,* Little, Brown and Company, Boston, 1964.
17. Rockefeller, Nelson A.: *The Future of Federalism,* Harvard University Press, Cambridge, Mass., 1962.
18. Senate Subcommittee on Intergovernmental Relations, *The Federal System as Seen by State and Local Officials,* U.S. Government Printing Office, Washington, 1963. Also see other publications by the subcommittee.
19. Vile, M. J. C.: *The Structure of American Federalism,* Oxford University Press, Fair Lawn, N.J., 1961.
20. *Virginia's Answers to Congressional Questions on State and Federal Authority,* Virginia Commission on Constitutional Government, Richmond, Va., 1963.
21. Weidner, Edward W.: *Intergovernmental Relations as Seen by Public Officials,* Intergovernmental Relations in the United States Research Monograph, No. 9, The University of Minnesota Press, Minneapolis, 1960.
22. Ylvisaker, Paul N.: *Intergovernmental Relations at the Grass Roots: A Study of Blue Earth County, Minnesota to 1946,* Intergovernmental Relations in the United States Research Monograph, No. 7, The University of Minnesota Press, Minneapolis, 1956.

CHAPTER

6

IDEOLOGY: THE FRONTIER FOUNDATION

People in all nations have an interest in political ideas and see them as important. But within each nation, citizens are able to conceptualize ideas only according to their own ability and education as shaped by the expectations of the culture. In some cultures, the number of people who are interested in ideas as such and discuss them as the bases for deriving political principles is high. France may be an example. In the United States, on the other hand, the culture does not seem to call for this kind of discussion. Most Americans prefer to discuss personalities and specific issues. Many people do not discuss politics at all and probably react on the basis of habits and attitudes that they are incapable of verbalizing.[1] But individual reactions to such political matters as civil rights and foreign aid policy often involve, unknowingly, bits of ideas that have been developed by systematic philosophers.

A HIERARCHY OF IDEAS

The Levels of Abstraction. Not all persons can think effectively in abstract terms. Most people require examples or practical illustrations before they can grasp an idea. Many Americans require even more. They want to be able to see how an idea or its practical application affects them personally before they consider it important. The number of persons who can think in terms of abstract, systematic ideas and who *act upon conclusions based on them* probably differs in accordance with the level of one's education and expectations of his culture. But whatever the balance, we can probably divide the use of ideas in politics into three categories along a continuum; one does not abruptly end where the next begins, but rather blends into the next along hazy lines. Let us look at the three levels of abstraction and rationality. We can classify them as philosophy, ideology, and symbolism.

Philosophy. Philosophy involves the *systematic development of ideas;* it is essentially an appeal to human reasoning ability. Its objective is to explain social phenomena in terms of ultimate

[1] V. O. Key, Jr., *Public Opinion and American Democracy,* Alfred A. Knopf, Inc., 1961, chap. 2.

causes and to develop logical relationships among the various observable phenomena. Plato, Aristotle, Thomas Aquinas, Immanuel Kant, Karl Marx, and John Dewey are among the host of philosophers who have written systematically about social phenomena. They have all concerned themselves with the state and the role and organization of government, as would be necessary if they were to have a complete philosophy.

America has produced relatively few philosophers, although many of our learned men have been concerned with philosophical problems, as we see in the account of their views by the great chronicler of American ideas, Vernon L. Parrington.[2] Perhaps one reason why we have not developed more philosophers is that Americans have always concentrated upon the empirical and practical. Most philosophers have used empirical evidence when convenient, but they have not regarded it as an essential basis upon which to build. Generally they have preferred to discover meaning through the use of logic. On the other hand, John Dewey, a famous American philosopher, based his thought system on *empirical* findings and the scientific method generally. The same basis undergirds the philosophy of "logical positivism," which, though it did not originate in the United States, has been strongly supported in this country. It, too, emphasizes the scientific method as the desirable approach to learning.*

***LOGICAL POSITIVISM. A school of philosophy that uses the concepts of science, logic, and mathematics. It views political and other social values as givens that cannot be proved or disproved, but that are nevertheless subjectively meaningful because they are accepted as real by individuals.**

Few Americans study the writings of philosophers of this or any other nation and hence are not in a position to use their ideas as criteria in evaluating political programs. Neither Jefferson nor Dewey is often read by Americans. These two writers express American views to the extent that they do because they reflect American folk values, not because citizens have read their writings and been impressed by their rationality.

The views of typical citizens are not the result of the influence of philosophers. They stem from more visceral impressions. After eliminating the few Americans who are committed to particular formal philosophies, we divide the remainder into two groups—those whose political reactions are guided largely by *ideology* and those who are guided by *symbolism*.*

***SYMBOL. Anything that is intentionally used to stand for or represent something else. (The definition is from David Krech, R. C. Crutchfield, and E. L. Ballachey, "Individual in Society," McGraw-Hill Book Company, New York, 1962.)**

---

[2] Vernon L. Parrington, *Main Currents in American Thought*, Harcourt, Brace & World, Inc., New York, 1930, is the classic study of American thought up to the coming of the New Deal. Parrington's personal views in support of populism and progressivism are evident in his writings.

Ideology. Ideology may be described as "folk philosophy." It is not as systematic or as sophisticated as philosophy, and it evolves gradually, with no single thinker as its source. In this sense, it resembles folk songs more than the works of serious composers.

Ideology is made up of a network of interrelated normative values that emerge from a particular life-style and environment. A set of values has been called a "myth" by Robert MacIver. He has pointed out that myths (or portions of an ideology) are "the value-impregnated beliefs and notions that men hold, that they live by or live for. Every society is held together by a myth-system, a complex of dominating thought-forms that determines and sustains all its activities. All social reactions, the very texture of human society, are myth-born and myth-sustained."[3] The term "myth," as used here and by MacIver, describes a concept designed to justify life-styles. It does not imply approval or disapproval, truth or untruth. It suggests only ideas that some people accept as a basis for judging the worth of political or social phenomena.

Perhaps the term "myth" is not a happy one, for most of us are accustomed to thinking of a myth as a bit of folklore that is untrue. Ideology has the disadvantage of being associated with Marxian concepts, but the definition used above is widely accepted by contemporary social scientists. In any case, folk philosophies may exist independently of their truth or falsity or of their relationship to the eternal verities. They are too general, too broad, too unscientific to be proved or disproved. They are accepted on *faith,* and when faith in their rightness fades away, belief passes into the shadow, except for its vestiges that are no longer recognizable in their original form. In response to changing economic and social conditions, new ideologies are created that may be antagonistic to and directly challenge old ones. On the other hand, old ideologies are frequently renovated in order to meet changing environments and may be applied to situations far removed from the situations that originally gave rise to the idea.[4]

The exact relationships among economic and social conditions, life-styles, and ideologies are not yet known by social scientists. Karl Marx believed that ideologies were merely superficial explanations of the economic system (Freud, a few generations later, would have said "rationalizations"). It seems likely, however, that all three interact upon one another in an as yet undelineated fashion. Ideologies, the authors here argue, are not simply distorted, stylized empirical theories. They are normative, or value-laden, theories about the environment and the nature of the "good life" within it. They stem from life experiences, but are not necessarily caused by them; and they tend to perpetuate life-styles even when the factors that accompanied their establishment have disappeared. Each drastic change in the environment of the citizen has been accompanied by a broad change in the belief system, but without destruction of all of the existing roots.

[3] Robert M. MacIver, *The Web of Government,* The Macmillan Company, New York, 1947, p. 4.

[4] *Ibid.,* p. 6.

There are vast differences in the life experiences of a farmer in the far reaches of Western Civilization, an immigrant worker doing a simple task in one of the new factories of an emergent industrial nation, a self-made millionaire who has contributed to the accumulation of industrial capital for a nation that has come to believe that industrialization offers the formula for a higher standard of living, the unskilled worker who has seen his neighbors laid off as the result of automation, and the organization man with job security and a comfortable home in the suburbs, where he is surrounded by persons having incomes, education, and interests similar to his own. Each set of life experiences is accompanied by a different, but historically related, life-style, social value system, and set of political propensities.

The two functions of ideology. While the ideologies of whole nations and their cultures have not been given much systematic study, the behavior patterns of social groups, which are much smaller, have been described in some detail by social psychologists. From their work, we know that an ideology consists of common beliefs, common values, and common norms (folkways and mores). The sharing of these permits the ideology to perform two major functions: It directs action toward the satisfying of wants; and it creates goals or wants for the group or, in this case, the nation. The first of these functions includes the procedures for action as well as the motivation to act; the second provides both a set of valued objectives and at least a rough ordering of their relative importance. And we know that:[5]

> The existence of a common ideology tends to minimize behavior differences due to different wants of different members. A common ideology does this by creating a core of *common wants* among the members and by inducing a *common method of expressing different wants.*

Hence ideology helps secure consensus on both procedures and goals, as well as voluntary cooperation with political institutions and voluntary compliance to its rules by most of the people most of the time.

The characteristics of ideology and some examples. One political scientist—instead of trying to define ideology—has called it a "body of concepts." These concepts have the following characteristics:[6]

1. They deal with the questions: Who will be the rulers? How will the rulers be selected? By what principles will they govern?
2. They constitute an *argument;* that is, they are intended to persuade and to counter opposing views.
3. They integrally affect some of the major values of life.
4. They embrace a program for the defense or reform or abolition of important social institutions.

[5] David Krech and others, *Individual in Society,* McGraw-Hill Book Company, New York, 1962, p. 402. Italics in original.

[6] Robert E. Lane, *Political Ideology: Why the American Common Man Believes What He Does,* The Free Press of Glencoe, New York, 1962, pp. 14–15.

5. They are, in part, rationalizations of group interests—but not necessarily the interests of all groups espousing them.
6. They are normative, ethical, moral in tone and content.
7. They are (inevitably) torn from their context in a broader belief system, and share the structural and stylistic properties of that system.

Most ideologies also have these qualities:

1. They are group beliefs that individuals borrow; most people acquire an ideology by identifying (or disidentifying) with a social group.
2. They have a body of sacred documents (constitutions, bills of rights, manifestos, declarations), and heroes (founding fathers, seers and sages, originators and great interpreters).
And all ideologies, like all other beliefs, imply an empirical theory of cause and effect in the world, and a theory of the nature of man.

Ideologies are accepted on *faith;* they cannot be proved or disproved. Who can prove, except to the satisfaction of those already convinced, that government should do only the things that cannot be done by individuals or private enterprise? Who can prove that a society in which "no one is either too rich or too poor" is better than one in which maximum profits are allowed to those who most satisfy the wants of other citizens?

What is meant, in any case, by "too rich" or "too poor"? The beliefs of one age may not be meaningful in a later age, but they tend to persist. For example, the beliefs of the frontier yeoman farmer were developed in an environment that is worlds away from that of the contemporary urban factory worker or organization man. Yet the frontiersman's love of freedom and individualism carries over today. Each new American ideology has been intended, within the existing environment, to improve the condition of the average man. Each one has been an expression of a meaning of social justice within a given environment. The frontier farmer wanted individualism because he thought that government could do little to help him clear the stumps from his homestead and that increased taxes would only serve to diminish his profits (if any), without any commensurate benefit. Furthermore, he suspected, even after the Jacksonian Democrats took power, that governments tended to benefit the wealthy and the urban businessman rather than the farmer.

In contrast, the small-business man of today favors individualism because he believes that it will give him the greatest possible freedom in making his own decisions. He may also believe that government regulations will make it more expensive for him to engage in business (by raising sanitary or safety standards, for example, or by placing a minimum under wages). He may also see the increased taxes that are necessary to pay for increased governmental services as additional costs that will not be equaled by the services provided. Thus, ideas born in one age may be accepted for different reasons in another.

And, of course, changing economic circumstances may produce relatively new ideologies. The Great Depression that began in the fall of 1929 produced or accentuated economic insecurities; over the following decade, acceptance of the idea that government should aid the individual and the economy in times of stress and reduce certain kinds of widely shared insecurities was brought about. The ideas and programs of the resulting social service state stood in sharp contrast to and in conflict with the earlier ideas of self-reliant individualism. But, as always when the dominant ideology changes, some persons remained committed to older beliefs. With the passage of time, their numbers have become smaller and their plight more desperate.[7]

There normally exists, however, an ideology that is accepted by a dominant group of citizens. Politicians are both captured by it and able to condition their appeals to meet its expectations.

A further point about ideologies should be made: Their relationship to the environment is something like that of the chicken to the egg. Existing

[7] See Daniel Bell (ed.), *The Radical Right,* Doubleday & Company, Inc., Garden City, N.Y., 1963. See especially the article by Talcott Parsons.

Figure 6-1

Every Era Has Its Causes

"Please, Lady, you're making it very difficult!"

Drawing by W. Miller; © 1962, The New Yorker Magazine, Inc.

ideologies condition emerging political, social, and economic circumstances; persons experiencing these circumstances, in turn, modify existing ideologies. Ideas and the environment in which they exist are hence independent, each affecting the nature of the other.

Political Organization and Ideology. A number of ideologies dealing with domestic and foreign concerns have been dominant at one time or another in America. Each has *gradually* shaded into the next, with the older ones living on in vestigial form.

Political parties at any time in history are necessarily concerned with making appeals to the existing ideology or ideologies. As a new value system begins to develop out of the old—or as a replacement for it—one political party or another may be expected to try to gain votes by espousing the new ideology. The winner is likely to be the party in power at the time an ideology is generally accepted. Hence, *the public tends to associate the prevailing ideology with a particular political party,* which becomes the majority party. Except in strictly single-party areas of the nation, one party claims to "own" the ideology; and as long as that ideology is dominant, that party will be dominant and can expect to win most elections. The history of the Presidency, Congress, and the governments of most states is not one of two closely balanced organizations frequently exchanging control of public office; it is one of long control by a single party, perhaps for many decades with only occasional interruptions.

If one party, through the life of a particular ideology, tends to win control of Congress and the Presidency most of the time, why does it not win *all* of the time? Ideas, social forces, and interests are stable. They do not change rapidly. But personalities in politics do; campaign incidents do; discrete events in individual lives do; the balance of forces among the cross pressures upon the individual do; and individual perceptions of the critical issues of the moment do. Thus a person may believe that the Republicans are more likely to avoid war than the Democrats, but that the Democrats are more likely to ensure prosperity for the typical citizen. He might well reach one conclusion in 1948 (for the Democrats), when his major concern was for preserving prosperity; he might reach another (for the Republicans) in 1952, when anxieties about the international situation were overwhelming to him. In 1960, he might have an extremely difficult time deciding and might not have voted for either major candidate.[8]

The "out-party," which in American politics plays the special role of serving as a vehicle of *protest,* is constantly faced with the dilemma of pursuing a policy of "Me too," that is, "We support the prevailing beliefs but think we can do a better job, especially since the other party has been in too long." Or the party pursues a policy of "Not me." In the latter case, the party embarks upon a politics of nostalgia in which an older myth is held to be better and to be still "really accepted" by the people.

[8] See Angus Campbell and others, *The American Voter,* John Wiley & Sons, Inc., New York, 1960. See especially p. 16.

Once a substantial number of people have lost faith in an ideology, they are not likely to return to it again. We can, therefore, answer the question so often asked by members of the minority party: Is the me-too or the not-me policy most likely to be successful? Ordinarily, the only hope is to take a me-too position, no matter how unpalatable. Except in times of rapid and dramatic change (when it might conceivably be possible to market once again a previously rejected ideology), it is not feasible to attempt to change the values or the expectations of the electorate. It is necessary to gain their votes within the limits of their belief system.

The two parties are thus under strong pressure to take approximately the same general position when they take stands on issues at all. The role of the program-oriented reform party has been played most of the time by third parties in America. These parties have generally either favored ideologies of the past or ideologies that have not yet gained much acceptance. Therefore, they can rarely expect to win elections.

Propaganda and Ideology. Propaganda, whether used in a political campaign or at some other time, makes no sense to the general public unless it is designed to appeal to the prevailing belief systems. It is sometimes considered necessary to seek public support for a proposal under circumstances that will not permit a forthright explanation of the reasons. For example, in the 1940 negotiations between Prime Minister Winston Churchill and President Franklin Roosevelt for the trading of fifty old four-stacker destroyers for bases in the West Indies, Roosevelt presented the transaction to Americans and to Congress as a good bargain by which we would greatly improve our home defense position in return for a handful of obsolete destroyers. His appeal was in terms of personal interest and safety, although his actual objective was to help keep Britain from collapsing under Nazi pounding.

Simultaneously, Churchill was telling Parliament that the destroyers were vital (which was true) and that Britain was surrendering nothing permanently, only granting leases to a nation that would further Britain's interests. If he had presented the transactions as a trade of destroyers for part of the Empire, he would have encountered strong opposition.[9] Thus each chief of government appealed to the beliefs and concerns that would most likely produce a favorable reaction in the popular assembly and among the citizens of his nation. A simple argument that "we will gain in the long run from this deal" would probably have been ineffective.

Public Policy and Ideology. Every act of politics is conditioned by the ideology that is dominant in the officeholder's constituency and by the officeholder's individual ideology. As a result, what the President does may not always seem rational if we use as a criterion his or the nation's advantage in terms of a power struggle. Similarly, an action of the President, the Secretary of

[9] The interpretation is that found in Winston S. Churchill, *Their Finest Hour,* Houghton Mifflin Company, Boston, 1949, book 2, chap. 5.

State, a congressional investigator, or a segregationist leader may not necessarily be highly regarded by non-Americans. He may not meet the expectations of foreigners, though what he does may satisfy his own conscience or the expectations of his constituents.

As an example of this, we might look to the U-2 incident in May, 1960, near the end of the Eisenhower administration. After an American aircraft on a photographic intelligence mission over the Soviet Union was shot down and the pilot captured, the President candidly admitted that the plane was American and that it was indeed on an intelligence mission. Many members of the public undoubtedly approved of this action, believing that the President had done the "right thing" in telling the truth. (Remember the comment in Chapter 2 about the moralizing tendencies of Americans.) Yet in his frank confession, the President was violating the established principles of espionage, which hold that the spying nation never admits to the identity of any of its agents and does not concede publicly that it engages in espionage of any kind. (All major nations do, of course, engage in espionage, and the United States some years ago publicly admitted to the general purposes of the Central Intelligence Agency.) The President's action caused leaders of friendly nations and specialists in international relations and espionage to conclude that he—and also perhaps the typical American—was naïve. Yet he was meeting the expectations of most Americans. To them, he was acting in an honorable way.

The governmental leader, hence, is faced with making policy within the framework of the existing ideology or, more accurately, with explaining his acts in terms of the dominant ideology. In the above case, Eisenhower could almost certainly have found some way of explaining away the incident without being candid. In choosing forthrightness he gained in the eyes of most Americans, but lost in the eyes of intelligence and diplomatic specialists around the world. The fact that he acted as he did is probably a reflection of the fact that ideology does not merely condition the rhetoric that is used in campaigns and in public explanations of political acts; it also assumes reality in the eyes of the decision maker, and his personal beliefs help to shape the decision that he makes. President Eisenhower probably believed that he ought to make the decision he did make because it was the moral thing to do.

Symbolism. An elaborate system of symbols prevails in politics as in all organized human activity. These symbols have meaning both because they appeal to the emotions and because they are the outward, shorthand expressions of the loosely clustered ideological values that hold society together and enable the political system to function. An ideology always includes a package of value-colored symbols, for the manifest form of ideas "is nothing more than a conglomeration of symbols."[10]

[10] Harold D. Lasswell and others, *The Comparative Study of Symbols,* Stanford University Press, Stanford, Calif., 1952, p. 65.

All people react to symbols and make use of them. This is as true of the highly educated, very intelligent person as it is of the individual of little schooling and subnormal intelligence. Because this is the case, symbols reach many more people than do discussions of ideology. The individual whose knowledge of and interest in politics is marginal may not be able to verbalize much about America's democratic traditions or any of the ideologies that are discussed below, but he is likely to feel an emotional response to the flag, the national anthem, and a military salute. More importantly for the political candidate or the officeholder, he also responds to many verbal symbols that abbreviate involved concepts which could not be explained to or understood by him.

Look at some examples. "Law" symbolizes much more than the statutes defining crime and describing rights and privileges of individuals. In all the dominant American ideologies, it has also symbolized social stability, confidence in a way of life, and protection against arbitrary action. As such, it can be used in propaganda against a political opponent: "I stand for a return to a government of laws. I deplore my opponent's belief in a government of men."

Similarly, "the people" does not mean simply the voters or the citizens of the nation collectively. In symbol, it stands for "the side of right," "the good," and even "wisdom." Hence, "The voice of the people is the voice of God."

Thousands of terms are used in connection with ideologies, terms that are symbolic in character and therefore produce either favorable or unfavorable emotional responses in the target person—the dignity of the individual, self-reliance, the public interest, our forefathers, the national defense, the welfare state, big business, labor bosses, politicians, full employment, free enterprise, States' rights, or socialized medicine, to name but a few.[11]

People in many cultures apparently feel the need to explain the symbols of an ideology in terms of ultimate, not simply adequate, sources. In America, we associate popular opinion with the will of God. The ancient Jews attributed the Book of the Law (which we know as Deuteronomy) to Moses. They did this much as we say that a Supreme Court decision represents the "real meaning" of the Constitution, the one intended by the Founding Fathers. The Jews were not satisfied to say the law was *in the spirit* of Moses. In the same way, Americans have generally not been satisfied to say that a Supreme Court decision is *one plausible interpretation* of the Constitution. We feel more secure if we see the Supreme Court as a living symbol of the Constitution itself; if we can accept its decisions

[11] According to some social scientists, so many citizens react only to habit and attitude, are so inarticulate, and their values so inconsistent, that the term "ideology" is not appropriate. See Robert G. McCloskey, "The American Ideology," in Marion D. Irish (ed.), *Continuing Crisis in American Politics,* Prentice-Hall, Inc., Englewood Cliffs, N.J., 1963, pp. 10–25, and his citations.

not as a *possible meaning,* but as *the meaning* of the Constitution. It did not seem to bother the ancient Jews that the Book of the Law included an account of the death of the man who was said to be its author. Similarly, it does not matter to most Americans that some of the Founding Fathers said that their Constitution could not foresee all future needs and that it was not designed to do so.

Historical evidence that would damage the perfection of a symbol is often ignored in our desire to achieve and retain confidence in the symbols that are meaningful to us. For example, President George Washington once asked the Supreme Court for an advisory opinion (a legal interpretation, but not one in which an actual case is involved). Chief Justice John Jay told the President that the writers of the Constitution had not intended to have the Supreme Court offer such opinions to the executive branch. Yet Washington had been the President of the Constitutional Convention and presumably should have known as much as anyone about the intentions of the framers. Jay had not even been a delegate. If Washington did not know the intentions of the framers, did Jay? Because the ritual of accrediting particular interpretations of the Constitution to the intentions of those who met at Philadelphia was thus established so early in history (1793), it seems likely that the image of the Constitution as a symbol of American unity, unbroken in its history from that summer of 1787, is extremely basic to our belief system.

Actual facts are not important where symbols are involved. We believe the images that the symbols produce in our minds, not the historical facts that are available to those who trouble to investigate.

COLONIAL ORIGINS OF AMERICAN IDEOLOGY

Why should the United States have differed so much in its pattern of development from the nations of Central and South America? What is the driving force behind the efficient exploitation of natural resources, the sharp and continuing increase in the American standard of living? Some have said that America simply had greater natural resources, including soil, than most nations. But this is only a part of the story. Many other nations in the world have great resources but a much lower standard of living. It seems likely that ideology is at least a partial explanation of what has happened in the United States.

Some have argued that ideology is responsible, and they have found the explanation in the free enterprise system in which they believe. This is probably a part of the story, but free enterprise—in *fact* as distinguished from *symbol*—has been much less important in America than folklore would have it. Through the colonial and frontier periods, Americans were committed to the idea of "Let's try whatever seems to work," rather than to a rigid belief in free enterprise as such. And after American industry began to grow rapidly in the 1880s, price competition declined in many components of the economy, being replaced by advertising competition.

Scholars are not in agreement as to the causes for America's spectacular history or of how its various parts fit together, but many of them agree that a particular point of view—that is, an ideology—is in part responsible. One has said:[12]

> Capitalist economic development, the basic argument runs, had its greatest opportunity in a Protestant society and created the burgher [urban middle] class, whose existence was both a catalyst and a necessary condition for democracy. Protestantism's emphasis on individual responsibility furthered the emergence of democratic values in these countries [the United States and those of northwest Europe] and resulted in an alignment between the burghers and the throne which preserved the monarchy and extended the acceptance of democracy among the conservative strata. Men may question whether any aspect of this interrelated cluster of economic development, Protestantism, monarchy, gradual political change, legitimacy, and democracy is primary, but the fact remains that the cluster does hang together.

The teachings of Calvinistic Protestantism in the two centuries before the Declaration of Independence were important. They were not restricted in their influence to members of one religious group, however. Jews, Catholics, and agnostics alike seem to have accepted the ideas of individual responsibility, hard work, and thrift and to have fitted themselves into the American system of government and economics. We need only look at the way in which the pattern was adopted by the Irish, the first great Catholic immigration. (There were, of course, many Catholics in this country at the time of the War for Independence; one of them, John Carroll of Carrollton, signed the Declaration of Independence.) Coming in huge numbers beginning in the 1840s, the Irish were at first despised and forced to accept a social position not unlike that of the Puerto Ricans in New York today. But by accepting what has sometimes been called the "Protestant ethic," while at the same time remaining devoted to their own religion, the Irish in a few generations rose rapidly in terms of both status and wealth. In a sense, the Irish-Catholic Kennedy family, one of whose third-generation members reached the highest office in the land, epitomizes the American devotion to the idea of advancement through individual responsibility, hard work, and the reinvestment of one's profits.

Whatever the source of the ideas, there is no doubt that by the time of the War for Independence, Americans, Calvinist Protestants, and others alike, believed that acquiring wealth was ethically permissible and that there was virtue in thrift and saving (necessary, incidentally, for a new nation that needed to accumulate wealth for capital expansion).

Acquisition was accomplished through individual effort—at least in the early days of capitalism. Thus emphasis was placed upon the individual's obligation to work out his own problems and upon his need for self-

[12] Seymour Martin Lipset, *Political Man,* Doubleday & Company, Inc., Garden City, N.Y., 1960, p. 71.

reliance. The individual was expected to be responsible for his own welfare, although this view did not arise until after the free enterprise doctrine began to be coupled with the ethic toward the end of the eighteenth century. Work itself came to be viewed, not as a necessary evil, but as a moral obligation. Hard work, especially physical work, was regarded as good for the soul. One additional belief had been borrowed from Calvinism and was important in the development of America: the idea that a man's station in life is the result, not of assignment to a certain status by tradition and accident of birth, but of his own efforts. So Americans early believed in the possibility and ethical acceptance of an open class system of the type that has long characterized the culture of this nation.

THE IDEOLOGY OF FRONTIER INDIVIDUALISM

From the time the Constitution went into effect until after the Civil War, the prevailing American ideology reflected the life-styles of the yeoman farmer and the small-town merchant of the frontier. After Washington's terms as President, the office became partisan in character. The political party which first captured the Presidency was the class-oriented Federalist party, to which many of the Founding Fathers had belonged. But the Federalists could not reelect John Adams in 1800—significantly he lost to Thomas Jefferson, who stood for agrarian egalitarianism—and the party died out in a short time. Meanwhile, Jefferson and others busied themselves in the construction of the first typical American party of broad appeal that was based on the ideology of the average man. The author of the Declaration of Independence "gathered behind him the great mass of small farmers, mechanics [skilled tradesmen], shopkeepers, and other workers" who, collectively came to make up the Republican party. In the 1820s, that party was retitled the Democratic-Republican party and, after Jackson made the term "democratic" acceptable, the party was again renamed and became the Democratic party in about 1830.[13]

During this important formative period, several things about the nation are important in addition to those noted above:

1. Approximately 97 per cent of the American people lived on farms and in small towns at the time of independence.

2. Unlike the pattern in Europe, where land was often held by large landowners but was worked by peasants, the great bulk of American farmland was worked by the farmer and his family. He either owned his farm, was buying it, or hoped to buy it. If he had a hired man, that man was usually only working for a few years in order to accumulate enough money to begin farming for himself. The yeoman farmer—the exception in

[13] Quotation from Allan Nevins and Henry Steele Commager, *The Pocket History of the United States,* rev. ed., Pocket Books, Inc., New York, 1951, p. 144.

Europe—was the key person in the American economy. He was neither very rich nor very poor, and around him arose the concept of the common man.

3. The frontiersman was not dedicated to the doctrine of free enterprise. Farming, by it nature, encouraged belief in self-reliance, but the colonists had been accustomed to the mercantile system that was then popular in England. In brief, the mercantilists permitted a great variety of governmental regulatory activities in the economic realm. They providėd a basis for a tradition that later helped to encourage the farmer to seek government aid for himself and to regulate the businesses that affected farming most directly—particularly credit and transportation.

The Beliefs of the Frontiersman. What were the beliefs about government organization and programs that followed from the frontiersman's faith in hard work, thrift, individual responsibility, the competence of the common man, and the possibility of economic and social advancement? The following are the most important:

1. *Any man is as good as another man in public office.* Jefferson had implied this in the Declaration of Independence (1776), and Jackson had made it explicit in his first message to Congress (1829). One of the objectives of the Jeffersonians and Jacksonians had been to replace the aristocratic Federalists in the bureaucracy with persons who believed in their version of democracy. By the 1830s, the spoils system, by which Federal bureaucrats were selected on the basis of party loyalty, was well established. The system was logical if we assume, with Jackson, that the few qualifications needed in order to run a government are widely distributed throughout society and that those who carry out the policies of Congress and the President ought to believe in those policies.

The principle of universal manhood suffrage came of the frontier, following logically from egalitarianism. It was necessary to the development of Jacksonian thought. Furthermore, it was the natural result of the effect of inertia upon the already existing tendency to broaden the electorate—a tendency that had begun before the Revolution. It appears that at the time of the war with England, about 90 per cent of the rural dwellers of Massachusetts could vote, but there was a possibility that property requirements might disfranchise a considerable portion of the urban working class which began to emerge in considerable numbers after the War of 1812. Changes tending toward the elimination of property requirements took place at a great rate during the 1830s especially, and by 1850, virtually all property restrictions had disappeared from voting requirements. Universal manhood suffrage had been achieved—though only the visionary extended the concept beyond the white man. Thenceforth, the general public—the vaunted common man—possessed the potential for the control of government in its own interest.

2. *To the frontiersman, the election rather than the appointment of government officers was a mark of democracy.* This view had an enormous impact upon the writing of state constitutions from the 1830s through the 1850s, particularly in the development of the long ballot.

The United States Constitution, written by aristocrats rather than frontiersmen, had sought to minimize the participation of the voter. The Jacksonian view, thus, became dominant too late to have drastic effects upon the Federal pattern of administrative organization. However, the reduction of the Electoral College to a routine, and its replacement with selection virtually by popular vote, fitted the frontier beliefs. So did the direct election of senators, but this did not come until the Progressive movement of several generations later.

3. *A pragmatic approach.* On the question of how much the Federal government should be involved in the economy, the frontiersman could choose between the mercantilist's belief that the job of government was to assist in the expansion of the economy and the stump-clearer's conviction that things were not likely to get done unless he did them himself.

In general, pre-Civil War Americans took the position that government could help with a number of things that would benefit them. In particular, they supported the use of state and Federal funds for such things as canal building and the construction of the first "U.S." highway—the National Road from the Cumberland Gap to south-central Illinois (beginning in 1808). Even earlier—in 1787—under the Articles, Congress had provided the first and historically one of the most significant grants to local governments by giving land to help establish public school systems in what was then the Northwest territory.

On the other hand, by and large, the functions of the state and Federal governments in the domestic sphere remained small, and Jacksonians were quick to oppose legislation that they thought would benefit only a favored class. Jackson himself vetoed (1830) the bill for Federal aid to the Maysville Road in Kentucky because he was convinced that it was designed more for a few businessmen than for ordinary citizens.[14]

The frontiersman was a practical type: he was willing to accept governmental aid when he saw that it could help him, but—given his particular environment—most of the time he saw little that it could do for him.

The Frontier in Full Command

The prototype politician. A distinction has been made between the philosophy of Jefferson, the man of reflection, and the ideology of the Jacksonian frontiersman, the man of action. It has been said that Jefferson sought the ideal of equality in order to develop individuality, while the Jacksonian frontiersman sought the same ideal as a means of providing opportunity for ambition and a chance to climb the ladder to wealth and power.[15]

[14] See Glyndon G. Van Deusen, *The Jacksonian Era: 1828–1848,* Harper & Row, Publishers, New York, 1959.

[15] J. C. Livingston, "Alexander Hamilton and the American Tradition," *Midwest Journal of Political Science,* 1:209–224, November, 1957.

Jefferson was an intellectual who loved humanity, but he had less direct contact with individual common folk than did the Jacksonian politician of the following generation. The frontier campaigner concentrated on exploiting the commonly shared values of his constituents and especially on the use of political symbols. He did not seek to make philosophers out of them or to teach them the alleged beauties of individuality. In this sense, he became the prototype of nearly all subsequent American politicians.

A prototype campaign. In the presidential campaign of 1840, Martin Van Buren, seeking reelection, was opposed by General William Henry Harrison. This campaign may be regarded as the prototype of all subsequent campaigns in America.

Martin Van Buren had been Andrew Jackson's personal choice as his successor in the White House. He served out one term and came up for reelection in what might be regarded as the campaign in which "the formula" for American politics based on symbolic appeals was first applied in its modern form. It has not changed appreciably to this day, despite developments in means of communication, levels of education, and a vast increase in the number and quality of functions of government.

Van Buren, a Democrat, was opposed by the Whigs, an agglomerate group led by conservatives from the East, such as Daniel Webster, and those from the newer lands, such as Henry Clay. Unable to agree among themselves, the Whigs adopted no platform at all in 1840; instead, they approached the campaign on a "me-too" basis. They sought to show that they were the true friends of the common man, especially the frontiersman. For President they nominated a folk hero, General William Henry Harrison, and called him by the affectionate nickname of "Tippecanoe" (after the site of one of his victories over that frontier villain, the Indian). For Vice President, they selected a renegade Democrat, John Tyler. Harrison, who came from an aristocratic Virginia family and lived as a country gentleman on 2,000 acres outside Cincinnati, was sold to the public as a true frontiersman. His supporters toured the country, wearing coonskin caps, speaking from the porch of a log cabin mounted on a wagon, with a hard cider jug conspicuously near the door. Harrison had been in public life very briefly and was not on record on any of the day's major issues. His party offered the working people of the frontier a real he-man; the expanding urban working populations were offered something too—"Two dollars a day and roast beef."

Meanwhile, an effort was made to show that Van Buren did not deserve the vote of the common man. He was an Eastern aristocrat (actually, his father had been an upstate New York saloonkeeper) who lived like a king in the White House and who—of all disgraceful things—put cologne in his beard. Obviously, if the people wanted a real successor to Jackson in the White House, the Whig "frontiersman" was their man. Harrison won the election.

It seems likely to historians, however, that the really controlling factor was a sizable skeleton in the Democrat's closet—the financial panic of 1837. Characteristically, the voting public blames the incumbent group for whatever misfortunes may have taken place during its term in office—the question of actual responsibility is quite irrelevant. Later, voters seeking simple solutions to complex problems unrealistically blamed President Herbert Hoover for the Great Depression and President Franklin D. Roosevelt for the postwar expansion in Soviet power.

In its use of generalities, irrelevancies, and emotional appeals in preference to rational argumentation on the questions of the day, the campaign of 1840 set the pattern for American politics. Such a pattern is, perhaps, dictated by universal suffrage, combined with an open class system that makes little provision for political leadership from an educated upper class to which the average voter will defer.

Two Agrarian Traditions. There have been two agrarian traditions in America, not one. The tradition of the yeoman farmer that is emphasized here probably represents the mainstream of American ideological development, but it had a competitor:[16]

> Their inherent opposition to one another was to become clearer with each passing decade until it reached a climax during the 1850s in the contest for control of the territories beyond the Mississippi. Each of these new agrarianisms found expression in imaginative and symbolic terms: that of the South in a pastoral literature of the plantation, that of the Northwest in the myth of the garden of the world with the idealized Western yeoman as its focal point. The Southern social ideal owed nothing to Western experience. Its emphasis was upon the settled patterns of life in the older slave states along the Atlantic seaboard rather than upon the newer, rawer Southwest. The main tradition of Western agrarianism was developed north of the Ohio River and thence transported into the trans-Mississippi region as a consequence of the Northern victory over the South in the Civil War.

The differences produced by these two traditions have, of course, had enormous political consequences. The great plantations were generally broken up after the Civil War, but the tenant farmer system that followed resembled the European rather more than the Midwestern approach to agriculture. Accompanying this system was the tradition of government by the Bourbon aristocracy, a group that had no counterpart in Indiana or Nebraska. The same could be said for the class-and-caste system which gave uneasy order to the South after the great conflict. Later, when the white tenant farmers sought to join the mainstream of the American life-style (in the Populist movement at the end of the nineteenth century), and still later, when the Negro sought to do so, the social conflict was enormous.

[16] Henry Nash Smith, *Virgin Land: The American West as Symbol and Myth,* Harvard University Press, Cambridge, Mass., 1950, chap. 12. (Reprinted in paperback by Vintage Books, Random House, Inc., New York.)

FOREIGN POLICY AND THE FRONTIER NATION

Foreign policy, like domestic policy, may be treated as something that is developed as a response to a particular ideology. Indeed, the popular press is more likely to discuss foreign relations matters in terms of belief systems than any other aspect of public policy.

It has sometimes been said that the United States, unlike Great Britain, did not attempt to develop a coherent foreign policy until after World War II. To a considerable extent, the statement is probably correct. American policy prior to the First and Second World Wars was confused, inconsistent, and of indifferent public support. If we go back to the nineteenth century, it would be even more difficult to find a positive statement of beliefs and policies concerning our relationships with other nations.

An Ocean for Insulation. Even though their foreign policy could not be expressed in positive terms concerning the things they would want to do to other nations, or with them, nineteenth-century Americans had a belief system relative to foreign policy. It was the *ideology of isolationism,* as we shall call it. It reflected the wishes of a people who had abandoned their complex and often troubled homelands in order to be left alone. Many immigrants had left "the old country" to escape military service. To one degree or another, they were pacifists. To them, alliances for defense implied potential militarism, to which they were opposed.

Other immigrants came to this country because they saw opportunity here. They felt that others who wanted to live and advance as they did could join them. It is a short step from this assumption to the notion that Americans have no obligations to people in other countries: "They are still there, so they must like it—and they must like the troubles and wars, too."

With the means of transportation and communication slow and the Atlantic Ocean vast, Americans could see little reason to become involved in the complex intrigues of European nations, and they repeated over and over again that "all we want is to be left alone." Out of these desires came the fundamental ideology of isolationism—one that held sway with little modification until the time of World War I. It was based on three essential concepts: (1) the avoidance of entangling alliances that could bring America into Europe's wars; (2) an extension of the American defense perimeter to include all of North and South America; and (3) a doctrine of limited expansionism.

Washington's Farewell Address. George Washington, on leaving office after having declined to run for a third term, submitted a lengthy statement to his countrymen concerning his view of the relationship of America to other nations. He urged the preservation of the institutions that had been developed, and the foreign policy views he expressed became a cornerstone of American faith, perhaps because they so well fitted the views of a newly independent and isolated people. Many Presidents and members of Congress have since echoed them.

Washington (1797) warned against "sympathy for the favorite nation, facilitating the illusion of an imaginary common interest in cases where no real interest exists." And he said that we should avoid "participation in the quarrels and wars" of other nations. His view, which was very popular at the time and long remained so, was that we should extend our commercial relations with other nations, but have as little as possible to do with them politically.

He warned that "real patriots who may resist the intrigues of the favorite [nation] are liable to become suspected and odious, while its tools and dupes usurp the applause and confidence of the people to surrender their interests."

If this statement seems to have a remarkably contemporary ring, it is because the threat of foreign infiltration remains a fear of many Americans, particularly those who still believe essentially in the ideology of isolationism. Indeed, terms such as "patriot" and "dupe" are still part of the rhetoric of isolationism. The very term "isolationism" has had an unhappy fate, having been used in ways that cast disfavor on it in the propaganda of those who reject the isolationist ideology.

Washington believed that "Europe has a set of primary interests which to us have none or a very remote relation," and that "it is our true policy to steer clear of permanent alliances with any portion of the foreign world."

Yet the Father of his Country did not follow this ideology blindly or without concern for the reason for its public popularity. "Our detached and distant situation," he noted, "invites and enables us to pursue a different course" from the European system of mutual defense alliances. It would thus be a mistake to assume that Washington would have taken the position that he did in an age of radio communication, jets, and ballistic missiles. We do not know what he would advise today; but in his day and throughout the following century, his view was overwhelmingly accepted by Americans.

The Monroe Doctrine. The simple idea that "you leave us alone and we will leave you alone" probably suited the frontiersman just fine, but it did not meet all of the needs of the President and the spokesmen of the State Department in the formulation of policy. They had to decide practical questions within the framework of the ideology of isolationism. What, for example, was the Secretary of State to do about the claim of Imperial Russia for the Pacific Coast territory south of Alaska (which it owned) down into what is now southern British Columbia? What about the desires of antidemocratic imperialists who wanted to help Spain restore her crumbling empire by retaking the newly freed nations of South America? Did isolationism dictate that we ignore these developments?

The answer was "No." And the answer contained ingredients of both the desire of those responsible for the nation's defense to have some breathing space in which to operate, and the first glimmer of an American feeling of responsibility for preserving independence in the New World and the wish to retain a preferred position in relation to other American nations. These views were expressed in the Monroe Doctrine (1823), which the President announced, largely on the advice of the Secretary of State, John Quincy Adams. It held that no European nation should henceforth be permitted to create new dependencies in the Americas or to interfere with or threaten the independence of a nation of the New World; we, in turn, would not interfere in quarrels among European nations.

The policy received rapid and widespread acceptance. It became a part of the ideology of isolationism, probably its most enduring part.

A God-favored Nation. As the nineteenth century advanced, Americans moved ever westward. They moved into Oregon, which was territory disputed with Britain; into Texas, which was Mexican; and into California, which was under weak Mexican control. As they carried along their belief in progress, growth, and government under law, Americans came into conflict with the Spanish-American culture, which was radically different. So Americans in the new territories talked much of wrongs against their property, of capricious laws that did not give them equal protection, and of hostile actions against them. Many of them felt an obligation to "civilize" and "develop" the raw land of the West, just as their parents had done in the area between the Alleghenies and the Mississippi. So in short order, we reached agreement with Britain on dividing up the Oregon country; in 1845, we annexed Texas, which had earlier become an independent nation; and in 1847, we went to war with Mexico, ostensibly over a dispute concerning the southern border of Texas. When the fighting ended, the United States secured not only California, but all of the great Southwest. Americans felt all the more that they had a "manifest destiny."

The Years of Energy and Enthusiasm. The first half of the nineteenth century was a period of rapid growth in population and wealth by a young nation that was protected by vast oceans from the threats and fears of other nations. Enormous enthusiasm and self-confidence were generated during this period, and Americans, not surprisingly, often concluded that their land was particularly blessed by Providence. President James Knox Polk spoke for much of the nation (1847): "An all-wise Creator directed and guarded us in our infant struggle for freedom and has constantly watched over our surprising progress until we have become one of the great nations of the earth."

The idea of a nation especially favored by the Almighty was, of course, not unique in America, but it has continued throughout the country's history and remains very much alive today. It has led us to believe that we cannot lose a war or fail to solve a domestic crisis. Our traditional viewpoint, like that of the New York Yankees, gives us a self-confidence that helps us to reach our goals. But it leaves us unprepared for possible eventualities. Most Americans probably cannot conceive of our losing a war, and it was a great shock to us when the Soviet Union, in the postwar years, began to beat us at our own game by scoring a number of firsts—orbiting a satellite, putting the first man into space, and establishing relationships with new nations as "the friend of the little fellow." As times change, our self-image may change, and the resulting dislocation may be a psychological problem for the nation as a whole. But the attitudes formed in the green years of the Republic have provided, and continue to provide us with a confidence that sometime annoys the citizens of other nations, but often stands us in good stead in times of stress or threat.

SELECTED BIBLIOGRAPHY

The folk beliefs of the period between Jamestown (1620) and the beginning of the Civil War (1861) can be recaptured today only by the genius of the historian and the recorded thoughts of the writers of the day; it is too late to conduct public-opinion surveys or record ad-libbed speeches. There is much to guide us, however, in seeking to understand the belief systems of the early years.

The classic study of American ideas for this period is that of Parrington [18], but it should be remembered that he was a product of the progressive period and tended to romanticize the yeoman farmer. Many others have covered this same ground, often from differing points of view [3, 4, 5, 6, 9, 11]. Some of the pre-Independence and non-American thinkers whose ideas were reflected by frontiersmen are discussed by Mayer [13] and Weber [28].

De Tocqueville [5, 6], the brilliant French observer, can be read in the original or in translation. His writings about American democracy not only reflected the age, but were probably also reflected by Americans who sought to live by the image he described. There has always been in America both a liberal and a conservative tradition. The former is described by Hartz [7], the latter by Rossiter [21] and Morris [16]. The basic economic ideas of the period are restated and recommended for today by Hayek [8]. Many history books and journals are useful in outlining the ideas and value system of the period.

Jefferson can, of course, be read in the original. Every library contains books of his letters, speeches, and messages (see, for example [17]). The traditions of his era are developed by Wiltse [29]; the ways in which various groups, from reactionaries to Communists, have sought to use his words and high status for propaganda purposes are discussed by Peterson [19].

The next great wave of democracy, Jacksonianism, is the subject of another large bibliography. Jackson's own First Inaugural Address is a good place to begin reading, and this text might be followed by that of Schlesinger [23]. Many others deal with the subject, although not all share the same perspectives [1, 10, 14, 15, 26].

Americans in this early period had an ideal model or dream that they pursued. Sanford [22] describes the idea of progress toward a utopian goal; Smith [25] shows how the West served to keep the dream alive; Warner [27] discusses the rags-to-riches story in the analytical framework of the social scientist. MacIver [12] tells us that these daydreams or images help to hold a society together and give the citizen some criteria by which to evaluate proposed governmental policies. The special views of the South need to be examined separately, as they are by Cash [2] and Sellers [24]. The actual life-style of the period, as distinguished from the romanticized image, is discussed in many history books and journal articles. See, for example, Riegel [20]. White [30, 31, 32] has written about the process of policy development and execution and ideas on bureaucracy that prevailed from the days of Washington to the Civil War.

No first-rate description of the gradual stagnation of the ideas of the first half of the nineteenth century exists, but those trapped by it outside the mainstream of American society have been the subject of a great many novels and plays, such as Sinclair Lewis's *Main Street* and Erskine Caldwell's *Tobacco Road.*

1. Blau, Joseph L. (ed.): *The Social Theories of Jacksonian Democracy (1825–1850),* The Liberal Arts Press, Inc., New York, 1960.
2. Cash, Wilbur J.: *The Mind of the South,* Alfred A. Knopf, Inc., New York, 1941.
3. Curti, Merle E.: *The Growth of American Thought,* 2d ed., Harper & Row, Publishers, New York, 1951.
4. De Grazia, Sebastian: *The Political Community,* The University of Chicago Press, Chicago, 1948.
5. De Tocqueville, Alexis: *Democracy in America,* New American Library of World Literature, Inc., New York, 1960. (Other paperback and hardbound copies available.)
6. De Tocqueville, Alexis: *Journey to America,* Yale University Press, New Haven, Conn., 1963 (paperback).
7. Hartz, Louis: *The Liberal Tradition in America,* Harcourt, Brace & World, Inc., New York, 1955.
8. Hayek, Friedrich A.: *The Constitution of Liberty,* The University of Chicago Press, Chicago, 1960.
9. Hofstadter, Richard: *American Political Tradition,* Vintage Books, Random House, Inc., New York, 1961 (paperback).
10. Hugins, Walter E.: *Jacksonian Democracy and the Working Class,* Stanford University Press, Stanford, Calif., 1960.
11. King, Wendell: *Social Movements in the United States,* Random House, Inc., New York, 1956.
12. MacIver, Robert M.: *The Web of Government,* The Macmillan Company, New York, 1947.
13. Mayer, Milton (ed.): *John Locke, Adam Smith and the Federalist,* Oceana Publications, New York, 1960.
14. Meyers, Marvin: *The Jacksonian Persuasion, Politics and Belief,* Vintage Books, Random House, Inc., New York, 1960.
15. Miles, Edwin A.: *Jacksonian Democracy in Mississippi,* The University of North Carolina Press, Chapel Hill, N.C., 1960.
16. Morris, Richard B. (ed.): *Basic Ideas of Alexander Hamilton,* Pocket Books, Inc., New York, 1960.
17. Padover, Saul (ed.): *Thomas Jefferson on Democracy,* New American Library of World Literature, Inc., New York, 1961.
18. Parrington, Vernon L.: *Main Currents in American Thought,* Harcourt, Brace & World, Inc., New York, 3 vols., 1930.
19. Peterson, Merrill D.: *The Jefferson Image in the American Mind,* Oxford University Press, Fair Lawn, N.J., 1960.
20. Riegel, Robert E.: *Young America: 1830–1840,* University of Oklahoma Press, Norman, Okla., 1949.
21. Rossiter, Clinton: *Conservatism in America,* Alfred A. Knopf, Inc., New York, 1955.
22. Sanford, Charles L.: *The Quest for Paradise: Europe and the American Moral Imagination,* The University of Illinois Press, Urbana, Ill., 1961.

23. Schlesinger, Arthur M., Jr.: *The Age of Jackson,* Little, Brown and Company, Boston, 1945. (Available in paperback.)
24. Sellers, Charles G., Jr. (ed.): *The Southerner as American,* The University of North Carolina Press, Chapel Hill, N.C., 1960.
25. Smith, Henry Nash: *Virgin Land: The American West as Symbol and Myth,* Harvard University Press, Cambridge, Mass., 1950. (Available in paperback.)
26. Van Deusen, Glyndon: *The Jacksonian Era: 1828–1848,* Harper & Row, Publishers, New York, 1959.
27. Warner, W. Lloyd: *American Life: Dream and Reality,* The University of Chicago Press, Chicago, 1953.
28. Weber, Max: *The Protestant Ethic and the Spirit of Capitalism,* George Allen & Unwin, Ltd., London, 1930. Translated by Talcott Parsons.
29. Wiltse, Charles: *The Jeffersonian Tradition in American Democracy,* American Century Series, Hill and Wang, Inc., New York, 1960.
30. White, Leonard D.: *The Federalists, 1789–1801,* The Macmillan Company, New York, 1948.
31. White, Leonard D.: *The Jacksonians, 1829–1861,* The Macmillan Company, New York, 1954.
32. White, Leonard D.: *The Jeffersonians, 1801–1829,* The Macmillan Company, New York, 1951.

CHAPTER 7

IDEOLOGY: CONFLECTS IN AN INDUSTRIAL AGE

The two rural traditions, those of North and South, became the basis upon which ideas about government were built after America began to industrialize and move toward becoming an urban nation. Rapid change took place in the years immediately following the Civil War. It was during this period that the financing and productive techniques of the large corporation emerged as the effective processes for the accumulation of national and personal wealth. America could not become a rich nation so long as it was primarily an agricultural one. But urban industrialization was a way of life drastically different from what Americans were accustomed to; when it arrived, our government was not only structured for an entirely different way of life, but the ideas as to what government's role should be were based on the earlier and different rural way of life.

The problems of an industrial age were not problems of whether the government could aid the frontier farmer in his routine labor, but whether the individual farmer could get a fair hauling rate from a huge railroad corporation; not whether the small-town merchant would deal fairly with his small-town and farming neighbors, but whether a nationwide manufacturer of canned goods would sell products that would not poison those who bought them; not whether Uncle Hiram could find a job as a farmhand through the slack winter months (his brother would take him in and let him eke out an existence cutting timber on the back forty), but how thousands of factory workers would support their families if a management decision closed a plant for three months; not whether the one-room school that was educating the next generation of farmers should buy a new heating stove, but whether a different curriculum was needed in order to prepare a generation of professional specialists of all kinds; not whether the United States should send a high-ranking member of the administration to attend the coronation of a European monarch, but whether it was possible to prevent the thermonuclear destruction of the world.

In this new age, we could expect that changing life experiences and life-styles would change the public's concept of the proper function of government in helping individuals toward the good life as redefined in the new environment. But these changes would not be at a uniform rate.

THE IDEOLOGY OF INDUSTRIAL INDIVIDUALISM

The coming of big business with its large capital investments, high degree of mechanization, and impersonal conditions of labor, produced a political ideology for the times, the ideology of industrial individualism. It was a modified and modernized ideology of frontier individualism, moved into the small towns and emerging cities and made to fit a new pattern of life. In the place of the frontiersman, the new hero was the self-made man of industry in the Horatio Alger tradition. In the place of the long-dominant Democratic party, the new Republican party emerged from the Civil War as—except in the South—the strongest political coalition and the one that successfully associated itself with the new ideology. While Congress had been dominant in the past, the judicial branch gradually became the strongest of the three. It served as the energetic protector of the new ideology. Through the Fourteenth Amendment, which was originally adopted in an effort to give the freed slaves equal status as citizens, economic individualism was written into the fundamental law of the land by using the concept of "due process of law" to resolve conflicts in favor of property rather than governmental regulation. Americans, with varying degrees of clarity, recognized that the future wealth and power of the nation lay in rapid industrialization.

Poor Boy Becomes Millionaire. No one reads the works of Horatio Alger today. His more than 100 stories won no literary prizes and made sense only in the spirit of the times in which they were written. But they reflected the folklore of an emerging industrial nation by telling the nineteenth-century youngster that opportunity was his for the taking, that success can be measured in terms of material accomplishments, and that success results from virtue and hard work. Perhaps not every boy believed that he could become another Vanderbilt or Carnegie by this simple formula, but he was constantly bombarded with such propaganda by newspapers and magazines that were controlled by persons whose interests coincided with those of the new titans of business and industry. Undoubtedly these teachings profoundly affected Americans, urban and rural, rich and poor; they had much to do both with conditioning American behavior and with the way in which citizens accepted business as the most important institution in our society and permitted the new giant corporations to create "clusters of private government which first neutralized state powers and then overcame them."[1] And inspiration for the golden age of individualism came not just from dime novels and the press: During World War I, for example, the number of millionaires in the United States more than doubled.

The new ideology included the idea that business (including industry) was the nation's most important institution; that what was good for business was good for the nation; that other institutions, social or political, should play a secondary role and not interfere with the activities of the business community. Free enterprise and *laissez faire* became key symbols; government was regarded as inefficient, and its control over business was held to be not only a threat to the progress of the nation, but in fact immoral.

The Federal and state courts became guardians of free enterprise and the dominant ideology. When these were threatened by Federal regulation, the courts turned to the theory of States' rights, and at the same time, they set aside state regulation as interference with the interstate commerce power of the Federal government. With the courts the dominant of the three branches of government, the Constitution came to be revered more than

[1] Robert J. Harris, "States' Rights and Vested Interests," *Journal of Politics,* 15:461, November, 1954.

Figure 7-1

The Formula Fiction of Horatio Alger Portrayed the Ideology of an Age—Although J. Wesley Was Slow to Understand It

"Why don't you do a story about me, Mr. Alger? How I inherited this business from my father and..."

By permission of Burr Shafer.

ever. In the folklore of the day, it was given a spirit of its own. It was treated as if it existed apart from the interpretations of it. And although the judges often made use of their personal philosophies in interpreting the document, their decisions were written in a ritualistic language which suggested that it was the duty of the judges not to use their own values in interpreting the document, but to seek to "discover" its true intent. The "intention of the framers" was found to have been the doctrine of free enterprise, even though the men at Philadelphia were not in fact committed to that doctrine, rather they were mercantilists.

The people accepted these ideas in general, but as always, their attitudes were ambivalent. They believed in hard work; they believed that it would be rewarded. They believed government should not interfere with their efforts. But where these beliefs failed to help individuals in their time of troubles—as was the case with the farmers toward the end of the nineteenth century—they also continued to accept the frontiersman's pragmatism. They would seek help wherever they could find it.[2]

Agrarian Radicalism. As America matured, changing from a frontier nation of farmers to an industrial nation of urbanites, life experiences changed; there was a gradual shift in basic ideology from opportunity to security, from individual to collective activity. It is perhaps ironic, though understandable, that the first significant efforts at collective action came from the farmers, the very men who were thought to represent, in Charles Beard's phrase, "rugged individualism." Agrarian radicalism did not have as much support in the commercial farming areas of the corn belt as it did further west and south in the marginal cash-crop areas.

The farmer, through neglect of the political arena as a medium for protecting his interests, had gradually fallen into an impossible economic position and had lost his political dominance by the end of the nineteenth century. "His was the only considerable economic group that exerted no organized pressure to control the price he sold for or the price he paid."[3] He had voted away the public domain to the railroads in his desperate need for transportation facilities—and the railroads were now repaying him with excessive freight charges.[4]

> He took pride in the county-seat towns that lived off his earnings; he sent city lawyers to represent him in legislatures and in Congress; he read middle-class newspapers and listened to bankers and politicians and cast his votes for the policy of Whiggery [property rights and *laissez faire*] that could have no other outcome than his own despoiling.

[2] This section borrows from Charles R. Adrian, *State and Local Governments: A Study in the Political Process,* McGraw-Hill Book Company, New York, 1960, chap. 4, where further development of the ideology of industrial individualism is presented.

[3] Vernon L. Parrington, *Main Currents of American Thought,* Harcourt, Brace & World, Inc., New York, 1930, vol. 3, p. 262.

[4] *Ibid.*

Both the farmers and the business corporations, especially the railroads, established professional lobbies in Washington. The conflict between the farmer and his historic business-world enemies came about in the years that followed, when the railroads developed rapidly and came virtually to monopolize control over the transportation of the farmers' products. At the same time, the great industrial trusts began to control the productive and consumer goods the farmers needed. Grain elevators, too, were essential to the farmers' welfare, since they controlled the sale price of his cash products and the conditions under which he could sell them—and these were owned by absentee landlords in cities miles from the farmers who used them. Bankers controlled credit, and their policies encouraged a continuing deflation of the currency, which forced upon the farmer unbearable long-term debts.

The governmental programs demanded by the farmer have come to be known as "Granger" legislation because the National Grange carried much of the farmers' political burden in the last part of the nineteenth century. Most of these demands were upon state governments,[5] but some were directed toward Congress. A major victory for the farmers came in a Federal commitment to control railroad rates in interstate commerce after the Supreme Court had held that the states could not do so. (The principle of "dual federalism" was invoked to claim that the national government had exclusive jurisdiction over such commerce.)[6] The Act to Regulate Commerce provided for restrictions upon the activities of railroads and established what was to become commonplace in later years, a quasi-legislative body to administer the act—in this case, the Interstate Commerce Commission. The act was a landmark in legislation; it was the forerunner of what was to come.

The Worker and Individualism. The American trade union movement is about as old as the country itself. Serious efforts at unionization of the skilled trades were made in Andrew Jackson's time, though they were not the first. The number of working people had increased enough in the Eastern cities by the 1830s for leaders of protest to demand a change in the ancient common law concept of a strike as an illegal conspiracy. Jackson, who had gotten the votes of the factory workers, established a ten-hour day for civilian workers in the Navy's shipyards (1836). This was at a time when most factory workers spent twelve and more hours at the job each day. So unionization movements and demands for better wages, hours, and conditions of labor date from the days when most of America was frontier country, or only slightly removed from it. These movements began before the heyday of industrial individualism and have continued to the present.

Yet the era of powerful trade unions, enjoying governmental protection

[5] Adrian, *op. cit.*, gives an account.

[6] *Wabash, St. Louis, and Pacific RR. Co. v. Illinois,* 118 U.S. 557 (1886).

and possessing considerable political power, began, essentially, only two generations ago. There were several reasons for this slow development. In the first place, unionization of workers was slowed by the constant job threat posed by immigrants from abroad and migrants who began the rural-to-urban trek early in our history. With the very real threat of importing new and cheap labor, it was difficult enough to organize skilled workers and virtually impossible to organize the unskilled. If this was not reason enough, there was the hostile attitude of the courts, in which many of the judges were former corporation lawyers. Judges, in any case, by and large accepted the doctrine of *laissez faire*. The many legal weapons of the judiciary made organization difficult, and appeals to the legislative branch of government to change the rules were largely unsuccessful. The legislators, too, generally believed that the progress of business was more important to the country than the welfare of an individual worker. Furthermore, in the 1870s and 1880s, the bottom dropped out of traditional morality so far as business relationships were concerned. Some of the business leaders of the day made use of tricks, market manipulations, spies, sabotage, bribery, and other practices that would have been considered criminal in an earlier or a later America. Whole legislatures and many congressmen were in the pay of corporations. Had working people made a serious threat to get the law changed, they would quickly have been outbid in their efforts to elect sympathetic congressmen.

Labor leaders in the earlier years were often immigrants who could be denounced as not being "true Americans." Furthermore, the dysfunctionality of the ideology of frontier individualism under conditions of industrialism created a partial vacuum that was temporarily filled by the already existing working-class concepts of Europe. Many labor leaders embraced frankly radical philosophies. They were therefore, not seen as contributing to the mainstream of American social development; rather, they were regarded as a threat to it. Finally, the general public was basically committed to the doctrine of individualism. A nation of yeoman farmers and their descendants tended to identify with the employer—in contrast to the European tenant farmer, who was more likely to see himself as a laborer. If efforts to bargain collectively were coupled with the threat of coercion through a strike or boycott, workers were even less likely to earn public sympathy. And the farmer, as always, saw higher urban wages as a threat of a higher cost to the things he had to buy, a threat to his standard of living. So urban labor remained largely unorganized for economic or political action until after the Great Depression began.

Urban labor did, however, influence elections. For example, some historians believe that Benjamin Harrison failed to gain reelection in 1892 partially because of the unpopularity of his running mate, Whitelaw Reid, among the working people of New York City and other Eastern cities. (Reid's newspaper had been openly antiunion.) The workingman himself was probably strongly committed to individualism and belief in opportunity for economic advancement during this period, but being an empiricist like the farmer, he was beginning to look to collective action through the trade union and the local political machine as a means for reducing his greatest anxieties and insecurities.

The Small-Business Man: Adherent to an Eclipsed Ideology. As political ideology undergoes gradual modification, individuals do not all adjust to changes in the same manner. Some are out leading the parade and demanding that the public recognize the need for a new point of view. Others seek to manipulate the symbols of a popular ideology. Still others accept new ideas passively, but without much hesitation if they seem to fit the current environment. Still others accept change very slowly or not at all. This is the case with individuals in every group in society. There is a great range in the beliefs of farmers, workers, and businessmen. When we lump them together, we can do so only in a statistical sense and we can talk only about *dominant* beliefs. Yet the distribution of beliefs within groups is not the same in each case; it is probably safe to say that businessmen, and especially small-business men, have most strongly preserved their belief in the concepts of industrial individualism.

Most small businesses are service or distributive rather than productive operations. They are intensely competitive (about 400,000 small businesses are started annually; only 20 per cent of them survive for ten years). They struggle against one another, against the large corporations that supply them, and against the potentially more efficient corporate form of organization of their businesses, as in the case of the large chain supermarkets that have left so little room for the traditional corner grocer. In these circumstances, it is understandable that the small-business man would continue to believe in the values of the American agrarian frontier. To him, success is still not to be found so much in luck or in environment as it is in self-reliance, hard work, and thrift. He recognizes that big business, big labor, and subsidized farming pose serious threats to him by raising both his business costs and (part of the same thing) his taxes.

In an effort to cling to a fading part of the American way, "the thinking and temper of the small businessman indicates a profound ideological attachment to the values of a preindustrial order—indeed, he has become a contemporary advocate of the spirit and virtues of agrarianism."[7] Because he is suspicious of all the many things alien to the world in which he lives and to his idealized version of the same, he is especially distrustful of foreign ideologies, internationalism, the upsetting of established traditions, cosmopolitanism, urbanism, and collectivism.

[7] John H. Bunzel, *The American Small Businessman,* Alfred A. Knopf, Inc., New York, 1962; Arthur J. Vidich and Joseph Bensman, *Small Town in Mass Society,* Princeton University Press, Princeton, N.J., 1958, pp. 116–117; and Alpheus T. Mason, "American Individualism: Fact and Fiction," *American Political Science Review,* 46:1–18, March, 1952.

He is concerned about possible monopoly practices in big business. He fears the expanding power and activity of organized labor. He views activities on behalf of the consumer, the urban worker, or big business as costs that he has to share without any equivalent benefit. With the ambivalence typical of political value patterns, the small-business man does favor government legislation that will improve his economic lot, but most of what he is interested in involves local and sometimes state governments. He is not convinced that the Federal government can do much to help him. There are some exceptions, of course. Persons in the building trades benefit from the policies of the Housing and Home Finance Agency, for example. But despite its name, the Small Business Administration (SBA), which was created from the remnants of the Reconstruction Finance Corporation in 1953, offers little to the typical small-business man. Most Federal government programs, in fact, are not aimed at him. More than the farmer—Americans, after all, still need food and fiber—he is expendable today, and he knows it. And since virtually all programs under the social service state are seen as costing him more than he gains from them, he becomes an advocate of minimal governmental "interference" in business, of free enterprise, and of States' rights constitutionalism.[8]

Congressmen have long been concerned because small-business men seem to feel divorced or alienated from the mainstream of American political action, for they are always concerned about the anxieties of constituents. Furthermore, a basic rule of politics is to provide something for every major interest in society. Politicians assume it to be better to satisfy many persons in part than to satisfy a few completely. As a result, congressmen have long been desirous of "doing something for small business." What that something is, given the realities of economics, is not clear. But the House and Senate have both established small-business committees. The committees have not come up with detailed legislative programs in the postwar years, however. At times, they have investigated the effects of big business as a stifling influence on small business (e.g., a 1952 Senate committee report, *Monopoly and Cartels*), and they have sought support for legislation that would assist small business. At other times, they have inquired into the way in which government competes with business or how government red tape has been an obstacle to small-business men and has raised costs (e.g., the 1957 Senate committee report *Government Competition with Private Business*). In both cases, the reports have reflected different sets of concerns of the small-business man.

Congress has sometimes acted on behalf of the small-business man, as it did in permitting states to adopt fair trade laws, that is, laws that permit the manufacturer to fix the price of his product and thus to reduce price competition among retailers. Similarly, the Robinson-Patman Act of 1936 sought to prevent vigorous price competition by prohibiting the selling of

[8] John H. Bunzel, "Comparative Attitudes of Big Business and Small Business," *Western Political Quarterly,* 9:658–675, September, 1956.

the same product under different brand names and made other provisions for limiting price competition. Yet not much effective help has come to the small-business man, and he is himself doubtful if government can help him, except perhaps by curbing big business, big labor, and big government.

The SBA was established in response to concerns about the monopolistic powers of big business. It offers loans and loan guarantees (up to $350,000) to small business, aids it in getting government contracts, and offers advice about new products. The second Hoover Commission, which was deeply concerned about efficiency and economy in government and business, took a dim view of the agency, particularly of its practice of granting loans at interest rates that did not repay the costs of the SBA. But Congress, concerned with an important segment of the economy and with a group of politically active constituents, made the agency permanent in 1958. It has not, however, the resources or the kind of program that can have a substantial effect upon the profit levels of small business, on its ability to compete with big business in cost terms, or its ability to get government contracts. The small-business man is perhaps the most frustrated person in the American political arena because government can neither help him substantially with his own problems, nor does it put a stop to the trends that he sees as a threat.

The Business Propagandist. The small-business man represents a considerable segment of the economy. The number of businesses he operates is huge in total, and many people are engaged in them. But they are not the dominant portion of the business world and have not been for several generations. The views of the small-business man are, however, reflected for him by other parts of the business sector of society.

Business journals and the bureaucracies of some big-business organizations, such as the Chamber of Commerce of the United States and the National Association of Manufacturers, tend to give continued support to the ideology of industrial individualism, but their views appear to be considerably more conservative than those of typical members of large corporation bureaucracies. This is so because journal editors, chamber of commerce secretaries, and the like, see themselves as responsible for propagating the symbols of the business world. They become attached to the symbols they use, and whatever the individual businessman may believe, the symbols he is expected to endorse are those of individualism. His trade associations meet these expectations. Furthermore, in testifying before congressional committees, these groups often find that it is easier to get consensus among their leaders on what to oppose than on what to take a positive stand. As a result, business groups often give the impression of being more negativistic toward governmental programs than may actually be the case.

In any event, the conservative writers in business journals rather consistently see expanding governmental activity as leading to socialism or even communism. Government is seen as inefficient and enmeshed in red tape, and corruption is regarded as a natural and perhaps certain result of large budgets. Government is portrayed as an impersonal, rather sinister institution that stands outside and above the social order, threatening it rather than serving it.[9]

The Organization Man: The Businessman's Transition to a New Ideology. The large industrial firm is as alien to fundamental American traditions as the trade union. Americans are happy to have its products, but the large, formal organizations and the potential for control over the market leave us with mixed feelings. Furthermore, the big-business bureaucrat, named the "organization man" by William H. Whyte, Jr.,[10] has views and interests that are very considerably different from those of the small-business man. Whyte has pointed out that the corporation executive lets the personnel and financial departments of the company handle his savings for him, that the advertising agency for the company is busy convincing people to spend, not to save. The business bureaucrat, unlike the small-business man, usually has opportunity for advancement in both pay and status by moving up the organization ladder. He does not see the firm's market as fixed, but rather as having room for expansion. His annual income is not usually dependent on the rate of profit of the firm. Taxes are not a cost of business to him unless he happens to be in the department responsible for paying them, and labor relations are handled by specialists in a similar way.

The big-business bureaucrat, therefore, does not have the strong motivation of the small-business man to fight the social service state. Of course, he does not reject the language of individualism, and he probably believes in it in principle. This particular set of symbols is especially important to the public relations department of the firm, for it can be useful in seeking to preserve the traditional, if uneasy, political alliance between the small proprietor and the large business firm; in seeking to prevent the adoption of proposals for governmental policy where those policies would threaten the company welfare; and in making good-will appeals to the public, which still sees the symbols in a favorable light, whether it lives by them or not.

In terms of both his immediate economic interests and the social pressures upon him, the organization man has less reason to be a conservative than does the small-business man, and his political views may vary considerably according to his background and interests. Being better educated than the typical small-business man, he may have broader and more sophisticated views of economic and social issues. He will probably conform to expectations in reflecting traditional individualist rhetoric, but he has far less incentive to take political action in support of these views than the small-business man has. And if his personal avocational interests should

[9] Marver H. Bernstein, "The Political Ideas of Selected American Business Journals," *Public Opinion Quarterly,* 17:258–267, Summer, 1953.

[10] See William H. Whyte, Jr., *The Organization Man,* Doubleday & Company, Inc., Garden City, N.Y., 1957.

lead him to become active in an interest group seeking appropriations for some expensive program—expanded foreign aid for the African nations, say, or urban renewal—his hobby will probably not cost him his job.

THE IDEOLOGY OF THE SOCIAL SERVICE STATE

As the nation changed from an individualistic, rural society to an economically interdependent and urban one, much social dislocation took place. When industrial individualism failed to meet felt needs, people turned to collective effort through government. Americans today are still overwhelmingly committed to the idea that the individual should be left alone to do as he pleases wherever possible. But increasingly, groups have seen the government as the best, or perhaps the only available umpire to settle disputes between clashing interests (small business versus big business, workers versus employer, one trade union versus another, farmer versus big business) or as the only perceived institution that can help to relieve the fears and worries of the contemporary urbanite. The pattern first followed by the farmer was later taken up by the workingman and many businessmen.

The New Ideology. The shattering experience of the Great Depression, which began in the fall of 1929 and lasted until the nation began to prepare for World War II a decade later, convinced many that job security, guaranteed payments in the event of unemployment or industrial accident, government assistance in preparing for retirement, help in finding a job, and other hedges against starvation were more important than opportunity or the abstract principle of freedom from government control.

As the *Nation* noted in 1868, "If the doors of the future are once thrown open to what are called 'the masses,' and they catch even one glimpse of the splendid possibilities which lie within it, it is in vain to close them again. The vision never leaves their minds."[11] And indeed, in a series of movements—the farmers' activities beginning in the 1870s, Theodore Roosevelt's Square Deal, Robert LaFollette's Progressive movement, Woodrow Wilson's New Freedom, and others—the common folk had come to realize that government was potentially a powerful weapon in their hands and that each of them had a vote equal to that of any banker or corporation president. By the 1960s, the idea of minimal government had "almost vanished from the mind" of the ordinary urban citizen.[12]

These doors for political action did not open as suddenly as many Americans seem to believe. The basic ingredients of the social service state

[11] Quoted in Alan P. Grimes, *The Political Liberalism of the New York Nation,* The University of North Carolina Press, Chapel Hill, N.C., 1953, p. 40.

[12] Robert E. Lane, *Political Ideology: Why the American Common Man Believes What He Does,* The Free Press of Glencoe, New York, 1962, p. 188.

concept were offered more than half a century ago in one of Theodore Roosevelt's most famous speeches—to the G.A.R. (Grand Army of the Republic) encampment at Ossawattomie, Kansas, on August 31, 1910. The ideas were not original with Roosevelt—third parties had been urging them for years—but he lent to them the prestige of an ex-President, one of the most popular political heroes of the twentieth century. T.R. talked of his Square Deal and of his New Nationalism, and much of what he said was later reflected in the programs of Wilson, Eisenhower, Kennedy, and his fifth cousin, Franklin D. Roosevelt. Here are some highlights from that speech:[13]

> We are face to face with new conceptions of the relations of property to human welfare, chiefly because certain advocates of the rights of property as against the rights of men have been pushing their claims too far. . . .
>
> The State must be made efficient for the work which concerns only the people of the State; and the nation for that which concerns all the people. There must remain no neutral ground to serve as a refuge for lawbreakers, and especially for lawbreakers of great wealth. . . .
>
> [The New Nationalism] is impatient of the utter confusion that results from local legislatures' attempts to treat national issues as local issues. . . .
>
> [The New Nationalism] regards the executive power as the steward of the public welfare. It demands of the judiciary that it shall be interested primarily in human welfare rather than in property. . . .
>
> The National Government belongs to the whole American people, and where the whole American people are interested, that interest can be guarded effectively only by the National Government. . . .
>
> I do not ask for overcentralization [a term that can, of course, mean anything to the particular individual]; but I do ask that we work in a spirit of broad and far-reaching nationalism when we work for what concerns the people as a whole. [T.R. would probably have been as much opposed to the big labor of today as he was to big business. He reflected nicely the long-standing American belief that a public policy can always be found that is fair to everyone—the revered "public interest."]
>
> I stand for the Square Deal. But when I say that I am for the square deal I mean not merely that I stand for fair play under the present rules of the game, but that I stand for having those rules changed so as to work for a more substantial equality of opportunity and of reward for equally good service.

T.R. then proceeded to recommend many policies that have since been adopted: government supervision of corporate stock issues, a graduated income tax, the conservation of natural resources for the benefit of all instead of for the profit of businessmen, comprehensive workmen's compensation laws, the regulation of child labor and of women in industry, and government enforcement of safe and sanitary factory working conditions.

Here we see the first President to assert that national economic organization could be checked only by national government action; that the Presi-

[13] Many of his ideas were published in Theodore Roosevelt, *The New Nationalism,* The Outlook Company, New York, 1911.

dent is the one most likely to offer policy leadership as the functions of the Federal government expand; and that government's role in an urban society would have to differ from its role in a rural society. But he insisted, in line with traditional American ideology, that large organizations are untrustworthy and require government control and that he wanted no more government than was necessary in order to ensure "substantial equality of opportunity and of reward."

But Roosevelt's view did not come to dominate national government politics until the mid-1930s. Franklin D. Roosevelt was elected on a platform that repeated the values of industrial individualism rather than those of the social service state. But depressions, increasing urbanism, and increasing complexity of society brought about ever-stronger demands for governmental action. Furthermore, each interest group tended to ask for those things it felt most in need of without consideration of the overall effect of new programs on the size of government or on the traditional concept of individuality as the supreme goal in America.

Of course, it was not only the workingman who sought government support for himself and protection for his labor union. In the 1930s, farm organizations, if not all farmers, for the first time came to fully understand the techniques of political activity. Businessmen turned to government for credit when they could not get it elsewhere; the builder of homes sought government aid for his business; the transportation industry sought government subsidies.

Wherever the hopes of men had been frustrated under industrial individualism, people were now able to turn to government to bridge the gap between what a person could provide for himself and what he needed in order to possess a reasonable degree of physical and psychological security. Even those who sincerely believed in individual self-reliance—and they were many—came to recognize that the great bulk of the breadwinners worked for someone else who decided, almost arbitrarily, whether they were to be hired, fired, promoted, transferred, or raised in pay. Under such circumstances, the ideal way of life might lie beyond one's grasp, and governmental activity in some areas might be a necessary evil in order to give the individual protection that the corporate system did not provide.

Bank deposit insurance: An example. When Franklin D. Roosevelt took office, the nation was at the very bottom of the Great Depression. The banks were in deep trouble. Long lines of depositors appeared before opening time each day, bent upon withdrawing their accounts so as to hoard them. A run on one bank or reports of the failure of another further undermined the public's trust and confidence in these institutions. Roosevelt, once in office, sought to put a stop to the mounting panic by closing all banks. After a short time, those found to be in sound condition were permitted to open again. But people still remembered that friends had lost their life savings by the failure of a local bank. Something more than the assurance of auditors that the banks were sound seemed to be needed.

The legislation that was proposed called for the establishment of a

Federal government corporation, a publicly owned insurance company. It would insure both banks organized under the national banking laws (which were required to join in the plan) and those organized under state laws (if they met certain conditions). The proposal for the Federal Deposit Insurance Corporation (FDIC) was introduced in Congress with bipartisan support. It was strongly opposed by the American Bankers' Association. Leaders of that group argued that the act would encourage greater government supervision of banking and hence "government control." But at the moment, people had more confidence in government than they had in banks, and the act passed. (Banks had already been subject to government control, of course, through the Federal Reserve Act of 1913, but that act had been supported by banking interests and was drawn up so that the Board of Governors of the Federal Reserve System was dominated by bankers. The act had been designed to overcome the problems of bankers, not depositors.)

After more than a generation of its existence, it is interesting to review the FDIC record. No depositor in a member bank has ever lost his deposit within the guaranteed amount. (Today, it is $10,000.) The requirements of the FDIC have added to the bookkeeping tasks and red tape of member banks, but the government corporation has not taken over policy making and has not produced intolerable governmental interference, as was feared in 1933 by the American Bankers' Association. The plan has been widely regarded as a success, and American banking has expanded and prospered under the plan. Bankers themselves now overwhelmingly accept it and mention it in their advertising.

Rural versus Urban Social Systems. Perhaps the most important factor making for collective action in the modern era has been the trend toward an urban nation. The farmer or small-town dweller of the past provided most of his own household services. His garden, wood lot, and large frame house provided the resources for a self-contained family-welfare system. He had room enough to care for retired parents (physical disability was the only basis for retirement, and it usually came gradually, without the shock of today's sudden and required retirement at the age of sixty-five), and for widowed or orphaned relatives. If a farmer or small-town merchant became ill, his relatives and neighbors saw to it that his work was carried on for him until his health was restored. Involuntary unemployment was unknown except for the village idiot or the family black sheep.

With urbanization, society totally changed. Water and sewage-disposal systems could no longer be provided on an inexpensive and simple basis. Houses were smaller and more expensive—there was no longer room for retired parents, widowed sisters, or orphaned nephews. Relatively few people found that they could provide adequately for their own retirement independently of their children. Yet the children often could afford neither to feed nor house their parents, not at least, if they were to maintain what had come to be the conventional standard of living. And even the elderly person who was willing to work found that there were no jobs to be had—he was too old.

Illness or injury now spelled economic disaster to the factory worker or the white-collar clerk, whose pay offered little opportunity for saving. Certainly, friends or relatives could not take over his job for him temporarily—and business and industrial leaders refused to consider such personal tragedies as a social cost chargeable to the firm. Unemployment of an involuntary nature became not merely a potential threat—it became commonplace. A man who worked for another man, or worse, for an impersonal corporation, might be laid off at any time for being ill too much of the time, for growing too old, because the nature of the business was cyclic or seasonal, because of a depression or financial panic, or even because of a personality conflict with the foreman or personnel officer.

The individual no longer felt confident in his ability to control his own destiny or his environment. The large, impersonal corporation with a bureaucracy, highly specialized and expert at passing the buck, was more than he could comprehend. Urban society had produced interdependence where independence had once existed. It had produced insecurities nearly

Figure 7-2

Industrial Individualism Took a Narrow View of Production Costs

"A vacation? You mean you actually want me to pay for three days when you won't even be here?"

By permission of Burr Shafer.

unknown in an agrarian society. These circumstances caused people to look around for a social institution to help them regain the stability and security that had slipped away from them. The most likely—perhaps the only—candidate was government.

The Return of the Democrats. The Democratic party is one of the oldest in the world, dating from the 1790s. (The Republican party is also a veteran, having a continuous existence of well over a century.) It had been powerful and accustomed to victory throughout the first half and more of the nineteenth century. Then it fell upon hard times, being associated in the minds of many Northerners with rebellion. It had no claim on the prevailing ideology of America's industrializing years. But the Democrats regained power in 1932 on a massive protest vote, and they came, in the decade that followed, to be associated with the new ideology of the social service state.

The complicated and elaborate system of government that resulted, together with the need for policy leadership, resulted in a renewed emphasis upon the executive branch of government and a decline in the power of the judiciary (as Theodore Roosevelt had foreseen). As the locus of power shifted, so did the popular hero. The self-made businessman was not rejected, but he was pushed from center stage and in his place has come the "common man," who is something of an urban reincarnation of the frontiersman. And for the middle class, the suburbanite conformist became the model. The emphasis, in other words, shifted from an individualistic to a pluralistic society; to use Kluckhohn's terms, the society shifted from one of "strictly personal values" to one of "group values."[14]

How long the present ideology will retain its vitality or how it might be modified with the passage of time, no one can anticipate. But it is significant that many Republicans, including some who are conservative by personal conviction, have talked of "modern Republicanism" and have decided that, in most parts of the United States, elections can be won only by a basic acceptance of the social service state.

ISOLATIONISM AND INTERNATIONALISM TODAY

The basic pattern of attitudes toward foreign relations was developed at the time of our War for Independence and immediately afterward. These ideas were developed in detail and applied to a variety of changing world conditions in the last half of the nineteenth century, but they were not fundamentally important prior to the time of our entry into World War II (1941).

[14] Clyde Kluckhohn, "Shifts in American Values," *World Politics,* 11:252–261, January, 1959.

Our Period of Expansionism. After America had healed her Civil War wounds and gone through a rapid period of industrialization, her people began to look beyond the immediate borders for additional frontiers. Americans were and always had been a restless people, and this restlessness was combined with a desire for spreading to others what were considered the benefits of the American way of life. (It apparently seldom occurred to leaders during this period that others might see this as imposing our will and cultural values upon others.) In the case of the Spanish-American War (1898), we Americans combined this zest for living with a desire to help a New World nation free herself from the colonialism of a European power. It is perhaps significant that this new move, which made the United States a world power with far-reaching possessions, took place only eight years after the frontier had been formally closed.

For decades America had had to import funds from Europe to finance her industrial expansion. Now we began to invest American funds in Central and South America especially, but also as far away as China. Although a great many citizens probably thought that we were helping these nations to trail along in our footsteps (missionaries of many faiths, for example, often followed the dollar), these essentially profit-seeking undertakings usually left the economy of the other nation dependent upon us and its common people no better off than before. In this respect, Americans were probably no worse—and no better—than Europeans.

The American people never supported the theory of empire or of colonialization, however. The great bulk of the citizenry would no doubt have argued, had there been a Gallup poll in 1900 or 1920, that our ultimate aim was to make our possessions either free nations or states of the Union with full status. But whatever the ordinary citizens may have believed our goals to be, and however good their intentions, America during this period came to be associated among nationalist leaders around the world with the old exploitative policies of the European nations. And our investors abroad were exploitative, sometimes even in defiance of official American policy.

This period in our history is little understood by most Americans. It was explained away as something of an international do-good project that would bring to other nations the blessings of American wealth and liberty. But the story is now used against us by the Communist bloc to our great disadvantage. We are often pictured in their propaganda as the worst of all imperialists—a good demonstration of the point that it is the *image* rather than the *fact* of history that is important in shaping the minds of people.[15]

[15] Many historians argue that the "facts" of history, much less their meaning, can never be fully known and that each generation rewrites history to reflect its own values and purposes. The implications of this cannot be examined here, but the more serious reader may wish to keep it in mind as a problem connected with our efforts to understand the social process. See C. Vann Woodward, "Our Past Isn't What It Used to Be," *The New York Times Book Review,* July 28, 1963, pp. 1ff.

Isolationism and Expansionism. As we noted in the previous chapter, expansionist philosophy was early coupled with the ideology of isolationism. Indeed, the two have been combined as parts of a general ideology of nationalism—emphasis upon patriotism, the American way of doing things, the assumption of the superiority of American institutions and processes.

Historically, the term "isolationism" has been applied only to relationships with European nations.[16] These countries have been seen as the villains, the competitors. And, of course, exponents of nationalism long ago realized that we could not move into Europe, but rather would have to expand into the Americas, the Pacific, and Asia. Yet our expansion beyond the continental limits of the United States inevitably brought us into the conflicts of the world and into closer contact with the distrusted European nations. As a world power, we had worldwide responsibilities and interests, and the results of this brought us out of our shell. So the ideology of nationalism, as is the case with so many ideologies, contained within it conflicting goals and interests. Unless we chose to return to pristine isolationism, our expansionist policies would eventually bring us to the point where we would need to construct working relationships with other nations, and our power and wealth would make us an actor on the international stage. So the descendants of the nineteenth-century isolationists ended up in a decision-making arena which their grandparents had originally set out to avoid.

The Ideology of Internationalism. When World War I broke out in Europe (1914), Americans applied their usual criteria, by then more than a century old, and decided that the war was none of their affair, although we were sympathetic toward the democratic nations. And we did become involved three years later.

We entered the war, but not because the bulk of the American people had been converted to the idea of a worldwide obligation that required a preservation of the ways of life most like our own. And we did not enter to redeem President Wilson's naïve pledge to make the world safe for democracy. The fighting had started in Europe not because of an essential conflict in ideology, as was the case in World War II and would probably be the case in a third world war, but rather because of conflicts of economic interest and traditional commitments to a balance of power in Europe. The effective appeals for intervention centered on traditional American values: objections to interference with American shipping and trading; the death of Americans aboard foreign vessels that were sunk by submarines under conditions that seemed to violate our traditionally strong sense of fair play; the arrogance of the German leaders, and American resentment of the idea that Germans thought Americans could be "pushed around."

[16] See Bernard Fensterwald, Jr., "The Anatomy of American 'Isolationism' and Expansionism," *Journal of Conflict Resolution,* 2:111–139, June, 1958.

These were some of the major reasons why we finally—and with many doubts—entered the war. We did "show the Kaiser," but we did not convince ourselves that our decision was the right one.

The war and the peace that followed were disillusioning to the great bulk of Americans. They had followed Wilson when he appealed to their nationalistic pride, but they failed to understand his insightful arguments that the future peace of the world depended upon the character of the treaty that ended the war. European leaders did not understand him either and insisted upon a traditional "divide-the-spoils" treaty of the type that Americans associated—unfavorably—with Europe. When the debacle was over, isolationism seemed stronger than ever. The Senate would not permit America to join the League of Nations—Wilson and those who still remained loyal to his leadership, saw this as a disaster—and isolationism remained our foreign policy throughout the 1920s and well into the administration of Franklin D. Roosevelt. (Roosevelt and Cordell Hull, his Secretary of State, emphasized a good neighbor policy with the other Americas that was in the best tradition of America, but it was largely ignored by American investors using traditional procedures in the nations where Hull was seeking to make friends.)

The negativism, idealism, and emphasis upon honor as the only basis for war was exemplified by the great isolationist leader of the 1920s and 1930s, Senator William E. Borah of Idaho. He was one of the leaders in opposing American participation in the League of Nations and the World Court:[17]

> Acceptance, then, of membership in any international organization meant to Senator Borah "nothing less than a complete surrender of the traditions and principles which have made us the most powerful nation and the happiest people in the world today. . . . In this conflict," he concluded, "those who are not for Washington's policies are against them. . . . On another occasion he remarked: "If the Savior of Men would revisit the earth and declare for a League of Nations, I would be opposed to it."

The views of Borah were based upon the oldest of American traditions. But these views assumed that there was a pattern of world conflict involving essentially matters of economics and pure power interests. World War II, which began in 1939, was based essentially upon ideology. The threat that Wilson had seen to democracy in World War I was very real indeed in World War II. Many Americans were deeply concerned about the threat to democracy that was implied in the hatred and power of Nazism. Others—and not only Jews—were horrified by the racial theories and policies of the Nazis. The Japanese presented a somewhat similar threat, although here the concerns were more economic and nationalistic, so far as America was concerned. Despite Roosevelt's efforts to convince the American people that the war being fought by Britain and the under-

[17] Charles W. Toth, "Isolationism and the Emergence of Borah: An Appeal to American Tradition," *Western Political Quarterly,* 14:555–568, June, 1961. Quotation from p. 562.

ground movements in a dozen European democracies was also their fight, we probably would not have entered World War II except for the same reason that we entered the first—honor. The Japanese leaders decided that war was the only way by which to reach their goals and attacked Pearl Harbor—a decision that was not discouraged by American tactics at the time.

During the war, Americans did not deviate far from their traditional concern with personal material welfare. Less than 15 per cent of the respondents during wartime polls considered international relations issues (other than winning the war) as matters of top concern. Yet the extreme isolationism of Americans diminished greatly during this period. Between 70 and 80 per cent of the people indicated that America "ought to play a larger part in world affairs than was the case in the past."[18]

In the years following the war, Americans have generally accepted the role of world leader with reluctance. But they have accepted it. The great bulk of the people, according to the polls, support our membership in the United Nations and accept the necessity for America's active involvement in world politics.

As one specialist in American foreign policy has observed:[19]

> Thus the rigidity of isolationism has been replaced by a newer plasticity. But this readiness to support an active world role has to be qualified in a number of ways. The undertow of withdrawal is still very powerful. Deeply ingrained traditions do not die easy deaths. The world outside is still remote for most Americans; and the tragic lessons of the last decades have not been fully digested. Readiness to participate and to sacrifice appear to be unstable [and are obvious only in the presence of a perceived threat]. They are based not on a mature fear of the consequences of irresponsibility, but more on immediate anxieties which rise and subside with fluctuations in international tension.

Furthermore:[20]

> When a sample of American respondents is offered a "gift package" like "keeping peace in the world," they express an enormous interest in foreign affairs. They are interested if the issue is formulated in simplified, panacean terms.

It appears, too, as if the voters have begun to view the Presidency as the institution to guard them against external threats. "Congress looks inward toward the nation; the President looks outward to the world. . . . The President is the custodian of popular safety, national destiny, the conscience of the people."[21]

[18] Gabriel A. Almond, *The American People and Foreign Policy,* Harcourt, Brace & World, Inc., New York, 1950, p. 76.

[19] *Ibid.,* p. 85.

[20] *Ibid.,* p. 79.

[21] Lane, *op. cit.,* p. 149.

Until after World War II, probably only the elections of 1916 (Wilson over Hughes by an eyelash), 1920 (Harding over Cox by a landslide), and 1940 (Roosevelt over Willkie by a comfortable margin) centered around issues of foreign policy. But in 1952, the people swept Eisenhower into office by a tremendous vote that was a reflection of anxieties caused by six years of seemingly endless cold war and a struggle in Korea that was not understood as to purpose and to which no end seemed in sight. Eisenhower avoided domestic policy leadership and was reelected four years later in the widespread belief that he was America's best bet to contain the Russians. Both Kennedy and Nixon emphasized foreign policy in 1960. It seems likely that in the immediate future, presidential races will center around foreign policy issues, while voters will continue to elect congressmen and senators primarily on the basis of domestic policy or on personality and other intangibles. Of course, in a close election domestic issues may remain the determining factor, and foreign policy issues sometimes mask domestic clashes of interest.

There is some indication from the polls that Americans—perhaps in reaction to anxieties concerning the threats of nuclear warfare and communism—are becoming more concerned about international problems. Wilber M. Brucker, Secretary of the Army under Eisenhower has noted, however, that Americans "seem always to wait to be shocked into action. . . . There is a fatalistic belief in this country that right will prevail without the necessity of making sweeping decisions. Unfortunately, right may not prevail."[22]

OUTSIDE THE MAINSTREAM

The Small-town Dweller. The ideas of the more or less typical person who lives in a village or small city cannot, in one sense, be considered outside the mainstream of present-day ideology, for his beliefs come out of the principal channels of our widest ideological rivers. Furthermore, he has influence beyond his numbers in the selection of congressmen, legislators, and political party officers. Yet his ideas are now only a reflection of America's past. They are minority views. Perhaps more important, the small-town dweller often sees himself as surrounded by the hostile world of the big-city urbanite, a world he does not approve of or understand. His views represent a blend of those of Calvinism, the lower middle class, and the small-business man. They extend the blanket of legitimacy only over policies that are inadequate or inappropriate for present-day metropolitan America.

Even the vocabulary of the small-towner differs from that of his urban brother. To him, a member of an ethnic group is a "foreigner"; an alcoholic is a "drunk." The highly skilled professional specialist of the city is some-

[22] Associated Press dispatch, July 17, 1961.

one he cannot understand, someone who does not fit the jack-of-all-trades tradition of the village. In an age when most Americans stress democratic sharing in decision making, he finds meaning and comfort in authority. So he demands punishment rather than rehabilitation for criminals and juvenile delinquents. He believes in the use of force rather than "hand holding" in international relations. He opposes the "coddling" of children in elaborate school systems. He sees drunkenness as a sign of moral weakness, not of emotional illness, and he still believes in custody for the "insane" and "feeble minded" rather than treatment for the "mentally ill" or "retarded."[23]

His emphasis upon saving and thrift fit nicely into this overall view of social policy. He can in good conscience argue for inexpensive punishment rather than expensive rehabilitation; for hunting down and imprisoning Americans whose loyalty is suspect, rather than paying the heavy expenses of a foreign-aid program designed to stop the spread of communism abroad; and for modest programs in the fields of education, welfare, and others where he often sees policies advocated by professionals in those areas as "loaded with frills."

The American small town is the bastion of conservative thought. Although its values are a declining influence, they remain important as a brake upon the principal trend. They force us to go slower than some exponents of the social service state would prefer and to reexamine each new departure in terms of our oldest traditions.

Ethnic Groups. Ethnic groups are important politically because their members are generally desirous of social and economic advancement. They see government—where each man has one vote—as a means for gaining assistance toward their goals of equality of opportunity and for social acceptance. These perceptions give ethnic ideologies a special character, as does the fact that their members often have a nostalgic feeling for "the old country" from which their ancestors came. They often favor policies that would benefit these lands or want liberalized immigration quotas from them. Jews were among the leaders in denouncing Hitler and the Nazi policies in Germany. Members of Polish, Czech, and other ethnic groups whose ancestral homelands are behind the iron curtain responded hopefully to 1952 Republican statements that it was America's duty to push back the curtain. Some Irish-Americans still call for the United States to help unite Northern Ireland with Eire.

Like all ideologies, those of ethnic groups vary according to the case. Some people carried to this country political traditions that the mainstream American regards as radical; others have as part of their normal way of life certain behavior patterns that are illegal here. Some come out of cultures with a traditional government and others feel more dependent

[23] See Charles Press and Charles R. Adrian. "Why the States Are Sick," *Antioch Review*, 53:100–120, June, 1964.

upon it than do most Americans. The sharp decline in immigration since World War I is making ethnic group politics less important with the passage of time. But it is still a part of the American political scene and a force to reckon with.

Negroes. Because of a background of slavery and systematic exclusion from the political process, Negroes, although they have long constituted roughly 10 per cent of the American population (slightly more today), have until recently been almost completely apolitical. Negroes have had a high crime rate, both because crime often results from economic disadvantage, and because Negroes long considered it impossible to obtain justice in the "white man's court." So they often took the law into their own hands. Unable to apply any considerable pressure in politics, they built a life-style that often included a view of government and its agents as the enemy to be avoided or defied. But gradually Americans became more concerned about equality; at the same time Negroes moved into the Northern industrial cities, where politicians recognized the potential value of their votes. As a result, Negro politics began to follow the same pattern as that of ethnic groups. Indeed, Negroes may be regarded as members of an ethnic group, since they share a generally definable subculture, even to an emerging interest in the new nations of Africa and demands for additional assistance to them.

The South. It was noted above that the agrarian tradition of the South is different from that of other regions of the United States. Obviously, the South differs from much of the rest of the nation in many ways: in its attitude toward the Negro; in its conservatism despite economic conditions that might indicate a favorable climate for government participation in the economy; in its slower rate (until recently) of urbanization; in its lower educational levels; in its relative poverty (now changing, too); and in dozens of other ways. Yet the political views and life-styles of the South stem from values as old as those of the North.[24] Its ideology has, however, been colored by preoccupation with matters of race and by the inferiority- and persecution-creating myth of the Lost Cause. Because of such factors as urbanization, the ideology dominant in the South will in the future come closer to that of the industrial North.

CONTEMPORARY IDEOLOGY

In the 1960s, the ideologies of the social service state and internationalism were dominant, but both had changed gradually in the postwar years. The social service state had developed out of the terror and desperation of the Great Depression. It contained both emergency and reform characteristics

[24] See Charles G. Sellers, Jr. (ed.), *The Southerner as American,* The University of North Carolina Press, Chapel Hill, N.C., 1960, and the many histories of the South.

and incorporated many of the long-standing demands of farmers, working-class people, and even businessmen.

Since the war, the notion of the state performing social service functions has expanded slowly and cautiously. Now there are a number of different approaches to it, particularly those of organized labor and the middle-class, typically suburban, organization man. Differences, however, are more in degree and type of emphasis than in kind. Labor seeks to expand the veil of protection given to all who are threatened with loss of income, but its program tends to be centered more and more on a class-oriented basis. Labor does not dominate in either major political party and, as a self-conscious minority, it tends to use bombastic tactics and to accentuate conflict and competition. This is a rational technique for seeking support by dramatizing differences among the various groups in the political structure. But the emphasis upon political in-fighting stands in sharp contrast to the preferences of the dominant person in the formation of American ideology today—the organization man. He seeks to take the

Figure 7-3

The Problems of Bureaucracy Are Universal in Our Society

"Is there anyone I could tell I was disappointed in some romaine lettuce?"

politics out of politics, or at least to make it as bland as possible. He wishes to have government assist in the search for security and care for the maladjusted, but he wants to find the way of doing this in consensus rather than conflict (see Chapter 20).

The principal characteristics of the ideology of internationalism also change as time passes. Postwar adaptations that predominate in the 1960s are outlined in Chapter 21.

A Closing Note. The precise way in which life experiences, life-styles, ideology, and governmental policies and processes are interrelated is not yet precisely known.[25] Yet the observations made in the last two chapters, as well as in Chapter 2, are critically important in an analysis of politics. They provide a basis upon which to build a meaningful interpretation of behavior in the political process.

SELECTED BIBLIOGRAPHY

Most of the items cited at the end of Chapter 6 are also relevant for this chapter. They are not repeated here.

The coming of industrialism and the making of business, rather than farming, a central concern had a great effect upon American attitudes, though earlier values continued to be important. We see this reflected in the writings of Hays [14] and Sutton [23]. The Horatio Alger myth developed and persisted [10], but both the common man and the intellectual continued to view the city with suspicion [25]. The importance of rhetoric and conventional wisdom to the acceptance of the ideology of industrialism is indicated in a classic study by Arnold [1].

The Populist and Progressive reform movements developed early and were persistent counterpoints [20] to the principal movement toward business orthodoxy, as Hofstadter has shown [15]. These protests were vigorous and sometimes intolerant [9], and they were also related to support for America's development into a world power [7, 8]. The progressivism and expansionism of the period has been amply recorded by Beale [2], Mowry [21] and Link [19], among many others.

Goldman [11] is among those who have described the rise of the social service state; Berle [4] shows why New Deal liberals disliked big business, despite its great contribution to a high standard of living. Rossiter, cited at the end of Chapter 6, offers a summary of the conservative view throughout our history. His work is supplemented by Kirk [17], who is less objective but more vigorous. Goldwater [12] states the position of a contemporary conservative, and Buckley [5] speaks for the right wing. Greene [13] presents thirteen articles on the current status of American ideology, Bell [3] discusses the lack of systematic ideas as a basis for contemporary politics, but Lane [18], using the depth interview techniques of psychiatry, shows that there is at least a latent ideology of the American common man.

Bunzel [6] describes the ideological conflict within the business community, and Prothro [22] relates the values of contemporary businessmen to the total

[25] Technically, the problem is that research techniques have not yet been devised by which to operationalize the study of ideology and to show its causal relationship to political motivation.

American ideological tradition. The views of the alienated and insecure small businessmen are reflected in the House and Senate committees on small business (for example see [16]).

1. Arnold, Thurman: *The Folklore of Capitalism,* Yale University Press, New Haven, Conn., 1937.
2. Beale Howard K.: *Theodore Roosevelt and the Rise of America to World Power,* The Johns Hopkins Press, Baltimore, 1956.
3. Bell, Daniel: *The End of Ideology: On the Exhaustion of Political Ideas in the Fifties,* The Free Press of Glencoe, New York, 1960.
4. Berle, Adolf A., Jr.: *Power without Property,* Harcourt, Brace & World, Inc., New York, 1959.
5. Buckley, William F.: *Up from Liberalism,* Hillman Books, New York, 1961.
6. Bunzel, John H.: *The American Small Businessman,* Alfred A. Knopf, Inc., New York, 1962.
7. Dulles, Foster Rhea: *America's Rise to World Power, 1898–1954,* Harper & Row, Publishers, New York, 1955.
8. Faulkner, Harold: *Politics, Reform and Expansion, 1890–1900,* Harper & Row, Publishers, New York, 1959.
9. Ferkiss, Victor C.: "Populist Influences on American Fascism," *Western Political Quarterly,* 10:350–373, June, 1957.
10. Ginzberg, Eli, James K. Anderson, and John L. Herma: *The Optimistic Tradition and American Youth,* Columbia University Press, New York, 1962.
11. Goldman, Eric F.: *Rendezvous with Destiny,* Vintage Books, Random House, Inc., New York, 1961.
12. Goldwater, Barry: *The Conscience of a Conservative,* Hillman Books, New York, 1961.
13. Greene, Lee S. (ed.): "Conservativism, Liberalism, and National Issues," *Annals,* vol. 344, November, 1962.
14. Hays, Samuel P.: *The Response to Industrialism: 1885–1914,* The University of Chicago Press, Chicago, 1957.
15. Hofstadter, Richard: *The Age of Reform,* Vintage Books, Random House, Inc., New York, 1961.
16. House of Representatives, Committee on Small Business, *Mergers and Superconcentration,* 1962.
17. Kirk, Russell: *The Conservative Mind, from Burke to Santayana,* Henry Regnery Company, Chicago, 1953.
18. Lane, Robert E.: *Political Ideology: Why the American Common Man Believes What He Does,* The Free Press of Glencoe, New York, 1962.
19. Link, Arthur S.: *Woodrow Wilson and the Progressive Era: 1910–1917,* Harper & Row, Publishers, New York, 1954.
20. Madison, Charles A.: *Critics and Crusaders: A Century of American Protest,* Frederick Ungar Publishing Co., New York, 1961.
21. Mowry, George E.: *The Era of Theodore Roosevelt, 1900–1912,* Harper & Row, Publishers, New York, 1958.
22. Prothro, James W.: "Business Ideas and the American Tradition," *Journal of Politics,* 15:67–87, February, 1953.
23. Sutton, Francis X., and others: *The American Business Creed,* Harvard University Press, Cambridge, Mass., 1956.
24. White, Leonard D.: *The Republican Era: 1869–1901,* The Macmillan Company, New York, 1958.
25. White, Morton, and Lucia White (eds.): *The Intellectual versus the City: From Thomas Jefferson to Frank Lloyd Wright,* Harvard University Press, Cambridge, Mass., 1962.

CHAPTER 8

INTERESTS AND INTEREST GROUPS

On September 12, 1960, a Cincinnati drug firm applied to the Food and Drug Administration for a permit to market a German drug called Thalidomide, which would be used to induce sleep. The company said it had conducted research on the drug for twenty months. After considering the application for several months, Frances Oldham Kelsey, a medical officer of the Food and Drug Administration, denied the application. In the next fourteen months, the company continued to press for a change in the ruling, but Dr. Kelsey was supported by her administrative superior, and Thalidomide was never marketed in the United States, although it was distributed to physicians for experimental use.

Meanwhile, a subcommittee on antitrust and monopolies of the Senate Judiciary Committee, headed by Senator Estes Kefauver (Democrat, Tennessee), had been investigating prices charged for "miracle" drugs. Findings of the committee suggested to Senator Kefauver that drug firms were charging what he considered exorbitant prices. The root of the trouble, in his opinion, was the patent system that permitted a monopoly for the production of newly developed drugs. Drug firms argued that prices were reasonable, considering the costs of research and development of new drugs. Some critics said that Kefauver, faced with a tough reelection fight at home (where he was accused by some opponents of being "soft" on desegregation), was using the issue merely as a campaign gimmick.

A bill prepared by the Senator in March, 1962, was, over his objection, referred to the whole Judiciary Committee, chaired by Senator James O. Eastland (Democrat, Mississippi). Action there, in Kefauver's view, greatly weakened his bill, so much that he had doubts about supporting it. The Kennedy administration gave Kefauver little hope of securing a stronger measure and advised support of the parent-committee version.

The United States has a long tradition of food and drug regulation that began during the period of the Progressives and muckrakers at the beginning of the century. It was discovered that some patent medicine manufacturers were putting habit-forming drugs, such as opium, into their products to encourage their continued use. At about the same time, conditions in Chicago packing houses were found to be highly unsanitary. (The socialist

Upton Sinclair wrote a famous exposé novel *The Jungle.*) The food commissioner of North Dakota once reported that his state alone was consuming ten times more "Vermont maple syrup" every year than the state of Vermont produced. The first Pure Food and Drug Act was passed at the urging of President Theodore Roosevelt and became law in 1906. It sought to prevent the misbranding or adulteration of foods and drugs.

The act had established the principle of Federal regulation, but it did not result in the control of useless patent medicines or the abolition of lurid advertising. The manufacturer was required to show that the drug would not cause injury, but he was not required to prove that it would perform as claimed. Postmaster-General Arthur Summerfield, who served in the Eisenhower administration, once commented that more money is being made in medical quackery than in "any other criminal activity."[1]

Sales of ineffective patent medicines were largely to low-income persons of little education, and the public attitude generally was one of live and let live, so long as a drug did not hurt its user. (Medical men pointed out, however, that the availability of quack remedies sometimes resulted in the individual not seeking competent aid until it was too late.) Among the politically effective portions of the community, patent medicines were little more than an annoyance that interrupted television programs with diagrammatic displays of man's inner organs. Many efforts were made in the years following adoption of the original act to secure more effective regulation of "ethical" (i.e., prescription) drugs as well as of patent medicines.

The picture changed suddenly with the first reports that the drug Thalidomide, which was being used experimentally by human beings, very probably was responsible for birth deformities. It was believed to have caused deformities in some 5,000 infants, most of them in Germany. Over 15,000 patients had used the drug in the United States. This information was anxiety-producing for all who could read or hear. It dramatized what seemed to be extreme laxity in the control of drugs. Many citizens were shocked—they had assumed that Federal law and United States government experts were protecting them from such threats. Yet this drug was nearly placed on sale, and it might have been, save for a conscientious technician and a courageous supervisor. The revelation and continued

[1] James Harvey Young, *The Toadstool Millionaires,* Princeton University Press, Princeton, N.J., 1961.

repetition of the story in the newspapers and particularly in women's magazines created a groundswell of demand for stricter regulations.

Dr. Kelsey was awarded the Gold Medal for Distinguished Federal Civilian Service on August 17, 1962. At about the same time, the President recommended stronger controls. The Senate passed a control bill the same

Figure 8-1

AMERICAN DRUG FIRMS HAVE CONTRIBUTED TO THE NATION'S HEALTH
Industry Develops Effective Drugs for Major "Killer" and Crippling Diseases

Disease	Drugs developed
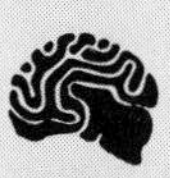 Mental illness	Twenty-five major tranquilizers, all developed in 1950s
 Heart	More than twenty drugs in use, all developed since 1939
 Infectious diseases	More than two dozen antibiotics since 1939
 Cancer	Twenty compounds now used in various treatments
 Inflammatory diseases	Twelve to fifteen major steroids now in use

The Better Life, *Pharmaceutical Manufacturers' Association, Washington, 1961.*

month, 78 to 0. Kefauver, still trying to salvage one of his original purposes, to prevent what he considered to be excess profiteering, attempted to insert a provision that any drug firm charging profits of over 500 per cent above production costs, including research, would lose its patent in three years rather than seventeen. His motion was defeated 53 to 22. The House passed a bill prepared by the administration, which had now decided the time was ripe for stiffer controls. In October, a conference committee largely accepted the House version. The revised drug control bill was passed unanimously in the Senate on October 3, 1962, and in the House on the following day. The President signed it into law. The provisions were far stricter than any ever proposed by Kefauver or any included in the substitute bill. Companies would henceforth be required to show drugs to be effective for the purposes claimed on the basis of substantial evidence before they would be allowed on the market. The Food and Drug Administration was empowered to withdraw any drug immediately if it posed an "imminent hazard" to public health. Manufacturers were required to register with the Administration, and other controls were tightened. Positive government approval was to be required for marketing. Previously the government was only given the opportunity to disapprove, and if it did not act, the firm could proceed. Labels were required to show the drug's generic name as well as its trade name. (One of the causes, Kefauver claimed, for high prices was that physicians prescribed by well-known trade names when the same product could sometimes be obtained more cheaply.)

In the fall elections one month later, both Democratic and Republican candidates pointed to the new drug control act as a measure they had supported. There was probably no need to do so, but in order to drive home the point, they emphasized the benefits to the consumer in the new law.

INTERESTS AND THE POLITICAL PROCESS

The above story of the proposed introduction of Thalidomide into the American drug market demonstrates some of the complexities of the political process by which public policy is made. The process is one by which wants, ideological or economic, of individuals in society become reflected in the law. In this illustration, wants expressed by organized groups were important. Organized groups generally possess a great advantage over unorganized opponents, and they seldom encounter serious resistance unless the opponents gain the advantage of vast supporting publicity, publicity that makes effective appeals to the prevailing ideology. The pharmaceutical firm in our case study is an example of such a group. So is the national association of pharmaceutical firms. These groups were both supported and opposed by other organized groups whose own particular interests were also involved in the issue. All of these groups either maintain permanent lobbies in the nation's capital or lobby on a temporary basis in order to make their influences more strongly felt on a particular issue.

Not all individual wants are formally or permanently organized, however. But the unorganized interests are not powerless: the candidate for office may seek to gather their support for his own goal of securing election, while offering in exchange his support for their goals. In our example, members of Congress and the President sought to strengthen their own campaigns and perhaps to improve their images as guardians of the people by revitalizing and passing amendments to the Food, Drug and Cosmetics Act, amendments that placed stricter controls on the manufacture and marketing of drugs on the American market. From the point of view of the typical citizen, this was a desirable step toward providing additional protection.

This case study also indicates the conditions under which the decision-making process is most responsive to pressure. The organized group could ordinarily have been expected to prevail. But it may not do so at times when a dramatic event publicizes the need (in cultural terms) for governmental action and when an election is approaching. An individual decision maker is most receptive to pressure when he has ambitions for advancement to higher office or is, at least, concerned about possibly losing the one he currently holds.

The reader may wish to refer back to the case study occasionally, since

Figure 8-2

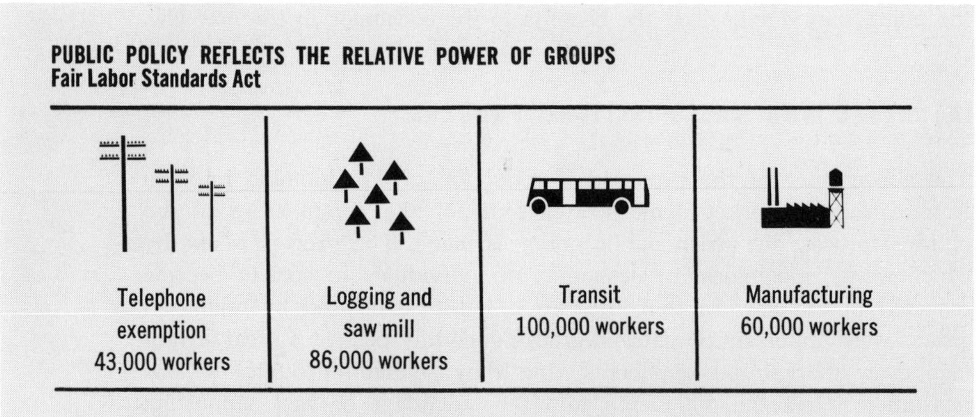

Various interests have secured exemption for themselves from the national minimum wage law.
(Better Minimum Wage for More American Workers, *AFL-CIO, Washington, 1960*).

it points up many characteristics of the political process in a pluralistic society. The authors, to avoid monotony, will use examples from other events in the discussion that follows.

The Function of the Group. An interest group, according to the leading authority on the subject,[2] is a collection of individuals who, "on the basis of one or more shared attitudes [common habits of response], makes certain claims upon the other groups in the society for the establishment, maintenance, or enhancement of forms of behavior that are implied in the shared attitudes." Groups often deal with one another directly, as when the steel industry and steelworkers' union engage in collective bargaining over wages, hours, and conditions of labor. America's pluralistic society is, despite a trend toward increased governmental activity, still one in which the small private governments of interest groups make many of the rules that guide the behavior of members—as when the bar association enforces upon lawyers its views of what constitutes ethical practice. Groups also engage in negotiations with other groups on behalf of their memberships. When a local branch of the National Association for the Advancement of Colored People (NAACP) negotiates with the local association of restaurant owners for the desegregation of lunch counters in the community, leaders in the two organizations are performing functions that might, and. in some nations would, be performed by governmental officials.

In an increasing variety of circumstances, American governmental officials have become involved in the policy process. This is so today not just in cases where other negotiations fail, as when there is a hopeless impasse over wages in the steel industry, but often almost as a routine procedure whenever a group seeks social change. Groups thus become *political-interest* groups, making their claims directly upon government or indirectly upon other groups through government. This may be true of any group in society, but is especially true when the routine of a group is threatened by change.

An unorganized interest group has less protection in the political process than one that is organized—it may have to depend on the chance that a political candidate will provide assistance. Therefore, there is a tendency for people who share an interest to organize into groups if they have not already been organized for other economic, social, or religious purposes. (Organization, or a move into the political arena by an existing group created previously for another purpose, may take place at the instigation of either a political or a nonpolitical leader.) Formal organization is of value in that it concentrates resources that may be used profitably in the policy-making process. Organized groups may also form alliances and associations in order to pyramid resources. Such alliances often develop

[2] David B. Truman, *The Governmental Process,* Alfred A. Knopf, Inc., New York, 1951.

among groups that share the same ideology. In the example that headed this chapter, many other lobbies with no interest in pharmaceuticals joined the drug company group because they also opposed government regulation.

The relative strength of each organized group is determined by its wealth, size of membership, degree of cohesiveness, and salience to the social system. Wealth, in terms of money, is easily converted into other resources. Members are normally also potential voters, and thus the strength of a group may be related to its size. A high degree of cohesiveness permits the group to present a united front and may add to the intensity with which it lobbies. But size and cohesiveness tend to be reciprocal—as size increases, cohesiveness declines, and vice versa. Salience varies with the culture. In a devout society, religious groups are of central importance; in another society, such groups may be virtual outcasts and the opinions of their leaders considered unimportant or perhaps even subversive. A society that emphasizes the desirability of accumulating material goods produced by private capital and of "progress" will pay serious heed to business interests. One devoted to the contemplative life and stability in life-styles may regard the interests of tradesmen as trivial.

Other resources are a function of the age and social status of a group, the ability of its leadership, specialized knowledge, skill at lobbying, inside connections, intensity of interest, and willingness to expend scarce resources. The last of these is probably often determined by the importance of an issue as measured in terms of the group's goals or reason for existence. The most successful group is the one having an "optimum mix" of various resources.

Other Considerations in Interest-group Formation. Four additional points should be made distinguishing interests from organized interest groups before we attempt to examine in detail groups in the political process:

1. Persons may or may not possess an awareness of mutual interests; they may or may not be in communication with one another; they may or may not be formally organized. Individuals committed to a particular interest may include public officials as well as laymen. No single interest is ever completely represented by a single group or alliance of groups, for every organization contains dissenters. Many supporters of a cause refuse to join groups, but prefer to remain fellow travelers. *Interests,* therefore, exist independently of *interest groups.* Organized labor cannot rally all of its members in opposition to the Taft-Hartley Act, nor does all opposition come from organized labor.

2. As children, we learn that there are two sides to every question and to think of things in terms of black and white, interesting or uninteresting, good or bad. Actually, the old cliché is quite wrong: there are not two sides, but many sides, to every question. Almost every American would support the principle of high agricultural production, but the number of possible national agricultural programs is almost infinite. Some persons may agree on a subsidy program, but have different goals in mind; others may disagree on the desirability of subsidies, but agree on the preferred structure of organization for agricultural production, for example.

3. The combination of individuals constituting an interest varies with each issue. This is true even in relation to similar controversies. For example, the persons opposing desegregation of restaurants are not the same ones who oppose desegregation of schools or residential subdivisions.

4. Although a great many persons may be concerned about a particular political issue, large numbers of people are always unaware of it, or unconcerned. This is true even when an issue may in fact affect them, although, if the implications of possible policies were explained to them, they might be activated and expend resources.

The Purpose of Interest Groups. In any nation of millions of people, the typical individual cannot expect to have much influence upon governmental policy if he acts alone. Only the most exceptional individual—the Bernard Baruch or Albert Einstein—could hope to do so. Others accept as effective spokesmen for their interests the leaders of groups to which they belong or with which they identify. Many formal groups, among other activities, engage in lobbying as a means of gaining access to decision makers.

To gain his desired objectives in public policy, the individual who is deeply concerned about an issue may choose to work through a political party. When the party takes a stand for a definite set of principles, this approach is rewarding. This is a common occurrence in European democracies. In the United States, however, political parties are loose coalitions, each covering a great variety of political viewpoints. The individual belongs to a political party for a variety of reasons that are connected largely with family tradition, economic status, and geographic location. However, he can seldom go to the polls and vote for a major party that will behave with internal consistency so that the issue he favors will be supported by all leaders of the party he favors.

He may choose to become active in a political party, of course, and seek to influence its policies. But by the simple act of voting for the slate of a particular party, he will not be able to assure himself that he has selected a group of public officials who are ideologically in accord with him. If he wishes to influence public policy, therefore, he will usually find it more expedient and fruitful to join forces with like-minded persons in an interest group.

The Advantages of Organization. We have already noted that persons sharing an interest may be willing to expend resources—particularly, money and votes—toward the achievement of a specific policy goal. But an organized interest possesses the additional advantage of a system of communication that may be effective with both its membership and outsiders.

The communications net serves as an information channel, keeping

Figure 8-3

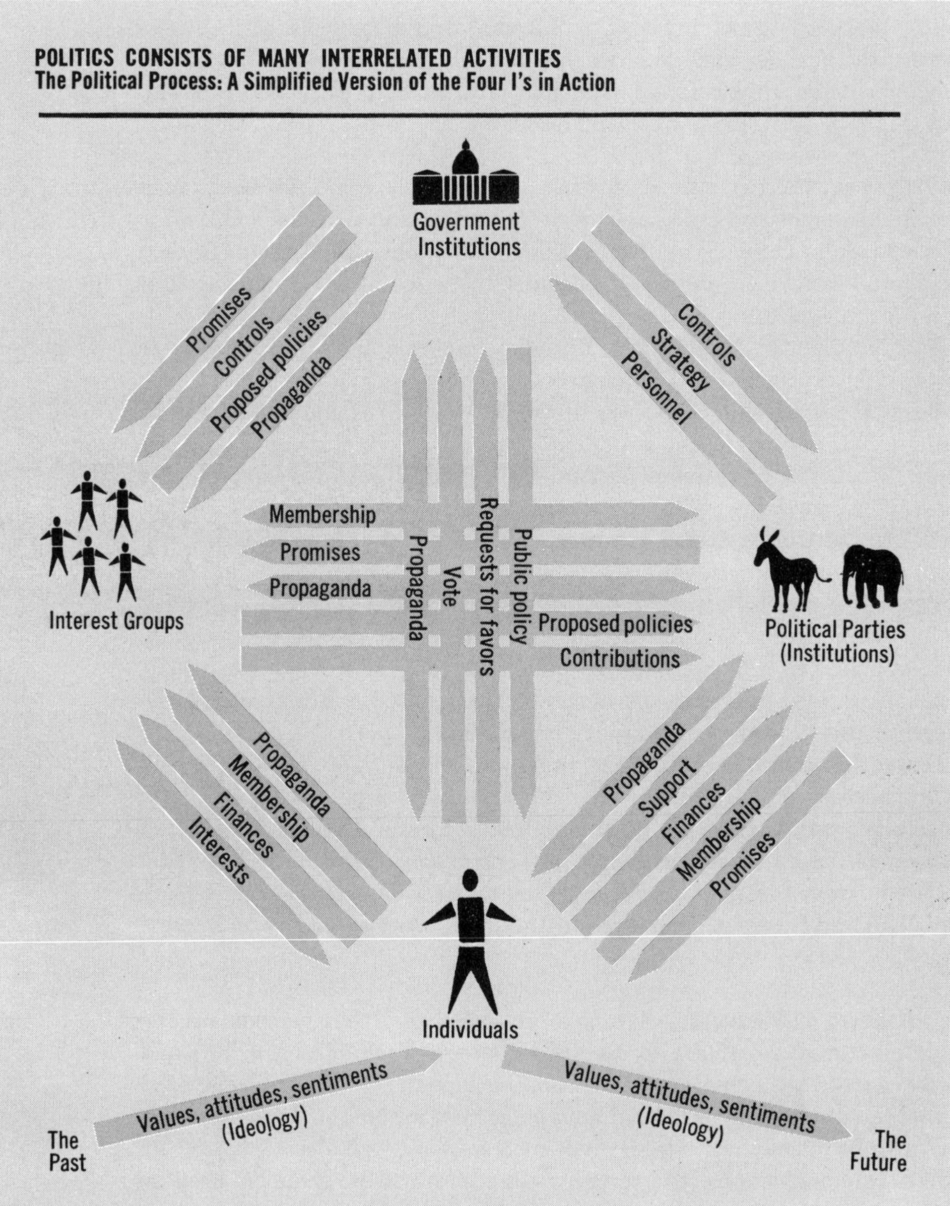
POLITICS CONSISTS OF MANY INTERRELATED ACTIVITIES
The Political Process: A Simplified Version of the Four I's in Action
Government
Institutions
Promises
Controls
Proposed policies
Propaganda
Controls
Strategy
Personnel
Membership
Promises
Propaganda
Propaganda
Vote
Requests for favors
Public policy
Proposed policies
Contributions
Interest Groups
Political Parties
(Institutions)
Propaganda
Membership
Finances
Interests
Propaganda
Support
Finances
Membership
Promises
Individuals
Values, attitudes, sentiments
(Ideology)
Values, attitudes, sentiments
(Ideology)
The
Past
The
Future

members informed about matters in which they share a concern. Such information may not otherwise be easily available. For example, the National Municipal League exchanges information among members on local government reform activities. Stamp collectors' groups share information on new Post Office policies and proposed stamp issues. The communications issued are normally colored by the policy positions of the leadership of the group. The leadership uses the communications net to promulgate innovations in order to show that it is, in fact, leading and, perhaps, to maintain or expand its power. It seeks support for itself and the organization by informing members of recent problems and events (e.g., civil rights groups point out flagrant cases of discrimination), and victories for some group-sponsored cause (e.g., stamp collectors got the Post Office Department to set up a special window to service collectors in the larger post offices). The leadership sees one of its functions as getting deviant members to conform to organization policy and uses the communications system to this end. Thus the American Medical Association leaders seek to keep physician-members from supporting compulsory government health insurance plans.

The existence of a communications net also enables the leadership to mobilize political-action groups on short notice. This is often done in order to push for or block a bill pending before Congress, for example. The leadership also strives to improve the image of the group in the eyes of nonmembers by such tactics as planting favorable stories whenever possible in newspapers, magazines, or on radio and television.

An organized group has machinery that may be used to get out the vote or raise funds for political-action purposes. It can also make labor available, some of which may be highly skilled and specialized. Thus the AFL-CIO, through an allied organization (COPE), can help get voters to the polls, raise campaign funds, and provide labor for such routine but necessary activities as envelope stuffing. Business firms and associations do the same sort of thing. A firm may, for example, loan its highly skilled public-relations men to assist on a political campaign or a propaganda effort on behalf of a cause. The American Medical Association once assessed all of its members $25 in order to fight a particular bill in Congress—the assessment was technically voluntary, but the social pressure to conform was considerable. Only a pre-existing organization with a sense of *esprit de corps,* a communications system, and a policy strongly supported by the leadership can act promptly and effectively in emergency situations or in times of serious threat to a particular interest.

Interest Groups Distinguished from Political Parties. Interest groups differ from political parties chiefly in that they do not seek to capture offices for members, but attempt to influence public policy. They also differ from most political parties in the United States in that they are made up of persons who have basically the same interests and viewpoints—they are normally much more ideologically cohesive than political parties.

GROUPS AND SOCIAL NORMS

Much has been said of the evil influences and dangers of interest groups in politics. Congress has begun to control their lobbying activities and expenditures somewhat. Some critics have even suggested that groups, or at least their lobbying activities, be legally abolished or stringently controlled. Most such suggestions are, however, naïve. If we had two or more political parties, each standing upon a definite platform to which it could be held, interest-group activities would take place largely within the party structures, since control of platforms and policy directives would be important. Such is not the case in the United States, however. Interest-group representatives are active within political parties, of course, for it is to their advantage if nominations go to persons who favor their position, or if they can build up social capital (good will) by supplying campaign funds. But such activities do not necessarily provide a strong voice in the decisions of the nation, and without lobbying, congressmen might be free (and perhaps irresponsible) agents. Even with lobbying before Congress and activity at election time, interest groups are probably not as influential as is popularly believed. During the 1920s and 1930s, when the American Legion was presumably a powerful political force, party affiliation and popular swings between parties were so important that the Legion's support or opposition in a particular congressional campaign had only a slight bearing on the fate of the incumbent seeking reelection.[3]

The Ethics of Lobbying. Individual interest groups no doubt sometimes go beyond the bounds of what society would consider as acceptable behavior. They sometimes fail to give an accurate picture of the interests, desires, and aspirations of their individual members and otherwise act irresponsibly, but most of them are kept in check—to a considerable degree, at least—because they are ordinarily opposed by competing groups having an interest in containing them, or by unorganized groups that may be mobilized during a campaign.

There have often been claims and occasionally evidence of wholesale vote buying and corruption under the capital dome. But conventional wisdom offers an exaggerated picture of the character of lobbying and does both the lobbyist and the congressman a disservice. During the 1880s, when the activity of the industrial robber barons may have brought public morality to its lowest ebb, Frank Carpenter, who was Washington correspondent for the *Cleveland Leader,* made observations similar to those of many observers of Congress today.[4]

[3] V. O. Key, Jr., "The Veterans and the House of Representatives: A Study of a Pressure Group and Electoral Mortality," *Journal of Politics,* 5:27–40, February, 1943.

[4] Frank G. Carpenter, *Carp's Washington,* McGraw-Hill Book Company, New York, 1960, p. 279.

Figure 8-4

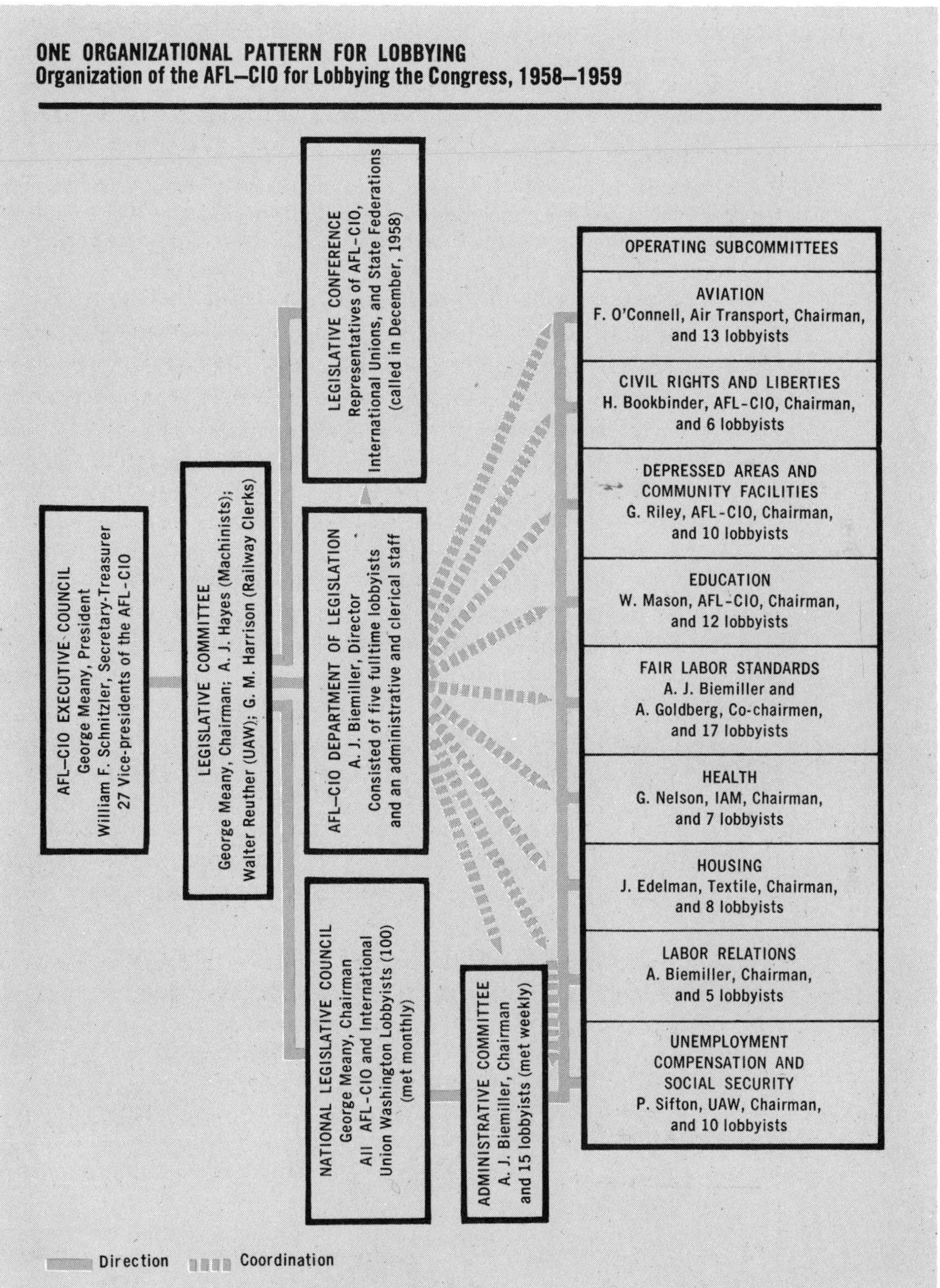

Courtesy of Samuel C. Patterson, State University of Iowa.

> Scandals . . . have given the people of the United States an exaggerated idea of the extent of lobbying in Washington. Congressmen do not often sell their votes for actual money, and much of the lobbying here is legitimate and honorable. A man who seeks to influence legislation by convincing Congressmen of the best way to vote, by arguments only, is also called a lobbyist. During the agitation about the wool tariff this year, many prominent men in that business were here lobbying, among them little Dave Harpster of northern Ohio. No one would ever think of accusing Farmer Dave of anything shady, and the large part of the Washington lobbyists are just as honorable as he. Of the hundreds of pension lobbyists, national bank lobbyists, mail contract lobbyists, etc., nine-tenths are sound businessmen who would not think of trying to buy votes in Congress.

Senator Paul Douglas of Illinois once announced that he would not accept a gift worth more than $2.50. Other congressmen permit lobbyists to buy them dinner or to entertain them. Most frequently, though, the large gift comes as a contribution to a political campaign or for expenses in office. As Senator, Richard M. Nixon accepted an $18,000 personal fund from interest groups in California to help defray the expenses of his office. Senator Francis Case of South Dakota, on the other hand, once assumed that a contribution of $2,500 to his campaign fund by the oil and natural gas interests was an attempt to buy his vote on a natural gas regulation bill. Ironically, he already favored the petroleum industry side of the issue, but by baring his conscience in public he killed the bill. During the Billie Sol Estes inquiry of 1962, Senator Ralph Yarborough of Texas was found to have accepted contributions from Estes for a series of radio broadcasts. Colleagues who knew of the Senator's integrity and were aware of the expense of campaigning openly sympathized with the Senator on the Senate floor.

Perhaps the point most frequently overlooked when lobbying activities are considered is that most congressmen are firmly committed on most important issues. Lobbyists can often spend their money better by trying to defeat congressmen for reelection than by trying to change their minds.

Efforts at Lobby Control. In general, lobbying regulation has taken two forms: prohibiting certain activities as improper and providing publicity about all lobbying.

Congress has tended to require higher standards of the executive department than of its own members. Thus when Charles E. Wilson, the president of General Motors, became a member of the Eisenhower Cabinet, he was asked to sell his stock lest a conflict of interest might make him, in effect, a lobbyist for General Motors. No similar expectation applies to successful congressional candidates.

Congress has done little to prohibit lobbying practices that are unethical but not generally regarded as criminal. The Hatch Act of 1940 placed controls on campaign contributions (see Chapter 12), but in general, this has done little to inhibit interest-group activities in campaigns.

Another method of controlling lobbies and lobbying is by publicity. As early as the 1920s, utility companies and agencies of foreign powers who lobbied before Congress were required to register. Since the Regulation of Lobbying Act of 1946, agents representing groups whose principal purpose is to influence legislation have been required to register with the Clerk of the House and the Secretary of the Senate. They must disclose the individual or group who employs them, how much they are paid, how much they spend and for what purposes. About 400 lobbyists, who represent over 1,000 organizations, file such quarterly reports, and they are listed in the *Congressional Record*.

There have been several major difficulties with the publicity method. An agent may claim: "It is not the *principal* purpose of my group to influence legislation. Our principal purpose is the manufacture of widgits. We do not have to register." Using such an argument, a number of groups have not registered. A second factor is that when the act was tested in the Supreme Court in 1954, it received a narrow interpretation; lobbying before Congress was covered, but not "educational campaigns" that were directed at the voters. Thus millions may be spent on pamphlets, newspaper ads, and television broadcasts, with no accounting required. The act is also weakened by the fact that no agency is in charge of enforcement.

Despite these problems, the public now has more information than it previously had, even though the nation's newspapers seem reluctant to publicize the registrations. The provisions for fines and even prison sentences stand as a warning against flagrant lobbying activity. And there is always the possibility that the law will be enforced, as it was in 1956, when representatives of the Superior Oil Company of California were fined $2,500 each for not registering and the company itself was fined $10,000. This case grew out of disclosures relative to a bill to regulate natural gas producers.

The Current Image of the Lobby. The lobby still is suspect in American folklore. Most congressmen and the President recognize that the right to petition is a legitimate one and find that some lobbies are helpful in providing them with needed information and political ammunition. The problem with lobbies probably is not so much one of improper activities; it is the fact that the segments of American society that are sufficiently organized to protect their interests through lobbying give a distorted image of the electorate and public demands as a whole. One political scientist, examining the range of registered groups, concludes that the pressure system has a business and upper-class bias so that the system actually represents only about 10 per cent of the nation's citizens.[5] Lobbyists do, however, indicate when an important represented group feels that a proposed change is of sufficient importance for it to spend resources for its defeat or passage.

[5] E. E. Schattschneider, *The Semi-sovereign People: A Realistic View of Democracy in America,* Holt, Rinehart and Winston, Inc., New York, 1960, chap. 2.

VARIETY IN INTEREST-GROUP PATTERNS

The organizational and operational patterns of interest groups offer almost endless variety. Some of them are especially created for the single purpose of lobbying; for others, lobbying is only a side line. Some are temporary organizations created for a special problem; others are permanent groups. Some have stable memberships over a long period of time; others enjoy far less loyalty from their rank and file. Some are always present and active at the seat of government; others lobby only when a matter of particular interest is under consideration. The Anti-Saloon League, for example, was created specifically for political action to prohibit the sale of intoxicating beverages; lobbying is only one of many activities of the Automobile Manufacturers' Association. A temporary organization may exist for a highly specific purpose, perhaps "to repeal Section 12a of the Interstate Commerce Act." (In registering as a prerequisite to lobbying activity, groups sometimes list their purposes very specifically.) The large manufacturing, labor, and farm organizations have enough interest involved to maintain large permanent staffs in Washington, but temporary groups and some permanent ones seek to apply pressure only occasionally, whenever a particular decision affecting their membership is pending.

Interest groups endlessly realign their forces as expediency demands. Politics is not simply business versus labor, though that is a part of the story, and businessmen do not always work together. Groups operate in both temporary and continuing alliances with other groups. The fluidity of the interest-group system is one of its principal characteristics. For example, trucking industry lobbyists join with other business lobbyists against organized labor on many matters involving proposed changes in the Taft-Hartley Labor-Management Act, but they join in coalition with the independent Teamsters' Union in seeking more favorable competitive conditions for the trucking industry as compared with the railroads. And although the Teamsters and the AFL-CIO are in frequent ideological and jurisdictional disputes, they join in opposing legislation, such as the Landrum-Griffin Act of 1959, that they see as a threat to all organized labor or as an effort to increase government control over its decisions. Some businessmen's groups have opposed expanded foreign economic aid; others have favored it. The latter have found themselves in general alignment with organized labor on that point. The variety of combinations is great. Ours is a dynamic system.

Although many groups active in the political process confine themselves to action on a fairly narrow front, quite a number of organizations demonstrate a great breadth of interests. In general, the large farm organizations take a position on any major issue of public policy if it may be said to affect the welfare of farmers. This means that they are free to take positions on all issues. The same is true of the general labor unions and businessmen's groups. Thus we find that the American Farm Bureau Federation, the AFL-CIO, and the National Association of Manufacturers all hold positions on Federal aid to education and on foreign economic aid. Veterans' organizations also have broad legislative programs, as do some church, fraternal, and other groups.

Status and Group Power. The character of a group varies according to its status in the culture and the degree to which it is viewed as having a legitimate right to influence a particular type of decision. Similarly, the techniques available to a group are limited by the self-image of the leadership relative to "proper" conduct and by the nongovernmental role of the group. Thus a religious organization will not likely get involved in "gutter politics," a labor union might feel less constrained. One group may be able to get away with something that would produce highly unfavorable publicity for another. The American Medical Association, in lobbying against compulsory national health insurance during the 1950s, took advantage of the high status that physicians enjoy in our society. The deference people pay physicians enabled their pressure group to engage in tactics that might have been roundly criticized if they had been used by, say, the United Steel Workers, a group of considerably less status. On the other hand, the American Medical Association must act in accord with its image of dignity and responsibility, while the steelworkers and their representatives can act in a more free-swinging style—people are not surprised at them under such circumstances, but physicians feel they cannot afford to do violence to their public image.

COHESIVENESS OF GROUPS

The Interest Group Is Not a Monolith. Interest groups are internally more consistent as to ideology and public policy preferences than are the two major political parties, as was noted above. The more consistent the views of the membership, the more politically effective the group is likely to be, but the membership is rarely in unanimous accord.[6] There are several reasons why this is so:

1. Groups, especially those that are active in national politics, may have members from a large part of the nation or all of it. The larger the membership and the greater the geographic area that it is drawn from, the more likely it is that there will be some differences of opinion about political goals and the means to them. The large group gains strength from membership, but the small one has an important advantage too: It is likely to be more cohesive as to ideology and goals and hence able to take an unequivocal stand on issues. The Chamber of Commerce of the United States cannot gain consensus on some tariff questions, but the association of American watch manufacturers can stand firmly in favor of high tariffs on Swiss imports. If the political efforts of the organization are not favored

[6] Truman, *op. cit.*, chap. 6.

by some part of the membership, whom does the group represent? How is it possible for the rights and interests of the minority to be protected or furthered?

2. Large groups depend for day-to-day operations upon a professional bureaucracy at national headquarters and in Washington. This raises the old question: Does the tail wag the dog? The professionals in Washington normally know a great deal more than the membership about subjects of interest to the group, the political climate, and lobbying strategy. They are relied upon heavily for advice. Under the circumstances, the professional leaders may have great influence over the legislative program. They can push hard for what they want and nail down other parts of it. They can include items that are tangential to the main concerns of members and that members might not agree with. And because it is generally easier to gain support through opposition than through consensus to favor, some professionals spend much of their time lobbying against proposed legislation and neglect the development of a positive program. The bureaucracy of a group serves as a general propaganda agency for the group and the leaders sometimes become closely attached to the symbols they use, which leads them to make stronger commitments to ideological positions than a majority of their members seem to. The prcfessional leaders of the Chamber of Commerce of the United States and the National Association of Manufacturers appear to be much more committed to the doctrine of industrial individualism than a great many members. Similarly, the leadership of the AFL-CIO is more aggressively liberal than much of the membership—at least concerning certain programs such as public housing, urban renewal, and civil rights.

3. The national and local aims of members may conflict. The political climate may be different, or the goals may be essentially different, or there may be a difference between the principle in the abstract and its application in the community. Thus in the postwar years, while the Chamber of Commerce of the United States has urged that urban renewal be conducted without Federal aid and has opposed expanded Federal aid, affiliate members have been busy at the local level, devising plans for urban renewal, often deliberately building them around Federal aid. And in an almost identical reversal of positions, the AFL-CIO leadership has pushed for expanded Federal urban renewal programs, while the membership at the local level has often opposed such plans, especially if they involve areas where members live or if a project threatens to alter racial living patterns of the community.[7]

4. People join groups for many reasons that need not include support for their legislative goals. This is true particularly because the groups themselves often exist for many purposes other than political action. A member of the AFL-CIO may have joined the organization in order to get

[7] See Oliver P. Williams and Charles R. Adrian, *Four Cities,* University of Pennsylvania Press, Philadelphia, 1963, chap. 7.

better wages, hours, and conditions of labor. He may or may not see a connection between these goals and a broad union social action program. Or he may have joined the union merely because the firm where he was able to get work had a union-shop contract that required him to join. He may or may not have information about the AFL-CIO position on the most recent foreign-aid bill. If he does know that the union has a position and if he knows what it is, he may approve or disapprove or simply not care.

Similarly, the American Farm Bureau Federation, which is generally regarded as the spokesman for the nation's more successful commercial farmers, may include persons who joined for a host of reasons. Some may approve of the Federation's legislative program and may have joined in order to develop and support it. Others may have found it personally advantageous to join, but may disapprove of one or more points in the Federation program. A third group may have joined simply because they could not say "no" to the organizer, or because they wanted to please a friend, or in order to conform to neighborhood expectations, or for the sake of the group's social activities. It is never easy to say who is speaking for whom in politics.

Cross Pressures on the Individual. The individual normally belongs to a number of groups, not all of which have like views toward the same questions of policy. This pattern of overlapping memberships produces *cross pressures** on the individual.

***CROSS PRESSURE. Social and psychological forces upon the individual that partially cancel one another out. They result from overlapping organizational memberships or psychological identifications. Cross-pressured persons tend to withdraw from political participation.**

For example, Oswald Torkelson may belong to a labor union that has strong views about expanding foreign aid; to the American Legion, which has grave misgivings about the way such programs have been conducted; and to a church that favors economic aid, but opposes use of taxes for armaments. The local chamber of commerce, to which Torkelson does not belong (the individual is not likely to belong to directly countervailing secondary groups, such as trade unions and business associations), may have still another view. It may want the foreign-aid bill to require most foreign-aid materials to be purchased in the United States, and the chamber secretary may argue that this will help guarantee Torkelson steady employment (if the firm he works for is engaged in certain kinds of production). Yet a requirement of domestic purchase where possible may work to discourage the advancement of industry in underdeveloped countries and hence work against one of the very purposes for which Torkelson's tax money is being spent. Again, it is difficult to determine who is representing whom and precisely how.

We know from a number of studies that cross pressures on the citizen (see Chapter 9) tend to discourage him from voting. In a similar way, cross pressures on the citizen through membership in a number of groups tend to drive him toward the middle of the road. If he happens to belong to a radical group on the left or a reactionary group on the right, his other group memberships will tend to pull him away from the extremes. The fact that the individual is subjected to the propaganda of the various groups to which he belongs or with which he psychologically identifies is another factor that contributes to the tendency for American politics to be characterized by relatively small deviations from the norm, that is, small deviations from the middle of the road. Cross pressures resulting from overlapping memberships tend to keep the differences between liberal and conservative rather small in America, as compared with some European democracies.

MOTIVATIONS FOR GROUP ACTION IN POLITICS

Not only do groups vary in type of organization and degree of internal cohesiveness; they also vary in the techniques they use in seeking to influence public policy and the selection of elected officeholders. There are many bases for the political motivation of groups. For example, organizations may seek to use the sanctions of government to support their own battles for economic advancement or to reduce their anxieties concerning competition. Thus the interests that in the past supported a Chicago-to-Gulf Waterway or those that wanted expanded Federal programs to aid irrigation in the West were not so much concerned with the principle of "comprehensive water development and resource management" as they were in the opportunities for profits that these proposed Federal programs offered.[8] And liquor dealers in the District of Columbia, represented by the Washington Retail Liquor Dealers' Association, want Congress to permit distillers to set the price of their products so that they will not be determined by competition.[9] (These same small-business men, however, probably also favor the doctrine of free enterprise and applaud when it is called "the system that made America great.")

Ideology as Motivation. Ideology is sometimes a powerful factor in encouraging political activity even in cases where no economic payoff can be seen. Thus the Foreign Policy Association is involved in seeking to influence State Department policy, and the Society for the Prevention of Cruelty to Animals is concerned about the humane slaughter of animals in

[8] Norman Wengert, *Natural Resources and the Political Struggle,* Doubleday & Company, Inc., Garden City, N.Y., 1955, p. 24.

[9] *The New York Times,* Mar. 28, 1960, p. 49.

packing plants. In neither case do members expect to gain economically from the policies they support. One step lower on the scale of rationality is symbolism, which may also serve as an effective motivating force. Thus various groups lobbied a few years ago to have Congress add the words "under God" to the pledge of allegiance. This symbolic goal, too, had no economic payoff. It fulfilled an ideological need.

The Search for an Arbiter as Motivation. In some cases, interest groups become involved in public policy because they feel a need for an arbiter to provide stability in situations in which they would otherwise be in constant conflict with another interest group. Agriculture and conservation groups, for example, may see government regulation as a means for reducing conflict over land use by defining hunting areas and seasons. In some circumstances, business and labor may both welcome the government's mediators.

Marginality and Motivation. One way of identifying highly motivated groups is to imagine the existence of a sphere of activities in which behavior is governmentally regulated. Outside this sphere there is consensus that there should be no government regulation. Near the center, there is consensus on at least broad governmental policies for regulation. Along either side of the circumference of the sphere is a marginal zone of uncertainty in which the public is indifferent or undecided about how much regulation or vigorous enforcement there should be. Within this marginal zone, we normally find highly specific policy issues rather than broad, sweeping conceptions of policy.[10] To the person not directly involved, the issue may often seem trivial, and the marginal increment of change in policy almost unnoticeable although it may have an overwhelming effect upon certain persons or institutions. For example, if oil-depletion allowance for tax purposes had for years been established at 27.5 per cent (as has been the case), most citizens would accept the principle of allowances, but the specific rate would be quite meaningless to them. If a proposal to reduce the rate to 20 per cent were then made, most persons would not perceive that anything of importance was at issue, but the effect on companies engaged in oil drilling exploration would be great, and in some cases, it could make the difference between a marginal or a profitable firm. The change would also inferentially raise the possibility of further changes.

One might generalize that *the political activity of any group is proportionate to its stake in the marginal definition of legality and of law-enforcement levels.* That is, it is relative to how close the group believes the boundary between legality and illegality is, or is likely to be, to its

[10] The authors are indebted to Richard H. McCleery of Antioch College, whose concept of marginality was a basis for this section.

own activities. For example, persons who hold radio and television licenses must be concerned both with the personnel and the policies of the Federal Communications Commission and with proposed changes, even in small details, in the Federal Communications Act, for these can affect them in important ways, even to the extent of forcing them out of business. Likewise, exponents of conservation policies and of retaining natural beauty spots for public recreation sites must be concerned with the governmental process if they wish to achieve their goals. Government is their last, best hope, since the vistas they wish to preserve are rapidly disappearing. And aviation and electronics firms, to cite still another example, depend to a large extent upon government contracts for their profits. They must be concerned about defense policies, contract-award policies, business-cost policies, and many other decisions that are made either in Congress or the Pentagon.

The typical white-collar citizen who performs some specialized task in a corporate bureaucracy may be interested in politics as a hobby or as a civic responsibility, but he is not intensely involved in politics, except by choice. He is not likely to be in trouble with the law, nor is his perceived welfare especially dependent upon legal decisions. The importer of narcotics for use by addicts is also not likely to be politically active. His job is so far outside the law that he cannot hope to secure governmental sanction.

This last case offers a possible illustration of how almost any group may become politically active. Some specialists in the treatment of narcotics addiction have recommended that the government supply drugs under medical supervision to addicts under treatment. If such a policy were seriously considered, illegal narcotics importers might well surreptitiously support the advocates of a "get tough" policy who oppose this approach, for it would threaten their profit potential.

Time and Marginality. The pattern of marginality varies through time. Once public servants holding office by political appointment were highly active in politics—they had to be. Today they have protection from arbitrary dismissal through the procedural requirements of the Civil Service Commission. Their path has been away from the margin and toward stability and acceptance. Not only have they moved away from political activity, but the Hatch Act actually prohibits most Federal employees from engaging in partisan political activity. On the other hand, many Negroes who once thought they could not make economic or social progress through political action now find that they can. As a result, they have changed their behavior pattern from almost total political apathy to intense activity.

The degree to which American citizens and interest groups engage in political action largely depends upon whether or not they see their social and economic welfare as immediately related to governmental decisions and whether they think they can possibly shape the significant policy.

GROUP ACTIVITIES IN OTHER BRANCHES OF GOVERNMENT

Interest groups do not concentrate their attention exclusively upon the legislative body, although that is where much of the policy they are concerned with is formally adopted or killed. It is, therefore, a major focus of attention.

Pressures on the Bureaucracy. The arenas of decision making in American government are many. In addition to Congress and political parties, interest groups seek to influence a number of governmental agencies. The independent regulatory commissions have enormous powers; many of their decisions have the force and effect of law. Railroads, for example, must persuade the Interstate Commerce Commission to give favorable consideration to policies they want. Users of atomic energy for nonmilitary purposes must bring their cases before the Atomic Energy Commission. A broadcasting firm cannot go on the air without Federal Communications Commission approval, and the granting or withholding of a television license may make the difference between poverty and wealth for such a firm.

Groups must also deal with bureaucracies in the regular Federal government agencies. For income tax exemption, a private charitable foundation must have approval of the Internal Revenue Service, for example. Private firms must also have rulings from time to time from that agency, rulings that may greatly affect their profit margin. The Department of Commerce grants export licenses for certain kinds of goods; the Department of Agriculture grants import permits for others.

As government has grown more complex, detailed legislation has become less practicable. Congress leaves large areas of detail to administrative discretion, and this increases the urgency with which interest groups lobby the bureaucracy.

Pressures on the Chief Executive. Even the President is subject to constant pressures. But he is subjected to a greater variety of pressures than a member of Congress. The latter is often in a poor position to resist pressure; but those on incumbents in the White House are countervailing, that is, they tend to balance one another off. In a sense, the only significant persons to the President are the writers of history. But he must also consider retribution at election time, or the wishes of his friends or those whom he admires or who, he believes, do things "the right way."

Every highly motivated group seeking legislation attempts to influence the President as well as members of Congress. This pressure is usually directed through the White House staff. Even the President's wife may be approached by interest groups. Mrs. Franklin D. Roosevelt often transmitted to her husband the concerns of liberal groups and actively championed their causes. Similarly, a university president, Milton Eisenhower, was often approached by those seeking his intercession on their behalf when his brother was President.

Pressures on the Courts. Groups also seek to advance their interests through action before the courts. They do not lobby judges in the same way they lobby senators. Private approaches to judges outside the courtroom are rare and a violation of prevailing norms of behavior. They probably do take place, but the lobbyist who uses this approach risks a contempt citation and heavy penalties. The more usual approach is to lobby in the selection of judges or to appeal to the values of the judiciary and the traditions of the law in open court. The procedures are different, but the goal is the same—a favorable decision.

In the years before the Great Depression, strategists for corporations often found that the courts offered the best chance for them to forestall interests that were seeking to control corporate activities—interests that sought the support of the legislative and executive branches. Thus in the early years of this century when interests concerned with the health and welfare of bakers prevailed upon the New York legislature to pass a law forbidding employees to work in a bakery for more than ten hours a day or sixty hours a week, proponents of *laissez faire* prevailed upon the United States Supreme Court to kill the legislation, using the legal argument that it interfered with the right of workingmen freely to contract for their labor. Justice Rufus W. Peckham went so far as to suggest that such "meddlesome interferences with the rights of the individual" would have to be stopped, or all citizens would be placed "at the mercy of legislative majorities."[11]

Recently, advocates of the extension of equal rights to all have generally found the courts the most favorable arena in which to seek their goals.[12]

Seeking Access. Interest groups approach whatever arenas of decision making most welcome them and are most likely to be sympathetic. They use whatever techniques seem called for under given circumstances, provided that society approves of, or at least is tolerant of them. And, of course, in the major conflicts in America's history, the legislative, executive, and judicial branches all are likely to be approached. This has been the case with both sides in the school desegregation controversy.

Supporters of an interest move from one decision-making arena to another if their cause is not supported. A group losing an administrative decision commonly appeals to a higher administrative officer and may move from there to the courts. It it still loses, the group may ask Congress to change the law or ask the President to issue a directive overruling an agency bureaucrat, or it may seek to infiltrate and control the agency involved. In extreme cases, a group may seek a constitutional amendment. There is almost no end to the possible choices of strategies.

[11] *Lochner v. New York,* 198 U.S. 45 (1905).

[12] See Harmon Zeigler, *Interest Groups in American Society,* Prentice-Hall, Inc., Englewood Cliffs, N.J., 1964, chap. 11.

GROUPS AND THE PUBLIC INTEREST

When any group announces a policy position, it seeks explicitly or implicitly to associate its stand with "the public interest." In fact, virtually every politically active individual or group claims—often in sincerity—to be acting for the public interest. On the other hand, critics of the stand taken by a particular pressure group commonly complain that it is selfish and that members ought to act in the public interest. With everyone using the term "public interest," it becomes useless as an analytical tool. Yet it is a basic part of the belief system of democracy to say that public policies are—or should be—in the public interest. As such, the concept may serve a useful function in encouraging compliance with the law; in turn, this compliance is an important device for achieving a stable society. The term is also useful as a symbol to remind legislators and administrators that no matter how many groups they may have listened to before making a decision, other unrepresented or underrepresented groups and individuals will also be affected by the decision. As one writer on the subject has said:[13]

> Instead of being associated with substantive goals or policies, the public interest better survives identification with the process of group accommodation. The public interest rests not in some policy emerging from the settlement of conflict, but with the method of that settlement itself, with compromising in a peaceful, orderly, predictable way the demands put upon policy.

But even this description is somewhat inadequate as an analytical tool in that it gives us no basis for measuring whether there is consensus on substantive policy, and the definition itself probably could not find much support among those who use the term. One political scientist who has catalogued and analyzed the many ways in which the concept has been used concludes that "there is no public-interest theory worthy of the name."[14]

When he sees the term "public interest" the citizen should keep in mind that it is probably being used as a glittering generality to support the particular writer's personal value preferences. We are a nation with a vastly diverse collection of cultural subgroups, with important regional, group, and even class differences in values and behavior patterns. It is difficult to secure consensus on goals. Even when we do (dominant American opinion favors material "progress" and the defense of the nation against foreign challenges, for example), we lack consensus as to means. Many political writers have bemoaned our nation's inability to achieve consensus and the rejection by many Americans of particular concepts of

[13] Frank J. Sorauf, "The Public Interest Reconsidered," *Journal of Politics,* 19:616–639, November, 1957.

[14] Glendon A. Schubert, Jr., *The Public Interest,* The Free Press of Glencoe, New York, 1960. By permission of the publisher.

the public interest. But whether this lack of overriding agreement is good or bad, it appears to exist, and most public policy is *in fact* (and irrespective of whether it *should be*) the result of compromise among conflicting interests. Much legislation is important to particular groups, but not to society as a whole. The American system of government is based largely upon satisfying the demands of particular groups that are concerned about particular wants.

CLASSIFICATION OF INTEREST GROUPS

Interest groups may be classified in a great number of ways. We have suggested several in this chapter. Groups differ according to *technique,* which may range from an underworld spokesman's crude threats to uncooperative local officials or those of an "old-school" union leader or business executive to seek defeat for a congressman coming up for reelection, to the dignified, rational arguments some groups place in Sunday *New York Times* advertisements. Techniques include marching with placards before the north portico of the White House, bringing cases to the courts (as the NAACP and the Jehovah's Witnesses have done with special effectiveness), routine lobbying, and such direct-action techniques as the sit-in and the prevention of administrative officials from carrying out their assigned duties (as in farmers' actions to prevent court-ordered sales of land on which there are defaulted mortgages—a technique dating back to Shays' Rebellion in 1786). These are only a few examples. Possibilities are nearly infinite in number.

Groups also differ according to *resource base* or dependency. That is, some groups depend primarily upon sheer numbers in their membership (e.g., the AFL-CIO); others, on wealth (e.g., a manufacturers' association); still others, on intimidation potential (e.g., an underworld organization); and some, on the cohesiveness of the group membership (e.g., physicians or dentists).

Groups may also be classified as to type, whether they are public (e.g., the Department of the Navy, the U.S. Forest Service), semipublic (the Federal Reserve Board, the state bar of Ohio), or private (the American Legion, United States Steel Corporation, the Northern California Committee Against Reapportionment, the National Anti-Monopoly League).

The *internal* structure is also significant. Groups may range from relative democracy in leadership policies to a high degree of autocracy. One example of the former is the International Typographical Union, which is a democratic government in microcosm with elections involving competing political parties.[15] Many groups seek cohesiveness and attempt

[15] Seymour Martin Lipset and others, *Union Democracy,* The Free Press of Glencoe, New York, 1956. By permission. (Available in paperback through Anchor Books.)

to avoid conflict. Among the many ways by which to further this goal is to elect officers one year before they take office, as does, for example, the American Political Science Association.

Types of Interest Groups. Hundreds of interest groups are active in Washington. Probably more than 1,000 persons are active lobbyists at any session of Congress if we count those who are registered and add those who need not register under the law—lobbyists for various government agencies, or top staff people of various interest groups who prepare data to be used by the front man, for example. We also find businessmen seeking favors from agencies, journalists with axes to grind, writers of letters to congressmen, and others whose activities might be classified as lobbying.

The groups for which lobbyists work are enormously varied. They include the well-known agricultural, business, and labor groups. Just as well known, but perhaps less frequently thought of as lobbyists, are the representatives of government agencies (see Chapter 17). But we only scratch the surface in mentioning these major broad-gauge groups; there are many more which subdivide themselves until the most specific and highly focused of them are interested in legislation of such detail that its technical complexities cannot be comprehended by most of us.

Farm groups consist not merely of the conservative American Farm Bureau Federation, the Patrons of Husbandry (the National Grange), and the more volatile Farmers' Union, but also of their state branches and specialized groups, such as the Crop Quality Council, the National Milk Producers' Federation, and the California Fruit Growers' Association. Sometimes farmers organize for direct action in seeking to raise prices. They did so through the Farmers' Holiday Association of the 1930s and the National Farmers' Organization of the 1960s.

Business groups are represented by familiar organizations, such as the Chamber of Commerce of the United States and the National Association of Manufacturers. But these offer just a hint of the depth of the iceberg that confronts opponents. Chambers of commerce groups have both state and local organizations and each may have different or at least more specific positions from those of the national body. National organizations exist for many particular types of business (e.g., bearing manufacturers, coal producers, or shoe retailers), regional organizations (e.g., the Atlantic, Gulf and Great Lakes Shipbuilding Association, the Southwestern Peanut Shellers Association), and spokesmen for particular firms (e.g., the Bangor and Aroostook Railroad, the Boeing Company). The firm need not be a large one—Avon goes calling on Capitol Hill and so does a representative of David Burpee, the well-known seed grower. And the interest may be highly specific: some years ago, for example, the B.H.C. Spinks Clay Company, Inc., of Paris, Tennessee, was registered for the avowed and sole purpose of "retaining the present depletion allowance for ball and sagger clays."

Labor groups include not only the AFL-CIO and the large independent unions, such as the railroad brotherhoods and the Teamsters (truck drivers), but more focused groups, such as the United Automobile Workers, the United Steel Workers, the Amalgamated Meat Cutters and Butcher Workmen of North America, and the International Union of United Brewery, Flour, Cereal, Soft Drink, and Distillery Workers of America. There may also be temporary alliances of unions that are normally in conflict, if the cause is one in which their shared interests exceed their differences (e.g., the Joint Minimum Wage Committee).

Varieties of Interests. In addition to the various groups that speak for business and manufacturing firms, organized labor, agriculture, and government agencies, there are many others. They include Federal government employees, state government agencies, local government agencies, the professions, charitable organizations, religious groups, veterans' organizations, ethnic groups, and special-cause groups.

Without giving examples, it is difficult to portray the fantastic variety of interests that are represented before Congress (or, for that matter, a state legislative body). The Regulation of Lobbying Act, through its requirement of registration, gives us some idea of that variety.[16] In every Congress, there are such groups as the Committee for Collective Security, the Council of Conservationists, Inc., the Committee for Effective Use of the International Court by Repealing the Self-judging Reservation, the Committee to Support the U.S. Congress Bill Creating a Commission on Obscene Matters and Materials, the Home Town Free Television Association, and dozens of others.

Liberal groups include the Americans for Democratic Action and the Committee for the Nation's Health; right-wing groups include the Daughters of the American Revolution and the National Economic Council, Inc. We find also the National Committee for Effective Design Legislation, the Estate of Edward F. Pipe (probably involved in estate- and inheritance-tax problems), the National Tax Equality Association, the American Israel Public Affairs Committee, the American Justice Association, the Christian Amendment Movement (which favors a constitutional amendment declaring that the United States is a Christian nation), the Family Tax Association, the United World Federalists, Inc. (which wants to create a federal government for all of the planet), the Townsend Plan, Inc. (with a generation-old plan for aid to the retired), the Rust Prevention Association (interested in plant-disease control, not iron oxide), and the Propeller Club of the United States (concerned not with model airplanes, but with merchant marine matters). Any citizen who believes that he has an interest to protect can lobby before any of the three branches of government, and he can do so whether the forum he chooses is the one that has the legal power to act in his case or not.

[16] Reports filed by lobbyists are listed in the *Congressional Record* each March and thereafter quarterly.

The fact that "this is still a free country" was testified to a few years ago, when registered lobbyists included a representative of the American League for an Undivided Ireland (which has been interested in "any legislation which may help to effectuate the unification of all Ireland") and a citizen of Georgia (a one-man "group"), who registered stating that he was "interested in Federal legislation to prohibit unbonded, unelected, irresponsible city policemen from being armed with deadly weapons . . . or otherwise to require them to be underwritten by solvent bonds, as is required of elected and bonded responsible high sheriffs."

A Closing Note. This chapter has been concerned with interests and the groups that are formed around many of these interests. The materials presented relative to interest groups will be developed further in later chapters. Special attention to interests in the foreign and domestic policy-making arenas will be given in Chapters 20 and 21.

SELECTED BIBLIOGRAPHY

A vast literature exists on interest groups and interest-group theory. The former exists because Americans generally, and political scientists in particular, have long been interested in the way that groups pressure government and because the group has often been treated as a villain, a seeker after "special privilege." The latter represents a major—and highly controversial—attempt to build a general theory of political decision making.

The pioneer study on group theory was done by Bentley in 1908 [2]; another classic work is that of Truman [38]. Herring [19] was also an early contributor; others who have supported the general theory have been Gross [15], Hagan [16], Latham [23], and Zeigler [45]. Critics have wondered how much of political action can be explained by the theory and have pointed out that it does not explain political motivation at all. For example, see Rothman [31]. Kariel [20] adds the question as to whether bigness in government, business, and labor may not have destroyed the meaningfulness of the group-interaction concept for American politics.

Some persons have argued that special interests should be subordinated to the "public interest." The content of meaning for this elusive term is examined by Schubert [33], Smith [35], and Sorauf [36].

The problems of leadership within groups are treated in public administration textbooks and by Selvin [34]. Perhaps no discussion of the bibliography listed here and at the end of Chapters 6 and 7 relative to specific kinds of groups is necessary. Some of these works are simply descriptive, others attempt to relate their findings to a theory of groups. Zeigler [46] does an especially good job in doing this.

1. Baker, Roscoe: *The American Legion and American Foreign Policy,* Bookman Associates, New York, 1954.
2. Bentley, Arthur F.: *The Process of Government,* 4th ed., The Principia Press of Illinois, Evanston, Ill., 1955. (Originally published in 1908.)
3. Blaisdell, Donald C.: *American Democracy under Pressure,* The Ronald Press Company, New York, 1957.
4. Boyer, William W.: "Policy Making by Government Agencies," *Midwest Journal of Political Science,* 4:267–288, August, 1960.

5. Cleveland, Alfred S.: "NAM: Spokesman for Industry?" *Harvard Business Review,* 26:353–371, May, 1948.
6. Dahl, Robert A.: "Business and Politics: A Critical Appraisal of Political Science," *American Political Science Review,* 53:1–34, March, 1959.
7. Dearing, Mary R.: *Veterans in Politics: The Story of the GAR,* Louisiana State University Press, Baton Rouge, La., 1953.
8. Dillon, M. E.: "Pressure Groups," *American Political Science Review,* 36:471–481, June, 1942.
9. Dowling, R. E.: "Pressure Group Theory: Its Methodological Range," *American Political Science Review,* 59:944–954, December, 1960.
10. Eldersveld, Samuel J.: "American Interest Groups: A Survey of Research and Some Implications for Theory and Method," in Henry W. Ehrmann (ed.), *Interest Groups on Four Continents,* The University of Pittsburgh Press, Pittsburgh, Pa., 1958.
11. Engler, Robert: *The Politics of Oil,* The Macmillan Co., New York, 1961.
12. Gable, Richard W.: "NAM: Influential Lobby or Kiss of Death?" *Journal of Politics,* 15:254–273, May, 1953.
13. Garceau, Oliver: *The Political Life of the AMA,* Harvard University Press, Cambridge, Mass., 1941.
14. Golembiewski, Robert T.: "The Group Basis of Politics," *American Political Science Review,* 54:962–971, December, 1960.
15. Gross, Bertram: *The Legislative Struggle,* McGraw-Hill Book Company, New York, 1953.
16. Hagan, Charles B.: "The Group in Political Science," in Roland Young (ed.), *Approaches to the Study of Politics,* Northwestern University Press, Evanston, Ill., 1958.
17. Hamilton, Walton, H.: *The Politics of Industry,* Alfred A. Knopf, Inc., New York, 1957.
18. Hardin, Charles M.: *The Politics of Agriculture,* The Free Press of Glencoe, New York, 1952.
19. Herring, E. Pendleton: *Group Representation before Congress,* The Johns Hopkins Press, Baltimore, 1929.
20. Kariel, Henry S.: *The Decline of American Pluralism,* Stanford University Press, Stanford, Calif., 1961.
21. Kesselman, Louis C.: *The Social Politics of FEPC,* The University of North Carolina Press, Chapel Hill, N.C., 1948.
22. Kile, Orville M.: *The Farm Bureau through Three Decades,* The Waverly Press, Baltimore, 1948.
23. Latham, Earl: *The Group Basis of Politics,* Cornell University Press, Ithaca, N.Y., 1952.
24. Lear, John: "Drugmakers and the Government—Who Makes the Decisions?" *Saturday Review,* 43:37–42, July 2, 1960.
25. Miller, Robert M.: *American Protestantism and Social Issues, 1919–1939,* The University of North Carolina Press, Chapel Hill, N.C., 1958.
26. Odegard, Peter (ed.): *Religion and Politics,* Oceana Publications, New York, 1960.
27. Pinner, Frank A., and others: *Old Age and Political Behavior,* University of California Press, Berkeley, Calif., 1959.
28. Reagon, Michael D.: "The Political Structure of the Federal Reserve System," *American Political Science Review,* 55:64–76, March, 1961.
29. Riggs, Fred W.: *Pressures on Congress,* King's Crown Press, New York, 1950.
30. Riker, William H.: *The Theory of Political Coalitions,* Yale University Press, New Haven, Conn., 1963.

31. Rothman, Stanley: "Systematic Political Theory," *American Political Science Review*, 54: 15–33, March, 1960.
32. Schriftgeisser, Karl: *Business Comes of Age*, Harper & Row, Publishers, New York, 1960.
33. Schubert, Glendon A., Jr.: *The Public Interest*, The Free Press of Glencoe, New York, 1960.
34. Selvin, Hanan C.: *The Effects of Leadership*, The Free Press of Glencoe, New York, 1960.
35. Smith, Howard R.: *Democracy and the Public Interest*, The University of Georgia Press, Athens, Ga., 1960.
36. Sorauf, Frank J.: "The Public Interest Reconsidered," *Journal of Politics*, 19: 616–639, November, 1957.
37. Tomasek, Robert D.: "The Migrant Problem and Pressure Group Politics," *The Journal of Politics*, 23: 295–319, May, 1961.
38. Truman, David: *The Governmental Process*, Alfred A. Knopf, Inc., New York, 1951.
39. Tucker, William P.: "The Farmers Union: The Social Thought of a Current Agrarian Movement," *Southwestern Social Science Quarterly*, 27: 45–53, June, 1946.
40. Tussman, Joseph: *Obligation and the Body Politic*, Oxford University Press, Fair Lawn, N.J., 1961.
41. Velie, Lester: *Labor U.S.A.*, Harper & Row, Publishers, New York, 1959.
42. Vose, Clement E.: "The National Consumers' League and the Brandeis Brief," *Midwest Journal of Political Science*, 1: 267–290, November, 1957.
43. Wengert, Norman: *Natural Resources and the Political Struggle*, Random House, Inc., New York, 1961.
44. Wildavsky, Aaron: *Dixon-Yates: A Study in Power Politics*, Yale University Press, New Haven, Conn., 1961.
45. Zeigler, Harmon: *Interest Groups in American Society*, Prentice-Hall, Inc., Englewood Cliffs, N.J., 1964.
46. Zeigler, Harmon: *The Politics of Small Business*, Public Affairs Press, Washington, D.C., 1961.

PART II

THE POLITICAL PROCESS

How do

institutionalized

allocations of power

shape American

political action?

Actors in the political process range from the public official to the nonvoter. Voting behavior of the individual is shaped by a variety of legal, social, and psychological considerations. In making decisions he takes cues from his experiences, habitual attitudes, opinion leaders, and the reference groups with whom he identifies. *(Chapter 9, The Voter Who Decides.)*

The American party system is more frequently used by political actives to secure election than to offer public-policy positions to the voter. The formal, highly decentralized organization, the lack of effective competition in many areas, and the sometimes conflicting coalitions of interests within each party encourage ideological diversity and decentralized power. *(Chapter 10, Political Parties.)*

Election procedures are shaped by officeholders to maximize their chances of election. But the American ideology and characteristics of the voter also affect the choice of election machinery. Primaries and conventions are unique American compromises for recruiting candidates. Political actives can generally, but not always, manipulate choices toward their own preferences. *(Chapter 11, Nominations and Elections.)*

The candidate views the campaign as an instrument for securing votes and not necessarily one for informing the voter. He relies principally on a variety of propaganda techniques in seeking to build a favorable image. Increasingly the public-opinion poll is relied upon in making decisions about strategy and tactics. *(Chapter 12, Election Campaigns.)*

All political institutions require leadership. But the style of that leadership varies with the demands imposed by the institutional situation. The shape of the job screens applicants so as to favor different social backgrounds for different leadership positions. *(Chapter 13, Public Leadership.)*

Congressmen are recruited according to characteristics valued in constituencies that overrepresent rural and small-town America. But the institution itself also subtly shapes the attitudes of members through norms of the legislative body, committee experience, the system of advancement, and partisan and presidential demands. *(Chapter 14, Congressmen and Their World.)*

The rules of procedure provide congressmen, especially the leaders, with numerous opportunities for shaping or blocking legislation. Built-in vetoes are common. The investigative technique often provides an alternative to legislation in that it is an effective weapon with which to influence public opinion and thereby the other branches of government. *(Chapter 15, Congress at Work and Play.)*

The Presidency is an institutionalized office of leadership, greater than any individual. The office possesses vast formal powers, but these can be invoked only under special circumstances. The incumbent is constantly challenged to combine his legal resources with a skillful cultivation of public support and thereby maximize his influence on policy making. *(Chapter 16, The Presidency.)*

Public policies are both influenced and executed by professionally trained administrators. The bureaucratic environment affects the attitudes, procedures, and goals of administrative personnel. The expertise of bureaucrats provides a powerful weapon in the interaction among a governmental agency, its public, and other branches of government. *(Chapter 17, Administration and Bureaucracy.)*

The legal myth holds that courts do nothing but apply the law. But in fact in interpreting legislation or exercising judicial review, the Supreme Court is always to some degree a political body that makes public policy. The justices are influenced by procedures that encourage neutrality, informal relations among themselves and other Federal and state legal officers, as well as by pressures from outside the court system and the ideologies to which they personally subscribe. *(Chapter 18, Law and the Judiciary.)*

CHAPTER

9

THE VOTER WHO DECIDES

The American voter is eulogized in folklore and in election-day editorials. He is interviewed, analyzed, and reported on by pollsters. Pundits comment on his current mood and thought. Interest-group spokesmen seek his support. Politicians woo him. Those who do not receive his approving smile sometimes damn him. He is courted because he can open doors that many persons would like to enter.

The popular image of democracy, as was noted in Chapter 3, portrays the voter as a rational being who tests the statements of rational candidates seeking public office on the basis of meaningful platforms based on current policy issues. We have seen that, while rationality is advantageous to effective democratic government, it is not absolutely essential. The image is useful. It helps the average citizen in his quest for confidence in his government and those who run it. But the student of politics should be as much concerned with reality as he is with the image projected by an ideology.

THE VOTER: ANOTHER POLITICAL ACTOR

One of the four I's of the political process that we discussed in Chapter 1 is the *individual.* The individual may play a number of roles. He may be:

1. An elective public official
2. A political or career official or government employee
3. A political party leader
4. An interest-group leader
5. An opinion leader not identified with a particular group
6. A voter
7. A nonvoter

The political process involves the interaction of all of these persons. Each one, even the nonvoter, is a political actor, for his actions or failures to take action affect the outputs of the process.

Individuals in politics play such different roles that it would not be feasible to treat all of them in a single chapter. In the following material we therefore restrict ourselves to the last two categories, the voter and the nonvoter. A large number of citizens never or only rarely vote. Among the politically active, the great bulk never do anything other than vote. It is to these political actors that we now turn.

SOME CHARACTERISTICS OF THE VOTER

Social scientists, historians, and journalists have been studying the voter in his native habitat for many years. They have made some general observations that we might consider before proceeding further. The voter, in a collective or generic sense, is characterized by instability, short memory, lack of information, ambivalence, emotionalism, ethnocentricity, pluralistic views, and skepticism.

Inertia. The voter is known for his conservatism. This is generally true in all nations. The ordinary citizen is likely to prefer what he has to what he might get in the event that some complex and poorly understood political stratagem were to succeed. Only in times of desperation and despair is he likely to favor change openly; and after an episode characterized by experimentation, he takes what seems to work best and establishes a new conservatism based upon it. Thus the public supported the experimentation of the New Deal during the mid-1930s out of a sense of urgency in the search for work and security. After certain new functions of government were found acceptable, these became a basis for a new conservatism, and the typical voter became skeptical or apathetic about proposals for further moves in the direction of the social service state.

In foreign policy matters, Americans are generally little interested, except for a persistent wish that the tensions of the cold war would somehow go away. Yet the citizen may suddenly become vitally interested in a particular aspect of foreign policy and demand sudden and decisive action. Americans, for example, paid little attention to deteriorating American-Japanese relations in the late 1930s until the gunboat *Panay* was sunk by Japanese bombs. The public was suddenly outraged, and had the United States gone to war at that point on a matter of honor and in order to "teach them a lesson," the action would probably have been highly popular. Yet after a few weeks, the incident was nearly forgotten, and attitudes returned to their position of equilibrium; Americans were once again in the mood to consider Japanese imperialism in the Orient "none of our business."

Similarly, in October, 1945, just two months after World War II had ended and when the nation was faced with the need to work out its postwar relationships with the Soviet Union, only 7 per cent of a Gallup poll sample saw foreign policy as the most vital problem facing the United States. A year later, the figure was still only 22 per cent. But by March, 1947, with the cold war beginning to drop below the freezing point, 54 per cent saw foreign problems as most vital.

Figure 9-1

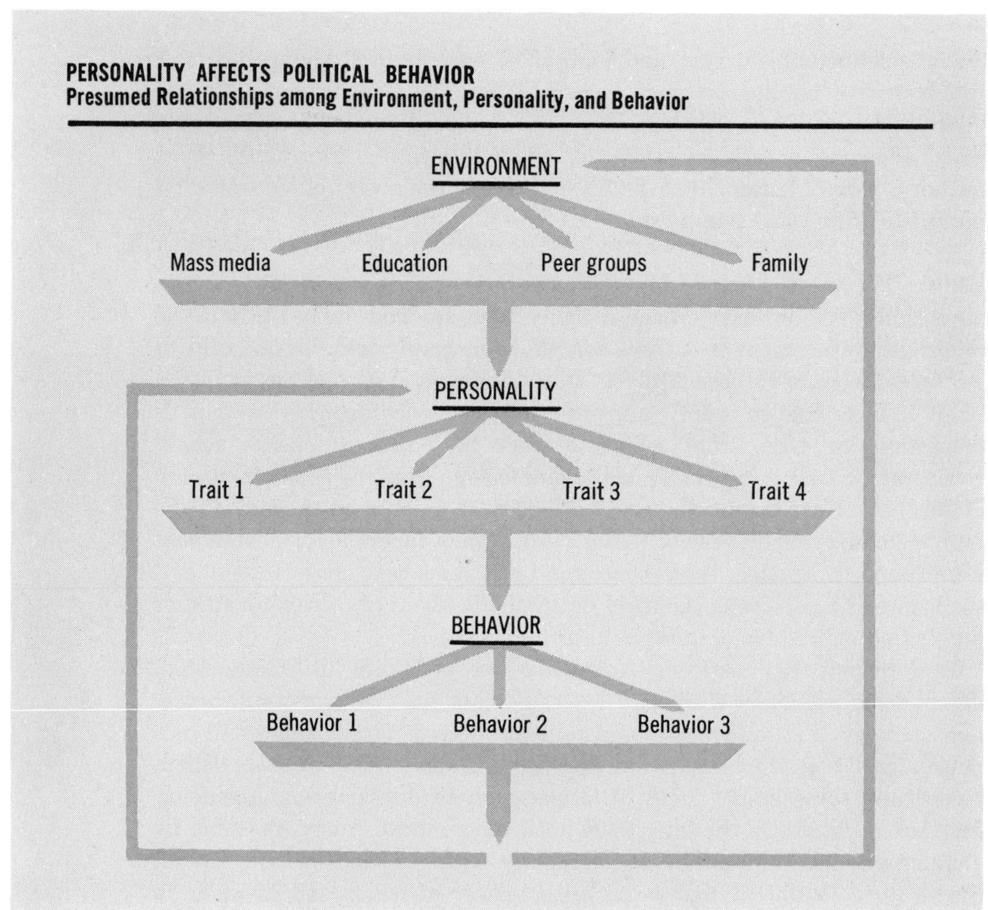

Lewis A. Froman, Jr., "Personality and Political Socialization," Journal of Politics, *vol. 23, fig. 1, May, 1961.*

The voter usually sees issues as short-range problems, not as part of a larger picture. Most of the time he is apathetic about them. If they are not dramatized in terms of human interest and personal involvement, he is not likely to be interested. In the 1952 presidential contest, when Americans seemed to be deeply concerned about the cold war and the stalemate in Korea, and when a large number (by American standards) of voters went to the polls, only 37 per cent of the public was "very much interested" in the campaign. Another 34 per cent said they were "somewhat interested," and 28 per cent, despite social expectations that citizens should be deeply interested in elections—said they were "not much interested."[1]

Short Memory for Details, Long Memory for Traumatic Events. During the years since 1946, when the iron curtain clanked down, relations between the United States and the Soviet Union have traced the path of a pendulum. The deliberate Soviet policy has been to "talk tough" for a time, then to withdraw for awhile and give the impression that the two countries might work out their differences. These pulsations are reflected in the polls. Each time the Soviets lower the cold war temperature a few degrees, a substantial number of Americans indicate to the pollsters that they believe the nation might be at war within six months. Yet as soon as the Communists permit a moderating breeze to flow across the world, citizens seem to forget their apprehensions, lapse into apathy, and fail to support all-out defensive or economic-aid measures that might require sacrifices in their standards of living.

Candidates for public office live in fear of events that might damage their chances taking place near election time. Yet such an event (for example, a dramatic disclosure concerning the candidate's past) is likely to be forgotten after a month or two. It is thus common policy for a candidate to put on the table at the beginning of a campaign any of his cards that are soiled or might be made to appear so by opponents. Conversely, he avoids using what he thinks will be his most effective charges against his opponent until near election day (unless they are to be the theme of the entire campaign).

In contrast to these reactions on details, however, voters react for generations to the salient events in our history. Even today, some people still, in effect, vote for Lincoln or against Hoover, for these men symbolize two of our greatest and most memorable national experiences.

Lack of Information. The civic leader, the well-educated citizen, the editor, the person who makes politics an avocation—members of what has been called the "attentive publics"—can be considered a reasonable approximation of the informed, rational man who is pictured as the typical citizen in the ideal model of democracy. Such persons are, of course, not typical at

[1] Angus Campbell and others, *The Voter Decides,* Harper & Row, Publishers, New York, 1954, p. 34.

all, and the average voter is actually in possession of very little factual knowledge as he makes his decisions about politics.[2]

Stories about the uninformed voter are legion. Even the information he does possess often represents folklore that cannot be supported by facts or empirical analysis. Both systematic polls and informal polls of the man-on-the-street type regularly show, for example, that relatively few voters can name their congressmen. A somewhat larger number of persons can usually name at least one of their United States senators. But 2 per cent or more of the nation's adults cannot even name the President. A few years ago, voters in one Illinois congressional district renominated the man who had held the office for several terms—but he had died almost three months before. Commenting on this, a *Detroit Free Press* editorial writer complained: "You can't expect good government when voters are so uninformed as to the record of their own Congressman that they don't even know whether he is alive or dead."

During the 1948 presidential campaign the *Minneapolis Tribune* sent a reporter around the country to get the flavor of public opinion as reflected by bus riders. (Buses, it might be noted, are most likely to be used by relatively low-income persons with relatively low levels of education.) Here were some of the comments he elicited or overheard:[3]

> A plump, jovial housewife: "I really don't know who's going to win the election. I suppose folks talk about it, but I just never listen."
>
> A clerk: "I don't know who our congressman is from here. We've got a representative, but I don't rightly know how he stands. I suppose a person ought to brush up on that sort of thing, but it seems everybody is so busy making a living they don't pay much attention to politics."
>
> A hospital technician demonstrated that many people want to talk about the things that cause them anxieties and that threats to one's health may be more important by far than politics. She said: "I saw something in the papers today about that Russian spy investigation in Washington. It's quite interesting, isn't it? Did you happen to notice that Babe Ruth died? Ruth, the one who used to play for that baseball team? Died of cancer. Cancer's a terrible thing."

In that year, with the cold war already begun and the atomic bomb making war seem a more terrible threat than ever, 27 per cent of the voters in an interview sample said they had no information concerning American foreign policy, and another 23 per cent indicated only a low level of information.[4]

The cult of the average man leads us to poll citizens about all sorts of technical matters over which they could not be expected to possess enough knowledge to make a meaningful decision. And folklore is often reported,

[2] See Bernard Berelson, "Democratic Theory and Public Opinion," *Public Opinion Quarterly,* 16:313–330, Fall, 1952.

[3] Jack Wilson, *The Minneapolis Tribune,* Aug. 20, 1948.

[4] Angus Campbell and R. L. Kahn, *The People Elect a President,* University of Michigan, Survey Research Center, Ann Arbor, Mich., 1952, p. 56.

as if, because it is believed by the average citizen, it were worth publishing. The Gilbert Youth Research Company, for example, regularly reports to its subscribing newspapers the views of teen-agers on a variety of complex subjects ("Teeners Favor Speed-up in U.S. Space Program"[5]).

Pollsters ask a cross section of the public what should be done about some particular problem, such as a depression or an international crisis. These polls are, of course, valuable as a guide to the public's mood which, in turn, tells decision makers what degree of support or opposition to expect in relation to proposed policies. But the newspapers frequently report them as if they should be the *basis* for public policy making. Furthermore, newspapers (with the exception of a few with a select clientele, such as the *New York Times* or the *Christian Science Monitor*) print in their letters-to-the-editor columns all types of communications, whether they are based on reason and factual knowledge or are almost totally irrational. Since the editor usually refuses to help the reader separate folklore from knowledgeable opinion (he often sees this position as part of the notion of freedom of the press), he contributes to the image of the average man as the possessor of plausible solutions to technical and complex issues.

Ambivalence. The attitudes of the average citizen are characterized by ambivalence, that is, by conflicting beliefs. We are often unaware of these internal inconsistencies in our value systems and use one notion at one moment and a contradictory one at another. This ambivalence is partly the result of the fact that the processes of logical thought are not understood by most citizens. For that matter, many philosophers or social scientists, when depending upon logical derivations for the development of a concept, find that colleagues criticize their work for logical inconsistencies. So perhaps we must expect this ambivalence.

It is likely that our choices between alternatives represent, in part, the difference between ideal and practice, between what we ultimately believe in—what we would accept in the absence of social pressures, economic interests, status anxieties (fears of loss of face), and other challenges—and what we do in fact accept, given those challenges. For example, the Swedish social scientist Gunnar Myrdal sees America faced with a dilemma caused by the difference between our ideal of the equality of man and our practice in the treatment of the Negro.[6] The individual often reacts differently when faced with the ideal as compared with what he sees as a threat resulting from the Negro's wishes for economic and social equality. Similarly, Americans believe in the principle of freedom of expression, but many citizens are likely to be willing to take a generous view of the meaning of the phrase only when they see no ideological threat to themselves or the country. The individual believes in the ideal, but he

[5] Headline in *The State Journal,* Lansing, Mich., Mar. 6, 1960.

[6] Gunnar Myrdal, *An American Dilemma: The Negro Problem and Modern Democracy,* Harper & Row, Publishers, New York, 1944.

also believes in curbing those who would use it to spread ideas he regards as subversive to basic American beliefs and his own interests.

Let us look at a few examples of our ambivalent attitudes so that their inconsistencies will be clearer in our minds:

Americans say	**But Americans also say**
"It's a free country."	"If they don't like our ways, why don't they go somewhere else?"
"Every man is created equal."	"The trouble with the Negro is that he doesn't know his place."
"Americans work too hard. They never stop to relax and enjoy life—all they get is ulcers and heart attacks."	"Americans don't work the way their grandparents did. All they want is shorter hours, more coffee breaks, and a chance to goof off from work."
"The trouble in Washington is that government is controlled by pressure groups and vested interests."	"Someone should get up a petition and send it to our congressmen and senators."
"Public policy should be based on the public interest, not special interest."	"Employees should be represented on government retirement boards—it's their pensions that are involved."
"Americans are too concerned about appearances. They overdress their wives, buy a new car for its flashy chrome, and manicure their front lawns."	"Americans have ruined the appearance of everything they've touched. They have spoiled the countryside with billboards and fringe-area slums, and hideous electric lines dot the landscape when they could easily be put underground."
"A man's home is his castle."	"The judge shouldn't have let that crook go just because the police didn't have a search warrant."
"Congressmen should make the laws, not the bureaucrats."	"How can those congressmen claim to know more than the experts?"
"The voice of the people is the voice of God."	"The masses are asses."

What the public-opinion polls show often does not accord with what people actually do in the voting booth. This is sometimes a result of sampling error—mistakes made in selecting the cross section to be interviewed. But it may also be, in part, a result of differences between what we say for public consumption, what we feel we *ought* to say, and what we say when there is no social pressure.

In 1957, a Gallup poll indicated that 63 per cent of the American voters favored open-shop or right-to-work laws.[7] The next year, voters had an

[7] The poll reported in August, 1957, asked this question: "Some states have passed right-to-work, or open-shop laws that say each worker has the right to hold his job in a company, no matter whether he joins the labor union or not. If you were asked to vote on such a law, would you vote for it—or against it?"

opportunity to vote on state constitutional amendments to protect the "right to work." The voters in the less industrialized states generally approved such legislation, but it was defeated in California (although the Gallup poll had indicated that 61 per cent of the people in the West favored such legislation) and by 2 to 1 in Ohio (56 per cent in the Midwest favored the legislation). What was remarkable about the Ohio vote was that not only working-class people, but middle-class and rural people also opposed the proposal.[8] Why the apparent discrepancy? A poor job of polling? Probably not. The chances are that most Americans feel that they are *expected* to favor freedom to work without the requirement of joining a specified union, and most of them probably are in favor of such a right *in principle.* But the Ohio vote analysis clearly shows that people—once inside the society-shielding curtain of the booth—voted what they conceived to be their interests and their beliefs *in the context of their everyday lives,* in their particular firms and in their particular communities. In addition, political leaders may have played a significant role in pointing out to individuals the personal and logical implications of proposed policies.

The ambivalence of the voter probably cannot be explained entirely in terms of failure to think logically or in the difference between ideal and practice. It is probably also, in part, a result of the anesthetizing influence of the advertising copywriters of Madison Avenue. Commercial advertising, especially as it is used on television and radio, is deliberately designed to dull one's reasoning ability and regularly presents conflicting claims. The public is apparently unconcerned about it. Thus, the citizen is not troubled if in one week he is told that "Zilch's beer, because of a new miracle process, is better than ever," and a few weeks later learns that "Zilch's beer uses the same great formula that was brought from Germany in 1848." And of course, the recent tendency has been to rely heavily on commercial advertising techniques in "selling" political candidates.

The voter is also ambivalent because he is subject to cross pressures from the communications media and the various groups to which he belongs or with which he identifies. Both his daily newspaper and his trade union may present plausible appeals to him, thus creating confusion. (Cross pressures are discussed on pp. 221–222.)

Emotionalism. Earlier chapters have noted that symbols, sentiments,* and emotions are important in shaping the citizen's view of political campaigns and events. So are superficial impressions and professionally produced

---

***SENTIMENT. A disposition to act in a particular way that results from an individual attitude.**

---

[8] See John H. Fenton, "The Right-to-work Vote in Ohio," *Midwest Journal of Political Science,* 3: 241–253, August, 1959.

candidate images (see Table 9-1). Politicians, of course, work hard to rouse emotions, and they are experts at ringing the changes on the symbols that bring about visceral responses. They work harder at gaining emotional responses than they do at making rational appeals simply because they believe that they get a greater payoff in this way. A political rally is carefully staged to arouse the audience. Flags are plentiful. So are pictures of the party's heroes. A band may play martial music. The main speaker is often preceded by so many middleweights that the audience is too

TABLE 9-1

CITIZEN OPINION ON CANDIDATE LIABILITIES, 1960 PRESIDENTIAL CAMPAIGN

Kennedy's liabilities		Nixon's liabilities	
As seen by Democrats	**Per cent of sample**	**As seen by Democrats**	**Per cent of sample**
Catholic	28.7	Republican	31.0
Inexperienced	15.8	Views (foreign affairs)	14.9
Views (domestic affairs)	12.2	Doesn't represent the common man	12.5
Too young	11.5	Not independent	10.5
Humility	5.7	Not sincere	9.0
Affiliations	5.7		
	$n = 139$		$n = 522$
As seen by Republicans		**As seen by Republicans**	
Views (domestic affairs)	18.9	Views (foreign affairs)	33.3
Inexperienced	16.7	Not independent	10.0
Spends too much	12.9	Past record and performance	6.7
Democrat	11.8	Less capable than Kennedy	6.7
Too young	11.8	Personality	6.7
		Religious slander used in campaign	6.7
		Too fast	6.7
	$n = 185$		$n = 30$
As seen by Independents		**As seen by Independents**	
Views (domestic affairs)	19.1	Views (foreign affairs)	22.0
Spends too much	16.5	Not independent	17.8
Catholic	14.7	Not sincere, honest	10.2
Inexperienced	13.0	Past record and performance	9.3
Can't do what he promised	7.8	Republican	8.5
	$n = 115$		$n = 118$

SOURCE: Courtesy of Roberta S. Sigel, Wayne State University, taken from a study conducted in Detroit, 1960. Totals do not equal 100 per cent since "no opinions" are omitted.

exhausted even to try to analyze the reasoning or factual content of his talk. Besides, most of them came to cheer rather than evaluate the speaker anyway. National conventions are, of course, the greatest of these events and are planned by professional showmen with the greatest care for their dramatic interest and emotional impact. This has been particularly true since the coming of radio and especially television. (See Chapter 12, "Election Campaigns."

A few additional points might be made about emotionalism as a factor in politics:

1. Feelings may run very high. People often become as ego-involved with a particular party, political figure, or ideology as they do with their alma mater's football team. On the day that President Franklin D. Roosevelt died, a Texas conservative held a cocktail party to celebrate the event, and offered a toast: "Let's drink to the – – –, now that he's dead."[9] And on hearing of the death of Senator Joseph R. McCarthy, who considered ridding the government of Communists to be his mission and who many considered a true patriot, a Midwestern liberal growled bitterly: "It's his most patriotic act to date." The inhibitions of our culture would cause most of us to regard such manifestations of feelings as being in extremely bad taste. Yet they are not uncommon and indicate the emotional impact that politics has on many.

2. We seem to feel a strong need for folk heroes and father images to reinforce our confidence in the nation, the party, or our way of life generally. As has been noted in earlier chapters, the appearance of things is often more important than the reality, the image more important than the historical record. General George A. Custer is a folk hero, and regarded as a great, if unfortunate, Indian fighter. Yet his own serious mistakes led to his death and that of his soldiers. And practically no American recognized the name of General Ranald Slidell MacKenzie until he became the hero of a television series, although he was perhaps the most effective of all Indian fighters.

The desire for a father image as a motivating factor in voter decision appears to be accepted by some psychiatrists, at least.[10] Probably a great many citizens during the cold war have viewed the President as the one person who must be counted on to save them from immediate annihilation in thermonuclear war. In times past, and to a considerable extent in the 1960s, citizens have looked for comfort and security not to a single father image, but to the United States Supreme Court as an institution. The citizen has had faith in the Court as an instrument to correct the mistakes they expect that governors, congressmen, the bureaucrats, the President, and even the voters themselves will make.

[9] Quoted in John Bainbridge, *The Super-Americans,* Doubleday & Company, Inc., Garden City, N.Y., 1963, p. 187.

[10] Franz Alexander, "Emotional Factors in Voting Behavior," in Eugene Burdick and Arthur J. Brodbeck (eds.), *American Voting Behavior,* The Free Press of Glencoe, New York, 1958, p. 302.

When the voter is not eyeing folk heroes and father images, he is likely to be interested in colorful personalities as a desirable ingredient in a campaign. We have elected Presidents who lack flair for the dramatic, who are colorless (James Monroe, Benjamin Harrison). And many members of both houses of Congress fit this category. Sometimes one rises to great eminence in that body despite lack of color (Senator Robert A. Taft of Ohio, for example). But political leaders who choose candidates look for dramatic ability, for the "crowd pleaser." They have good reason. During the 1952 presidential campaign, 53 per cent of the voters in a sample survey indicated that they would be willing to vote for the opposition if their own candidate had an unattractive personality.[11]

Ethnocentricity. Oliver Wendell Holmes once said that the earth's axis is driven through the center of every small town in America. He was referring to a common social phenomenon that is called *ethnocentrism.**

***ETHNOCENTRISM. The practice of judging other cultures and subcultures by the values and standards of the culture of the person doing the judging. It almost necessarily results in the conclusion that one's own community, nation, or way of life is superior to all others.**

Ethnocentrism is widespread in the world, a nearly universal trait, and it is an extremely strong factor in the American culture. It serves a socially useful purpose in helping members of a group, community, or nation to work together and to assume responsibilities, and it provides them with a frame of reference for evaluating events. But it is also "at the heart of group conflict. Exaggeration of the importance of one's own group at the very least implies a superior attitude toward other similar groups; very often ethnocentrism is charged with hatred for other communities, other tribes [or races], and other nations."[12]

Persons in the mainstream of American culture look with disapproval upon immigrants. Middle-class persons find it difficult to sympathize with the strivings of working-class persons, in part because they consider their life-style to be inferior. It is then but a short step to considering their political goals undesirable.

In relation to foreign affairs, ethnocentrism is a powerful factor conditioning attitudes. Americans find it difficult to believe that fighter pilots of France or the Soviet Union can be on a par with those of America, even harder to believe that Chinese pilots could be. It is almost inconceivable to many Americans that Italian diplomats could be as skilled as American. (More wily perhaps, never as skilled.) It is common folklore that America "pulled the British and French chestnuts out of the fire" in World War I,

[11] Campbell and others, *op. cit.*, p. 95.

[12] Arnold W. Green, *Sociology*, 4th ed., McGraw-Hill Book Company, New York, 1964, p. 49.

and it easily follows that we therefore made the greatest sacrifices. In fact, France had eleven times as many deaths of personnel in the armed services as did the United States, and their nation suffered enormous physical damage, while we had none. We often believe that if other countries would adopt the "free enterprise system" or would "work as hard as we do" or would otherwise accept our cultural values, the Communist threat to such nations would disappear. We sometimes suspect that other countries do not adopt our economic and political systems out of stubbornness or ignorance. And we are simply outraged when a Frenchman assumes, as a matter of course, that his nation has a superior culture, or when the Soviet Premier says that his nation intends to surpass American productivity in *x* years.

Perhaps the most significant effect of ethnocentricity on foreign policy making lies in the fact that Americans are accustomed to thinking of public policy in terms of their personal concerns about economic and social status. As a result, questions of foreign policy that do not directly involve the American economy are difficult to conceive of, and until the tensions of the cold war began to infiltrate every household, Americans were wont to be apathetic about foreign policy and to regard it as generally unimportant.[13] Even today, Americans find it difficult to think of foreign policy in terms other than dealing with inferior peoples who will not accept our values and way of life, of programs that drain away billions of dollars annually in taxes, or of problems of the competition of cheap foreign goods and labor.

Pluralistic Views. The American distrust of centralized power, which dates from the days of colonial rule and the isolation of the frontier, still reflects itself in the average voter's preference for a multiplicity of nuclei of decision making. There has never been any grass-roots support for a party system such as that of England or for transferring technical functions to a professional bureaucracy in Washington. (The expansion of Federal domestic programs appears to result primarily from slowness or incapacity of state and local governments in meeting new demands; also, the Federal government can raise money and achieve uniformity in programs more easily than can other government units.) We believe that, even within the Federal structure, where the President has enormous administrative powers, certain functions should enjoy a considerable degree of independence.

So we support the idea of the independent regulatory commissions (such as the Interstate Commerce Commission, the Federal Trade Commission, or the Federal Power Commission), even though these agencies sometimes have the effect of turning control of a function over to those who supposedly are being controlled by the agency (as has been the case in the

[13] This point is developed in Gabriel A. Almond, *The American People and Foreign Policy,* Harcourt, Brace & World, Inc., New York, 1950.

Interstate Commerce Commission during much of its history). Support for these agencies, which are essentially independent of both the President and Congress, comes in part from a romantic desire to take certain functions out of politics. Most Americans do not trust politics and politicians, and so they tend to look for ways of eliminating the decision-making powers of those who are chosen to rule, ways of putting decision-making on a "businesslike" basis. So to most Americans, setting up a commission whose members can be removed only with the greatest difficulty and whose powers are not easily diminished by Congress seems like a good way to get decisions out of the hands of politicians, rather than a way to create an autonomous locus of power responsible to no one—except perhaps to the interest groups most concerned with its activities. We distrust special interests, but we approve of a policy of decentralization that increases their influence on public policy making.

Skepticism. Americans are not cynical about government to the extent that they lose faith in democracy, but they carry their skepticism about those in power and their motives to the point where their confidence is high only in times of great and clearly perceived dangers. People placed their faith in Franklin D. Roosevelt during the Great Depression and in Dwight D. Eisenhower during eight fear-ridden years of the cold war. At such times, many go to the opposite extreme: hero worship. But this is the exception.

The typical citizen is quite cynical about politicians—at least, this is the case by the time he reaches voting age. Children, before they are fully politicized, are singularly lacking in this trait.[14] Although the adult feels himself competent to make rational judgments about complex political issues, he fears that the politician will take advantage of the naïveté and lack of knowledge of *other* citizens. He recognizes that politicians do successfully exploit anxieties (of others), and he often sees them as happy-go-lucky, gregarious, irresponsible persons who have no principles and will promise anything to anybody. But in fact, while some politicians no doubt fit the stereotype and are themselves cynical about the intelligence of those who elect them, most live according to the values that influence other citizens, and they are limited in their behavior accordingly.

The politician has low status in America. The very word is a term of opprobrium. Presidents, senators, and governors enjoy high prestige in their social roles as leaders of the state, but when they go out on the hustings to campaign, they are immediately reduced in status as they take up the politician's role.

"It's just politics," is a favorite American expression. The ordinary citizen probably does not understand the content of the term—it has been repeated for generations without much analysis—but in most cases it

[14] Fred I. Greenstein, "The Benevolent Leader: Children's Images of Political Authority," *American Political Science Review* 54:934–943, December, 1960.

probably means, "I don't understand it, but I'm suspicious of the motives of those involved."

The low esteem in which political figures are held is revealed in the following excerpt from a letter to the editor:[15]

> One foundry worker, or as far as that goes, any American worker, produces more real wealth in one hour than all the congressmen during an entire session, or any number of sessions. Both parties will agree that nothing of any social significance has been accomplished in Washington for years. But there is ample evidence all around us that the American worker has been on the job.
>
> When a congressman sits down to eat there is evidence before him that work has been done, even though the food is about to be wasted.

The lack of belief in the political process as the decision-making machinery that matters in American society was reflected in two kinds of responses to questions asked of a sample of voters during the 1952 campaign. At that time, 30 per cent of the respondents said that they cared little or not at all who won the Presidency, and no less than 72 per cent believed that it would make little or no difference to the country which of the candidates won.[16] Of course, in the latter case, the respondents may have been quite right, for policy in America is usually decided by the balancing off of the various effective interests before the decision-making persons or agencies of government, rather than by the election of a party that stands on a specific platform of proposed public policies (see Chapter 8).

In Summary: The Voter and Democracy. We should repeat here a central point made in Chapter 3: The empirical evidence on what the voter is actually like differs widely from what he is like in the ideal model based on the rational-man theory, but democracy nevertheless operates satisfactorily most of the time. Problems arise for decision makers because the typical voter has a short memory but persistent habits, and because he is usually apathetic, but sometimes mercurial, uninformed, ambivalent, emotional, ethnocentric, distrustful of power holders, and skeptical. But leaders in all types of governments have problems in their relations with ordinary citizens. Furthermore, in grave emergencies the American people have strongly tended to provide the support needed to sustain the highest law of government—the survival of the nation.

We might note, too, that we do not conclude that the voter *ought* to have the characteristics reported in studies, or that some of these characteristics cannot be changed through education. Our observation is that, despite the qualities of voters that deviate seriously from the ideal model, democracy still works.

[15] *The Minneapolis Tribune,* May 12, 1949.

[16] Campbell and others, *op. cit.,* pp. 36–38.

PERSONALITY AND POLITICS

No systematic approach to the relationship between personality and politics can or need be attempted in a book of this type, but a number of observations on their relationship might be made here. Thomas Hobbes in the seventeenth century and Harold Lasswell in the twentieth, both political scientists, have commented on the importance of politics as a device for the gratification of personal psychological needs. Both have agreed that man uses politics and the sanctions of government in order to gain—in Hobbes's terminology—safety, income, and deference. That is, man sees politics as a means by which to increase his personal safety as well as his economic and social standing. Politics may be used for personal psychological ends by (in the psychologist's definitions) both normal and abnormal persons. In the following discussion, we have in mind mildly and moderately neurotic personalities and particular manifestations of "normal" personalities much more than psychotic personalities.

The person who chooses to become active in politics seeks to achieve this triumvirate of goals—safety, income, and deference—through public office itself. Others see government as a supplemental means of achieving them. But government and politics may be more than this, or more accurately, the quest of these goals may take many forms. A few of them are particularly important in their implications for the functioning of our governmental system.

Tolerant and Authoritarian Personalities. Different personality types react differently to political stimuli. The following points seem especially important to the understanding of politics:

1. Leaders in democratic societies tend to have more tolerant personalities than do nonleaders, and this applies to political and nonpolitical leaders alike.[17] It is likely that persons with highly authoritarian personalities cannot succeed as leaders in American groups, except in the case of the extremists of the radical left and the ultraconservative and reactionary right. A leader must work with a variety of people of differing

[17] This section is based on research reported in Seymour Martin Lipset, *Political Man,* Doubleday & Company, Inc., Garden City, N.Y., 1960, chap. 4; Gabriel Almond, *The Appeals of Communism,* Princeton University Press, Princeton, N.J., 1954; Samuel Stouffer, *Communism, Conformity, and Civil Liberties,* Doubleday & Company, Inc., Garden City, N.Y., 1955; Herbert McClosky, "Conservatism and Personality," *American Political Science Review,* 52:27–45, March, 1958; James G. Martin and Frank R. Westie, "The Tolerant Personality," *American Sociological Review,* 24:521–528, September, 1959. See also Theodore Adorno and others, *The Authoritarian Personality,* Harper & Row, Publishers, New York, 1950. Some important questions about the classic Adorno study are raised in Angus Campbell and others, *The American Voter,* John Wiley & Sons, Inc., New York, 1960, pp. 512–515; and in Christie R. Jahoda and Marie Jahoda (eds.), *Studies in the Scope and Method of "the Authoritarian Personality,"* The Free Press of Glencoe, New York, 1954.

and conflicting views. He must have a personality that permits him to tolerate these differences and to respect the rights of individuals to them. The leader also must be able to tolerate the demands for change that come out of most groups in America, for these groups are often organized for "progress" toward goals they have established. Progress nearly always means change, and it often implies the need for compromise with those who will be affected unfavorably by that progress.

2. There are fewer authoritarian personalities* among the middle class than among the working class. This is probably related to differences in

---

***AUTHORITARIAN PERSONALITY.** A cluster of traits found in some persons. It includes a high degree of conformity, dependence upon authority, overcontrol of feelings and impulses, rigidity of thinking, ethnocentrism. David Krech, R. C. Crutchfield, and E. L. Ballachey, *Individual in Society,* McGraw-Hill Book Company, New York, 1962.

Figure 9-2

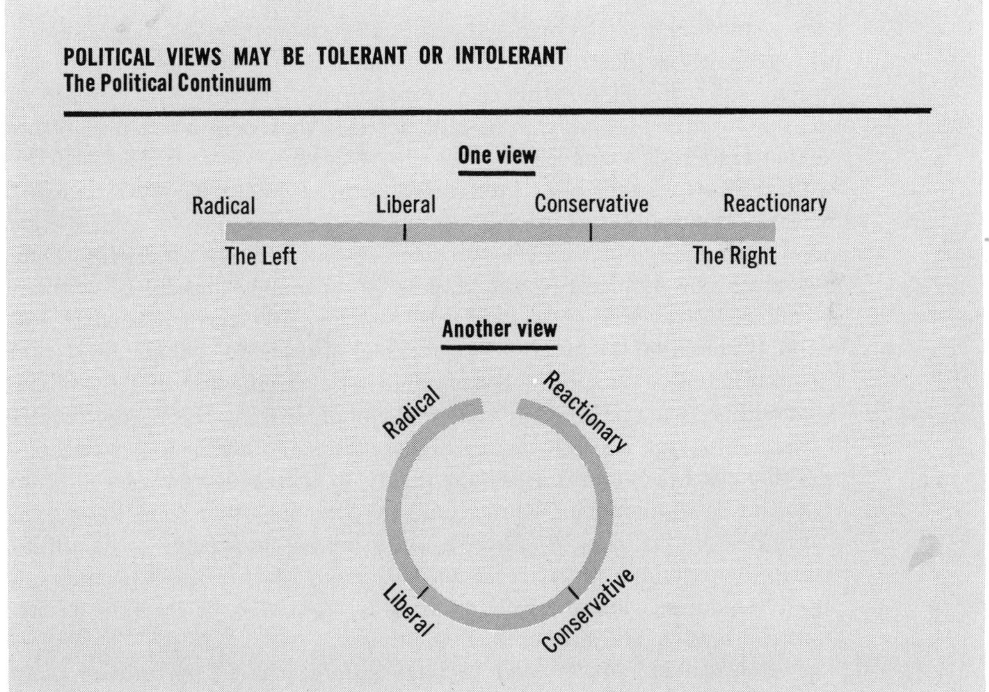

The extremists in politics tend to be authoritarians and sometimes jump from the far left to the far right or vice versa.

TABLE 9-2

PROPORTION OF MALE RESPONDENTS WHO ARE "MORE TOLERANT" WITH RESPECT TO CIVIL LIBERTIES ISSUES

Occupational category	Percentage
Professional and semiprofessional	66
Proprietors, managers, and officials	51
Clerical and sales workers	49
Manual workers	30
Farmers or farm workers	20

SOURCE: Samuel A. Stouffer, *Communism, Conformity and Civil Liberties,* Doubleday & Company, Inc., Garden City, N.Y., 1955, p. 139; Seymour Martin Lipset, *Political Man,* Doubleday & Company, Inc., Garden City, N.Y., 1960, p. 104.

child rearing, life-styles, and sense of security. The lower middle class—the white-collar workers and clerks who barely qualify as members of the class and are often determined to keep a distinction between themselves and working people—is also an insecure group, and personality development of members seems to follow more authoritarian lines. In general, the better education and the higher status in society one has, the more tolerant his personality is likely to be. (The self-made man is often an exception—he may enjoy the high status that comes from his wealth and position in life, but he may be highly intolerant of ideas that were not a part of his particular formula for success.)

Table 9-2 indicates that intolerance is most likely to prevail among farmers. They have traditionally emphasized conformity to conservative views. Urban manual workers also seem to be relatively intolerant. They and their parents have faced threats of economic insecurity without respite. A factory worker, at least until very recently, has not been able to permit his children the luxury of tolerance or of ideas that compete with and threaten his own. As a result, some studies have indicated that the somewhat authoritarian personality is normal among working-class people, while it is abnormal and neurotic among higher-status and higher-income people. Working-class people are especially likely to take a narrow view of civil rights, to be intolerant of ethnic and racial groups other than their own, and to be skeptical concerning the effectiveness of democracy or its ability to help the individual with his wants.[18] Seymour Martin Lipset has pointed out that persons who are isolated socially, spatially, or by type of job generally tend to be less tolerant than others.

3. Political extremists tend to have authoritarian personalities more commonly than moderate liberals or conservatives (see Table 9-3). Persons who feel highly insecure seek to overcome their insecurity by finding

[18] In addition to the above citations, support for this paragraph may be found in Arthur Kornhauser and others, *When Labor Votes,* University Books, Inc., New York, 1956, pp. 198–200.

TABLE 9-3
POLITICAL EXTREMISM AND AUTHORITARIAN VIEWS

Statement	Percentage agreeing with statement	
	Liberals	Extreme conservatives
Duties are more important than rights.	32	63
The world is too complicated to be understood by anyone but experts.	26	51
You can't change human nature.	30	73
People are getting soft and weak from so much coddling and babying.	31	68
The heart is as good a guide as the head.	22	58
We have to teach children that all men are created equal, but almost everyone knows that some are better than others.	35	73
No matter what the people think, a few people will always run things anyway.	33	63
Few people really know what is in their best interests in the long run.	43	77

NOTE: A comparison between extreme radicals and moderate conservatives would probably have produced similar results. The definition of "extreme conservative" was drawn from the characteristics of conservatives delineated by self-classified conservative writers, as interpreted by McClosky. For a criticism of this method, see Willmoore Kendall, "Comment on Herbert McClosky's 'Conservatism and Personality,'" *American Political Science Review,* 52: 506–510, June, 1958.

SOURCE: Herbert McClosky, "Conservatism and Personality," *American Political Science Review,* 52: 27–45, March, 1958.

a firm rock for a foundation.[19] Democracy is anxiety-producing in that it forces us to face up to decisions; it does not give us the One Grand Solution that would tell us in a trice what is right and what is wrong. It asks us to work out the answers for ourselves. Some types of personalities cannot bear the strain of such expectations; their possessors are hence tempted to look for political ideologies that provide them with instant ready-made answers to the political questions they ask. Communists and some of the more doctrinaire Socialists on the left, as well as fascist-like and other antidemocratic or nondemocratic groups on the right, have a special appeal to those who place certainty, predictability, and simplicity above personal responsibility and personal choice.

Anxiety and Politics. Like all psychological phenomena mentioned in this book, anxiety cannot be examined in any detail as to its effect upon

[19] Milton Rokeach, *The Open and Closed Mind,* Basic Books, Inc., Publishers, New York, 1960.

politics. But a few factors are of great importance and are mentioned here for that reason.[20]

Learning theorists point out that two different kinds of learning lead to different behavior patterns. In one case, a stimulus leads to behavior that helps to satisfy the felt need or want of the individual. Thus a Coca-Cola sign suggests the desire for a cold, energy-filled drink. The drink tends to satisfy the individual's feeling of thirst and hunger. A second drink is less interesting and desired, a third still less. Soon the individual wants no more—until he gets hungry and thirsty again. The reaction of lessening interest here is the one the economist talks of in discussing the law of diminishing marginal utility.*

***THE LAW OF DIMINISHING MARGINAL UTILITY. As the amount of a good that is used increases, the marginal utility of the good—the additional usefulness or satisfaction added by its last unit—decreases.**

In another kind of learning, the stimulus produces a response that does not diminish or satisfy the felt need or want. These nonsatisfying responses are, in the individual, neurotic in character and the product of anxieties, that is, of vague, unfocused fears. Whatever the source of the anxiety, it produces a compulsion toward some type of action. The action may have no effect upon the source of the anxiety, but it may create a habitual response. When the action does not make the person feel more secure, he repeats the act, and each failure may intensify both the anxiety and the next response. Thus the person with an anxiety neurosis may feel a need for social acceptance, but he does not overcome the anxiety, no matter how many prestigeful people accept his dinner invitations. Or if he fears communism, no number of espionage convictions will convince him the government service is free of spies.

A policy based on anxiety responses means that the addition of another hydrogen bomb or intercontinental missile to America's arsenal does not diminish our fear of Soviet power.[21] We cannot gauge whether such addition reduces the threat that we feel, and so there "appears to be no point at which the acquisition of more security is not worthwhile. For the object of the defense effort is not just a reasonable security level, but the avoidance of any possibility of defeat." This feeling of insecurity does not end even when we possess enough nuclear armament to destroy the entire population of the world.

Anxiety appears to be a reaction characteristic of group behavior in relation to government. Almost every group collectively feels that, no matter what governmental policies are adopted, it has not fully

[20] This section draws upon Frank A. Pinner, "Notes and Method in Social and Political Research," in Dwight Waldo (ed.), *The Research Function of University Bureaus and Institutes for Government-related Research,* University of California, Bureau of Public Administration, Berkeley, Calif., 1960.

[21] See *ibid.,* pp. 191–192.

achieved what it wants. It seeks more. The individual often feels the same. Even if his attitude is not caused by neurotic anxiety, he has difficulty seeing cause-and-effect relationships concerning governmental policy. So if he is concerned about Communist infiltration, or the political power of labor bosses, or monopoly control by big business, no amount of government activity, even of the kinds he specifically has called for, will convince him that he need no longer be concerned with the problem. He wants not merely to reduce the threat he perceives, he wants it totally eliminated and it is almost impossible for him ever to believe that it has been totally eliminated.

So we see that the political system is one in which groups demand action from government, but their demands are not satisfied even by policy decisions in accord with their demands; in addition, the anxieties of individuals are a basis for demands for governmental action, but even if the demanded action is forthcoming, the vague fears and concerns of the individual are not extinguished. Certain policies, it might be noted, may at least temporarily and sometimes permanently *diminish* anxieties and hence demands for action, but this is not likely to be the case—and these policies (so far as we know) cannot eliminate the anxieties and the demands they generate.

The Paranoid in Politics. Paranoia is a symptom, not a disease. It is associated with a variety of neuroses and psychoses, mild and serious. In general, it refers to systematic delusions involving feelings of persecution. The individual often suffers great mental anguish because of his belief that "everyone's against me." His behavior toward threatening stimuli, commonly father or authority figures, is often aggressive and hostile. In rare instances, especially in the extreme case of paranoid schizophrenia, the person may resort to violent action. The man accused of the assassination of President John F. Kennedy, for example, showed such behavior patterns.[22]

This particular psychological phenomenon is of importance in politics for a number of reasons, even if we discount the fact that much of the critical mail received by congressmen and the President has pronounced paranoid overtones and that these correspondents can be a considerable nuisance to the public official and his staff. In particular, paranoid attitudes make it impossible for the individual to reason as other people do. He has a set of "facts" and a method of logic all his own, and explanations of political phenomena that satisfy others therefore will not satisfy him. Furthermore, his paranoia may also involve neurotic anxieties, so that his complaints, fears, and demands cannot be sated, no matter what his public officials do about whatever it is that concerns him.

All kinds of people, institutions, or recurring events can be the focus of paranoid concern. Most of us are familiar with the fact that persons with serious mental illnesses often believe that "they want to kill me." The typical paranoid is, however, only a neurotic person who is quite capable

[22] See "Portrait of a Psychopath," *Newsweek,* Dec. 16, 1963, pp. 83–84.

of serving society usefully and living a reasonable approximation of a normal life. But in regard to certain kinds of things, he reacts in a special way. Let us look at a few implications of this for politics.

In cases of paranoia that are quite extreme, something like mass paranoia may be experienced. In Germany between the two world wars, the Jews were blamed—were made the scapegoats—for all kinds of difficulties that the nation was experiencing. The delusion that the Jews were at the root of every problem spread from a few paranoic rabble-rousers to so many people that the idea was almost converted into a piece of folklore—believed even by persons who did not suffer from paranoia. This development had cataclysmic political effects, as we know, resulting in the deaths of millions of persons.

Other views of politics are more common and less drastic in their effects; for example, the small-business man who thinks that government will not aid him because it is dominated by "labor bosses"; or the manual worker who attributes all of his troubles to the influence of big business in government; or the farmer who explains everything with "Wall Street runs the government."

The threat of communism to our way of life is the kind of anxiety-producing situation that is likely to trigger paranoic responses that lead, in turn, to a search for scapegoats and to the assumption that the threat must be overcome at all costs, including even the loss of individual freedoms and the tolerance of dissent. Paranoia in the case of the Communist threat—and it should be clear that the threat is very real, very great, and that there has been some Communist infiltration of American government in the past and no doubt continued efforts at infiltration today—centers on blaming the Communists for every problem and expecting to find Communists or Communist sympathizers in almost any governmental post. Some people, for example, have opposed the addition of cavity-decreasing fluorides to public water supplies on the suspicion that it might be a Communist plot to poison the people. Some have accused liberals and even conservatives of being Communist dupes because, in their positions of responsibility, they have not succeeded in reducing the anxieties concerning the threat of communism. (Note that it was pointed out above that rational, serious efforts to overcome a genuine threat, even when they are highly successful, are not likely to reduce the level of the anxieties that exist.) Sometimes it is said, in effect, "Of course, he doesn't *act* or *look* like a Communist or a Fronter, but that's just part of the scheme!" which is a classic paranoid reaction when the observable conditions do not appear to fit the suspicions.

Those minorities who believe that an enemy is hiding behind every door and appearing in every disarming disguise are especially important politically because the strategies they would like to use to fight the enemy are certain to be rejected, and this will create in them enormous frustrations. Furthermore, because their behavior is neurotic and largely irrational, governmental policies will not satisfy them, no matter what the policies or who the policy makers are. And because their beliefs very powerfully possess their minds, they are likely to react more violently and more bitterly than other citizens when they are faced with political frustration.

Alienation and Anomie. In a day of large, impersonal social organizations, many people feel that they have lost the ability to control their environment. This is especially significant because of America's traditional ideological emphasis upon man's ability to do exactly that. At the same time, people may also have the feeling that they cannot understand the value system on which the political apparatus is built and political decisions are made. The former is referred to by the term "alienation," the latter by "anomie." The two are related and may exist in addition to the problems of personality discussed in the three preceding sections.

In the case of alienation, the individual is likely to believe that he is not a part of the political process.[23]

> The politically alienated believe that their vote makes no difference. This belief arises from the feeling that political decisions are made by a group of political insiders who are not responsive to the average citizen—the political outsiders. Political alienation may be expressed in feelings of political powerlessness, meaninglessness, estrangement from political activity, and normlessness.

The individual, in other words, may feel that he cannot affect political decisions; that government is not controlled by the voters, but rather by a handful of powerful persons; that his vote will not make any difference in the way government is operated and that one candidate is about the same as another; that there are no ethics in the political arena; and that he receives no gratification of his sense of civic duty or of the fulfilment of the dream of democracy by participating in the political process.

As to the effect of feelings of alienation upon the American political process, studies tend to indicate that they are most pronounced among lower-income, lesser-educated, older, and minority peoples.[24] Feelings of alienation are likely to be increased by the growing sense of the impersonalness of life in a day of big business, big labor, and big government and by the increasing complexity of government, with its many functions. But we may also note that Americans have always griped about politics and spoken cynically of politicians. They no doubt tend to do so when they are interviewed about an election—it is simply American custom.

Anomie, the feeling of rootlessness because the values of contemporary society are not understood or because there appear to be none, is another result of a complex society. In medieval times, persons knew little of the world beyond their own manor or town. Aside from the nobility and their entourages, few went abroad. In any case, the life-style and the deep belief

[23] Murray B. Levin, *The Alienated Voter,* Holt, Rinehart and Winston, Inc., New York, 1960, chap. 4. Quotation from pp. 61–62.

[24] *Ibid.* Also see Wayne E. Thompson and John E. Horton, "Political Alienation as a Force in Political Action," *Social Forces,* 38:190–195, March, 1960; and Kornhauser and others, *op. cit.*

in religion and its threats and promises scarcely differed from one place to another in Europe. And life changed little from one generation to the next. It was easy for people to know how they stood in relation to one another and to distinguish right from wrong; a pervasive consensus shrouded European man. But such is not the case today in either Europe or the United States. Dozens of belief systems are alive in America. There are dozens of subcultures and religions, all of them less a center of life than they once were. What one man regards as proper action, another believes to be wrong, and a third says, "I wouldn't do that, but let each man lead his own life."

So without the solid rock of a stable society, many are left with a sense of anomie, which is "associated in persons with an anxiety characterized by feelings of isolation and pointlessness and in communities with the breakdown or absence of common values or beliefs."[25]

It is possible that an absence of shared beliefs will produce serious social problems because of a lack of confidence in the holders of public office, but we do not know how important this threat is in America. Undoubtedly, anomie is related to any lack of a sense of national purpose; it may be either a cause or effect (or both) of our tendency to think of public policy in the narrow terms of our own interests as we see them, rather than in terms of what is desirable as an overall policy. The latter is possible only when a pervasive consensus exists.

In Summary. Political problems are not typically the result of personality abnormalities, and the layman cannot easily become a do-it-yourself psychologist, analyzing the personality maladjustments of politicians and voters. It would be easy to reach conclusions that are entirely erroneous if we sought to do so. But we know that personality does have an influence on politics. We can understand the behavior of both politicians and those whose support they seek if we understand, for example, that anxieties are not wiped out by the simple passage of a law, that authoritarian personalities want simple, direct action and are little interested in dispassionate analysis of the available facts, and that the paranoid may be both unreasonable and unrealistic in his demands upon officeholders.

THE VOTER HAS HIS REASONS

The model of democracy as it developed in the seventeenth and eighteenth centuries was described in Chapter 3. This ideal model has become a part of the folklore of democracy, so that politicians commonly act *as if* it fitted reality, and newspapermen despair in their editorial columns about the "uninformed" electorate or the nonvoting habits of Americans ("Ameri-

[25] Sebastian de Grazia, *The Political Community: A Study of Anomie,* The University of Chicago Press, Chicago, 1948, p. 6. De Grazia draws upon information from psychology and psychiatry, for the most part, in developing the concept far beyond what is noted here.

TABLE 9-4
RELATION OF DEGREE OF INTEREST IN CAMPAIGN TO VOTING TURNOUT, 1956 (In per cent)

Voting behavior	Degree of interest		
	Not much	Somewhat	Very much
Voted	58	72	87
Did not vote	42	28	13

SOURCE: Adapted from Angus Campbell and others, *The American Voter,* John Wiley & Sons, Inc., New York, 1960, table 5-4.

cans in frightening numbers fell down on the job last Tuesday"). Superficially, a case can be made in support of the alarmed editorials. In one sample survey, 34 per cent of those interviewed, choosing from among offered alternatives, thought the Electoral College was "a special school for congressmen's children," and in some congressional elections only one-third of the eligible voters go to the polls.

Instead of assuming that voters cast their ballots on the basis of a rational and dispassionate evaluation of the issues and the candidates' positions, or that voting is always better than nonvoting, we might examine the empirical evidence available. What do we know about why people vote—or do not vote?

Why a Citizen Votes. A summary of research on voter motivation indicates that the following are the primary indicators of whether or not a particular citizen is likely to vote.[26] He will be likely to vote:

1. *If he believes his interests are strongly affected by governmental policy.* In other words, he tends to vote if he believes he has a personal economic, social, or ideological interest in the election (see Table 9-4). Farmers, for example, know that they have a stake in price-support policies. This gives them a strong motive for being interested in an election. Forty-one per cent of the eligible women, who are generally less interested in politics than men, failed to vote in the 1948 election. But that was a time of peace and prosperity. Four years later, the threats presented to them and to the very lives of their husbands and sons by the Korean conflict brought them out in much larger numbers, though 31 per cent did not vote even then. (Women supported Eisenhower in a significantly larger proportion than did men.)

2. *If he understands the relationship of the election to his own interests.* A person may be profoundly affected by government policies, but if he does not recognize that his personal interest is at stake, they do not exist for him, and he may be blithely apathetic. In general, therefore, the better

[26] Seymour Martin Lipset and others, "The Psychology of Voting: An Analysis of Political Behavior," in Gardner Lindzey (ed.), *Handbook of Social Psychology,* Addison-Wesley Publishing Company, Inc., Reading, Mass., 1954.

informed and educated a person is, the more likely he is to vote. Alternatively, a dramatic event, such as the Thalidomide scandal (see Chapter 8), by expanding the arena of the concerned, may temporarily increase the number of politically interested persons. But people frequently do not perceive their interests, not even their most narrow and personal interests, and they habitually discount the future very heavily; if the threat to their interests is not immediate, it may not be regarded as a threat at all. The editor of the *New York Times* Sunday magazine has noted that "the euphoria that numbs the voters to reality obscures the fact that probably the number one problem of the time is American public opinion."[27] If only 30 per cent of the potential voters can identify the major foreign policy issues of the moment, and only 20 per cent can be classified as "reasonably well informed"—as the polls show—it is clear that people will not necessarily recognize a matter that affects their future when confronted with it.

3. *If he is subjected to social pressure to vote.* Upper-middle-class persons are more likely to be expected to vote by peer groups than are working-class members. A small-town dweller whose daily activities are highly visible is more likely to be subjected to social pressure to vote than an apartment dweller, who is shielded by the relative anonymity of the large city. Some parents teach their children that voting is a social obligation, others make no such effort. A few religious groups are opposed on principle to voting.

These pressures are subject to change, however, as are all aspects of the political process. When Negroes thought—as they did for generations—that political action for them was futile, political instruction was not a part of child rearing in their homes. But it may become an important part—as it long has been in many Irish-American homes—as this access to economic and social advancement becomes increasingly important to Negroes.

4. *If he is not subjected to cross pressures.* If the various factors listed above do not tug the citizen in opposing directions, he is more likely to vote than if they do. If one of his interests (say, his religion, which may be the same as that of a major candidate) conflicts with another (say, his business, which he believes would be most helped by a different candidate), he may not vote at all. Similarly, what he reads in his union newspaper may conflict so forcefully with what he reads in his daily newspaper that he may give up any attempt to understand and so not vote. He may have grown up in a family of Democrats but is now surrounded by Republican neighbors. Or he and his wife may not be able to agree, which tends to disrupt the political convictions of both.[28] The conflicts that he feels may be so great that he cannot bring himself to vote for candidates of either major party.

[27] Lester Markel, "What We Don't Know *Will* Hurt Us," *The New York Times Magazine,* Apr. 9, 1961.

[28] William A. Glaser, "The Family and Voting Turnout," *Public Opinion Quarterly,* 23:563–569, Winter, 1959.

Four categories do not exhaust the factors that may possibly be relevant to voting, of course. Social scientists have collected a great many voting statistics and taken many sample surveys, but much remains uninvestigated. For example, to the above should probably be added personality and fortuitous factors. Almost any inconvenience will discourage the marginally motivated: complex voting laws or machines, a rainstorm, a long ballot, or a waiting line at the polling booth. A person with pronounced aggressive paranoid tendencies is likely to be strongly motivated to vote, even though his desire to do so may be confounded by his dissatisfaction with all candidates. A person may also be discouraged by a fear of the consequences of political activity or by the belief that voting is futile and will not affect the election.[29] It is possible that a person who, as a child, had all of his decisions made for him by a parent will tend to be more apathetic about voting than persons with different experiences, other things being equal.[30] But the points already made are sufficient to indicate that people make decisions about voting (and other political participation) much as they do about other things that affect them: they use *their own perceptions* of reality as a frame of reference and then decide whether voting is worthwhile as a means of achieving or protecting desired goals.[31]

Who Fits the Voting Categories? Looking at the above analysis from a different perspective we may ask: What kinds of people are most likely to fit into the above categories? Here are some examples:[32]

1. Women seem to feel less social pressure to vote and perhaps see fewer interests at stake in elections than do men. This has been so since women were given the vote nationally after World War I (1920). Most women continue to allow leadership in political orientation to come from men, although the right of the man of the house to make the family political decisions varies somewhat by issue.[33] Collectively, women are less well informed about politics than men; they are more suspicious of organized politics; they are more interested in the personal qualities of a candidate than in his program; they are more parochial in their views and give less support to international involvements in particular; and they tend to be more conservative than men.[34] There are probably good reasons

[29] Morris Rosenberg, "Some Determinants of Political Apathy," *Public Opinion Quarterly,* 18:349–366, Winter, 1954–1955.

[30] Lewis A. Froman, Jr., "Learning Political Attitudes," *Western Political Quarterly,* 15:304–313, June, 1962.

[31] Concerning the way we react to social phenomena, using as a basis our *image* of the phenomena, see Kenneth E. Boulding, *The Image,* The University of Michigan Press, Ann Arbor, Mich., 1961.

[32] Data chiefly from Campbell and others, *The Voter Decides;* Campbell and others, *The American Voter.*

[33] See, for example, James G. March, "Husband-Wife Interaction over Political Issues," *Public Opinion Quarterly,* 17:461–470, Winter, 1953–1954.

[34] Philip K. Hastings, "Hows and Howevers of the Woman Voter," *The New York Times Magazine,* June 12, 1960.

why all this is so. As the guardians of society's morals, for example, women are likely to be concerned about the personality and behavior of a candidate (and perhaps whether he has the qualities one would like in a father or a son-in-law). A good-looking candidate under fifty, who has a "nice family" and all of the outward appearances of respectability makes more impression than one who, lacking these qualities, offers a fuller dinner pail. Similarly, the suspicions many women have about international involvements probably reflect their concern with the threat of war and their dislike of aggressive behavior, as well as the practical concerns of providing for the family rather than seeking to save the world.

Women generally seem to fear personal involvement in politics. They are suspicious of party leaders and, even more than men, think highly of the congressman who "thinks for himself" instead of hewing the party line (when there is one). They think of politics as "dirty" even more than men do and fear social disapproval if they were to become directly involved.[35]

The difference in political behavior between women and men is likely to continue indefinitely because the political attitudes of women seem to be related to the fact that their social roles are different from those of men. The training of a female child is different from that of a male, and as early as the fourth grade there are measurable differences between boys and girls in their political knowledge and points of view.[36]

2. The more income an individual has, the more he is likely to vote. In 1952, only 53 per cent of those earning less than $2,000 a year voted; of those earning over $5,000 a year, 88 per cent voted.

3. Professional and executive personnel are more likely to vote than white-collar clerks; in turn, white-collar clerks are more likely to vote than unskilled manual workers (see Table 9-5).

4. Older people are more likely to vote than younger people. A person in his early sixties is more likely to vote than people in other age groups; 82 per cent did so in 1952 and 1956. Only 53 per cent of the persons in their early twenties voted in those elections. Again, this is probably a function of perceived interests. Young people presumably have not yet become as aware of the interests that affect them as they will be later. And perhaps, as an individual grows older, he becomes more concerned about security and the preservation of what he possesses. Shortly after the age of sixty, voter participation declines again, largely because of the infirmities of old age.

5. Conservatives are more likely to vote than liberals. Perhaps this is because higher-income persons and those with more education—people in high-participation categories—also tend to be conservative. Republicans are also more likely to vote than Democrats, in part because these same

[35] Hilda Cole Espy, "Why Are Women Afraid of Politics?" *Woman's Day,* November, 1959, pp. 38ff. A summary of empirical data is given here.

[36] Fred I. Greenstein, "Sex-related Political Differences in Childhood," *Journal of Politics,* 23:353–371, May, 1961.

persons are likely to be Republicans. In 1952, 8 per cent of the "strong Republicans" failed to vote; the figure for "strong Democrats" was 24 per cent.

Not all categories can be easily identified as to voting habits. Some studies show small-town dwellers and farmers as voting in greater percentages than urbanites, others do not. Negroes vote in much smaller percentages than whites, but this is partly the result of disfranchisement in much of the South. The lack of a tradition of political activity among Negroes and their generally disadvantaged status in terms of education and income add to their tendency not to vote, however. Yet in some metropolitan areas, Negro turnout is higher than that of whites of equal income and job status.

The Voter's Guides. What has been said so far in this chapter might seem to indicate that the typical voter has no guidelines upon which to act. Such is not the case. He does have considerable information that he can take into

TABLE 9-5

NONVOTING IN THE UNITED STATES (From among total eligible)

Population category	Percentage not voting	
	1948	1952
Men	31	21
Women	41	31
Whites		21
Negroes		67
In metropolitan areas	17	21
In towns and cities (other than metropolitan areas)	37	27
In rural areas	59*	32*
Professional and managerial persons	25	12
Other white-collar workers	19	19
Skilled and semiskilled workers	29	26
Unskilled workers	50	40
Farmers	58	33
Foreign-born American citizens (white only)		19
Second-generation citizens (white only)		14
Third-generation citizens (white only)		16
Fourth-generation or more citizens (white only)		29†
Total	49	38

* This category is probably skewed by the disproportionate representation of rural population in the South where there are many low-participation categories. Other studies show higher participation in rural than in urban areas.

† This figure would appear to fall outside the general pattern. Assuming the sample was valid, the higher percentage here may result from the fact that many white Southerners and hill folk, who fit into low-participation categories, are largely centered in this group.

SOURCE: Angus Campbell and others, *The Voter Decides*, Harper & Row, Publishers, New York, 1954.

Figure 9-3

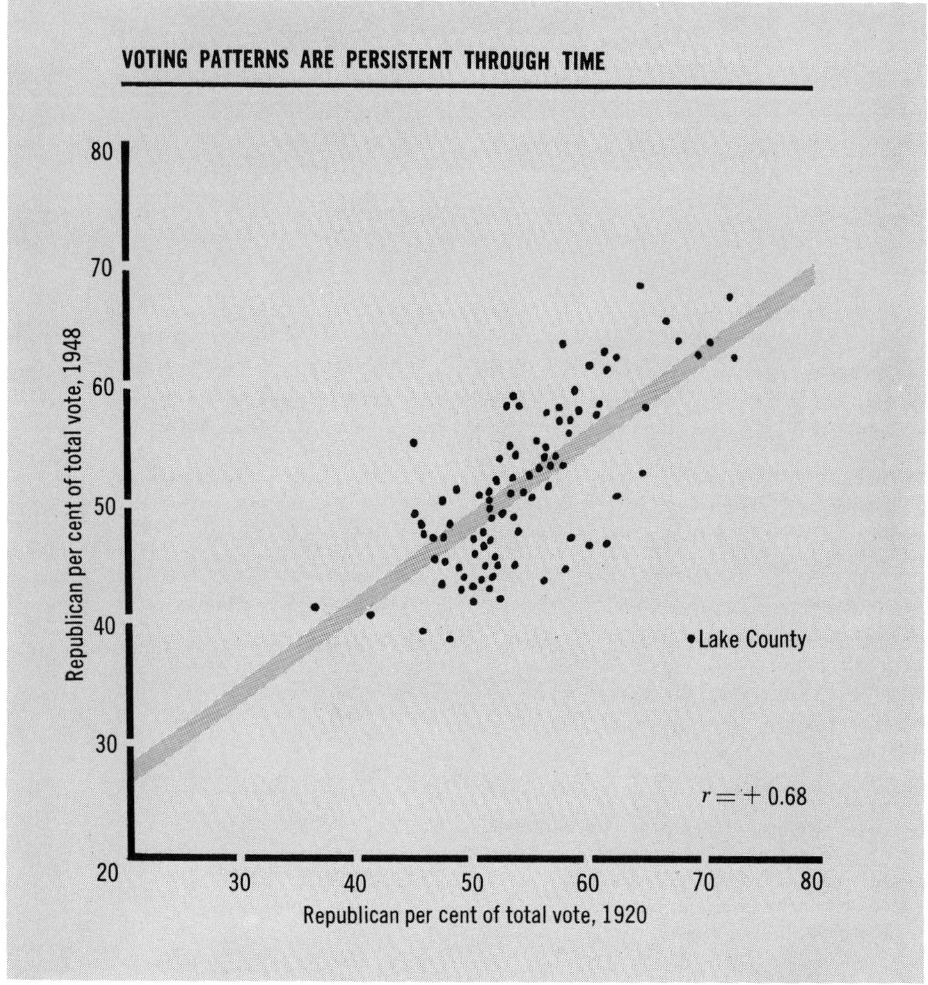

This scattergram shows dispersion around a trend line; the trend line, in turn, shows the typical relationship between 1920 and 1948 Republican voting in Indiana by counties. The farther from the line, the less typical the change in the county. In the twenty-eight-year period, Republican voting strength declined by one-third, on the average, in the typical county; but in Lake County (Gary), it declined from 69 per cent to 38 per cent. [V. O. Key, Jr., and Frank Munger, "Social Determinism and Electoral Decision: The Case of Indiana," in Eugene Burdick and Arthur J. Brodbeck (eds.), American Voting Behavior, *The Free Press of Glencoe, New York, 1958, fig. 15-2.]*

TABLE 9-6

EXTENT OF FAMILY SHARING OF POLITICAL VIEWS, USING SIMPLE CORRELATIONS

Attitude object	Mothers vs. fathers	Mothers vs. children	Fathers vs. children
	*r**	*r**	*r**
Capital punishment	.63	.57	.43
Labor unions	.84	.74	.47
Social security	.70	.71	.51
Unemployment compensation	.69	.58	.74
New Deal†	.95	.70	.57
Farm subsidies†	.75	.57	.55
Old-age assistance†	.54	.46	.08

* The *r* (rho) symbolizes the Pearsonian coefficient of correlation. Correlation is a statistical measure of relationship between two or more variables. The closeness of relationship (in this case, the amount of agreement on political views) increases as the positive number approaches 1.00 and declines as it approaches zero. The former expresses complete agreement, the latter no pattern of relationship, while −1.00 represents total disagreement. Much general information about attitudes and family relationships, and by generations can be gained from a study of this table.

† Using data from 1934–1935.

SOURCE: Based on H. H. Remmers, "Early Socialization of Attitudes," in Eugene Burdick and Arthur J. Brodbeck (eds.), *American Voting Behavior,* The Free Press of Glencoe, New York, 1959, table 2.2.

account. In particular, he has personal experiences, habits, and personal contacts or reference groups to guide him.

The voter early learns his family's general point of view, if it has one, on major issues of the era, and its party affiliation, if any. He is likely either to accept these as basic guidelines or to rebel against them deliberately if he is resentful of parental control. A man who could not identify the party affiliation of Theodore Roosevelt or the approximate period in history when he was President may have a clear recollection of the party allegiance of his mother and father, and their salient life experiences, such as their accounts of the years of the Great Depression. The teachings of one or both parents are often important guides to the voter (see Table 9-6). Although children, whose life experiences differ from those of their parents, may reject parental teachings, as many young people did during the early years of the New Deal, they are more likely to agree with their parents than with friends.[37]

In addition, each individual has a wealth of personal experiences. He

[37] Eleanor E. Maccoby and others, "Youth and Political Change," *Public Opinion Quarterly,* 18:23–39, Winter, 1954–1955; Herbert McClosky and Harold E. Dahlgren, "Primary Group Influence on Party Loyalty," *American Political Science Review,* 53:757–776, September, 1959.

may make a rough correlation between them and political activities. He does not need to rely entirely on the vague promises of politicians. To some degree, at least, he knows of specific kinds of governmental programs or policies that seem to have aided or injured his interests. He may be right or wrong in attributing causes, but he is likely to have some basis for using this relationship in making decisions on voting. He also has his own general feeling of well-being or dissatisfaction.

The voter is ordinarily a member of or able to identify with a number of organizations, and he can take his political cues from these reference groups, or from individuals he respects. He may not know the name of the congressman from his district, how he voted on issues, or his party affiliation; but if he is at all interested in the election, he is likely to know which candidate or party his union shop steward or business association secretary is supporting. This information, in itself, may be all he feels he needs to know in order to vote his own interests. Views expressed by such leaders are an important part of the political process, for the cues from trusted interest-group spokesmen are often a substitute for class or even party leadership to Americans. One study of voting found that a number of persons on every level of society, because of their role or as the result of personal motivation, become opinion leaders in politics. Just as women take fashion cues from women who are seen as style leaders, opinion leaders give political cues to other citizens.[38]

In addition, interest-group leaders who are highly visible even to the casually interested may provide the necessary cues for the assumption of a stand on a public issue. When Martin Luther King announces his position on a civil rights measure pending in Congress, both integrationists and segregationists are helped to decide how they stand on the matter. Similarly, although few people have any accurate knowledge of the contents of the Taft-Hartley Act, if Walter Reuther takes a public position on a proposed amendment to it, large numbers of people can instantly make up their minds on their own position and how their own interests would be affected by the proposed change.

Finally, habit is the most important influence of all on voter decisions. In many, perhaps most elections, the individual need only decide whether he is going to continue to support the party or candidate he has been supporting or whether he is going to cast a protest vote. Unless he is consciously dissatisfied, he may almost automatically cast his vote in terms of his allegiances.

The Vote as Safety Valve. We have seen that people tend to vote in the way and to the degree that they perceive particular interests affecting themselves. The result of this, together with perhaps less social pressure than exists in some countries, is that Americans vote in much smaller numbers than do the citizens of other democracies. Is this a sign that democracy is

[38] Paul F. Lazarsfeld and others, *The People's Choice: How the Voter Makes Up His Mind,* 2d ed., Columbia University Press, New York, 1948.

TABLE 9-7

RELATION OF SENSE OF CITIZEN DUTY TO VOTING TURNOUT, 1956 (In per cent)

Voter turnout	Sense of citizen duty				
	Low				High
Voted	13	42	52	74	85
Did not vote	87	58	48	26	15

SOURCE: Adapted from Angus Campbell and others, *The American Voter,* John Wiley & Sons, Inc., New York, 1960, table 5-7.

ill or failing in this country? Quite likely not. The person who stays away from the polls "tends to be a person of lower involvement, whose emotional investment in politics and its partisan decisions is on the average much less than that of the voter."[39] People thus stay away from the polls deliberately. They are not interested and they feel that voting in the particular instance will avail them nothing (see Table 9-7).

Should we then be alarmed, as editors often are, when we note that a 60 per cent turnout of the eligible voters is very high for a presidential election? Or that voting is still lower for congressional and statewide offices? And still lower, in the typical case, in local elections? Many political scientists answer in the negative, citing the "safety-valve" theory. The theory holds that:[40]

> Participation in elections varies generally with the anxiety level of the voters. A moderate turnout . . . or for that matter a poor one, indicates a fairly satisfied electorate, one that either sees no important controversy as existing, or that does not think the election will contribute to the settlement of existing controversy. A very large turnout, however, might indicate serious anxieties among voters, and a feeling of desperation. Far from being a healthy sign, such a situation might be one ripe for a demagogue or for hasty and possibly imprudent action.

The important question is not whether people *do* vote, but whether they *may* vote if they choose. There are still some significant barriers to voting in the United States. For example, although the Negro is gaining access to the polls in the South, he is still systematically excluded in many sections, especially in rural areas (see Chapter 19). A few non-Southern states continue to require a literacy test (a barrier originally designed to inhibit big-city machines in their use of immigrant support), and a handful of states restrict certain bond-issue questions to property owners. A major inhibition to voting, and one often unrecognized, is the complexity of registration and voting procedures. Any restrictive conditions on access to

[39] Campbell and others, *The American Voter,* p. 111.

[40] Charles R. Adrian, *Social Science and Community Action,* Michigan State University, Institute for Community Development, East Lansing, Mich., 1960, p. 1.

the polls, such as registration requirements (which are designed to provide honesty in elections and ensure that no one votes more than once) will tend to some degree to discourage voting, and they will disproportionately discourage those in the low-participation categories discussed above. Similarly, complex voting procedures, such as the long ballot and voting machines, discourage participation. The voting machine, which provides efficiency in the tabulation of the vote, is a confusing and even frightening device to many voters. A Michigan study indicated that a 1958 referendum question on holding a state constitutional convention would probably have passed if voting machines had not been concentrated almost exclusively in urban areas, which were the centers of support for the proposal. An examination of one county indicated that:[41]

> The level of participation among machine precincts in the county was highest in Ann Arbor's third precinct of the second ward, where 88.4 per cent of the voters participated in the referendum. This precinct includes much of the most expensive residential housing in the city. At the lower end of the participation scale in Ann Arbor was the second precinct of the first ward, which has a predominantly Negro population with much sub-standard housing and low income and educational levels.

When an issue that the citizen considers important arises, he will go to the polls if he is eligible. Typically, the marginal voter—one whose interests are slight, and who does not participate regularly—will go to the polls to *protest;* and he will usually do this when a crisis can be conceived of in terms of human interest and personal involvement.

There is, of course, one important concern that must be borne in mind when we say that the "shoe-pinches" approach to voting seems to permit a functional democracy. That is the problem of the frequent inability of the voter to perceive his interests, to understand the many complex events going on about him, and his unwillingness to give very serious consideration to emerging problems and to the future generally. Democracy is a special kind of government with which mankind has had little experience. It has had some close calls—Winston Churchill's warnings to the British people in the late 1930s barely set the stage in time for saving British democracy. He was listened to with only half an ear; it was nearly, but not quite, too late when he finally was permitted to lead. Yet democracy, whether through its inherent character or through luck, has survived many crises.

A Closing Note. The problems of democracy can be overcome—and in the past have been overcome—by the assumption of responsible leadership by public officeholders and by keeping open the information channels that permit our leaders, in and out of office, to warn the public of what may be

[41] John P. White, *Voting Machines and the 1958 Defeat of Constitutional Revision in Michigan,* University of Michigan, Institute of Public Administration, Ann Arbor, Mich., 1960, p. 30.

headed its way. Modern democracy, after all, does not ask the public to rule, but only to choose its rulers.

There are some exceptions, of course. In an effort to achieve the literal democracy—government by the people—of primitive societies and of the New England town, reformers of a few generations ago urged the use of the initiative and referendum, both of which permit the voters to decide directly on issues of public policy. Although they were widely adopted at the state and local levels and are especially important at the local levels, neither is used in connection with national-government questions. And at all levels, ours is essentially a representative democracy that does not ask as much of the people as does direct democracy. But what it does ask is quite a bit when considered in the context of the many other matters that compete for the attention and evaluation of the citizen.

SELECTED BIBLIOGRAPHY

The citizen's concept of politics and the ways in which his attitudes can be manipulated have been of interest to students of politics since ancient times. Aristotle, Machiavelli, and Hobbes were all concerned with the actual, more than the ideal, citizen. Wallas [45] offered a pioneer study (1909) showing the fallacy of traditional belief in the voter as a rational man. Mencken [34], a famous American journalist of the 1920s, discussed the same subject, as did Lippmann [27, 28].

The *Public Opinion Quarterly,* published since 1937, is a journal specializing in voter attitudes. The Survey Research Center has reported on the views of a sample of the electorate in each presidential election since 1948 [6, 7, 8]. Berelson [4] and Lazarsfeld [25] were pioneers—but not political scientists, incidentally—in seeking to learn how the voter makes up his mind. Lane [22] and McPhee and Glaser [32] have examined the same subject, while Rogers [35] has criticized the pollsters for seemingly implying that the voters' opinions *ought* to be accepted and used as the basis for policy. Key [20], a leading figure in political science in the postwar period, has effectively placed public opinion in its political context, and Lane [23] provides a convenient summary of why people get involved in politics.

Personality, as it relates to politics, has been studied a great deal since about 1945. Rigid and authoritarian personalities have been of special interest [1, 11], as were hostility [38] and anxiety [10, 44]. Many have written on the general subject of personality [16, 18, 19, 42, 43]. Alienation and anomie have also been accepted as important concepts [12, 15, 26]. Psychological components of voter attitudes have been further developed by Dorsey [14], who discusses the psychological need for the individual in a democracy to identify with his government, and by Lasswell [24], a pioneer in relating psychological theory to politics.

Political behavior cannot be completely explained by psychological factors, as Miller [33] and the Survey Research Center data have shown. And some political scientists, using such data as those of Scammon [39], have been content to describe voting aggregates without seeking to explain their causes. Others have concentrated on impressionistic interpretation of the data, as has the journalist Lubell [29, 30].

Voters do not all react in the same way. Gallup and other pollsters, therefore, often report findings according to regions of the country or by religion. Working-class people have special characteristics [21], as do Jews who, incidentally, support liberals and Democrats more consistently than do members of any other group [17].

1. Ainsworth, L.: "Rigidity, Stress, and Acculturation," *Journal of Social Psychology,* 49:131–136, May, 1959.
2. Almond, Gabriel A.: *The American People and Foreign Policy,* Harcourt, Brace & World, Inc., New York, 1950.
3. Bain, Henry M., and Donald S. Hecock: *Ballot Position and Voter's Choice,* Wayne State University Press, Detroit, Mich., 1960.
4. Berelson, Bernard R., and others: *Voting: A Study of Opinion Formation in a Presidential Campaign,* The University of Chicago Press, Chicago, 1954.
5. Burdick, Eugene, and Arthur J. Brodbeck (eds.): *American Voting Behavior,* The Free Press of Glencoe, New York, 1958.
6. Campbell, Angus, and others: *The American Voter,* John Wiley & Sons, Inc., New York, 1960.
7. Campbell, Angus and R. L. Kahn: *The People Elect a President,* University of Michigan, Survey Research Center, Ann Arbor, Mich., 1952.
8. Campbell, Angus, and others: *The Voter Decides,* Harper & Row, Publishers, New York, 1954.
9. Cantril, Hadley: *Human Nature and Political Systems,* Rutgers University Press, New Brunswick, N.J., 1961.
10. Chodorkoff, Bernard: "Anxiety, Threat, and Defensive Reactions," *Journal of General Psychology,* 54:191–196, April, 1956.
11. Christie, Richard and Peggy Cook: "A Guide to Published Literature Relating to the Authoritarian Personality," *Journal of Psychology,* 45:171–199, April, 1958.
12. De Grazia, Sebastian: *The Political Community: A Study of Anomie,* The University of Chicago Press, Chicago, 1948.
13. Dewey, John: *The Public and Its Problems,* Henry Holt and Company, Inc., New York, 1927.
14. Dorsey, John M.: "A Psychoanalytic Appreciation of American Government," *The American IMAGO,* 18:207–233, Fall, 1961.
15. Farris, Charles D.: "Selected Attitudes on Foreign Affairs as Correlates of Authoritarianism and Political Anomie," *The Journal of Politics,* 22:50–67, February, 1960.
16. Froman, Lewis A., Jr.: "Personality and Political Socialization," *Journal of Politics,* 23:341–352, May, 1961.
17. Fuchs, Lawrence H.: *The Political Behavior of American Jews,* The Free Press of Glencoe, New York, 1956.
18. Hennessy, Bernard: "Politicals and Apoliticals: Some Measurements of Personality Traits," *Midwest Journal of Political Science,* 3:336–355, November, 1959.
19. Hoffer, Eric: *The True Believer,* New American Library of World Literature, Inc., New York, 1961.
20. Key, V. O., Jr.: *Public Opinion and American Democracy,* Alfred A. Knopf, Inc., New York, 1961.
21. Kornhauser, Arthur, and others: *When Labor Votes,* University Books, Inc., New York, 1956.
22. Lane, Robert E.: *Political Ideology,* The Free Press of Glencoe, New York, 1962.
23. Lane, Robert E.: *Political Life,* The Free Press of Glencoe, New York, 1959.
24. Lasswell, Harold D., and Abraham Kaplan: *Power and Society: A Framework for Political Inquiry,* Yale University Press, New Haven, Conn., 1950.

25. Lazarsfeld, Paul F., and others: *The People's Choice: How the Voter Makes Up His Mind,* 2d ed., Columbia University Press, New York, 1948.
26. Levin, Murray B.: *The Alienated Voter,* Holt, Rinehart and Winston, Inc., New York, 1960.
27. Lippmann, Walter: *The Public Philosophy,* New American Library of World Literature, Inc., New York, 1961 (paperback).
28. Lippmann, Walter: *Public Opinion,* The Macmillan Company, New York, 1922.
29. Lubell, Samuel: *The Future of American Politics,* Anchor Books, Doubleday & Company, Inc., Garden City, N.Y., 1960.
30. Lubell, Samuel: *Revolt of the Moderates,* Harper & Row, Publishers, New York, 1956.
31. McClosky, Herbert, and Harold E. Dahlgren: "Primary Group Influence on Party Loyalty," *American Political Science Review,* 53:757–776, September, 1959.
32. McPhee, William N., and William A. Glaser (eds.): *Public Opinion and Congressional Elections,* The Free Press of Glencoe, New York, 1962.
33. Miller, Warren E.: "The Socio-economic Analysis of Political Behavior," *Midwest Journal of Political Science,* 2:239–255, August, 1958.
34. Moos, Malcolm (ed.): *H. L. Mencken on Politics: A Carnival of Buncombe,* Vintage Books, Random House, Inc., New York, 1960.
35. Rogers, Lindsay: *The Pollsters,* Alfred A. Knopf, Inc., New York, 1949.
36. Rokeach, Milton: *The Open and Closed Mind,* Basic Books, Inc., Publishers, New York, 1960.
37. Rovere, Richard H.: *Senator Joe McCarthy,* Harcourt, Brace & World, Inc., New York, 1959.
38. Saul, Leon J.: "Hostility," *The American Behavioral Scientist,* vol. 4, supplement, June, 1961.
39. Scammon, Richard M.: *America Votes: A Handbook of Contemporary American Election Statistics,* The Macmillan Company, New York. (Biennial since 1956.)
40. Schattschneider, E. E.: "Intensity, Visibility, Direction and Scope," *American Political Science Review,* 51:933–942, December, 1957.
41. Schattschneider, E. E.: *The Semi-sovereign People,* Holt, Rinehart and Winston, Inc., New York, 1961.
42. Smith, M. Brewster: "Opinions, Personality and Political Behavior," *American Political Science Review,* 52:1–17, March, 1958.
43. Stanton, Alfred H., and Stewart E. Perry (eds.): *Personality and Political Crisis: New Perspectives from Social Science and Psychiatry for the Study of War and Politics,* The Free Press of Glencoe, New York, 1951.
44. Stein, Maurice, and others (eds.): *Identity and Anxiety,* The Free Press of Glencoe, New York, 1960.
45. Wallas, Graham: *Human Nature in Politics,* University of Nebraska Press, Lincoln, Nebr., reissued 1962. (First published, 1909.)

CHAPTER

10

POLITICAL PARTIES

A political party is a group of people banded together for the purpose of seeking elective public offices. As such, it differs from an interest group, which is a collection of people banded together for the purpose of promoting or protecting social, economic, or ideological interests.

Of course, a political party may be ideologically cohesive—its members may all have basically the same values and the same attitudes toward issues of public policy. This is true in authoritarian countries, inevitably, because acceptance of a particular set of values is a prerequisite of admission to party membership. It is also generally true of the multiparty democracies of Europe—France, Scandinavia, and the Low Countries, for example. It is to a considerable degree true of Great Britain, which is essentially a two-party nation, although it does have the Liberals, a respected but quite weak third party (it has seldom held the balance of political power).

But agreement on values is not a characteristic of the major parties in the United States. Throughout history—excepting only the Federalist party at the beginning of the nineteenth century—our parties have been based on geography rather than ideology. Whereas European parties have usually centered around socio-economic classes, parties in the United States have included persons from all social classes.

THE TWO-PARTY SYSTEM

All democracies have political parties. In each case, the parties have generally had their origins in custom; only in modern times have they been institutionalized through formal legislation regulating their operations, and this regulation controls only a portion of their activities. Parties are functional in the democratic political system in that they provide a practical, effective means through which elective public offices may be filled. Parties also have been widely accepted as having a legitimate social function, for they are useful to the political system, to candidates, to the party worker who seeks status and recognition through noncandidate political activity, and to the individual citizen.

Parties are useful to candidates in several ways. In some cases, they provide financial support. They offer a reservoir of experienced and talented people and willing workers. The former can provide useful advice; the latter can carry out useful routine functions, such as mailing or distributing door to door or encouraging potential supporters to register so that they will be eligible to vote. Perhaps most important to the candidate is the fact that if he secures the party's nomination he automatically garners the votes of those who habitually vote for that party and potentially those of persons who lean toward it, for he has gained legitimacy in their eyes.

To the active participant in politics, the party offers a chance for recognition through the formal offices it has to offer as well as an opportunity for status advancement, for no matter how humble an individual's origins, a party office or a public office may be offered to him as a reward for loyal service. The party may provide a chance for advancement that prejudice or social custom might otherwise deny him, or its needs may be especially in harmony with his particular talents.

The individual citizen often finds the party meaningful in that it provides a focus for his emotional reactions to the social and economic forces that act upon him. It also offers a frame of reference to use in judging political events: If his parents identified with a particular party, he is likely to do so too, and if he does, the public positions taken by party leaders whom he respects are likely to be accepted as his own. The party leaders become his personal reference group and his guides in the formulation of political opinion.

If Parties, What Pattern? A nation may have a single political party. If that party is totalitarian in character, it will express the dominant ideology of the leaders. If the party is democratic, it will probably be divided into factions, as the Democratic-Republican party was in the United States after the death of the Federalist party and before the rise of the Whig party, or as a single party is today in many parts of the nation where the two-party system does not prevail. On the other hand, a democracy may have a two- or a multiparty system.

If there are two national parties, as has been the case in the United States, this may indicate either that there are essentially only two significant ideological positions on public issues, or that a variety of ideological positions are blended into two-party confederations. The latter is the case in the United States, where the two parties are decentralized both organizationally and on issues.

Why Two Parties? Empirical evidence is not adequate to permit a confident answer. A two-party system is certainly traditional in the United States, stemming from the natural division between those who favored and those who opposed first the revolt against Great Britain and later the adoption of the Constitution. Historical accident may also have played a part, for it happened that the class-oriented Federalists were opposed by the class-neutral Jeffersonians in the early nineteenth century, and this presented another dichotomy.

Subsequently, the structure of the young nation's political system tended to reinforce and institutionalize the two-party system. Members of the House of Representatives were elected from single-member districts. This produced a winner-loser situation. Had there been multimember districts, especially if more than two were to be chosen from a single district, as has been the case in some European democracies, a multiparty system might have been encouraged, for lesser parties would have had a chance to win some seats. In addition the Electoral College came to be selected on the basis that the party getting most votes in the presidential contest would get all the electoral votes in a state because the electors were chosen at large rather than by districts—if one member of the party was a winner, all were winners. If election were by districts, lesser parties would be encouraged. They would be helped even more if each party were to receive a proportion of the electoral votes of a state equal to its proportion of the party vote, but no such tradition developed.

The two-party system has been further supported by the desire for Federal patronage. A third party could not expect to win the Presidency except under most unusual circumstances and would therefore rarely receive any of the patronage that is the goal of some party workers.

Similarly, the custom in Congress of awarding chairmanships only to members of the dominant party in each house has supported the two-party system. A minor party could not expect to hold a plurality of seats in either house and, consequently, could not look forward to the prestigeful and powerful chairmanships of committees. During the period after the Civil War, Southerners were discouraged from creating a third party by these considerations. In addition, the rules of the Democratic National Convention were helpful in keeping Southerners within the fold, for they required a two-thirds vote of the delegates in order to nominate a candidate for President or Vice President. This Southern veto power was not lost until 1936, when it was abandoned in favor of a simple majority vote.

As we shall see in this chapter, the American system of politics involves two parties only in a special sense. The two are not effectively competitive in most parts of the country, and a system of factions is the more common arrangement. Even at the national level, there is a considerable difference between the presidential party, with its national and particularly urban orientation, and the congressional party, with its statewide or parochial orientation.

The Decentralized Party Structure. Each party in the United States is decentralized in an organizational sense. There are several reasons. Each party must accommodate itself as an institution to the Federal system of government, and in recognition of the fact that there are separate constituencies for each elective office. Furthermore, the legal rules reflect the prevailing value patterns and their emphasis upon the man rather than the party, thus making it relatively easy for almost anyone to become a candidate if he is politically attractive, irrespective of his standing with the regular party organization.

Issues are oriented to the particular campaign for the particular office rather than to the party as a national entity. This is the case because of the decentralized organizational pattern; because of the individual's relatively easy access to party candidacy, irrespective of his ideological position; and because each party in each constituency seeks the support of the same uncommitted voters that its opponents are wooing. This makes it necessary for the individual candidate to be concerned not with a national party ideology, but with the expectations of the uncommitted voter of his constituency.

THE AMERICAN PARTY PATTERN

The political party may be viewed as a particular type of interest group, since its members have a collective interest in capturing public office and in the patronage and other perquisites that follow. Yet an authority on American parties, V. O. Key, Jr., has noted: "Perhaps only by courtesy may a party be designated as a group. Among its members the sense of belonging, the awareness of shared concern, and the impulse to action in the same direction may be scarcely discernible."[1] This statement requires some explanation: In the conventional wisdom of the voting public, a party probably seems to be a group of people who think and act alike; the "good" party is the one whose members are believed to think and act as does the particular individual citizen who is doing the evaluating.

Actually, American parties do not consist of ideological groupings. Instead, they are loosely coordinated federations of persons whose primary mutual interest—for many, the only mutual interest—is winning elections. But the party also is important in the political system because it performs the functions listed at the beginning of this chapter. Several features of the American party system may help to clarify the picture.

[1] V. O. Key, Jr., *Politics, Parties, and Pressure Groups,* 4th ed., Thomas Y. Crowell Company, New York, 1958, p. 180.

Membership. Party membership in the United States has only a vague meaning, except to the very few individuals who participate directly in partisan campaigning. Perhaps 10 per cent of the adult public is active in a presidential campaign in any way that extends beyond voting and television viewing. In 1956, only 10 per cent of those interviewed in a representative sample said they had contributed money or bought tickets or done "anything" to help the campaign of one of the parties or candidates. In 1952, only 4 per cent claimed to have done these things. In each election, 7 per cent had attended political meetings or other assemblies, and 3 per cent had done "other work" for a party or candidate. Only 2 or 3 per cent of the persons over twenty years of age considered themselves to be members of a political club or organization.[2]

With the exception of an occasional minor party, no one is elected to membership or expected to hold certain beliefs in order to be accepted for membership in a party. Joining is commonly restricted to taking the oath of party allegiance, which is required in many states in order to secure a primary ballot, but there is rarely an attempt to restrict primary participation to devoted members through this procedure. Ordinarily, dues are not collected, although some major party organizations have experimented with voluntary dues as a fund-raising technique. But persons who do not pay dues are not excluded from the party through identification.

Members, therefore, range from loyal doorbell ringers, envelope stuffers, and confirmed partisans who always vote for the party ticket and for the primary-election candidates who have the support of the leaders in control of the party machinery, to the independents who reluctantly register as party members only because they must in order to vote in the primary election—often the decisive election in American politics. A more meaningful concept than party membership is party identification, a concept examined later in this chapter.

Parties as Confederations. In many democracies, a party is a monolithic organization existing on a national basis. Although there may be internal factions, as there are in the British Labour party, for example, most of the significant parties in European democracies are national structures. There may be struggles for control of the machinery, but the victorious group is in a position to speak on more than a provincial basis so long as it wins mandates at the formal party convocations. In America, however, we scarcely even pretend that this is the case.

In the United States, there is a formal party organization in every state, and each state organization operates quite independently of the others. The state groups get together every four years in order to nominate candidates for President and Vice President and to piece together a conveniently vague platform. Each state party, in recognition of the

[2] Angus Campbell and others, *The American Voter,* John Wiley & Sons, Inc., New York, 1960, table 5.1.

confederate nature of the national organizations, has one male and one female national committeeman. (In recent years, the Republicans have given a third seat to each state carried by the party in the last presidential election. This seat is occupied by the state chairman.)

Issues. State campaigns for the United States Senate are conducted on various issues, or no issues at all, depending upon local circumstances. A candidate may be called upon to defend the national or state record of his party. A few issues involving national policy may be central in a campaign, but they are not necessarily related to national party platforms. Contests for the lower house of Congress are usually still more parochial.

Even the Presidency is not necessarily fought over on the basis of issues on which the parties divide (see Chapters 11 and 12). A very few issues, for example, separated the presidential candidates in 1952, 1956, and 1960, so far as their own speeches or the written words of the party platforms were concerned. In 1952, the major platform difference seemed to be over what should be done with oil under the seas within the 3-mile limit of the mean low-water mark of the shoreline. The issue was important to the oil companies concerned, and to some who saw it as a symbolic issue of Federal versus state control. Viewed in the latter sense, it acted as a cue to businessmen and labor leaders who inferred that positions taken by party leaders on this matter might indicate their positions on other issues. But most of the public probably decided how to vote that year in response to habits and feelings resulting from six years of a stalemated cold war and the Korean shooting war, which had not been made meaningful to the average citizen whose sons were there.

In terms of stated policy, there was little to distinguish the two parties, so far as their approach to these issues was concerned. To the citizen, however, one was the in-party and responsible for what had happened. The other was the out-party and an object of hope for solutions that would alleviate anxieties. We thus restate a point that has been made in earlier chapters and will be repeated later in other contexts: Campaigns do not normally center on rational discussions of public policy, and the parties, hence, do not normally divide on such a basis. Instead, the two-party system of the United States tends to cause both parties to seek the middle of the road and to compromise between the extreme points of view in order to maximize their attractiveness to the voters by seeking the most common denominator of appeal. The alternative is electoral disaster.

Factions. Two or more, sometimes many more groups or factions in any given state may use the same party label, although these groups may be as competitive with one another as if they bore different labels. Thus politics in many Southern and Border States center around a number of factions, each using the label of the Democratic party. Factions are found in both major parties in all parts of the nation. The primary-election process has tended to encourage factionalism, and the result is that the

United States does not have two parties, but rather dozens of them, perhaps hundreds. Yet we commonly think that there are only two parties because nearly all political groups call themselves either Republicans or Democrats. (In this book, "party" specifically refers to all factions grouped under a single label.)

Significance of factions. The real struggle in any state for control of public office is often between factions, rather than between Republicans and Democrats. In the 1960s, only about one-fourth of the states were genuinely competitive between the two major parties for statewide elections in the sense that either party could win the major offices. In only about two-thirds of the states did the second party have any real chance of winning control even under unusual circumstances. In the one-party states, the biggest party problem may not be how to win the election, but how to persuade someone to serve as candidate.[3]

Interfactional issues. Conflicts between factions may or may not be based on issues, just as is the case with parties. Sometimes a single party label may serve as an umbrella for two important factions, one liberal and the other conservative, as has been the case in a number of states for many years. This division upon ideological lines, and sometimes on the basis of specific major issues, may exist in either one- or two-party states. The division is likely to exist in one-party states because the only hope for political success lies with the single party; all must crowd under the same tent and then divide themselves up. Hence, in the Border States, one Democratic party is the party of the gentry and conservatism on business and racial issues; another Democratic party is the refuge of urban Negroes, coal miners, urban workers, and farmers.[4]

In two-party states, liberal and conservative factions are likely to develop as a result of the conventional accommodation practices of the American party. Thus in Minnesota, conservative Irish-Catholic politicians from small cities and towns have tended to become a minority faction as the liberal urban groups have come to dominate the Democratic-Farmer-Labor (DFL) party. At the same time, the successes at the polls of Farmer-Laborites in the 1930s and later of the combined DFL party, produced a demand for more moderate candidates in the Republican party in the hope of a return to power. The rise of the moderate wing of the party, beginning in 1938, forced old-time conservatives more and more into a minority faction. The factions then were required to struggle against one another, while at the same time the parties were locked in a struggle between those who, in each party, emerged victorious in the factional fights.

[3] See, Key, *op. cit.*, chap. 11; V. O. Key, Jr., *American State Politics*, Alfred A. Knopf, Inc., New York, 1956, pp. 97ff.; Austin Ranney and Willmoore Kendall, "The American Party Systems," *American Political Science Review*, 48:477–486, June, 1954; and Warren E. Miller, "One-party Politics and the Voter," *American Political Science Review*, 50:707–725, September, 1956.

[4] John H. Fenton, *Politics in the Border States*, The Hauser Press, New Orleans, La., 1957, p. 208.

Factional fights need not involve ideological differences; they may center on power considerations. It is common for gubernatorial and senatorial candidates to lead separate factions within a party. Each seeks to operate the party machinery. The senator frequently controls important Federal patronage as a resource if he is a member of the President's party; the governor has state patronage and the advantage of being on the scene.

Factions are sometimes relatively permanent. In North Dakota, two factions in the Republican party competed continuously from 1916 to 1956. In Louisiana, the Long and anti-Long factions were identifiable from the early 1930s until the 1960s. In contrast, factions in Florida have been highly transitory.

Factional competition. Factional competition should not be equated with two-party competition, even when factions are well defined within a one-party state and survive for considerable periods of time. For example, an examination of the Long and anti-Long factions in Louisiana reveals actions that would be improbable, if not impossible, in a two-party state. Candidates switched from one faction to the other without regard to previous alignments. Candidates for United States Senate and the House of Representatives paid little attention to factional lines. If members of either faction won such offices, they were generally renominated without contest. Linkage to presidential politics was also weak. Factions did not always remain loyal to the ideological issues that ostensibly divided them. Voters sometimes had difficulty distinguishing between factions because occasionally a slate would be incomplete and, in effect, a candidate would become the nominee of both factions. In addition, local party leaders switched their following from one candidate to another, often for a price, in a way that would be impossible in a two-party state.[5]

According to some democratic models, two-party competition is supposed to result in each party making bids to the unorganized voters. Thus the average voter holds a power in politics similar to the power he holds in the marketplace, where competition between two firms for the same customer results in attempts of each to better serve the customer at cheaper prices.

Two-party competition does not, of course, always fit the model. For example, one study of three counties with varying patterns of factional and two-party competition found that, in the most competitive two-party county, the fight was largely over traditional issues having little relationship to present-day events.[6] However, a study that used three different measures found competition within the states to be somewhat related to policy payoffs; that is, as states became more competitive, they also had higher average old-age-assistance payments and made higher expenditures on

[5] Allan P. Sindler, *Huey Long's Louisiana,* The Johns Hopkins Press, Baltimore, 1956, pp. 248–286.

[6] Edwin H. Rhyne, "Political Parties and Decision Making in Three Southern Counties," *American Political Science Review,* 52:143–152, December, 1958.

welfare.[7] (However, the wealth of the particular state accounted for an important part of the difference.) In his study *Southern Politics,* V. O. Key, Jr., argued similarly that North Carolina was a leader among Southern states in many functional areas because it has always had a Republican party enclave that consistently challenges the dominant Democratic party.[8]

American Parties: Loose Confederations. We have seen in this section that American parties are loose confederations of persons who often hold to conflicting ideologies. Parties are often divided by factional differences of considerable magnitude. We now turn to the question of why parties exist. What do they do for and to the social system, the party leaders, the candidates, the citizen?

THE FUNCTIONS OF PARTIES

Persons active in party leadership are fundamentally interested in winning office, and all other considerations are likely to be secondary. But political parties do perform a number of other functions. They recruit candidates from among those who have been successful in other fields, potentially effective campaigners who have not been active in the party—Dwight D. Eisenhower and Ulysses S. Grant are obvious examples. Parties finance campaigns and present candidates to the public for consideration. They restate values, goals, and conventional knowledge to the public, reminding citizens of their basic beliefs. They stimulate interest in political campaigns and in the great issues that divide legislative bodies. They serve as constant critics of public and private decision makers.

When the two-party system first began to appear as a result of conflict over the adoption of the Constitution, and when it later reached full development in the Jacksonian period, the party was expected to coordinate administrators. It was looked to as a means for bringing about interrelated efforts by the three branches of government, and within them, it was looked to for coordination of the two houses of a legislative body and the various administrative officers of the executive branch.

At the state and local level, a number of factors have limited party effectiveness in the performance of these functions. In particular, there are the use of the primary election (which permits each candidate to be independent of the others), nonpartisan elections (which have the same effect), and the widespread existence of one-party politics.

[7] Thomas Casstevens and Charles Press, "The Context of Democratic Competition in American State Politics," *American Journal of Sociology,* 68:536–543, March, 1963. Also, Richard A. Dawson and James A. Robinson, "Interparty Competition, Economic Variables and Welfare Policies in the American States," *Journal of Politics,* 25:265–289, May, 1963.

[8] V. O. Key, Jr., with Alexander Heard, *Southern Politics,* Alfred A. Knopf, Inc., New York, 1949, p. 208.

At the national level, the enormous appointive powers of the President and a short ballot have prevented power from drifting into as many independent loci as is the case at the state and local levels, but coordination is limited by the independence of members of Congress from the national party structure and by the fact that the parties are loose confederations rather than national organizations.

PARTY STRENGTH—A RELATIVE MATTER

Although we have so far spoken of one- and two-party states and the lack of effective competition between parties in most of the states, accuracy requires a more complete and precise statement of the pattern. After all, although Democrats won all but one of the elections in Mississippi between 1914 and 1960, their opponents (including third parties) received at least 40 per cent of the vote in nearly 3 per cent of the elections. And although the Republicans lost only one statewide election in Vermont over the same period, their opponents received at least 40 per cent of the vote in about 18 per cent of the elections; in over one-half of the elections, the opponents received over 30 per cent of the vote.[9] A state such as Iowa is "normally" Republican, but it cannot be dismissed as a one-party state, for the Democrats win about one-fourth of the statewide elections, which are sometimes crucial in helping to determine domination of Congress and the White House.

The principal "swing" states—states that can go to either party in a presidential or senatorial contest or elect a majority of its congressmen on either ticket in any election—may be defined in a number of ways. A taxonomy is difficult to develop because the voting pattern differs for each office. In fact, one study has concluded that it is not meaningful to talk of competitive states, but only of competitive offices within states. The offices of senator and governor are the most party-competitive.[10]

The classification shown in Figure 10-1, which attempts to list states by competitiveness, lists over one-half in a two-party category. This study considers all states in which the smaller party wins at least 27 per cent of the time to be competitive. Another classification, which shows that competition varies by office, is illustrated in Figure 10-2. Figure 10-1 also shows that there are a number of "modified one-party" states that lean heavily in the direction of a single party, but cannot be considered certain. Only the

[9] Recomputed from Ranney and Kendall, *op. cit.* See also Joseph A. Schlesinger, "A Two-dimensional Scheme for Classifying the States According to Degree of Inter-party Competition," *American Political Science Review,* 44:1120–1128, December, 1955; and Robert T. Golembiewski, "A Taxonomic Approach to State Political Party Strength," *Western Political Quarterly,* 11:494–513, September, 1958.

[10] Joseph A. Schlesinger, "The Structure of Competition for Office in the American States," *Behavioral Science,* 5:197–210, July, 1960.

states of the Confederacy (excluding North Carolina) can be considered safely Democratic, and even among these states, the Republicans won some electoral votes in the elections of 1928 (Hoover-Smith) and in those since 1952. Only Vermont is a "certain" Republican state, and even there, the Democrats appear to be gaining somewhat. They captured a congressional seat in 1958 for the first time in a century, elected the governor in 1962, and won the electoral votes in the 1964 presidential contest. Nevertheless, in only about one-fourth of the states (those in which either party can expect to win some major offices at least 40 per cent of the time) does a competitive two-party system exist.

Figure 10-1

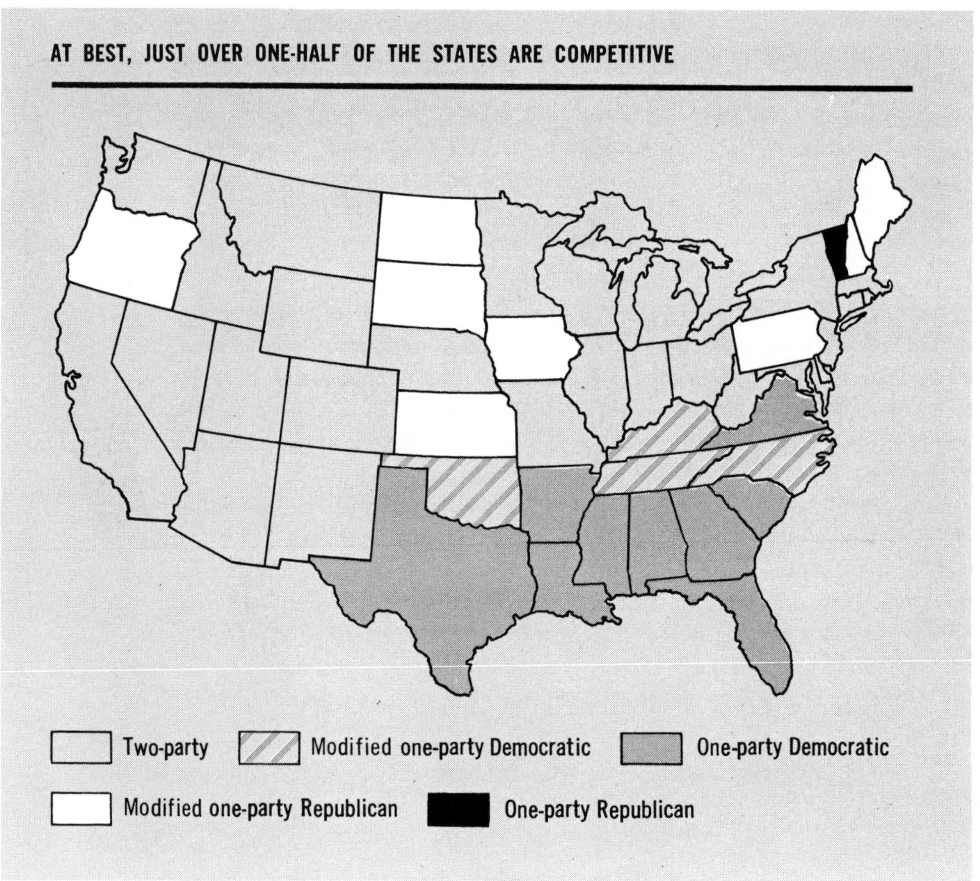

Austin Ranney and Willmoore Kendall, "The American Party Systems," American Political Science Review, *vol. 48, fig. 1, June, 1954.*

Figure 10-2

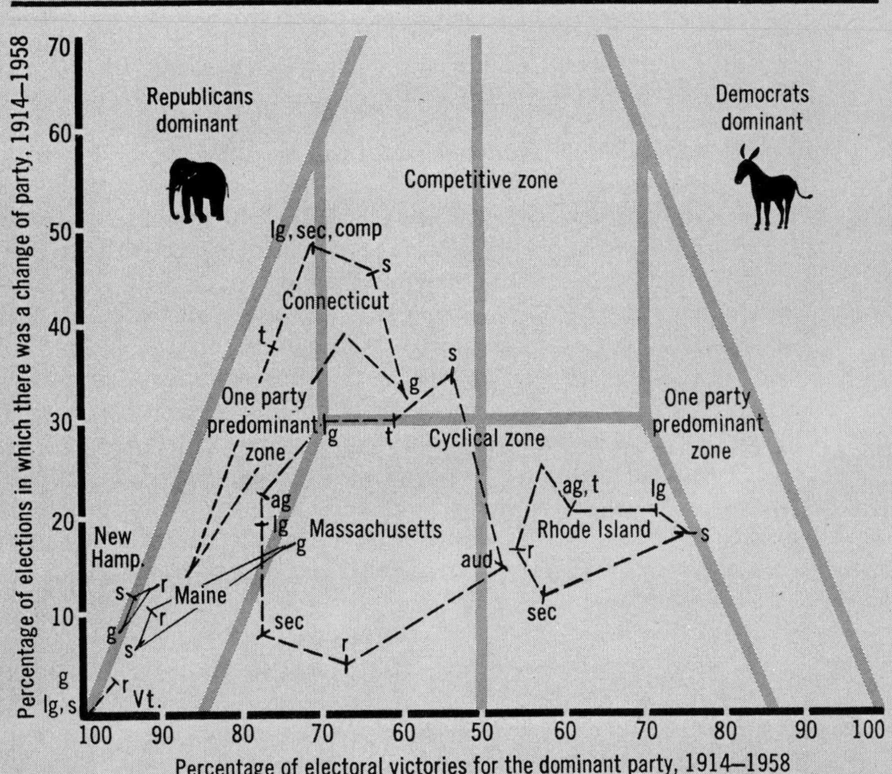

Office key

g: Governor
s: Senator
r: Congressmen
lg: Lieutenant Governor
sec: Secretary of State
ag: Attorney General
aud: Auditor
t: Treasurer
comp: Comptroller

In some states (e.g., New Hampshire), there is little competition by party. In others (e.g., Massachusetts), some offices can go to either party in any election. (Adapted from Joseph A. Schlesinger, "The Structure of Competition for Office in American States," Behavioral Science, *5:197–210, July, 1960.)*

PARTY ORGANIZATION

The formal structure of American government encourages factionalism and decentralization in the major political parties. The federal system divides parties between state and national levels, and the separation of powers within each level encourages further divisions. Various groupings exist in both major parties; under each organizational roof, many factions flourish. The loose confederations that are the American parties are mirrored in organizational structure.

National Organization. The national chairman of each party is its organizational head. He is formally selected by the national committee, although in presidential years he is actually selected by the presidential candidate because his major duty is running the presidential campaign. This arrangement weakens rather than strengthens party organization. In the losing party, the chairman is the choice of a defeated candidate, and thus he automatically faces criticism and opposition. Even in the winning party, the chairmanship generally changes after the campaign, since the victorious strategist often is given an important appointment. Party organization at all levels centers around candidates in competitive races.

The national committee members are formally chosen by the national party convention, but in reality, that body only ratifies the choices made by the state delegations. The committee becomes a council of ambassadors, each of whom is generally an important leader back home. Identification remains local. Meetings occur infrequently, normally only about twice a year. Because state representation is not based on population, the large urban states are drastically underrepresented on the national committee. As a rule, this results in a group that is more conservative than the presidential candidate or his choice for the national chairmanship, a fact that does not augur well for organizational unity. (In 1956, Democratic Chairman Paul Butler created the Democratic Advisory Council, a body of liberal Democrats whose statements on policy were designed to contrast with the conservatism of the National Democratic Committee.)

Duties of the national committee are few. As in every organization, members speak only for themselves—not for the whole party. The national committee is expected to raise funds for the campaign and to pay off any debt remaining afterward. It makes arrangements for the national convention, including the crucial selections of speakers and the temporary chairman. (In 1952, the Taft-controlled Republican National Committee selected convention officers and speakers who opposed both Eisenhower and any platform concessions to the large urban areas, a tactic that was effectively turned against them at the convention by a "fair play" campaign of the Eisenhower supporters.)

The national committee is also in charge of the national office. Until 1928, the parties closed up shop between presidential campaigns. After their landslide defeat of that year, the Democrats maintained the national

Figure 10-3

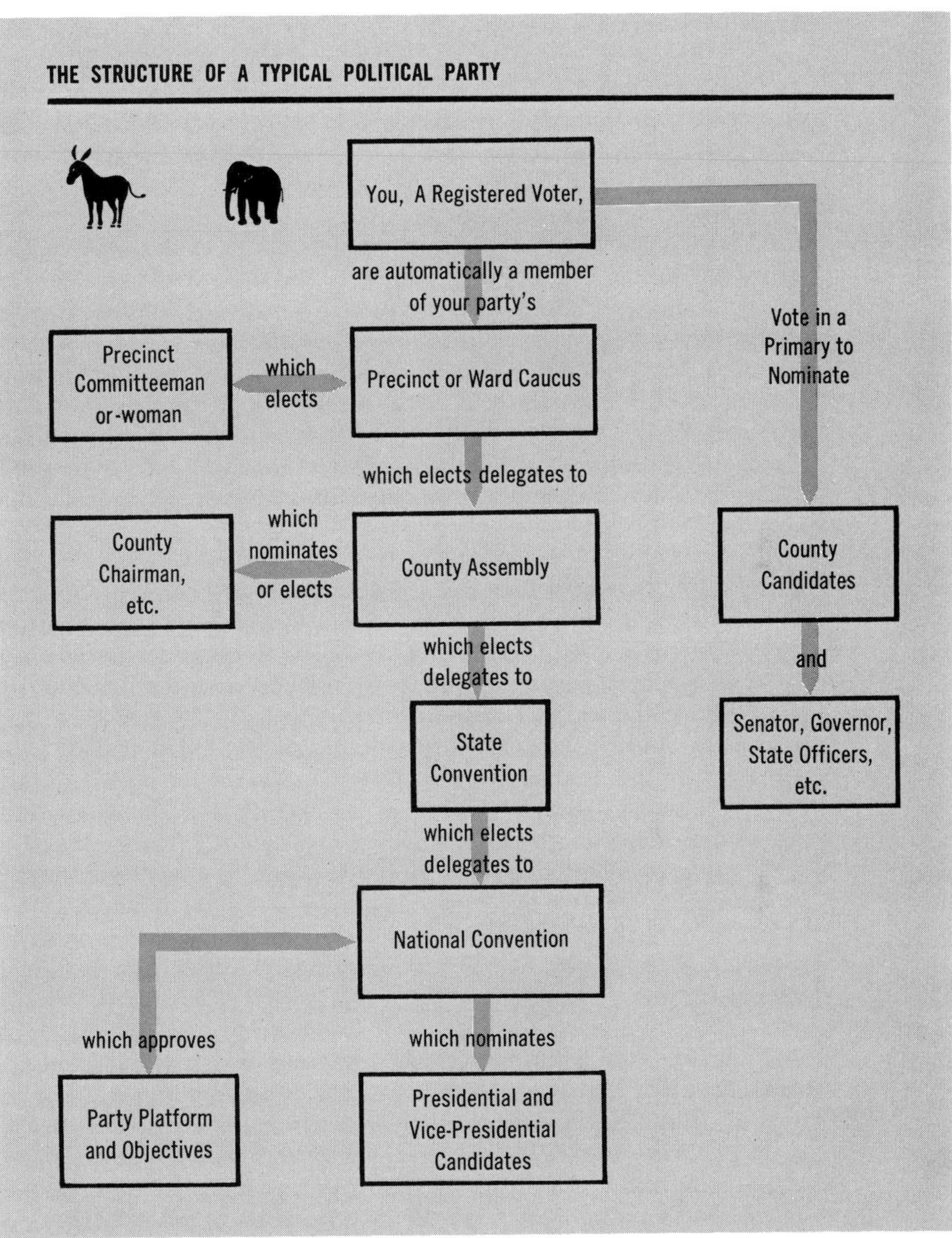

Based on data from the Committee on Political Education, Labor and Politics, AFL-CIO, Washington, 1960.

office to help rebuild the party. They established a steady drumbeat of criticism of President Hoover as the Depression deepened, and they thus demonstrated the political value of a full-time national office. The national party offices now engage in year-round research, speech writing, and publicity activities. Staff members have successfully helped local candidates plan their campaigns, supplying them with much useful information. Research arms of both parties give advice about candidate chances that is based on more than hunches, and thus funds may be spent where the greatest return may be expected.

As each national office has been given more duties, some observers have hoped that greater overall party consistency and unity would emerge. This has not happened. The national office of the party in possession of the White House distributes national committee funds to needy candidates who have supported the President. For the out-party, the national office remains of little importance. In both cases, the principal function of the national office is party publicity rather than participation in particular campaigns. The overall pattern is historically familiar: Locally, power is stable; nationally it is held by a temporary grouping around a presidential nominee.

Senatorial and Congressional Committees. Two committees in each party at the national level work to reelect incumbent congressmen and senators. Secondarily, they help to elect party nominees in states or districts held by the opposition. These committees are responsible to legislators of the party, not to the national committee: this has been the case since their origination in 1866 by Republican legislators who were feuding with President Andrew Johnson. Generally they do not become involved in the primary election (though revelations in 1958 showed the Republican committee had made "loans" to primary candidates). The existence of these committees encourages further rifts within national parties; the congressional arm of each party (represented by the committees) is unwilling to trust its fortunes to presidential leadership (represented by the national committee) or for that matter, even to the other branch of the legislature.

State and Local Party Organization. Party organization is determined at the state rather than the national level. The result is endless variety. Generally there is some kind of state committee (which may vary in size from a handful of party leaders to a group large enough to fill an ordinary movie theater) and a state chairman. The chairman is normally the gubernatorial nominee's choice, no matter how he may be officially selected. He faces competition, however, and may not be the real leader of the party organization. Continuing conflict may exist between him and the national committeeman from the state. The separate election of executive officials such as the attorney general or secretary of state, as well as of the party representatives in legislatures that markedly overrepresent rural areas, encourages factionalism and opposition to the gubernatorial wing of the state party. Again, built-in constitutional provisions encourage divisions.

Below the state level, the basic organizational unit is normally the county or, within metropolitan centers, the congressional district. The minor levels of organization within cities are the ward and precinct. Generally, local party workers are chosen by party caucuses of voters or local primary elections. In either case, selection is often a formality. Because of low interest and turnout, the choice is normally made by party leaders or by self-recruitment. In some states, the local nominees for county office make the choice. The usual pattern is for other party offices to be filled at conventions at the county or congressional district level and then at the state level (if there is a state convention). A few states have elections for these offices.

Actual organization throughout a state may vary from the old-style machine, with its errand-boy precinct committeeman (Chicago is one of the few surviving examples), to little more than a list of names. Outside of the few highly organized machines in low-income wards, parties generally have large gaps in their actual organization at local levels. Prosperity and the absence of patronage discourage recruitment of precinct captains or block workers. In some suburban areas, a new type of organization is developing that has more in common with the March of Dimes than with the traditional party machine. Using the techniques of tea and coffee parties, "issue schools," or "Know Your Candidate" programs, volunteers, particularly women, spread propaganda or raise funds. Generally the most active organizations are built around candidates facing stiff competition.

New-style Political Organizations. In several states, extralegal party organizations have won considerable power. Generally, these are dominated by good-government, white-collar types. The Independent Voters of Illinois (IVI) has normally supported liberal Democratic candidates in the Chicago area, although in several elections the group has given support to Republicans and thus encouraged ticket splitting. In California, the Republican Assembly and the California Democratic Council have organized to control the choices of their parties in the primaries by making preprimary endorsements. Reform Democrats in Manhattan, in coalition with Mayor Robert F. Wagner's followers, took over control of the organization from the orthodox Tammany Hall group. Sometimes these organizations have even recruited candidates. They have generally been devised to permit a faction to take control of one of the major parties and they are particularly likely to exist where the major party is still controlled by old-style ward heelers.[11]

On the national level, the League for an Effective Congress is typical of the new-style independent group. It is organized to support liberal candi-

[11] See James Q. Wilson, *The Amateur Democrat,* The University of Chicago Press, Chicago, 1962.

dates of both parties. Citizens are solicited to contribute to a national fund, and these moneys are "invested" where the group's national board feels they will provide the largest payoff for those desiring liberal senatorial and congressional candidates in each party.[12]

Party organization is probably entering a new phase in the electronic age, but one study of New Jersey party officials found that while old-style methods were slowly dying out, there was still a place for them in low-income Negro and Puerto Rican wards. In addition, the role of party leaders as expediters between the public and a confusing bureaucracy was found to have taken on new importance. Specialized information about government, theoretically available to all, appeared to be as highly prized as old-style political favors once were. The author concludes that, despite changes, some old-style organization is likely to continue in many urbanized areas for some time to come, since it continues to satisfy a widespread need.[13]

The Questions of Strong Party Organizations. The signs should point to a strengthening of overall party organization as the nation becomes more urbanized and sectional differences diminish. Thus far, however, not even the high prestige of the President can enforce cooperation among party groups. Cooperation is still the result of bargaining among independent units.

The "loyalty pledge" of the 1952 Democratic convention highlights the difficulties. It was adopted after considerable handwringing, but did no more than state that delegates would agree to use every "honorable means" to ensure that the nominees of the convention would be designated on their state ballots as the Democratic party nominees. Even this modest proviso was bitterly opposed by the Southern minority within the party.

PARTIES AS COALITIONS OF INTERESTS

All political parties throughout history have been concerned with interests of one kind or another. In some nations, interests have tended to organize their own structures, but in the United States parties consist of *coalitions* of interests,* some of which are antithetical in character. Thus the Demo-

---

***COALITION.** **An alliance of individuals, factions, or parties for political-action purposes. It is usually temporary and may be for some particular purpose rather than for all types of political activity.**

---

[12] Harry M. Scoble, "Political Money: A Study of Contributors to the National Committee for an Effective Congress," *Midwest Journal of Political Science,* 7:229–253, August, 1963.

[13] Richard T. Frost, "Stability and Change in Local Party Politics," *Public Opinion Quarterly,* 25:221–235, Summer, 1961.

cratic party includes both the extreme segregationists of the Deep South and many of the leaders of the movement toward desegregation and racial equality. The Republican party has been the home of many advocates of *laissez faire,* but it also housed the Non-partisan League leaders in North Dakota in the period around World War I when that group advocated state ownership of various businesses as part of a program of agrarian socialism. More recently, it has included such liberals as Governor Nelson Rockefeller of New York.

Liberals and Conservatives. Parties derive most of their support from considerations other than rational programs of proposed governmental policies or ideological positions. (Both major political parties include persons who range along the political continuum from ultraconservative to extreme liberal.) In the image outside the South, the Democratic party consists of those who favor the continued extension of the New Deal policies of the 1930s. There are indeed many such persons within the party. They dominate it in most large Northern industrial states. But the relative conservatism of Democratic majorities in Congress should in itself be enough to warn the careless observer against easy generalization. Congressmen and Presidents have different constituencies, and hence, they have different patterns of political behavior. Some of the most conservative persons in America are Democrats: Senator Harry F. Byrd of Virginia and Senator Frank J. Lausche of Ohio are examples. Although such liberal senators as the senior Robert F. Wagner of New York in the 1930s, and Hubert H. Humphrey of Minnesota and Paul Douglas of Illinois in the 1950s were Democrats, so were such conservative senators as Price Daniel of Texas and Pat McCarran of Nevada, along with many moderates.

At each presidential nominating convention when the renomination of the incumbent is not automatic, there is usually an array of possible nominees who hold various general outlooks on politics. In 1960, persons considered for the Democratic nomination included Hubert H. Humphrey, who was commonly pictured as a liberal, and Lyndon B. Johnson, whose image was somewhat more conservative than that of John F. Kennedy, who got the nomination.

The top leaders among the Democrats in both the House and Senate tend to be conservatives, and are often but not always from the South. Because of the seniority system, many congressional committee chairmen come from noncompetitive, "safe" districts and are more conservative than the Presidents of the same party (see Chapter 14). For example, President Roosevelt's "court packing" plan of 1937, in which he proposed to overcome Supreme Court opposition to the New Deal by enlarging the membership of that body, was defeated by conservative Democrats in Congress. Similarly, President Truman's proposals for admitting large numbers of European refugees after World War II was largely frustrated by the implacable resistance of Representative Francis Walter, a conservative Democrat from Pennsylvania who headed the House Immigration and Naturalization Committee.

The same general pattern prevails among Republicans, even though many Americans think of the GOP as representing a conservatism that is somewhat to the right of center. In the 1960 nominating convention, Richard M. Nixon fitted that stereotype and received the nomination. But there were many Republicans who would have preferred Governor Nelson Rockefeller of New York who, like the Republican senators from that state in recent years, is a liberal and regarded by many conservatives as a Republican New Dealer. There were also many Republicans who would have preferred the ultraconservative Senator Barry M. Goldwater of Arizona. In 1964, they dominated their party convention when no liberal or moderate other than Rockefeller was willing to make a concerted effort. The result was the candidacy of a right-winger whose limited appeal resulted in a heavy defeat for the party.

Whichever party occupies the White House, the President is likely to find his congressional leaders to be more conservative than he is (see Chapter 14). Thus President Dwight D. Eisenhower learned that such Republicans as Senator Joseph R. McCarthy of Wisconsin, Representatives Daniel A. Reed and John Taber of upstate New York and Speaker Joseph W. Martin, Jr., of Massachusetts gave him almost as much trouble as did the Democrats. President John F. Kennedy's majority leader in the House was the leading opponent of his proposal for Federal aid to education.[14]

In comparing parties as they range along the liberal-conservative continuum, perhaps the most that can be said is that the Democratic candidate in any given presidential or congressional contest will nearly always be further to the left than the Republican candidate. If the Republican takes a liberal position, the Democrat will take a still more liberal position. If the Democrat is conservative, his GOP opponent will be still further to the right. In New York, a liberal Republican can expect to face a still more liberal Democrat; in Texas, a conservative Democrat will find his Republican opponent still further to the right.

If all factors are considered, the balance of factions within the Democratic party lies somewhere to the left of that in the Republican. Some observers expect this gap to widen as America shifts from parties based on the sectional or geographically defined interests of a rural society to parties based on the class interests of an urban economy. If this is the case, party competition should increase. Another theory holds, however, that differences in class interests will be overbalanced by desire of both parties to gain support from the undecided moderates, who will hold the balance of power in the elections for many offices. Evidence pointed to in support of either theory includes: (1) the increasing number of states that are be-

[14] See James McG. Burns, *The Deadlock of Democracy,* Prentice-Hall, Inc., Englewood Cliffs, N.J., 1963.

coming competitive for major offices; (2) a Republican breakthrough in the South—they elected a governor in Oklahoma and almost took a senatorial seat in Alabama in 1962; (3) voting in metropolitan areas, which shows a steady rise in the percentage of Republican vote if precincts are arrayed according to income or social status.

THE GREAT COALITIONS: THE DEMOCRATS

We have seen, thus far, that parties in this country are loose confederations. We have examined their functions, the way in which they are organized, and the coalitions of interests that are joined in the confederations. The analysis can be further illustrated through a brief survey of party history.

The first parties in the United States formed around the question of the Constitutional adoption. Those who favored the new plan of government called themselves Federalists and, after securing its adoption, they became

Figure 10-4

Each Party Is a Grand Coalition

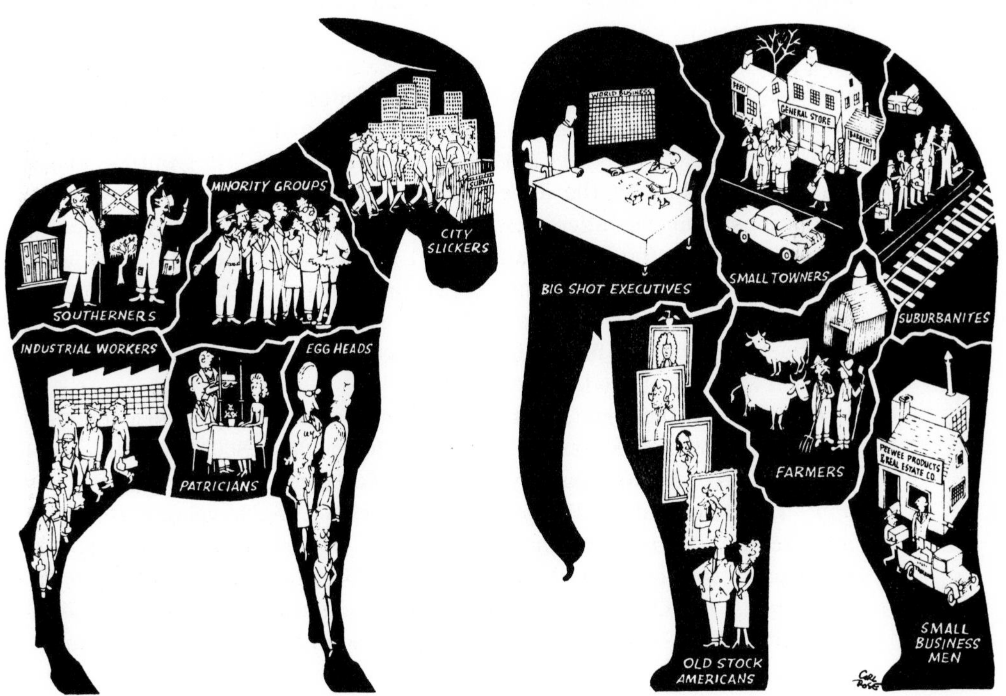

The New York Times Magazine, Nov. 4, 1962.

the political party that supported strong central government and the encouragement of commerce and manufacturing as a basis for the development of the new nation. Their opponents were at first known simply as the Antifederalists. They opposed some of the important provisions of the new Constitution or bemoaned the omission of certain things they regarded as imperative, such as a bill of rights, or they believed that the Articles of Confederation could be made adequate. They were dissatisfied with the *status quo* and concerned about the domination of public policy making by an economic elite and the preservation and expansion of the ordinary citizen's opportunities to have access to and representation in democratic government. Thus, from the earliest days of the Republic our two political parties have tended to divide at least partly on the question of property interests versus the rights of the ordinary citizen. The Federalists and their successors tended to emphasize—though not to the exclusion of other considerations—the interests and importance of private property and private decisions about property as an instrument for economic growth. The Antifederalists and their successors tended to emphasize—though not to the exclusion of other considerations—the rights of the ordinary citizen. This emphasis served as a check upon what its members considered excessive concern with the importance of property and privileges for those who controlled it. But as we shall see, this was only a general and very broad truism subject to many qualifications. Virtually from the beginning, the parties were, and still are essentially grand coalitions of persons who have diverse interests.

The Founding and Development of the Party. The Federalists had no chance for a permanent life. They created a class party in a nation that was increasingly subjected to the egalitarian influences of the frontier. While they were looking to the advancement of commerce, industry, and the plantations, Thomas Jefferson, with the help of others, was busy building a party (to become the Democratic party) of yeoman farmers, skilled tradesmen, shopkeepers, and others of modest means. These people were gradually molded into a budding party of the common people which did not reach its complete flower until three decades later in the age of Andrew Jackson who was elected in 1828.

The Democratic party lost the Presidency only twice between the election of Jefferson (1800) and the election of Lincoln (1860), each time to a military hero who was portrayed as a typical frontiersman, after regular opposition candidates (Whigs) failed to win. The Democrats stood for grass-roots popular government, the plantation system in the South, and the yeoman farmer of rural America in the North. It also appealed to the propertyless urbanite in an emerging industrial system. The party not only dominated the Presidency, but Congress as well, most of the time. It possessed an unbeatable combination until the centrifugal force of the slavery issue caused it to fly apart in the 1850s.

After the Civil War, the Democrats had to bear the burden of being the party to which most of the Confederates had belonged. The Republicans waved the bloody shirt of patriotism with great success. Even so, elections for the Presidency and Congress were close for two decades, beginning in 1876 (the disputed Hayes-Tilden contest); a number of them turned on the outcome in New York, a closely balanced state. In the meantime, the Democrats were building up the potential for a new winning combination: the Solid South (where the Republican party symbolized Southern humiliation), and the urban workingman, who was rapidly increasing in numbers. The latter group consisted largely of immigrants. Although the Republicans courted them in some cities (notably Chicago, Cincinnati, and Philadelphia), immigrants moved into the Democratic party for the most part. With a strong grass-roots tradition and less orientation toward middle-class values than the Republicans, this party became the home of most of the big-city machines that flourished between the 1870s and World War II. The urban workingman, constantly faced with the threat of unemployment that was not his own fault, a legal system that was oriented toward the needs of business leaders, and a multitude of personal problems for which government offered little assistance, found the big-city machine a useful and often essential instrument for his own security and even survival.[15] Although the political leaders ("bosses") were often personally interested in wealth or profit, they did provide important social assistance, and the loyalties they built up paid off importantly for the party. The roles played by the Democrats during this period aided the party in gaining the support of many ethnic groups that became, and still are an important source of electoral strength.

By 1932, folklore and history had relegated the Civil War to the background of the party's image. In that year, Franklin D. Roosevelt was the Democratic candidate for the Presidency. In the midst of the Great Depression, he reaped the harvest of his party's history of nurturing the urban workingman, the individual who suffered greatest during the years of widespread unemployment. In a desperate protest vote, others joined with him in rejecting the long-dominant Republican party. The age of the social service state had arrived, and the Democrats, who benefited from the protest vote of 1932, could claim to be the guardians of the new political ideology. Between 1932 and 1964, the Democrats won seven out of nine presidential elections. In the same period, they controlled fifteen out of seventeen Congresses. How long the Democrats will remain the majority party in the United States cannot be predicted, but the coalition that has been its principal source of power for a generation—Southerners, Negroes, urban working-class families, marginal farmers, and a relatively small but influential group of intellectuals—was still producing winners in the 1960s.

[15] On the social function of the boss and machine, see Charles R. Adrian, *Governing Urban America,* 2d ed., McGraw-Hill Book Company, 1961, chap. 6; and Robert K. Merton, *Social Theory and Social Structure,* rev. ed., The Free Press of Glencoe, New York, 1957, pp. 71–81.

THE GREAT COALITIONS: THE REPUBLICANS

The contemporary Republican party represents a traditional coalition and is a descendant of the Federalists of Revolutionary days. In most democracies since the seventeenth century, business and industrial leaders have favored a strong central government committed to the idea that the most

Figure 10-5

PARTY STANDING CHANGES OVER TIME

YEAR	1800 – 1830 – 1860	1860 – 1890 – 1930	1930 – 1960 – ?	
Prevailing Domestic Ideology	Frontier individualism	Industrial individualism	Social service state	?
Prevailing Foreign Policy Ideology	Isolationism		Internationalism	?
Dominant Political Party	Democratic	Republican	Democratic	?
Victories in Presidential Elections by Dominant Party	13 of 15	13 of 17	6 of 8 (through 1960)	?
Hero of the Age	Frontiersman	"Self-made" businessman	Common man (working class) Organization man (middle class)	?
Dominant Branch of Government	Legislative	Judicial	Executive	?

important social institution is business. The Federalist party endorsed this concept and so long as the developing business and financial groups of the Eastern seaboard dominated the national government, they wanted it strong. But when the Jeffersonians and Jacksonians, appealing to the common man, took control in Washington, businessmen found themselves no longer able to dominate public policy. They gradually abandoned their earlier position and took refuge in the Whig party, which stood somewhat vaguely for decentralized power (in opposition to the strong populistic leadership of Andrew Jackson). And they came increasingly to doubt the efficacy of the Federal government as an agent for the needs of business. After the Civil War, most businessmen endorsed the philosophy of *laissez faire* and advocated minimal governmental activity, except in relation to the protective tariff.

The Republican Heyday. The Whig party, unable either to gain mass support (even after electing the folk heroes William Henry Harrison and Zachary Taylor) or to take a popular stand on the slavery issue, died in the 1850s. It was succeeded by the Republican party, which inherited most Whig loyalties and later added to them popular appeal based on having saved the Union and resolved the slavery issue in the Civil War.

The Republican party began its efforts in 1856 by seeking to imitate the old Whig formula. It nominated a colorful military hero, John C. Fremont, for the Presidency, but he could gather a mere one-third of the vote. In the next election, Abraham Lincoln did only slightly better with 40 per cent, but a divided Democratic party gave him the victory. He barely survived his campaign for reelection in 1864 against General George B. McClellan.

Following the 1864 election, Republicans emerged as the majority party. They could not only make their claims about the war, but they became the spokesmen for the emerging American industrialist and the ideology of industrial individualism (see Chapter 7). Between 1860 and 1932, the Republicans won fourteen of eighteen Presidential elections and controlled Congress the great bulk of the time. (The party lost twice to Cleveland, a conservative Democrat, and twice to Woodrow Wilson. One of the Cleveland victories, according to the historian Charles A. Beard, may have been the result of the stuffing of New York City ballot boxes by Tammany Hall. The two Wilson victories may be attributed to the split in the Republican party between the followers of Theodore Roosevelt and those of William Howard Taft.)

From the 1870s through the 1890s, however, the two parties were closely balanced in strength. In 1876, Samuel J. Tilden, a Democrat, received more popular votes than did Hayes, the winner, and Cleveland out-polled Harrison in losing the 1888 election. Four years earlier, Cleveland and Harrison had received almost identical voting totals, with the former the winner. Between 1896 and the Great Depression, however, the Republicans were clearly dominant.

A Minority Party. Since 1932, the Republican party has been definitely a national minority party. In the late 1950s, it could count on the basic loyalty of only about 33 per cent of the eligible voters nationally, as against about 54 per cent for the Democrats. (The remaining 13 per cent were apolitical persons or true independents, the latter constituting a much smaller percentage of the actual voting population than is recognized by conventional wisdom.) Between 1932 and 1960, the Republicans won the Presidency twice, but only by siphoning off Democratic voters by running a war hero who was not identified in the public mind with the party. Eisenhower was seen as the *individual* who represented the best available person to end the Korean conflict and prevent a third world war.[16]

In 1960, Richard M. Nixon narrowly missed victory, though the election apparently would not have been very close had John F. Kennedy not been a Roman Catholic.[17] Between 1932 and 1964, the Republicans won control of Congress only in 1946 and 1952.

The post-Civil War magic formula for the Republicans lasted only so long as the typical citizen agreed that business was the most important social institution. When an industrial system with its enormous insecurities brought demands for a type of governmental action that the Republicans had never supported as a national party, and when the pervasive 1929 depression swept the land, the Republicans found themselves saddled with an image that made repeated victory dependent upon special conditions at election time, as has always been the case of the minority party in American politics.

PARTY IMAGES AND IDENTITIES TODAY

In 1956, President Eisenhower easily won reelection, but Republicans failed to gain a majority in either house of Congress. A large number of voters:[18]

> Still approved of the Democratic party and disapproved of the Republican Party on the basis of the groups each was felt to support. . . . The Democrats were still thought to help groups primarily of lower status: the common people, working people, the laboring man, Negroes, farmers. . . . The Republicans, on the other hand, were thought to help those of higher status: big businessmen, the upper class, the well-to-do. This facet of public attitude is undoubtedly strongly colored by the past.

But both parties experienced difficulty in projecting an image. In 1961, 45 per cent of the youth of high school and college age had no image of

[16] Data from Angus Campbell and others, *The American Voter,* John Wiley & Sons, Inc., New York, 1960, chaps. 3 and 4.

[17] According to the data of the University of Michigan Survey Research Center, Ann Arbor, Mich.

[18] Campbell and others, *op. cit.,* p. 47.

either party,[19] although the figure would certainly be smaller among older persons.

The parties do not take firm positions on many issues, and they do project blurred images. Nevertheless, the party labels should not be dismissed as meaningless. Party identification is still the best predictor of how a congressman will vote.[20] Interest-group leaders often prefer to seek access in one party as against another, and they must believe that there is an advantage in doing so. And there is something of a party vote that shows up in the "coat-tail effect"—in 75 per cent of the two-party congressional districts, the party that wins the Presidency gains in the percentage of its share of the congressional vote.[21]

Democratic Support Groups. In the 1960s, certain groups provided the basic source of voting strength for both parties. For more than a century, the Democratic party has appealed to those who stand outside the mainstream of American ideology:

The Solid South. It had been breached by Herbert Hoover in 1928 and by Eisenhower twice. Nevertheless, the South was still fundamentally dependable for local offices, even though in national elections it is in a state of change.

The working classes of the Northern industrial cities. Only about one-third of the nation's skilled and unskilled manual workers normally vote Republican.

Ethnic minorities. These groups are Democratic in large measure because their members immigrated fairly recently and tended to move to the larger cities rather than into rural areas. They were befriended by the Democratic machines in cities. Having had less time than earlier immigrants to become amalgamated into the American culture, they are still identifiable as Polish, Italian, Bohemian, or Japanese. Their children are, however, losing their distinct identity and are moving to the suburbs after having received good educations; many of them are now voting Republican—as conforming middle-class citizens are expected to do.

Religious minorities. Religious minorities—Roman Catholics and Jews, in particular—are also chiefly from the late immigrations, having arrived between 1890 and the closing of the main gates of immigration after World War I. These groups, who came principally from Southern and Eastern Europe, developed alliances with the Democratic urban organizations.

In recent years, Catholics, who have lost their ethnic identity, have tended to imitate the behavior of their peer groups. Thus working-class Catholics remain Democratic, but middle-class Catholics tend to be-

[19] George Gallup and Evan Hill, "Youth, the Cool Generation," *Saturday Evening Post*, Dec. 30, 1961, p. 78.

[20] David B. Truman, "Federalism and the Party System," in Arthur W. Macmahon (ed.), *Federalism, Mature and Emergent,* Doubleday & Company, Inc., Garden City, N.Y., 1955, pp. 115–136.

[21] Charles Press, "Presidential Coattails and Party Cohesion," *Midwest Journal of Political Science,* 7:320–335, November, 1963.

come Republicans; at least, this was the case prior to the candidacy of John F. Kennedy, who had a strong appeal for Catholics as Catholics, an indication that status anxieties remain just below the surface among people who have until recently been regarded as members of minority groups.

Jews were traditionally Republican (being overwhelmingly middle class) until about 1936. A great many of them then became concerned that isolationists in their party lacked an understanding of Adolf Hitler's threat to democracy in general and to European Jews, with whom they identified, in particular. As a result, Jews became staunch internationalists and among the most loyal of Democratic voters from that time onward. In 1952, 1956, and 1960, they were the most dependable of Democratic voters.[22]

Racial minorities. Negroes were fundamentally Republican until the Great Depression. When they voted—and relatively few did in the South, where they were discouraged from voting by a number of techniques, and in the North—they voted for the party of Abraham Lincoln and those who had succeeded in abolishing slavery. But the Depression brought insecurities, wartime and postwar urban conditions provided for economic advancement, and Negroes began to vote for New Dealers and their ideological successors in the Democratic party. Today Northern Negroes are much more inclined to vote Democratic than are Southern Negroes; in the South, many Negroes still consider the Democratic party to be that of the Bourbon aristocracy, which has kept them economically deprived, and the segregationists, who have kept them socially and politically deprived. But even in the South, Negroes have come to view Democratic presidential candidates as the candidates most likely to advance their cause.

Republican Support Groups. For the Republicans, the principal support groups in the 1960s were the following:

The lower-middle-class small-business men. This group is perhaps the most conservative in America (as was seen in Chapter 7). Its members identify strongly with middle-class values and seek to separate their identity from that of the urban working class, an identification they see as a major threat. The group is Republican by tradition, and this preference is reinforced by the increasing identity of urban workers with the Democratic party.

Businessmen and industrialists. In 1956, this group voted 75 per cent Republican in the presidential contest, while Eisenhower was winning by 57 per cent. Higher-income persons generally tend to vote Republican. They appear to view the party as one symbolizing middle-class respectability, greater conservatism, and a commitment to the furtherance of business generally.

[22] Data chiefly from the University of Michigan, Survey Research Center, Ann Arbor, Mich.

Small-town dwellers. The Republican party receives heavy support from the residents of the small towns of America (outside the South), but this is an area of declining importance. The party has also been powerful in New England, although not in the more industrialized parts of it. It could once count on the support of farmers (outside the South), but this group has been about evenly divided between the two parties in the postwar years.

Suburbia. The growing middle-class suburbs are the party's greatest source of power today and the one area in which it is increasing in strength. The middle class has expanded rapidly in the postwar years; while not all who are absorbed into the middle class vote Republican, a great many do—support for the party remains part of the normal behavior pattern of the organization man.

The Position of the Two Parties Today. The above groups support the Republican organization and keep it alive and vigorous; but they are not, taken alone,

Figure 10-6

The Republican Party Is One of Middle-class Respectability

"Do you have to tell everyone you're a Democrat and create those awful silences?

Drawing by Stan Hunt; by permission of the Saturday Evening Post.

enough to give Republicans control of Congress or the Presidency. A strong protest vote against the majority party is necessary for them to capture Congress as they did in the discontented year of 1946, just after World War II, and in 1952, when voters protested against the apparently meaningless (to most of them) Korean conflict. A man of great popular appeal, a folk hero, or a charismatic personality would seem to be required if Republicans are to capture the Presidency for they must win nearly 20 per cent of the balance of the electorate while keeping all of their own members in line in order to win the White House—and more than one-half of that 20 per cent must come from among persons with pronounced tendencies to vote Democratic.

The task of the Democrats is easier, of course, except that many of their supporters are not as reliable as voters, often having to be convinced that they should bother to vote. Republicans have a significantly lower percentage of nonvoters and persons with low-turnout propensities. The principal Democratic areas of support—the South and the industrial urban areas of the North—are still vigorously expanding in population. The party has the fundamental loyalty of a majority of the national electorate, and there were no signs in the mid-1960s that the party's basic appeal was on the wane. It will, if earlier party patterns are maintained, eventually lose its favored position, but just when this will be—just when a newer ideology with perhaps another party associated with it will come to a position of dominance—is not known and is not now predictable.

PARTY IDENTIFICATION

The support groups of the two parties each consist, of course, of individuals, each of whom has his reasons for offering support. Let us examine some of those reasons. Party membership in the United States, as we have already noted, is not a meaningful concept if we use such criteria as campaign activity, financial contribution, or formal enrollment. It is probably most useful if we think of party "identification" rather than membership, that is, if we switch from a legal to a psychological concept. The term "party identification" refers to "the extent to which an individual considers his membership in categorical political groups (e.g., a national, ethnic, or religious minority; social class; political party) as part of his self-image."[23] We know from several studies that political party identifications are acquired early and tend to be passed along from one generation to the next within a family. Party affiliation, though according to conventional knowledge a result of deliberate rational choice, is actually

[23] Frank A. Pinner and Henry F. Cooke, "Political Identifications—Some Data and Reflections," a paper delivered at the Midwest Conference of Political Scientists, Columbia, Mo., May, 1961.

TABLE 10-1

DIFFERENCES IN VOTING BEHAVIOR BY RELIGION (URBAN CATHOLICS AND PROTESTANTS), 1948 (In per cent)

Socioeconomic status	Religion	Voting Republican Elmira, N.Y.*	Voting Republican Philadelphia, Pa.
High	Protestant	98	88
	Catholic	50	85
Middle	Protestant	83	77
	Catholic	31	39
Low	Protestant	66	41
	Catholic	31	18

* Data from Bernard L. Berelson and others, *Voting,* The University of Chicago Press, Chicago, 1954.

NOTE: The same pattern was found in each city. Voting patterns are related to values learned in various social relationships.

SOURCE: Derived from Oscar Glantz, "Protestant and Catholic Voting Behavior in a Metropolitan Area," *Public Opinion Quarterly,* 23:73–82, Spring, 1959.

in large measure inherited as a family heirloom, much as is religion or citizenship[24] (see Table 10-1).

Frank A. Pinner and Henry F. Cooke, in a study of "rather bright [third-grade] children in an upper-middle-class suburban community" found that:[25]

> Of the twenty-two children in this class, fifteen proclaimed themselves Republicans and three, Democrats. The remaining four were in doubt but were able to report one day later that they had questioned their parents about their party affiliation and had found that they were political independents.

A larger study by Fred I. Greenstein, of 659 fourth- to eighth-grade children in New Haven, Connecticut, found that "from remarkably early ages boys and girls parallel men and women in the ways that their political responses vary."[26] In this study, one-third of the fourth-grade girls and 41 per cent of the fourth-grade boys could name at least one political party leader; 12 per cent of the girls and 15 per cent of the boys named a political news story when asked to pick out a news item that was

[24] Campbell and others, *op. cit.,* pp. 141–143; Herbert McClosky and Harold E. Dahlgren, "Primary Group Influence on Party Loyalty," *American Political Science Review,* 53:757-776, September, 1959; Fred I. Greenstein, "Sex-related Political Differences in Childhood," *Journal of Politics,* 23:353–371, May, 1961.

[25] Pinner and Cooke, *op. cit.,* p. 3.

[26] Greenstein, *op. cit.,* p. 353.

"interesting"; and 23 per cent of the girls and 39 per cent of the boys named a political figure as a famous person they wanted to be like.

Persons are most likely to acquire their party identification from their parents. Other factors of special, but lesser, importance include the area of the nation in which one was raised (any Southerner is likely to be a Democrat, any nonurban New Englander, a Republican), income level (the higher it is, the more likely the individual is to be a Republican), religion (Jews and Catholics are likely to be Democrats, Protestants are more likely to be Republicans), and occupation (blue-collar persons are likely to be Democrats, white-collar persons to be Republicans). But these are only tendencies derived on a statistical basis. Any individual may not fit the pattern—there are, after all, Protestant New England businessmen who are Democrats, Catholic factory workers who are Republicans, and a very few in every category who vote for third parties.

Not all persons feel a sense of sympathy with a particular political party. In a mobile society, intermarriage among persons from differing backgrounds is not uncommon, and the children of such marriages are

TABLE 10–2

DISTRIBUTION OF PARTY IDENTIFICATION, 1952–1960 (In per cent)

Political party	Oct. 1952	Sept. 1953	Oct. 1954	April 1956	Oct. 1956	Nov. 1957	Oct. 1958	Oct. 1960
Strong Republican	13	15	13	14	15	10	13	14
Weak Republican	14	15	14	18	14	16	16	13
Independent Republican	7	6	6	6	8	6	4	7
Independent	5	4	7	3	9	8	8	8
Independent Democrat	10	8	9	6	7	7	7	8
Weak Democrat	25	23	25	24	23	26	24	25
Strong Democrat	22	22	22	19	21	21	23	21
Apolitical ("Don't know.")	4	7	4	10	3	6	5	4
Total	100	100	100	100	100	100	100	100
(Total number of cases)	(1,614)	(1,023)	(1,139)	(1,731)	(1,772)	(1,488)	(1,269)	(3,021)

SOURCE: Survey Research Center, University of Michigan, Ann Arbor, Mich.

subjected to cross pressures that may make them true independents (see Chapter 9). As a result, many of them will also have a relatively low interest in politics. They are likely to be nonvoters—after all, a major factor encouraging interest in politics is emotional identification with one of the teams or parties, just as is the case with a football or baseball team. A person whose mother came from a family of Democratic Eastern factory workers and whose father was the son of a Republican grocer from the Midwest is likely to be a true independent, for the cross pressures he feels will tend to balance one another, and he will probably be left with no emotional loyalties.

One other point should be made: People *do* sometimes deliberately change their party affiliation. An individual may, largely by inheritance, identify with one party through his college years or until he achieves a certain position in society. Then, after evaluation of where he believes each party within his locality or state stands on issues he considers to be important, he may become an independent or begin to identify with another party. Yet it is easy to confuse rational decisions about parties with the social and economic pressures that guide the individual toward new identifications. The son of a Democratic factory hand may work his way through college while still identifying with the cause of the working-man and believing in liberal programs, but as he begins to rise to highly paid technical or administrative positions in a business firm, he is subjected to many overt and covert pressures that may gradually change his point of view and his identification. Almost without realizing it, his party identification changes. He decides one year that this time he is going to support the Republican candidate; before long, he is doing so regularly, perhaps even becoming active in support of the party. A similar transition in the Democratic direction may be made, for example, by a Southern Negro Republican who moves to a unionized industrial city in the North.

MINOR PARTIES

Americans think of party politics almost exclusively in dichotomous terms—there are two parties; if any others appear on the ballot, they should be ignored because a minor party vote is a vote wasted. Despite this attitude, other party names do appear on the ballot. But their candidates are rarely successful. In 1948, for example, eleven parties theoretically were in the presidential race, although many of them could not qualify for a place on the ballot in most states. The Progressive Citizens of America ran Henry A. Wallace on a platform calling for liberal reforms and a *rapprochement* with the Soviet Union. The States' Rights Democratic party or Dixiecrats, a Southern splinter group, opposed the strong civil rights plank that was in the Democratic platform for the first time that year. The Socialist party, for the last time ran its veteran candidate Norman Thomas, who had by then almost achieved a middle-class respectability. The minor or "third" parties also supported Socialist-Labor and Socialist Worker (Trotskyite) candidates; a Vegetarian; a Prohibitionist; a Greenback party candidate, who called in nineteenth-century fashion for the total abandonment of the gold standard, an issue by then incomprehensible to most of the American public. There was also the Christian Nationalists' Crusade, a rabble rousing, anti-Catholic, anti-Semitic, arch-nationalistic protest group that appealed chiefly to the alienated among the lower middle class. The States' Rights Dixiecrats carried four states in the Deep South, and Wallace received about 2 per cent of the vote. The other parties received few votes. Throughout most of American history, the race has been almost exclusively between two major parties. Through time, the formal legislation relative to parties and elections has reinforced tendencies in this direction.

There have been some third-party successes, in the sense that such groups have occasionally received a substantial number of votes. In 1892, 1912, 1920, 1924, and 1948, individual minor-party candidates received over 1 million votes each time. In 1914, the Socialists and Progressives together pulled over 1.5 million votes in congressional elections. But the only third party in American history to displace a major party and become one of the "big two" was the Republican party, which first ran a candidate for the Presidency in 1856.

Despite the general unwillingness of Americans to vote for third parties, these organizations do play an important part in American politics. They serve two principal functions. First, they offer "spectacular criticisms of the party in power which often the major opposition party fails to provide."[27] Unlike the major parties, which are at least as fearful of alienating regular supporters as they are anxious to gain new ones, minor parties stand on specific principles and can therefore be outspoken.

Second, minor parties have frequently been the innovators of new issues and new governmental programs. The graduated income tax, railroad and banking regulation, unemployment compensation, the popular election of senators, the primary election, old-age pensions, and many other policies that are now commonplace and that neither major party would oppose in principle, were first suggested by minor parties. This has been the great contribution of third parties—to bring to the forefront emerging public demands. But it has also been a source of their frustration, for whenever their proposals have gained much public acceptance, one and shortly both of the major parties have taken from them the enticing bait. So they almost never gain general popular acceptance and must instead be content to serve as the hair shirt of the political system.

Although third parties have been important as innovators, it should not be assumed that they develop only farsighted, responsible policies that are then stolen from them. Innovation is not an efficient activity. Most creative

[27] Hugh A. Bone, *American Politics and the Party System,* 2d ed., McGraw-Hill Book Company, New York, 1955, p. 303.

proposals are rejected by the decision makers of society. They are found to be "impractical," or they may be so deviant from dominant values as to be wholly inappropriate. Often new ideas result from the fact that social change does not follow a measured course. People who are affected by economic change or new life-styles earlier than others may form protest organizations, including third parties, ahead of others. They seem to be anticipating trends, although in fact they may only be among the first to be affected by them. Thus, the LaFollette Progressives of 1924 drew some of their support, at least, from farmers and others who were affected by the beginnings of the Great Depression, beginnings that occurred long before the stock market crash of 1929.

Third parties vary greatly in their reasons for existence; hence the chances that some of their policies eventually may be adopted also varies. Some parties are highly doctrinaire (Communist, Socialist Worker, American Nazi), with a persistent, well-developed ideology. Others reflect the emotional thrashings of the alienated, often taking extremely intolerant views and concentrating on finding scapegoats (the Know-Nothings, the Christian Nationalists' Crusade) or demanding economic reforms for those who feel unfairly deprived (Populists, Greenbackers). Still others result from deliberate ploys when secession from the major party is threatened and finally carried out in an effort to force the dominant leaders to negotiate (Theodore Roosevelt's Progressives, the Dixiecrats). From these varied groups have come such improbable proposals as these: abolish the United States Senate; amend the Constitution to prohibit all non-Christian religions; abolish the Federal income tax; prohibit all secret lodges and clubs; and permit the voters to overrule decisions of the United States Supreme Court by popular referendum.

THE AMERICAN PARTY SYSTEM: CRITICISMS AND AN EVALUATION

Politicians and political parties have been subjected to considerable criticism over the years from a variety of sources. They must, of course, constantly live with the chronic tendency of Americans to view politics as evil and politicians as untrustworthy. Politicians probably live by basically the same rules as do business executives, farmers, or labor leaders. But the parties and their leaders are quickly criticized by persons who are quite patient with the deviousness, slowness, indecisiveness, and ambivalence of nongovernmental leaders in our society. Apparently, our values lead to expectations that politicians hold to *higher* standards of behavior than do businessmen, farmers, or union leaders.

Parties are also criticized for knuckling under to every discernible pressure; for being made up of all persons who claim membership, whether they are loyal to the party or not; for having leaders who make careers of their jobs and show no responsiveness to the members' wants unless votes are at stake; and for failing to take firm stands on issues. But to the degree that these criticisms are valid, the characteristics did not emerge from nowhere to spite society; they are primarily the result of applying American social values to the political system.

Americans generally do not like the idea of parties being closed except to those who can pass certain tests for membership. They are apathetic about party activity, and hence, they often permit the leadership of the parties to become self-perpetuating bureaucracies. And the lack of ideological cohesiveness in our parties is to a considerable degree a result of having a two-party system in a land which—unlike some democracies, such as the United Kingdom—consists of a very large number of subcultures and where no simple arrangement of the belief systems exists upon which to build public policy.

The Function of Effective Criticism. A common and perhaps especially serious criticism of our party system is that the party out of power does not provide the responsible but effective criticism needed to protect the interests of the minority and to prevent irresponsible action by the "ins." Some years ago, a committee of political scientists commented:[28]

> The fundamental requirement of accountability is a two-party system in which the opposition party acts as the critic of the party in power, developing, defining and presenting the policy alternatives which are necessary for a true choice in reaching public decisions. The opposition most conducive to responsible government is an organized party opposition.

The parties do not, however, often have clearly defined differences in policy positions, as has already been noted. Furthermore, the out-party often does not lead the opposition to the in-group. Indeed, it generally allows the party in power to generate its own internal opposition whenever possible. Thus:[29]

> The actions of the Republican party during the conflict over President Roosevelt's proposal to enlarge the Supreme Court supply the most notable example of this failure of responsible, partisan opposition in recent political history. That legislative battle was probably the most crucial of the New Deal era, but it was publicly fought within the Democratic party, while the Republicans maintained a stony, official silence. . . . So far was the American public from accepting the role of a responsible opposition that Republican Congressional leaders dared not oppose the plan, fearing that opposition bearing a Republican label would lead both electorate and legislators to assume the existence of hidden values in the proposal of the Democratic President.

[28] American Political Science Association, Committee on Political Parties, *Toward a More Responsible Two-party System, American Political Science Review,* 44: Supplement, September, 1950, pp. 1–2.

[29] Karl A. Lamb, "The Opposition Party as Secret Agent: Republicans and the Court Fight, 1937," *Papers of the Michigan Academy of Science, Arts, and Letters,* 46:539–550, 1961.

Franklin D. Roosevelt, on February 5, 1937, proposed to Congress a modification of the Supreme Court structure that, he said, would permit the supplementation of elderly justices with younger and more vigorous men who could maintain a faster pace and help clear up the Court docket. In fact, his intention undoubtedly was to secure a majority that would sustain New Deal legislation, which had suffered a number of defeats in the preceding term of the Court; in some decisions important policies had been held unconstitutional, several by 5 to 4 votes. The next evening, John D. M. Hamilton, the Republican national chairman, gave a speech in Pittsburgh:[30]

> Hamilton had chosen to define for the men of Pittsburgh the duties of the opposition party. During the course of his meal, Hamilton was called to the telephone. Senator [Arthur H.] Vandenburg, calling from Washington, told Hamilton that a meeting of three Republican Senate leaders that afternoon had decided that vigorous Republican opposition was the only possible influence which might cause the President's plan for "packing" the Supreme Court to be passed. There were enough Democratic votes to kill the measure, Vandenburg said, and the Senators had decided to allow the Democrats to lead in opposing the plan, rather than establish an opposition that might unite the Democrats behind the President. Vandenburg asked Hamilton to refrain from mentioning the Court plan in his address that evening. . . .
>
> Hamilton . . . returned to the banquet room and told [his audience] that the function of the opposition party was to formulate alternative solutions to the recognized problems, rather than to indulge in indiscriminate criticism.

The Leaderless Opposition. Although the party in possession of the White House has a clear spokesman and considerable national patronage, the opposition party does not. The losing presidential candidate, by his very defeat, may not be popularly accepted as a party spokesman. Furthermore, leaders of his party in Congress often resent his efforts to speak for the party, claiming that right for themselves as incumbent officeholders. The party out of power is hence often badly divided. The national chairman who remains from an unsuccessful campaign or his successor, who is a compromise choice made by national committee members, is usually a weak rather than a strong leader. The leaders in fifty states are faced, after each defeat, with building a new coalition that will have a chance to win the White House the next time.

A Closing Note. Our parties remain what one political scientist has called "a mystic maze."[31] We do not seem, as a people, to expect them to assume the role that parties play in Great Britain, where each stands for election on a quite precise set of proposed policies and where each is expected to criticize the actions of the other in a rational, responsible manner.

[30] *Ibid.*, p. 540. Lamb's description of the incident is based on an interview with Hamilton.

[31] Stephen K. Bailey, *The Condition of Our National Political Parties*, The Fund for the Republic, New York, 1959, p. 7.

The American party pattern is one that has accommodated itself to a federal system of government, the separation-of-powers principle, and a society that consists of many subcultures. Its heterogeneity is reflected in the preference for localized, parochial domination of party machinery. State and local patronage, to the typical party worker, is more important than national patronage, especially in one-party states.[32] This patronage allows local organizations to be independent of the national committee both for manpower and for finances. Even national government patronage, when it is available, is dispensed primarily by congressmen or senators with regional or statewide constituencies, rather than by the White House staff or the national committee. National party organizations are therefore, except for the presidential campaigns, almost nonexistent. The pattern is one in which the federal system of government "tends to encourage confederation in the party's government."[33]

SELECTED BIBLIOGRAPHY

In addition to the citations for Chapters 9 and 11, there are many works dealing specifically with American parties. They are cited in the textbooks in the field. We have relied particularly on the work of Key [8, 9, 10]. These writers also offer criticisms of the party system as did the Committee on Political Parties [4] which hoped for a "responsible two-party system." More recently Bailey [1] has reexamined the matter. Writers have used a variety of values and assumptions in developing models for a party system.

Some examination of party patterns has been made by regions of the nation, particularly by Key [10] in a classic study of the South, Fenton [6] for the Border States, and Lockard [11] for New England. Nash [14] offers a convenient study of third parties.

1. Bailey, Stephen K.: *The Condition of Our National Political Parties,* The Fund for the Republic, New York, 1959.
2. Boorstin, Daniel J.: *The Genius of American Politics,* Phoenix Books, The University of Chicago Press, Chicago, 1960.
3. Brogan, D. W.: *Politics in America,* Anchor Books, Doubleday & Company, Inc., Garden City, N.Y., 1960.
4. Committee on Political Parties, American Political Science Association: *Toward a More Responsible Two-party System,* Holt, Rinehart and Winston, Inc., New York, 1950.
5. Duverger, Maurice: *Political Parties,* John Wiley & Sons, Inc., 3d ed., Science Editions, 1963. Translated by Barbara North and Robert North, with a foreword by D. W. Brogan.
6. Fenton, John H.: *Politics in the Border States,* The Hauser Press, New Orleans, La., 1957.
7. Hicks, John D.: *Republican Ascendancy, 1921–1933,* Harper & Row, Publishers, New York, 1960.

[32] V. O. Key, Jr., *Politics, Parties, and Pressure Groups,* 4th ed., Thomas Y. Crowell Company, New York, 1958, p. 368.

[33] *Ibid.*

8. Key, V. O., Jr.: *Politics, Parties, and Pressure Groups,* 5th ed., Thomas Y. Crowell Company, New York, 1964.
9. Key, V. O., Jr.: "Secular Realignment and the Party System," *The Journal of Politics,* 21:198–212, May, 1959.
10. Key, V. O., Jr., with Alexander Heard: *Southern Politics,* Alfred A. Knopf, Inc., New York, 1949.
11. Lockard, Duane: *New England State Politics,* Princeton University Press, Princeton, N.J., 1959.
12. Lubell, Samuel: *The Future of American Politics,* Doubleday & Company, Inc., Garden City, N.Y., 1956.
13. Milbrath, Lester W.: *The Washington Lobbyists,* Rand McNally & Company, Chicago, 1963.
14. Nash, Howard P., Jr.: *Gadflies of American Politics: A Short History of Third Parties,* Public Affairs Press, Washington, D.C., 1956.
15. Prothro, James W., and others: "Two-party Voting in the South," *American Political Science Review,* 52:131–139, March, 1958.
16. Schlesinger, Joseph A.: "The Structure of Competition for Office in the American States," *Behavioral Science,* 5:197–210, July, 1960.
17. Silva, Ruth C.: *Rum, Religion and Votes: 1928 Reexamined,* The Pennsylvania State University Press, University Park, Pa., 1962.
18. Standing, William H., and James A. Robinson: "Inter-party Competition and Primary Contesting: The Case of Indiana," *American Political Science Review,* 52:1066–1077, December, 1958.
19. Wilson, James Q.: *Negro Politics,* The Free Press of Glencoe, New York, 1960.
20. Zariski, Raphael: "Party Factions and Comparative Politics," *Midwest Journal of Political Science,* 4:27–51, February, 1960.

CHAPTER

11

NOMINATIONS AND ELECTIONS

An election, in a democracy, distributes public offices of power and prestige. In doing so, it performs a vital function in the political system. It determines who is to reach the winner's circle and is therefore to make decisions that affect the lives of millions.

To be effective in the political process, an election must:

1. Be accepted as the legitimate method of choice by a dominant portion of society
2. Provide an effective means of recruiting candidates
3. Provide machinery for the final choice of the person who is to assume office

The United States has many one-party areas where the candidate of that party can ordinarily expect to win office. Elsewhere, the candidate of one of two parties can nearly always expect to win. For these reasons, the selection of the party candidate is often the critical choice.

In this chapter, it seems appropriate for us to ask who selects the candidates, who is advantaged, and how, by a particular method of selection. Party leaders have more influence than others over selection, but they cannot always control it. Outsiders who run for office can sometimes capture the imagination of the electorate, and if they succeed, the skepticism and reservations of the professional party actives may not be enough to prevent their selection.

The nomination process in America involves the use almost exclusively of either the convention or the primary-election technique, both of which are essentially American in origin. In most democracies, political party leaders generally have firmer control over nominations than is the case in the United States. Since the time of grass-roots Jacksonianism, the American emphasis has been upon finding ways by which to reduce the power of the party's professional oligarchy and to increase popular participation in the nomination process. In part, this tendency has been encouraged by the widespread existence of one-party politics, but it is also a function of the abiding faith Americans have in the common man and in his ability to make the right decisions without direction from professional specialists.

The election campaign, too, differs in the United States from that in most other democracies. It tends to be longer, less oriented toward specific issues, and is based more upon the candidate's personal appeal than upon that of the party.

THE CHOICE OF CANDIDATES

Since the 1820s, American nomination machinery has had to be accommodated to a number of particular characteristics of American democracy. We have noted the importance of the concept of the average man and of his right to participate in all steps of the selection process. In addition, the many persons who are directly chosen at the polls—far more than in any other democracy—must somehow be selected in a manner that produces satisfactory officeholders. Furthermore, these persons, are often chosen at the same election, for it is not uncommon in the United States to have simultaneous voting for, say, the President, members of Congress, state officers and legislators, and county, school, and township or municipal officeholders. There has been, however, some tendency in recent decades toward the separation of elections for the several levels of government.

Early Nomination Devices. In colonial times, when social institutions could be simple, a man commonly became a candidate for office by self-announcement. Voters knew candidates personally or by reputation. When a local squire decided that he had matured enough in terms of experience and social standing to present himself as a candidate for justice of the peace or for the legislature, he expected that his constituents would evaluate him in terms of their image of him in relation to what they expected in the particular public office.

Quite commonly, it was expected that the office should seek the man, and the individual was either genuinely drafted or arranged for what could be made to appear to be a draft. Much of this early attitude remains with us still. Persons are often urged by their neighbors and friends to become candidates for the school board or suburban council or for township and county offices in rural areas. Even in the case of the exalted office of President, the ritual has long required the candidate to deny that he is seeking the job, then later to state that he is doing so at the urging of friends and national leaders. (A newsman of the day stated that the first indications he had that Zachary Taylor wanted to be President in 1848 came when the general, on duty in Mexico, began writing letters to editors denying that he was a candidate.)

The caucus, the oldest institutional device for nomination in the United States, consisted originally of an informal meeting. It rose to importance as political parties became organized, but existed even in colonial days. John Adams, in 1763, gave one of the earliest descriptions of the smoke-filled room:[1]

> There they smoke tobacco till you cannot see from one end of the garret to the other. There they drink flip [spiced and heated hard cider], I suppose, and there they choose a moderator, who puts questions to the vote regularly; and selectmen, assessors, collectors, warden, firewards, and representatives are regularly chosen before they are chosen by the town.

In America's early days, the caucus members could print a ballot and distribute it themselves, with citizens who approved of the list carrying it with them to the polling place and simply dropping the premarked ballot in the box.

With the growth of cities, the caucus became large and unwieldy. To overcome this problem, the convention method came into use. Nominations were made at formal meetings after the convention delegates had been chosen by caucus at the precinct—or smallest political subdivision—level.

The widespread development of citywide or statewide political machines in the nineteenth century made this method subject to corruption. The machine controlled the precinct caucus by excluding unwanted persons. This could be done through trickery by keeping secret the time and place of meetings, by threats, by better strategic planning, and other devices. And whoever controlled most of the precinct caucuses controlled the convention. In one-party areas, the machines often controlled elective offices simply by controlling the nomination process.

Reforms in Nomination. Around the beginning of the present century, the reform movement produced a change in nomination procedure. The direct primary election was substituted for the caucus and convention. It is now almost universal in the United States. There are a few exceptions, the most important and dramatic of which are the nominations for President and Vice President of the United States, candidates whose selection is described below.

Strictly speaking, a primary election is nothing more than a non-assembled caucus. In an earlier day, every eligible voter was entitled to take part in the selection of candidates. Later, part of this job was turned over to those who were theoretically his representatives acting at a convention. When the convention proved to be unrepresentative and class- or boss-dominated, the primary election was devised to return nominations

[1] From the diary of John Adams, quoted in a number of sources.

"to the people." The plan in large measure transfers control of the nomination machinery from the party to the state, all parties choosing their candidates on the same day under the supervision of public election officials, with ballots standardized and printed at public expense (except in a few Southern states) and with a secret ballot (in contrast to most caucus and convention systems).

The direct primary was first used by the Pennsylvania Democratic party in the 1840s. It gradually spread throughout the country, with Connecticut (1955) the last state to accept it as a nomination device. It began to be used for statewide nominations in the 1890s, and Wisconsin (1903) was the first state to establish compulsory primary elections for all state elective offices.

The leadership in Wisconsin probably can be attributed to the great reform zeal generated by Governor Robert M. (Fightin' Bob) LaFollette. But it was in the South, where one-partyism prevailed, that the primary system of nomination first came into general use, apparently as a result of efforts on the part of excluded groups and classes to overcome potential domination by a party oligarchy.[2] In rough terms, the primary was adopted first in the one-party states and later in the competitive two-party states. After the South, the West picked up the plan, then the Midwest, and finally the East, where the leaders of old and well-established party structures delayed its acceptance.

The Primary Election. Primary elections are of two types, partisan and nonpartisan. In both types, candidates seeking nomination usually qualify for a place on the primary ballot by securing a required number of signatures of qualified voters on a petition.

The nonpartisan primary is actually an elimination contest. Names appear on the ballot without party designation. The usual practice is to eliminate all but two candidates on the first balloting. Political parties may or may not be active in nonpartisan elections. Usually they show little or no activity, preferring to concentrate on those elections in which partisan designation on the ballot assures the party leaders of influence over the outcome and probably over the nominee. Nonpartisan elections are used primarily in municipal and state judicial elections. The Nebraska and Minnesota legislatures are also selected on a nonpartisan ballot, but this device is not used in the selection of the President or members of Congress.

The partisan primary, in which candidates' affiliation do appear on the ballot, may be *open* or *closed*. An open primary is open to any eligible voter, regardless of his party affiliation or whether he is a party member or a confirmed independent. All voters are given the ballots of all parties, though they may vote for the nominees of only one party (except in the state of Washington). In a closed primary, the voter must have registered

[2] V. O. Key, Jr., *American State Politics,* Alfred A. Knopf, Inc., New York, 1956, pp. 87–97.

as a member of the party or must declare his affiliation at the polling place, and he is given only the primary ballot of his party.

The closed primary is the more common, but in some states a voter needs only to declare that he is affiliated with a particular party in order to get its ballot. In some cases, in fact, the election clerk simply inquires, "What ballot do you want?" without suggesting that allegiance to the party is a technical requirement. In a few states, transferring from one party to another in the primary is relatively difficult, and a real effort is made to keep the process of nomination within the control of persons who actually identify with the party.

About one-fourth of the states use the open primary, which seems to have received much popular acceptance because the voter need not reveal his choice of party and the secret ballot is thus fully preserved. Perhaps the open primary would be adopted in more states if party organization leaders did not see it as making identification of supporters more difficult or fear "raiding." That is, that supporters of Party A may, if they have no significant contests of their own, vote in the primary of Party B, seeking to nominate weak candidates. In fact, however, this is quite rare in states that are party-competitive, at least, in Michigan, Minnesota, and Washington, probably because leaders of both parties are anxious to make a strong showing in the primary for its favorable psychological effect in relation to the general campaign and because it would be difficult to organize an effective raid in any case.[3] In the 1964 Wisconsin presidential preference primary, however, many Republicans (who had no intraparty contest) apparently voted for Governor George C. Wallace of Alabama on the Democratic ticket in order to embarrass President Lyndon Johnson, who was then urging Congress to adopt a civil rights bill.

For the most part, the notion of party membership is lightly regarded in the United States, and the typical citizen neither understands nor accepts the theory of the primary as being a device by which party members choose the candidates of *their* party. Instead, many Americans believe that one should vote for the man rather than being concerned with the welfare of a political organization. Voters hold to this belief, even though most of them are committed to a particular party by custom. Furthermore, in practice the critical decisions about public office are usually made in the primary rather than in the general election—even in two-party states, a great many cities, counties, and congressional districts are one-party-dominated. As a result, the concept of party membership is minimized and the concept of the primary as an integral part of the process by which public officials are selected is emphasized.

The Runoff Primary. The tendency in all states is for popular interest to concentrate on the primary of the stronger party. As the chances for the

[3] Research on Michigan and Minnesota by the authors; on Washington, see Daniel M. Ogden, Jr., "The Blanket Primary and Party Regularity in Washington," *Pacific Northwest Quarterly,* 39:33–36, January, 1948.

minority party to win elections decrease, popular participation in that party's primary also decreases, but at an even faster rate.[4] In the South, the advantage to the Democrats has been so great that eleven states have tried to ensure majority choice for public office by requiring a runoff primary in all cases where no candidate wins a majority in the first primary. The runoff is usually conducted between the two candidates who receive the most votes in the first primary. This method is used to prevent the manipulation of the results by flooding the ballot with a multiplicity of candidates, something that can be done, for example, through the adroit use of "name candidates." The runoff ensures that the candidate who finally wins is acceptable to a majority of those voting, though he may not be their first choice.

States that have adopted the runoff primary have frankly recognized that the primary is the actual machinery through which elective officers are selected. In many other states, however, the primary is normally also the effective decision-making locus.

Preprimary Conventions. A few states have party conventions before the primary. The purpose of these is to reduce open intraparty conflict by permitting faction leaders to work out compromises in advance of voting. It may also be used to weaken the chances of a popular campaigner who is, however, unacceptable to the dominant leaders of the party. On the primary ballot, the endorsed slate may be starred to indicate the candidates who are the choice of party leaders. This method does not always succeed. In 1950, four members of the Democratic slate in Minnesota were defeated by unknown candidates, all of whom had Irish names. Democratic voters in St. Paul, which is heavily Irish, were probably responsible for the slate defeat in a light primary vote. The advantage of the preprimary convention to party leaders is that it encourages greater party cohesion. Colorado, Massachusetts, New Mexico, Minnesota and Utah have all used variations of this endorsement procedure.

The Presidential Primary. Reformers in the early twentieth century not only advocated the primary as a means of letting the voters choose the party candidates for Congress and state offices, they also argued that the principle should be applied to the choice of President. As a result of reform pressures, about one-third of the states have provided for presidential primaries. These are of two types: (1) those in which voters choose the state's delegates to the national conventions; and (2) those in which voters indicate their preference among the candidates who have chosen to enter the contest in that state. A few states provide for both.

In most states, delegates to the national convention are chosen by state or district conventions or by party committees; but about one-third of the delegates to recent conventions of both parties have been selected by

[4] Key, *op. cit.*

popular vote. In a number of states, including several with very large representation (California, New Jersey, Ohio, Pennsylvania), the delegates are, or may be, instructed by primary or state convention as to how to vote on the early ballots. In most states, the delegate is a free agent or carries with him no more than a feeling for the general preference of those who sent him to the convention.

Although opinion polls indicate that the general voting public believes it should have a greater voice in the selection of the President—a viewpoint we would expect—the presidential preference primary has not been a great success even though a number of states have used it for several decades. The major difficulties in the use of the primary for indicating preference are several.

First of all, in most states, the primary is not a contest between leading presidential candidates. The important candidates sometimes refuse to enter, particularly in cases where they believe that their strength is sufficient to win without taking the risk of the primary or where they do not wish to be measured against a local favorite. Usually, the candidate can himself decide whether to enter, although in Oregon all candidates considered significant by the secretary of state are entered unless the individual withdraws by affidavit. (Persons not included by the secretary may be entered by petition.)

Second, politicians often enter "favorite sons" from their own or neighboring states, men who may have little chance of winning the big prize. Thus, in 1964, it was difficult to evaluate the victory of Henry Cabot Lodge in New Hampshire. Was he a man with great voter appeal? Was he merely being honored by proud fellow New Englanders? Or was he getting mainly anti-Rockefeller and anti-Goldwater votes? If a favorite son is supported in a particular state, the meaningful result may be that the delegates of the state become free agents after he is eliminated. Their activities may be of a sort that cannot be predicted in advance and may bear little relationship to second-choice preferences of the state's voters.

Third, in states where convention delegates are elected and a presidential preference primary is held, a majority of the winning delegates may not be supporters of the winner, with a resulting confusion as to the meaning of the voting results. In some states, the delegates are pledged to support the candidate who polls the highest vote, but this is not always the case.

The preferential primary cannot be dismissed as unimportant, however. It has been especially effective in eliminating possible presidential nominees. The 1952 contest between General Dwight D. Eisenhower and Senator Robert A. Taft probably convinced many Republican delegates that, whatever their personal preference, the former was far more popular with voters than the latter and hence had a far better chance to win in November. In 1960, Senator John F. Kennedy of Massachusetts, a Catholic and a middle-of-the-roader, demonstrated in West Virginia, an overwhelmingly Protestant state with a chronically high unemployment level, that he had greater voter appeal than did Senator Hubert H. Humphrey of Minnesota, a Protestant who was perceived as a liberal. The outcome of that primary election, which Kennedy won easily, probably convinced many delegates that they should support the man who eventually was elected President that year.

The future of the presidential preference primary remains uncertain, but it appeared in the 1960s to be gaining support, both from professional politicians and from rank-and-file voters.

Criticisms of the Primary. Although it is the dominant form of nomination for office in the United States, the primary election has never been well understood by most Americans. Voters are annoyed by the long "bedsheet" ballot with which they are confronted. They resent the fact that they must usually reveal their party preference in order to vote. And even when the open primary is used, they become incensed to discover that splitting the ticket, that is, selecting candidates from more than one party, is not permitted (except in the state of Washington).

Even though the primary is frequently the arena in which the real decision as to who will occupy a public office is made (see Chapter 10), the typical voter has never considered the primary to be as important as the general election. The difference in rate of turnout, with few exceptions, is great. The primary often has less than one-half the participants of the general election. The result is that the candidate's constituency is quite different in the two elections. There are three other principal differences between the primary and the general election:

1. Highly motivated interests are likely to have a disproportionate advantage in the primary, for their supporters will probably go to the polls, while the person with a marginal interest in politics (but probably a deep stake in political decisions) will tend not to vote.

2. Conservative candidates have a greater advantage than do liberals in the typical primary. Studies show (see Chapter 9) that conservatives are much more likely to vote than are liberals, especially in routine or undramatic elections. This phenomenon is partly responsible for giving both the House of Representatives and the Senate a conservative cast.

3. The absence of symbols or any indication of the factional or other group association of the individual candidate in the primary tends to encourage support of "name" candidates among the uninformed voters. Any candidate whose name resembles that of someone who has recently been a page-one newspaper figure is advantaged in the primary, even in cases where in a convention he would have no advantage at all over his opponents.

The primary is expensive for those who must campaign against competition for the nomination, and the goal of making all interested and qualified persons easily available for the public to nominate is frustrated by the fact that only the wealthy or those financed by a party or interest groups can afford to enter. Furthermore, the necessity for mounting a systematic campaign in order to gain the nomination discourages many individuals from entering the lists or even from indicating that they would be available for nomination. The need to conduct two campaigns rather than one is also discouraging to the marginal politician who is not sure that he wants to undertake the difficult burden of seeking public office in an arena in which, he often feels, there are no holds barred.

Whether financial incapacity, fear of the campaign, or lack of interest is the cause, the fact that so many primary elections have little competition itself indicates a failure on the part of the system to produce the type and number of candidates its originators intended. In many areas of the nation, the candidates are still determined by the party machinery, a fact that is not necessarily bad, but is not in the spirit of those who sponsored the plan. In such cases, the primary only ratifies the decision of the party leadership.

The primary has not greatly changed the kinds of persons nominated for office, as its originators hoped it would, though it may contribute to the nomination of publicity lovers and demagogues, while discouraging less exhibitionistic types. Because voters are not always acquainted with the candidates, it promotes the selection of persons with "political" names, names that sound like those of persons already widely known in the community or state, and of persons who happen to have a spot at or near the top of a long ballot.[5] It discourages party responsibility and the development of slates of candidates who collectively take meaningful positions on the issues of the day. It encourages intraparty rather than interparty conflict, thus probably contributing to the maintenance of one-partyism with its factional jungles that are so incomprehensible to the typical voter. The primary adds to the confusion of the American campaign by permitting it to be used for irrelevant purposes: Persons may file with no hope or perhaps even with no desire for victory; their purpose is to gain personal attention or, especially in the case of lawyers, to advertise their business or professional firms.

We cannot be sure, however, about the net effect of the primary upon the American political system, for too many variables are involved, as the social scientist is wont to apologize when he is not sure of his ground. For example, although the primary surely works to sustain one-partyism, it is quite possible that other factors would have prevented the widespread development of a two-party system in America. Had this been the case and the old caucus and convention system been retained, the typical voter would probably be even more frustrated than he is today, for under such conditions he would have a voice in neither the nomination nor the election.[6]

[5] Henry M. Bain and Donald S. Hecock, *Ballot Position and Voter's Choice,* Wayne State University Press, Detroit, 1957.

[6] See Key, *op. cit.*

However valid the arguments concerning the primary may be, it is an entrenched bit of Americana and is and probably will long remain the mechanism through which a great many of the actual decisions in the selection of persons to public office are made. Perhaps changes in it can be devised so as to make it a more effective contributor to the democratic process, but changes in the electoral system in this country have historically been made not so much in order to make it more nearly resemble some currently fashionable model as to provide immediate advantages to a dominant party or faction. Differences in party structure and election machinery from one state to another are in part, at least, a function of the desire of a group in power to strengthen its ability to stay in power. If changes in the nomination process are to be made, they must be made within the political environment as it exists in each state. The primary election itself was advocated for idealistic reasons, but it was often adopted for the practical political reason that it increased the political power of those advocating it.

THE NATIONAL CONVENTION—THE GREATEST SHOW ON EARTH

The huge hall is prepared to meet the needs of the great broadcasting networks. The city in which it is located was determined by vigorous bidding, with the winner paying a large sum of money to the party treasury, a sum collected from merchants who expect to profit from the delegates, technicians, and visitors during the week of the convention.

In making the physical arrangements for a convention, the convenience of the delegates is a secondary consideration. This is essentially a show, and so it is fitting that the layout should be one most appropriate for the staging of a telecast. The actors perform on the podium, so it gets special attention. The ordinary delegates are more members of the audience than of the show. Just as the members of the studio audience of a Bob Hope program are expected to laugh and applaud on cue, the delegates are expected to vote and applaud on easily recognized signals from the podium. No one holds up an applause sign, as they do for Bob Hope's studio audience, but the time-honored ritual of convention speech makes this unnecessary. Oratorical inflections and cue words do the job.

As with any carefully staged high-budget television show, the convention moves according to a script written by professionals highly skilled in their trade. They know that it is foolish to have the first major speech, or keynote address, in the daytime hours when most male and many female voters are away from their TV sets. Similarly, they would not permit the eventual presidential nominee of the convention to make his formal acceptance speech at other than prime viewing time. And they insist that he accept using a carefully prepared script in which, by the ritual, he says that he is humble in the thought of the great responsibility that is thrust upon him (this may be true, but most successful politicians are vain, not humble, men); that he has secured the nomination without having made a single commitment to any other person (almost certainly not true); that he is prepared to give his all in the cause of victory (true); that winning will depend on the good teamwork by all persons devoted to the party (true in a close race); and that the future survival of the nation and our way of life depends on the party winning in November (quite surely not true).

The script is designed for variety, for the convention is the first really big barrage of the election campaign. As such, heavy artillery is called for. There is the hoary veteran of many a campaign. The late President Hoover performed this role for many years at Republican conventions. The Democrats have used a number of persons. In 1960, they had Sam Rayburn of Texas, Speaker of the House for longer than any other man in history. Comic relief is provided by some well-known professional who roasts the other party with satire and sarcasm. Clare Boothe Luce did this at the 1948 Republican convention, for example.[7] There is the bright young "comer," sometimes in the role of keynoter. Harold Stassen, whose early flowering produced poor political seed, played this part for the Republicans in 1948; Governor Frank Clement of Tennessee did so for the Democrats in 1956; Governor Mark Hatfield of Oregon fitted the role for Republicans in 1964.

A movie star is also a staple for a relatively dull moment when the housewives of America need to have their interest renewed. In 1960, Ronald Reagan appeared in this role for the GOP, Peter Lawford for the Democrats. Selected representatives of all significant wings of the party are also allowed to make their appearance on the platform and the left- and right-wing representatives are given their chance to say that, while the candidate does not represent all they had hoped for, they believe him to be better than whatever might be offered by the other party. Governor Nelson Rockefeller (liberal) and Senator Barry M. Goldwater (arch-conservative), played these roles for the Republicans in 1960. The nominee is, of course, ordinarily from the moderate portion of the party—the 1964 Republican candidate apparently was a rare exception—and hence the symbolic laying on of hands by the defeated is important for the cause of party solidarity. The liberal and conservative wings, doomed to seeing their candidates lose (gracefully of course, as the script requires), need to be given their moment for heartfelt cheers.

The speeches follow a set form, especially the "man-who" nominations, in which tradition requires that the name of the nominee, known to all in advance, is not mentioned until the very end of the speech. At that time, in a thunderous climax, it serves as the signal for a boisterous demonstration, professionally planned and staged by persons hired and rehearsed for the job.

[7] An excerpt is reproduced in Edward R. Murrow and Fred W. Friendly, *I Can Hear It Now* (Columbia record ML 4261), vol. 2.

Figure 11-1

Politicians Play a Particular Social Role and They Act Out the Part Expected of Them

"You can relax, Senator. They've switched to Betty Furness."

As soon as all nominations have been made, the moment of highest drama arrives. The secretary of the convention calls the roll of the states, and the chairman of each delegation responds, often with a brief preliminary commercial message ("The great state of Idaho, the land of snow-capped mountains and the world's finest potatoes, casts 5½ votes for . . . "). As the choices are reported, TV announcers give a running total and indicate how near the leader is to victory. Often the outcome is anticipated far in advance and there is only one ballot, but some conventions are badly divided and many ballots are required. The time between roll calls is one of intense activity by the managers for various candidates. Those for the front runner will try to prevent delays, while other managers may ask that the convention recess until the next day so that they may have time to try to make deals. After a ballot, delegations may switch their votes, and each state tries to be the one that will gain the honor of putting the winner over the top. When a nominee is finally announced, pandemonium breaks loose. After order is restored, which will be whenever the chairman believes the TV audience is tiring of the show, the chief manager for the runner-up will usually move that the nomination be made unanimous. This results in more frenzied cheering.

After following a somewhat abbreviated version of the same procedure in selecting a vice-presidential candidate (usually chosen by the presidential candidate); loudly adopting a platform drafted by a committee that did its work even before the convention met or the nominee was known, and which few delegates have read or will read; adopting a variety of resolutions, including one relative to the "wonderful hospitality" of the host city and approving several items of housekeeping procedure proposed by the national committee staff; the work of the convention is finished. After a final flurry of oratory in which victory is predicted and the future of the nation is painted in the most simplistic terms—the party will provide strong leadership in the name of humanity and will lead the nation to peace, prosperity, and plenty while the opponents will be weak, indecisive, and dominated by special interests and will threaten us with war, depression, and relative poverty—the weary delegates go home. The television networks then return to their viewer-preferred normalcy, and the candidates find some hideaway to rest up for the exhausting grind ahead. After the convention is over, the typical citizen probably feels that he has been a spectator at a great show, reformers denounce the convention as inadequate for modern needs, and professional politicians usually feel that the most acceptable men, all factors considered, emerged from the skirmishing. There were highly dissatisfied pros after the GOP conventions in 1912 and 1964, however. (Postconvention activities are covered in Chapter 12.)

Development of the Convention. After the campaign, citizens vote to indicate their preference. But the formal choice is made by the Electoral College, which votes in each state about a month after the popular balloting. The number of electors in any state is equal to that state's total number of senators and representatives. In addition, three votes are allotted to the District of Columbia.

When they set up the Electoral College, the Founding Fathers assumed that the electors, acting as free agents, would choose the President and Vice President. But by custom, the votes are nearly always cast as a bloc vote for whichever candidate has a plurality of the popular vote in each state. Thus, whoever gets one more vote than any other candidates in a given state gets *all* of the state's electoral votes.

The Founding Fathers assumed further that outstanding citizens in each state would be chosen for the College and that they could be counted on to look for someone who would be perceived by most persons as one who would act for the people.

The assumptions implicit in this plan were invalid because they ignored the importance of cleavages created by conflicting interests, and the plan worked only for the selection of George Washington. It limped along through the choice of John Adams in 1796, but failed to meet the crisis of 1800, when party issues were clearly joined.

In order to provide for such contingencies, members of Congress began to assemble every four years in a nominating caucus to choose the persons they wanted electors from their party to vote for. This plan worked for a while, but suffered from the deficiency that it did not give representation in the nomination caucus to states that had no members in the House from the party doing the nominating. Since the objective of a party was—and is—often to capture the electoral vote of the states it lost the last time, particularly those it lost by a narrow margin, this could sometimes be a serious liability. Political leaders who had no voice in selecting a candidate might not show much enthusiasm for him.

In 1824, another crisis arose in connection with the structural arrangements for nomination. William H. Crawford of Georgia was the presidential choice of the Democratic-Republicans. But the Federalist party was dead, and with only one party in the field, state legislative leaders were not willing to concede the office by acclamation. Andrew Jackson of Tennessee, John Quincy Adams of Massachusetts, and Henry Clay of Kentucky were nominated by state legislatures, some of which declared that the congressional caucus had no right to nominate the party candidate. In the Electoral College voting, Crawford ran last; the House of Representatives, which under the Constitution chooses the President when no candidate has a majority of the electoral vote, selected Adams (although Jackson had a plurality of the popular and electoral vote).

The uproar created by the 1824 election led to further changes. The Jacksonians in particular argued that the congressional caucus was undemocratic. They felt that it had unfairly deprived them of the Presidency. In 1831, the first national presidential nominating convention was held by the Antimasonic party; in the following year, both the Jacksonian Democrats and the National Republicans (soon to be known as the Whigs)

Figure 11-2

THE ELECTORAL COLLEGE SYSTEM GIVES THE KEY TO LARGE STATES
1960 Electoral Map of the U.S.

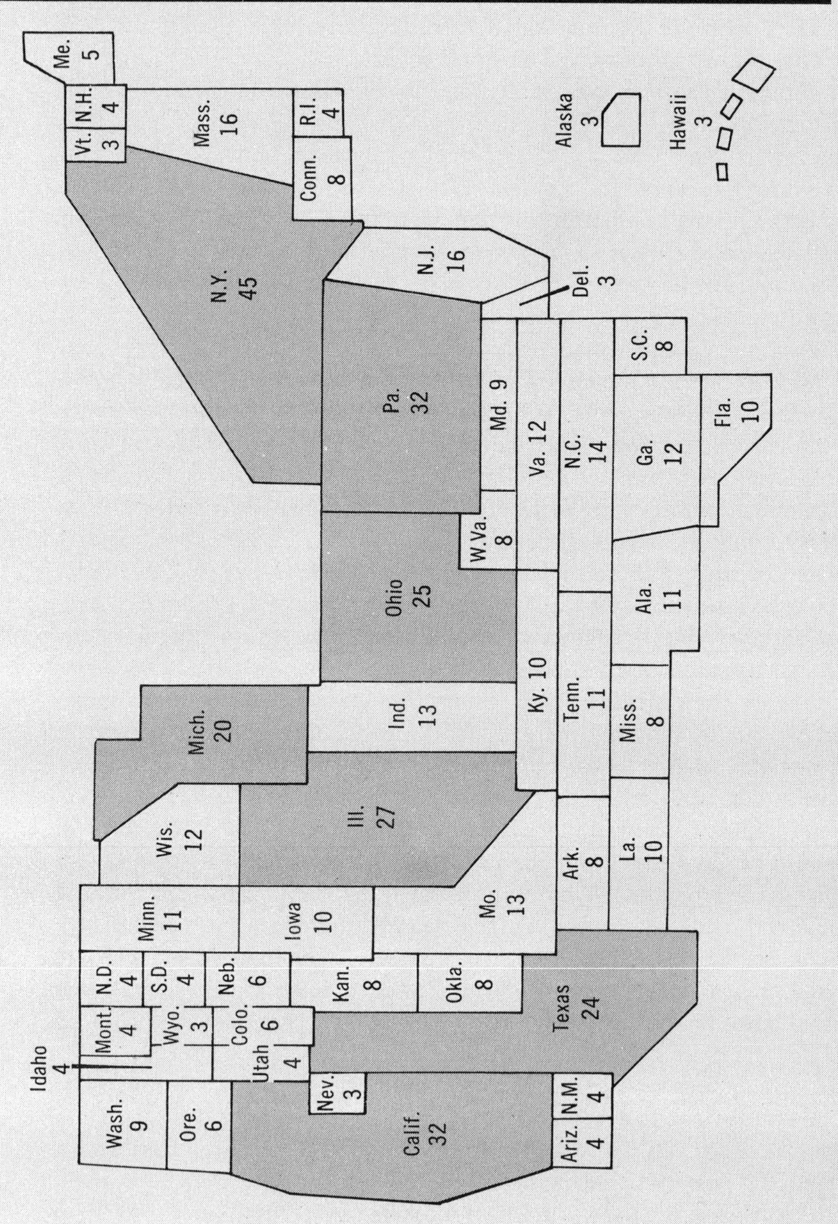

used the method. The basic structure of the convention has not changed from that time to the present.

Conventions were, from the 1830s until the twentieth century the principal device for nominating members of the House of Representatives, as well as state officers and legislators (United States senators were selected by legislatures until 1913). Today they have been generally replaced by primary elections. Only Connecticut, New York, and Indiana still make important use of the convention for major offices, and they too depend upon the primary for filling most state and local government offices as well as for the nomination of congressional candidates.

The Convention at Work. A convention, formally, is a large collegial body. Any such group must in practice be divided into leaders and followers, however. Furthermore, the convention floor is such a picture of confusion, noise, and interrupted conversations that the recognized leaders could not possibly carry on their work there. So they do it in the smoke-filled room.

Most of the leaders at a convention are known well in advance of the first day of sessions. Each major candidate for office has his spokesmen. Each delegation has a few leaders. The top leader of a state delegation may be the governor or a United States senator. Other leaders may also include persons in formal party leadership positions within the state and perhaps a financial angel or two. The top leader normally has shown his organizational ability in the past, has demonstrated that he can win elections, and controls important patronage.

The term "smoke-filled room" was coined in 1920 by Harry F. Daugherty of Ohio, who predicted that the three principal candidates for the Republican nomination would be deadlocked and that Warren G. Harding, an obscure Senator from his state, would emerge from such a room as the party's compromise choice. In most conventions, unlike that of 1920, there are no more than two principal candidates; the task of candidate spokesmen, in off-the-floor discussions, is to encourage delegate leaders to believe that their man has a good chance both for nomination and election. The delegation leaders are, of course, anxious to pick the winner and to pick him early. To do so will maximize their influence in the campaign and in the selection of the principal officeholders if the candidate is elected. In only about two conventions in five is there serious conflict over the nomination; and in many of these cases, the conflict is resolved before the actual

The total number of electoral votes is now 538, so the majority required to win is 270. In 1960, the seven largest states, shown in dark shading on the map, had 205 votes. Of them, the three largest states, New York, Pennsylvania, and California, had 109. Electoral votes are shown in boxes on each state, and the area of each is distorted in proportion to the number of its votes.
(The New York Times, *Nov. 6, 1960.*)

balloting begins. The problem of identifying the probable winner is not very often a serious one, and for a number of reasons:

1. The incumbent President automatically gets renominated for a second term if he wants to run again, for refusing to support the party leader is tantamount to an admission of poor performance, and this would contaminate the whole party, making the task of winning difficult for any substitute who might be chosen. In 1948, the Democrats nominated Harry Truman, even though he was not popular with either the liberal or Southern wing of the party. He had not been selected initially for President, but had succeeded to the office only on the death of Franklin Roosevelt, and many delegates did not believe he could win. The party's slogan, wags said, was "I'm just mild about Harry."

2. The incumbent President may choose his party's next candidate. Jackson chose Van Buren in 1836, Theodore Roosevelt chose William Howard Taft in 1908, and Truman had great influence in the selection of Stevenson in 1952. The incumbent is able to do this because of his high status as President and because large numbers of party leaders are indebted to him for past patronage and other favors. The power of the President works both ways, however. In 1960, Eisenhower—typically—refused to try to name his successor; by his vagueness and hesitancy, he threatened Richard M. Nixon's candidacy, even though it is generally believed that Nixon was highly acceptable to the President.[8]

3. The most popular candidate, the one with the greatest chance of winning, may emerge from the presidential preference primaries, as Eisenhower did in 1952 and Kennedy in 1960, thus simplifying the politicians' problem of picking a winner. The primaries may narrow the field sharply by eliminating potential candidates long before the convention meets. Thus Wendell Willkie, Republican nominee in 1940, withdrew from the 1944 race after being badly defeated in the Wisconsin primary. Sometimes the party will choose a candidate who did not do well in the primaries, as the Republicans did with Hoover in 1928 and the Democrats with Stevenson in 1952 (he was not entered in any of them), but this may be an increasingly uncommon exception to the pattern.

4. One man may be so outstanding as a leader and the kind of man the professionals trust and want that he has little competition. This was true of Hoover in 1928 and Nixon in 1960.

The Republican conventions were "cliff hangers" during the 1940s; so was that party's contest in the early months of the struggle for delegates between Eisenhower and Taft (1952). The Democrats have not had an equally uncertain situation confronting them since Franklin D. Roosevelt won the nomination over stiff competition in 1932, at which time he had to depend on the great political skills of James Farley in order to get the

[8] See Richard M. Nixon, *Six Crises,* Doubleday & Company, Inc., Garden City, N.Y., 1962.

nomination. (Prior to 1936, the Deep South had a veto over proposed nominees in the Democratic party, for it took two-thirds of the delegates to nominate. The Republicans have always used a simple majority.)

Yet we should not assume that the typical delegate today is a placid party hack, willing to follow the leader in exchange for the freedom to have a good time and enjoy someone's free food and drink during convention week. American politics today is as different from that of the 1890s as is the first automobile from that of today's carefully tuned sports models. Political scientists have noted differences that have emerged in the last two generations or so:

1. Delegates, far from being hacks, are typically important public officeholders, community leaders, business executives, labor leaders, or professional persons. They are well educated and have been successful in their chosen fields.[9]

2. The old-fashioned political boss and machine are no longer of much importance in America. Only a few cities have anything resembling the nineteenth-century political organization. As a result, the cigar-smoking, amiably corrupt boss is more easily found in cartoons and in popular folklore than in smoke-filled convention back rooms. Although the public may picture the leader of Tammany Hall pulling strings from behind the scenes, he is actually much too busy trying to keep some semblance of influence to attempt to control a delegation.[10]

Such string pulling has been further reduced by the changes in Southern patterns of voting and in convention rules. Thus, Southern delegates to the Republican convention once constituted a large bloc of uncommitted votes from states that never gave a majority to the Republican candidate. Frequently they were controlled by presidential patronage, or they might be for sale to the highest bidder. The voting power of this bloc was reduced after World War II by giving substantial increments of votes at the convention to states that had supported the Republican ticket in the previous election. At the same time, a number of Southern states have become genuinely competitive in recent presidential races.

3. Except when the incumbent President desires renomination by his party, "no one man, no single group, controls the convention."[11] We have already noted that the American political party system is at least as federal in character as is our governmental system. There is no meaningful national political party organization, except as it is molded by the incumbent President with his patronage and other sanctions. Each state has dozens of elected officials and non-office-holding party leaders, each a

[9] See Paul T. David and others, *The Politics of National Party Conventions,* The Brookings Institution, Washington, D.C., 1960. (Paperback edition edited by Kathleen Sproul.)

[10] This section borrows in part from James MacG. Burns, "Inside View of the big Powwow," *The New York Times Magazine,* July 10, 1960.

[11] *Ibid.*

power in his own right, each with a number of persons, often including delegates, beholden to him. Hence:[12]

> There is not one center of power in the convention, or even a dozen, but hundreds. Some centers of influence are, of course, much greater than others, but power is spread widely among a host of little clusters of leaders and followers in a complex and ever-changing web of influence. Most of the delegates are subjected to such a profusion of political pressures within their states that on the important ballots they simply cannot be switched from one candidate to another by the dictates of one leader.

Ultimately the delegate decides on the basis of such practical considerations as the known or strongly suspected preferences of most of the members of his party in his district; his personal preference, selected because he believes the candidate shares his ideological beliefs; temptations in the form of patronage or promises of help in his own campaign for office; the dictates of strategy required in order to help defeat a rival party faction in his own state; or perhaps simply a desire to pick the right (i.e., successful) candidate at the right moment and hence enjoy the pleasures of riding with the winner.

The Functions of a Convention. A national nominating convention secures its television and press attention because it nominates a man who may become the next President of the United States. But it has three other important, if somewhat less-publicized, functions:

1. It nominates the Vice President, a man who normally gets much less publicity than the Chief Executive. The vice presidency has been the butt of many jokes. ("A woman had two sons. One went away to sea, the other became Vice President. Neither was ever heard from again.") In fact, however, the office is "one heartbeat away" from the most powerful position in the democratic world. Its importance has been demonstrated many times: Of the twenty-six men who have become President without succeeding on the death of the incumbent, four have died in office of natural causes, and four have been assassinated; in nearly one out of three cases, then, the Vice President has become President. In political terms, the vice presidency is an important prize, an honor to be distributed in such a way as to balance the ticket geographically and, if possible, ideologically and a basis for bargaining in gathering support for presidential candidates at the convention.

2. The convention also adopts a platform that is ostensibly a statement of the position of the party on the issues of the day; in most cases, it is little more than a collection of clichés designed to have a favorable emotional appeal to as many groups as possible, while alienating as few other groups as possible. A platform is not this alone, of course. The parties

[12] *Ibid.*

do, sometimes, take unequivocal stands on issues, especially when they cannot easily avoid doing so or when they believe that survival requires it. Sometimes dominant forces on the resolutions (platform) committee impose upon the convention and the presidential nominee a more definite position than they might prefer. Thus in 1948, a liberal-dominated committee proposed a strong plank on civil rights; it had not been urged by President Truman, and it caused a great deal of conflict. (Truman, accepting what had become an accomplished fact by the time he arrived at the convention arena, campaigned hard in support of the plank and later came to be identified with it, although he had probably preferred that it not be adopted.) In 1960, the Republican platform reflected neither the wishes of the resolutions committee nor of the convention delegates, but was essentially a statement agreed upon by Richard M. Nixon and Nelson Rockefeller, the dominant figures in the convention.

3. The other major function of the convention is to draw up the basic rules that control the operations of the national party organization. Because the party is not a single structure but, in reality, an alliance of fifty state organizations, the powers to be granted to the national committee, to the national chairman, and to special committees are important, and they must be approved by a majority of the state delegations to be effective.

Do Conventions Make Sense Today? In 1952, the esteemed English publication the *Economist* commented favorably on the quality of the two presidential nominees, Eisenhower and Stevenson. It then added that "Europeans, viewing the clumsy chaos of the nominating conventions . . . will be moved once more to reflect that God moves in a mysterious way his wonders to perform." Many an American would add his "Amen." But the sophisticated student of our political system ought not either blame or credit the Almighty or believe that the results are to be attributed to America's storied good luck. In fact, what is widely considered the high quality of the candidates for the Presidency fundamentally results from the convention system, not in spite of it.

In the early twentieth century, the British political scientist James Bryce complained that great men were not chosen President.[13] His criticism would probably not be repeated today. In the intervening years, governmental activities and responsibilities have expanded greatly. In recent decades, both parties have almost without exception sought the kind of men Bryce wanted, those "of education, of administrative experience, of a certain largeness of view and dignity of character." The Presidency, in fact, has generally been filled by a man who fits the spirit and demands of the time (greatness for Lincoln, reform for Theodore Roosevelt, idealism for Wilson, mediocre normalcy for Harding, daring experimentation for

[13] James Bryce, *The American Commonwealth,* The Macmillan Company, New York, 1911, chap. 8.

Franklin Roosevelt, sturdy calmness for Eisenhower). Bryce's complaint failed to recognize that, in the years between Lincoln and T.R., Americans did not want superior men in the White House. Since the Great Depression, the kind of men he wanted have been sought by the convention leaders and have been available.[14]

Would nationwide primaries, the popular plan for the selection of candidates, be a superior means of reflecting the demands of the times or providing the candidate required at a time when a serious mistake could bring disaster both to the nation and to the democratic nations of the West? We cannot answer with certainty, but it seems unlikely that the reply would be "Yes." The leaders of conventions are keenly aware of the need to nominate the right man for the time, and they want a President who can perform creditably. They screen out the rabble-rousing demagogue—an Adolf Hitler might appeal successfully to a deeply anxious public, but he could not get past the major party pros. After all, as Governor Theodore Christianson of Minnesota once said, the party has "a past to honor and a future to protect." The calculating professional is far more likely to choose a man who can perform those functions than is the sentimental, impressionable voter.

Even if we assumed that the public could choose from among the many candidates in a way that would select one of a type needed for the times, there would be many problems:[15]

> If a choice among all the noteworthy alternatives were to be submitted to a primary election in which all party voters could take part, the winner in the first election, more likely than not, would still be only a minority choice. . . And inherent in almost any conceivable kind of primary is the risk that the most attractive candidate [and the most qualified] may not even be on the ballot, and the further risk that the turnout of voters may be too low to insure representation of actual party sentiment about the candidates who do happen to be on the ballot.

In practice, the national party conventions, for all of their brassy ostentation and blatant appeal to the emotions, do produce candidates appropriate for the expectations of the culture and for the preservation of the nation's highest ideals. It seems unlikely that a change will be made from the present system in the near future. It is also unlikely that such a change would produce candidates more representative of the wants and needs of the citizenry, if we measure those wants and needs in terms of the requirements for the longer-range demands of the survival of the nation and its ideals. To say this is not to suggest, of course, that the present method of nomination is either ideal or impartial as it affects various hopefuls.

[14] On the way in which availability differs according to perceived needs in different conventions, see Dwaine Marvick and Samuel J. Eldersveld, "National Convention Leadership: 1952 and 1956," *Western Political Quarterly,* 14:176–194, March, 1961.

[15] David and others, *op. cit.,* p. 250.

VOTER ELIGIBILITY

For more than a century, democratic theory has generally accepted the idea that nearly all adults should be permitted to vote. American ideals are in accord with this, but in practice a considerable number of persons are excluded from voting. There is no Federal law on voting. Eligibility in presidential, congressional, as well as local elections is a matter of state law. Reformers who wish to eliminate residential, literacy, and other restrictions favor a Federal law for national elections. This has not been supported in Congress, especially not by Southerners, but Congress did submit for the approval of state legislatures a constitutional amendment outlawing poll-tax payment as a prerequisite for voting (discussed later in this chapter).

Residence Requirements. The usual prerequisites for voting include American citizenship; a minimum age of twenty-one (less in four states); a minimum period of residence in the state, county, and polling district; and registration. The high level of mobility in the American population makes residence requirements especially significant as factors barring persons from voting. The number disqualified by the legal provisions on residence is probably high, especially among urban workers and middle-class organization men.

Residence requirements are, to a degree, vestiges of an earlier theory of voting and are not in accord with that of universal suffrage. In particular, they reflect the ideas of an age when local elections were regarded as more important than national; an established residence was considered necessary in order for the voter to have a sufficient interest in public issues to vote responsibly. This notion is by no means dead today, but it is less accepted. The rules continue in force, however, and residence requirements vary from six months in many states to two years in Mississippi.[16]

Literacy Requirements. In an effort to reduce the once important political influence of the foreign-born and the city political machines that generally enjoyed their support, opposing political interests in some states succeeded in securing literacy requirements, beginning in New England in the 1850s. Elsewhere, the same type of literacy test has been used to discourage Negro voting. Some form of the test is still used in about one-third of the states.

[16] See the *Book of the States,* Council of State Governments, Chicago. (Published annually.) See also Morris S. Ogul, "Residence Requirements as Barriers to Voting in Presidential Elections," *Midwest Journal of Political Science,* 3:254–262, August, 1959. The basic historical reference is Kirk H. Porter, *A History of Suffrage in the United States,* The University of Chicago Press, Chicago, 1918. See also Chilton Williamson, *American Suffrage from Property to Democracy,* Princeton University Press, Princeton, N.J., 1957; and recommendations for changes in registration and voting laws in the 1963 report of the President's Commission on Registration and Voting Participation.

In Northern states, the test is now administered with varying degrees of strictness and is designed chiefly to debar the illiterate. But its traditional function in political battles remains important in New York, where the Democrats have sought a change in the state law in order to enfranchise Spanish-speaking Puerto Ricans. This ethnic group is numerous in New York City and represents a large reservoir of potential Democratic voters. Republican leaders have opposed a change in the law, using the standard argument that a knowledge of the English language is a prerequisite to informed voting.

Restrictions on the Institutionalized. There is a general rule that an individual may not vote so long as he is an inmate of a public institution. The rule applies to the mentally ill and to those incarcerated in jails and prisons. Laws vary from state to state, however, as to the conditions under which an individual's voting privilege is restored once he is released from an institution. There is a widespread popular notion that persons convicted of a felony lose their citizenship. This is a misconception, although in some states such persons do lose certain civil rights permanently, including the right to vote. In other states, however, the individual may vote if he is not actually incarcerated.

The rules against permitting the institutionalized mentally ill to vote have not been revised in the light of modern research into mental illness. It seems unlikely that institutionalization itself is an adequate criterion, and psychotics may not have particularly impaired political judgment. In one study of nonchronic, young adult psychotics in an intensive-treatment hospital, these persons, when compared with a control group, were found to have the same degree of interest in public events, their preferences for presidential candidates were logical, given their ideological beliefs, and they were equally willing and able to respond to questions. The patients responded differently from the nonpatients in only one important respect: They were less concerned with international tensions and tended to see the United States as a father image for the world, thus showing a significantly greater feeling of security in the strength and invincibility of the United States. The patients were found to be no more "illogical, inconsistent, or unprepared to fulfil their obligations as citizens than a similar group of individuals who are not identified as emotionally unstable."[17]

The Poll Tax. Payment of a poll tax was still a prerequisite for state and local voting in five Southern states as of 1964. In that year, the Twenty-fourth Amendment outlawed the poll tax as a prerequisite for voting for Federal office. Through being tied in with eligibility to vote, the tax has served as a method for keeping control of governments in the hands of the

[17] Marguerite R. Hertz and others, "Mental Patients and Civil Rights: A Study of Opinions of Mental Patients on Social and Political Issues," *Journal of Health and Human Behavior*, 1:251–258, Winter, 1960.

prosperous and the politically motivated. It has served to disfranchise white and Negro persons alike in Southern states.

The tax is simple in concept—a head tax of a few dollars on each adult (or male) within specified age groups. But by various devices—requiring the payment of all past-due taxes in order to be eligible to vote, deliberate failure to send out bills or notices of the tax, making payments of the tax due long before election, for example—the less literate, less politically conscious, and low-income people were easily made ineligible to vote.

In the years following World War II, the tax developed a special notoriety that was probably responsible for its repeal in nine states. The adoption of the constitutional amendment in 1964, prohibiting its use in establishing eligibility to vote in national elections, was to be expected. Elimination of the poll-tax requirement will, however, do more to destroy a *symbol* of discrimination against Negroes (and low-income whites) in voting than it will to eliminate their exclusion from the polls. Many other techniques, such as selective enforcement of the literacy test or intimidation, remain available as weapons.

Registration. Registration refers to the act of placing one's name on the roll of voters. It is required today in nearly all urban and many rural areas of the United States. Registration is not in a legal sense an additional qualification for voting, but only a mechanism for determining that those who cast ballots are actually qualified.[18] The device has been used as a means of reducing fraudulent voting, and it was especially supported in earlier decades by reformers seeking to control the free-wheeling activities of big-city machines. In the South, registration has been an effective device for controlling access to the polls. It can be decided at registration, for example, that a Negro (in former days, not infrequently a low-income white, as well) cannot meet the literacy requirement or cannot "correctly interpret" portions of the state or Federal constitution.

There are two types of registration. Periodic registration requires reregistration after a certain period of time (perhaps every two or four years); permanent registration does not, although a variant of this type provides that one must vote at least once within a given period of time (perhaps two years) or his name is dropped from the voter rolls.

Periodic registration is more expensive to administer, and it tends to discriminate against the less well-informed politically and those with low political motivation. Such persons may forget to reregister and may not read the notices that would remind them. It serves to minimize fraudulent voting by eliminating from the rolls persons who have moved out of the voting district or died.

Permanent registration minimizes the demands upon the citizen; once

[18] See Joseph P. Harris, *Registration of Voters in the United States,* The Brookings Institution, Washington, D.C., 1929; and the *Book of the States, op. cit.*

registered, he remains eligible to vote so long as he does not change residence or, in some states, fail to vote within a specified period of time. Permanent registration makes fraudulent voting easier, for the voter rolls at any given time include the names of persons who have died or lost their eligibility.

The political significance of formal rules relative to voter registration is demonstrated by an example from Michigan. In that state, permanent registration was the law during the period between 1949 and 1963, when the state had Democratic governors. The voter's name stayed on the register, provided he voted at least once in four years. In 1963, however, the Republicans controlled the governorship and both houses of the legislature for the first time in fourteen years. The law was promptly changed to require voting at least once in two years in order to remain on the register. The significant consideration was that the Democrats had far more persons in the low-information, low-motivation categories than did the Republicans; the Democrats would thus be deprived of more potential supporters by the law change.

NEGRO VOTING

In 1960, there were about 10 million Negroes of voting age in the United States, approximately one-half of them in the eleven states that once made up the Confederacy. In these states, there was a high inverse correlation between the percentage of the state population that was Negro and the percentage of eligible Negroes who were registered to vote. Specifically, the Spearman rank-order correlation was .84, which means that roughly 70 per cent of the question of whether or not a Negro could vote was explainable in mathematical terms according to the relative size of each state's Negro population. Only Virginia differed sharply from the others. That state ranked eighth in percentage of Negroes within the old Confederacy, but fourth lowest in percentage registered. This difference could perhaps be explained by the enforcement of the poll tax, the enduring strength of Southern traditions in Virginia, and the effectiveness of the Byrd machine as a political organization. (With Virginia excluded from the calculations, there was an extremely high rank-order correlation of .93 between Negro population percentage by state and lack of Negro registration for voting.)[19]

Prior to 1944,[20] there were few Negroes registered in any of the states that had once belonged to the Confederacy, and these few were nearly all in the Republican party, where they were ineffective and their wants were

[19] Calculations based on data from the U.S. Bureau of the Census and the Southern Education Reporting Service.

[20] See H. D. Price, *The Negro and Southern Politics,* New York University Press, New York, 1957.

ignored by a party that had long regarded them as a captive vote that had nowhere else to go. But in that year, the United States Supreme Court ended the so-called "white primary" by declaring that the primary election was an integral part of the election process and, as such, could not be closed to Negroes on the excuse that the party is a private association and the primary a private matter.[21] This rule had the immediate effect of permitting a great increase in the number of Negro registrations in most Southern states. Since the end of World War II, and particularly since about 1954, there has been a continuing increase in the percentage of Southern Negroes who vote. The number is larger in urban than in rural areas; in some communities, the Negro vote has become the balance of power, so important that politicians must woo it. It will become even more important in future years.

THE BALLOT

The form of the ballot is important to campaign strategists. Legal provisions make a difference as to the timing, techniques, content, and personnel to be involved in a campaign.

In the early years of the Republic, voting was oral; the elector simply told the election clerk his preference, which was duly recorded. In contested precincts where the various parties had both the desire and the ability to guard their own interests, party observers sought to keep the tellers honest. They were not necessarily successful. Later, each party or faction printed its own ballots. By using distinctive colors, it was easy to determine how each elector voted—a useful bit of information, especially in checking on persons who had committed their vote or were viewed by party representatives as having an obligation to them. With no standardized ballot, it was also easy to devise ways by which to stuff the ballot box—by printing premarked ballots on thin paper so that a party stalwart could drop in a number of votes while seeming to cast but one, for example.

The Secret Ballot. Beginning in 1888, American states one by one began to adopt the "Australian" or secret ballot, which was uniform in size, shape, and color, printed at government expense, and available only at the polling place from an authorized election official. As the principle of secrecy became fully established as a part of the American political system, the possibilities for tampering with the outcome of elections by placing pressure on the voter were diminished. But the blatant forms of pressure used by the nineteenth-century political machines of the cities and the social pressures for conformity in rural precincts were not the only devices available to resourceful politicians anxious to maximize their chances of victory.

[21] *Smith v. Allwright,* 321 U.S. 649 (1944).

Ballot Form and Election Outcome. Once again, we emphasize the important relationship between governmental structure and decisions about "who gets what, when, and how." As the Australian ballot developed, political party interests indicated support for a plan that would permit straight party voting. This could be accomplished quite easily by providing at the top of the party list of candidates a large circle that, if marked, would indicate that the voter wished to support all candidates of that party.

It was also in the party interest to have an easily recognizable symbol for those who could not read or were not certain of the party title. Hence the parties encouraged the use of such symbols, a donkey or a picture of Franklin D. Roosevelt for the Democrats or an elephant or a picture of Abraham Lincoln for the Republicans, for example. This kind of a ballot came to be known as the "Indiana" ballot.

Reformers, beginning in the late nineteenth century, were concerned about the "follow-the-leader" characteristics of a great many voters. They had observed that large-city machines had corralled many voters who had little knowledge of politics, and, in the case of immigrants, of the English language. These persons, who had been helped by the political organization in times of need, were willing to repay favors by turning over to their benefactors one of the few assets they possessed—their vote. To many an immigrant or other big-city unskilled and relatively uneducated voter, this seemed a fair exchange. To reformers, who came from the prosperous, well-educated middle class and still held to the eighteenth-century concept of the rational man, it was shocking. They felt that the voter should be informed on the issues of the day and about the individual candidates on the ballot. The result of this belief was a ballot on which there was no circle for straight party voting, names were listed by office in alphabetical order rather than by party, and there was no symbol under the party label to guide the illiterate or those unskilled in the English language. (During the reform period, a Birdless Ballot League was formed to lobby for the elimination from the ballot of images of eagles, chickens, or other fowl that could assist the uninformed voter.) This was the so-called "Massachusetts" ballot. Reformers continue to advocate it. Its effect is to weaken the political influence of the less-educated, less-informed, lower-income persons and their leaders.

Ballot Rules as Campaign Resource. What is one person's gain is often another person's loss in politics. Leaders who are in a position to influence the formal rules of the political game tend to restructure the law to their advantage, within the limits of what the public will accept as reasonably fair. In this sense, party influentials make rules in much the same way as do the owners of professional baseball clubs. Some "purists" believe that baseball would be a better game if the "dead" ball were used, and bunting, skillful base running, and defensive play were emphasized. Pitchers would like to use the spitball and other "doctored" balls. But the owners are the effective decision makers with regard to the rules of the game and their objective is to make profits by maximizing attendance. This is not done by making the rules fit the preferences of the *cognoscenti,* but by attracting the marginal fan, who knows little of the nuances of the game, but gets excited by a crackling double off the center field fence and believes that hitting a ball completely out of the park is more impressive than stealing second base.

The same considerations are involved in making the rules concerning who gets nominated for office and who gets elected from among those on the ballot. Those in a position to influence the outcome do not direct the rules toward the interests of the informed minority or those who support the eighteenth-century rational-man theory about "good" politics directed toward "educating" the general voter. They want home runs—victories made possible by dramatic politics that culminate in a voting procedure simple in character and designed to help the entire party ticket.

In most states, the rules have been changed from time to time to meet the exigencies of the moment with no consideration of their long-range implications. And it is not easy to anticipate the kinds of changes that may benefit the dominant group. In Ohio, a switch was made in 1950—by party leaders—from the Indiana ballot, which such leaders usually favor, to the Massachusetts ballot, which leaders have usually regarded as a device desired by the antipolitics good-government or "goo-goo" groups. The change was helpful to the Republicans in the particular campaign, and that was reason enough to make the switch. In Minnesota, the direct primary election was adopted in 1913, not because it was regarded as a better or fairer method of nomination, but because the incumbent governor thought it offered him a chance for renomination while the existing party convention system did not. He took advantage of reformist sentiments in the legislature and the state at large and thus helped to keep himself in office. A. B. (Happy) Chandler aided his drive for the governorship of Kentucky in the same fashion in the 1930s. As lieutenant governor, he called the legislature into session one day when the governor was out of the state and asked that it make mandatory the use of the primary election. It had previously been optional with the party organization. Chandler, correctly it would seem, guessed that he would have a better chance for the gubernatorial nomination in a primary than in a state convention. The legislature passed the wanted legislation. The incumbent governor promptly returned and complained to the state supreme court. But it held that the change was an accomplished fact. Soon Chandler was governor.

On the other hand, the dominant groups cannot do as they please. The existing rules are usually regarded as legitimate and are hence relatively inelastic. Sometimes long-run rather than immediate advantages are sought, as in deals over congressional redistricting, where leaders of one party or faction may accept a plan that will not give them an increase in victories at once. But they may recognize that ecological trends indicate that they can win new seats in the near future under the plan. And changes for immediate advantage sometimes backfire a few years later. In the

1950s, the Republican-controlled Michigan legislature moved the September primary back to August, which had the effect of preventing Governor G. Mennen Williams from trying for a place on the Democratic national ticket and, failing this, exercising the option of running again for governor. By 1964, however, the timetable thus established worked against Governor George Romney exercising the same option in Republican politics.

ELECTIONS: THE EFFECTIVE DECISION-MAKING LOCUS

Election systems are a product of the goals of the dominant groups in society. But the methods and procedures selected by leaders of these groups do not necessarily lead to the ends they desire. As a result, (1) no nonnormative system is the "correct" means by which to nominate and elect those who are to rule in a democracy; (2) the devices developed to increase popular participation in the nomination process do not necessarily have the effects intended; and (3) the effective choice of the voters—the point at which the ordinary citizen can influence the determination of those who are to hold office—may occur in a number of different places.

We have emphasized throughout this text that models of a political system or any part of a system reflect the preferences and purposes of those constructing the model. Hence the notion of what is best may differ according to whether the person making the evaluation is, for example, a professional party leader, an officeholder, a devotee of eighteenth-century concepts of the rational man, a subversive bent on destroying the system, or an advocate of equal voting opportunities. Our purpose here is to describe and analyze the system, not to evaluate it.

A few generations ago, reformers sought to establish the direct primary as the fairest and most effective means by which to choose those who were to serve as candidates for office. But as a leading authority on the American party system once noted:[22]

> The primary mode of nomination gives free play to forces that make it difficult for the party hierarchies to do much by way either of good or evil. The observation that such consequences tend to prevail should not be interpreted as an argument for the return of the old-style convention system, which had its erraticisms as well. The point is rather that under the processes of the primary we have a wide range of consequences . . . more or less totally unforeseen by the architects of this system of nomination.

Earlier, we made the point that in a democracy an essential consideration in determining if a nation has a democratic form of government is whether it has a system by which a genuine choice between competing candidates exists. Some critics of the American system of politics have

[22] V. O. Key, Jr., *op. cit.,* p. 168.

assumed that the effective choice must be made in a general election and must be made between competitors from two or more political parties. The meaningful choice need not, however, be made through party conflict or at the general election.

In a minority of states, the general election is the crucial decision-making arena. In others, it is the primary that is fought out in hard and desperate fashion by those who seek office. Although even in one-party states, the voter does not pay much attention to the primary, he does have the opportunity to participate; this is the critical factor in determining whether a democracy exists.

The effective decision in politics is rarely a simple thing and it is hardly ever a single act. Even though the voter has a choice at the primary or general election, he can in practice choose only from among those whose names are on the ballot. A write-in candidate rarely can win. Thus the individual's announced decision whether or not to run for a particular office may be critical in helping to determine what kind of person will appear on the ballot and, finally, fill that office. The same is true of the party leaders' decision as to whether or not to allow wide-open competition for the nomination and of the convention's decision (where a convention exists) as to which person it will permit the voters to consider. In the final decision as to who is to occupy a particular office, a great many decisions are involved—by the individual potential candidate and the party leaders, by those who make the rules under which the political game is played, and by those who go into the voting booth and choose between or among actually competing candidates. The outcome is affected by the kinds of persons who are willing to make themselves available, the rules under which they must play in seeking office, the expectations of the public concerning the social function of the particular office at the particular time, and the way in which the campaign for office influences those who have the meaningful choices to make. There is no guarantee that the man who wins the office will fill it in a manner that meets public expectations or the demands of the times or that he can cope with the particular issues that accidentally come to that particular office for decision during his tenure.

To date, the outcome of candidate selection has been such as to permit our system of democracy to continue to function in a fashion that is at least generally acceptable to a substantial portion of the public. Much more than this probably cannot be expected of democracy.

SELECTED BIBLIOGRAPHY

Nominations and elections are covered, for the most part, in the literature cited for Chapters 10 and 12. Traditional party structure and behavior is described in Adrian [1] and Kent [8]. Newer patterns of political organization are the subject of two articles in *Life* [5, 10]. The systems of nomination in states that may have either one-or two-party structures are described by Key [9] and voting patterns by Scammon [14]. Wilson [16] describes the rise of amateur clubs and discusses their relative assets and liabilities to the party professionals. Harris [6], in an old but still basic study, looks at the problems and practices of election administration.

1. Adrian, Charles R.: *Governing Urban America,* 2d ed., McGraw-Hill Book Company, New York, 1961.
2. Akzin, Benjamin: "Election and Appointment," *American Political Science Review,* 54:705–713, September, 1960.
3. Bain, Henry M., and Donald S. Hecock: *Ballot Position and Voter's Choice,* Wayne State University Press, Detroit, 1961.
4. David, Paul T., and others: *The Politics of National Party Conventions,* The Brookings Institution, Washington, D.C., 1960.
5. Hall, Leonard W.: "An Old Pro Describes How Politics in the U.S. Has Changed," *Life,* Apr. 25, 1960.
6. Harris, Joseph P.: *Election Administration in the United States,* The Brookings Institution, Washington, D.C., 1934.
7. Janowitz, Morris, and Dwaine Marvick: *Competitive Pressures and Democratic Consent,* University of Michigan, Institute of Public Administration, Ann Arbor, Mich., 1956.
8. Kent, Frank R.: *The Great Game of Politics,* Doubleday & Company, Inc., Garden City, N.Y., 1923.
9. Key, V. O., Jr.: *American State Politics,* Alfred A. Knopf, Inc., New York, 1956.
10. *Life,* July 4, 1960. (The entire issue is devoted to politics in America.)
11. Macrae, Duncan, Jr., and James A. Meldrum: "Critical Elections in Illinois: 1888–1958," *American Political Science Review,* 54:669–683, September, 1960.
12. McClosky, Herbert, and others: "Issue Conflict and Consensus among Party Leaders and Followers," *American Political Science Review,* 54:406–427, June, 1960.
13. Press, Charles: "Voting Statistics and Presidential Coattails," *American Political Science Review,* 52:1041–1050, December, 1958.
14. Scammon, Richard M.: *America Votes,* The University of Pittsburgh Press, Pittsburgh, Pa. (Biennial since 1955.)
15. Seligman, Lester G.: "Political Recruitment and Party Structure," *American Political Science Review,* 55:77–86, March, 1961.
16. Wilson, James Q.: *The Amateur Democrat: Club Politics in Three Cities,* The University of Chicago Press, Chicago, 1962.

Case Studies

Blaisdell, Donald C.: *The Riverside Democrats,* Eagleton Institute, New Brunswick, N.J., 1962. Case no. 18.

Carney, Francis: *The Rise of the Democratic Clubs in California,* Eagleton Institute, New Brunswick, N.J., 1958. Case no. 13.

Ernst, Harry W.: *The Primary that Made a President: West Virginia, 1960,* Eagleton Institute, New Brunswick, N.J., 1963. Case no. 26.

Hamilton, Charles V.: *Minority Politics in Black Belt Alabama,* Eagleton Institute, New Brunswick, N.J., 1962. Case no. 19.

Hapgood, David: *The Purge That Failed: Tammany v. Powell,* Eagleton Institute, New Brunswick, N.J., 1959. Case no. 15.

Hennessy, Bernard: *Dollars for Democrats, 1959,* Eagleton Institute, New Brunswick, N.J., 1962. Case no. 20.

Holtzman, Abraham: *The Loyalty Pledge Controversy in the Democratic Party,* Eagleton Institute, New Brunswick, N.J., 1962. Case no. 21.

Lockard, Duane: *Connecticut's Challenge Primary: A Study in Legislative Politics,* Eagleton Institute, New Brunswick, N.J., 1959. Case no. 7.

Munger, Frank: *The Struggle for Republican Leadership in Indiana, 1954,* Eagleton Institute, New Brunswick, N.J., 1962. Case no. 23.

Smith, Rhoten A. and C. J. Hein: *Republican Primary Fight: A Study in Factionalism,* Eagleton Institute, New Brunswick, N.J., 1958. Case no. 11.

Vines, Kenneth N.: *Two Parties for Shreveport,* Eagleton Institute, New Brunswick, N.J., 1959. Case no. 12.

Wilder, Philip S., Jr.: *Meade Alcorn and the 1958 Election,* Eagleton Institute, New Brunswick, N.J., 1959. Case no. 6.

CHAPTER

12

ELECTION CAMPAIGNS

Political campaigning is essentially a matter of communications. It always has been. The way in which the problem has been attacked has varied through time, however. In the nineteenth century, campaigning was based on face-to-face relationships in which the worker in the precinct, township, or other local area contacted the individual voter directly. This is still the case to some extent, but today campaigning relies increasingly on the media of mass communications—newspapers, radio, and television. With changes in technology, the techniques have changed, but the objectives are still largely the same. They are not primarily to inform the citizen and to give him a rational basis for supporting a particular party or candidate, but rather to secure, by whatever appeals will be effective, the support of enough voters to win.

OLD AND NEW CAMPAIGN STYLES

In days when the newspaper alone provided a basis for mass communication, political leaders found it desirable to build organizations that were structured all the way down to the level where they could reach the ordinary citizen in his home or at his regular recreation haunts (the church social, the Fourth of July celebration, the beach, the county fair). Today, they visit the nearest radio or TV studio in order to tape a message that can be repeated as often as financial resources will permit and that brings the actual voice and physical image of the candidate into the home.

The Boss and Machine. The boss of yesteryear and his organization or machine did not exist in spite of society or even because of apathy on the part of voters. They existed because they performed an important welfare function in a day when unskilled urban workers and marginal agricultural workers received little help from an unconcerned society or from a minimally active government. The machine provided food for the destitute, jobs for the unemployed, English instruction for the foreign-born, entertainment for the poor, burial for those lacking the wherewithal, activities for a potentially delinquent youth, church contributions for the centers of worship in the slums, bail bonds for those in trouble, a marriage brokerage for young hopefuls, and protection for the weak and obscure against a legal and social system that favored those who were socially and economically advantaged. The machine obtained the money for these expensive services (and sometimes for the pockets of its leaders) from those who had it—the merchants, manufacturers, and the underworld.

The machine extracted money by acting as a broker for governmental services. The organization raised funds in a great variety of ways. It made available for a price all types of licenses and permits, utility franchises and ordinances that might be helpful to a business. Sometimes it resorted to simple blackmail or the shakedown racket. Much money was made through contract rebates: Contracts were granted to a firm that was working closely with the machine with the understanding that part of the profit would be returned to the organization. Owing to the once common belief that it was cheaper to buy off the machine than to fight it, the business community often worked closely with the machine. So did the illegal business community, the underworld, which needed governmental cooperation and was willing to pay for it. The funds raised by the machines were often enormous, but so were the costs of the social services they provided.[1]

Campaigning under such circumstances involved providing entertainment, reassurance, and hope to the common man, a man who had little interest in issues or in furthering the image of democracy as an institution based on rational decisions made by rational men.

How did the politician of two generations ago garner votes? By promising "two dollars a day and roast beef." By taking the factory workers' children on picnics. By appealing to patriotic symbols with long, colorful Fourth of July orations, by handshaking, and even by baby kissing. He also was often a part of an organization that had professional or part-time semiprofessional workers in every neighborhood. A continuous politics of welfare services was more important to him than one of major issues. A farmer wanted clear title to his property? A young widow needed food and coal for herself and her small children? A son was in jail on a minor charge? The politician or his representative could be called on

[1] For more on bosses and machines, see Charles R. Adrian, *Governing Urban America,* 2d ed., McGraw-Hill Book Company, New York, 1961, chap. 6, and items cited there.

for help. Often he cut red tape or put the citizen in touch with the effective decision maker or, by adding the weight of his power, changed the balance of forces in the political arena so that the citizen, if his request was not unreasonable, could satisfy his particular need.

This kind of politics is not dead today. But it is much less important than it once was, and for many reasons. For example, social welfare services have been highly professionalized, and the rules of eligibility for such services have been made predictable by being assured without the intervention of a political machine. Americans have more reason than ever to need individual decisions from government, but they increasingly rely on the lobbyist, on the attorney or other spokesman for an interest group, or on their own attorney in making the contacts and in negotiating. Perhaps above all, mass communication has made it less necessary to use face-to-face techniques of campaigning and, indeed, has placed a premium on having the politician reach vast numbers of people rather than a few as the most efficient use of his time.

The Contemporary Pattern. Mass communication is the key to political success today. A campaigner can reach millions of voters by radio and television with no more effort than was once required to harangue the county fair grandstand crowd. Of at least equal importance is the fact that the candidate can quickly communicate, through radio and television, with opinion molders. Every chamber of commerce secretary, union shop steward, and local party worker can evaluate the candidate for himself and receive cues as to how to present his arguments in political talks and discussions.

Means of transportation have improved along with means of communication. The jet airplane can move man about with such great speed that a candidate can give talks at opposite ends of the nation a few hours apart and the public has come to expect such performances. Abraham Lincoln did not leave Springfield in 1860 or make a single speech. William McKinley conducted his 1896 campaign principally from his front porch in Canton, Ohio. Many nominees have made extensive use of the train, the "campaign special." Franklin Roosevelt introduced the airplane in 1932.

The broad sweep of the campaign trails of Vice President Nixon and Senator Kennedy shown in the map indicate the change the jet age has made. In previous years, even with air travel, itineraries were planned on a region-by-region basis, with a candidate covering one area before moving on to the next. Now the reduced travel time of jet aircraft allows the candidates to use the "scatter" technique—hitting three and four regions per day, often in widely spaced parts of the country. The goal is to keep the candidate's presence felt and to get a continuing big play from regional press, radio, and television. The theory is that local outlets tend to ignore a candidate unless he is on the scene. (The New York Times, *Sept. 18, 1960.*)

Figure 12-1

JET AIRCRAFT HAVE DRASTICALLY CHANGED CAMPAIGN STYLES
Presidential Campaign: Two Weeks of the Candidates' Travels

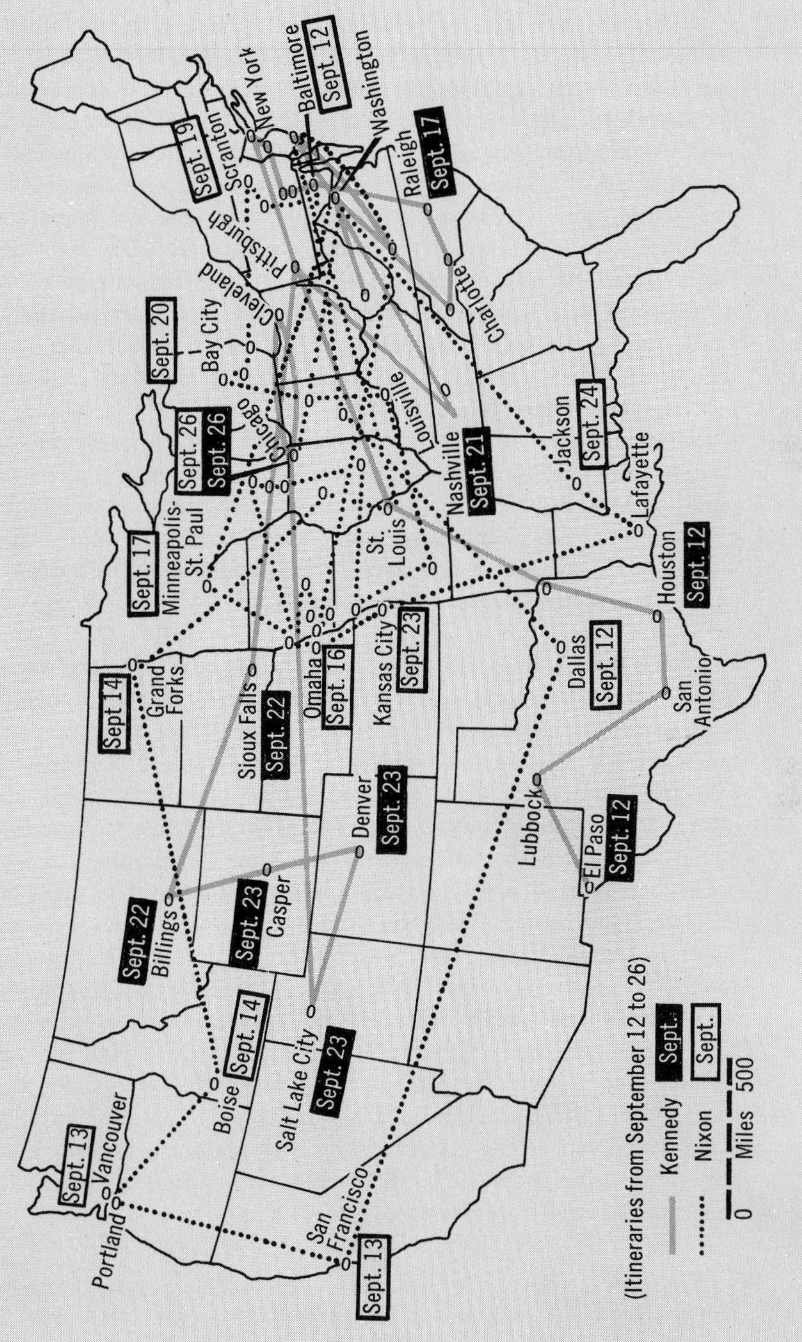

He flew from Albany to Chicago to accept the Democratic nomination for President. By 1960, the jet had become standard campaign equipment. John F. Kennedy traveled 44,000 miles, made 360 speeches in 43 states; Richard M. Nixon, 212 speeches in all 50 states. He traveled over 65,000 miles.

While the candidate once planned the campaign, the tactics for a given appearance, the content of a speech, and almost every aspect of the campaign, he today has the assistance of a variety of technical experts, specialists in public relations, specialists in organizing and managing volunteer workers, specialists in speech writing, indeed, specialists in every aspect of the job. The problem of financing has become bigger than it once was—costs have increased greatly, while there are few impelling reasons for persons to contribute more heavily to the campaign chest. But if the job is important enough and the candidate is highly enough regarded and is conceived of as a possible winner, adequate funds can usually be found. Furthermore, the major candidates can often find volunteers for much of their work. They are still faced, however, with the high cost involved in purchasing radio and television time.

Americans have often sought to imitate the corporate way of doing things. They did this in developing the council-manager plan as the closest parallel to be applied in the governing of cities, for example. Similarly, the corporate method of creating demand was borrowed for use in politics. Commercial advertising has become the model, and its techniques have become the methods for modern political campaigning.

Mass Media and the Public-relations Man. Since the old-style political campaign has declined in importance, and the mass media of communications have reduced the effectiveness and need for the part-time precinct worker, it is not unnatural that in the years after World War II political campaigns have more and more been turned over to public-relations specialists who have increasingly put political advertising on the same basis as commercial advertising and have tended to use the same techniques.

Democrats were highly critical of their opponents in 1952, when the GOP virtually turned direction of the Eisenhower-Nixon campaign over to a well-known Madison Avenue advertising firm, and Time, Inc., released some of its skilled writers to help elect the ticket by writing speeches in a style newspapers would like. But such techniques became standard for both parties starting with the 1956 election and are likely to remain so.

Some public-relations gambits have undoubtedly violated the highly prized American concept of fair play; and a good deal of moral indignation is expressed concerning alleged cynics who would try to sell candidates or buy votes, using the same sordid techniques as those used in advertising. One critic has put it this way:[2]

[2] Frank H. Jonas, *Western Politics and the 1956 Elections,* appended to the *Western Political Quarterly,* vol. 10, p. 17, 1957.

> Descending frequently on the voter in an unrelenting barrage of propaganda and hitting him from all sides over a period of time, the verbal and written guided missiles of the public-relations counsel, aimed at a very low intellectual level in order to reach everyone in the mass-media-consuming public and intended to arouse the stay-at-home voter mainly by appealing to fear and anger [anxieties], have the effect of dulling not only his senses so he can hardly tell truth from error but also his moral sense so he can hardly tell right from wrong.

A relevant criticism, no doubt. Yet one wonders. It was not the Madison Avenue public-relations counsel who thought up the idea of aiming at a low intellectual level, and the cause of the problem—if there is one—lies not so much with him as it does with the inherent characteristics of the institution of universal suffrage. The prototype campaign of "Tippecanoe and Tyler, too," in 1840 set the pattern that is still used.[3]

MASS MEDIA IN THE CAMPAIGN

Radio and Television as Entertainment. *Meet the Press* has been on radio and television since 1945. When it completed its fourteenth year on television in 1961, Laurence E. Spivak, who runs the show, said its success formula was based on the fact that:

> We recognized from the first that our job was to inform and that the necessary elements for a successful program were these—a guest important in the news, the right time for him, and challenging questions by an informed, responsible, and fair panel of reporters.

In fact, however, *Meet the Press* has never been designed primarily to inform, and fairness does not appear to be a central concern of the reporters. The program instead uses the fox-and-hounds formula that has always been successful on American radio and television, whether the program involves football, a detective story, or the interviewing of political leaders. The objective of the reporters is not to inform the public, but rather to put on a show in which the reporters seek to elicit from the interviewee things he does not wish to say and the interviewee tries to say what he wants to say in his own style. True public-information programs on radio and TV are rare, for they are considered dull by producers. News and public-policy issues are treated by radio and TV as entertainment items. The policy makers for these media of communication do not wish to jeopardize listener or viewer loyalty at prime viewing times by offending the typical citizen with educational efforts.

The Importance of Television Today. Evidence as to the effectiveness of television upon a campaign is conflicting. One study (made in 1952) expected

[3] See above, pp. 170–171.

to find that (1) areas with television coverage would have a larger voter turnout than areas without it and that (2) there would be an increased awareness of the party issues involved in the campaign in areas reached by television. Neither expectation was supported by the evidence, however. The researchers in this case offered the guess that the hypotheses failed because interest in the campaign was already at a high level of intensity.[4]

Perhaps television has merely become a substitute for the more traditional media. Auto workers rated TV as the most important source of information for them in the 1952 campaign. It far outranked newspapers, radio, personal talks, speeches, mailed leaflets, or other media, so far as their opinion of the trustworthiness of information was concerned. (Newspapers were at the bottom of the list of trusted sources.) When union members were asked for their most common source of information, however, they named newspapers.[5]

The Manipulation of the News. Experienced politicians have this general rule about reporter relations: A politician should always try to control a news story that affects his political status. He should try to control the timing, the content, the slant, and other relevant aspects of the story. He thus necessarily devotes a good deal of time and thought to the task of beating competitors to issuing a story, to the wording of a release, and to covering all important aspects of the story so as to minimize the danger of unexpected questions from reporters at the time the release is given to them.

The President has great powers to control news flow, of course. He releases news by announcement at press conferences or at other times as he chooses. He can be sure of maximum news media coverage. If he chooses, he can appear on nationwide radio and TV to present a matter of importance.

Until Franklin D. Roosevelt's day, a "White House spokesman" issued all presidential news releases. The President could not be questioned by newsmen and could not be quoted, except when the news release contained a quote or when he issued copies of a speech. Roosevelt, who understood the value of publicity and had a highly effective radio personality, devised the "fireside chat" as a technique of direct reporting to the people, that is, of securing popular support for his programs. He returned to the practice of regular press conferences that was originated by Woodrow Wilson but had then fallen into disuse during the 1920s. F.D.R. agreed to be directly questioned (in a polite and proper manner, of course). He could still not be quoted without specific permission. Later, President Eisenhower (on advice from his press secretary, James Haggerty) permitted filmed or

[4] Herbert A. Simon and Frederick Stern, "The Effect of Television upon Voting Behavior in Iowa in the 1952 Presidential Election," *American Political Science Review,* 49:470–477, June, 1955.

[5] Arthur Kornhauser and others, *When Labor Votes,* University Books, Inc., New York, 1956, chap. 3.

taped portions of his press conferences to be released after editing, and he dropped the restriction on quotations. President Kennedy went still further and permitted some of his conferences to be broadcast live by radio and TV. The increasing demand for information and the need to preserve public confidence in the nation's top decision maker have thus gradually brought the President away from his former position, which was as isolated and protected as that of a European monarch. Reporters now complain that the publicity function of the conference has reduced the ability of the individual reporter to determine the questions to be asked and hence to use the traditional journalistic technique of catching the interviewee off guard.[6] President Lyndon Johnson, at the beginning of his administration, attempted to restore the "snap" conference, which was relatively informal but did not allow reporters time to plan hostile questions.

The President can use his ability to command the attention of the press in many ways. In the guise of President, he can aid his own campaign for reelection or that of congressmen or of the successor his party has chosen. He can refuse to hold conferences over a long period of time, as Eisenhower sometimes did, if he wishes to avoid being questioned. He can release items, not in person, but through his press secretary if he does not want to be questioned about them. And he can always say "No comment," a statement that is less safely used by any other American political figure.

Members of Congress and the candidates for their seats have less ability than the President to control what goes into the press concerning themselves, but they are influential in affecting the way news is handled. The high status of a United States senator helps him to get press coverage. Congressmen tend to emphasize parochial interests, which are also concerns of the newspaper editors in their districts. A congressman from Hawaii denounces sugar quotas favorable to other areas; one from southern Michigan demands the repeal of the Federal tax on new automobiles; another from Massachusetts calls for additional defense contracts in labor-surplus areas.

The unskilled politician who does not anticipate news events, is inept at the timing of statements to the press, allows opponents to break stories first, and waits for newsmen to come to him is at an enormous disadvantage in the battle for men's minds. And of course, manipulation of the communications media is not limited only to the campaign period. It is a constant process and essential to success in the political occupation.

Importance of the Newspaper. Although there is evidence to indicate that readers do not believe all they see in the newspapers, as was noted above, this medium is vitally important for a number of reasons. American families nearly all subscribe to newspapers, out of interest in local advertising and comics or out of habit, if for no other reasons. United States

[6] Worth Bingham and Ward S. Just, "The President and the Press," *The Reporter,* Apr. 12, 1962, pp. 18–24.

newspaper circulation exceeds that of every other nation in the world, save only the United Kingdom, Belgium, Australia, and the three Scandinavian countries—and of these, only the United Kingdom and Australia are considerably ahead on a per capita basis. American illiteracy (using a fifth-grade level of reading as a test of literacy) is under 3 per cent; outside the South, it is almost zero. This compares with 5 per cent in the United Kingdom, 19 per cent in the U.S.S.R, and 92 per cent in Bolivia.[7] Under these circumstances, it is understandable that heavy emphasis is placed upon the use of newspapers for political propaganda. Since newspaper sources are also generally used in radio and TV, a double-barreled effect is achieved by release of material to the press. The number of radios per 1,000 population in the United States far exceeds that of any other nation—701, as compared with 309 for second-ranked Sweden. The same is true of TV. The mass media are used to replace older campaign communications techniques, partly because they are almost ubiquitous.

The Newspaper Editor as Educator. Newspaper editors have traditionally claimed responsibility for keeping the public informed, but in practice they base their policies upon certain conventional practices of journalism that in some circumstances inhibit the dissemination of meaningful information. In particular, editors commonly make their stories conform to the expectations of conventional wisdom, even in cases when knowledge based on sound research techniques is available. This practice probably helps promote circulation and it provides the reader with the kind of information he *expects* to receive, but it does not *inform* him in the sense of providing information based upon the best available scholarly or scientific study.

Newspaper editors will, for example, write about "public opinion" relative to a particular issue even when no measurement of opinion has been made, or when a poll has revealed a finding different from what the editors describe it as being. Or they will report praise of Politician A by Politician B without indicating that the two have a working alliance. Or they will quote a statement by a politician or other opinion leader relative to some matter of economics without indicating whether or not the economic assumptions in the statement are plausible. An announcement full of platitudes and glittering generalities will be reported without comment or explanation of its routine, ritualistic character. Political charges are commonly presented with no guide to the reader as to their nature, purpose, or plausibility and without a hint as to whether they are made by responsible persons who can reasonably be supposed to know something about the subject or by crackpots. Editors of daily newspapers continue to assume that they have no more obligation to make sense out of a reported item than does a tape recorder. They just "print the facts." For many a reader, such an approach to reporting does little to help him understand what is happening in the political world.

[7] William Albig, *Modern Public Opinion,* McGraw-Hill Book Company, New York, 1956, table 4.

CAMPAIGN RESOURCES

Party Workers: A Critical Campaign Resource. Relatively few Americans take an active part in political campaigns and in transmitting our political culture. Young people are not encouraged to believe that such activity is important. One study found that 83 per cent of high-school- and college-age Americans had no intention of entering politics;[8] another that only 2 per cent of the high school girls and 14 per cent of the boys would admit to interest in someday running for public office (see Table 12-1).

One can be politically active without running for office, of course. In fact, the largest portion of the actives prefer to be simply party workers. Both parties rely upon a relatively small number of volunteer workers to help the even smaller number of professionals. In the 1952 presidential contest, 27 per cent of the eligible voters said that they talked politics and tried to persuade others to vote for their candidates, and 11 per cent engaged in some kind of organized party activity. In this category, 3 per cent said they did some party work, such as stuffing envelopes; 7 per cent said they attended political meetings, rallies, picnics, and the like; only 4 per cent contributed money or bought tickets to fund-raising events. Some people, of course, were active in all three types of activity.[9]

In a postelection sample survey in the same year, 9 per cent of the United Automobile Workers' membership claimed to have been active in the campaign in such things as handing out leaflets, displaying posters, and the like. Another 17 per cent said they had talked politics during the campaign, but 73 per cent stated that they had done nothing active.[10] A somewhat higher proportion of high-school-age citizens, representing a

[8] George Gallup and Evan Hill, "Youth, the Cool Generation," *Saturday Evening Post,* Dec. 30, 1961, p. 78.

[9] Angus Campbell and others, *The Voter Decides,* Harper & Row, Publishers, New York, 1954, p. 30.

[10] Kornhauser and others, *op. cit.,* chap. 1.

TABLE 12-1

POLITICAL ATTITUDES OF HIGH SCHOOL STUDENTS (In per cent)

Attitudes and activities	Girls	Boys
Democratic preference	55.6	53.2
Republican preference	27.8	24.6
Other preference	5.6	9.0
Undecided	11.0	13.2
Have taken part in politics	26.0	22.0
Expect to work in politics	37.0	27.0
Expect to run for office	2.0	14.0
Have been contacted by local party organization	37.0	20.0

SOURCE: Adapted from Gilbert Youth Research Company, syndicated report of July 28, 1963.

TABLE 12-2

EFFECT OF DIFFERENT COMMUNICATIONS TECHNIQUES ON VOTING BEHAVIOR, 1953 AND 1954*

Contact	Number of voters	Voter turnout (per cent)
Personal		
1953	20	75
1954	122	25
Mail		
1953	22	59
1954	81	10
No contact†		
1953	21	33
1954	187	6

* Study conducted in Ann Arbor, Mich.

†Control group.

NOTE: The 1953 election was a municipal and statewide election. Differences in response are statistically valid by chi-square test.

SOURCE: Samuel J. Eldersveld, "Experimental Propaganda Techniques and Voting Behavior," *American Political Science Review,* 50:160, table II, March, 1956.

cross section of the total population, have reported active participation in politics or the intention to participate as adults (see Table 12-1). Whether the parties need more volunteer participants than they have is uncertain. Professional organizers argue that they can use all the volunteer help they can get. At some point, however, the addition of workers would probably result in the sharp reduction of their marginal utility values. Even though the number of workers in a campaign may not be what campaign managers would wish, it may be adequate for needs, given the present-day style of campaigning and the reliance of the typical voter on professional and amateur opinion molders. In any case, we have no basis for concluding that the system suffers from lack of personnel. We do know, however, that large numbers of persons with varying degrees and types of skills are necessary to every campaign that involves a congressional district, a state, or the Presidency, and that personal contacts—the most time-consuming kind—are still the most effective in getting out the vote (see Table 12-2).[11]

Persons of many types with many motivations make up the active work force of a political party. Individuals may be classified by motivation into several categories:

[11] Phillips Cutright and Peter H. Rossi, "Grass Roots Politicians and the Vote," *American Sociological Review,* 23:171–179, April, 1958; Samuel J. Eldersveld, "Experimental Propaganda Techniques and Voting Behavior," *American Political Science Review,* 50:154–165, March, 1956.

The ideologues. Some people become active in party affairs because they believe that this is a form of political action by which they can push forward their own ideological beliefs. But at the local level the party active is likely to have a constituency more homogeneous than that of the party leader at a higher level. The active who has strong ideological commitments is, therefore, less likely to climb from local ranks to leadership positions in the party than the more tolerant moderate, who is motivated by other considerations. Persons with strong ideological beliefs are the least flexible and hence the least likely to be successful if they seek to become leaders,[12] but this may not be important to them. They may be willing to labor patiently in the political vineyard so long as they are able to make a psychological association between the party and their personal ideological goals.

The hobbyists. Politics is, to many people, an interesting hobby. With increasing amounts of leisure time available to many persons and with parties chronically in need of manpower, politics has come to be viewed as a hobby. As such, it competes for attention with skiing, motorboating, gardening, charity drives, and hundreds of other activities. Middle- and upper-class women in particular have leisure time to devote to party activities and are increasingly performing routine tasks. In addition, many qualified women are moving into leadership positions, partly because of social acceptance of them in this role and partly because they have built up claims on party offices through years of loyal service in menial positions.

The job seekers. The opportunity to find a job that paid better than any that an individual could qualify for in private business was once an important motivation for going into politics. In addition, a person might seek a part-time government patronage position that would supplement his income, or he might want to increase his family's income by getting a government job for his wife. This type of interest in politics has been dulled somewhat by the increasing scope of the merit system of civil service and by plentiful private jobs for skilled persons, but it is still important.

The status and publicity seekers. Traditionally, politics has offered an opportunity for members of numerous, but socially inferior, ethnic groups to advance in terms of status. In seeking status advancement a member of an ethnic group in the nineteenth century was often limited to becoming a businessman catering primarily to other members of his group, becoming a clergyman, joining an underworld organization, entering the sports or entertainment world, or seeking political party or public office. Politics still provides a ladder for status strivers. All socially and economically deprived groups, and Negroes in particular, still see this type of activity as offering opportunity. In addition, any person who sees his ordinary

[12] See Edmond Costantini, "Intraparty Attitude Conflict," *Western Political Quarterly,* 16:956–972, December, 1963.

career blocked may turn to an alternative career in politics. The truant officer in the school system who concludes he will never become a principal or an assistant superintendent may, through years of hard work in the party, become a party candidate for the state legislature or a statewide elective office. The mayor's chauffeur, through similar activity, may become his party's county chairman. Both find themselves the recipients of publicity and the possessors of more power and higher status than would otherwise ever have been possible for them.

One may become active in politics because of a psychological need for attention. The ordinary, obscure person who works for the party may be able to hobnob with front-page personalities. He may come to be on a first-name basis with the governor. Or, he may want publicity for his business. The party active, through personal publicity, may attract customers. This can happen in connection with any business or profession, but political activity is most helpful to attorneys. The obscure lawyer can attract clients to his office through other party actives or because people believe he may have greater influence with decision makers than do other lawyers, or he may become a candidate for public office and thus receive free and ethical professional advertising.

Mixed motives and changing actors. The individual party active need not, of course, be driven by a single motive. Most probably he is not. The hobbyist, for example, may have chosen this particular hobby because he sees the party as a means to further his personal beliefs. He may also be aware of the possibility of higher status and personal publicity through party activity, and it is not unlikely that he might accept a government job for himself or a member of his family if it becomes available. Motives are often supportive of one another rather than in conflict.

Party workers are not a particularly stable group, however. Some of them are attached to a faction or individual; they remain active only so long as their lodestar is in the ascendant, for campaigns commonly are arranged around a candidate, rather than the party itself. Others, in our mobile society, move out of the district and are lost to the organization. Others become disillusioned. Many take part in one type of campaign but not in another: A party active may work hard on behalf of the candidate for United States senator, for example, but do nothing for the campaign of his party's candidates for governor, the House of Representatives, or the state legislature (see Table 12-3). Furthermore, many workers devote only a part of their time to party activities (see Table 12-4). The professional party worker has largely been replaced by the amateur. With the decline of the old-fashioned machine and the rise of the hobbyist, this is typically the case. Even the full-time worker often fits the professional category only temporarily during a campaign, having been released by a loyal party member from a government job, a law firm, a business organization, a labor union headquarters, or some other institution for the duration of the campaign.

TABLE 12–3
ACTIVITY OF CAMPAIGN WORKERS (In per cent)*

Duration of activity	Democrats (150)†	Republicans (124)†
Two campaigns	24	16
One campaign	27	42
Inactive	49	42
Total	100	100

* Study conducted in three state assembly districts, California, 1948 and 1953.
† Number of workers surveyed.
SOURCE: Adapted from Dwaine Marvick and Charles Nixon, "Recruitment Contrasts in Rival Campaign Groups," in Dwaine Marvick (ed.), *Political Decision Makers,* The Free Press of Glencoe, New York, 1961, table 3.

Party personnel today are commonly transitory, amateur or semiprofessional, largely nondependent upon the party leadership for economic survival, and in general a very different type from the personnel of a few generations ago. But they are the people who operate the party apparatus, and in this sense, they *are* the political party.

Money: A Critical Campaign Resource. Jet travel, prime television time, staff specialists essential to the presentation of the candidate in his best light, printed literature, and other essentials in a modern campaign are enormously expensive. Some of the cost can be absorbed outside the budgets of the principal campaign organizations; a newspaper or magazine may release a reporter for speech writing or a private firm may absorb the cost of political television time into its regular advertising budget (this is tech-

TABLE 12–4
WORKING TIME CONTRIBUTED BY CAMPAIGN VOLUNTEERS (In per cent)*

Portion of time volunteered	Democrats (168)†	Republicans (131)†
Full time	16	25
Half time	32	38
Part time‡	52	37

* Study conducted in three state assembly districts, California, 1956.
† Number of workers surveyed.
‡ Less than half time.
SOURCE: Adapted from Dwaine Marvick and Charles Nixon, "Recruitment Contrasts in Rival Campaign Groups," in Dwaine Marvick (ed.), *Political Decision Makers,* The Free Press of Glencoe, New York, 1961, table 4.

nically illegal, but a charge would be difficult to prove in court). But even with help of this sort and with much volunteered time, the direct outlays of money by political organizations are enormous. Their sources are so many and so obscure that the actual amount contributed to and spent on a state or national campaign is never fully known.[13] In the 1952 political campaign, expenditures were estimated at $140 million for nominating and electing all officeholders selected that year.[14] Though this may seem high, it is unlikely that the amount being spent on campaigning is increasing faster than the gross national product.

At one period in American history, campaigns were paid for, in large part, by a few very large contributors. In 1896 and 1900, the Rockefeller-controlled Standard Oil Company gave a quarter of a million dollars to the McKinley campaign treasury—a great deal of money in those days. In 1904, Perry Belmont and Thomas Fortune Ryan together paid most of the costs of the losing Democratic candidate, Alton B. Parker. Alexander Heard, a leading authority on campaign costs, believes that the number of direct financial contributors was much smaller in those days as compared with the post-World War II period. Even so, only about 5 per cent of those who actually vote contribute any money at all during campaigns; of these 3 million or so persons, few make contributions of over $100, and most of them give only a dollar or two. One reason so few contribute "has long been the lurking suspicion that contributing to political parties is somehow a shoddy business."[15] Yet parties are essential to a large democracy, and they cannot operate without money.

In recent years, political leaders have increasingly called for contributions. Many ways to increase them have been suggested, such as permitting contributions to be deductible from income taxes (up to a certain amount) and providing for more complete disclosure of contributions so that people may be less apprehensive about contributing.[16] Some specialists have suggested that Congress appropriate the funds for the national campaigns, thus reducing the problem of candidates' dependence on those seeking to gain influence through contributions.

Who contributes and why? In 1956, according to the Senate Privileges and Elections Subcommittee, there were only 7,751 contributions of over $500 to Republican and 2,663 to Democratic campaign organizations seeking to elect persons to national offices. Yet in each election year, roughly two-thirds of campaign expenses come from these contributions. Some pay-

[13] For examples of obscure sources, see *1961–1962 Campaign Contributions and Expenditures,* Congressional Quarterly Service, Washington, D.C., 1963.

[14] This section borrows generally from Alexander Heard, *The Costs of Democracy,* The University of North Carolina Press, Chapel Hill, N.C., 1960, and *Money and Politics,* Public Affairs Committee, Inc., New York, 1956.

[15] President's Commission on Campaign Costs, *Financing Presidential Campaigns,* 1962.

[16] *Ibid.* See also Herbert E. Alexander, *Money, Politics and Public Reporting,* Citizens' Research Foundation, Princeton, N.J., 1960.

ments are very large indeed. In 1956, members of the du Pont family gave $248,000 to the Republicans. (The Hatch Act of 1940 limits *individual* contributions to $5,000.) The second largest family contribution came from the Pews of Pennsylvania (oil); it was $216,000. The largest contributor to the Democrats was the Reynolds family of North Carolina (tobacco); $49,000. The Democrats, incidentally, must always operate on

Figure 12-2

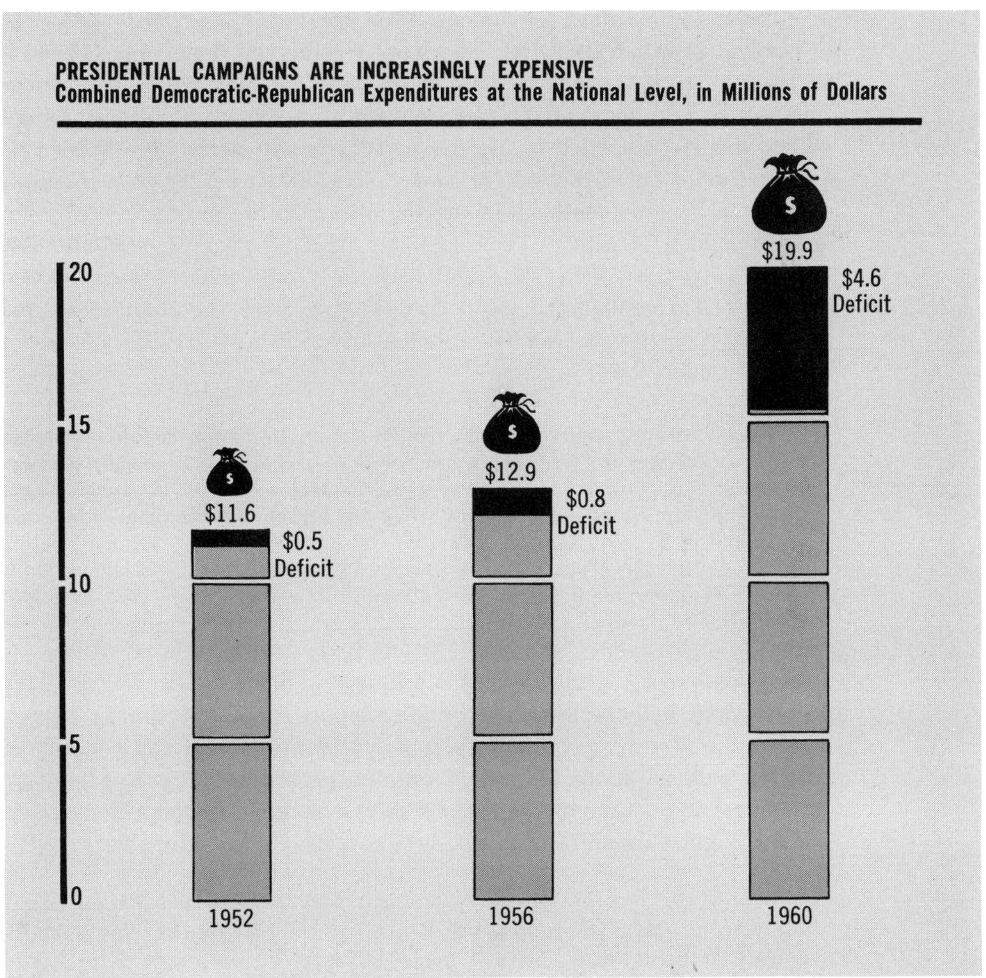

This money was actually spent by committees operating in more than one state, not including money transferred to other organizations. (Financing Presidential Campaigns, *Washington, 1962, p. 10.*)

a smaller budget than the Republicans, though the difference is less than is popularly supposed. In 1960, the Republican National Committee spent $10.1 million on the national campaign; the Democratic committee, $9.8 million. But the Republicans collected all but $700,000 of their amount before Election Day, while the Democrats had a deficit of nearly $4 million.[17]

Both parties, but particularly the Democrats, concentrate on trying to expand the number of small contributors, those who give less than $100, even though these are expensive collections in terms of the administrative costs involved in proportion to the total received. It does the party little financial good to collect $5 if it costs $4 to do so, but the contributions do provide an important psychological linkage.

Why do people contribute? For many reasons, no doubt. Some believe that in doing so they are "buying democracy," or they regard a contribution as a social obligation. Others are deeply interested in politics or some policy and feel impelled to aid the persons or the party they believe in. Others cannot bring themselves to say "No" when asked by a friend or coworkers. The big contributors are the ones who are most suspect by the general public, of course. Why should a man or couple contribute, say, $5,000 to a party? Why should at least forty-nine persons have hedged their bets and contributed more than $500 to *both* the Republican and Democratic parties in 1956? In anticipation of a direct payoff? Alexander Heard has concluded:[18]

> What contributors buy is not as tangible as is often supposed. Mostly what they buy is "access." . . . The main result of access, said a former national treasurer noted for his persuasion with the fatter cats, is to "speed things up." The number of cold bargains that are struck for campaign funds are negligible. The real influence derived from big contributions is a latent one. . . . But large contributions pave a sure road to the decision-making centers of government for those who want to present their case, which is often all they need.

The great cost of campaigning is a long-standing problem that is likely to get worse, and there is little public support for the parties or for permitting the wealthy people or business corporations and labor unions to pay the bulk of campaign costs. Thus the problem of financing political campaigns is another of the serious issues testing American democracy, but the public shows little interest or sympathy. One observer has noted:[19]

> It is moot whether the financial base will broaden sufficiently before government subsidies are voted to help meet campaign costs. The public is quickly aroused when "fat cats" or special interests are exposed for having

[17] Herbert E. Alexander, *Financing the 1960 Election,* Citizens' Research Foundation, Princeton, N.J., 1962, table 1.

[18] Heard, *Money and Politics, op. cit.,* pp. 14–15.

[19] Alexander, *Financing the 1960 Election,* p. 92.

undue influence in government decision-making, yet only a small proportion of the electorate support their parties and candidates with even modest contributions.

Either the establishment of government subsidies or the voluntary broadening of financial constituencies would herald democratic changes as significant as those brought about by the broadening of electoral constituencies.

Sample Surveys: A Useful Campaign Resource. Since the 1930s, the pulse of the public has been taken during each political campaign, usually by a number of polling organizations. Most polls operate on a profit-making basis by selling their information to newspapers or political party leaders. Editors have found that their readers are intrigued simply by the experience of learning prior to the election how their fellow citizens are supposed to view the contest and who the winner is likely to be. But the polls have a more immediate campaign function. Political leaders have come to make extensive use of them in plotting their strategies. The information they provide, especially those conducted privately for a party or candidate, provides a basis for major campaign decisions.

Polls and their predecessors. From 1912, when Wilson defeated Taft, until 1964, the major-party candidate with the longer surname won the Presidency. Does this mean that a bet on the man with the longer name is a safe one in the next election? It does not. Occasionally an editor asks his readers to return a coupon in the newspaper stating their candidate preferences. Is the totaled result an indication of who is likely to win? It is not. In neither case is the finding based on a sound measurement of what mathematicians call "statistical probability." The former case is mere coincidence; the latter encourages only the highly motivated to respond. At the polls, votes count equally, regardless of how interested or emotionally involved in politics a person may or may not be.

A somewhat better barometer is the experienced politician who listens carefully and weighs the reports he receives. Some become very skillful in judging probable outcomes, including the critical question of probable turnout levels. In 1936, James A. Farley, chairman of the Democratic National Committee, predicted that Franklin D. Roosevelt would carry all states except Maine and Vermont. Many thought he was joking, but he was totally accurate. In the confusing 1948 campaign, President Truman sent his old, experienced friend Leslie Biffle, the secretary of the Senate, on a tour of Midwest farm states. Biffle traveled in the disguise of a chicken buyer, talking with all types of farmers. In August, when the polls showed the Midwest a tossup, Biffle reported to the President that he would carry enough of the Corn Belt to win reelection. Truman thought his conclusions more dependable than those of the pollsters. Like other citizens, however, professional politicians sometimes confuse wishful thinking with reality. A study of confidential predictions of their own districts made by county and precinct chairmen in the 1928 presidential campaign showed the Democrats off by 18 per cent and the Republicans by 7 per cent.[20] In 1932, a dozen Republican senators, listening to the radio broadcast of the Democratic National Convention, concluded that Franklin D. Roosevelt was the weakest candidate the Democrats could have nominated. "The Senators said he did not have an appeal to the mass of voters and wasn't likely to catch fire."[21]

The polls remain the most accurate measure of voter sentiment, however, and professional political leaders themselves commonly hire private pollsters to help them in strategic planning. The professional pollsters, although they are often criticized for one reason or another, have a fine record for accuracy. In 1948, the Gallup poll, which is the best known and has the best long-term record, had its worst experience. It was 4.4 percentage points high in its estimate of the Dewey vote—not an error of gigantic proportions. What caused so much difficulty was that it reported Dewey as the probable winner. In reporting results, Gallup probably made some technical errors, according to critics, and he failed to point out that the figure, within the limits of possible statistical error, might permit either candidate to win. In later campaigns, he was more cautious.

The basis of polling. Polling techniques are derived from a finding of statistics: A small cross section, or sample, of the total population one is concerned about, if properly identified, will show within very small possibilities of error the characteristics of the whole population. The major problem is to find the right persons to fit the requirements of the sample. Highly refined techniques for doing this have been developed. Another problem, not yet solved, is to determine the level of voter turnout and to identify citizens who are likely to vote or to stay at home. A skewed (unbalanced) pattern in the actual turnout can produce a result that is different from the one expected when persons go to the polls in the proportions represented in an opinion sample.

In addition to indicating voter attitudes toward candidates and parties, the polls are commonly used to sample grass-roots opinion on current issues of public policy. Newspapers purchase results of such polls because many of the readers probably believe that the views of the common man are indicators of what policy ought to be. Politicians use them for hints on methods of increasing their popularity—knowledge that may have an important payoff in the next campaign.

THE TECHNIQUES OF CAMPAIGNING

In 1948, when Harry Truman was running for reelection, he campaigned hard against the Taft-Hartley Labor Relations Act, making its repeal one of his principal campaign promises. Yet in that same year, pollsters found

[20] Claude E. Robinson, *Straw Votes: A Study of Political Prediction,* Columbia University Press, New York, 1932, chap. 1.
[21] Joseph W. Martin, Jr., *My First Fifty Years in Politics,* McGraw-Hill Book Company, New York, 1960, p. 68.

that 37 per cent of the voters had never heard of the act, and another 29 per cent had no opinion concerning its merits.[22] Truman sought to make an issue of a matter that apparently caused little excitement among rank-and-file voters. Why? Probably because in doing so he mobilized on behalf of his campaign the trade union leaders of the land—a large and powerful resource. When Eisenhower talked of the importance of a balanced budget in 1952, he may have bored most of his listeners, but he rallied bankers—high-status and influential opinion molders—to his support. The need in a campaign is to activate latent support; the conversion of nonbelievers is secondary.

Sometimes the telling issue is not the subject of debate in the campaign at all, and there may be many reasons why this is so; for example, it may be politically disadvantageous to mention the item (e.g., the need for a tax increase), or the problem might be too complex to translate into the effortless symbolism of a campaign (e.g., the question of giving foreign aid to a particular uncommitted nation).

Politics as a Game of Strategy. Since issues are often complicated and anxiety-producing, the typical voter may not wish to face them. He is, therefore, more likely to respond to symbols than to rational arguments, and campaigns tend to become games of strategy, similar to chess, bridge, or war. Game theory can easily be applied to campaigns: Boards of strategy for both teams seek to plan their moves in advance, to anticipate the moves of the opposition, to devise open moves and secret moves, to bluff, to bargain, to form coalitions (especially in primary-election campaigns), and in general to try to maximize the payoff, which is the chance of winning or the size of the margin of victory.

Of course, the abilities of professional politicians, relying principally upon experience in testing public reactions, vary greatly with the individual, and monumental blunders are sometimes made. The amount of strategic planning that is done in advance varies greatly too, as does the quality of the vitally important staff work in a major campaign. In addition, a candidate's performance is limited by time and budget.

Choices of Strategies. The political strategist has a surfeit of strategies to choose from. His problem is in determining which to use and how best to use them. In making decisions, he must take many factors into consideration. For example, the strategy he decides to use may depend upon his own oratorical abilities as compared with those of his opponent, upon his estimate of whether issues or personalities will be more important in the campaign, upon the image that already exists before the public both of himself and of his opponent, and upon many other considerations.

The candidate may choose to take a position of aloof indifference toward

[22] Angus Campbell and R. L. Kahn, *The People Elect a President,* University of Michigan, Survey Research Center, Ann Arbor, Mich., 1952, p. 56.

his opponent, coupled with a "nonpartisan" posture concerning political conflict, as did Thomas E. Dewey in 1948 and Dwight D. Eisenhower in 1952. To do this, he will probably have to feel that he is considerably ahead of the pack. A congressional candidate may choose to give his opponent the silent treatment, but before he does, he must feel quite sure that he is vastly better known or better respected than his opponent. He may have to select defensive strategies too. Although a general political rule holds that the best defense is a strong offense, some of his opponent's shots may score, especially if he has a political past to defend. He may try to drive a wedge between his opponent and his followers, and he may even decide upon a deliberate smear campaign. Of course, the best approach is usually a mixed strategy, employing several of the above.

The Image of the Candidate. Because the art of propaganda involves not only the adroit handling of issues of policy, but also the presentation of a personality to which the voters will probably react favorably, a major political problem lies in the need to construct an image of the candidate. If the candidate and the voter meet only at the secondary level, the voter has no chance to know the candidate as a whole personality. Instead, he gets only fleeting, carefully selected impressions of the man who wants his vote.

The candidate, therefore, seeks to create a synthetic personality for himself and to sell it to the public; at the same time, he and his supporters try to create an image of his opponent that will dampen the enthusiasm of anyone less closely related to him than his mother. The politician has many different choices as to the type of person he wants to have the public think he is, and the picture he will settle upon will be the one he thinks best suits the particular needs of the day. Later he may want to modify the image somewhat and may or may not find it possible to do so. There are always limits to what he can do.

Although the candidate has options that he can exercise to show himself to be a man of daring, of caution, of liberal experimentation, of sharp business acumen and conservatism, of gentle patience, or of firm decisiveness, certain items appear and reappear in political images, and all of them reflect enduring social values and expectations. These items differ according to the office sought, but some of them are as follows:

1. The candidate is a family man and devoutly religious. Frequently he tries to associate himself with that symbol of goodness and morality, the small town. In 1940, Wendell Willkie, long a prominent New York utilities executive, arranged to formally accept the presidential nomination in his boyhood home of Elwood, Indiana. (Secretary of the Interior Harold Ickes, unimpressed, dubbed him "the barefoot boy from Wall Street.")

2. He is in good health. Even minor illnesses, such as head colds, are kept from the press, if possible. In 1944, Franklin Roosevelt was rumored to be in bad health. To demonstrate his vigor, he rode through a driving autumn rain the length of Manhattan. In 1960, Candidate Nixon went to

special efforts to get medical evidence to show that a knee damaged during the campaign was not disabling.

3. He has done something especially patriotic—usually he has uncovered a "Red plot," or was awarded several battle stars for military action.

4. He has vast energy and works a twelve- or fourteen- or sixteen-hour day—and takes home a briefcase full of papers to browse through during odd moments of the evening. But we are also told that he is hardly ever home evenings because he averages five dinner speaking engagements a week. Incidentally, he gets to the office at eight each morning, if not sometimes earlier.

5. He is exceptionally intelligent—not highbrow, of course, but he reads everything from *Little Orphan Annie* to Tolstoi. He also reads several daily newspapers, including the *New York Times,* and a few weeklies.

6. He likes whatever the typical citizen likes—old-time favorite tunes, for example. (Franklin D. Roosevelt complained about the frequent renditions of "Home on the Range" to which he was subjected after he was

Figure 12-3

Rational Discussion May Be Dysfunctional for the Candidate

"That's an excellent question, sir, and I'm going to give it the respect it deserves by not attempting a quick, superficial answer here. Instead, I'd like to say that if I should be elected, I plan..."

The politician sometimes uses the "bait-and-switch" technique of the salesman. He encourages questions from the floor but answers the ones he wants answered. (Drawing by Stevenson; © 1960, The New Yorker Magazine, Inc.)

mistakenly specific in answering a newsman's question concerning his favorite melody.) He likes Western and detective stories, TV, and for that matter, anything else the bulk of the public likes. Presidents have served hot dogs to visiting royalty, and Nelson Rockefeller, aristocrat, has been careful to be photographed eating blintzes and other favorite proletarian ethnic foods.

7. He is fond of sports and is quite a sportsman himself. He played some football or baseball in school and loves to hunt and fish.

8. He writes his own speeches—usually in longhand. (Actually, almost no important politician does this today. He simply would not have the time. His role is to deliver them publicly.)

9. His wife does all or most of the shopping and the housework, and there is a mortgage on their modest home.

In fact, if the reader of the human-interest stories that relate such items were to do a bit of calculating, he would find that either public-relations counselors for political candidates have a tendency to exaggerate or politicians live in a world that has a day of more than twenty-four hours. Of course, many politicians do lead strenuous lives and work far harder at their jobs than the typical citizen does.

The image that is to be portrayed is polished constantly and not just through "planted" human-interest stories. The candidate works on it during personal and TV appearances, when receiving visitors, and on every other occasion. The image that the voter holds of him is one of his most important assets—or liabilities.

Some Rules of Political Campaigning. In every campaign, and for officeholders between campaigns, there are certain general rules to be followed. These are established on the basis of empiricism. We cannot list them all, but they include the following:

1. Avoid the defensive; take the offensive and, when you lose it, use the first opportunity to resume it. If you have bad news that cannot be kept a secret (and few secrets are possible in political campaigns), release it under the least unfavorable conditions. If possible, do not let your opponents announce it. A Friday afternoon statement is often the least bad, for the Saturday newspapers are the smallest and the least carefully read.

2. Always keep statements simple and easily understood. Put the emphasis on the manipulation of symbols rather than on rational explanations. Never attempt a complex, detailed explanation unless it is in your interest to confuse the issue or to be deliberately vague. Because Americans react more quickly in opposition to policies than in their support, spend more time criticizing the opponent than in promoting a positive program. At the same time, work to develop a personality image; give this a higher priority than program development.

3. Do not create a martyr for the opponents to exploit. Any behavior that the public considers unfair, or undue harassment, may react to the advantage of the victim.

4. Never intervene in an intramural battle within the opposing party. While the opponents are fighting among themselves, they are helping you; even though you may sympathize with one side, it is to your advantage to remain silent. Organize the discontents to your support. [Hence in 1964, there were Citizens for Goldwater (Democrats) and Citizens for Johnson (Republicans).]

5. Never introduce a campaign gambit if it is likely you will abandon it. Be as certain as possible that you know what the next two or three steps in your procedure are and that you understand the countermoves available to the opposition. This is essentially the rule of a boy's play group: Don't start anything you can't finish.

6. Never "cop a plea"; that is, never concede the validity of a charge by the opposition. To do so is to place yourself on the defensive, a violation of the first rule. Always have an explanation that will seem plausible for any party defeat, for every decision, and for any matter that affects you and may become a matter of newspaper attention.

7. Never put anything in writing that you are not willing to see in the newspaper the next day. There are many possible leaks to the press by the discontented and the opportunistic, and politicians generally assume that

Figure 12-4

"Mud Slinging" through Rumor Works Both Ways

"I could dig up some hot stuff from his past if I were sure he wouldn't retaliate."

By permission of Burr Shafer.

if more than two persons have knowledge of a particular matter, it is potentially public knowledge.

8. Always expect rumors in a campaign and try to control them by starting some that will benefit you. Every rumor deliberately started is a danger, however. It may backfire.

9. Make few concessions to groups that have "no place to go." Concentrate on the marginal groups and voters. Concessions to them may have the greater payoff.

10. Beware of the efforts of interest groups to trap you into commitments. Such commitments may be in the interest of a candidate, but they may also be unacceptable to most of his constituents or result in entrapment between rival groups of near-equal power—a dangerous position in most campaigns.

According to the rational-man theory, the politician "should owe his office to his ability to persuade an informed electorate of his qualifications for office and of the wisdom of his policies, and to that ability alone."[23]

[23] Stanley Kelley, Jr., *Political Campaigning,* The Brookings Institution, Washington, D.C., 1960, p. 1.

Figure 12-5

The Voter Often Responds Better to Appeals to Vote against the Incumbent than to Positive Action Proposals

"Don't bother to outline a program—just criticize the previous administration."

By permission of Burr Shafer.

To the politician, however, the campaign is not primarily a device to inform the public, but rather to persuade the voter to support him and his party. Informing the voter and seeking to secure his support are not the same thing.

CAMPAIGN APPEALS

Any communication designed to create a desired effect, impression, or opinion is propaganda. It is not necessarily either bad or good, since it can be used for either good or bad ends. It is simply a communications technique that is used when one individual or group seeks to affect the attitudes of other individuals or groups. Propaganda may be obvious or subtle, open or concealed, crude or polished. The student of politics should be able to understand something of its character and to recognize certain types of propaganda when they are encountered. It will not be possible in this book to provide more than an introduction to the subject.[24]

[24] For further reading, see A. M. Lee, *How to Understand Propaganda,* Holt, Rinehart and Winston, Inc., New York, 1952.

Figure 12-6

Is This Next? Probably Not.

Drawing by Dove; © 1962, The New Yorker Magazine, Inc.

How to Read an Editorial. With some practice, following a political campaign in the newspapers can be interesting and informative. A knowledge of propaganda techniques is useful, as is a knowledge of the words and symbols that are frequently used by politicians, reporters, and editors.

The following "translation" of the types of terms frequently found in newspaper editorials gives some idea of the process of interpretation, although the words of one editor do not always coincide with those of another. These are some possible interpretations, depending upon the biases, interests, and goals of editors:

Editorial quotation	Possible meaning
"He is a clear-thinking public servant."	He holds views with which the editors agree.
"He is a fuzzy thinker."	He holds views with which the editors do not agree.
"He is a statesman."	He is any political figure with whom the editors agree.
"He is a politician."	He is any political figure with whom the editors disagree.
"He will serve without favor to anyone as a servant of all the people."	He has no strong convictions about anything. Or perhaps: He will support the editors' views.
"The people demand action."	The editors demand action.
"He gives the people the facts."	He says what the editors like to hear him say.
"He is independent and level-headed."	He is on the editors' side.
"If the voters are as well informed as we think they are, he will emerge the victor."	His chances aren't very good. Or perhaps: The election is a tossup.
"He is running in response to a great ground swell of popular demand."	He is running as the choice of politically important individuals and has announced his candidacy after a carefully staged publicity campaign masquerading as grass-roots spontaneity.

Types of Propaganda. In order to give a better idea of the manner in which propaganda is used, a few illustrations might be offered of types by which some—not all—propaganda might be classified.[25] Many types are used simultaneously, however; they are not mutually exclusive.

Name calling. This represents an attempt to associate the opposition candidate or an undesired proposal for public policy with words and

[25] This is the typology used by the Institute for Propaganda Analysis. See A. M. Lee and E. B. Lee, *The Fine Art of Propaganda,* Harcourt, Brace & World, Inc., New York, 1939.

symbols that produce an unfavorable response in the mind of the listener.

Common barbs hurled at opponents are spender, radical, reactionary, "pinko," bumbler. Opponents are said to be fuzzy-thinking servants of Wall Street or special interests, soft on communism, Pollyannas, or lacking in the will to win. President Truman called conservatives "Neanderthals."

Politicians are usually careful to avoid personalities in name calling and restrict this device to use of symbols and slogans. There are many exceptions, however. Truman occasionally called a critic a liar. Republicans called him "High-tax Harry." Winston Churchill, more skilled in language usage than the typical politician, once said that his opponent, Clement Attlee, was "a sheep in sheep's clothing."

Transfer. The campaigner tries to transfer the authority or prestige of a high-status symbol to himself. In particular, he likes to use religious references. The rabble-rouser Gerald L. K. Smith called his magazine, *The Cross and the Flag*. William Jennings Bryan said he wanted to keep the common man from being *crucified* on a *cross* of gold. Willkie (1940) and Eisenhower (1952) did not conduct political campaigns; they led *crusades*.

Glittering generality. This is similar to the above, except that a phrase of vague and general meaning is used to produce a favorable response toward the candidate or his program. Examples include references to the good life, the dignity of man, fair play, a program based on morality, a positive policy, patriotism, statesmanship, independent and nonpartisan service. Campaign slogans often fall into this category: "Two dollars a day and roast beef" (Whigs, 1840); "A chicken in every pot" (Republicans, 1900); "You never had it so good" (Democrats, 1952).

The glittering generality is a tried-and-true ingredient for every political party platform. Governor "Pa" Ferguson of Texas, in fact, once described a platform as being "like the hoop skirt which covers everything and touches nothing."[26]

Testimonial. There has scarcely been a political movement of any consequence in the years since the Civil War that has not asserted that its philosophical roots may be found in the ideas of Washington, Jefferson, and Lincoln. Quotations are easily lifted from context as supporting evidence. Another use of the testimonial is to get motion picture or sports stars to give public support to a candidate, seeking to transfer the popularity of the one to the other. This type of approach—it can be used equally well by Communists, Socialists, moderates, conservatives, or reactionaries—is simply the testimonial. It is frequently used in commercial advertising and is regarded as a basic device in political campaigns.

Plain folks. Nearly every candidate since the coming of universal suffrage has sought to show that he is really a plain, ordinary sort of person, not much different from the voter to whom he is appealing. When Terrill Sledge ran for the United States senatorship from Texas, he used a ten-

[26] S. S. McKay, *Texas Politics,* Texas Tech Press, Lubbock, Tex., 1952, p. 131.

year-old car with a sign painted on it: "This ain't no helicopter, folks. This is your flying fortress." He promised to use it to bomb the three "big-money candidates" (name calling). But Sledge was no semiliterate. He was, in fact, a Phi Beta Kappa and a Rhodes scholar.[27] He was, however, no winner, either.

Famous usages of the plain-folk appeals were made by both Franklin D. Roosevelt and Richard M. Nixon. The former, in 1944, said that his opponents were not satisfied with attacks on his wife and children: "They even attack my little dog, Falla." The President indicated that while he could take the criticism (the Republicans had claimed that Falla had been forgotten on an Aleutian Island by F.D.R. and that a destroyer or cruiser had been sent for him), the dog, a Scotty, resented the implication that he would allow taxpayers' money to be wasted. The Falla speech took the voters' attention away from the issues of the day and focused it upon a small, innocent dog, an animal that most Americans love.

This successful gambit was imitated by Republican vice-presidential candidate Nixon in 1952. Senator Nixon had been accused of having accepted from various sources contributions for a special campaign fund. (Such funds are common among politicians of both parties.) Nixon, called upon to explain his financial condition, appeared on television to explain that his was an ordinary family with ordinary financial problems and ordinary interests. He pointed out that his two little girls had been especially pleased with a dog, Checkers, that had been sent to them from admirers in Texas (ordinarily a Democratic state). He also asserted, with synthetic determination, that even though some might regard this as an improper gift, the family had decided to keep the dog. The speech was a great success. The fact that it had not explained any of the sources of the campaign fund was apparently lost upon nearly all the viewers.

Politicians seek to show that they live ordinary lives, that they worked hard in their youth, that they are educated but not overeducated, that they have ordinary tastes, and that they are not aristocratic in bearing or attitude. Richard Nixon, in 1952, emphasized that his wife's coat was cloth, not fur. Earl Long once urged rural voters in Louisiana to "vote for a good old country boy from over here in Winn parish that thinks and smells like you on Saturday."[28] He was elected governor.

Card stacking. In a sense, all propaganda falls into this category; it involves simply the selected use of and the selected emphasis upon the multitude of facts available. In card stacking, the candidate may tell the truth and nothing but the truth, but he does not tell the whole truth. He tells as much as he wants to in the manner he wants to. By skillful use of words, he may also seem to be saying something that he is not actually

[27] S. S. McKay, *Texas and the Fair Deal,* The Naylor Co., San Antonio, Tex., 1954, p. 216.

[28] A. P. Sindler, *Huey Long's Louisiana,* The Johns Hopkins Press, Baltimore, 1956, p. 148.

saying. The selective use of information is as important in political advertising as it is in commercial advertising.

Band wagon. In a day when conformity is especially prized, it is understandable that candidates should try to create the impression that large numbers of voters are turning in their direction. Perhaps the most pervasive use of this device took place in the 1948 presidential election, when most of the newspapers of the nation consciously or unconsciously contributed to a general impression that only institutionalized idiots and favor seekers were supporting Harry Truman and that others would vote for Thomas E. Dewey. But the band-wagon technique depends upon social pressure, and that pressure may disappear in the secrecy of the voting booth, so the device did not work that time. Still, a politician finds it useful in creating a favorable atmosphere. He especially likes to use it in primary-election campaigns by getting a sequence of well-known politicians to endorse him or his slate, thus creating the impression that anyone who counts is coming to recognize the meritorious candidate.

CAMPAIGNING MAKES A DIFFERENCE

Politicians act as if a political campaign is a crucial variable in the outcome of elections. They appear to believe that they will win or lose according to the manner in which they conduct their campaigns. Yet political scientists have long wondered if any opinions are actually changed by the millions of words uttered and dollars expended during the months preceding an election. Some studies indicate that most people make up their minds early as to how they are going to vote and then do not change their positions. In the 1948 presidential contest, for example, 37 per cent of the voters had decided how to vote even before the nominating conventions, and another 28 per cent had decided by the time the conventions adjourned. Thus in an election that is often said to have turned on last-minute decisions, only 12 per cent of the voters decided in the last two weeks, including 3 per cent on Election Day.[29] In 1952, 47 per cent of the voters had decided on the party they would vote for before the presidential candidates were named; another 35 per cent had decided at the time of nomination or shortly thereafter. Only 18 per cent decided in the last twelve weeks before election, and 5 per cent in the last two weeks.[30]

Is it really worth all the strain of an exhausting campaign if there are so few voters to convince? In answer, two points should perhaps be stressed. One is that the 12 per cent who decided in the last two weeks of

[29] Angus Campbell and R. L. Kahn, *The People Elect a President,* University of Michigan, Survey Research Center, Ann Arbor, Mich., 1952, p. 9.

[30] Arthur Kornhauser and others, *When Labor Votes,* University Books, Inc., New York, 1956, p. 36.

the 1948 campaign and the 5 per cent who did in 1952 could more than make up the margin of victory or defeat in any reasonably close campaign, and if there is a hard core of last-minute deciders, they are worth courting. Any congressional or presidential candidate who receives 55 per cent or more of the vote can be sure that the press will report his victory as a landslide, and one who wins by 52 per cent is likely to feel that he had a comfortable margin.[31] The second point is that polls such as those just cited give no indication as to what the potential voter turnout might be. Veteran politicians know that no matter how much they win or lose by, there will always be enough stay-at-homes to have produced a different election result. The candidate, therefore, aims much of his campaign at persons who already agree with him: His object is not to change opinions, but to stir his potential supporters sufficiently to cause them to register and vote. The ability of the campaigner to mobilize his latent vote on Election Day is probably the real key to success or failure in campaigns. It is true that the candidate will talk as if he were trying to sway people from the paths leading to error—that is, support of the opponent—but his real purpose is to light fires under his own supporters. In any case, the campaign is of crucial importance to the politician. He cannot afford to regard it with anything less than the utmost seriousness.

SELECTED BIBLIOGRAPHY

The bibliography for the two preceding chapters is also applicable to this chapter in general. Political campaigns are given general treatment in the textbooks dealing with political parties.

Mass communication as it affects modern campaigns is the subject of books by Berelson and Janowitz [4], Klapper [14], who evaluates research to date, and Thomson [29]. The Langs [15] examine the effect of voter images of presidential candidates as influenced by the Kennedy-Nixon debates of 1960.

Propaganda by which the candidate seeks to influence the voter is explained by the Lees [16, 17], who develop the propaganda categories used in this chapter, and by McWilliams [18], who links propaganda to the techniques of mass communication. Actual political strategies have not been extensively studied by political scientists, although Key [13] is an exception, and Reston [24], an outstanding journalist, raises questions about them. Kelley [12] sees strategies in terms of the eternal problem of creating an informed electorate.

Presidential campaigns have been examined in a number of studies. As examples, Bagby [2] reports on that of 1920, Thomson and Shattuck [30] on 1956, and White [31] on 1960. Images of what the public has expected of presidential candidates at different periods of history are reflected in campaign biographies as reported by Brown [7].

Opinion polls are discussed by Key [13] and criticized by Rogers [26]. Robinson [25] presents a pioneer study.

Politicians and their recruitment is discussed by Jacob [11], Marvick [19],

[31] This point is made in Harold F. Gosnell, "Does Campaigning Make a Difference?" *Public Opinion Quarterly,* 14:413–418, Fall, 1950.

and Matthews [21]. The financing of campaigns has been reported on by a President's Commission [23], Heard [10], and Shannon [27].

There are many political novels and an important literature dealing with the political novel. Blotner [5] discusses the subject. Snow [28] uses the politics of a small group as the basis for a novel. The self-selection of a leader in this group offers a problem similar to that confronting a political party when it selects a chairman or a presidential candidate.

1. Albig, William: *Modern Public Opinion,* McGraw-Hill Book Company, New York, 1956.
2. Bagby, Wesley M.: *The Road to Normalcy: The Presidential Campaign and the Election of 1920,* The Johns Hopkins Press, Baltimore, 1962.
3. Bell, Wendell, Richard J. Hill, and Charles Wright: *Public Leadership in the United States,* Chandler Publishing Company, San Francisco, Calif., 1961.
4. Berelson, Bernard, and Morris Janowitz (eds.): *Reader in Public Opinion and Communication,* The Free Press of Glencoe, New York, 1950.
5. Blotner, Joseph L.: *The Political Novel,* Random House, Inc., New York, 1960.
6. Bogardus, E. S.: *Leaders and Leadership,* Appleton-Century-Crofts, Inc., New York, 1954.
7. Brown, William B.: *The People's Choice: The Presidential Image in the Campaign Biography,* Louisiana State University Press, Baton Rouge, La., 1960.
8. Davis, James C.: "Charisma in the 1952 Campaign," *American Political Science Review,* 48:1083–1102, December, 1954.
9. Gosnell, Harold F.: "Does Campaigning Make a Difference?" *Public Opinion Quarterly,* 14:413–418, Fall, 1950.
10. Heard, Alexander: *The Costs of Democracy,* The University of North Carolina Press, Chapel Hill, N.C., 1960. (Also in paperback.)
11. Jacob, Herbert: "Initial Recruitment of Elected Officials in the United States—A Model," *Journal of Politics,* 24:703–716, November, 1962.
12. Kelley, Stanley, Jr.: *Political Campaigning,* The Brookings Institution, Washington, D.C., 1960.
13. Key, V. O., Jr.: *Politics, Parties, and Pressure Groups,* 5th ed., Thomas Y. Crowell Company, New York, 1964.
14. Klapper, Joseph T.: *The Effects of Mass Communication,* The Free Press of Glencoe, New York, 1960.
15. Lang, Kurt, and Gladys Lang: "Ordeal by Debate: Viewer Reactions," *Public Opinion Quarterly,* 25:277–288, Summer, 1961.
16. Lee, A. M.: *How to Understand Propaganda,* Holt, Rinehart and Winston, Inc., New York, 1952.
17. Lee, A. M., and E. B. Lee: *The Fine Art of Propaganda,* Harcourt, Brace & World, Inc., New York, 1939.
18. McWilliams, Carey: "Government by Whitaker and Baxter," *Nation,* vol. 172, 1951. (Four articles, beginning April 14.)
19. Marvick, Dwaine (ed.): *Political Decision Makers,* The Free Press of Glencoe,New York, 1961.
20. Marvick, Dwaine, and Charles R. Nixon: "Recruitment Contrasts in Rival Campaign Groups," in Dwaine Marvick (ed.), *Political Decision Makers,* The Free Press of Glencoe, New York, 1961.
21. Matthews, Donald R.: *The Social Backgrounds of Political Decision-makers,* Doubleday & Company, Inc., Garden City, N.Y., 1954. (Also in paperback.)

22. Porter, Kirk H., and Donald B. Johnson (comps.): *National Party Platforms, 1840–1960,* The University of Illinois Press, Urbana, Ill., 1961.
23. President's Commission on Campaign Costs: *Financing Presidential Campaigns,* 1962.
24. Reston, James: "Our Campaign Techniques Reexamined," *The New York Times Magazine,* Nov. 9, 1952.
25. Robinson, Claude E.: *Straw Votes: A Study of Political Prediction,* Columbia University Press, New York, 1932.
26. Rogers, Lindsay: *The Pollsters,* Alfred A. Knopf, Inc., New York, 1949.
27. Shannon, Jasper B.: *Money and Politics,* Random House, Inc., New York, 1961.
28. Snow, Charles P.: *The Masters,* Charles Scribner's Sons, New York, 1951. (Also in paperback.)
29. Thomson, Charles A. H.: *Television and Presidential Politics,* The Brookings Institution, Washington, D.C., 1956.
30. Thomson, Charles A. H., and Frances M. Shattuck: *The 1956 Presidential Campaign,* The Brookings Institution, Washington, D.C., 1960.
31. White, Theodore H.: *The Making of the President, 1960,* Atheneum Publishers, New York, 1961.

CHAPTER

13

PUBLIC LEADERSHIP

Any social group needs leadership. The nation as a whole does; so does a political party, Congress, each administrative agency of government and the administration as a whole, and small groups of government workers, such as a handful of foresters in an Alaskan valley. Leadership involves "the art of coordinating and motivating individuals and groups toward desired ends."[1] It also involves responsibility for finding ways and means for accomplishing group goals and for choosing among these ways and means.

THE CHARACTER OF LEADERSHIP

According to conventional wisdom, leadership is natural and general, a function of personality. "A leader is a leader," it is said. Researchers are now convinced that there are no leadership types, although there are some nonleadership types. Some persons are not likely to become leaders under any circumstances—the totally unaggressive, contemplative, withdrawn individual or the person of below-average intelligence within the group. The evidence indicates that all effective leaders must have integrity (as defined by the members of the group) and the courage to defend the group if and when it is challenged. Appearance, weight, sex, age, and energy bear some statistical relationship to successful leadership.[2] But students of leadership today generally agree that leadership ability depends on the *situation*. A man who is excellent as a leader for an isolated research group of the U.S. Weather Bureau on Christmas Island might be a failure as director of the Bureau, and vice versa. A man regarded by his subordinates as a superior head of the U.S. Public Health Service might do a poor job as a senator or as President, or vice versa. The field general handling an emergency might be a failure in the patience-demanding job of long-range strategic planning.

Leadership varies with the values of the particular group, as well as with time and place. A woman would not, at this time, be

[1] John M. Pfiffner and Robert V. Presthus, *Public Administration*, The Ronald Press Company, 4th ed., New York, 1960, p. 92.

[2] *Ibid.*, pp. 97–98.

acceptable as President. A layman would not likely be accepted by physicians as head of the Public Health Service. A rough-and-tumble Tammany Hall political leader of the nineteenth century would be much less effective using today's more genteel political style.[3] A leader with a deep commitment to one of the ideologies described in Chapters 6 and 7 would not be effective in a group or with a clientele devoted to another ideology.

Leadership functions and expectations differ according to level of responsibility. Middle-management persons are expected to oversee the details of daily operations. The company commander in the Army, the county agricultural agent, the county chairman of a political party, or the district director of the Internal Revenue Service perform leadership functions very different from those of the President, the Secretary of State, a four-star general, or the Director of the FBI. While middle-management personnel must be adept in supervising routine operations, top management is primarily concerned with the protection of the values of the group (although middle management also has some responsibilities in this area) and with long-range planning. In order to be effective in these two roles, top-level administrators must be able and willing to delegate to others responsibility for making decisions on details.[4]

Given American cultural values, there is an emphasis in this country upon "democratic administration." Thus, in our society:[5]

> Authority seems to grow out of a dynamic, reciprocal relationship between leader and led, in which the values, perceptions, and skills of followers play a critical role in defining and legitimating the authority of organizational leaders. Acceptance of authority rests essentially upon four interlocking bases: the technical expertise of the leader; his formal role or position in the organization's hierarchy; his rapport with subordinates or his ability to mediate their individual needs for security and recognition; and the subordinates' generalized deference toward authority [their tendency to reduce personal anxieties by exchanging approval for conformity to authority], reflecting in turn the process of socialization.

Leadership within a given culture and at a given level of responsibility varies according to the expectations of one's peer group. A member of Congress is oriented toward the grass-roots values and goals of his constituents; the bureaucratic leader, toward the values and goals of the profession with which he identifies—values and goals that are probably also shared by most of the members of the agency. As a leader, an Army sergeant behaves differently from a captain, and the captain, in turn, behaves differently from a general.

[3] For studies, see Ralph M. Stogdill, "Personal Factors Associated with Leadership," *Journal of Psychology,* 25:60–62, January, 1948.

[4] See Philip Selznick, *Leadership in Administration,* Harper & Row, Publishers, New York, 1957.

[5] Robert V. Presthus, "Authority in Organizations," *Public Administration Review,* 20:91, Spring, 1960.

Leadership is much more complicated than it is considered to be in conventional wisdom or in some of the early writings in public administration and politics. But folk beliefs are powerful and persistent. Therefore:[6]

> There is an understandable inclination to think of leadership in a group or an organization as residing in one person. Perhaps the most extreme example of this is the tendency among many people to see the President as *the* U.S. Government, despite the fact that there are millions of civilian and military people who are direct participants in such a large undertaking. Belief in the idea of an individual leader has certain authoritarian overtones. It conveys the notion of an order-giver, a dominant individual, one who is playing all the important roles.

In fact, however, leadership is ordinarily shared by many persons. It is not an individual matter; rather, it is only one particular role among the many roles found in any organized group.

IMAGES OF THE LEADER

The leader is not perceived by all in the same way. His role is shaped by the expectations of followers. Most of them seem to perceive him as "first among equals," a power center, or as a father figure.

The First among Equals. Many leaders, especially in middle-management positions, are expected to be one of the group, and only slightly different in behavior or social distance from other members. All are colleagues. This is the pattern in many administrative positions and at the lower levels of political party organizations. The leader may lead—but not by too much. He is not expected to be a "hatchet man" who would drastically reorganize the group or change its goals.

When several areas in a Kentucky county were studied to determine the extent to which farmers had adopted twenty-one practices recommended by government agencies, it was found that leaders led, but not as modifiers of norms (see Table 13-1). In neighborhoods where farmers valued change, leaders helped them make changes. Where they valued the *status quo,* leaders joined in resisting change. In neither case were leadership norms different from those of the group. The leaders served primarily as defenders of prevailing values.

This kind of leader, the first among equals, is not necessarily viewed as a permanent leader. Within the political party, for example, formal positions of leadership may be viewed as temporary—for one campaign or a two-year term, perhaps. Informal or "natural" leadership also changes,

[6] John M. Pfiffner and Frank P. Sherwood, *Administrative Organization,* Prentice-Hall, Inc., Englewood Cliffs, N.J., 1960, chap. 19. Quotation from p. 354.

TABLE 13-1

RECOMMENDED-PRACTICE ADOPTION SCORES, LEADERS AND FOLLOWERS, BY HIGH- AND LOW-ADOPTION AREAS

Area	Leaders	All respondents
High adoption	66	48
Low adoption	37	32

NOTE: Leaders in low-adoption areas had lower scores than did followers in high-adoption areas. Their scores were also little different from those of their followers.

SOURCE: Adapted from C. Paul Marsh and A. Lee Coleman, "Farmers Practice Adoption Rates in Relation to Adoption Rates of 'Leaders,'" *Rural Sociology,* 19:180–181, June, 1954.

although it may be more enduring. Even so, when situations within the organization or in its external environment change, the type of leader wanted may also change. And in some organizations, including political parties, personnel is often transitory, so that the leader in one campaign may not be present for the next. Workers in a group recognize this type of situation and take it into account in dealing with leaders.

The Power Center. Whether the leader is seen as a colleague or a guardian, his power may be an important consideration, and sometimes it is the most important characteristic of his role. The "boss" of the nineteenth-century machine controlled sanctions that made him someone to be deferred to, if not feared. The same may be true of the President or may characterize the relationship between a junior congressman and the powerful chairman of a committee that acts on matters of importance to the congressman's district.

The Father Figure.* The leader may be seen as one who has a duty to make major policy decisions and give direction (and hence a degree of security) to all. Some psychologists have identified certain personalities as "authoritarian." Persons fitting this category are seen as supporters of strong, unequivocal leadership—and if they become leaders themselves, they expect unquestioned obedience from followers. A few people, whose personalities are highly intolerant of indecision, want a charismatic leader.[7]

***FATHER FIGURE. A person who provides for another a psychological substitute in the role of the father. In politics, such a figure may be perceived in the role of protector and provider for the people of a community, a political organization, a nation in general, or specifically for the individual.**

[7] James C. Davis, "Charisma in the 1952 Campaign," *American Political Science Review,* 48:1083–1102, December, 1954.

Other persons are merely attracted to a leader who, because of his personality, seems to have strong, magnetic qualities of leadership.

As social distance* between leader and led increases, the leader is more likely to increase in status and to have greater deference paid him. The President apparently is seen by many persons as a father figure. So are many heroes of the nation and the political party. Individuals who have dependent personalities and perhaps also those who feel helpless and deprived may also seek a father figure. Thus George McLain who, through his California Institute of Social Welfare, became a leader of a political-action movement for elderly persons, most of them old-age-assistance recipients, was seen by members as a friend, protector, or "good shepherd," rather than as a political leader.[8]

***SOCIAL DISTANCE. The degree of social intimacy an individual will accept between himself and a typical member of a social group.**

A study of presidential leadership images (which, of course, would not necessarily fit other leadership positions) indicated that people most wanted in the office a man of honesty (78 per cent), intelligence (55 per cent), and independence, "a man with lots of ideas of his own on how to solve problems" (45 per cent). The presidential role was not generally viewed as one to be occupied by a colleague—a first among equals—although a minority of respondents did want in him friendliness (8 per cent), humility (10 per cent), and "sympathy with the lot of the little man" (20 per cent). The image of the President as a father substitute and strong leader was shared by persons in all social, income, sex, age, and race categories.[9]

THE POLITICAL LEADER

The stereotype of the American politician is one of a simple-minded, happy demagogue who promises all things to all people. Some come close to fitting this mold, others are far from it. As is the case with many leaders in society, politicians may be gregarious or retiring, scholarly or almost unlearned, brilliant or of modest mental capacities.

Here are some significant points on political leadership:

1. Persons can lead only if others follow. They can secure a following only through either fear or faith. The former is not a strong reed upon which to lean, or a permanent one. Some tyrants have sought to use it,

[8] Frank A. Pinner and others, *Old Age and Political Behavior,* University of California Press, Berkeley, Calif., 1959. See especially pp. 179–183.

[9] Roberta S. Sigel, "Presidential Leadership Images," a paper presented at the 1962 annual meeting of the American Political Science Association, Washington, D.C. The sample used was drawn from the Detroit area.

and it can be used—especially in the form of terror—on a temporary basis. But as some of the notable tyrants in history—Adolf Hitler in Germany, for example—have recognized, long-term rule requires the ordinary citizen's confidence in the leader and a sense of his right to rule.

Political leaders in democracies can rule only if citizens have faith in them, so they must do what the typical citizen expects of his leaders. In playing for the support of the ordinary, poorly informed, modestly educated citizen, in trying to express in simple terms complex issues and problems, he gains the image that is expressed in the stereotype.

2. Politicians may be persons who have initially gained popular attention and support as leaders in business, the military, organized labor, or education. But in a day of specialization, politics is largely an *occupation* or profession engaged in by specialists who devote their lifetimes to seeking and serving in elective or appointive political offices. Some professionals are probably in politics out of a sense of obligation. Others were drafted in some manner and did not leave the field again, or they started out to get publicity for a legal or real estate business, for example, and stayed on. But most of them are probably, to a degree, like other professional actors, exhibitionists who crave attention and enjoy floodlights, cameras, microphones, and crowds, important decision-making positions of power, fawning deference from those who are dependent upon their decisions, and the thrill of victory in combat. Politicians also pay penalties, however—in long work weeks, public ridicule, low status as candidates if not in the public positions themselves, and the anxieties that accompany insecure nontenure jobs.

3. The politician is primarily a catalyst. He need not be an innovator, although this is expected of some political leaders. His job is to serve as a broker and a salesman. As a broker, he brings together those who have a mutual, but not entirely compatible, interest and seeks to arrange a compromise. As a salesman, he takes a proposed solution of some specialist or a compromise among the proposed solutions of specialists and seeks to convince the misinformed and the skeptical of the practicality and functionality of the solution. Experts in various fields are the principal innovators. These experts provide the grist for social change; leaders do the milling.

The task of those who follow politics as an occupation in a democracy is to link up the parts in the system: the economic, social, and ideological interests of citizens; the demands of those who have power resulting from publicity, wealth, or social position; the recommendations of the technical specialists; and the administrative bureaucracy. Their task is crucial in any political system.

The Recruitment of Leaders. Although many persons volunteer for leadership positions, their willingness is not necessarily a measure of ther acceptability. Every political system must contain institutionalized methods by which various leadership roles may be filled from among persons who come reasonably close to fitting the image of the role that is held by those who have an effective voice in the selection. Both the type of leader wanted and the process of recruitment vary with the office. Both are different for party leaders, agency heads, interest-group leaders, the Presidency, congressmen, and judges.

PRESIDENTIAL AVAILABILITY

Politicians speak of a candidate they regard as suitable for a particular office as being "available." What this consists of is well described in folklore.

The legal requirements for the Presidency are quite simple: The candidate must be at least thirty-five years old, a natural-born citizen, and must have lived at least fourteen years in the United States. The courts

Figure 13-1

A Convention Is Never Completely Predictable

"It's all set, boys—just one more speech by some fellow named Bryan, and our candidate gets the nomination."

In the Democratic convention of 1896, more astute persons than J. Wesley Smith failed to anticipate the nomination of William Jennings Bryan. (By permission of Burr Shafer.)

have never ruled on the meaning of "natural born," and the question of whether the son or daughter of an American citizen born outside United States territory but automatically a United States citizen under the law of *jus sanguinis* would be eligible. Michigan's Governor George Romney, who was considered by some to be available presidential timber in 1964, was born in Mexico of American parents. It was generally assumed that he would be eligible.

Who Can Play? The traditional formula of availability, according to the historian Sidney Hyman,[10] restricts the choice of our Presidents to a "natural aristocracy," which is "the residue of what is left when we subtract" the following groups:

1. All females from the total population. No woman has ever been seriously considered for nomination by a major party, although at least a dozen have been minor-party choices.
2. All males outside the age group, thirty-five to sixty-seven. The youngest nominee to date has been John F. Kennedy, who was forty-three. (Theodore Roosevelt became President at forty-two, but he succeeded on the death of the incumbent, William McKinley.) The oldest person to be nominated for the Presidency was William Henry Harrison, who was sixty-seven when first nominated (1840). He was drenched during the inaugural ceremonies, caught pneumonia, and was dead thirty days later.
3. All who were not born American citizens. A legal requirement.
4. All whose ethnic strain "is not compatible with that of the English alliance." This rule does not, however, exclude descendants of the early New York Dutch immigration, from whose membership three Presidents have come. All exceptions have been quite recent: Smith and Kennedy (Irish), Hoover (Swiss and German), Willkie and Eisenhower (German), and Goldwater (partly Polish).
5. All men who are ill.
6. All who have experienced well-publicized marital difficulties. A bachelor has been nominated only twice. Stevenson (1952) was the first divorced nominee of a major party.
7. All colored peoples.
8. All non-Protestants. Alfred E. Smith (1928) was the first major exception, and he was buried in the voting. Kennedy, the first Roman Catholic President (1960), still suffered a handicap as a result of his religion.
9. All Southerners. The last bona fide major-party nominee from the South was Zachary Taylor of Louisiana (1848). Woodrow Wilson was born in Virginia, but his education and job experience was in New Jersey. Lyndon B. Johnson of Texas inherited the job.

[10] The categories used here are from Sidney Hyman, *The American President,* Harper & Row, Publishers, New York, 1954, pp. 231–232.

10. All who come from small states. The nominee, it is hoped, will carry his own state; the larger it is, the more electoral votes he brings with him.

11. All who have been conspicuously identified with big-city life. Some, such as Theodore Roosevelt and William Howard Taft, were actually "big-city boys," but they apparently were not so perceived.

12. "All whose family origins cause unease to our middle and upper classes." This tends to exclude all who are closely identified with an incompletely acculturated ethnic group.

13. All lawyers conspicuously identified with a specialized clientele.

14. All individuals conspicuously identified with a special segment of the economic community. A person perceived of as a big-business executive or a professional labor union leader would have rough going. So would a professional politician, were he to be viewed as an interest-group spokesman.

15. Individuals lacking some experience in major civilian offices of government. More than one-half of the Presidents have served in Congress. Only two unsuccessful candidates have never held a political office: Horace Greeley (1872) and Wendell Willkie (1940). Only two Presidents have not held a civilian political office: Grant and Eisenhower. Washington had held no civilian office except that of a delegate to the Constitutional Convention.

Figure 13-2

The Governor of a Large State Is a Presidential Contender

"Why don't we just nominate the Governor of New York—whoever he is—and go home?"

By permission of Burr Shafer.

Millions are lopped off by each of the fifteen requirements; and what remains is less than 100 persons in any given election year. But as Hyman has suggested, all rules are not applied simultaneously or without exception. President Eisenhower, nominated because he was a war hero who had demonstrated ability to preserve his popularity, should not have been eligible because of his German ancestry (rule 4) or because he was deficient in experience with civil government (rule 15). When renominated in 1956, he was still recovering from a heart attack (rule 5). President Franklin Roosevelt had been badly crippled by polio (rule 5), and President Kennedy had to overcome handicaps (4 and 8).

Another group has been virtually excluded from availability: incumbent United States senators. Kennedy (1960) was the first Democrat to be nominated from the Senate in a century (Stephen A. Douglas of Illinois was chosen in 1860), and the Republicans did not go to the body until 1920, and then only to break a deadlock by nominating Warren Harding. The rule appears to be outmoded, however. The public now seems to view the President as, above all, the defender of the nation against foreign threats.[11] Under these conditions, nominations from the Senate may become common. When the office centered on domestic policy (prior to 1940), governorships were the usual immediate background of nominees.

The concept of availability changes with the times, for it is based on the contemporary image of the legitimate candidate for the particular job. In the relatively tolerant 1960s, the conservative Senator Barry Goldwater could receive the serious consideration of Republican delegates, even though a middle-of-the-roader is likely to displease fewer people than is an extremist, and even though he would once have been disqualified by three rules: rule 10 (he was from Arizona); rule 12 (his father was Jewish); and rule 14 (he was perceived as being especially favorable to the interests of business).

The Formal Rules of Recruitment. The above parlor game is based on significant formal rules that affect the recruitment of presidential candidates: (1) The initial selection is made by a party convention rather than by a primary; (2) the election is by the Electoral College rather than by a direct nationwide vote; and (3) citizens within a state elect the state electors on a winner-take-all basis.

The Party Interest. Professional politicians generally want to select a winner. Only when the potential winner threatens to upset current party organizational arrangements will they tend to pass him by for a less popular candidate. Theodore Roosevelt in 1912 and Estes Kefauver in 1952 were viewed in this way by many professionals of their own party. The professionals are also more likely than the voters to select a candidate having political experience. They view the Willkies and Eisenhowers with less

[11] Sigel, *op. cit.*

enthusiasm than popular senators and governors. This may in part be because many of the delegations to national conventions are controlled by sitting governors, and some of these inevitably become favorite sons, dark horses, or front-line contenders for the nomination. But there is also a political rule of thumb that says "Never nominate an outsider if an insider can win." People who have served the party long and faithfully are not only seen as more deserving, they are also regarded as more trustworthy in the sense that they can be depended on to make appointments and dispense patronage according to the understood rules of the club. The rule applies to all political offices, including the grandest prize of all.

THE CONGRESSMAN AS LEADER

Americans seem to expect a congressman to be simultaneously dignified, noncontroversial, reflective of the beliefs of the common man, a person of decisive action, and effective. If a congressman does not seem to act on a matter people are concerned about, he suffers in the next election. If he tries to act in a matter that he cannot actually influence, he is a "boob." If he is not concerned about a drought, he is callous. If he is, people snicker and ask when "the politicians" are going to begin their rain dances. If he is not concerned about the "humane" slaughter of animals or cooking of lobsters, he is again callous. If he is concerned, other constituents will wonder when he is going to stop being sentimental and become concerned about "serious matters." If he tries to be interested in all things, he is criticized for "grandstanding." If he refuses to pamper the sentimental, the advocates of folk wisdom, the crackpots, and instead seeks to concentrate on critical problems of foreign policy or the economy, he loses popular support. In a very real sense, the congressman "can't win," at least with all groups all of the time.

Does Mr. Smith Really Go to Washington? Not just any citizen is likely to be elected to Congress. The rules make it more likely that some persons will be elected than others. Some of these rules are found in the Constitution; others, probably more important rules, are enforced by custom. A few stem from the peculiar requirements of the congressional role.

The way these rules increase the odds for some over others is frequently quite obvious. For example, the Constitution says a senator must have been a citizen for at least nine years and a representative for at least seven. This legal rule puts a handicap on the naturalized citizen. But even without such rules, voters appear inclined to elect native-born legislators. Although 7 per cent of the white population was naturalized, only 2 per cent of the senators elected in a ten-year period following World War II were naturalized. These had been born in Canada, Great Britain, and Germany—nations to which a large portion of Americans trace their lineage. The formal and informal rules thus increase the favorable odds for the native-born or, if the successful candidate is foreign-born, for those whose national backgrounds are those of the large early immigrations.

Who Are the Leaders? In this section, we will examine how the rules operate to select individuals with special characteristics for Congress. Before beginning, an important distinction must be made. The average congressman is not the same as the typical congressional leader. The image of Congress that most Americans have is based on what they have read about congressional leaders, such as Sam Rayburn, Lyndon Johnson, Robert Taft, or Everett Dirksen and Charles Halleck (of the "Ev and Charlie Show"), or of chairmen of newsmaking investigating committees, such as Joseph McCarthy, Estes Kefauver, or Francis Walter. These images mislead because both houses of Congress have rules for selecting leaders that give advantages to some over others. These rules will be examined in Chapter 14. Here we will consider only what the average legislator is like.

Status: House and Senate. According to the Gallup polls, most Americans downgrade politics as a vocation. Paradoxically, the same polls report that those who are successful in politics are accorded considerable prestige. The apparent inconsistency is explained by the fact that citizens view differently the candidate ("politician") and the man who holds public office and exercises important powers.[12] The politician who has been elected to the House of Representatives receives some prestige and can call himself "the Honorable." The successful candidate for the Senate receives a good deal more prestige. Let us note how the rules of selection build up the Senate but keep the House in a more modest position.

To be elected a senator, one must have been a citizen for at least nine years; for the House, only seven. The same kind of subtle discrimination in favor of the Senate applies on age. Representatives must be at least twenty-five; senators, as befits their greater dignity, must be at least thirty years old. The Senate also has the advantage of being a smaller body, and it was so from the beginning. Today the Senate has 100 members; the House, 435. Each senator has his own desk on the floor; House members are so crowded that since 1914 they have had to file in and select their places from among the rows of 448 chairs, arranged as in a theater. None of the seats is reserved; it is first come, first served. This also has its effect on the status of the two bodies. A senator serves a six-year term; the House member must run for reelection every two years, an onerous chore for any legislator and a particularly trying one for a legislator whose district is half a continent away from Washington, D.C. The Senate is also a more difficult office to attain, since it requires a statewide race, which is apt to be expensive. In all but the most sparsely

[12] See William C. Mitchell, "The Ambivalent Social Status of the American Politician," *Western Political Quarterly,* 12:683–698, September, 1959.

populated states more House than Senate seats must be filled. Then too, the Senate has powers that the House does not have. Senators give "advice and consent" to Presidents on appointments, a power which Allen Drury made the theme of a dramatic political novel. Senators must also give their consent to all treaties, and this is a prerogative jealously guarded.

The picture that emerges from the formal rules is that of an upper house, the Senate, whose members assume considerable importance. Some have called it "the world's most exclusive club." Many men have used the Senate as a gateway to the history books or at least to *Who's Who*. By comparison, the House often appears to be a body of junior legislators, a kind of legislative body of jaycees. Such a judgment is overly harsh, but for the freshman representative lost among 434 other congressmen, and the prestigeful 100 of the Upper House, it contains more than a kernel of truth. It is not true, however, of those who have become leaders in the House. The Speaker is usually called the second most powerful man in Washington, second only to the President, and other House leaders have more power than some senators. But all senators, even freshman senators, are men to be reckoned with. The same is not true of all congressmen, though each gains a flash of the spotlight on occasion, when the leaders need his vote.

The Typical Lawmaker. What effect do these facts have on the recruitment of legislators? One result is that positions in both houses are political prizes at the top of the heap. Seldom are they won by nonprofessionals. There are very few senators who have not previously been elected to some state or national offices and only about one in ten representatives who have not. In 1962, about one-third of the senators were former representatives. The movement in reverse is rare; a recent history of the House of Representatives notes that only fifty men served first in the Senate and then in the House. Many of these men, like Henry Clay, lived in an earlier day, when the informal nomination of Presidents by congressional caucus gave House leaders a special advantage. A state governorship is often rated higher by politicians than a seat in the House, though the status varies with the size of the state. About one-fifth of the senators in recent Congresses had at one time held the office of governor.[13]

Age and wisdom. Senators, on the average, are older than representatives. The typical senator is in his late fifties and the representative in his early fifties. The average age of both is well above that of the average voter,

[13] The discussion of background characteristics of national legislators is based on the research of Donald R. Matthews, reported in *The Social Backgrounds of Political Decision-makers,* Doubleday & Company, Inc., Garden City, N.Y., 1954, and *U.S. Senators and Their World,* The University of North Carolina Press, Chapel Hill, N.C., 1960. Also see George Galloway, *A History of the United States House of Representatives,* H. Doc. 246, 87th Cong., 1st Sess., 1962.

who is forty-three. In a few cases, such as those of Henry Clay of Kentucky in 1806, Rush Drew Holt of West Virginia in the 1930s, and more recently Russell Long of Louisiana, men have been chosen as senators before reaching the legal age of thirty. Few have had to wait to take their seats for reasons of age, and Clay demonstrated how meaningless formal requirements may be by actually taking office before reaching the age of thirty. Occasionally, someone is elected to the House who is young enough to be mistaken for a page boy. Since the Civil War, and especially in the twentieth century, when the life span of the average citizen has been lengthening, the voters have been electing increasingly older men to both houses of Congress. The writers of the Constitution were young men, but today persons of their age seldom get elected to Congress.

Women. Neither branch of Congress contains many women, but the House of Representatives has more than the Senate. The first woman legislator was elected to the House in 1916 from Montana, a Western state in which an imbalance in the sex ratio perhaps led to accordance of greater status to the feminine sex than is the case in the more conservative East. Since 1920, the House has always had one or more feminine members. Margaret Chase Smith of Maine and Maurine Neuberger of Oregon are the only women in recent years to serve extended periods in the Senate. Mrs. Smith is the widow of a congressman; Mrs. Neuberger (since remarried) is the widow of a senator, as was true of the only other elected woman senator, Mrs. Hattie Carraway of Arkansas, who served prior to World War II. (Other women have been members of the Senate, but only for short interim appointments.) In the Lower House, the number of women has in recent years totaled fifteen or so, or about 3 per cent of the House membership. A number of these women have been widows of congressmen.

Education. Nine out of ten senators and eight out of ten representatives have had some college training. The Big Ten, the Ivy League, and other quality Eastern universities have contributed more than their proportionate share of graduates to the Senate in postwar years.

Race. No Negro senators have been elected since the period of Reconstruction following the Civil War, when a few served as Republican members from Southern states. The number in the House is generally around five (or 1 per cent), although more than 10 per cent of the national population is Negro. A majority of the Hawaii delegation has been and probably will continue to be Oriental.

Religion. In 1950, one-third of the members of Congress were Catholic, and about 5 per cent, Jewish. This proportionate overrepresentation probably results from ethnic status striving in the political arena. The high-status affiliations were proportionately overrepresented within the Protestant membership.

Social background. Judged by the occupation of their fathers, 95 per cent of the recent senators and 91 per cent of the representatives came from middle- and upper-middle-class backgrounds—groups the census classifies as professionals, proprietors, officials, and farmers. In 1890, the approximate time when most of the legislators who were serving at the time of a major study by Donald R. Matthews were born, these groups made up less than 40 per cent of the national labor force. If farmers are omitted from the high-status group, roughly 60 per cent of each house were sons of professional men, proprietors, and public officials. In 1890, these groups made up only 11 per cent of the national population.

The same kind of picture emerges when the occupational status of congressmen themselves is examined. In 1949, all members of the Senate and 95 per cent of the House members were of the census categories listed above, although only about 26 per cent of the national labor force fitted these categories. Congressmen thus overrepresent white-collar categories and are not representative of a cross section of the electorate. One should not assume, however, that Congress is a "millionaire's club," a charge often made in the days when state legislatures selected senators, a charge that at that time contained a great deal of truth. No one has collected figures on congressional income, but the general impression of observers is that most of our national legislators had incomes in the middle- and upper-middle range before their election. Every Congress, in addition, includes a sprinkling of very wealthy men, but very few directly from the working class.

In summary. The voters, recognizing the status of a congressional position and the competition among aspirants for these positions, have tended to drive the qualifications up far beyond the legal requirements. In general, those of higher-than-average status in the nation or the district they are to represent are selected. Of the two bodies, the informal requirements for the Senate are higher.

Job Risk and Political Availability. Let us next look at the political occupation from the view of a potential candidate and note how the formal rules and requirements tend to screen out applicants. Despite the glory and prestige, running for Congress is a rather risky business for most citizens. Few die-sinkers or plumbers can afford the luxury of a race, and for the average middle-income professional or business man, a campaign may be a costly vacation—and for his wife a senseless venture into fantasyland. Even if one is elected for a two-year term, he may then be defeated the next time. If he is, he has lost ground to his competitors in his business or professional career. He can pick up the pieces and try again in two years, but most vocations will not permit extended leaves or interruptions without putting the individual at a serious disadvantage. (The differences in the campaign environment help to explain why some categories—academicians, for example—are far more commonly found in the British Parliament than in Congress.)

The career that most completely harmonizes with the activities of politician and national legislator is the law. The subject matter overlaps so that a lawyer who has obtained a first-hand knowledge of the intricate aspects of legislation has added to his professional value rather than detracted from it. The law is also a career that, to some extent, may be left and then picked up again, particularly by one who has made many important contacts in a political career. Such a person would have enhanced his value to his profession. (Indeed, when a member of a law firm is elected to Congress, his erstwhile colleagues sometimes find themselves suddenly and without effort on their part placed on retainer by corporations or labor unions.) These values would not obtain for concert musicians, architects, physicians, actors, engineers, ministers, or the principal character in a postwar motion picture and stage play whose occupation before entering the Senate had been painting white lines in the center of streets. The initial campaign, which is normally a particularly difficult hurdle, can be viewed as an advantage for a young lawyer. Candidacy is a legitimate form of advertising, a way in which he can call attention to himself and his abilities. In addition, the lawyer has an opportunity to try for a host of offices that are held by members of the legal profession exclusively, such as prosecuting attorney, attorney general, or a judgeship. Some of these can serve as stepping-stones to a legislative career, helping a politician to get his name known before he tries for more important offices. Finally, if a lawyer has served in Congress for some period and then is defeated, he has a chance to be appointed to a judicial vacancy if one occurs while his party has an occupant in the White House.

In 1964, two-thirds of the Senate membership and 57 per cent of the House membership consisted of lawyers. Yet members of the legal profession in the national labor force totaled less than one-tenth of 1 per cent. The second largest vocational classification in each house was that of a heterogeneous grouping of businessmen and manufacturers, who collectively numbered about one-tenth of the membership. From time to time, some members have headed large corporations, as was the case with one-time Senator Homer Capehart of Indiana. Others have been only moderately successful in their business careers. Three other occupations are somewhat complementary to a legislative career—farming, education, and journalism. Each accounts for about one legislator in twenty.

Voluntary Association Memberships. National legislators share another characteristic with most other politicians: They are gregarious. Perhaps they find it politically advantageous to be associated with a number of organizations. Most postwar senators were found by Matthews to be above-average joiners. Over two-thirds of them belonged to five or more political organizations. On the average, about three in five were veterans and had joined one or more veterans' groups. Many were also Masons or members of the Knights of Columbus, and a large number belonged to fraternities. In addition, the legislator is commonly a member of a religious organization. (A person with little interest in religion not uncommonly finds the teachings of a church—or at least its activities—suddenly of great importance once he enters politics. Citizens, a great many of them themselves a bit weak on theological nuances, seem to expect it.) During his period of apprenticeship in politics, he may also have joined various lodges, service clubs, or professional associations. Whether the legislator is a joiner because he knows membership will gain him votes or one who enjoys such activity in any case is not clear. Perhaps both are factors. One need only review the biographies of legislators prepared by the congressmen themselves, however, to see that these men take organizational ties seriously.

POLITICAL PARTY LEADERSHIP

The types of persons who take an active part in political party organizations were discussed in Chapter 12. These persons are not necessarily leaders, for many of them merely work in the organization and do not have or want leadership responsibilities.

Party actives as a whole appear to have much stronger ideological commitments than do rank-and-file voters,[14] which would seem to indicate that party leadership is fundamentally different from organizational leadership, in which the leader differs only slightly in attitudes from the group membership. But major party leaders tend to be less rigid in their ideological positions than are minor local leaders.[15]

THE RECRUITMENT OF ADMINISTRATORS

Social Backgrounds of Administrators. The extremely high status enjoyed by the top members of the British bureaucracy stems in part from the fact that these men in the past were drawn almost exclusively from the upper classes and the most prestigeful universities. The pattern is changing somewhat in Britain, with more emphasis upon a broader recruitment base and better chances for advancement through the ranks.

In the United States, the bureaucracy has regularly been drawn from a much broader spectrum of the class structure than has been the case in Britain or in Congress and the American judiciary. Persons of humble background can and do reach the executive levels of the governmental bureaucracy even more often than they do in the American business corporation, which has also been stimulated considerably by the drive for position of the status-striving bureaucrat (see Table 13-2.) The government bureaucracy, in recent years, has tapped the talent resources of

[14] Herbert McClosky and others, "Issue Conflict and Consensus among Party Leaders and Followers," *American Political Science Review,* 54:406–427, June, 1960.

[15] Edmond Costantini, "Intraparty Attitude Conflict," *Western Political Quarterly,* 16:956–972, December, 1963.

TABLE 13-2

OCCUPATIONAL DISTRIBUTION OF ADULT MALE POPULATION (1920) AND FATHERS OF BUSINESS AND CAREER CIVIL SERVICE EXECUTIVES (In per cent)

Occupation	Adult male population (1920)	Fathers of contemporary business executives	Fathers of contemporary career civil service executives
Unskilled or semiskilled laborer	31	5	4
Skilled laborer	16	10	19
Small-business man	5	18	15
Clerk or salesman	10	8	10
Foreman	2	3	5
Executive, owner of large business	4	31	15
Professional man	4	14	16
Farm laborer	7	*	*
Farmer	20	9	15
Other	1	2	1
Total	100	100	100

* Less than one-half of 1 per cent.

SOURCE: W. Lloyd Warner and others, "A New Look at the Career Civil Service," *Public Administration Review* 22: table 5, December, 1962.

minority ethnic and racial groups. It has attracted their members because there is probably less discrimination in Federal employment than in any other large bureaucratic structure in the land.

The typical career civil servant at the executive level is today about fifty years old. He entered government service, usually by examination, at the age of twenty-seven and took more than seventeen years to reach his present position. He became an executive at a slightly older age than did his counterpart in the business corporation. Unlike the corporate or military executive or the civil servant in some European nations, he does not represent a family in which such service is a tradition. He tends to come from rural or large-city settings, rather than from middle-sized cities. He has shifted from one agency to another considerably more often than business organization men have changed firms (see Table 13-3), and he has much more education (see Table 13-4), which he probably secured with little help from his family.[16] He receives less pay for his responsi-

[16] Data from W. Lloyd Warner and others, "A New Look at the Career Civil Service," *Public Administration Review* 22:188–194, December, 1962, which compares data from W. Lloyd Warner and others, *The American Federal Executive,* Yale University Press, New Haven, Conn., 1963, with W. Lloyd Warner and James C. Abegglen, *Occupational Mobility in American Business and Industry,* The University of Minnesota Press, Minneapolis, 1955.

TABLE 13-3

NUMBER OF ORGANIZATIONS ASSOCIATED WITH DURING CAREER: GOVERNMENT AND BUSINESS EXECUTIVES (In per cent)

Number of organizations	Career civil service executives (1959)	Business executives (1952)
1	13	25
2	15	23
3	17	22
4	15	13
5	12	7
6	9	5
7 or more	19	5
Total	100	100

SOURCE: W. Lloyd Warner and others, "A New Look at the Career Civil Service," *Public Administration Review,* 22: table 3, December, 1962.

bilities than does the private business executive (see Table 13-5), but he is not likely to leave government service for a better-paying private occupation, even though he falls ever farther behind the organization man in pay as his responsibilities increase.

The Political Executive. The bureaucratic leader who achieves his position by political appointment rather than through the regular merit system is quite different from the man pictured by conventional wisdom. He is quite surely a person identified with the President's party, and in this sense he fits the popular stereotype; but he is not likely to be a small-to-middling

TABLE 13-4

EDUCATIONAL LEVELS OF FEDERAL EXECUTIVES, BUSINESS EXECUTIVES, AND ADULT MALE POPULATION (In per cent)

Education	Career civil servants (1959)	Political executives (1959)	Business executives (1952)	Adult males, 30 and over (1957)
Less than high school	*	*	4	46
Some high school	2	1	9	17
High school graduation	5	2	11	21
Some college	15	7	19	7
College graduation	78	90	57	9
Total	100	100	100	100

* Less than one-half of 1 per cent.

SOURCE: W. Lloyd Warner and others, "A New Look at the Career Civil Service," *Public Administration Review* 22: table 1, December, 1962.

TABLE 13-5

SALARY COMPARISONS BETWEEN FEDERAL CIVIL SERVANTS AND PRIVATE BUSINESSMEN DOING SIMILAR WORK, 1961

Federal employees		Business employees	
Salary grade	Approximate salary	Approximate salary	Percentage over Federal salary
GS-12	$ 9,735	$11,125	14
GS-13	11,415	13,500	18
GS-15	14,705	20,175	37
GS-18	18,500	32,400-45,000	115

NOTE: The salary comparisons were between individuals in the Federal classified civil service and persons doing "similar work" in a selected sample of business firms.

SOURCE: John J. Corson, "Comparable Pay for Comparable Work?" *Public Administration Review,* 21: table 1, Autumn, 1961.

businessman who has received his appointment through a large contribution to a party campaign fund or through someone who has done so or through devotion to routine party activities.

Between 1933 and 1963, only 14 per cent of all non-civil-service appointees had been delegates to national party conventions; only 13 per cent had made party contributions of $500 or more during presidential campaigns. Indeed, the largest single category of political appointees was persons named to office from positions in the civil service; more than 80 per cent of all political executives had had some Federal government experience before appointment. Thus, "in virtually every type of political executive position internal promotion is the most significant route to the top."[17]

THE JUDGES AS LEADERS

All Federal judges are appointed by the President and serve until they voluntarily retire or die or, in very rare cases, are impeached. The President's nominations must be confirmed by the Senate. These are the legal requirements around which have grown struggles over appointment, for as we have indicated, choices for office make a difference in policy making.

The Justices: A Collective Portrait. Studies of Supreme Court justices reveal most of the same familiar socioeconomic characteristics found for other decision makers. They are largely from middle-class and upper-middle-

[17] Dean E. Mann, *Federal Political Executives,* The Brookings Institution, Washington, D.C., 1964.

class backgrounds—out of ninety-one appointed from 1789 to 1960 only nine have been classified as "of essentially humble origin."[18] In the eighteenth and nineteenth centuries, their families were normally of the politically influential landed gentry; in the twentieth century, of the professionalized upper middle class. Two-thirds were from families prominent in politics, and one-third were related to other prominent jurists. Only one had not participated in practical politics. Most attended colleges and law schools of high standing.

The Constitution places no requirement on place of birth, but an overwhelming majority were native-born; the others were mainly born in northwestern Europe. A large majority of the justices were of the higher-status Protestant denominations. The tradition that at least one member of the Supreme Court be Catholic and one Jewish dates from the beginning of the twentieth century and has not always been followed.

A more informal portrait of the fourteen men who have served as Chief Justice of the United States finds that Earl Warren is the sixth without previous experience as a judge, the second born west of the Mississippi, and the first to play a clarinet. Three of the Chief Justices have served in the military, including one who was in the Confederate army (Edward White).[19]

The Recruitment of Judges: How a President Chooses. Students of the Court find that a justice's opinions do not correlate well with his party affiliation or even with the position of the President who appoints him. The deviation is usually assumed to result from the independence encouraged by the life tenure. President Truman, for example, expressed dismay to find that two of the justices he had appointed voted with the majority in declaring his seizure of the steel mills during a strike unconstitutional. Chief Justice Salmon P. Chase, in ruling on legal tender, declared unconstitutional actions he had himself previously taken as Secretary of the Treasury in Lincoln's Cabinet.

Nevertheless, Presidents play the averages. They generally appoint only members of their own party—there have been but twelve exceptions on the Supreme Court. Ninety-five per cent of all Federal judgeships filled by Presidents from Cleveland to Eisenhower were from the President's party.

Presidents also attempt to find nominees who reflect their own ideological viewpoint. Failures in this respect have been dramatic and so are remembered. President Theodore Roosevelt said of Justice Oliver Wendell Holmes that he could make a judge with a stronger backbone out of a banana. Holmes, in his first important decision after appointment by

[18] John Schmidhauser, "The Justices of the Supreme Court: A Collective Portrait," *Midwest Journal of Political Science*, 6:1–57, February, 1959. See by the same author, *The Supreme Court*, Holt, Rinehart and Winston, Inc., New York, 1960, pp. 30–64.

[19] *The New Yorker*, Oct. 10, 1953, pp. 29–30.

Roosevelt, had sided against the government in the Northern Securities antitrust case. Yet over the long haul, Holmes's great stature probably added to Roosevelt's—the appointment of one of the Court's giants was to his credit—and in most of his decisions, he probably shared with the man who appointed him the typical aristocratic emphasis upon honor, tolerance, and *noblesse oblige*. President Wilson appointed justices who took opposite viewpoints. Justice James C. McReynolds had, as Attorney General, handled the case against the tobacco trust, but on the Court, he was conservative and defended big business. He was anti-Semitic to the point that he would not for several years speak to another justice appointed by Wilson, the liberal Jew Louis D. Brandeis. As we have said, Presidents try to play the averages—if they make mistakes (from their viewpoint), it is not because they have not tried.

"With the advice and consent . . . ." The Senate also is influential in making its confirmations. Some judges have appeared before the subcommittee for questioning—generally with no help to their causes, since they may be asked embarrassing questions relating to pending cases. Refusals to answer look like sidestepping to legislators. In recent years, Southerners have questioned in detail justices who are expected to uphold the Court's integration position, but thus far have not blocked any such nominations. Senator James Eastland of Mississippi, as chairman of the Judiciary Committee, once attempted to devise his own oath that would determine the nominee's Americanism. (The Federal Bureau of Investigation does a check of all nominees.) The only rejection of a Supreme Court nominee in recent generations occurred in 1930. It was inspired by a coalition of Midwestern progressive Republicans and Democrats who were opposed to President Hoover. Impartial observers argue that a case can be made that the rejected nominee, John J. Parker, was subsequently more liberal as a lower court Federal judge than was Owen J. Roberts, the nominee who was accepted.

The Senate has also been partial to ex-legislators, particularly senators. Presidents faced with congressional criticism have occasionally selected their nominees from the Senate for this reason. Customarily, such nominations are not even reviewed by committee, but are automatically approved.

Additional factors. Other considerations that also influence the appointment may be paying off political debts, selecting friends, balancing the court geographically, the previously mentioned custom of Catholic and Jewish representation, and even, it has been claimed, ridding oneself of a potential political rival. In addition, Presidents generally prefer justices in their fifties—not so young as to be inexperienced or so old as to have a short tenure. President Franklin Roosevelt had a predilection for law-school professors. He appointed four to the Court.

The American Bar Association (ABA) has attempted to influence the selection of justices by urging that the association be given the opportunity of "rating" the nominees. President Eisenhower submitted his nominations to its leaders, and none was appointed without ABA approval. The Senate Committee on the Judiciary usually hears opinions from the association, too. President Kennedy, perhaps considering the conservative cast of the ABA and recognizing the importance of the justice's policy stand, was less inclined to give the A A a veto over selections. Southern attorneys have urged that Supreme Court justices be selected from among other judges with at least five years of experience. The hope appears to be that this would result in more conservative justices and perhaps more Southerners. Social scientists and legal scholars who have examined the evidence find that in some cases outstanding justices have had judicial experience and in some cases have not. The same is true of justices generally rated as not outstanding. There appears to be no relationship between having had previous judicial experience and being a superior Supreme Court justice.

A Closing Note. In this chapter, we have discussed some aspects of leadership in public policy making. The subject is too complex for full treatment here. We have emphasized that leadership is not the only relevant factor in decision making, but involves one particular role in the complex organizations involved in the American political process. Furthermore, it is not the same in its various manifestations.

Patterns of recruitment of leaders for different types of positions in government vary, for the type of person wanted depends upon how the particular role is structured and how it is perceived by clientele groups and constituents. Some of these patterns were described above.

SELECTED BIBLIOGRAPHY

The subject of leadership is complex, and a social scientific understanding of it has only recently begun to emerge. It is discussed quite fully in books on public administration and social psychology, where additional bibliography may also be found. For example, see Pfiffner and Presthus [16] and Krech, Crutchfield, and Ballachey [12]. Surveys of the literature on leadership are presented in Cartwright and Zander [4] and Stogdill [21]. For the especially interested reader, we cite a number of special studies. For example, Hamblin [7] shows that leaders are more effective in times of crisis than at other times; Gouldner [6] demonstrates that the father image of the leader increases with social distance between leader and led; Bennis [2] indicates that an important distinction exists between leadership and command; and Selznick [19] points out that the functions of middle and top management are very different. Dozens of biographies of Presidents exist. They are useful in seeking to understand the concept and style of leadership of these men, with their different personalities, life experiences, and problems. Irish [10] discusses the leadership style of Dwight D. Eisenhower.

For the social backgrounds of decision makers, we have relied principally on Hyman [9] for the Presidency, Warner [22] for the bureaucracy, Matthews [13, 14] for Congress, and Schmidhauser [18] for the courts.

1. Bell, Wendell, Richard J. Hill, and Charles Wright: *Public Leadership in the United States,* Chandler Publishing Company, San Francisco, Calif., 1961.
2. Bennis, W. G.: "Leadership Theory and Administrative Behavior," *Administrative Science Quarterly,* 4:259–301, December, 1959.
3. Bogardus, E. S.: *Leaders and Leadership,* Appleton-Century-Crofts, Inc., New York, 1954.
4. Cartwright, Dorwin, and Alvin Zander: *Group Dynamics: Research and Theory,* Harper & Row, Publishers, New York, 1953.
5. Gibb, Cecil A.: "The Principles and Traits of Leadership," *Journal of Abnormal and Social Psychology,* 42:231–238, Summer, 1947.
6. Gouldner, A. W.: *Studies in Leadership,* Harper & Row, Publishers, New York, 1950.
7. Hamblin, R. L.: "Leadership and Crisis," *Sociometry,* 21:322–335, September, 1958.
8. Haythorn, William: "The Influence of Individual Members on the Characteristics of Small Groups," *Journal of Abnormal and Social Psychology,* 48:276–284, Autumn, 1953.
9. Hyman, Sidney: *The American President,* Harper & Row, Publishers, New York, 1954.
10. Irish, Marian D.: "The Organization Man in the Presidency," *Journal of Politics,* 20:259–277, May, 1958.
11. Jacob, Herbert: "Initial Recruitment of Elected Officials in the United States—A Model," *Journal of Politics,* 24:703–716, November, 1962.
12. Krech, David, Richard S. Crutchfield, and Egerton L. Ballachey: *Individual in Society,* McGraw-Hill Book Company, New York, 1962. See especially chap. 12.
13. Matthews, Donald R.: *The Social Backgrounds of Political Decision-makers,* Doubleday & Company, Inc., Garden City, N.Y., 1954.
14. Matthews, Donald R.: *United States Senators and Their World,* The University of North Carolina Press, Chapel Hill, N.C., 1960.
15. Petrullo, Louis, and B. M. Bass (eds.): *Leadership and Inter-personal Behavior,* Holt, Rinehart and Winston, Inc., New York, 1961.
16. Pfiffner, John M., and Robert V. Presthus: *Public Administration,* 4th ed., The Ronald Press Company, New York, 1960. See especially chap. 5.
17. Pfiffner, John M., and Frank P. Sherwood: *Administrative Organization,* Prentice-Hall, Inc., Englewood Cliffs, N.J., 1960.
18. Schmidhauser, John: "The Justices of the Supreme Court: A Collective Portrait," *Midwest Journal of Political Science,* 6:1–57, February, 1959.
19. Selznick, Philip: *Leadership in Administration,* Harper & Row, Publishers, New York, 1957.
20. Simon, Herbert A.: *Administrative Behavior,* 2d ed., The Macmillan Company, New York, 1957.
21. Stogdill, Ralph M.: "Personal Factors Associated with Leadership," *Journal of Psychology,* 25:60–62, January, 1948.
22. Warner, W. Lloyd, and others: *The American Federal Executive,* Yale University Press, New Haven, Conn., 1963.

CHAPTER

14

CONGRESSMEN AND THEIR WORLD

"My fear," Senator Barry Goldwater of Arizona once said, "is that the legislature becomes nothing but a mill, the crank of which is turned by the other end of the street . . . and the laws become automatic."[1] In this sentence, the Senator dramatized the contemporary concern over the proper function of the popular assembly in modern society.

Relations between President and Congress have changed dramatically in the twentieth century. The prestige of the executive has steadily grown as America has become a first-rate world power and as the Federal government has assumed responsibility for national prosperity. Some observers now are apprehensive about and critical of this development lest Congress become merely a puppet, dancing as the President in the White House at the other end of Pennsylvania Avenue jerks the strings. But not everyone deplores the change. Indeed, some feel it has not gone far enough. Walter Lippmann in *The Public Philosophy* argues that even now the executive is enfeebled in handling foreign policy by the encroachments of an aggressive Congress.[2]

Whether a citizen believes the legislature is too strong or not strong enough depends on how he would answer the larger question: What is the function of a legislative body? At issue is the problem of the proper relationship in a democratic republic between the representative assembly and the executive (who is also a representative of the people). Americans, through trial and error, have fashioned an answer. It is a great deal like the answer found in most other democratic nations in the twentieth century, and in this chapter we explore its implications for American government.

[1] *Oil and Gas Lobby Investigation,* Hearings, U.S. Sen. Special Committee to Investigate Political Activities, Lobbying, and Campaign Contributions, 84th Cong., 2d Sess., 1956, p. 585. Quoted in David Truman, *The Congressional Party,* John Wiley & Sons, Inc., New York, 1959, p. 5.

[2] Walter Lippmann, *The Public Philosophy,* New American Library of World Literature, Inc., New York, 1955.

THE FUNCTION OF POPULAR ASSEMBLIES

Legislative bodies were reluctantly invented by kings to provide the crown with money and soldiers. At first only the nobles or peers were represented, but eventually, as the powers of the parliaments expanded, the base of representation also was enlarged. The functions of these first assemblies were to hear the king's requests and to act favorably upon them. Shortly, to the displeasure of the monarch, the legislature began to bargain for concessions by presenting grievances and withholding action on some proposals. Thus the traditional function of the legislature, as it evolved in English experience, was to consider the proposals of the executive, and force the king to listen to public criticisms before it agreed to provide the money to support royal programs.

American Historical Experience. The traditional function of legislative bodies was transplanted to the American colonies with little change. Colonial assemblies exercised their powers by providing funds for royal governors and by publicly investigating and vocally criticizing proposals and actions initiated by the executive. But after a while, they added an additional power, one that was also being claimed by the British Parliament at that time. Colonial legislatures argued that, as representatives of the people, they had the power to do more than act on executive proposals; they themselves could originate policy. Colonial legislatures became adept at avoiding the executive veto of their policies through such methods as creating legislative commissions to enforce laws, putting orders into effect pending the approval of the Crown, and threatening the governor with financial reprisals if he did not support their demands.

During the Revolutionary War, the colonists, freed of royal governors, established governments that either had no executive to bypass or had an executive who could be bypassed easily. The Articles of Confederation and state constitutions with weak executives were such experiments. Because of what some citizens regarded as the unhappy results of this system, the convention that created the Federal Constitution abandoned the trend and set up an executive office with strong powers, including a curb on the legislature through the veto.

The accepted doctrine of the United States during the nineteenth century, however, carried the theory of legislative supremacy to its logical conclusion—the legislature alone, it was claimed, should create policy. The job of the President, it followed, was merely to administer these laws. As a champion of this viewpoint, President Thomas Jefferson agonized over his decision to purchase the Louisiana Territory without specific authorization of Congress or the Constitution. He hoped that some way might be found, even through constitutional amendment, to bring his action into harmony with his theory. He understood that his act was a major policy decision and one that would change the destiny of a tiny nation and might enable it ultimately to become a world power. The

President also knew that he could not temporize, or the opportunity would pass. As Madison, Hamilton, and Jay had observed in *Federalist Paper 70,* an executive can act more effectively than a legislature in policy matters requiring secrecy, decision, and dispatch. Practice triumphed over ideal, and Jefferson pledged Napoleon the money.

During the nineteenth century, the ideal of the legislature as the center for policy innovation suffered other notable setbacks. Congress demonstrated that it could not effectively prosecute a war (the War of 1812) or set policy for a peace (the Reconstruction period following the Civil War). Its claim to be the sole representative of the people had been obliquely challenged by Jefferson, who coaxed Congress to adopt his program using the fiction that Congress itself had invented these policies. The issue was met head on by Andrew Jackson, who announced that he had been elected by all the people and thus was their spokesman. He championed a specific program that he felt the people had endorsed, and he was determined to get it enacted into law. Presidents who were like him—Polk, Lincoln, Johnson, Cleveland, and even McKinley—were described as "strong" Presidents, that is, Presidents who wanted to innovate policy. In the nineteenth century, they were the exceptions. But by the twentieth century, men of this type nearly always occupied the White House. During a hundred-year period, the innovating role of Congress had withered, despite the popularly accepted theory.

The twentieth century began with President Theodore Roosevelt, who proclaimed himself a "steward of the people" and boldly defended the policy-innovating functions of the President.* After the four-year interlude of William Howard Taft, Woodrow Wilson further strengthened the presidential office. Symbolically, he emphasized the initiative of the President in policy making by personally reading his State of the Union messages to Congress rather than presenting the legislature with printed copies. The practice was initiated by the first President, but abandoned by the third, Jefferson, who thought it smacked of the British speech from the throne. (Besides, Jefferson had a poor speaking voice.) Every twentieth-century President since F.D.R. has carried on this precedent.

***STEWARDSHIP THEORY. This theory holds that the President has something akin to inherent powers of office that permit or even require him to do anything necessary to protect the nation, so long as his acts are not unconstitutional. It is a theory also closely associated with the idea that the President has an obligation to provide leadership in policy development. The Whig theory, in contrast, holds that the President can do only those things clearly authorized by Constitution or Congress and should leave policy development to Congress.**

By the time of the Great Depression of the 1930s, the President of the United States was expected to support his annual State of the Union message to Congress with proposed legislation prepared by his staff. These bills were, of course, formally introduced by a sympathetic member of

Congress, but legislators were under no illusions concerning their source. President Roosevelt on one occasion neglected to provide a bill with his recommendation, and he was roundly criticized for this by the leaders of the opposition party. "What specific kind of legislation," they asked, "does the President want?"

Congress in Action Today. Congress thus has returned to the traditional role of popular assemblies, that of critic and investigator of the executive program. A statement by Walter Lippmann is a good summary of present practice: "The executive is the active power in the state, the asking and the proposing power. The representative assembly is the consenting power, the petitioning, the approving and the criticizing, the accepting and the refusing power."[3]

The congressional role is one of championing stability against change. Typically, congressmen questioning an executive official at a hearing try to make him justify the course he proposes rather than suggesting alternatives. The typical stance of Congress is "Go slow—until we are sure."

That such a function is needed in democratic policymaking is generally recognized—although observers disagree on how much or how little restraint is required. What has resulted in America is a rare blend of innovation and stability. The political scientist E. H. Carr has characterized this democratic goal as "peaceful change."[4] It is change that comes by increments—haltingly and, to some, frustratingly—through minor amendments and tinkering rather than through bold new policies.

The twilight of Congress? We should not assume that Congress performs only a "laying-on-of-hands" function. All Presidents, even the most unassertive, have received legislative scars demonstrating that Congress is not quietly acquiescent. Congress, they know, expects to be consulted on most important policy changes.

There are exceptions to the normal relationship. Sometimes Congress can be bypassed, but doing so invites retaliation. The Senate after World War I felt left out of the Versailles Treaty negotiations. Its response to Wilson's proposed peace treaty had a tinge of vindictiveness. It refused to ratify the League of Nations article and in the process discredited the President.

On rare occasions Congress has rubber-stamped executive proposals. During World War II, it took the word of the President and a few of its own leaders on the importance of the atomic-bomb project and, without knowing or asking what was happening, appropriated millions of dollars. During the first seven weeks of Lincoln's term and the first 100 days of Franklin Roosevelt's, Congress acted almost without question on proposals of far-reaching consequence. After periods of crisis, the traditional methods of open scrutiny and criticism have returned.

[3] *Ibid.*, p. 31.

[4] E. H. Carr, *The Twenty Years' Crisis, 1919–1939,* St Martin's Press, Inc., New York, 1949, chap. 13, pp. 208–223.

Some citizens like to think of Congress as a body of potential Mr. Smiths who went to Washington. In their fondest imaginative version of reality, congressmen are thought of as developing ideas for laws and then getting them accepted by other congressmen, the President, and the nation. This happens, but it is rare.

On several occasions Congress has made appropriations—as in the case of the long-range RS-70 bomber program—only to have the President refuse to spend the money. Infrequently, but on important policy matters, Congress has successfully designed a policy and overridden a President's veto (e.g., the Taft-Hartley Labor Relations Act or the McCarran-Walter Immigration Act). But all of the above examples are an unusual reversal of roles between President and Congress.

Because Congress controls the purse strings, its desires can never be wholly disregarded by the executive branch. Control over requests for new taxes was the original source of legislative power, and it still is the most important. Congress exercises influence by saying "No" or by threatening to say "No." This essentially negative function is important both from the standpoint of the status of Congress and for the health of a democratic nation.

Congress is not a mill that cranks out the laws the President wants. Most of the proposals concerning important issues are dropped into the hopper by the officers of the executive branch, but the legislative product that comes out of the other end of the policy machine, if anything emerges at all, is sometimes barely recognizable to its author. The congressional machinery almost always leaves its mark.

Symbols of legitimacy. In the democratic process of review, Congress as a group of representatives of all the people carefully examines proposed innovations. When it makes a law, its action legitimizes the innovation in the name of the people of the United States. A law becomes an acceptable declaration of policy. In order to perform this critical social role effectively, it is imperative that Congress be viewed by the public as having a *right* to declare the law. This right must be assumed no matter how simple or brilliant, selfish or altruistic the individual legislator and no matter whether members sit in rapt attention, put their feet up and read newspapers, or doze off during debate. As with the Presidency, the courts, or the bureaucracy, Congress seeks to ensure its image of legitimacy by following traditional ritual, by the use of symbols.

Senators bear ancient and honorific titles that date from the days of Rome's glory. Members of both houses are entitled to preface their names with the distinctive term "the Honorable"—usually noted merely as "Hon.," but still important in setting them apart. The opening of each session is marked by impressive ritual, including a prayer. Members speak of one another as "the distinguished member" (or senator), no matter how undistinguished, and the tradition is that remarks on the floor are never addressed in a personal manner to another member. All members are expected to behave with proper decorum.

Other important symbols are used: No one except members and legislative staff (and, in the Senate, former members) is allowed on the floor. Few members may be on the floor at any particular time, and they may be inattentive, but they are expected never to walk across the front of the rostrum. Spectators in the gallery are not permitted to talk or applaud. An affront to "the dignity" of either house is potentially contempt of Congress. The national popular assembly seeks always to maintain the ritual appearance of dignity and thoughtful reflection, no matter what the facts of the moment, because they symbolize its important democratic role.

Other functions. The institutional arrangements of Congress fulfil individual needs as well as important functions in the democratic policy-making process. As is the case in most institutions, the special needs that are satisfied often become primary in the eyes of participants.

For the citizen, Congress provides access to a complicated governmental system. The voter may want to complain about an income tax ruling, to

Figure 14-1

Congressmen Are Guardians of Parochial Interests

"It's intolerable, General Washington. The farmers of Valley Forge deserve more consideration. Drilling at all hours, drums scaring the livestock, and several chickens stolen. We have friends in the Continental Congress, you know..."

Both voter and congressman often see the "small picture" as their proper concern. J. Wesley Smith is not alone in overlooking the "big picture." (By permission of Burr Shafer.)

secure a copy of *Child Care,* to know if the government publishes figures on safety-pin sales, or to learn how to get a veteran's pension. When puzzled, angry, or helpless, he takes the advice: "Write your congressman."

If the citizen is also a representative of an organized group, his desire for access may result in a direct and continuing relationship with Congress. The group representative may appear as a witness, buttonhole congressmen privately, or prepare substitute bills.

For the party active, congressmen may provide patronage in jobs and favors that may strengthen the party machinery. Perhaps, for some party actives, a congressman personifies an ideological stand. Congressmen also help write the political rules for campaigning and generally devise them to advantage incumbents and often a particular party.

Finally, congressmen themselves may view the institution as a means to satisfy private ambitions, an arena in which to give service, a place where they may be fully challenged, or where they may argue for strongly held ideological beliefs or interest-group commitments.

Like all successful institutions, Congress thus satisfies many social and individual needs, some quite unrelated to its primary function as the legitimizer of the law. The recognition that such secondary functions exist and are important to participants broadens one's understanding of legislative behavior. If one assumes that congressional action is designed only to review executive policy, actions based on other responses are likely to be misunderstood or viewed as incomprehensible or improper. Some congressional behavior will always contradict the primary formal purpose of popular assemblies. But even such actions are understandable in the social context of politics.

THE CONGRESSMAN'S CONSTITUENCY

Possibly the most important of the legal requirements affecting Congress is one that is little appreciated because it is so completely taken for granted in the United States. Senators and representatives must be residents of the states they represent. Representatives may live in parts of the state outside the district they represent. They seldom admit that they do. Franklin D. Roosevelt, Jr., when he was a congressman from New York City admittedly lived a few blocks outside the district he represented. Other congressmen, in fact, have also lived outside their districts (perhaps especially when they represent working-class urban areas), but they nearly always maintain nominal and voting residences within their own bailiwicks. When Robert F. Kennedy announced that he would run for the Senate in New York, he was not a resident of the state and could not even make a pretense that he was. But his was a rare case.

Veteran members of Congress sometimes tend to drift away from their constituencies in both their actual physical residence and their psychological identification. Members of Congress who are defeated after many years of service often remain in Washington and never return "home." Some years ago a Midwestern congressman was defeated in the primary by an opponent who incessantly repeated the charge that the incumbent no longer lived in the district, that he was, indeed, "a Maryland dairy farmer." By custom that is almost never openly violated, a candidate for Congress must have lived in his district long enough to qualify to vote there, and must continue to at least pretend to be living there during his tenure of office. This simple fact has many important implications for the behavior of national legislators.

The Back-home Orientation. A national legislator is not selected by his national party. He is nominated in a primary election of the voters in his district or state. As a result, except for a desire to share in patronage decisions, he can easily choose to be quite independent of the President or the national chairman. Generally he can carry the primary if he is an incumbent. But he must still, of course, win the general election in order to stay in Washington. If he loses, he cannot be transferred to another constituency, as is common in Great Britain; he must try again from his home state or district or give up.

Because a congressman or senator loses his seniority if he is defeated, few return if electoral disaster strikes. A senator or congressman's motto is apt to be "You gotta get elected. Then you legislate your ideals." Issues can, of course, help a legislator get elected or reelected and so can campaigning. But most legislators are apt to conclude:

1. They must defend the interests of the district or state against all comers, including the President or a Supreme Court majority.

2. They must support the sentiment of the home district when it has been clearly expressed on an issue, irrespective of personal beliefs. Even liberal congressmen from the South normally oppose civil rights legislation. Congressmen from economically depressed areas support "job-creating" proposals even when they believe the schemes will not actually create jobs.

3. They must build support by doing favors or "cultivating the district." Since national surveys consistently show that only about two in ten persons can name their congressmen (the identification of senators is slightly higher), legislators feel that their best chance to make a lasting impression is when they respond to constituent requests.

United States legislative bodies, to a greater extent than those in other nations, have a "back-home" orientation. This orientation is so important to the shaping of the legislative product that we will return to discuss it again at a later point. Now we will note only that it is a prevalent characteristic of legislators, and one that is easily accounted for by the rules of selection.

Apportionment: Who Gets Represented and by How Much? Given this local orientation, the question logically follows: How are congressional seats allocated?* Geography becomes an important factor in determining the kind of men who become congressmen. Neither house of the national legislature was designed precisely to reflect population. Proportionately more congressmen come from the sparsely populated sections of the nation than from the densely settled areas. According to the 1960 census, the requirement that each state have two senators meant that the chances against a New York citizen being a senator were 8,391,152 to 1, as compared to chances in Alaska of 113,083 to 1. In a state of average population, like Iowa, the chances are 1,378,768 to 1. The most consistently overrepresented states in the Senate are those in the Rocky Mountain and upper New England areas.

***APPORTIONMENT. The allocation of legislative seats to constituencies. Apportionment may be done using a more or less permanent formula or on an ad hoc basis. The United States Senate is permanently apportioned, using a simple formula. The formula for apportioning the House dates from 1930. It leaves districting, or the setting of specific boundaries for the seats allocated, to the state legislatures.**

That the same kind of malapportionment, in terms of population, is found in the House of Representatives is less widely recognized. Each state receives at least one representative. This gives a slight bonus to the less-populated states, since crossing state lines would be necessary in order to give some districts a full quota of population. In 1960, five states had but one congressman.

An even more important factor in House malapportionment results from the rule that districts are created by state legislatures. In most states, the legislatures have considerably overrepresented the rural and small-town areas at the expense of the urban. For example, congressional districts varied in size of population from 236,216 to 634,864 in Alabama in 1960; in Michigan, from 177,431 to 802,994. In most states, some districts were three times as large as some others; but in six states, some districts had more than four times the population of others.[5] In *Colegrove v. Green* (1946), the United States Supreme Court ruled that legislative districting was a political question beyond the power of Federal courts to consider. *Baker v. Carr* (1962), however, ruled the opposite, although no guidelines were given on judging what might be classed as "invidious discrimination." In *Wesberry v. Sanders* (1964), the Court ruled that congressional districts must be relatively equal in population within a state and in *Reynolds v. Sims* (1964) that both houses of state legislatures must be similarly representative.

Legislatures have also constructed districts for rural and partisan advantage through the gerrymander. This is designing boundaries to odd shapes so that a favored group can maximize its potential voting strength,

[5] See U.S. Department of Commerce, Bureau of the Census, *Congressional District Data Book,* 1961, p. 150.

while the opposition's strength is minimized by being concentrated in a few districts.

The effect of these procedures for recruiting national legislators is to give the House of Representatives a definite small-town coloration. Paradoxically, the Senate, though it has never been based on population, is more big-city in orientation. The reasons are several. In a state with a large urban complex, like California, Illinois, or New York, a politician cannot usually be elected in a statewide race without support from urban areas. A person with an unmitigated small-town or rural image is apt to find himself at a disadvantage. Even a state like North Dakota, for example, that is more rural than metropolitan, has some urban areas and these make for heterogeneity in the senator's constituency. The urban vote may not by itself prevail, but a strong veto from urban areas may serve to leaven a candidate's ruralism. Not so for the congressman in the House. A classification scheme made in 1963, after most states had reapportioned, placed 46 per cent of the 435 districts in the "rural" category (areas having no city of 25,000 or more) and an additional 11 per cent in a mixed category.[6] Urban and suburban areas were underrepresented by 16 seats.

Members of the lower house are often nonurban in orientation, but the common belief that a great many national legislators are farmers is erroneous. Even in predominantly agricultural states and congressional districts, representatives are elected from the small town. The most rural state in the union, North Dakota, had no "dirt farmer" in either house in 1962. One study of places of birth of postwar senators found that cities between 2,500 and 50,000 population are overrepresented, while both the more rural and more urban areas are underrepresented.[7] It is the small town and its viewpoint that leaves its mark on the legislative process.

THE CONGRESSMAN'S WAY OF LIFE: THE JOB INFLUENCES THE MAN

It is an oversimplification to assume that congressmen are nothing other than small-town lawyers transferred to the national scene. This is only part of the truth. The other part was pointed out by the late Senator Richard Neuberger of Oregon in an article entitled "They Never Go Back to Pocatello." The job changes the man. After a number of years in Washington and at the center of things, it is often difficult for a congressman to leave. As Senator Neuberger observed, the legislator's wife and children also show a reluctance to return to the "boondocks." He reports

[6] *Congressional Quarterly Weekly Report,* Sept. 20, 1963, pp. 1642–1656.

[7] Donald R. Matthews, *U.S. Senators and Their World,* The University of North Carolina Press, Chapel Hill, N.C., 1960.

that the first senator elected by a direct vote of the people, Jonathan Bourne, Jr., never returned to Oregon because, he frankly admitted, "Washington D.C. seemed a whole lot more like home."[8]

Being in Congress grows on a man and gradually changes some of his original opinions. He becomes more like other congressmen and ex-congressmen, whatever their party, than like the other small-town lawyers who stayed back home. Imperceptibly, under the impact of the congressional role, some of his most strongly held opinions begin to change slightly. His fresh conceptions of what is proper behavior and the expectations of others about him shape his behavior.

Campaigning as a Way of Life. Senators and representatives, unlike Federal judges and bureaucrats, are elected, and that sets the stage for the kind of lives they must live. The job demands of most almost constant campaigning. Some representatives are fortunate—they do not have much competition in either the primary or general election. Usually this state of affairs is the result of long tenure and an unassailable reputation back home. A national legislative position is prestigeful enough so that we might expect almost certain competition, even if only from among those who disagree with the incumbent. This does, in fact, occur, except where local conditions make it difficult. In Southern states, there is a tradition not to file against an incumbent. The tradition is not sacrosanct, however, as Herman Talmadge demonstrated when he announced he would run against Walter George, who was viewed in Washington as one of the most important leaders in the Senate. Senator George, then an old man, decided not to make the grueling race.

The personal ambitions of would-be candidates are often held under temporary control if an incumbent seems invulnerable. When a veteran legislator announces voluntary retirement, however, a free-for-all scramble often results.

Errands are to be run. Since the possibility of competition is always present, the legislator constantly campaigns. A relatively simple, though expensive, way to do so is by answering mail and requests, entertaining visiting delegations of constituents, preparing newsletters, and perhaps having a radio program. Most congressional office forces are especially organized to handle such duties. The work of the legislative body is itself relatively unscheduled and unpredictable. Added to it are the never-ending requirements of what Senator Kefauver called the "messenger-boy role." Being a messenger means that a congressman's legislative work is subject to an unending series of interruptions in order to care for what seem to be trivia, and this is true even of congressmen who may wish to devote their time to the great issues of the day. Congressman Jerry

[8] Richard Neuberger, *Adventures in Politics,* Oxford University Press, Fair Lawn, N.J., 1954, pp. 152–63.

Voorhis of California once described the job as doing three things at once all of the time.

Publicity. The second way that a legislator campaigns effectively is through publicity. The congressional role demands that he get attention in one way or another. The "ink" he gets back home in the newspapers tells the voters who he is and that he is working hard for them. With some constituents, all he can hope for is that publicity will remind them of his name. If the legislator is on an important committee, he can sometimes make headlines. The temptation to do so has sometimes led senators and representatives into bullying committee witnesses and making unsubstantiated allegations. They hope that the dramatic charges will cause attention. More often, however, the legislator has to be content with such routine announcements as those of the names of local young men he has nominated for the Armed Forces academies, or of the impending visit of the President to the district. On a really good day, he may be able to report that some Federal project is to be built in his district—perhaps a new post office or even a missile base. He also will always be on the alert to introduce a bill that will make news back home. For example, if he is a Northern legislator, he can propose that certain practices used by Southern states to lure industry be outlawed. Some bills may have little hope of passing, but at least the newspapers back home will print the publicity release about it. Occasionally the legislator may make news by boosting some local product. This is the basis for the flowery arguments that sometimes have occurred over the value of, say, Idaho potatoes as compared to Louisiana rice. Debates on such weighty subjects usually are terminated by the legislators trading products—with appropriate photographs to local newspapers, of course. Such byplay generally occurs in the Senate, where there is unlimited debate. The House member has more difficulty in getting into the act. All such publicity is "free" in the sense that it is not directly paid for as advertising is, but someone has to take the time to plan it and to follow through on it. The staff member is painfully aware that it is not free.

The hard campaign. The legislator must also appear back home, and not only in the few weeks before election. The most effective time to campaign is when voters are not thinking about an election. At such times, they regard their congressman as a public figure—not a mere political candidate. This means airplane trips halfway across the continent or more if that is where the district is. On the other hand, if his is a district near Washington, the congressman is flooded with visitors and demands for speeches, so that each condition has its disadvantages. While back home, the congressman will be on a tight schedule. His local staff man will try to see that no minute is wasted, which means the congressman is likely to be short on sleep and will have to make it up on the airplane back to Washington. He is expected to wax enthusiastic nightly over chicken, mashed potatoes, gravy, and peas or spaghetti dinners. He will hear several times a day what to him must be the most irritating of all sentences: "I'll bet you don't remember me." He probably does not, but he has learned several gimmicks to disguise the fact. If it can be managed, he will talk to luncheon clubs and church groups as well as to party stalwarts. All this requires energy and endurance.

Meanwhile, Back at the Capital. . . . But what of his life in Washington? The nation's capital has an attraction for politicians that makes them loath to leave, even in defeat. The business of Washington is almost exclusively politics. Except for a baseball club that generally hovers just above the league cellar, a few art galleries, and the Smithsonian Institution, the city has no major industry or cultural attractions that are not "political." Senators are eternally surrounded by political gossip and intrigue. They are alternatively flattered and importuned for favors. Representatives generally live at a lower key, but nevertheless, they also get their full share of political life. The atmosphere is tiring to many, with its continual struggling for advantage, whether it be on the Senate floor or at a social gathering. But it is also exhilarating. It leaves its mark. As it drains energies, it changes a congressman's outlook.

Along with the social life, there is also the work load. Most national legislators believe there is not enough time to do what they are presumably sent to Washington to do, that is, to consider legislation and vote intelligently on it. One chore they face is to listen to long hearings, as each committee witness has his say. Senator Eugene McCarthy of Minnesota has proposed a reform that would help cut down the work load of those involved in budget hearings. "Let us require," he has suggested, "that each of the witnesses who testify be made to listen to every one of the other witnesses who will wish to testify on the subject." Most legislators require their office staffs to keep abreast of the details of the legislation in which they are most interested and depend upon other sources—party leaders, friends, other legislators, and lobbyists—for information on other bills. No man can read and study carefully every bill, even every bill that is reported out of committee. In addition to his "homework," the legislator will want to make occasional speeches on some subject or prepare material to insert in the *Congressional Record*.

The busyness involved in this work load is obvious. What is less frequently noted is the degree of uncertainty involved. The legislator can never be quite sure when something important for his political future may happen. Schedules may be changed rather quickly. He operates on a system very similar to that described in the Army phrase "Hurry up and wait." At times he simply wastes time listening to a speech concerning a bill on which he is already committed or waits for a roll call to be completed or attends a committee hearing at which a witness (who is too important to be ignored) is saying what three others have already said. At the same time, gnawing within him is the knowledge that he does not have time to waste; at any minute something important may be occurring, and he should be where it is most likely to happen. This is one reason why a legislator may be on the floor reading a newspaper or answering mail while he waits his turn to speak—the speech being made will not change his mind, and his speech will not change his colleagues' minds, but each speech must be given because of its potential impact among constituents. But the mail must be read and answered.

The High Cost of High Office. The legislative life involves expensive activities. Running errands, getting publicity, entertaining visitors, and campaigning all cost a great deal of money. In addition, the legislator is expected to have a residence in his district, even though his family is living in suburban Washington.

In 1952, the *New York Times* reported that on the average, representatives and senators were spending about $3,000 a year more than their salaries. Some were balancing their personal budgets through placing members of their family on the payroll. Others were charging high fees for speeches to organizations interested in particular pieces of legislation. The Billie Sol Estes case of 1962 revealed how commonly such activities as the recording of radio broadcasts or the financing of congressional campaigns were paid for by outright contributions. In 1952, it was revealed that a number of oil, aircraft, and other manufacturing concerns had set up an $18,000 kitty for Richard M. Nixon, who was then Senator from California, to defray office expenses.

Some legislators continue in their private businesses or remain as partners in law firms. The association of a prominent legislator with a particular firm is often found to help business, although some critics have questioned the ethics of the practice.

Until the twentieth century, congressmen often continued to practice law, even before the Federal courts. Daniel Webster, for example, made his famous plea in the Dartmouth College case while he was a senator, even though members of Congress vote on such things as the salaries and powers of judges. Such activity would not be condoned today.

Occasionally members of Congress gingerly approach the question of increasing their own salaries. But each time they attempt to do so, citizens have responded with a "Bundles for Congress" campaign, and congressmen have been called on to explain their action. In 1955, the President had recommended the pay raises; they were tied to increases for the high-status Federal judiciary, and a nonpartisan "blue-ribbon" citizens' committee was asked to make a study of the problem and give its recommendation. The result was an increase to $22,500 per year, with some extra allowances for stationery and travel. New York City judges make more than this; so do rather ordinary left fielders for the Baltimore Orioles and successful manufacturers' agents. Most qualified observers believe that if congressmen are to profit from their office, it must be after their term of service has ended, when they may act as lobbyists or "consultants" to firms that have interests at stake in Washington. In 1964, the congressional salaries were raised to $30,000; this was $9,500 less than an associate justice of the Supreme Court.

Occupational Hazards of the Men on the Hill. What, then, is the effect on the congressman of the world in which he lives? His experience tends to be as broadening as a good education or trip abroad is supposed to be. Back home in the small-town law office, one can say, "All this talk about aid to foreigners looks pretty simple to me." The congressman's milieu makes it less simple because he must associate and continually listen to people he partially or wholly disagrees with. Doing so educates him quickly to the subtleties of political questions. He must listen to voters, to groups from home, to professional lobbyists, to witnesses in committee, and particularly to the opinions of other congressmen. A Southern white and a Northern Negro congressman must recognize the right of one another to speak. Ardent New Dealers have offices next door to acknowledged members of the John Birch Society. The experience of the congressional world generally leads to a slight shift of viewpoint to the center, whether the legislator's position was originally on the right or left.

The Washington experience also presents moral dilemmas. We have already noted how the need for funds may lead to practices that, while legal and generally accepted in Washington, to the general middle class, border on the unethical. A few congressmen have moved from Capitol Hill to prison when such activity crossed the borderline. The ethical questions they must resolve also make them less rigid and more tolerant.

The Washington experience is also a physical and emotional drain. Congressmen cannot keep regular hours or count on being home for dinner. No one has compiled statistics on congressional divorces and compared them to the national averages, but a compilation might reveal significant relationships between marital breakups and the competitiveness of a congressman's home district. Congress does, of course, have exceptional members who manage to live in a relatively relaxed way. But many members are politically ambitious. If they want to get ahead, they must work hard. Even if they merely want to stay where they are, they have to work hard.

The typical congressman, after a few years in Washington, is not the same man he was when elected. He undergoes pressures that will tend to broaden his outlook, test his endurance, inflate his ego—and may harden his sensibilities when circumstances threaten to thwart his desire to keep his office or to advance beyond it.

THE INSTITUTION INFLUENCES THE MAN

The congressman is also molded by Congress as an institution. Its effect on him is of such importance as to deserve special attention.

The Legislature as a Private Club. All organizations, whether fraternities, glee clubs, medical societies, or labor unions, develop their own customs and traditions. An organization that requires its members to be in daily attendance is particularly likely to have a set of rules, written and unwritten, concerning what is acceptable behavior. Most of the effective group members conform to established norms and are accepted by fellow members. They are accepted after being tested. For the club, traditions serve to preserve and protect the group and to train new members for acceptable roles. As in a fraternity initiation, the process of applying norms selects those of whom the group genuinely approves. The Senate, because it is smaller and of higher status, is a more clublike body.

Group norms and social conformity. In the 1930s, at the Western Electric plant in Chicago, a group of sociologists headed by Elton Mayo found that small work groups tended to have unspoken rules concerning a day's work. They ostracized shirkers and rate-busters and generally harassed them by such methods as hiding lunch buckets or by the "silent treatment." On the other hand, if an employee were ill, other workers might help him fill his quota. Legislators also have their norms, and they also enforce them by harassing techniques. Rarely need they go as far as senators did in 1954 in respect to Joseph R. McCarthy of Wisconsin, who was censured for "failing to cooperate with" and for "abuse of" a Senate subcommittee, for actions tending "to bring the Senate into dishonor" and "to impair its dignity," and for behavior "contrary to the traditions" of the Senate. (He was not censured for what critics considered violations of the norms of society, but rather for violating those of the club.)

Pride of membership. Members of Congress expect other members to regard Congress as the world's greatest deliberative body and to be proud of their membership in it. More importantly, each house stimulates loyalty to itself. Practical reasons exist for this. When a member of Congress is attacked by an outsider, he can expect his colleagues to close ranks around him. Thus, congressmen permit some of their colleagues practices that would be vigorously attacked if found in the administrative branch. We have mentioned some, such as bullying witnesses before committees, making unsubstantiated charges, placing relatives on the public payroll, or doing business from a public office, among others. As a student of the subject has said:[9]

> It would be a simple matter for any of these legislators to rise in Congress, as is their privilege, and request an investigation of a colleague's alleged misconduct in order to preserve public regard for the House of which he or she is a member. But time after time, like schoolboys on the "honor system," who yet refuse to proclaim the identity of the classmate who cheats, these Congressmen persistently "look the other way."

Initiation into the club. Congress also has a system of norms designed to initiate new members. These can be succinctly summed up by the phrase "Children should be seen and not heard." A young legislator is expected to sit quietly and learn his trade. He is expected not to make a speech for

[9] H. H. Wilson, *Congress: Corruption and Compromise,* Holt, Rinehart and Winston, Inc., New York, 1951, p. 3.

the first year or two after becoming a member. He should not challenge his elders by such actions as objecting when a motion is made that requires unanimous consent. He should not seek national publicity or play to the galleries. Instead, he should methodically set to work learning well a specialized subject-matter area. Speaker Sam Rayburn once said it this way: "To get along, go along."

Reactions: The exceptions that prove the rule. Not all young legislators accept this advice. Some, like the late Huey Long of Louisiana, are so flamboyant that they are ostracized. Others, like Senator William Proxmire of Wisconsin, decide not to try for membership in the inner group that runs the Senate. They prefer the alternative role of critic. This role was played effectively by such famous senators as Robert LaFollette of Wisconsin, William E. Borah of Idaho, and George Norris of Nebraska. In the Senate, ex-governors are considered the hardest to break in—docility does not come easily to anyone who has been chief executive of a state. The other incorrigibles are those who have difficult campaigns to look forward to. They must begin immediately to make a record. Another eager group is made up of those with presidential ambitions. Senator Kefauver was able to make headlines. As a result, he was seriously considered for the top place on the 1952 Democratic ticket. Congressman Nixon's rise from the House to the Senate and the vice presidency in six years stemmed from his aggressive behavior as a member of the House Un-American Activities Committee at a time when that group was at the zenith of its public support. Senator Fulbright's rise from the House to Senate was made possible in part by his offering of a resolution calling on the United States to join an international organization (the United Nations) at the end of World War II. In general, however, it is harder for a House member to gain by nonconformist behavior than it is for a senator because House rules allow him less freedom.

COMMITTEE POLITICS AND THE COMMITTEE PECKING ORDER

Every piece of legislation is sent to a committee. A few important committees, like the Rules Committee and Ways and Means Committee, give the majority party a two-to-one edge. Membership in other committees is generally proportionate to party strength in the whole House. In the House, the decision on which committee will review a bill is made by the Speaker. This decision may be of the greatest importance in the exceptional cases where two or more committees have some claim to an interest, because one may view the legislation favorably, while another may kill it or "amend it to death."

A study of the Full Employment Act of 1946 concludes that one of the most crucial decisions was referring the bill to the House Committee on Expenditures in the Executive Departments rather than to the House Banking and Currency Committee or the House Labor Committee. A scale of liberal-conservative voting records used showed that fourteen of the committee members voted conservative and seven voted liberal. Of the conservatives, eight came from constituencies that had no city larger than 30,000; five of the liberals were from heavily urban areas in New York, Chicago, and St. Louis. The chairman was a Democrat from Alabama with a strong conservative voting record. As the author of the study states, "Granted the power of committees and committee chairmen in determining the fate of a piece of legislation, this referral was a major blow to the sponsors of S. 380 [the Full Employment Bill]."[10] This House committee prepared a substitute bill that dropped out some of the most important sections of the bill as it was originally passed by the Senate.

The makeup of committees not only reflects the small-town bias of the two houses, but also, the members of committees generally gain their seats by seniority. Thus the important committees are even more small-town oriented than is Congress as a whole.

Each Committee Has a Status Position. Some committees are, of course, more desirable than others. A legislator may wish to serve on a particular committee because it considers matters of interest to his constituency. For example, legislators from the rural Midwest may wish to serve on the agriculture committee, just as employers and congressmen from heavily unionized constituencies may wish to serve on the Labor Committee or Westerners on the Interior Committee, which considers legislation concerning natural resources.

In addition, there may be an interest in a particular committee because of profession or vocation. Lawyers commonly sit on the Judiciary Committee. Ex-teachers desire a position on the committees dealing with educational matters. Preferences are sometimes also based on the desire to become a committee chairman, a feat that is easier on one of the less prestigeful committees, and a member may elect to stay on such a committee for a long period rather than to move to another one that is considered more important. All of these selections are made on the basis of personal interests.

Most choices, however, are made in terms of the prestige of the particular committees. Committees, like university faculties, major league baseball teams, sororities, and chicken flocks, have an order of status importance or a pecking order.

Each representative generally serves on one committee, and each senator, on three. The original assignments are made on the basis of the slots available at the time and the preferences expressed by the legislator. Before assignments for newly elected congressmen are made, those with seniority generally are given the opportunity to shift committees. Then the positions that are left are apportioned among the initiates. Even here, a

[10] Stephen K. Bailey, *Congress Makes a Law,* Columbia University Press, New York, 1950, p. 151.

regional and state bias may enter, since it appears that the newer members representing states from which congressional leaders have come are more likely to get the best choice of what is left after seats have been allocated by the party's committee on committees. The latter is a body of the more experienced legislators of each party.

Lyndon B. Johnson, when majority leader of the Senate, broke this pattern of seniority by insisting that every freshman Democratic senator be assigned to at least one important committee. Such a rule does not exist in the House; indeed, sometimes representatives with several terms' experience still lack a really important assignment simply because the movement upward is slower in a body of 435 members. Nevertheless, a study of the process of assignment in the House concluded:[11]

> The most important single consideration . . . is to provide each member with an assignment that will help to insure his re-election. . . . The most impressive argument in any applicant's favor is that the assignment he seeks will give him an opportunity to provide the kind of service to his constituents that will sustain and attract voter interest and support. In distributing assignments, the party acts as a mutual benefit and improvement society.

Is there an empirical way by which the relative status of legislative committees can be demonstrated? The resignations from one committee to join another give an indication of which committees sit on which rungs of the ladder. Donald Matthews's study of the Senate breaks the committees into four classes: "top, interest [such as agriculture or labor], pork [patronage], and duty." He found the top committees to be foreign relations, appropriations, and finance. The first two tended to be made up almost entirely of senators who were also chairmen of other committees. The least desirable committees were those dealing with the post office and civil service and the District of Columbia. (Congress is the city council for Washington, D.C.)[12]

The Committee and Its Members. The committee system, by enshrining seniority, sets up additional little worlds that socialize the legislators who participate in committee deliberations. First of all, the committee serves an educative function. It is easier for an individual to learn by listening to boring witnesses recite statistics and by asking the expert an occasional question (much as students do in class) than to pore over large tomes of statistics and dig out the pertinent data or to read long memoranda from his personal staff.

Some members change their viewpoints very little during consideration of a bill, but others are more flexible. One study of the Senate Foreign Relations Committee concluded that perhaps the easiest way to change

[11] Nicholas A. Masters, "Committee Assignments in the House of Representatives," *American Political Science Review* 55: 345–357, June, 1961.

[12] Matthews, *op. cit.*, pp. 147–175.

an isolationist into an internationalist is to give him a seat on this important and prestigeful committee.[13] The researcher found that committee members tended to develop attitudes on foreign relations different from those of the rest of the Senate. No such studies of other commitees have been made. The extent of such influence may vary with committee subject matter. But it seems likely that a similar process of influence might occur, perhaps one that makes those with a liberal bent more conservative.

THE LEADERS

Two sets of leaders exist in each house: the officers of the house and the committee chairmen. Each group has separate sources of power that enable them to be relatively independent of one another, while their common party identification encourages a degree of cooperation. The complex interaction of these leaders among themselves and with the President frequently determines the fate of major pieces of legislation.

The Legislative Party Leaders. The Senate, with 100 members, is small enough to permit each member to receive important committee assignments and, though at times it is a strain on colleagues and newsmen, unlimited opportunity to speak. The House, with 435 members, would, without strict discipline, be a mob—or so its leaders claim. House procedure is much tighter, and its leaders come closer to being autocrats than is the case in the Senate.

Both legislative bodies officially revolve around political party identifications. The party having the most members elects the Speaker in the House and the majority leader in the Senate. (The Vice President is the presiding officer of the Senate.) These votes are, without exception, party-line votes. The chairmen of committees are also always members of the majority party.

The majority party caucus elects the Speaker of the House. He is the presiding officer—but not an impartial or neutral one. It also selects a majority leader. The minority party caucus elects its own leader, the man who will become Speaker if the majority shifts in the next election. The Speaker has more power than any other single legislator, even though in a major revolt in 1910, these powers were somewhat curtailed. He presides, recognizes speakers (exercising some discretion), prevents or encourages delaying tactics, refers bills to committee for consideration, appoints members to special and conference committees, and makes parlia-

[13] David N. Farnsworth, "A Comparison of the Senate and Its Foreign Relations Committee on Selected Roll Call Votes," *Western Political Quarterly,* 14:168–175, March, 1961.

mentary rulings. He can be overruled by the House itself but this rarely happens. He can also speak on bills, although he does this from the well rather than the rostrum, and he can vote. His chief assistant is the majority leader and under him is the party "whip." Under him are regional whips. Their job is to line up votes for the party position.

In the Senate, the presiding officer is the Vice President. Because he is not a member of the body or elected by the senators and may even be a member of the minority party, he has fewer powers than the Speaker and is generally more impartial than the Speaker. He may not speak, but may make rulings and vote in order to break ties. The majority party chooses the President pro tem, who serves in the frequent absence of the Vice President. The most important party officer in the Senate is the majority floor leader, who is assisted by a whip. The minority party has a similar organization.

Legislators bring different personal characteristics to leadership roles. Lyndon B. Johnson, as Senate majority leader, gained a reputation for adroit political maneuvering. Speakers like Sam Rayburn have sometimes dominated their party following. Others have been inept and colorless. Because of the formal powers and strategic position of the major legislative leaders, the skill with which they perform shapes the legislative product significantly. Even Presidents, when they can do so, circumspectly try to influence the choice of congressional leaders.

Legislative leaders and party. Congressional party leaders frequently have all of the personal characteristics of the typical congressman. If Democrats, they may be Southerners from politically safe districts. They may be small-town lawyers or businessmen with long seniority.

But leaders do not imitate a stereotype. They are influenced by their role, including their apprenticeship as whips. They find their power and challenges in operating in the no-man's land between President and Congress. They become partly identified—in their own eyes and in those of their colleagues—as presidential and party loyalists. The pressure of their actions, whether directed toward the President or their own party colleagues, is to shape a party position satisfactory to both.

Sometimes the President or his staff may feel the legislative leader is less influential than he might be on behalf of the President's program. This seems to have been the feeling of White House aides in the Eisenhower administration concerning the long-time Republican House leader, Joseph Martin. While administration members could not depose Martin, he argues in his memoirs that they gave aid and comfort to the Charles Halleck forces that did. Martin, furthermore, defends himself as having supported his President's program, even though many parts of it were personally distasteful to him. Thus, when President Eisenhower asked for an extension of the Reciprocal Trade Agreements Act, Martin loyally supported him in rounding up votes. But the then majority leader has since commented that "probably two-thirds of the Republicans in the

House were opposed to this program. In fact, it was none too easy for me, who had been one of the original opponents in the 1930s, to support it." He has added: "My decision to support the President was less than a popular one in Massachusetts. One of my old friends, a textile man who had contributed liberally to Republican campaigns over the years, wrote me an angry letter advising me to pack my things and return home."[14]

Committee Leaders. The other important leadership positions in both houses are those of standing committee chairmen. Chairmen have a number of veto powers that make them potentially powerful negative figures. Occasionally they have refused to call sessions of a committee or have called them at inconvenient times. Acting on their own, chairmen of committees have held hearings and issued "committee" reports with no support from other members. These are extraordinary actions. More commonly, they use their power to set the agenda, appoint subcommittees, and decide which bills are to be considered. Some committee chairmen become so powerful that they are shocked and react with pettiness if rebuffed. When the House Rules Committee was enlarged by three in 1961, over the objections of its chairman, Howard Smith of Virginia, the new members arrived to find that no leather chairs had been provided for them.

The security provided by a committee chairmanship or even by that of an important subcommittee offers opportunities to attack the President on ideological grounds as well as to engage in arbitrary conduct. Some chairmen do this, particularly if they come from small towns and are strongly opposed on ideological grounds to the President's wooing of urban, labor, and minority voters. Chairmanships also offer the opportunity for personal aggrandizement at the expense of colleagues, President, and party. No blanket generalization applies, but in terms of probabilities, these positions of power in the legislature are the most inviting for independent activity.

There are twenty standing committees in the House and sixteen in the Senate. Each considers legislation in a general subject-matter area, holds hearings, and may report out or pigeonhole bills. The committees in general parallel the organization of the Federal bureaucracy, so that a legislative committee in each house has a supervisory function in respect to a portion of the administrative branch. A reluctant committee may be forced to report out a bill if a majority of the members of the house concerned sign a discharge motion. This action is rarely taken. One of the last times it happened the result was the discharge of oleomargarine legislation from a House Agriculture Committee that was more friendly to the dairy industry than to the soybean growers.

The road to committee leadership. How do committee chairmen get to be leaders? By staying alive and getting reelected. This is called the seniority

[14] Joseph Martin, *My First Fifty Years in Politics,* McGraw-Hill Book Company, New York, 1960, p. 230.

system. The member with the longest uninterrupted service in the body generally has first choice for committee vacancies that occur for members of his party. The member from the majority party with longest service on a particular committee becomes its chairman. Cases of ties are broken in favor of the legislator whose name comes first in the alphabet or by drawing straws. The system is one of government by the length of beard, one that reflects both the idea of leadership by elders that is common in primitive societies and the "Wait your turn," that is common in the play groups of American children.

This system has resulted in some peculiar choices of leaders for the majority party if one takes the position of the President or the national party platform as indicative of party position. During the beginning years of World War II, President Roosevelt was confronted with a chairman of the Senate Foreign Relations Committee who was an isolationist. President Eisenhower was faced with a Ways and Means Committee chairman who refused to report a key measure of the presidential program.

On the other hand, the seniority system also has functional advantages. It guarantees experience in leaders and reduces tensions by avoiding politicking for position. The alternative to seniority is party government, and with this would come the risk, as seen by congressmen, that the President might in turn be able to dominate Congress by influencing the choice of its leaders. Legislators commonly begin their careers critical of the system, but as they gain in length of service, they become supporters of it.

Committee chairmen and party constituency. Given the localism of American politics, there is the danger of conflict between the Presidency and congressional leaders over party policy. This is so because of the differences in constituency. Presidents are elected by carrying the populous industrial states of the North, such as New York, Illinois, and California. Senators and representatives are elected by carrying their home constituencies, and as we have noted, many of these constituencies are small-town and rural in character. Potential conflict is heightened by the seniority rule of selection. Congressmen who advance under the seniority rule come from politically static districts, while men who advance to the Presidency capture the nation's most competitive constituencies.

Let us look at some examples: In the Democratic party, committee chairmen commonly are from the Solid South or, less frequently, from the overwhelmingly safe districts of large cities, such as New York, Detroit, and Chicago. Republican chairmen most frequently come from the safe districts of the small-town and rural Midwest. Presidential hopefuls who are popular with these congressional leaders generally do not get the nomination of their party. For example, in 1952 one study showed that Dwight D. Eisenhower was the overwhelming choice of Republican congressmen who had been elected in competitive districts, while Senator Taft had the support of those whose election was less in doubt. (See Figure 14-2.)

The seniority system also tends to discriminate against fast-growing areas. California congressmen collectively, it has been found, lose in average seniority after every apportionment. In other words, every time district lines are shuffled, a few congressmen who have been building up seniority are defeated. States in which district lines remain unchanged offer no such perils for the sitting congressman. He rises to chairmanships.[15]

Regionalism and committee leadership. Let us look at the committee chairmanships and ranking minority members. When the Republicans controlled the House during the Eighty-third Congress (1953–1954), the Midwest had fourteen of nineteen chairmanships; the Middle Atlantic states, four; and New England, one. When the Democrats had a majority in the Eighty-fifth Congress (1957–1958), twelve of nineteen chairmanships were held by the South and the others by men from large urban areas: four in the Middle Atlantic states, two in the Midwest, and one from the Pacific Coast.

The composite picture of a committee chairman is thus one of a man who is older than most members and from a static district that is generally outside of a metropolitan area. His constituency is the opposite of that to which the President looks for support.

Yet some committee chairmen may also be influenced by party and presidential loyalty in their leadership role. The study by Matthews found that moderate Democratic senators, when assuming committee chairman-

[15] David G. Farrelly and Ivan Hinderaker, "Congressional Apportionment and National Political Power," *Law and Contemporary Problems,* 17:338–339, 351–361, Spring, 1962.

Figure 14-2

COMMITTEE CHAIRMANSHIPS ARE NOT DISTRIBUTED EVENLY BY REGION
Standing Committee Chairmen in September, 1962 (Per Cent)

	Eleven Southern states	Eighteen North and Border states	Twenty-one Western* states
1960 population	24.1	50.1	25.8
Senate seats	25.0	36.0	39.0
Committee chairmen	56.2	0.0	43.8
House seats	24.3	51.2	24.5
Committee chairmen	50.0	35.0	15.0

* Includes Alaska and Hawaii.

Note: Both Houses had Democratic majorities in 1962.

ships, tended to vote in harmony with the program of their presidential leadership more frequently than before.

Chairmen versus Legislative Leader. The floor leadership is selected by caucus or party "conference." The committee chairmen, who exercise an important negative influence, are chosen through seniority. Which leadership is the ordinary member most likely to follow?

The committee chairmen generally have the advantage in the tactics of obstruction. Their districts tend to be more conservative than the nation as a whole. It is much easier to stop the passage of a bill than to get one passed. Much of the struggle that goes on within Congress is an attempt to override this built-in veto of conservatives. Individual members are loath to jeopardize their influence by frontal attacks within committee.

On floor action, the evidence is not clear as to which group is the more powerful. One study, however, concludes that when the party leader and a committee chairman are in conflict, the average congressman is more likely to follow the party leader, who is attempting to implement the President's program.[16] It should be added that on much legislation conflict may not exist. Not all committee chairmen battle their President on most issues. On some issues, genuine party unity exists.

Congressman Clem Miller described the leadership oligarchy that controls the House as following an overly timid strategy. It leads only when sure of winning. "Latent power, negative power, is much better than power committed that lacks victory as a capstone. Hence the legislative timidity . . . the great time lags . . . while the Leadership waits for the pressures to build."[17] Thus, he argues, what often occurs is a complex negotiation process among leaders. The party leadership will commit itself to a fight with committee chairmen only with reluctance. Compromise or delay are preferred strategies until victory is assured.

PARTY AND CONGRESS

It is well known that American legislative bodies, unlike those in other nations, do not generally vote along party lines. Each legislator is an independent because he owes his election to a local constituency and not to the President or the chairman of his party's national committee. But this is only part of the story. He is also a member of Congress, where legislative leaders seek to strengthen party identification. Democrats and Republicans sit on separate sides of the aisle, often in separate parts of the lunchroom, and have separate lounges. In addition, some rewards and sanctions can be applied to the congressman by other members of his party in the legislature. These appear in terms of campaign help or its absence,

[16] Truman, *op. cit.*

[17] Clem Miller, *Member of the House: Letters of a Congressman,* edited with additional text by John W. Baker, Charles Scribner's Sons, New York, 1962 (paperback).

Figure 14-3

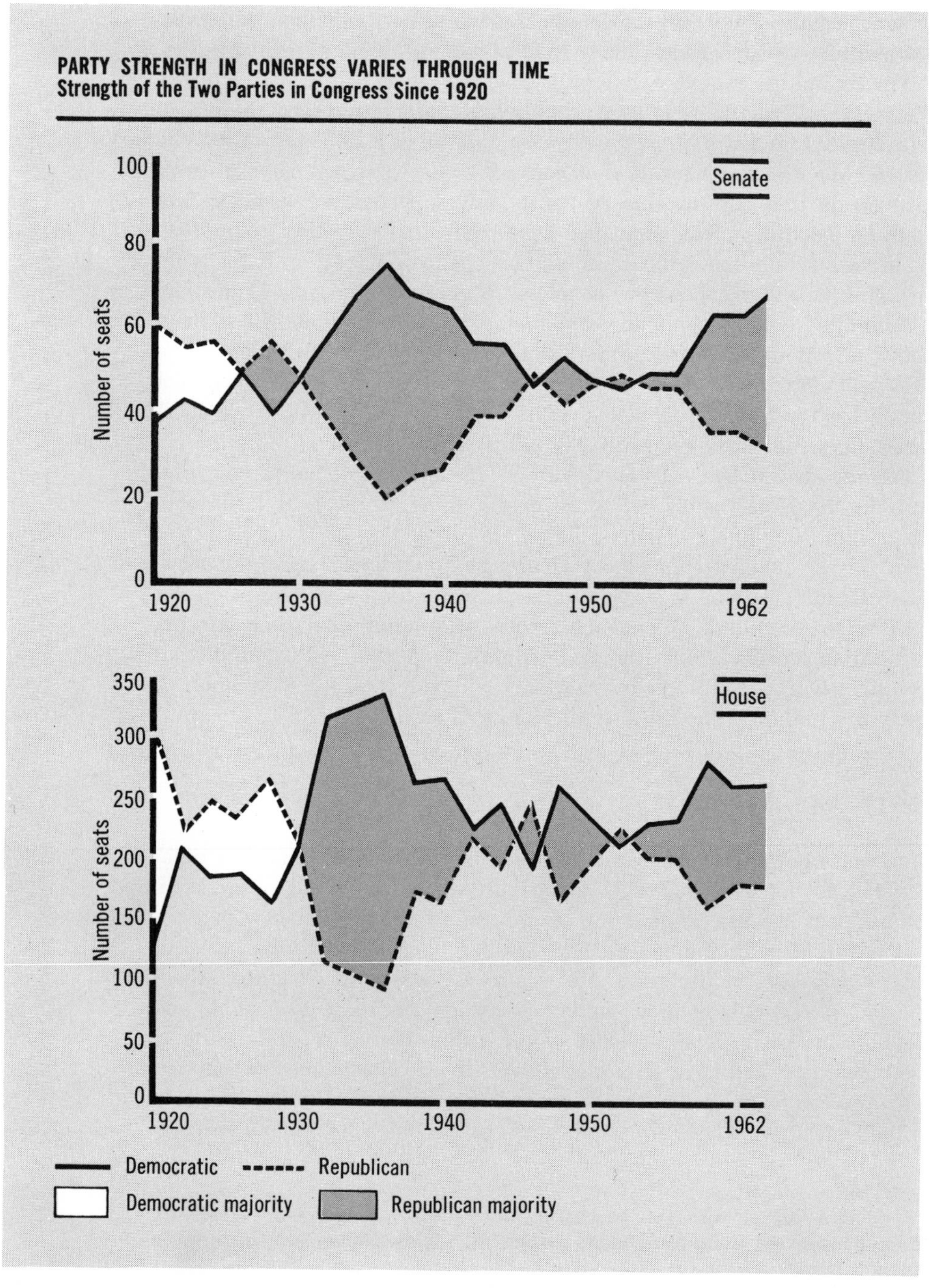

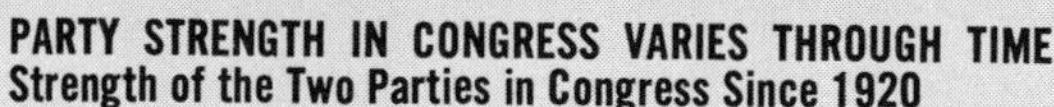

PARTY STRENGTH IN CONGRESS VARIES THROUGH TIME
Strength of the Two Parties in Congress Since 1920
Senate
Number of seats
100
80
60
40
20
0
1920
1930
1940
1950
1962
House
Number of seats
350
300
250
200
150
100
50
0
1920
1930
1940
1950
1962
Democratic
Republican
Democratic majority
Republican majority

and committee assignments (which are controlled by the party caucus and leaders).

The Task of Policy Innovation. Joseph Martin used to his advantage the tendency of party members to support the President of their party when he was minority leader in a Democratic Congress with a Democratic President. He observed that if a Republican sponsored a crippling amendment to a bill, it was not likely to receive support from dissident Democrats. He therefore sought to get a Democrat to offer the amendment.

On the other hand, a President can expect some opposition even from sympathetic members of the minority party simply because its members do not want to make an opposition President "look good." Joseph Martin again provides an illustration of an elementary game-theory tactic:[18]

> There was widespread public opposition to the extension of the draft [in 1941] . . . my position as Republican leader kept me on the alert for an issue that might yet funnel the winds into our sails and blow us back again to the commanding position the Republican Party had enjoyed in the 1920's. . . . The course I followed, therefore, was to court such popular sentiment as we could attract by opposing the bill, yet at the same time make no great effort to defeat it. . . . Thus, while as leader I voted against it myself, I hoped that it would pass. . . . When the voting began I was taken aback by the large number of Democrats who, under pressure from home, were lining up with Republicans against the bill. . . . I had the sinking feeling that I might have made a fatal miscalculation. Contrary to my wishes the bill might be defeated after all. Finally by a hair's breadth, it was passed 203 to 202. If I had wished, I could have got that one vote; when a leader comes that close he can always obtain an extra vote. But that was not my strategy. We lost, but won. Selective service had been extended, but the Republicans had made a record of keeping faith with the men who had been drafted for one year.

An even more subtle reason exists for a degree of party discipline. Legislators as individuals, because of their number, cannot fashion a legislative program. Senator Lyndon B. Johnson attempted to do so, with moderate success at best, when Democrats controlled both houses during the Eisenhower administration. However, even then the President's program was generally the agenda. Our parties do not fill the leadership gap for the reason that their platforms are designed more as sales documents than as programs. This leaves the President as the source of leadership. His program is the rallying point for the majority party and the focus of opposition for the minority. It is the President who brings up questions such as Federal aid to education or Medicare. Legislative leaders may bargain with him, or they may faithfully attempt to carry out his proposals. Sometimes the majority-party legislators balk, sometimes compromises must be made, but always it is this program that gives focus to

[18] Martin, *op. cit.*, pp. 97–98. Martin, in this quote, claims a leader can "always obtain an extra vote," but this works both ways—so can the opposing leader. The two may offset one another.

legislative deliberations and makes the role of legislative party leader meaningful.[19]

The Evidence of Party Voting. What evidence do we have that party voting does occur? Julius Turner, in his study of the effects of party as compared to constituency in roll-call voting, learned that party was a statistically significant factor in 90 per cent of roll calls. Few voted more often with the opposition than with their own party. Despite the importance of the coalition of Southern Democrats and Republicans in opposition to the programs of President Truman, only 5 per cent of the 1950 House members voted more often with the opposition than with members of their own party.[20] In the Turner study, issues causing sharp cleavage on the basis of party were found to be questions of the tariff, governmental action on economic matters, social and labor problems, and agriculture. On the other hand, questions in which there was little apparent party difference were those of veterans' benefits, women's rights, civil service, prohibition, and matters concerning the governing of the District of Columbia.

Another study surveyed 116 congressmen and a sample of voters in their districts in order to compare constituent opinions with roll-call votes.[21] The relationships were visualized as in Figure 14-4.

On social welfare questions, the congressman's own views correlated highly with his voting record and with the majority viewpoint in his district; that is, he was a representative of the dominant view of his party in his constituency. On foreign policy votes, there was little relationship with district or personal views. The authors surmise that such votes were influenced most by presidential pressure. On civil rights votes having to do with Negroes, the highest correlation was between roll-call vote and the representative's perception of prevailing views in his district rather than his own views. The authors conclude that the relationship between vote and constituency or party varies with the issue.

A study by Lewis Froman, Jr., emphasizes the degree to which constituency and party dominance are similar. Thus, when he examined Northern Republican and Democratic House districts, he found them to be markedly dissimilar in percentage of owner-occupied housing, nonwhite population, and population per square mile. Such social characteristics he regarded as useful indicators of local social organization. He found, in addition, that these and voting were related.[22] As in other studies, it was the congressman with the atypical constituency who was

[19] Truman, *op. cit.*

[20] Julius Turner, *Party and Constituency: Pressures on Congress,* The Johns Hopkins Press, Baltimore, 1951, pp. 29–32, 70–75.

[21] Warren E. Miller and Donald E. Stokes, "Constituency Influence in Congress," *American Political Science Review,* 57:45–57, March, 1963.

[22] Lewis A. Froman, Jr., "Inter-party Constituency Differences and Congressional Voting Behavior," *American Political Science Review* 57:57–61, March, 1963.

most apt to stray on party votes. Thus, while party alignments in the national legislature are far from perfect, a man's party—whether he is a Republican or a Democrat—is the best single predictor of how he will vote. The legislative leaders are constantly working to raise this ratio.

CONGRESS AND ITS CRITICS

One of the oldest traditions of our nation is that congressmen are fair game for crackerbarrel witticisms. "If you have a feebleminded citizen in your community," begins a newspaper editorial, "put him in the proper institution and cheerfully pay taxes for his support. Don't dodge the issue by sending him to Congress."[23]

[23] Quoted in Alexander Wiley, *Laughing with Congress,* Crown Publishers, Inc., New York, 1947, p. 3.

Figure 14-4

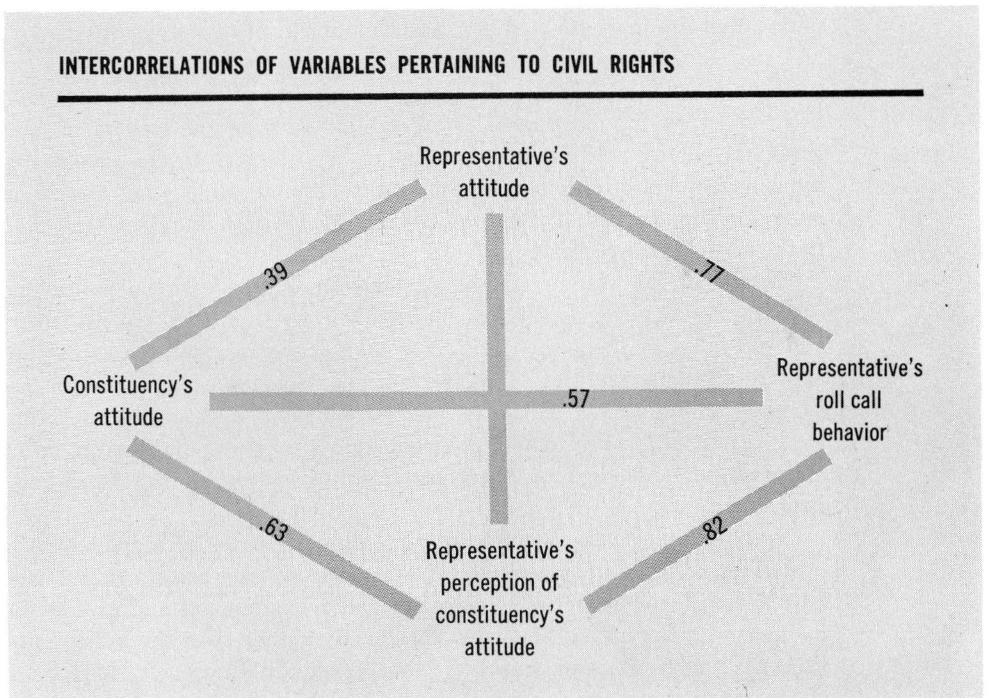

Note: Figures represent single correlations (Pearsonian rho). (Warren E. Miller and Donald E. Stokes, "Constituency Influence in Congress," American Political Science Review, *57: 45–46, March, 1963. From fig. 2.)*

Caricaturing congressmen has been a favorite routine of entertainers and an indoor sport for social critics. On the Fred Allen radio program of the 1930s, Senator Claghorn, an unreconstructed Southerner, always drew a laugh when, referring to the nation's laws, he would end his observation with the comment "I say, that's a joke, son." Will Rogers, the humorist, wryly claimed he didn't make up jokes; he only tried to report accurately what went on in Congress. Al Capp has popularized in his *Li'l Abner* comic strip some of the more unsavory activities of Congressman Jack S. Phogbound of Dogpatch. And the Pulitzer-Prize-winning editorial cartoonist Herblock portrays our nation's legislators as balding and amiable Katzenjammer kids who like nothing better (figuratively) than to use an ax or saw on the furniture or to set buckets of water on top of doors. George Lichty's Senator Snort, a pompous boob, is portrayed seeing himself as "staunch, fearless, atomic."

Two points are implied in these criticisms of Congress: Congress is not representative of the nation, and its members act irresponsibly. Congress was not originally designed to mirror the nation precisely. In the personal characteristics of legislators and in their belief systems, Congress is far from typical of a cross section of Americans. Rather, the strong tendency is for Congress to give the representational advantage to the parts of the nation that are least affected by the development of new ways of behaving and new ideas. The organizational rules also reward congressmen whose districts are the most static politically. The parts of the nation that have little effect on the election of the President provide the leaders of Congress. Given this advantage, congressmen who believe in the ideology of the small town do sometimes attempt to stymie what they regard as misguided majorities. To the majorities, such action may be viewed as the essence of irresponsibility.

This is not the whole of the story, however. As professional politicians, congressmen change. Sometimes they grow away from their constituencies and the ideas of their boyhood. As leaders, congressmen change as they explore the potentialities of their positions. Some take as their job the problem of building a legislative majority behind a defensible program. Generally it is the President's program that is taken as the starting point, and the party leaders of Congress faithfully serve as the President's lieutenants.

Congress sometimes permits antics resembling those of a spoiled child or actions of questionable ethics. No one can ever be certain that a wild outburst will not occur—the majority leader denouncing a President for his veto of a tax bill as "favoring the greedy rather than the needy" and then resigning (Senator Barkley versus Franklin Roosevelt, 1941); the charge that a respected general is the tool of traitors (Senator Jenner versus General Marshall in the 1950s); or the rider on a bill placing a prohibitive tariff on blue cheese (Representative Andresen of Minnesota versus the Kingdom of Denmark). The televised Army-McCarthy hearings in 1954 provided a glimpse of the extent to which irrationality and irresponsibility can go when individual legislators are permitted to act as they please.

Congress presents an incongruous picture of responsibility coupled with lapses of irresponsibility. Despite incidents out of keeping with national ideals, the nation has not floundered. Rather, the overview suggests that Congress has been able to rise to or be pushed to accept most of the big challenges of the twentieth century. It has performed a useful function as a critic and reviewer of executive action. Deadlock has not been the final result. The majorities that elect Presidents have generally achieved most of their goals in the end. Legislation to combat the Great Depression, to fight a war, and to participate in a cold war as donor of large-scale foreign aid has been adopted, even though it has represented sharp breaks with long-standing tradition.

Congress, like other legislative bodies, has its problems in finding an effective role in a complex modern society. But it continues to perform the vital functions of the popular assembly: debate, criticism, investigation, modification, and legitimation.

SELECTED BIBLIOGRAPHY

The bibliography of this chapter and the one that follows should be taken as one unit. No item is repeated. A number would be appropriate under both headings. In this listing, references that give an introduction to the political setting are stressed.

The best recent work on the United States Senate is by Matthews [24]. It portrays the atmosphere of this body as an institution and is analytical in its approach, attempting to describe who senators are and some of the reasons why they act as they do. A useful book that is more journalistic in treatment and much more pro-Senate in approach is by White [37]. A standard but now somewhat outdated work is by Haynes [14].

The House of Representatives has had few works devoted exclusively to it. The history by Galloway [10] and a study by MacNeil, chief congressional correspondent for *Time* [22], are the most recent and the best general works. Recently issued is a collection of articles on the House edited by Peabody and Polsby [25].

Works on the Congress as a whole have frequently taken on a reformist tinge. Among the best by scholars are those of Burns [3] and Young [39]. Legal treatments are those of Galloway [9], Griffith [12], and Riddick [27]. Members of Congress have also contributed to the literature. Robert Luce did a scholarly series of five works a generation ago, one of which is listed here [21]. Former Speaker Joseph Martin [23] is readable and candid. Senator Estes Kefauver, while a representative, prepared a book with a reformist tone [16]. Representatives Miller and Voorhis both set down their reactions to a stint in the House of Representatives, Miller as he was experiencing it [1] and Voorhis after the event [33]. T. V. Smith is a scholar-congressman whose reflections deal with the significance of the legislative process and, as he calls it, the legislative way of life [30]. Senator Joseph S. Clark and other senators comment and debate on the appropriateness of Senate procedures and leadership powers [5].

Several collections of essays and studies are available that discuss aspects of Congress. That of Wahlke and Eulau is concerned with legislative bodies in general and with empirical studies of legislative behavior [34]. Lowi's collection concerns only Congress and attempts to give background materials on the most important aspects of the national legislature [20].

A conservative viewpoint of the congressional role is expressed in Kendall's article on the two majorities [17], which discusses the differences in opinion between the congressional and presidential levels in terms of the differences in constituency of each. A scholarly analysis of the American system of government that contains many insights on the role of Congress is by Holcombe [15].

For students wishing to do term projects on the work of Congress, two general sources are invaluable. The first are the publications of the Congressional Quarterly Service, a private organization. These include the *Weekly Report,* a quarterly index, and the annual *Congressional Quarterly Almanac.* The other source of publications is the United States government itself. The *Congressional Directory* (issued for every Congress since the Tenth in 1807) and the *Congressional Record,* which is a day-to-day legislative journal (issued since the Forty-third Congress in 1873), are basic references for each Congress. (Unofficial records under other titles go back to the First Congress.) The appendixes of the *Congressional Record* contain a great deal of material inserted by congressmen. Also useful is *The Biographical Directory of the American Congress 1774–1961* (published in 1961). For those requiring more detailed information about congressional staff, including staff working for committees, see *The Congressional Staff Directory,* published by a private firm. For the Eighty-seventh and succeeding Congresses, the Bureau of the Census published a *Congressional District Data Book* [32], which gives detailed census breakdowns for each House district.

1. Baker, John W. (ed.): *Member of the House: Letters of a Congressman, by Clem Miller,* Charles Scribner's Sons, New York, 1962.
2. Burdette, Franklin L.: *Filibustering in the Senate,* Princeton University Press, Princeton, N.J., 1940.
3. Burns, James M.: *Congress on Trial,* Harper & Row, Publishers, New York, 1949.
4. Clapp, Charles L.: *The Congressman: His Perceptions and Problems,* The Brookings Institution, Washington, D.C., 1963.
5. Clark, Joseph S., and others: *The Senate Establishment,* American Century Series, Hill and Wang, Inc., New York, 1963.
6. Ewing, Cortez A. M.: *Congressional Elections, 1896–1944,* University of Oklahoma Press, Norman, Okla., 1944.
7. Ferris, Charles D.: "A Method of Determining Ideological Groupings in the Congress," *The Journal of Politics,* 20:308–338, May, 1958.
8. Froman, Lewis A., Jr.: *Congressmen and Their Constituencies,* Rand McNally & Company, Chicago, 1963.
9. Galloway, George B.: *The Legislative Process in Congress,* Thomas Y. Crowell Company, New York, 1953.
10. Galloway, George B.: *A History of the House of Representatives,* Thomas Y. Crowell Company, New York, 1961.
11. Goodwin, George, Jr.: "The Seniority System in Congress," *American Political Science Review,* 53:412–436, June, 1959.
12. Griffith, Ernest S.: *Congress: Its Contemporary Role,* New York University Press, New York, 1956.
13. Hacker, Andrew, *Congressional Districting: The Issue of Equal Representation,* The Brookings Institution, Washington, D.C., 1963.
14. Haynes, G. H.: *The Senate of the United States,* Houghton Mifflin Company, Boston, 1938.

15. Holcombe, Arthur N.: *Our More Perfect Union,* Harvard University Press, Cambridge, Mass., 1950.
16. Kefauver, Estes, and Jack Levin: *A Twentieth Century Congress,* Duell, Sloan & Pearce, Inc., New York, 1947.
17. Kendall, Willmoore: "The Two Majorities," *Midwest Journal of Political Science,* 4:317–345, November, 1960.
18. Kennedy, John F.: *Profiles in Courage,* Harper & Row, Publishers, New York, 1956.
19. Kraines, Oscar: *Congress and the Challenge of Big Government,* Bookman Associates, Twayne Publishers, New York, 1961.
20. Lowi, Theodore J.: *Legislative Politics U.S.A.,* Little, Brown and Company, Boston, 1962.
21. Luce, Robert: *Congress: An Explanation,* Harvard University Press, Cambridge, Mass., 1926.
22. MacNeil, Neil: *Forge of Democracy: The House of Representatives,* David McKay Company, Inc., New York, 1963.
23. Martin, Joseph: *My First Fifty Years in Politics,* McGraw-Hill Book Company, New York, 1960.
24. Matthews, Donald R.: *U.S. Senators and Their World,* The University of North Carolina Press, Chapel Hill, N.C., 1960.
25. Peabody, Robert L., and Nelson W. Polsby (eds.): *New Perspectives on the House of Representatives,* Rand McNally & Company, Chicago, 1963.
26. Polsby, Nelson W.: "Towards an Explanation of McCarthyism," *Political Studies,* 8:250–271, October, 1960.
27. Riddick, Floyd M.: *The United States Congress: Organization and Procedures,* National Capitol Publications, Manassas, Va., 1949.
28. Robinson, James A.: *The House Rules Committee,* The Bobbs-Merrill Company, Inc., Indianapolis, 1963.
29. Rogers, Lindsay: *The American Senate,* Alfred A. Knopf, Inc., New York, 1926.
30. Smith, Thomas V.: *The Legislative Way of Life,* The University of Chicago Press, Chicago, 1940.
31. Thomas, Norman C., and Karl A. Lamb: *Congress: Politics and Practice,* Random House, Inc., New York, 1964.
32. U.S. Department of Commerce, Bureau of the Census, *Congressional District Data Book.* First edition for 87th Congress, 1961.
33. Voorhis, Jerry: *Confessions of a Congressman,* Doubleday & Company, Inc., Garden City, N.Y., 1947.
34. Wahlke, John C., and Heinz Eulau (eds.): *Legislative Behavior: A Reader in Theory and Research,* The Free Press of Glencoe, New York, 1959.
35. Walker, Harvey: *The Legislative Process,* The Ronald Press Company, New York, 1948.
36. Wheare, K. C.: *Legislatures,* Oxford University Press, Fair Lawn, N.J., 1963. (Galaxy edition.)
37. White, William S.: *The Citadel,* Harper & Row, Publishers, New York, 1957.
38. Wilson, H. H.: *Congress: Corruption and Compromise,* Holt, Rinehart and Winston, Inc., New York, 1951.
39. Young, Roland: *This Is Congress,* Alfred A. Knopf, Inc., New York, 1943.

Cases Cited in Chapter 14:

Baker v. Carr, 369 U.S. 186 (1962).
Colegrove v. Green, 328 U.S. 549 (1946).
Gray v. Sanders, 372 U.S. 368 (1963).
Reynolds v. Sims, 12 L. Ed. 2d 506 (1964).
Wesberry v. Sanders, 376 U.S. 1 (1964).

CHAPTER

15

CONGRESS AT WORK AND PLAY

Not all that goes on in factories, offices, or even schoolrooms is work. Congress is no exception. As the business of lawmaking proceeds, congressmen find ways to make the environment a pleasant one. The "investigating" trip or the junket to the Panama Canal is the activity generally singled out by editorial writers as one in which the mixture of work and play is, in their opinion, too much in favor of the latter. The citizen should not expect that congressmen do nothing but work. Their extracurricular antics are a part of the job. Private house jokes, even practical jokes, help relieve tensions and boredom.

Congressmen "play" in a different sense as well—a form of play that is implicit in the phrase "the great game of politics." Influencing the actions of others without causing undue resentment is a delicate game. Politics of this type is a complex and fascinating game, often involving high stakes. It is a game demanding skill in which such gambits are used as trying to convince others that your real position is *A* but you will accept *B*, when *B* is what you really want. Congressmen thus play many roles; what they do or say is generally for the consumption of others. They act in anticipation of triggering certain reactions. They ask for more than they expect to get, trying to get as much as possible from a system in which teamwork and competition are the preconditions for getting anything. Successful politicking of this kind is ego-supporting in ways that few other activities can be.

For the student of game theory,* Congress offers many applications. Its organization and rules of procedure provide more opportunity for independent maneuver than is possible in most organizations. Each bill is potentially one that some member may view as a challenge for the exercise of his talents and powers. Some members seem to play for the sake of the game alone. Others combine a delight in the play with a genuinely serious purpose, such as protecting interests and ideologies.

***GAME THEORY.** An attempt to predict actions based on strategies used in games. The theory is conservative in that the tactics chosen will always be those guaranteeing minimal losses. It is based on the model of economic man.**

At any one time, a variety of moves in many separate games are occurring. Games are intertwined, as support in one game is traded for support in another. This is called "logrolling" or, in game-theory terms, "side payments." Thus the play is often more complex than the simplified mathematical models thus far developed. Information is incomplete and often inaccurate. Time is often short, since the participants are involved in so many separate games.

In the overview, the advantage in the game of politics is on the side of those who desire stalemate. When change occurs, it is likely to be a minor adjustment of what already is the law. Any innovation must be acceptable to a broad range of interests, and because the President's veto is equal to the votes of two-thirds of each house (the number that can override his veto), it must also be acceptable to the President. Building successful coalitions under these circumstances is the major game congressmen play, for without cooperation between Congress and the President, an attempt at change is likely to result in stalemate.

CONGRESS AND EXECUTIVE: COMPETITION OR COOPERATION?

Commonly, proposals to change a policy or create a new one come to Congress from outside its own membership. The annual State of the Union message of the President always contains suggested legislation, many of its proposals having originally been recommended to the Chief Executive by members of the bureaucracy. The other major initiators of new ideas are the interest groups that lobby before Congress.

A Two-way Street. Whatever the source of proposed legislation, if either the President or a coalition of congressmen takes a proposal seriously, it is a matter of great concern to the other and to the nation. Generally, a change in national policy is made by agreement between Congress and the President, i.e., by the passage of a law.

Alternative means for changing policy do exist: The Supreme Court may declare a law unconstitutional; the President can make an executive agreement, recognize a foreign nation, or issue an executive order based on a previous legislative act, for example.

But major changes occur when the action taken in committees and on the floor of the House and Senate is acceptable to the President. The halls of Congress are the principal battlefields of peaceful change.

Getting agreement between Congress and the President involves the consent of the President, the party's congressional leadership, and the leadership of the relevant committees. The process of bargaining is an unending struggle. Each bill is not an issue in itself, for one bill may help decide the fate of another through vote trading or logrolling. Thus President Kennedy in his first year in the White House did not energetically push civil rights measures lest doing so would alienate Southern Democrats and detract from support of other parts of his legislative program.

The contesting sides, furthermore, should not be regarded as monolithic groupings. An issue that splits Congress into coalitions may also pit executive agencies and presidential advisers against each other. Coalitions can include members of the executive agencies and of Congress. Strategy dictates that each group present a united front. While this is generally easier for the executive to accomplish, there may be serious disagreements among his principal advisers. A coalition must ultimately, however, secure the assent of the President (or he will veto the bill) or have an overwhelming majority in Congress. To survive without presidential support, a bill must be strongly pushed by congressional leaders, for a two-thirds vote is needed to override a veto. Coalitions of congressmen who support the President vary with the issues, although the interests of party and constituency appear to be the primary motivations for the formation of coalitions.

LAWMAKING PROCEDURES: A CONGRESSIONAL WEAPON

The passage of bills into law follows similar procedures in both houses. A bill is introduced and referred to a committee for consideration. If reported out of committee (and in the House, the Rules Committee), it is then placed on an agenda or "calendar." Some calendars are for noncontroversial bills, and these are scheduled for specific days.

Calendars and the Senate Filibuster. The Senate, for example, has a few days each session in which resolutions and bills having no opposition (generally private bills) may be voted on. A bill must have unanimous consent to be placed on this calendar. Other bills go on the regular Senate calendar. A bill of importance may be moved up on the agenda by a vote of the membership; in most cases, the motion of the majority-party leader initiates such a change. The House has several such calendars, depending on the nature of a bill. Bills are put on the consent calendar, providing there is no objection. Most are private bills relating to claims against the government, patent claims, and specific immigration cases. This calendar has been used, for example, as a means for expediting bills by which residents of the iron curtain countries who have special information have been admitted to citizenship outside regular quotas. Although they receive little floor consideration, private bills are given careful committee screening in both the House and Senate.

In recent years, the privilege of unlimited debate, or filibuster,* has been regularly insisted upon only in connection with civil rights legislation. By consent of two-thirds of those voting, however, the cloture* rule, which automatically shuts off debate at a specific time, may be applied. Southern senators long prevented the application of cloture on a succession of civil rights bills, but in 1957 and 1960 they did not resort to filibuster—probably because of the danger that they might be defeated, as they were in fact in 1964. During filibusters, the few senators on the floor and reporters in the press section have listened to long speeches that have included the reading of recipes, the poems of Lord Byron, and Margaret Mitchell's lengthy Civil War novel, *Gone with the Wind.* The Constitution is a favorite on such occasions. To deal with the problem, the Senate rules were amended in 1964 to require that at least three hours of each day's session be confined to the business at hand.

***FILIBUSTER. A technique of continuous speaking to prevent a vote from being taken. Applicable only in the United States Senate, not in the House of Representatives.**

***CLOTURE. A rule to close off debate in the Senate. A favorable vote of two-thirds of the senators voting is required. One-sixth of the membership can force a vote through petition.**

Filibusters are rarely broken, and an organized minority can continue for a considerable period, holding up vital legislation and delaying the adjournment of Congress. Sometimes even the threat of a filibuster is enough to encourage compromise. Cloture was invoked only four times between 1917 and 1927, on the Telstar bill in 1962, and for the Civil Rights Act of 1964. Democrats generally seek to avoid filibusters because they dramatically emphasize division within the party.

The Rules Committee. In the House, all bills reported out of committee are sent to the Rules Committee for placement on the agenda. Taxation and appropriation bills do not necessarily go through this procedure; they are "privileged" and may be called up at any time by a simple majority vote. The ostensible reason for having the Rules Committee is that the large size of the House requires a traffic bureau to guide bills to and into it. (The committee occasionally acts more like a jail warden than a traffic cop, however.)

The Rules Committee may lift an important piece of legislation out of order for immediate consideration if it wishes. It grants each bill a "special rule," or the bill will probably never be considered by the House. Some bills are given a rule with no privilege of amendment. The Rules

Committee determines the amount of time for debate on a bill. It also must approve proposed changes in the permanent rules of the House.

The powers this committee now holds were originally held by the Speaker himself. Before the "revolution" of 1910 he was the dominant member of the committee. The committee was redesigned then to permit the majority party, rather than an individual, to determine the agenda of the House. This is not the way it has functioned.

The transfer of agenda powers from the Speaker to this committee (he is no longer a member) meant a transfer of power from an officer selected by the majority-party membership to a committee whose membership is determined by seniority. As may be expected, this committee and its chairman have sometimes exercised their powers with vigor, as is the case in other committees. They have been most effective in vetoing legislation of which they disapprove. In 1937, three Democratic members joined four Republicans in blocking consideration of New Deal legislation. From the Roosevelt years through 1948, the Southern Democrat–Republican coalition worked best in this committee—more effectively there than on the floor itself.

Then in 1949, the victorious Democrats, with President Truman's encouragement, instituted a rule that a committee chairman could call up a bill that his committee had favorably reported if the Rules Committee had not reported it out within twenty-one days. An attempt to repeal this rule in 1950 failed. A substantial number of Southern Democrats voted for repeal, but sixty-four Republicans from urban constituencies voted for retention, against the wishes of their own party leadership. The anti-poll-tax bill was brought to the floor for a vote under this rule, as was legislation on housing and minimum wages, and statehood for Hawaii and Alaska. But in 1951, the discharge rule was repealed. The Rules Committee resumed its practice of occasionally bottling up legislation. Sometimes the committee has delayed legislation in order to bargain for modifications. For example, a bill authorizing the shipment of wheat to India was held up until it was amended to conform with the views of the committee majority.[1]

The battle over the Rules Committee continued under President Kennedy. The chairman, Howard Smith of Virginia, had been a target of liberals as far back as the 1938 primaries, when President Roosevelt attempted to "purge" antiadministration Democrats. In 1961, the Democrats held an 8 to 4 majority. Nevertheless, the committee threatened to bottle up major administration bills, including those for aid to distressed areas and minimum-wage legislation. The chairman and one other Southern Democrat almost always joined Republicans in voting. In the early days of the session, by a hairline vote, the Speaker succeeded in having

[1] George Galloway, *The Legislative Process in Congress,* Thomas Y. Crowell Company, New York, 1961, pp. 340–346.

the committee membership enlarged by three persons—two Democrats and one Republican. It was thought that these additional members would help get the President's program out of the Rules Committee. Soon after, however, the Kennedy aid-to-education bill ran into trouble when a Northern Catholic Democrat joined conservative Southern Democrats and Republicans in opposing the legislation.

The debate over the proper role of the House Rules Committee is likely to continue for a long time, since it clearly places in opposition the program of the national majority as championed by the large-city-oriented President and that of the legislative majority, which represents an ideology that is characteristic of small-town and rural America.

The Rules Committee, however, also serves functions that are favored by the majority of representatives. On most legislation, it acts as an efficient traffic director, preventing many bills of importance from being buried under trivia. Even when it sidetracks controversial bills, observers have argued that it is saving some congressmen, perhaps even a majority of congressmen, the embarrassment of taking a stand they wish to avoid.

Discharge of Bills.* In both legislative bodies, a majority of the elected membership may discharge a standing committee of a particular bill. Generally, however, this procedure is difficult. Members hesitate to offend a powerful chairman or his committee majority, and the required 218 signatures in the House and 51 in the Senate are not easily obtained. The Wages and Hours Bill of 1938, which set the forty-hour week, was brought up for consideration in this way, however. And the Civil Rights Bill of 1960 might have been thus discharged from the Rules Committee, but when the petitions were seven signatures short of the required majority, the committee surrendered the bill.

***DISCHARGE OF BILLS. A majority of the elected members of either the House or Senate may have a bill reported out of a committee automatically by signing a discharge petition.**

Shirtsleeve Work: Committee of the Whole. In conducting the ordinary business of legislation, the House generally resolves into the House Committee of the Whole. This is a procedure by which the whole body designates itself as a special committee. As such, it may debate matters without following all of the formal rules of parliamentary procedure. For example, the Constitution requires that a majority of the elected members be present to conduct business, but in Committee of the Whole, only 100 representatives need be present. An additional advantage is that roll-call votes—and this is particularly important on crippling amendments—are never taken. What happens to the bill in the Committee of the Whole determines its fate. When a bill is certain to pass, a member who has been fighting it in Committee of the Whole may wish to change sides so that he is on record as favoring it.

The debaters in Committee of the Whole are scheduled in advance, with those favoring and opposing the bill allotted specific time periods to use as they wish. Additional periods are set aside for comments from others, but these may be cut off at any time by moving "the previous question," i.e., that a vote be immediately taken.

Compromise: The Conference Committee. Bills must be passed in both houses of Congress in order to become law. This means that they will receive a thorough review in at least two committees. Appropriations receive reviews by both subject-matter and expenditure committees, four in all. Bills are usually passed in somewhat different form in each house. When they are, a conference committee from each House is needed to iron out differences. The Speaker appoints the members from the House, and the Committee on Committees appoints the members from the Senate. The chairmen, senior members of the committee concerned, and sometimes others favoring the bill are, as a rule, placed on the conference committee, but on some occasions the committee is stacked with opponents of the measure. The committee chairman and ranking minority member, in practice, generally select the other members. The conference committee reports back a revision which must be accepted or rejected in total. In the last days of a session, this may mean that the choice is between the conference committee version and no bill at all. Members of conference committees have taken advantage of this fact by writing new provisions into the bill or eliminating provisions that both houses have already agreed to. This does not occur frequently, but it is not rare.

Bills that survive committee review, passage by each house, and the conference committee are sent to the President. Even at the stage of transmittal, bills have been mislaid or found to be defective in some minor detail and thus killed. Such occurrences are rare today, however.

The "Rider" Gambit. The choices of the President in respect to a bill, once it has been adopted by Congress, are two. He must accept it or reject it. He cannot change it. A veto means there will probably be no legislation on the subject that year. This gives Congress an advantage. It has added to this advantage by permitting extraneous issues to be added as "riders" to another subject. Thus in 1943, Franklin D. Roosevelt found in an appropriation bill a rider that specifically forbade the government to pay the salaries of three men, who were identified by name. He argued the provision was unconstitutional (as a "bill of attainder"), and was later vindicated when the case went to the Supreme Court. At the time, he had the choice of creating financial confusion by vetoing the appropriation bill or accepting the rider with the rest of the bill. He chose the latter course, but recommended that Congress give to the President the power of vetoing items in appropriation bills, a power held by many governors. His successor, Harry Truman, also requested this power, but Congress has been reluctant to give up one of its weapons.

The Rules Are Not Neutral. The procedures of both houses of Congress have three major characteristics: First, they have sufficient complexity to offer advantages to those skilled through experience in their use. As in most bodies organized by their own rules, the neophyte is at a disadvantage for a considerable period. Those with seniority are also favored, as in the selection of committee chairmen or conference committee members. Second and more important, members of the legislature may twist the rules devised for a general purpose to serve their own particular ends. Finally, the rules preserve the independence of Congress vis-à-vis the executive. A fine balance of cooperation and conflict is preserved by which Congress can exercise its role of critic without being totally unresponsible for what occurs. The rules of procedure protect this independence, for seldom can a President treat congressmen as puppets.

Critics of the Minority Veto. The press of time has sometimes made it necessary to reduce some of the opportunities for obstruction. The ordinary House member has little opportunity to be an obstructionist. Even senators, who are proud of their right to unlimited debate, commonly acquiesce by unanimous consent to the ending of debate at a certain point. But the veto is still available for the individual senator and the leaders of the House. It also exists for any sizable minority that is determined to use any tactic of obstruction. Its most important aspects are the killing of legislation in committee, the special powers exercised by the House Rules Committee, and the Senate filibuster.

Criticisms are generally posed in terms of majority rule: Why should the majority of a legislature, wishing to take action, be blocked by a minority? An additional point: Should the majority be blocked by the very persons it has placed in positions of power? Finally: Should such members embarrass the President if he is of their own party?

Critics have generally proposed a number of specific reforms, such as permitting the discharge of bills with a smaller number of signatures than is now required, clipping the wings of the House Rules Committee further, providing for cloture by a simple majority vote; and, perhaps the most radical of all, elimination of the seniority system.

Reformers who argue, for example, that elimination of the powers of the House Rules Committee will expedite House action may be taking an oversimplified view of the realities of the power configuration of that body. A roadblock eliminated at one point might well reappear elsewhere. Perhaps significantly, the same effective veto for conservatives is provided in one house by the Rules Committee and in the other by a filibuster. Neither house has or perhaps, in the view of leaders, requires both institutional arrangements.

Congressional Review. The history of most pieces of successful legislation covers several sessions of Congress. Quick action has occurred, however, in genuine emergencies or on items in current vogue and hence helpful in congressional reelection campaigns.

The successful launching of Sputnik I in 1957 by the Soviet Union caused Congress to rush through greatly expanded appropriations for the missile program. A few months after the infant son of Colonel Charles A. Lindbergh was kidnapped in 1932, Congress had made several forms of kidnapping a Federal capital offense. The birth of a number of malformed infants (mostly in Europe) that resulted from inadequate testing of a new drug led to major changes in 1962 in the Food, Drug and Cosmetics Act.

New proposals are not generally passed the first time they are presented, however. The history of almost every successful policy is one of modifications made through the years. Even when a new policy is accepted, it is likely to function in the beginning on a modest basis. The Social Security Act provides an illustration. Many of its features, now taken for granted as a critical part of the program, were added by amendments to the original: expansion of the coverage, raising the rates and benefits, lowering the age of women to sixty-two, aid to the permanently disabled, special provisions for the hospitalized. Even after more than twenty-five years of experimenting with the program, there continues to be consideration of changes in the coverage and benefits.

Congress scrutinizes as much as it can and then generally acts reluctantly. Its machinery, especially the committee system, guarantees such a procedure on ordinary bills and places effective vetoes in the hands of those who need be least responsive to current political opinion—those from politically stable districts who are older men with long service.

Congressional review does at times help educate the nation. Congress can become a forum for those who have something to say on a proposal. A parade of lobbyists testifying before a committee strives to bring out the implications of the details of any proposal, as well as to indicate its sources of support and opposition. Congressmen themselves try to spotlight issues in speeches, many of which are reprinted from the *Congressional Record* for circulation back home.

This process of review is long and laborious and coupled with parliamentary maneuvering by skilled antagonists seeking either to kill or save a bill by the careful building of coalitions for or against it. Passage alone does not, however, ensure the launching or expansion of a program. Congress always separates the bill authorizing an activity from the one appropriating money to carry it out. Sometimes the dominant strategy takes the form of passing a bill and then making only a token appropriation or none at all.

The result of congressional review is that it generally takes more than a simple majority to put a program into actual operation. A determined minority, skilled in parliamentary techniques and placed in positions of authority can delay, amend, or kill a proposal more easily than a majority can get it passed.

Nevertheless, congressional machinery is, in the opinion of some observers, well suited for the "disjointed incrementalism"—marginal policy adjustment—that is characteristic of American political decision making. The argument is that procedures like those of Congress have a built-in rationality, considering that time and information costs are high and the full effects of any change are not completely predictable.[2]

OTHER POWERS OF CONGRESS

Congress's major effect on policy making is that of passing laws and thereby legitimizing change. Several additional legal powers aid one or the other branch of Congress in its bargaining with the President on the shaping of policy.

Constitution Making. The Founding Fathers gave Congress a legal way of bypassing the President. They permitted that body to propose changes in the Constitution through amendments. Such proposals must be supported by two-thirds of the members of each house and ratified by majorities in the legislatures of three-fourths of the states or, if Congress so specifies, by specially elected state conventions in three-fourths of the states. The bottleneck for amendments has been the two-thirds requirement in Congress (see Chapter 4). This almost always requires a bipartisan coalition, and because a constitutional amendment is involved, action is not taken lightly.

Some recent examples. In recent times, the amendment process has been at least twice used to attack the powers of the Presidency, once successfully. The successful move limited the President to two terms, a change achieved by a coalition of anti-Truman Southern Democrats and anti-Roosevelt Republicans during a Congress in which Republicans were in the majority.

The other attempt took place in the early days of the Eisenhower administration and was known as the Bricker amendment. Through the influence of the President, it failed of passage in the Senate by one vote. Its purpose was to limit the subject of treaties to matters over which the Federal government explicitly had power given it in the Constitution. Some Southerners, fearful that the International Covenant on Human Rights might be construed, if adopted, as giving the Federal government greater power in civil rights matters, joined isolationist Republicans in support.

[2] David Braybrooke and Charles E. Lindblom, *A Strategy of Decision: Policy Evaluation as a Social Process,* The Free Press of Glencoe, New York, 1963.

The amendment process can thus be used to attack the executive branch, but only under particular circumstances. A bipartisan coalition working against the Chief Executive is needed for success. Most Presidents have sufficient power and influence in Congress to gather one-third plus one of the membership to its position and thus block an amendment that is truly unwanted. On the other hand, Presidents cannot easily gather a two-thirds majority to make changes in the Constitution. In general, the balance of forces results in a standoff.

Congress, like the President, also has the power of informal interpretation of undefined terms in the Constitution. The Supreme Court, of course, usually has the final decision on this, but in many matters it is reluctant to act. Thus Congress largely does determine the procedures of its committees, even when it is argued that some of its procedures deprive citizens of constitutional rights. While constitutional interpretation is a real power exercised by Congress, it is most important in matters that might be called congressional housekeeping, that is, managing the details of congressional procedures. But even when congressional interpretation touches upon more general concerns, the Supreme Court is reluctant to overrule its interpretations.

Impeachment of Executive and Judicial Officers. The House of Representatives has the power to impeach the President, and once it did so. Andrew Johnson, Lincoln's successor, was acquitted of the charges and the conclusion reached by most observers was that impeachment was a clumsy blunderbuss when used against a President for policy reasons. The same conclusion had been reached in respect to the courts when, in 1803, President Thomas Jefferson encouraged Congress to attempt the impeachment of a Federalist judge. Today, the threat of impeachment is used only in cases of grave malfeasance. In all, twelve persons have been impeached, the last in 1933. Despite occasional demands, such as those by John Birch Society members, Congress is not likely to impeach the Chief Justice or associate justices of the Supreme Court or the President because of policy disagreements.

The procedure for removal is simple. The House decides on the indictment by majority vote. This technically is the impeachment. The Senate then sits as the jury and, to convict, must agree by a two-thirds vote. The Chief Justice presides if the President is being tried, because the Vice President, who normally presides, would have an obvious personal interest in the outcome.

Impeachment is not a practical weapon. If used only over policy disagreements, it would change our form of government from the presidential system with its independent executive to some hybrid of the parliamentary system, where the President could serve only at the pleasure of Congress. For that reason, it is a weapon akin to a machine gun or a cannon in a neighborhood brawl—too powerful to really be useful.

SPECIAL POWERS OF THE SENATE

The Senate has two main weapons exclusive to itself. They are (1) power to approve or disapprove many appointments of the President; and (2) power to decide whether or not a treaty is to go into effect.

Appointments. The Senate is asked to give "advice and consent" to the President on nearly all appointments. Today they exceed 100,000 in number. These include the Cabinet posts (and heads of most executive agencies), the Supreme and lower Federal courts, Federal district attorneys, diplomats, such as ambassadors and representatives to the United Nations, and members of governmental commissions. The great bulk of the appointees do not occupy major policy-making jobs, but are officers in the Armed Forces, postmasters, officials of the U.S. Public Health Service, and minor officials in the field, such as United States marshals.

The official executive family. A party coalition controls most nominations for positions that are part of the administrative family. The President is permitted to select whom he wants for his Cabinet and, generally, for important administrative posts. The political wounds need to be deep before senators will, as a body, desert a President of their own party. If an appointee faces a Senate controlled by the opposition, however, his chances are lessened. A Democratically controlled Senate in 1959, by the narrow margin of 49 to 46 rejected Admiral Lewis L. Strauss for Secretary of Commerce, the eighth man rejected for Cabinet office since 1787.

Some nominations have been rejected or withdrawn at the threat of rejection. The Progressive-Democratic coalition of the 1920s rejected Calvin Coolidge's nominee for the Supreme Court because it was contended that he had an antilabor record. The same group twice rejected his nominee for Attorney General. Later, President Roosevelt attempted to appoint a former Democratic national committeeman, Ed Flynn, as Ambassador to Australia and had to retreat before a coalition of Republicans and Southern Democrats who found the choice obnoxious. President Truman had to withdraw the nomination of a representative to the United Nations. Such rejections hinge on two circumstances: a bipartisan coalition in Congress that is unfriendly to the administration, and a plausible cause for rejection that can be dramatized as a policy position.

Senatorial courtesy. A different kind of coalition evolves when the Federal appointment touches local politics, as in Federal judgeships or United States attorneys. The nominee is normally expected to be of the President's party, a practice going back to Presidents Washington and Adams, who appointed only Federalists to the bench.

Exceptions are made for sound political reasons. Thus President Truman named Luther W. Youngdahl, Republican Governor of Minnesota, to a district court post at the urging of Democratic Senator Hubert H. Humphrey of that state. The Senator reportedly had good reason for supporting the move: He feared that Youngdahl might otherwise take his job away from him at the next election. But a few years later, President Kennedy, smarting under criticism from the American Bar Association (the organization had accused him of undue partisanship in judicial appointments), nominated a Republican for United States district judge in Illinois, the constituency of reform Democrat, Paul Douglas. The Senator was quick to protest: "I want to make it clear that I favor a Democrat. . . . Of the nineteen Illinois lawyers serving on the Federal District Court or Court of Appeals, ten are Republicans and nine are Democrats."[3]

The tradition of senatorial courtesy is followed when the President's party controls the Senate. The nominee must be acceptable to the senator or senators of the President's party (if there are any) from the state in which the appointment is made. The senator may, in effect, make the appointment or, at the very least, bargain with the President over who the nominee will be. If he fails to receive satisfaction, the magic formula is for the senator to appear before the committee or on the floor and say, "This nomination is personally obnoxious to me." Whenever these words are heard, other members of the majority party (and usually of the minority, as well) vote with him to reject the nomination. To do otherwise would be an affront to a member of the club.

This simple system leads to some results that could not easily be explained if the custom were not known to the observer. Thus, President Eisenhower appointed to Federal office in North Dakota, Democrats who had supported his opponent, but who also, because of their Nonpartisan League ties, had helped reelect maverick Republican Senator William Langer of that state. Similarly, Democratic Presidents have nominated Southerners who were generally out of sympathy with presidential goals to much-prized judgeships as well as to lesser offices.

Former members of the club. A third type of coalition occurs when the nominee is an ex-senator. Under such circumstances, opposition vanishes; approval is, by tradition, automatic—usually without even a hearing on the nomination. (There are a few exceptions. Ex-Senator Hugo L. Black, nominated to the United States Supreme Court by President Franklin Roosevelt in 1937, was closely questioned by the Judiciary Committee—but he was approved.)

Treaties. The second power held exclusively by the Senate is that of approving, by a two-thirds vote of those present, all treaties before they become effective. The Constitution says "with the advice and consent" of the Senate. Consent, in practice, is necessary. Advice is optional. The original upper house, then consisting of only twenty-six men, was conceived of as the equivalent of the colonial governor's council and hence

[3] *The New York Times,* Apr. 29, 1962.

was intended literally to advise the President. The first Chief Executive therefore dutifully went one day in 1794 to visit the Senate to discuss a treaty with Indian tribes. Washington was so outraged because of a motion to refer the treaty to committee for study that he said he would "be damned" if he would ever go back. For over a century thereafter, Presidents did not formally seek advice in advance of treaty submission.

The rejection of the League of Nations by the Senate in 1919 displayed the dangers of this policy, however. Yet since 1935, when the World Court was rejected, no major treaty has been disapproved. Franklin Roosevelt, more of a political realist and skillful politician than Wilson, successfully forestalled dangers that could be anticipated: He placed a senator from each party on the United States delegation to the first United Nations meeting and took them into his confidence at other times. Since then, ex-Senators such as Warren Austin of Vermont and Henry Cabot Lodge of Massachusetts have served on the United States delegation to the U.N. In recent decades, with leaders in both parties talking of a bipartisan foreign policy, the Senate's treaty power has become more of a latent threat than a power actively wielded. It seems likely that Presidents have learned the lesson: If the Senate leaders are not completely taken into his confidence, they are at least carefully cultivated on foreign policy matters and given a chance to have their say around the conference table or in the White House rather than on the Senate floor, where any act that is perceived as a personal affront to a senior colleague can make mincemeat of a fine roast the President and State Department may have carefully prepared.

A CONGRESS DIVIDED

To the careless observer Congress appears to be weak because it is divided into two chambers. In any battle, one may be played off against the other by a skillful President. The division is rarely bridged formally. Reformers have sometimes recommended joint committees, composed of members of both houses speaking with one voice. Except for the necessary conference committees to iron out disagreement on bills, only a few such committees exist, notably those for atomic energy and the economic status of the nation.

Evidence of a bitterness fostered by division also exists. In 1962, the underlying friction came to the surface in a somewhat trivial, but nevertheless significant, way when the eighty-three-year-old chairman of the House Appropriations Committee refused to meet in conference with members of the Senate Appropriations Committee, which was headed by an eighty-four-year-old chairman. Both were Democrats. House objections centered around three points: (1) Conference committee meetings were always held on the Senate side of the Capitol; (2) senators always were chairmen of conference committees, and the position was not rotated; and (3) the Senate too often restored cuts in the budget made by the House and then prevailed in conference committee.

The senators offered to move the conference room closer to the House side of the Capitol, but not to leave the Senate side. In an attempt at one-upmanship, they countered with a demand of their own—that, despite tradition that all revenue bills first be introduced in the House, the Senate Appropriations Committee be permitted to initiate money bills also. This squabble started in April and continued past the end of the fiscal year on June 30. Special action was needed to safeguard the payment of salaries to Federal employees.

The division of Congress that occasionally encourages each body to use strategies against the other permits the President to play one house against the other and frustrates the possibilities of members serving as leaders in proposing national policy. But national leadership is not, after all, a major legislative function. Division does, however, add to the power of Congress to delay and block. One house may pass a bill, while the other may kill it. Bills may even separately pass both houses and still not become law if an election intervenes, and two "Congresses" are hence legally involved. Thus even the weaknesses resulting from division may be used as a strength by political actors. On balance, they add to congressional ability to force the executive to justify his proposals. Division ensures that action will not be precipitate.

CONGRESSIONAL STAFF: ALLIES IN THE STRUGGLE

Some games, like chess and checkers, are played on an open board where all the players have perfect information about the pieces. In terms of game theory, the legislative struggle is more like warfare. Accurate information about opposition strength and strategy is scarce and valuable, and the costs of information gathering are high. Action is generally taken on the basis of incomplete information, but when information can be obtained, it can often quickly be transformed into a weapon.

Joseph Martin reports that in 1926, when he first joined the House Foreign Affairs Committee, the major debate, lasting for over one week, was whether Congress should appropriate $20,000 for an international poultry show in Tulsa, Oklahoma. Today the pace has quickened in the fields of both foreign affairs and domestic policy.

With the increased work load, the congressional attitude toward staff help and the information and skills they provide is changing. Traditionally, this attitude reflected the beliefs of the Jacksonian and small-town ideology: any man is good enough to do the job; and to make certain the help does not begin to feel it owns the jobs, there should be a complete turnover every time party control changes.

This attitude still holds for over 1,200 "housekeeping" employees who range from elevator operators to minor clerks. They are patronage appointments to be doled out to friends or deserving constituents of the more powerful legislators.

The old distrust of the expert is still found in the attitude toward staffs of standing committees. The Legislative Reorganization Act of 1946 permitted each committee a four-member research staff and six clerks. On some committees these jobs are still handed out to brothers-in-law or deserving widows from back home. The press of work on the most important committees has resulted in the retention of most of the trained staff when there is a change of parties because persons so expert are hard to replace. A number of committees still sometimes "borrow" experts from the bureaucracy. It is perhaps also significant that committee staff members are relied upon much less and have much less work to do than members of the legislators' personal staffs, who deal largely with patronage and political matters related to the political survival of the legislator.

At the time of World War I, Congress established the Legislative Reference Service as part of the Library of Congress in order to do research; a few years later, the office of the Legislative Counsel for bill drafting was added. The Reorganization Act of 1946 expanded both of these services so that within a few years the staff of the Legislative Reference Service more than doubled and its budget quadrupled. Thus Congress gradually accepted the complex conditions of modern lawmaking.

The Legislative Reorganization Act of 1946 expanded each representative's personal staff, allowing him a secretary and a few clerks. Every senator could hire an assistant and senators from larger states were given larger staffs with as many as ten clerks, plus an administrative assistant and a legislative assistant. Often congressmen handle staff positions as patronage, but some see the need for combining these considerations with those of professional competence.

Thus the congressional battleground is not without its experts on the side of Congress, but such skilled aides still lack the disciplined efficiency of the information-gathering corps supporting the executive. The development of a comparable corps that can keep information in the family is the key to congressional influence on policy making.

CONGRESSIONAL INVESTIGATIONS: A POWERFUL WEAPON

An ancient function of popular assemblies is that of investigation. Congress makes extensive use of the power. The official reason for committee investigations is fact finding so as to make possible better laws, but this is not the major reason for the activity. Investigations are the congressional answers to a President's fireside chats. They are an appeal to national public opinion over the head of the President—a most effective strategy for achieving policy or personal goals.

One Goal: Control. An investigation is one way by which Congress can attack the President and attempt to exercise control over the bureaucracy of the executive branch. Sometimes congressmen have usurped executive functions, as when Senator Joseph McCarthy made an "agreement" with Greek shipowners to get them to stop supplying Communist nations. Presidents commonly cooperate with congressional committees but have, since Washington's time, insisted that they do so voluntarily and on their own terms.

Congressional committees, of course, parallel the organization of the bureaucracy. Each committee has carved out its special sphere of agencies to oversee. In time, personal relationships with the bureaucrats become close. Given the power of the purse, coupled with that of investigation, Congress has a potential influence that has led to attempts by congressmen to directly supervise administration. This may consist of favoring particular individuals for advancement in the bureaucracy. In other cases attempts may be made to encourage or discourage energetic administration. A congressman with great seniority may have longer experience with an agency's activities than the President, agency head, or many of its employees. Congressional bypassing of the President directly to the administrative branch is a weapon with which a critical Congress can cripple a President's program at the administrative stage. It also permits bureaucrats who are out of sympathy with the President to convey their unfavorable viewpoints, sometimes with damaging effect, in committee hearings.

Presidents have occasionally invoked "executive privilege" and instructed the members of the administration not to give certain information, on the probable supposition that it would be used against them in Congress. This position is defended by use of the doctrine of separation of powers. Thus far, Presidents have always been successful, although investigating committees have put pressure on them to try to get a look at FBI files or the dossiers of public employees who were being investigated routinely for loyalty, for example. Following his term as President, Harry Truman was asked by the chairman to testify before the House Un-American Activities Committee. He refused on the basis that once such investigations were permitted, every retiring President would be threatened with harassment by unfriendly congressional committees, which would have a debilitating effect on the office of President.

Another Goal: Gaining Tactical Advantage. Congressional investigations are also undertaken to embarrass the administration. They may be launched either by members of the opposition party or by a dissident faction of the President's party. Thus Midwest progressive Republicans combined with Democrats to embarrass the Harding administration and, through the Teapot Dome investigation, in effect, to take the Secretary of the Interior out of the Cabinet and put him behind bars in a Federal penitentiary. More recently, conservative Republicans and Southern Democrats have cooperated. Other officials who have suffered a fate similar to that of Harding's Secretary of the Interior are Alger Hiss, some minor tax officials, and Harry Truman's appointments secretary. An investigation will not usually send an official to prison, but it may cause him to resign, as was the case with Sherman Adams, President Eisenhower's chief of staff. Even if an investigation does not accomplish this, it may succeed in harassing an official almost beyond endurance; this was the case with the attacks on Dean Acheson, the Democratic Secretary of State under President Truman, and David Lilienthal, who had at one time headed the Tennessee Valley Authority under President Roosevelt and was head of the Atomic Energy Commission under President Truman. Such attacks are in part inspired in the hope of gaining political advantage by the opposition or of raising the status of the congressional wing of the majority party at the expense of the presidential wing.

A By-product: New Policies. Congressional committee investigations may result in the molding of new policy. When Whitaker Chambers's allegations that Alger Hiss, a State Department career official, had passed secrets to the Communists were believed by a majority of Americans, it led to a complete reassessment of the Roosevelt-Truman loyalty policies for administrators and gave a strategic advantage to those making bitter attacks against the administration in hopes of changing its foreign policy.

A strategy for survival. A committee can conduct investigations only by the tacit permission of a majority of the House, and the level of its activity depends upon the amount of money made available. From its beginning in the 1930s, the House Committee on Un-American Activities, perhaps uniquely for a congressional committee, was subjected to criticism by various newspaper editors, clergymen, educators, and other persons, some of whom urged its abolition. In the early 1960s, the committee sponsored a film showing protests by students against a hearing the committee had held in San Francisco. The film was designed to attack the committee's critics and attempted to show that many of them were Communist-inspired or duped by Communists. The fact that critics were able to show that the film had been "doctored" in a number of respects by the committee staff took the edge off the charges. The gambit nevertheless serves as an excellent example of how an investigation can be used to further or continue in existence a committee at a time when its critics were many and perhaps interest in its activities was flagging.

Personal publicity: Goal and by-product. An investigation also projects committee members into the limelight if it attracts popular interest. Estes Kefauver, then an obscure senator, pushed himself into the presidential sweepstakes of 1952 by parading the stars of American gangsterdom across barroom television screens. (TV was in its infancy, and home sets were relatively few, but no bar was without one.) Senator Joseph R. McCarthy of Wisconsin made his name a household word with his traveling road show investigating alleged Communists in the early 1950s. More than any other legislator, his fame rested almost exclusively on his pyrotechnics as an investigating committee chairman.

Investigations and Social Values. A weapon as handy and useful as the investigation is likely to attract the interest of those who would abuse it. The early House Un-American Activities Committee set a style that many Americans interested in civil liberties objected to. Essentially, only the prosecutor's side of the case was heard. Committee members were seen by some observers as "hanging judges," who expected the witness to prove his innocence if he could, freely bullied witnesses, and released hearsay evidence without having carefully checked it. In the subversive-activities investigations, Communist turncoats were used to give evidence for pay. One such witness later created a tempest by reversing his testimony. Senator McCarthy initiated the technique of the closed hearing. After some of them, he gave to the press his own version of what had been said.

Criticisms have brought some changes in procedures, some announced in Supreme Court rulings in contempt of Congress proceedings (see Chapter 17), others made by Congress itself. In essence, these reform efforts attempted to reduce a congressman's freedom of action to conform to accepted American norms of fair play without reducing the effectiveness of the investigative weapon. The situation is similar to that of outlawing the beanball in baseball or declaring unnecessary roughness in football. Without some rules for its use in polite society, the weapon itself would finally be discredited. A short-run advantage could be turned into a long-run handicap.

But setting precise rules has not been easy because the short-run payoffs are so great. One method attempted to make a uniform set of procedural rules for all committees. The House in 1955 did issue such a set. It prohibited one-man hearings, for example. An additional difficulty with rules that attempt to apply procedures of the judiciary to the legislative process is that they may hamstring hearings and spin them out far beyond what is reasonable for a congressional fact-finding study.

The question of how responsible a congressional investigating committee will be is determined by the balance of pressures upon its chairman and membership. Committee staff members wish to please their bosses and will tend to behave according to what they believe will maximize their chances of doing so. Committee members want to be reelected or perhaps to go on to higher office as Richard M. Nixon did and Estes Kefauver tried to do. Some of them merely yearn for publicity. Some will tend to do whatever they believe will achieve these ends.

The controlling factor is the sophistication of the voter, for it is to his preferences, anxieties, and beliefs that the grandstand plays are made. Congressional investigators, in the past, have exploited anxieties concerning the threat to the nation posed by communism, the moral outrage engendered by the thought of the activities of professional gangsters, the suspicions people have of those who are in politics or possess power (e.g., the Teapot Dome, the "five percenter," and the Sherman Adams investigations). Committee members thus tend to behave according to what their constituents consider to be proper or, if not exactly proper, "necessary" under the circumstances as they are perceived by the dominant portion of the constituency. McCarthy could with impunity be rough on an ordinary witness and even a Cabinet member; on the other hand, attacks directed against the actions of President Eisenhower were not acceptable to most citizens.

What Gets Investigated? Reflecting the apportionment pattern in Congress, committee members perhaps most commonly tend to exploit the older American ideologies, or what is today the small-town viewpoint. Subjects concentrated on are most often those viewed with suspicion by the small-town resident—the "wicked" big-city people, movie stars, gangsters, labor union goons, college professors, and, most important of all, the officials of big government.

Insecure in a modern world, those who hold small-town views are prone to regard all change as close to treason and condemn it as such. Thus, the investigation of such contemporary issues and problems as the lot of Negroes is usually made by a commission appointed by the President. The conditions of migrant workers, Federal prison inmates, slum dwellers, or the permanently unemployable are less popular topics for congressional investigation, perhaps because they imply costly appropriations and are fairly irrelevant to an ideology that holds that people succeed to the extent of their effort and ability. The small-town viewpoint would, of course, be tempered if a change were made from the seniority system of committee selection or as House congressional district boundaries are drawn to reflect more closely population patterns.

Congressional investigations will continue to be criticized, but they are a traditional legislative function and will often serve useful purposes by revealing serious problems and testing public reactions. It is frequently argued that no new real information is turned up by committees, but that charge is incorrect. An investigation spotlights for the nation what only a few experts ordinarily know, and occasionally the hearings inform even the experts.

THE LEGISLATIVE STRUGGLE: A CASE STUDY

Each bill must pass through the same legal process. At each step strategic political decisions must be made. The legal or formal route is somewhat like the highway between New York and San Francisco, circa 1910. To describe the political process is to detail the adventures of those who attempt the trip. Some arrive, some break down along the way, and some limp in on three wheels. We will follow a bill as it jogs along through the maze.

First, however, we need an overview. Bertram Gross, a political scientist and experienced congressional staff member, lists the major points at which political decisions are crucial to the fate of a bill. We adapt his points and phrase them as questions and set them beside the formal legal steps.[4]

The legal route	Political decisions
The bill is introduced by a legislator.	Is the bill desirable now? Who should introduce it? What should it contain? What group will guide the campaign? What kind of educational campaign is needed?
The bill is referred to committee.	Which committee?
The committee decides if any bill is to be reported out.	Who will testify at hearings? Among possible committee decisions, which is now desirable?
The bill is voted on by the whole body.	What will be voted on and when? How should floor action be guided?

The bill, if successful, is sent to the other house. The same procedure is followed and, if the bill survives, the process continues as follows:

A conference committee is selected to compromise the versions of two houses.	Who is selected for the committee?
Both houses vote on conference version.	Should the conference version be supported?
The bill is signed or vetoed by the President.	What political considerations are more important to the President than to the two congressional majorities that have sent the bill to him?

Some bills are part of the President's "must" program. Of these, a few pass through Congress unscathed—more come through in a battered condition. Other bills are the product of congressional preferences, aided by supporting interest groups, and they may or may not be greeted with a presidential veto.

The Yellow Peril. The bill we will follow along its course into law was invented by and largely pushed along through the legislative route by a committee representing a particular combination of interest groups. It was not a bill of tremendous importance, but neither was it a negligible bill. It proposed to raise the number of the 400 million Chinese who could

[4] Bertram M. Gross, *The Legislative Struggle,* McGraw-Hill Book Company, New York, 1953, chaps. 9–19.

enter the United States on a permanent visa from zero to 105 a year. In practical terms, this meant very little; in symbolic terms it was very important to some United States citizens.[5]

A bill—now? From 1882 to 1943, Chinese could not enter the United States to become citizens. In 1942, a former United States consul sought out the editor of a magazine devoted to Asian affairs and suggested that the time was ripe for an article demanding repeal of the Chinese Exclusion Act. He argued that the Chinese were humiliated by the provision and were at that moment our ally in a massive war against Japan. (These were the days of General Chennault's Flying Tigers and "Vinegar Joe" Stilwell.) The American mood had shifted from looking at Chinese as sinister Dr. Fu Manchus to emphasizing the more amiable qualities exemplified by detective Charlie Chan or the wisdom of philosopher Lin Yutang.

The citizens' group decided the time was ripe for an attempt, though leads to the State Department indicated the latter did not want to put presidential prestige behind the effort. Its always cautious officials felt that a rejection or an acrimonious debate would be a disaster in relations with China.

Who is driving? The response to the article led to the organization of a citizens' committee to seek repeal of the Chinese Exclusion Act. No more than fifteen ever attended a meeting of the committee, although 250 letterhead members from forty states were listed. It was, however, a "blue-ribbon" organization, having the support of persons like Pearl Buck, the author of *The Good Earth.* The favorable groups were idealistic and religious, although some West Coast commercial interests having trade with China or hoping for it after the war, educators specializing in Chinese studies, Chinese-Americans, and Chinese nationals were included. This catalytic group formed itself into a steering committee to coordinate effort and made some decisions about its membership: Chinese would not be given leadership roles on the committee lest Congress regard it as a Chinese front group. Japanese groups were not encouraged to testify because of anti-Japanese feeling. Negro groups were not sought out, since they would antagonize Southern congressmen, who were a majority of the Democratic membership on the House and Senate Immigration Committees. Jewish groups were not sought out, since Jewish members might lend credence to a charge that repeal of the act was the beginning of the drive to weaken naturalization laws and admit greater numbers of Jewish refugees.

What's in the bill? The citizens' group also had to decide whether the bill would apply to all Asiatics and if so, under what conditions? Given the temper of Congress, the group decided to limit efforts to the Chinese alone and to seek to get the Chinese an immigration quota (although this would admit a mere 105 Chinese a year) and make them eligible for citizenship.

[5] The facts of this case study are taken from Fred W. Riggs, *Pressures on Congress,* Columbia University Press, New York, 1950.

These three goals were selected from a total of eight, which included repeal or prohibition of state laws against intermarriage between Orientals and Caucasians, allowing Hong Kong and South-American Chinese to enter under regular quotas, and other issues.

Who sponsors? Several bills had already been introduced; none had sponsors that would garner support. Representative Walter Judd, an ex-medical missionary in China, was strongly in favor of the proposal, but he was a freshman. One bill was by a New York Democrat, another by an American Labor party member who was suspected of Communist sympathies by many conservative members. Clearly the best bet was a West Coast representative, since opposition was supposed to be strongest there. At first, the citizens' committee decided to back the version of a Texas representative in hopes of getting Southern support. Unacceptable revisions of his bill turned the committee to others; it finally settled on Warren Magnuson of Washington, who also had introduced a bill.

What kind of educational campaign? The citizens' committee pegged its national campaign on two arguments: (1) It would help win the war, and (2) most people were not aware of this undemocratic clause and would want it changed if they knew about it. In Congress, their problem was to get Southern Democrats to regard the measure as a foreign policy issue rather than the domestic issue of alleviating conditions for a minority racial group. Some Republicans also would support the administration on a foreign policy, but not a domestic, basis.

The publicity campaign that sold these arguments cost the committee only a little over $5,000, but it included speakers on national radio public affairs programs, 30,000 mailings of a special booklet, 10,000 reprints of an article, 20,000 letters to select mailing lists, letters to newspapers, full-page advertisements signed by prestigeful people, a special celebration of China Day (July 7) and another celebration of Chinese Independence Day (October 10), and articles in the *New Yorker, Life, Reader's Digest, This Week,* and other magazines, and a broadside of favorable editorials sent to each congressman.

There was no doubt about committee referral, since each house had an immigration committee. The sponsors could, of course, have added material that would make most of the bill's content a matter for the Foreign Affairs Committee to decide. Such deviousness might have backfired. Besides, the sponsors were quite happy to have it go to the House Immigration Committee. The chairman of the House committee was a New York City Democrat who strongly favored the proposal.

Who testifies? The steering committee selected almost every person who testified for the bill. It chose a heavy West Coast representation, several congressmen, six Protestant clergymen and missionaries, three Roman Catholic priests, and a sprinkling of oil company representatives and educators. None of those testifying against were from the West Coast.

What now? At the close of the hearings, it was apparent that the forces favoring repeal of the exclusion clause had the votes, but no agreement could be reached on a quota system for admissions. Rather than reporting out the bill without a definite quota feature, the committee chairman decided to wait until after the summer recess. The steering committee began to work on opposition groups. The AFL was opposed, but in convention several of its member union spokesmen denounced international union policy, thus neutralizing this opposition. The same technique was successfully applied on the American Legion when the California and Massachusetts chapters came out for repeal. In this case, the efforts of Magnuson and some commercial interests hoping for trade agreements with China were especially helpful. Other favorable statements were secured in West Coast states from the California League of Women Voters, the Governor of California, the Seattle and other chambers of commerce, Congressman Will Rogers, Jr., of California, and the San Francisco and Los Angeles boards of supervisors. Further support was gained by Mme. Chiang Kai-shek's well-publicized tour of the nation in the late spring and early summer of 1943.

The Attorney General, whose department included the Immigration and Naturalization Service, was asked by the House committee for an opinion on two repeal bills. The reply, cleared by the President, was in favor of repeal. It appears that the President regarded this as a trial balloon. If the committee acted favorably, he would support the bill; if not, he would not, since it was not regarded by him as of high priority. He had just seen Congress override his veto on the Smith-Connally Act, and was not looking for another defeat, but he was thought to be personally favorable to repeal. Mrs. Roosevelt had been approached by the committee early in its efforts; she had, in fact, devoted a column of *My Day* to the subject as part of the July 7 promotion. Her plea for repeal was widely syndicated.

Within the Democratic majority of the committee, a debate raged between a member from Louisiana, who viewed the issue as affecting civil rights, and a representative from Texas, who did not. On the Republican side, four of the nine Republican members, including the ranking majority member and the nonvoting delegate from Hawaii, favored the bill; most of them on the basis that it was a "win the war" issue.

Who guides floor debate? The committee, after the recess, voted 8 to 4 to report the Magnuson bill. Eight members were absent. Immediately after favorable report to the floor, President Roosevelt sent a message to Congress endorsing the bill. The defeated Republican candidate for President, Wendell Willkie, had agreed with the steering committee to support the bill at the proper time. At this point, he gave his views to an off-the-record meeting of Republican congressmen. The House Immigration Committee chairman decided to delegate to the Texas representative authority to allot debate time among others instead of retaining it for himself, and this somewhat mollified skeptical Southerners. The bill successfully cleared the Rules Committee and shortly was passed on a voice vote.

What about "the other house"? In the Senate, the steering committee had received a fortunate break: Senator Andrews of Florida had, on his own initiative, introduced a companion bill. He was a Southerner and a member of the Immigration Committee, and its chairman, Senator Russell of Georgia, appeared to defer to his colleague's wishes. Senator Hiram Johnson of California, the member of the committee who was probably most opposed to repeal, was ill through most of the Senate action and, while registering his disapproval, did little else. As the Senate committee prepared to consider the bill, two important events occurred: The American Legion executive council reversed its stand and decided to favor the bill as part of the war effort, and the Attorney General and Assistant Secretary of State expressed approval of the legislation in letters to Senator Russell. The fact that Senator Russell visited Chiang Kai-shek in China in the summer of 1943 may also have helped gain his support. The committee held no separate hearings. It reported the bill out.

How about the President? The bill passed the Senate on a voice vote in the same version as it passed the House and was sent to the President's office. The central clearance procedure of the White House, administered by the Budget Bureau, asked the Secretaries of State and Labor and the Attorney General for their opinions; all approved. President Roosevelt signed the bill into law with the words "An unfortunate barrier between allies has been removed. The war effort in the Far East can now be carried on with a greater vigor and a larger understanding of our common purpose."

What next? The *ad hoc* Citizens' Committee for Repeal of the Chinese Exclusion Act disbanded.

Assessment. The repeal of the Chinese Exclusion Act was not an "administration bill," though in the final stages the administration and the President lent support to it. The bill was not particularly favored by the Republican–Southern Democratic coalition that controlled Congress on domestic issues. It passed because the sponsoring agencies correctly gauged the temper of Congress, saw to it that pressure reached Congress from effective sources, and framed the issue in ideological terms as one affecting foreign affairs rather than domestic policy.

At every step, the sponsoring citizens' committee had luck or fashioned their own luck. A few years before, repeal would not have been possible; five years later, as the Communists swept across China, it would have had no chance. Given an unfriendly committee chairman in either house, it might have been pigeonholed. Had the committee reached for dropping all barriers against Asiatics, as some of its members wished, possibly no bill would have emerged. Had the citizens' committee not offset the regional-deference practices of Congress—that is, the inclination to act in accord with the preferences of the representatives of the region most affected, in this case, the West Coast—they would have failed. Given the inclination of a President to look at the Chinese Exclusion Act as a nuisance that complicated foreign relations, the committee correctly judged that they would receive presidential aid if there was hope for congressional success.

All of these decisions were part of the political strategy and tactics of converting personal and group values into public policy. Other bills require somewhat different strategies and decisions. For some, the presidential veto is the stumbling block. For many more, securing release from committees is the crucial step. All bills have an individual political history, though the formal steps of bill passage remain unchanged.

PRESIDENT AND CONGRESS: A NATURAL ANTAGONISM?

In Congress, the President faces a will that he cannot dominate. The organization of Congress is designed to encourage the independence of its senior membership. Both houses are elected separately from the President and have different constituencies. They possess powers that can be used as effective weapons against any President.

All of this suggests an institutionalized, or built-in, antagonism between Congress and the President, and, to some degree, such is the case. One need only turn to today's newspaper or the back issues of the *New York Times* to find examples of sniping between individual congressional leaders and the President. Most of this is quickly forgotten, but at the time, it is considered serious and tends to give a permanent cast to the coloration of their relationships. A President knows that he cannot, except at great cost, openly defy Congress. If he does so, he invariably invites a pitched battle with professionals who are highly skilled in the art of politics. He may win an initial battle or two but lose the campaign. Most Presidents begin their terms enjoying a "honeymoon" with Congress, during which they press for crucial legislation while they still have social capital to expend. But they frequently leave the office with recriminations for their congressional colleagues.

Yet if there is a mutual antagonism, there must also be a basis for compromise and agreement. Somehow a President must help build coalitions of congressmen and executive officials behind policies he considers important. Problems must be handled. The decisions that are made generally are compromises. Presidents are often disappointed with the result—but then, so are many congressmen.

SELECTED BIBLIOGRAPHY

As the chapter title indicates, this section stresses studies of Congress in action. The earliest listed here is a classic written three-quarters of a century ago by a young professor of political science who later became President, Woodrow Wilson [38]. It is still relevant because it stresses the role of the committee system in all congressional deliberations, a theme never since absent.

Previous to World War II the early studies of Congress and interest-group pressures were published. Representative of this group are studies by Herring [21] and Schattschneider [29]. Postwar studies of the same topic dealing with the general interest-group activity rather than activities specific to one bill or one group were those of Truman [34] and Gross [19]. A recent study of lobbyists as political actors is that of Milbrath [25]. Several examples of interest-group literature of the scare type are also included [5, 10, 30].

The first statistical studies of congressional behavior were of congressional roll calls, to discover their influences on congressmen. That of Turner [35] established that party considerations on many issues were more important predictors of roll-call votes than constituency. In *The Congressional Party* [33], Truman studies roll-call votes to determine the influence of party leadership and presidential preference on voting. MacRae's study of roll-call votes, using scaling techniques [24], reveals two major scales, one on foreign affairs and another on domestic policy.

Other outstanding congressional studies are hard to categorize and can perhaps best be handled with a comment about each. Dahl [11] is particularly good in discussing the pressures and information converging on the representative that affect his opinion and his views of reality as well. Young [39] in his more recent work applies ideas derived from systems theory. Freeman's short study [15] is an excellent review of interactions between Congress and executive. Carroll [8] concentrates on a specialized topic of foreign affairs and discusses the major committees of the House in respect to it. The analysis has relevance to congressional action on domestic policy as well. Harris [20] provides a thorough study and the standard work on the "advice and consent" powers of the Senate on presidential appointments.

Recently, critics of American government have argued that congressional-executive relations are out of balance. For the view that Congress has permitted the Presidency to usurp policy innovation, see Burnham [6]. A contrary view by Acheson [1] argues that Congress is in fact usurping the President's role, particularly in foreign policy making. A concise summary of executive-congressional relations is found in Egger and Harris [14]. For a discussion of the question of representation; whether a congressman votes as his constituents wish or as his conscience dictates, see Gosnell [17] and De Grazia [18]. A fictionalized version of the moral dilemmas faced by congressmen will be found in the novel *Advise and Consent* [13].

1. Acheson, Dean: *A Citizen Looks at Congress,* Harper & Row, Publishers, New York, 1956.
2. Barth, Alan: *Government by Investigation,* The Viking Press, Inc., New York, 1955.
3. Bauer, Raymond A., Ithiel de Sola Pool, and Lewis A. Dexter: *American Business and Public Policy: Politics of Foreign Trade,* Atherton Press, New York, 1963.
4. Beck, Carl: *Contempt of Congress: A Study of the Prosecutions Initiated by the Committee on Un-American Activities 1945–57,* The Hauser Press, New Orleans, La., 1959.
5. Blaisdell, Donald C.: *American Democracy under Pressure,* The Ronald Press Company, New York, 1957.
6. Burnham, James: *Congress and the American Tradition,* Henry Regnery Company, Chicago, 1959.
7. Carr, Robert K.: *The House Committee on Un-American Activities, 1945–1950,* Cornell University Press, Ithaca, N.Y., 1952.
8. Carroll, Holbert N.: *The House of Representatives and Foreign Affairs,* The University of Pittsburgh Press, Pittsburgh, Pa., 1958.
9. Chamberlain, Lawrence H.: *The President, Congress and Legislation,* Columbia University Press, New York, 1946.
10. Chase, Stuart: *Democracy under Pressure,* The Twentieth Century Fund, New York, 1945.

11. Dahl, Robert: *Congress and Foreign Policy,* Harcourt, Brace & World, Inc., New York, 1950.
12. Donner, Frank J.: *The Un-Americans,* Ballantine Books, Inc., New York, 1961.
13. Drury, Allen: *Advise and Consent,* Doubleday & Company, Inc., Garden City, N.Y., 1959.
14. Egger, Rowland, and Joseph P. Harris: *The President and Congress,* McGraw-Hill Book Company, New York, 1963.
15. Freeman, J. Leiper: *The Political Process: Executive Bureau–Legislative Committee Relations,* Random House, Inc., New York, 1960.
16. Gibson, Frank: "A Bloody Tenet Washed and Made White: An Answer to a Proposal to Give Congress More Control over the Budget," *Midwest Journal of Political Science,* 4:76–82, February, 1960.
17. Gosnell, Harold F.: *Democracy, the Threshold of Freedom,* The Ronald Press Company, New York, 1948.
18. De Grazia, Alfred: *Public and Republic,* Alfred A. Knopf, Inc., New York, 1951.
19. Gross, Bertram M.: *The Legislative Struggle,* McGraw-Hill Book Company, New York, 1953.
20. Harris, Joseph P.: *The Advice and Consent of the Senate,* University of California Press, Berkeley, Calif., 1953.
21. Herring, E. Pendleton: *Group Representation before Congress,* The Johns Hopkins Press, Baltimore, 1929.
22. Kofmehl, Kenneth: *Professional Staffs of Congress,* Purdue University Press, Lafayette, Ind., 1962.
23. Lattimore, Owen: *Ordeal by Slander,* Little, Brown and Company, Boston, 1950.
24. MacRae, Duncan, Jr.: *The Dimension of Congressional Voting,* University of California Press, Berkeley, Calif., 1958.
25. Milbrath, Lester W.: *The Washington Lobbyists,* Rand McNally & Company, Chicago, 1963.
26. Munger, Frank, and Richard F. Fenno, Jr.: *National Politics and Federal Aid to Education,* Syracuse University Press, Syracuse, N.Y., 1963.
27. Murphy, Walter F.: *Congress and the Courts,* The University of Chicago Press, Chicago, 1962.
28. Rourke, Francis E.: "Administrative Secrecy: A Congressional Dilemma," *American Political Science Review,* 54:684–694, September, 1960.
29. Schattschneider, E. E.: *Politics, Pressures, and the Tariff,* Prentice-Hall, Inc., Englewood Cliffs, N.J., 1935.
30. Schriftgiesser, Karl: *The Lobbyists,* Little, Brown and Company, Boston, 1951.
31. Steiner, Gilbert: *The Congressional Conference Committee,* The University of Illinois Press, Urbana, Ill., 1951.
32. Taylor, Telford: *Grand Inquest,* Simon and Schuster, Inc., New York, 1955.
33. Truman, David B.: *The Congressional Party,* John Wiley & Sons, Inc., New York, 1959.
34. Truman, David: *The Governmental Process,* Alfred A. Knopf, Inc., New York, 1953.
35. Turner, Julius: *Party and Constituency,* The Johns Hopkins Press, Baltimore, 1951.
36. Wallace, Robert Ash: "Congressional Control of the Budget," *Midwest Journal of Political Science,* 3:168–187, May, 1959.
37. Westerfield, Bradford: *Foreign Policy and Party Politics,* Yale University Press, New Haven, Conn., 1955.

38. Wilson, Woodrow: *Congressional Government,* Meridian Books, Inc., New York, 1956 (paperback). (Originally published in 1885.)
39. Young, Roland: *The American Congress,* Harper & Row, Publishers, New York, 1958.

Law Cases

Barenblatt v. United States, 360 U.S. 109 (1959).
Watkins v. United States, 354 U.S. 178 (1957).

Case Study Materials

1. Bailey, Stephen K.: *Congress Makes a Law,* Columbia University Press, New York, 1950.
2. Bailey, Stephen K., and Howard D. Samuel: *Congress at Work,* Holt, Rinehart and Winston, Inc., New York, 1952.
3. Berman, Daniel M.: *A Bill Becomes a Law: The Civil Rights Act of 1960,* The Macmillan Company, New York, 1962.
4. Brown, MacAlister: "The Demise of State Department Opinion Polls: A Study in Legislative Oversight," *Midwest Journal of Political Science,* 5:1–17, February, 1961.
5. Latham, Earl: *The Group Basis of Politics,* Cornell University Press, Ithaca, N.Y., 1952.
6. McDonnell, Timothy L.: *The Wagner Housing Act (of 1937),* Loyola University Press, Chicago, 1957.
7. Odegard, Peter H.: *Pressure Politics: The Story of the Anti-Saloon League,* Columbia University Press, New York, 1928.
8. Price, Hugh D.: "The Congress: Race, Religion and the Rules Committee," in Alan Westin (ed.), *The Uses of Power,* Harcourt, Brace & World, Inc., New York, 1961.
9. Redford, Emmette S.: "A Case Analysis of Congressional Activity: Civil Aviation, 1957–58," *The Journal of Politics,* 22:228–258, May, 1960.
10. Riggs, Fred W.: *Pressures on Congress,* Columbia University Press, New York, 1950.
11. Scher, Seymour: "Congressional Committee Members as Independent Agency Overseers: A Case Study," *The American Political Science Review,* 54:911–920, December, 1960.
12. Schuman, Howard E.: "Senate Rules and the Civil Rights Bill: A Case Study," *The American Political Science Review,* 51:955–975, December, 1957.

CHAPTER

16

THE PRESIDENCY

Eight inches of driving snow fell on Washington, D.C., on pre-inauguration night, 1961, while impressarios Frank Sinatra and Peter Lawford wondered if their star-studded gala would be a catastrophe. Entertainers as varied as opera singer Helen Traubel and crooner Nat "King" Cole were to perform. Leonard Bernstein was to give a tribute to the President-elect, Laurence Olivier would speak for the British, Fredric March would read from Lincoln, and Milton Berle would tell jokes. It was the beginning of a great American pageant: the inauguration of a new President.

Although there were empty seats, the gala was a success. With the President-elect and his wife in attendance, ticket sales raised $1.25 million for the Democrats. At eleven o'clock the next day, the President-elect called at the White House, and the official ceremonies began as he and the retiring President rode together to the Capitol. Prayers were offered by clergymen of the major faiths. At one point, the lectern caught fire. Poet Robert Frost, eighty-six years old, read a special composition for the occasion, the Chief Justice administered the oath of office, and the new President gave his Inaugural Address ("Let us never negotiate from fear, but let us never fear to negotiate"). After luncheon at the Capitol, the President began the procession back to the White House and took his place on the reviewing stand as a mammoth parade passed before him. Spectators shivered in the 28-degree temperature through long hours of baton twirlers, model PT boats, horseback-riding cowboys, floats from every state, Armed Forces units, and marching bands. The evening was devoted to a series of inaugural balls. Meanwhile, following the Inaugural Address, the retiring President had lunch with a few friends and quietly left the city to be driven to his farm in Gettysburg, Pennsylvania.

Thus John Fitzgerald Kennedy became the thirty-fifth President of the United States with a pomp and ceremony and political hoopla reserved for that office alone. The ceremony was unique in some respects, but also typical of those before and those to follow. The new President had called the occasion a celebration of freedom. Others were reminded of a coronation. To all, the two-day inaugural signified that the office of President was unlike any other in the United States in power and prestige.

PRESIDENTIAL FUNCTIONS

Americans distrust both a strong executive and a strong Congress. Their distrust is, in fact, of strong government itself. Yet Americans have permitted the building of a powerful central government—one of the most powerful in the world. Some citizens have thought that this has happened by accident as the nation has grown from a small cluster of former colonies into a world power. In the process, all governmental branches have gained in power, but the executive branch has been the major beneficiary of the trend.

The Growth Pattern. The growth in presidential power has been unplanned and sometimes haphazard. Like most evolutionary processes, it has not resulted from a neat theory; rather, it has been a pragmatic response to events that radically disturbed and altered accepted patterns of behavior for most Americans—rapid industrialization and urbanization, worldwide wars and threats of war, and worldwide economic depressions.

The twentieth century, for the United States, has been a period of more or less peaceful revolution and continuing readjustment. As old ways of controlling social and economic conditions have proved ineffective, new ideologies have evolved. Those of the twentieth century have encouraged government action and control through the national bureaucracy. The institution of the Presidency has been at the center of the controlling process.

The reactions to crises of past Presidents have contributed to the powers of present officeholders in a number of ways. One of the most significant ways has been through presidential interpretation of the meaning of constitutional clauses. Some interpretations are never challenged in the courts (e.g., Jackson's argument that the President could veto legislation he disapproved of, not merely legislation he thought unconstitutional). Other interpretations have been challenged, but generally they have been upheld by the courts.

New interpretations have grown out of crisis situations. As Presidents have struggled to forestall what seemed to them impending disaster, they have often added to the powers of their office. Some, like Theodore Roosevelt, have argued that it was the President's duty as steward of the people to use every power not specifically denied him by the Constitution. Others, like William Howard Taft, have viewed the President as limited to those powers expressly mentioned in the Constitution. But both men added to the powers of the office. The President's legal powers have grown through new interpretations of old powers, but also by new grants of power.

Andrew Jackson, faced by a threatened secession in South Carolina, mobilized an army of 35,000. Abraham Lincoln, with insurrection confronting him, set up a blockade of Southern ports and virtually declared war on those in rebellion. Theodore Roosevelt, faced by a coal strike that would paralyze the nation, threatened to seize the mines. Under Woodrow

Wilson, government and presidential power expanded further as America waged World War I. William Howard Taft, distressed with the "You scratch my back and I'll scratch yours" methods of budgeting, argued that waste and haphazardness would be reduced if the President, rather than Congress, drafted the national budget. Wilson supported his proposal, and the power that some regard as among the most significant held by the President was adopted in the administration of Warren G. Harding. Franklin D. Roosevelt added to the President's power to fight a depression and wage global war. Harry S Truman faced the problems of inflation while conducting a fighting war in Korea and a cold war elsewhere, and was given new powers to meet these. Even Dwight D. Eisenhower, who took the office believing presidential power must be diminished, eventually lashed out with vetoes and recommendations to Congress in a fashion that suggested America could never return to the calm and peaceful days of Rutherford B. Hayes.

The Buck Stops Here. The powers of the President have frequently been attacked as undemocratic. It is not only twentieth-century Presidents who have been accused of being dictators. Writing at the end of his first four years in office Washington said, "Every act of my administration [has been] attacked in such exaggerated and indecent terms as could scarcely be applied to a Nero." Jackson, who presided over the political maturation of the frontier, was called "King Andrew." John Wilkes Booth convinced himself that he was assassinating a despot when he shot Lincoln in Ford's Theater.

Why has the concentration of presidential power been so necessary to American government? The evolutionary process of crisis and response described above is not a complete explanation. The office was important when America had a two-ship navy and the ink on the Constitution was hardly dry.

American government, like all others, requires leadership. Democratic governments try to keep such leaders responsible to the led, but they cannot continue without leadership. The function of the democratic leader as President is to speak for all—to defend those values that, in his eyes, are in the broad political interest of the nation. In the process the President may attempt to educate the nation (as Franklin Roosevelt did concerning the menace he perceived in Hitler), or he may be educated by it (as Franklin Roosevelt was in respect to his 1937 plan to alter the institutional framework of the Supreme Court). The primary protagonists of the President in this policy-shaping process are Congress, primarily, but also the Supreme Court. The final court of appeal is national opinion—if it can be reached.

The role of national leader thrusts upon the President the necessity to innovate as well as to coordinate, and he is expected to perform both tasks symbolically as well as in fact. It requires of him a timeliness that flows out of a sensitivity to the ideology of today's political majority.

For the man who is President, for those who serve as his aides and advisers, and for his wife, the office functions as a supreme challenge. The opportunity for creating new patterns in American life is greater in the Presidency than in any other office in the nation. Citizens may imitate much that they see in the White House, from playing golf to adopting the First Lady's coiffure. The office is creative in another sense because a President works within a system of severe limitations. Opportunity is coupled with checks in a way that requires political creativity. The office is the top one in the exacting profession of politics.

The Presidency also serves a function for Congress. That body, organized to reflect the diversity of the nation, also requires a sense of national direction. The history of the nation since Washington suggests that the President alone can provide that direction. Only when he does can the critical faculty of Congress, with its intensive screening and testing of ideas, lead to something more than stalemate.

For the average citizen, presidential leadership provides a focal point in a complex governmental process, someone who is responsible for what happens. Even in periods of calm, such a focus is a necessity. In crisis (the common condition of twentieth-century America) what Sidney Hyman in his study of the Presidency has called a "common reference point" is constantly needed if citizens are to gain any sense of having policy responsive to national opinion in a government of separated powers and checks and balances.

The Presidency is the major means through which general public opinion is channeled into the policy-making process. Like congressmen, citizens require a focus for their criticism. President Harry S Truman had on his desk the motto "The buck stops here," which gets to the root of the President's function for citizens. He is nominally in charge, and the nation expects him to lead. Ever since their inception during Franklin D. Roosevelt's first administration, public-opinion surveys have revealed a typical pattern: When there is a recession, a crisis like the meat shortage of 1946, a debilitating strike, a military action in which the United States suffers reverses, or a diplomatic defeat in the cold war, the President and his political party, even if they do not control Congress, are criticized and held responsible. The President's popularity drops most sharply when the calamity is directly and immediately felt by American citizens, as when sons and fathers are drafted for military action in foreign lands or are laid off from their jobs.

A President is sometimes blamed for what is not his fault. Herbert Hoover was savagely criticized in 1932 for his actions in the early period of the Great Depression. Shack towns built by the unemployed were called "Hoovervilles." On the other hand, a President may receive credit that he does not wholly deserve, as in 1928 when Herbert Hoover was publicized as the engineer of the prosperity of the 1920s. In either case, it is he—not Congress, the Supreme Court, or the bureaucracy—who is ultimately held responsible. Leadership is the President's job.

Symbols of Legitimacy. As with Congress and the courts, symbol and ritual have developed over the years in order to preserve and reinforce, in the eyes of the people, the legitimate right of the officeholder to "execute the office of President of the United States," to use the "soft-sell" language of the Constitution.

The President lives in a museum so famous that any third-grader can recognize a picture of it, and in a tourist attraction so important that for many hours a week the public rooms are not available to the occupant. A

Figure 16-1

Symbols of Status Help to Order Society

"How about that for a status symbol?"

Drawing by Richard Decker;
© The New Yorker, Inc.

trip through the White House is designed to inspire awe and, through the use of many pictures, to remind the citizen of the nation's history.

The President has his own anthem, "Hail to the Chief." The piece has no legal standing (Mrs. John Tyler liked it and decided it should be used to signal the arrival of the Chief Executive), but it is now considered poor taste to use the tune for any other purpose. As a result, it is so seldom heard that most people probably could not whistle it if asked to, yet the *maestoso* cadence makes its symbolism evident to all attending any public meeting.

Despite the love politicians have for overly lengthy introductions (or perhaps because of it), tradition requires that the Chief Executive be introduced only by a formula that is majestic in its very simplicity: "Ladies and Gentlemen, the President of the United States!" Similarly, and in contrast to some early efforts to find an elaborate designation for him, he is addressed only as "Mr. President." When he enters a room or hall, every man, woman, and child stands; when someone comes into his presence, he need not stand, not even for a lady, unless the person is also a chief of state—for no one else is his social equal.

The President has an escort wherever he goes, a special seal of office, a ritualistic incantation by which he is vested with his powers, and an elaborate ceremonial to accompany it. In other words, he is surrounded by American adaptations of the symbols of the king. Indeed, like the king, he is above the law and cannot be arrested (however, should he break the law while President, he could be arrested and tried in ordinary court once he leaves office). All of the pomp that accompanies the President and his family in their almost totally public lives is intended, through emotional appeal, to *legitimize* his functions, to make it seem *right* that the power and the glory are his, to make it seem *proper* that his decisions be accepted or at least given the most serious consideration, not only by the bureaucracy, Congress, and the courts, but by citizens at large, even those who have not supported him at the polls.

Not all citizens are affected by or perhaps even aware of these symbols, and some do not accord deference to the President. When John F. Kennedy was assassinated in 1963, the empathetic reaction to his death was enormous, but the National Opinion Research Center discovered that 8 per cent of the adults in their sample felt no sorrow for his wife and children and 12 per cent felt none that "a strong young man had been killed at the height of his powers." While his funeral was pending, all radio and television entertainment programs were suspended—and one San Francisco television station received over 800 telephone calls in three days protesting the interruption of regular programing. Most Americans, however, see the President as more than just another man—he is the living symbol of the nation.[1]

[1] See Paul B. Sheatsley and Jacob J. Feldman, *The Assassination of President Kennedy: A Preliminary Report on Public Reactions and Behavior,* National Opinion Research Center, Chicago, 1964.

THE PRESIDENCY INSTITUTIONALIZED

The Presidency has always been more than simply the one man occupying it. The office is a complex organization of men acting within a set of traditions and citizen expectations. Some parts of it operate with only occasional direction from the man who is President.

Yet the office cannot operate entirely on an automatic pilot. It needs direction. The central question about a President is: How much capacity has he to command the resources of power within the institution of the Presidency in such a way as to exercise effective influence on the process of decision making? His has never been an easy task.

President James K. Polk (1845–1849) gave this opinion:[2]

> No president who performs his duty faithfully and conscientiously can have any leisure. If he entrusts the details and smaller matters to subordinates, constant errors will occur. I prefer to supervise the whole operations of the government rather myself than entrust the public business to subordinates, and this makes my duties very great.

Polk had been a political confidant of Andrew Jackson, Speaker of the House, and Governor of Tennessee. When he campaigned for the Presidency, he pledged himself to but one term. In his diary, he listed four major goals, including the annexation of Texas. Historians agree that, unlike most Presidents, he achieved what he sought, although he did so at great cost. In his first year he permitted only three social calls and forbade serving wine and card playing in the White House. After a time, the press of work became so great that his wife became his secretary. In the fourth year of his term he took his first vacation. Three months after he left office, he died at his home in Nashville. His age was fifty-three.

The record of more recent Presidents, excluding the special case of John F. Kennedy, has shown that the duties of office have taken their toll: Harding and Franklin Roosevelt died in office, Wilson suffered a stroke and died a few years after retirement, Coolidge died of heart disease a few years after completing his terms, and Eisenhower had a heart attack in office. During this period, only Hoover and Truman have seemed to have suffered no direct loss of good health.

Assistance for the President. George Washington was the first President to recognize that the burdens of the office of President are too great to be borne by one man alone. But getting assistance, as he found in his dealings with Hamilton and Jefferson, is not a simple matter. Many matters of concern to the Presidency cannot legally be delegated. If the President is to lead, he must also decide.

Assistance rendered to the President is of six types. It includes (1) re-

[2] Amy LaFollette Jensen, *The White House: And Its Thirty-three Families,* 2d ed., McGraw-Hill Book Company, New York, 1962.

lieving him of unimportant details of the office, such as personally signing commissions (although President Truman estimated he nevertheless signed his name 600 times a day); (2) preparing memoranda and speeches and locating information; (3) help and advice in the making of large decisions; (4) administration of policy; (5) legislative liaison; and (6) campaigning. The first two of these are generally welcomed; the last four are more difficult to delegate if the President wishes to preserve his leadership role.

Prior to the administration of Theodore Roosevelt, Presidents depended to a large extent for staff work upon Cabinet officers and other department heads. This arrangement suffered from serious limitations. Presidents can rarely be completely sure of any other man, who may himself yearn for the Presidency. Nearly all Presidents have learned that some Cabinet officers or Vice Presidents have dreams of greater glory. Under Franklin Roosevelt, there were Hopkins, Farley, Garner, and Hull; under Truman, there were Wallace, Barkley, and Harriman; under Eisenhower, there was Nixon. A lieutenant who himself wishes to assume the office may hesitate to support a President on controversial policy lest it hurt his chances of

Figure 16-2

The President's Aides Are Vulnerable

"Oh, Washington himself is all right. It's the men around him like Jefferson and Adams and..."

It has always been possible to attack the President through those around him. (By permission of Burr Shafer.)

succession. Most of those named above served their Presidents in situations that grew more tense as the end of term approached. Some resigned or were, in effect, dismissed.

A President cannot completely depend upon department heads in policy matters even when they have no presidential ambitions because he is seldom the only source of political pressure upon them. Ours is a government of pluralistic powers, which encourages individuals to act independently. Heads of departments must placate congressmen and interest groups who are vitally concerned with their departments. In the process of battling for political survival, an agency head may drift away from the President. While the President may legally remove a Cabinet officer, the political costs may be too great to be worth it.

The Executive Office. Aiding the President are a personal staff and a number of specialized agencies that have gradually been added to the Executive Office. These form the institutionalized Presidency. By 1965, the Office had over 1,000 employees.

The White House office. President Theodore Roosevelt (1901–1909) was the first President to realize that the job required a truly professional staff and that it was too confidential to be delegated to Cabinet officers. He added to his personal staff and had a wing built onto the White House to provide needed space. But staff aid for the President on a large scale dates from 1939, when the recommendations of the Committee on Administrative Management, composed of three political scientists, were adopted. The essence of the proposals was to give the President all the staff help he wished and permit him to organize it in the way he wished. He was given six major assistants and as many as 300 others. They now serve in capacities related to public relations, speech writing, patronage, legal advice, ceremonial military duties, legislative liaison, civil defense, and the budget. Some, such as the press secretaries, have become familiar figures to the readers of news (Early, Ross, Haggerty, Salinger). Most others, as the committee recommended, are expected to have a passion for anonymity.

The Bureau of the Budget. The Bureau, with some 500 employees, was established in 1921 in the Treasury Department. It was moved to the Executive Office in 1939. Its purpose was to coordinate budget requests. Today it helps the President prepare a telephone-book-sized document by screening requests from agencies and attempting to achieve the balance that the President wishes. The Budget Director thus becomes a key administrative and political lieutenant, for the level of spending the President recommends indicates the kinds of programs he wishes to emphasize. Seldom does Congress increase presidential budget requests. What the Budget Director recommends to the President is generally the maximum that can be hoped for by an agency. The Director of the Budget is appointed by the President without the consent of the Senate and serves at his pleasure.

In the twentieth century, events are controlled, if they are controlled at all, by the actions of the bureaucracy. A President's major goal is to exercise maximum influence over the hundreds of departments and agencies that carry out and often make policy. He wants to be sure he is consulted; he needs several sources of information so that he can be more than the prisoner of a single interest; and he must be able to pick out particular actions he considers important enough to merit wide attention. In all these aims, the Bureau of the Budget helps him.

The Bureau also acts on a day-to-day basis to coordinate and control administrative practice to try to make it conform to presidential wishes. From the Bureau's financial powers has grown the task of chief planning and management agency for the whole bureaucracy. It engages in studies whose impact is felt throughout the administrative branch—studies of efficient methods of business operation and of organizational structure within units. All questionnaires sent to individuals by any government agency must be cleared by the Bureau for form, content, and avoidance of duplication.

The Bureau also operates as the major legislative clearinghouse for the President. It examines all legislative proposals, clears them with affected agencies, and transmits agency opinion, with its own recommendations, to the President. It screens all agency legislative proposals to ensure their consistency with presidential policy and prepares suggested veto messages for the President to consider whenever congressional action is at variance with executive policy.

A large part of the President's capacity to exploit his potential powers for influencing policy rests on the actions of the persons in the Bureau of the Budget. They operate within a complex bureaucracy and have a special influence on it. Their authority rests formally upon legislation enacted by Congress and, more informally, upon the power, administrative style, and historical objectives of the President.

The Council of Economic Advisers. This body was established by the Full Employment Act of 1946. It consists of three members who, with the aid of a staff of experts, inform and advise the President on the health of the nation's economy. They also prepare an annual report for Congress. Members have frequently been economists with high academic status. Their recommendations have the advantage of cutting across the activities of all departments, and in this sense, they combat departmentalism by fashioning suggestions for a coordinated policy.

Office of Emergency Planning. This agency was established within the Executive Office when civil defense functions were transferred from an independent agency to the Department of Defense. In an effort to strengthen the civil defense program, in which the public had little confidence, President Kennedy placed major responsibility for it in the Department of Defense, but he added a planning and advisory agency to the Executive Office so that advice and long-range planning could be conducted under his direct scrutiny. One of the agency's functions is to plan for the coordination of the economy in the event of war (price control, priorities, rationing).

The National Security Council. The Council was created in 1947 to coordinate military and diplomatic programs. It is not formally a part of the Executive Office, but its staff work is invaluable to the President (see Chapter 21). Its members, besides the President and Vice President, are the Secretary of Defense, the Secretary of State, and the Director of the Office of Emergency Planning. Others may be invited to attend, including the Joint Chiefs of Staff, the United States representative to the United Nations, or Cabinet officers, such as the Secretary of Treasury. In effect, members of the group, aside from the President and Vice President, are ambassadors from the major administrative power complexes concerned with defense problems. Their collective decisions are not necessarily binding on the members.

The Central Intelligence Agency reports to the National Security Council, but it is now part of the Executive Office. Two other agencies are connected largely with defense needs, and are part of the Executive Office; they are the National Aeronautics and Space Council and the Office of Science and Technology.

The Institutionalized Presidency in Action. Presidential staffs have been organized in different ways. Under President Eisenhower great responsibility rested on his chief of staff, Sherman Adams—so much so that journalists occasionally argued that Adams was in many respects the actual chief. Sometimes the President in news conferences seemed unaware of the implications of policy matters that he presumably had under consideration. Adams shielded the President from outsiders, particularly after his illnesses, and during a serious illness, the office of the President operated smoothly while the Chief Executive convalesced. Following Adams's retirement (which took place under congressional pressure), the President assumed greater personal responsibilities and, in the opinion of most observers, showed a surer grasp of the policy questions he dealt with. Under President Kennedy, the office was staffed with a kind of academic brain trust (Arthur Schlesinger, Jr., Walter W. Rostow, McGeorge Bundy, and, temporarily, Richard Neustadt). This organization was designed to allow each aide easy access to the President. President Kennedy directed that any memorandum that carried with it action requirements should include a list of possible alternatives. For Eisenhower, on the other hand, memoranda were not to be over one page in length and were to contain one specific action recommendation. Eisenhower organized his staff as a military hierarchy; Kennedy established (on advice from political scientist Neustadt) a "flat" organization, which encouraged competition among essentially equal staff members. Franklin D. Roosevelt also preferred the latter arrangement. In addition, F.D.R. felt totally free to ignore both personal staff and Cabinet advisers, bypassing them altogether or sometimes making decisions directly on matters a staff member thought he was assigned to investigate.

Hence, the Presidency is today an institution rather than a single man. It is many things and it performs many roles, among the most important of which is representing the President as chief policy maker and chief administrator. Without a staff of hundreds of persons whose fundamental loyalty is to the President and whose professional status is measured largely by his successes or failures, the President's office would be a captive of Congress and the bureaucracy.

The President is provided with ample staff. Its members serve as trouble shooters and do the spadework necessary for policy formulation. He also has a choice of experts for advice on the most pressing technical problems facing him. From these, the President can build a team that operates as an extension of himself. The Presidency is thus more than a single man—it is an organization with institutionalized roles. The President does not read all his mail or dictate all the replies. No longer need he plot legislative liaison down to minute details. No longer need he write his speeches. Staff members can make the Chief Executive seem omniscient regarding current events and policy recommendations, tenderly solicitous on the death of the wife of an old party warhorse, thoughtful and inspiring in proclaiming Armed Forces Day or in opening the Red Cross fund drive, aware of intrigue in a major agency, or two strategic steps ahead of his opponents. The Executive Office operates as he wishes and it saves his energy—it anticipates his wishes on the basis of past positions he has taken. When the President is absent or ill, it may even, under trusted aides, operate for a time as if the President himself were in active command.

But exercise of political power cannot be extended indefinitely. The ultimate power source is the President, and without his active and relatively direct support, a staff member lacks power.

Staff members are loyal because they owe their positions entirely to presidential choice. They have no outside sources of political support. For this reason, while they have been highly useful as trouble shooters, they are less effective in achieving policy objectives. Normally, the only political influence they possess is that provided by the President himself. Staff helps the President to make effective use of the power resources he already possesses, but it alone is not enough to enable the President to achieve his goals. He also needs the help of others who possess power in their own right.

POWER AND RESPONSIBILITY

While he generally must take responsibility for what happens, the President does not have a neat and logical package of legal powers sufficient to deal with every problem that arises. In some cases, he is checked on what seem to be points of relatively minor importance, while on other matters of crucial importance, he acts with a free hand. The power to veto any single item, set up to prevent legislative riders to appropriation bills, is held by forty-one state governors and was given to the President of the

Confederate States, but is denied the President. Yet the same President can, without consulting anyone, decide that the United States will recognize a new government abroad or will send troops into an area of the world where their presence may threaten war. President Truman alone decided to drop the atomic bomb and to send troops into Korea, yet he was denied by the Senate his choice for representative to the United Nations. President Eisenhower, acting unilaterally, sent troops to Lebanon, but was denied his first choice in seeking to fill a vacancy for Secretary of Commerce.

Legal powers are not the only powers, nor are the legal checks the only checks on the President. President Eisenhower's warm smile, which added tremendously to his voter appeal, was perhaps as important for achieving his aims as some of his formal powers. But a national wave of criticism of "payola" was to deprive the President of his right-hand man, though legally the President had the power to retain him in office and, in fact, announced that he wished to do so.

The President, being held responsible for national security, is generally among the first to want action when trouble threatens. Congress legally holds the initiative, but informally it looks to the President for initiative. On the other hand, Congress can permanently block the President's program, as it has on domestic issues for many Presidents. It can override his veto and, through this negative behavior, make policy. It has done so several times in history—on such important issues as the Taft-Hartley and McCarran-Walter Immigration Acts during the Truman administration. A government of checks and balances, such as ours, is balanced in favor of preserving the *status quo*. Innovation must prove itself. The President, who generally campaigns for change, is thus at a disadvantage.

The President's Many Hats. In describing the President's formal powers, it has been customary to say that he wears several hats: the Homburg of the ceremonial Chief of State, the peaked hat of the Commander in Chief of the Armed Forces, the top hat as chief diplomat, and other hats as chief legislator, chief administrator, political party chief, and chief citizen of the United States.

This is a convenient way of sorting out the list of the President's legal or informal powers, but it also tends to obscure presidential activity. The President is still a man, not a sociological concept that flits from role to role. He frequently is skillful enough to use one role to achieve a goal under another, for example, to use his role as Commander in Chief to gain a domestic goal. Thus Franklin Roosevelt used the war power to set up a Federal Fair Employment Practices Commission to discourage job discrimination because of race. The roles may also be in conflict in a given situation, and the President must choose the one most suitable to his goals.

The importance of the role concept is that these roles are recognized as legitimate ones for a President. When the President figuratively strikes a stance and talks in the accustomed phrases of a particular role, what he says has a familiar ring of authority. His power to act in this role is accepted by Americans as legitimate. These roles, with their formal powers, are something like masks. Behind each mask is a very human person manipulating the roles and the powers associated with each to achieve the very human ends he desires.

Chief of State. The President is the equivalent of a king—the father image for his countrymen. He is the ceremonial head of the nation, who proclaims its national holidays, receives its distinguished guests, grants special recognition to its heroes, and inspects its achievements. In this role he formally represents the whole nation and is therefore above politics. These responsibilities of the office may be a trial, as Herbert Hoover noted when he complained of a swollen right hand after several days of greeting citizens. They may also be politically useful. One of the weapons used by President Eisenhower against Senator Joseph R. McCarthy was to refuse him invitations to White House social affairs. Louis Adamic was so pleased with his invitation to the White House for dinner during World War II that he wrote a book about the event. Presidents have skillfully used the White House inspection tour to repair political fences and build up support for their programs or for their reelection. They find dams to be dedicated each election year and take advantage of Fourth of July addresses to put in plugs for treasured legislation bottled up in Congress. President Roosevelt fed the King and Queen of England hot dogs, and somehow this seemed to symbolize the growing together of the United States and Great Britain in the dark days before World War II.

These are but a few examples of the possibilities of this official role. A complete listing of its legal components could hardly reveal its political potentialities. The ceremonial and social aspects of this role are often nuisances that take the President from more important things, but they also provide occasions for furthering his goals. And always, no matter what the circumstances, he is the President of the whole nation, to some degree above politics, a solid rock in time of crisis, a symbol of unity against the enemies of the Republic, the guardian of our most cherished values.

Chief legislator. The President is deeply involved in the legislative process and is, indeed, judged by his ability to secure enactment of a legislative program. He has a veto that can be overridden only by a two-thirds vote in both houses of Congress. With this weapon, he can do more than threaten to block action. He may bargain, threatening a veto unless changes are made in pending legislation. He may also write messages that can be used as campaign fodder. Congressional supporters of Andrew Jackson moved that 15,000 copies of his veto of the national bank charter be printed. These were used in his reelection campaign. President Truman made similar use of his Taft-Hartley rejection in 1948. The veto may also be used to harass or to remind congressmen of presidential power. President Franklin D. Roosevelt is reported to occasionally have asked the Bureau of the Budget to find some bills of particular importance to individual congressmen for him to veto. A legislator who continually annoys the President may find none of his bills of parochial concern becoming law.

Most of the policy that interests the President concerns broad national issues, for these are the interests of his constituency. In this respect the congressman is vulnerable, for his paramount interest is his own career and his district. Presidents have often openly bought support, as Grover Cleveland did when he exchanged some patronage appointments for three votes on a tariff measure. Another technique is to use or threaten to use the big stick, as in this case from the Kennedy administration:[3]

> Representative Gerald R. Ford, Michigan Republican, and other Republican lawmakers said defense contractors from their districts had called them to suggest they vote for the higher debt limit (requested by the President) so the Defense Department would not have to cut back on contracts. The contractors were given to understand that their contracts would be the ones to suffer unless their Congressmen voted "right" on the issue.

The congressman is especially vulnerable when he introduces private bills or runs errands for his constituents that require cooperation of the executive department. Action can be expedited if the right contact is made. "One day I told him [President Franklin Roosevelt] that I needed a new road in the southern part of my district," Joseph Martin, the Republican floor leader of the House and bitter critic of the Democratic President, has written. "He called in Louis McHenry Howe. 'Louis' he said, 'Call MacDonald [Thomas H. MacDonald of the Bureau of Public Roads] and tell him I am sending down a black Republican and I want him to give him a road.' And I got it."[4]

The President also has the choice of allowing a bill to become law without his signature, thus expressing his displeasure with and lack of responsibility for it. Or he may let a bill passed near the end of the session die without any action. This is called the pocket veto.*

***POCKET VETO. Disapproval of a bill passed in the last ten days of a session. No veto message is required. The President simply does not sign it.**

The President may call Congress into special session at his discretion. President Truman recognized the political potential of this power when he called back a Republican-dominated Congress after the Republican National Convention had met and dared it to adopt legislation called for in the platform its party had just adopted. He was attempting to convince voters that liberal platform planks were merely window dressing so far as Republican congressmen were concerned.

[3] "Debt Bill Brings 'Blackmail' Cry," *The New York Times,* June 14, 1962.

[4] Joseph Martin, *My First Fifty Years in Politics,* McGraw-Hill Book Company, New York, 1960, p. 71.

Since 1921, the President has been responsible for the preparation of a budget that is submitted to Congress as his recommendation for expenditures. Items that are omitted can only with some difficulty be added. Those with low requests can seldom be raised unless there is a special reason for widespread congressional support. (Such agencies as the FBI and the National Institutes of Health have had their appropriations raised by Congress.) But usually Congress attempts to reduce the requests; in doing so, it must justify itself in the face of presidential arguments. The major advantage for the President lies in the fact that a budget is necessarily also a major policy statement. In making recommendations for expenditures, the President maps out a political program that forms the basis for congressional debate. It may be rejected in part, but the initiative for overall policy remains in the hands of the Chief Executive.

The annual State of the Union address to Congress (and the nation) in which he lists his recommendations for legislation and points with pride to claims of accomplishments is a major presidential lever. Since Franklin Roosevelt, Presidents have come to Congress in person. Presidents may also deliver special messages on particular topics, and these are frequently followed by specific bills that are introduced by friendly congressmen.

In sum, the President and his administration prepare a program that is the point of departure for almost every policy discussion in Congress. For the good of the party in the next election, party members will tend to rally around the President and attempt to give him something of what he asks for. While he is never wholly supported, he is seldom completely abandoned. Many of his suggestions may be rejected outright, but they can seldom be ignored—and the very fact of negative action gives the President and his supporters an issue with which to go to the people.

Chief administrator. In a complex society, extensive powers are placed in the hands of the government bureaucracy. In American government, this bureaucracy is nominally under the formal control of the President, whose very title is Chief Executive. However, counterforces also play on bureaucrats, encouraging their independence, sometimes of all arms of government, more frequently of the President. The President is legally responsible for the acts of most of the bureaucracy (President Kennedy was blamed for the activities of Billie Sol Estes in relation to the programs of the Department of Agriculture). But the President is far from having absolute power over government agencies.

The efficient exploitation of administrative powers is, nevertheless, a major source of presidential influence. Through such authority, major policy has been implemented. Thus Presidents Roosevelt, Truman, Eisenhower, Kennedy, and Johnson, faced with a Congress reluctant to extend rights for minority groups, extended such rights through full-employment commissions, government hiring and contract policies, appointment of Negro administrators, government loan policy, and other procedures.

The President is given the power to appoint the administrative heads of the major government departments, but usually only with the consent of the Senate. He may remove these officials simply by dismissing them. This is the principal legal basis of his administrative power. In the case of the regulatory agencies that have powers of a somewhat judicial or legislative character, such as the Interstate Commerce Commission or the Federal Power Commission, the President also makes the appointments with Senate approval. But his authority to remove such officials is generally limited by legislation. Even when it is not so limited, the Supreme Court has ruled that members can be removed only for cause and after notice and hearing on charges of improper actions. (*Humphrey's Executor v. United States.*) In a third category, the President is authorized to appoint many minor officials, and thus controls patronage that is of interest to congressmen.

The power of budget preparation gives the President another effective power over administration. Few agencies have enough support in Congress to secure appropriations higher than those requested in the presidential budget. Administrators know very well that, with few exceptions, if the President opposes them, their chances of securing financial support are markedly decreased.

Since President Franklin Roosevelt's administration, the Budget Bureau has been responsible for central clearance procedure for all proposed legislation from Federal agencies. Before a recommendation receives the President's blessing, it must pass this clearance. Agencies may informally bypass the process if they are asked questions in congressional hearings, but can seldom hope for success if they do. Such action invites presidential pressures against a proposal. Affected agencies are also asked to comment on all legislation passed before the President acts. He is free to ignore their comments, but the procedure is useful in building up support for him and in planning the budget that invariably must follow the next year.

The power to alter the formal pattern of the agencies of government by approving plans for reorganization submitted by departments and presenting them to Congress also belongs to the President. In most cases, a change must be made by a regular act. However, since 1939 and especially in connection with the recommendations of the two Hoover commissions, Congress has provided a unique procedure and has extended it from time to time: If the President's recommendations for reorganization are not rejected in sixty days in either house, they become effective. This power can represent life or death for an agency. It may also determine program emphasis. For years, as his diaries testify, Secretary of Interior Harold Ickes schemed to have the Forest Service transferred from the Department of Agriculture to his department. Franklin Roosevelt was said to have retained Ickes's support in part because he always held out to the Secretary the possibility of a reorganized Department of Conservation. For bureaucrats, the threat of a reorganization, with its implications for new and unpredictable relationships, budgets, and powers can seem like a nightmare. They prefer to initiate proposals for such plans and hence to control change.

By constitutional mandate, the President has the traditional administrative powers of inspection and requiring reports. These may be combined with his command of the headlines to create acute embarrassment for an administrator—or to make him a hero.

But these powers are not absolute for, in our pluralist system, the President is not the only source of power. Some agencies, such as the Air Force and the Veterans Administration, have made end runs around the President to secure increased appropriations from Congress. A few individuals, such as J. Edgar Hoover of the FBI, have such personal prestige that they could be dismissed only at great political cost by a President. Some agencies are exceptionally cross-pressured. Their heads know that if they administer a law as vigorously, weakly, or prejudicially as the President desires, they may be penalized because Congress disagrees with him. Congressional disapproval may be shown by the cutting of appropriations, by reducing agency powers, or even by eliminating the agency.

To summarize, administrators commonly respect presidential desires, but they know that the President is not the only source of political power. Support in Congress, by powerful interest groups, or through popularity among the general citizenry can serve as a wall behind which an administrator can partially protect himself from the claims or wants of the President. As General Douglas MacArthur discovered, however, Presidents can seldom be successfully and openly defied even by national heroes, much less by more commonplace administrators.

Commander in Chief. The President is head of all armed services. Despite occasional "Great Debates" in Congress, he may legally dispatch them where he wishes. Theodore Roosevelt sent the Navy halfway around the world and left it up to Congress to appropriate funds to get it back home. Abraham Lincoln, as a congressman, faced the frustration of opposing President James Knox Polk's war with Mexico, but having to support appropriations to ensure victory. Once fighting has begun, the congressman must help preserve the nation's honor.

Decisions by Eisenhower to send troops to Lebanon, by Truman to use atomic bombs on Hiroshima and Nagasaki, and by Franklin Roosevelt to name Eisenhower rather than other generals of greater seniority to head the Normandy invasion, were all made by Presidents in their role as Commander in Chief. Such decisions have great political implications, as the first administrations of our nation indicated. In those days, a major question dividing the parties was whether to wage war against France. Under Thomas Jefferson, the Democratic-Republicans favored neutrality. John Adams's Federalist administration had waged undeclared sea war with France. Franklin Roosevelt, in arranging a trade with Great Britain of "over-age" destroyers for leases on military bases, illustrated the political potential of the role. Domestically, Grover Cleveland's use of Federal troops to protect the mails ("The mail must go through") broke the 1894 Pullman strike led by the Socialist leader Eugene Debs.

As Commander in Chief, the President protects the democratic principle of subordinating the military to the civilian government. Presumably, he could have designed for himself an elaborate uniform and could take personal command of armies in the field. No President has done so, but both Lincoln and Franklin Roosevelt involved themselves in military-strategy decisions.

Sometimes the role of Commander in Chief has proved useful for achieving nonmilitary ends. Abraham Lincoln, involved in a close fight for reelection, suggested to General William T. Sherman that, if possible, troops from Indiana be furloughed in time for the state's elections. Sherman found it possible. Overall, however, the power has been used less in domestic policy battles than in backing the administration policy in foreign affairs.

Chief diplomat. In addition to the constitutional power to make treaties with foreign nations, which require ratification by a two-thirds vote of the Senate, the President may enter into less formal executive agreements. President Roosevelt's destroyer deal with Great Britain fitted into this category; so did Monroe's plan to disarm the border with Canada. Executive agreements may be used to avoid bringing the Senate into the decision-making process, but they may be repudiated by Congress if an appropriation is required to carry them out.

The President also sends and receives representatives to and from foreign nations. This is the power that enables him to recognize or break off diplomatic relations. His choice of diplomats must be ratified by the Senate, but most of them are accepted with little debate.

These powers, combined with the role of Commander in Chief, make the President an impressive representative in foreign negotiations. He cannot declare war, but he can involve the nation in actual fighting and can follow a policy with potential enemies that makes war almost certain, as did Polk, Lincoln, McKinley, Wilson, and Franklin Roosevelt. Only in the War of 1812 was congressional initiative important to the beginning of hostilities. He also guides peaceful relations, and given the reluctance of Americans to repudiate their representative in such negotiations in recent times, his policies are generally accepted. In modern diplomacy, disaster would often threaten the nation if the President were not given support by most congressmen and citizens when he is actually engaged in delicate dealings with allies and antagonists.

A series of Supreme Court decisions has recognized the President's primary responsibility in the conduct of foreign relations. Political realities, however, make it necessary for him to carry the Congress with him, since its role in respect to implementing policies through appropriations is of major importance.

Unofficial roles. Two roles are played by the President that are not based on legal powers or duties of the office: chief party leader and chief citizen.

Chief of the party. The President has only one important formal power in respect to his party. By custom, he has the right to select its national chairman, who functions generally as his spokesman. But the President's real influence depends on his position as a national leader affiliated with a political party. National prestige can be used to persuade congressmen or the confederation of state party groups that is called the national party to support his position. His sources of power are rooted in the favors he can grant, in patronage, and in his usefulness to candidates as a party symbol. Many Presidents have indicated their displeasure with particular local party chieftains by channeling patronage around them. There are limits to this technique when the state party has elected a United States senator, however. President Eisenhower made effective use of himself as party symbol when he invited selected Republicans to come to the White House and have pictures taken with him—pictures that could be useful in a campaign. Obstructive Republicans were not included on his list. Since about three-fourths of all congressional nominees increase their margin of victory when their presidential nominee wins, the coattails of a likely winner are significant. This is particularly true if it is evident that the candidate is more popular than his party. In 1952, Candidate Eisenhower for a while avoided endorsement of Senator William Jenner of Indiana. When Eisenhower did appear in Indiana, reporters said Senator Jenner followed him around all day "like a bird dog."

The President also has the power to put pressure on the party, for most party candidates feel that, if they are to win marginal races, he can hardly be openly repudiated. Thus most Presidents can secure a second-term nomination even in the face of opposition, as President Truman did in 1948, and can have an effect on the platform provisions and occasionally some influence on nominations even after leaving office. Theodore Roosevelt and Andrew Jackson were able to select their successors and get them nominated. Other Presidents have been less successful, but their endorsement is still prized. President Truman's endorsement of Averell Harriman in the 1956 convention did not give Harriman the nomination, but it did spotlight his candidacy. Four years earlier, as President, Truman's not-quite-open support of Stevenson gave the latter's reluctant candidacy all the boost it needed. In 1960, Richard M. Nixon was annoyed and confused by Eisenhower's reluctance to "interfere" in the process, even though Nixon was "acceptable" to him. Nixon feared this unusual laissez-faire approach might encourage potential competitors.[5]

Yet the President has very little party power where he desires it most—in the nomination of senators and representatives. Every President has to contend with members of his own party who are intent on scuttling his program. Many of them come from static districts and are not worried

[5] Richard M. Nixon, *Six Crises,* Doubleday & Company, Inc., Garden City, N.Y., 1962.

about the President's refusal to campaign for them. Some Presidents have been tempted to intercede in the primaries. The last full-scale attempt was in 1938, when President Roosevelt sought to purge certain Democrats who had consistently opposed his program. His only success was in his home state of New York. President Truman interceded in Kansas City and in a Missouri senate race with little success. (In one case, the Democrat was purged, but a Republican won the general election.) The prohibition against outside interference tends to boomerang against any candidate the President openly endorses against an incumbent. People are inclined to feel, "The selection of a congressman from this district is a matter for the people of the district."

Chief citizen. Of every President that historians have later called great, it can be said, as it was of George Washington, "He was first in the hearts of his countrymen." Great Presidents somehow achieve a symbolic status as spokesmen for the average citizen. The President's voice is the voice of the people. Washington, Jefferson, Jackson, Lincoln, Theodore Roosevelt, Woodrow Wilson, and Franklin Roosevelt all had this quality above others, and these are the Presidents whom historian Arthur Schlesinger, Sr., places at the head of his list of great Presidents. Few would dispute his selection at this level.

A President achieves the chief citizen role primarily by keeping close to the public mood. Thus Lincoln preferred to keep official visitors waiting while he talked to his wife's relatives from the South. Franklin Roosevelt cultivated a sense of intimacy with citizens through his radio fireside chats—the very name chosen for these addresses symbolized the relationship he was attempting to establish. (It is the image conjured that is important—in 1933, not many Americans had fireplaces and no one huddled near a space heater would say that he was at "the fireside.") The task is not easy, however. Kennedy complained, after one year in office, that he learned nothing directly, that he was isolated, and that all of his information was filtered through the bureaucracy and his personal staff.

The role of chief citizen requires more than a sharing of information. As Theodore Roosevelt said, the President holds an office of moral leadership. (The Presidency, he said, "is a bully pulpit.") He must dramatize that leadership. Citizens regard him not only as a symbol of the norm, but as one of their dominant aspirations. The effective President somehow voices the idealism of the nation, a vision of what the nation should be. But he walks a fine line because whenever he converts ideals into specific policy proposals, he leaves the role of chief citizen and becomes a party spokesman and a center of controversy. He performs the role best when he congratulates an astronaut on his latest achievement; or dedicates a hydroelectric dam, which, to millions of power users, will represent "progress"; or declares that Americans want happiness and prosperity for all mankind; or denounces those who somehow have been caught making "outrageous" profits; or speaks in favor of motherhood, childhood, full employment, and adequate security in "the golden years"; or assures the world that America wants nothing more than peace, but that she will not stand idly by if her honor is at stake.

REMOVAL AND SUCCESSION

The President can, as noted in the previous chapter, be removed from office by the slow and agonizing process of impeachment. The original intent of this provision, however, was only to rid the nation of a Chief Executive guilty of "high crimes and misdemeanors," neither of which is likely to be committed by a person who has survived the screening process that has been established for the job (see Chapter 11). The power of impeachment, in any case, was never intended to be used to remove a person who is physically or mentally incompetent or to get rid of a President with whom the leaders of Congress disagree politically. Other than in the rarest of circumstances, as discussed below, future Presidents will be removed only by the voters at election time, by retirement, or by death.

Presidential Incapacity. The question of determining when a President is too incapacitated to handle his duties is unsolved. To permit someone else to make this decision is to hold a political club over the President. To make no provision opens up the possibility of the nation having no actual President, with the President's staff or some self-appointed group making the decisions. This has happened in the past, during the period of President Eisenhower's heart attack, during the long period when President Wilson was recovering from a stroke, and during the four months that President Garfield languished after being shot by an assassin. For a time, the Presidency as an institution can continue to function when the individual himself is incapacitated. But this time period is surely a limited one. No President has ever gone insane or become senile, and perhaps the method of selection makes such eventualities unlikely, but they could happen. Such things have happened to kings, prime ministers, congressmen, and Supreme Court justices. Any citizen can, with little effort, mentally picture some of the problems that might arise if a man who holds vast powers relative to the domestic economy and who is the nation's most important single shield against the threat of nuclear warfare should become psychotic but refuse to resign. (No President has ever resigned, but it is generally believed that there is nothing in the Constitution that prevents him from doing so.)

The only suggestion relative to the problem that has substantial political support calls for a special council consisting of congressional leaders and Supreme Court justices to rule on the President's competence, but whether a regency would be permanent or only until the President recovered his faculties has not been explored. Thus far, Americans have been content to leave to each President the procedures he wants followed should he become incapacitated or be reported missing, as could happen in time of war. Both Presidents Eisenhower and Kennedy had written understandings with their Vice Presidents that called for mutual agreement as to the passing of responsibility. The transfer of power was to be temporary and to end by the unilateral decision of the President. This type of agreement is satisfactory for many hypothetical situations, but it does not solve the problem when a President is comatose or psychotic or when, as was the case under Johnson after the assassination of President Kennedy, there is no Vice President. Nevertheless, two students of the Presidency, Richard Neustadt and Sidney Hyman, in testimony before a Senate committee in 1964 recommended that Congress sanction the idea of such informal agreements rather than the adoption of constitutional procedures that might prove too rigid in specific situations.

The Heir Apparent. One observer, seeing the Vice President who served under Grover Cleveland said, "There goes the Vice President of the United States with nothing on his mind but the health of the President." Times have changed and the Vice President has become busier, but the statement still contains an essential truth. The Vice President's major function is to be ready to take over—and eight of our thirty-five Presidents have succeeded from the lesser office. Seven of our Vice Presidents have themselves died in office.

The Vice President is not generally selected for his qualities as a successor, however. And those who would succeed to the office if both President and Vice President should die are even farther removed from the general electorate or from selection for the strenuous duties of the Chief Executive. No one but a Vice President has ever moved up, but one would have, had Wendell Willkie and his running mate, Senator Charles McNary, won in 1940. Both were dead in less than four years. During President Truman's first term, in the year 1947–1948, the successor to the office would have been Speaker of the House Joseph Martin, who was of the opposite party. If the Speakership is vacant, the succession passes to the President pro tempore of the Senate. Following these officials are the members of the Cabinet, beginning with the Secretary of State and proceeding in the order in which Cabinet posts were created.

Between 1878 and 1947, the succession after the Vice President was to the Secretary of State, a prestigeful person whose views on at least some matters would be similar to those of the late President. Truman, however, wanted the heir to be an elected officeholder. Whether it is more democratic to choose a man from a politically noncompetitive district (as is almost always the case with the Speaker's constituency) who may have views far different from those of the dead President than to choose the late leader's trusted aide is perhaps a moot point. It would certainly be difficult to argue that the representative of a suburban constituency in Massachusetts (Joseph Martin) or of South Boston (John McCormack) was also representative of what Americans wanted in the White House. Congress, in any case, was glad to give precedence to some of its own members over Cabinet officers. After President Kennedy was assassinated in 1963, ex-President Truman continued to argue for the act he had asked for in 1947, while ex-President Eisenhower argued for a return to the act of 1878.

The Founding Fathers debated long on how to find a successor for the Presidency and decided on the office of Vice President only in the last weekend of the convention. Some have suggested that, rather than being elected for a four-year term, a Vice President serve only until the next election of House members, a maximum of two years, after which time the Speaker would become the first in line. Perhaps the reason for the lack of concern about the problem is that the Vice Presidents who have succeeded to the Presidency have not been failures as Presidents. Some, like Theodore Roosevelt, Calvin Coolidge, Harry Truman, and Lyndon Johnson, have been able to claim that they were successful, at least in the minds of many citizens, because they were subsequently elected in their own right. Others, like Tyler, Fillmore, Arthur, and Andrew Johnson, are ranked by historians as better than or at least no worse than those who either preceded or succeeded them.

The President Needs Help—Political Help. The unevenness of the President's great legal powers, the importance of informal powers and checks, and the President's desire for action make the presidential office one that requires political artistry if its occupant is to achieve many of his aims. Each President faces the problem of somehow matching his responsibilities with effective action, using whatever tools are at hand. His job is one of building coalitions through compromise and bargaining.

The President operates in a pluralistic system—much of what he wants to accomplish must be approved by Congress. Finding someone who has influence with congressional committee chairmen and who will at the same time be loyal to the President is difficult. Regular candidates for the role—depending on the issue and situation—are the Vice President, members of the Cabinet, and the elected congressional leaders (the Speaker and party leaders in both Houses). The President usually must act according to the issue that faces him. He will rarely be completely bereft of support by all of the above officials, but at crucial points he may feel himself to be abandoned.

THE VICE PRESIDENT AS POLITICAL AIDE

The Founding Fathers intended the vice presidency to be an important office, and after the first three presidential elections, it was. The Vice President was the candidate receiving the second largest number of electoral votes, and the two men to occupy the office, Adams and Jefferson, later became Presidents. Then in 1800, Thomas Jefferson and Aaron Burr, running as a political team, received the same number of electoral votes; and a great battle to break the tie followed in the House (see Chapter 4).

The Twelfth Amendment was designed to accommodate the constitutional system to the realities of party politics. From that time onward, the number-two man was not the candidate of the opposite party who had just been defeated for the Presidency. The electors were required to vote for President and Vice President as a team.

The candidate for the vice presidency was generally chosen by the presidential nominee to pay off a political debt or gain campaign votes. Occasionally, the office has been given to the runner-up at the party convention or to a representative from a party faction other than that of the presidential nominee; to an old man in order to balance a young one or, vice versa; or to a man from the West if the chief nominee came from the East. Nominee Kennedy, who had had a strained relationship with Lyndon Johnson, defended his selection of a running mate to the aghast Adlai Stevenson: "Because I want to win, and Lyndon can carry the South."

There has been a gradual change in the office since World War I, a change stressing the Vice President's potential as an assistant in policy matters. Wilson asked his Vice President to attend Cabinet meetings, and since Franklin Roosevelt's time, this custom has been firmly established. In 1928, Congress gave the Vice President some patronage in appointments to the Armed Forces academies. In 1949, he was made a member of the National Security Council; the office permits him to become acquainted with the most important military matters being discussed within the administration, information that is of great importance should he suddenly be called upon to assume the top spot, as was Lyndon Johnson.

The Vice President's official duty is to preside over the Senate, and by his rulings he has often helped the President's program. John N. Garner, formerly Speaker of the House, in the first days of the Roosevelt administration was especially effective in shepherding New Deal legislation through the Senate. (In Roosevelt's second term, a disillusioned Garner was effective in helping to block the President's program.)

Presidents have added other duties to the Vice President's role. Richard Nixon indicated that less than 10 per cent of his time was spent in presiding over the Senate. Garner was the first Vice President to make a good-will tour abroad as a presidential emissary, an assignment each successor has accepted. The Vice President is also useful for ceremonial functions at home as the official representative of the President. Franklin Roosevelt experimented by giving Henry Wallace administrative responsibilities as head of war agencies and, for a short period, an office designed for coordination of the administration. The latter experiment was not a success, but subsequently Presidents have placed Vice Presidents in charge of some administrative functions. President Eisenhower added to the Vice President's duties those of campaigning for Republicans in mid-term elections. His lack of success may discourage other incumbents from accepting this burden.

The limitations of the Vice President as a political aide are several. Although he often owes his original selection to the presidential nominee, sometimes it is a choice severely limited by a convention agreement, as was the case with Garner and Truman under Roosevelt, or by the political demands of the campaign as was the case with Johnson under Kennedy. The product of such calculations could conceivably be a political enemy later, as was the case with Dawes under Coolidge. The Vice President is also independent in that he has a four-year term and thus cannot be dismissed by the President. The Vice President also has one foot in Congress. This can be an advantage to the President, but it can also be a disadvantage, depending upon which group the Vice President identifies with in the case of a showdown. Despite these limitations, Presidents have increasingly attempted to win over the Vice Presidents as their supporters and have made them members of their official families.

CABINET MEMBERS AS POLITICAL AIDES

The heads of ten government departments are by tradition regarded as the Cabinet. The name of the body comes from the committee of the majority party (or sometimes, coalition) in the British Parliament, a group that heads the major departments, dominates policy making in the legislative body, and includes most of the important party leaders. It is crucial to the British constitutional system. The American Cabinet, on the other hand, is not mentioned in the Constitution and is not important today even in the unwritten Constitution. It has no legal existence at all. It was created informally by President Washington to provide him with a body of advisers.

The members serve at the pleasure of the President and meet only at his call. In some administrations, the Cabinet has met twice a week, but often Presidents have permitted long periods to elapse without a session. Under Kennedy, there were only fifteen meetings in the first year of his administration. He placed less value on this body as an advisory group than did Eisenhower. In order of their relative prestige (roughly the chronological order in which their positions were created and their rank in presidential succession), the members are the Secretaries of State, Treasury, and Defense, the Attorney General, the Postmaster General, the Secretaries of Interior, Agriculture, Commerce, Labor, and Health, Education, and Welfare. The permanent representative to the United Nations was also given Cabinet status at the request of Adlai Stevenson as a condition for taking the job. Other executive officials also regularly meet with the Cabinet, including the Budget Director, Chairman of the Council of Economic Advisers, special assistants to the President, and sometimes heads of important agencies not considered to be at Cabinet level.

What Is the Cabinet? The Cabinet is commonly thought of as the President's official family, which helps him in coordinating administration and gives him advice. It has not always worked out this way. The Cabinet is, first of all, a creature of the President; it has no independent status or collegial responsibility, although the Chief Executive is not the only influence on its membership. This fact may be observed in connection with Warren Harding's administration: A number of Cabinet members resigned under fire, and one was subsequently imprisoned, but this had no effect on the prestige of those who were not involved and therefore blameless.

The President is limited in Cabinet selection by political rather than legal considerations. First of all, the man he wants for a specific post may refuse to accept, and he may have to act quickly to close the gap. This happened in the case of Harold Ickes, Secretary of the Interior under Franklin Roosevelt. His only ambition was to be Commissioner of Indian Affairs. After the refusal of several others, Roosevelt selected him for the Cabinet post on the basis of a single short meeting. A Cabinet post may entail financial hardship and does not usually offer the opportunity to rise. Few congressmen return to Congress from the Cabinet, as Clinton Anderson did. Few Cabinet members become President, as Herbert Hoover did. Most drop away into obscurity.

The President's Team? The President's choices are also limited by considerations of political balance. He may wish to represent members of opposing political factions. President Kennedy chose Orville Freeman for Secretary of Agriculture, even though Freeman was a strong ally of his convention rival, Hubert Humphrey. President Lincoln named Seward and Chase to key positions. They had wanted the Presidency. More simply, the Cabinet spot may be given to pay off political debts, particularly those made to secure the nomination. Geographic consideration also counts. The Midwest expects to control Agriculture; the West, Interior. Businessmen want a businessman in Commerce and the Treasury, and unions want at least a veto over the choice for Labor. The political party organization wants to select the Postmaster General. The department once offered vast patronage, still supplies some, and frequently the national committeeman serves as Postmaster General. It is considered good strategy to appoint a woman to a major post, to select from a number of religious and ethnic backgrounds, and to include several ex-congressmen in order to keep in the good graces of that body. Under some conditions, it may be wise to select members of the opposition party, as Franklin Roosevelt did during World War II, and Kennedy did in selecting a Secretary of Defense and of the Treasury. Johnson retained both.

Sometimes a Cabinet member, because of such considerations, can operate in virtual independence of the President. For example, Jesse Jones served as businessman-representative in the Franklin Roosevelt administration for over ten years. He was particularly important to the President because of his political influence with congressmen and businessmen. On a number of occasions he differed openly with the President, although serving as his Secretary of Commerce. Roosevelt could not, however, afford to have him resign because Jones had important political supporters.

Josephus Daniels, an aide to Franklin Roosevelt, described the independent position of some Cabinet members as follows:[6]

> Half of a President's suggestions which theoretically carry the weight of orders, can be safely forgotten by a Cabinet member. And if the President asks about a suggestion a second time, he can be told that it is being investigated. If he asks a third time, a wise Cabinet officer will give him at least part of what he suggests. But only occasionally, except about the most important matters, do Presidents ever get around to asking three times.

Following the 1944 election, Jesse Jones was dismissed because Roosevelt was convinced that Jones had worked to throw the Texas delegation against him. Nevertheless, the quotation illustrates how, under certain conditions, a powerful President may be confounded by a sometimes useful Cabinet member.

Why Ten Agency Heads? An additional weakness in the Cabinet as an institution results from its somewhat arbitrary makeup. The Post Office, Interior, Commerce, and Labor departments were once among the principal agencies shaping governmental decisions. Today there are many newer agencies, some of them large in personnel, that probably have an impact as great or greater than that of the Cabinet on the American economy and way of life, although they are not represented in that group. Some of them are the Central Intelligence Agency, the National Aeronautics and Space Administration, the Federal Reserve Board, the Housing and Home Finance Agency, the Veterans Administration, for example.

When the government accepted responsibility for the policing of labor-management relations during the Franklin Roosevelt administration, the task was assigned to a new and independent agency, the National Labor Relations Board (NLRB). (Congressional leaders feared the Secretary of Labor was too often beholden to big labor and hence not a "neutral referee.") The Secretary of Labor continued in his historical role of presiding over what was essentially a data-gathering and publishing agency. But the Secretary, not the chairman or general counsel of the powerful NLRB, continued to attend Cabinet meetings. Heads of non-Cabinet departments are sometimes invited to attend meetings, but only at the whim of the President and under conditions that do not permit them to offer advice freely and confidentially.

When the President has achieved the proper balance from among those men who are willing to serve, he may have something less than the council of advisers he would select under ideal conditions. Experience suggests that most Presidents have found this to be the case. For example, President Calvin Coolidge said of his Secretary of Commerce Herbert Hoover: "That man has offered me unsolicited advice for six years, all of it bad."

[6] Josephus Daniels, *Frontier on the Potomac,* The Macmillan Company, New York, 1946, pp. 31–32.

Cross Pressures on the Cabinet. The Cabinet is also weak in that it is subject to cross pressures from other sources. Congressional liaison must be maintained or the Cabinet member will find his department nearly dismantled, as did Secretary of Commerce Henry Wallace under Roosevelt. Keeping good relations may result in an undercutting of the President. The Secretary also becomes subject to the interests of his department's professional bureaucracy and clientele groups. Secretary of Labor Mitchell under Eisenhower often espoused programs more liberal than those favored by the President. He needed to do so to retain the confidence of labor union leaders, who represented the major clientele of the Department's services. The tendency to take the side of the department against all comers, including the President, has been called "departmentalism." No Secretary is immune to it, and the extent to which he is captured by departmental interests weakens his usefulness to the President, though it will also tend to strengthen his importance and usefulness to the departmental bureaucracy and to raise its morale.[7]

The Decline of the Cabinet Function. Generally, because of departmentalism and the personal vagaries always to some degree implicit in selection, the Cabinet has been found to be of little use in coordinating administration or helping to formulate policy. Cabinet members have, because of the nature of their positions, preferred to deal directly with the President rather than thrashing out differences with other members in meetings. Presidents have found their Cabinets useful as sounding boards for ideas, for building *esprit de corps* and enthusiasm, and, to a certain extent, for information briefing. The report of members, however, has been that Cabinet meetings have often been a waste of time, filled with telling stories or speculating off the cuff on the news of the day. Because the President cannot completely trust every member, he may be loath to discuss policy questions that might be leaked to the press.

There is thus evidence that an institution that was of central importance in Washington's day has shot its bolt. With the rise of a personal staff and a vastly more complex bureaucracy, the Cabinet appears to have become more of a historical curio than a central gear in the executive machinery.

Inner Cabinets, Kitchen Cabinets, and Confidants. One way around the Cabinet problem is to select certain members of the Cabinet as an inner advisory Cabinet, or to avoid the Cabinet altogether and set up a kitchen cabinet.*

***KITCHEN CABINET. An informal group of advisers to the President. The members may hold positions on the White House staff, other positions in government, or no formal office at all. The term has been common since Andrew Jackson's time.**

---

[7] Material in this section was borrowed from Richard F. Fenno, *The President's Cabinet,* Harvard University Press, Cambridge, Mass., 1959.

The first method was used by Harding and the second by Franklin Roosevelt with his "brain trust." Both methods create ill feeling within the Cabinet, for they spell out the pecking order in painfully obvious fashion. Each method depends on the improvisation of the presidential incumbent.

Under Roosevelt, Harry Hopkins came to stand in a special position. For a time, he even moved his family into the White House. Franklin Roosevelt, in defending the choice of Hopkins to Wendell Willkie said:[8]

> Some day you may well be sitting here where I am now as President of the United States. And when you are, you'll be looking at that door over there and knowing that practically everybody who walks through it wants something out of you. You'll learn what a lonely job this is and you'll discover the need for somebody like Harry Hopkins who asks for nothing except to serve you.

This kind of relationship cannot be institutionalized; it must always be fortuitous. Its weakness for the President is similar to that of the personal staff: the adviser generally brings no independent source of political power to the administration. Nevertheless, among Presidents after World War II, special reliance has been on their personal staffs rather than on politicians or bureaucrats, who need be only partly committed to the Chief Executive.

PRESIDENTIAL INFLUENCE

We return to the questions asked early in this chapter: Does the individual holding the office of President have the capacity to command the resources of power within the Presidency in such a way as to exercise an effective influence on the processes of decision making? Can he give the nation's citizens the feeling that policy has overall direction that is responsive to national opinion? Can he encourage innovation sufficient to meet broad national wants as expressed in the dominant contemporary ideology? While Presidents may possess almost identical legal powers, they are not equal in stature and influence because their informal powers and their ability to exploit legal powers vary.

The President and His Worlds. Presidents, to be successful, must be sensitive to many publics and many constituencies. Popular opinion is all-important, but it alone does not suffice. Many actions a President desires are relatively uninfluenced by popular opinion; for example, a President's success may hinge on how he is viewed by the heads of other nations or their citizens. Presidential good-will tours thus have a definite purpose. Washington, where politics reigns supreme, also presents a special con-

[8] Robert Sherwood, *Roosevelt and Hopkins,* Harper & Row, Publishers, New York, 1948, p. 3.

stituency. If politicians and political observers sharply discount the President, his influence with congressmen, bureaucrats, or even his own staff may be too weak to permit him to achieve his goals. President Truman's image when he became President by succession (1945) provided such a case. Congress effectively overrode his veto on several major bills. Cabinet members, such as Henry Wallace, made speeches that were critical of the President on major policy issues. Dissident members of his own party openly sought other candidates for the Democratic nomination in 1948.

The President must also be concerned about the image of him held by important sectional, social, or economic interest groups. President Eisenhower appointed to his Cabinet a labor leader who had supported the opposition candidate; President Kennedy appointed some Republican businessmen as chief aides. When a President acts, he is judged in many constituencies. Political capital that he sacrifices in respect to one public is spent on behalf of another. Many specialized publics keep close watch on his actions and frequently reassess his activities. Since his power is not absolute, these assessments are an important determinant of the influence he can actually wield.

Presidential Command. The President's great legal powers are not enough to ensure his effectiveness as a leader. On occasion, the President may command and his order will be immediately obeyed. This was the case when President Truman dismissed General MacArthur as commander in Korea, and when President Eisenhower dispatched troops to Little Rock to ensure that Central High School would be integrated and remain open. Richard Neustadt, an assistant to two Presidents, argues that these examples of a President's strength are really examples of his relative weakness. President Truman permitted General Douglas MacArthur to criticize and ignore presidential policies over a long period of time, and he urgently attempted to persuade the general to comply with administration policy, for he did not wish to lose the general's military skills or bear the criticism that would follow dismissal. Similarly, before he took action, President Eisenhower announced that he could foresee no circumstance that would require him to send troops to Little Rock, and he met with Governor Orval Faubus of Arkansas, hoping that some solution to the difficulty might be found. Both Presidents delayed as long as possible. In the end, each took decisive action reluctantly and after other methods had failed. Each acted in the face of what he regarded as defiance, and while achieving his end, each paid for it dearly in recriminations leveled against him. Perhaps each also suffered losses in overall status.[9]

Neustadt argues that the President rarely commands, and that he does so only when five conditions are present: (1) The President clearly has

[9] This section is based on Richard E. Neustadt, *Presidential Power,* John Wiley & Sons, Inc., New York, 1960.

issued an order; (2) the meaning of the order is unambiguous; (3) the order is widely publicized; (4) the men who received the order have the means to carry it out; and (5) the President's authority to issue the order is clear.

A President will carefully weigh the debits and credits before he exercises his formal power. Every presidential act that is, in effect, a command given to people who are unwilling or reluctant to carry it out costs the President some enemies and engenders increased opposition. It is much better, when any of the above conditions is not met, to achieve what he wishes by the gentler art of persuasion, mixed with occasional goads and some rewards. This means occasionally using men he actively dislikes, even cajoling them, to achieve political ends he values. Like research psychologists, Presidents have learned that the carrot usually influences more than does the stick. President Truman expressed it this way, "I sit here all day trying to persuade people to do the things they ought to have sense enough to do without my persuading them."

Public Support for the President. In 1947, when President Truman spoke to the nation, his radio Hooper ratings reached some all-time lows. Yet immediately after the 1948 election, the President's pronouncements were listened to with a certain amount of deference. Why the change? The answer is that after 1948 he was elected in his own right rather than only succeeding to the office on the death of the elective President. A President ultimately derives his power from the people. This is the source of his persuasive influence, even when it must be combined with occasional threats or rewards for full effect. When it appears that the President no longer holds the confidence of the nation, senators from his own party may be emboldened to suggest that he resign, as Senator William Fulbright of Arkansas did following the Democratic party disaster in the 1946 elections. On the other hand, when he can demonstrate to congressmen by the contents of their mailbags that his appeal to the nation has met an enthusiastic response, as President Roosevelt did with his fireside chats, his influence is enhanced.

Public support can be dissipated like gas escaping in all directions from a leaky balloon or it can be skillfully managed by the President so that it comes to bear at the proper moment on the proper persons, by which one generally means Congress. One day in 1935 on the way to a racetrack with staff members, it occurred to presidential adviser Harry Hopkins that Franklin Roosevelt's public support was at its height and would probably within a short time decline. Robert Sherwood reports this comment: "Boys—this is our hour. We've got to get everything we want—a works program, social security, wages and hours, everything—now or never. Get your minds to work on developing a complete ticket to provide security for all the folks of this country up and down and across the board." That evening they went to work in the Walker-Johnson Building and the St. Regis Hotel to prepare a program. The President later adopted much of the program, agreeing with his aides that, given the victory of 1932 and the unprecedented vote of confidence in the midterm elections of 1934, his public prestige was at the highest, and this was the time to skillfully make use of it.[10]

The best judges of a President's political skill in exploiting public support are the professional politicians and those who report on government activities. They daily observe actions of the President, trying to understand how he will act in specific situations: Will he stand firm, compromise, or back down? Will he throw away an advantage or pull a rabbit out of his sleeve? Does he know what the score is on an issue or is he a political babe? President Truman was rated slightly above President Eisenhower by these experts. The latter occasionally confessed his lack of knowledge about an issue in press conferences and, in one case, permitted his Secretary of the Treasury to attack his budget the day it was issued. To the political professionals, this seemed sheer ineptness. On the other hand, the political maneuverings of both Roosevelts were treated by their associates with considerable respect. These Presidents were master politicians in relations with public or Congress and usually played their hands in a way that took in every possible trick.

But the general public does not usually judge a President in terms of his political skill. They give support presumably because they trust a President as a man and continue such support until their confidence is shaken. Harry Truman never achieved the degree of public support given Dwight Eisenhower or Franklin Roosevelt. Historians may or may not agree with contemporary estimates of a man—Coolidge, for example, is regarded as one of the weakest of Presidents by historians, though his personal public support during his administration seems to have been exceptionally high. But whatever the historians conclude later, public support when it is given is a precious commodity that forms the basis for much of a President's influence and persuasiveness.

A Summary Statement. The power and influence of a particular President thus depend on three factors: (1) his legal powers, which provide him with a bundle of sticks and some bunches of carrots that may help him in his dealings with Congress, the courts, or the bureaucracy; (2) his support by the public as demonstrated by letters, crowds, books, and articles about him and, ultimately, by votes; (3) his skill as a politician in cultivating public support and joining it with his legal powers.

No President has been a dictator, no matter how often he may have been called one in the heat of political debate. He is given great legal powers to fit his responsibilities, but he is also checked by other legal powers. His ultimate influence depends on his ability to mobilize and also follow public

[10] Sherwood, *op. cit.,* pp. 64–65.

opinion and skillfully use it to achieve the goals he has set for his administration. If he fails to mobilize public opinion or if he is inept politically, he will probably accomplish little in terms of political change despite his legal powers, because the Constitution created a government that is always to a degree organized to block or retard proposed changes. Only in times of extreme crisis, such as the early days of the Civil War or in the first hundred days of the Roosevelt administration during the Great Depression, have Presidents been able to act free of the usual checks and approach the powers wielded by dictators. At other times, they are forced into the role of persuader, bargainer and compromiser, which is the role of master politician.

SELECTED BIBLIOGRAPHY

The office of the Presidency is a patterned role to a greater extent than any other American office, excluding perhaps those of the court system. The American nation has expectations and norms that citizens apply to any presidential incumbent, and to some degree, these always determine his conduct. About some Presidents it has been said that the office made the man.

Given the institutionalization of role, one approach to the subject is that "the President wears many hats." Rossiter's excellent survey of the office [32] is the most explicit in using this framework. Other studies such as those by Binkley [2], Brownlow [4], Hyman [18], Laski [25], and Tugwell [40] fall within the scope of this approach.

An allied way of examining the office is historical or biographical. Such studies stress how one or sometimes several Presidents interacted with the requirements of the office when facing major and minor crises. Johnson's study [21] discusses the development of the office from Hoover through Eisenhower. Several biographies about or autobiographies by twentieth-century Presidents have been written [5, 6, 10, 28, 35, 38, and 39]. An account of presidential-congressional relations from the earliest administrations is found in Binkley [3]. The development of legal powers of the Presidency is covered best in Corwin [8], a standard reference.

The work by Neustadt gives greater attention to the President as decision maker [30]. Its viewpoint is that of the incumbent and his staff, whose problem is persuasion rather than command, using the tools of popular prestige and political skill to attain the President's objectives. Of interest on this point is the argument of Finer [12], who attempts to show in a scholarly way that the job of trying to guide American policy singlehandedly is now too big for one man; the shared responsibility of a Cabinet system that gets its power from the House of Representatives is his recommendation.

There have been several recent studies of excellent quality on the President's aides and the vice presidency. All have become standard works. For the Cabinet, see Fenno [11], now in paperbound edition; for the vice presidency, see Williams, [42, 43]; and for a description of presidential confidants and trouble shooters, see Koenig [23]. A handy, though somewhat prejudiced, presentation of President Kennedy's initial team, many of whom continued to serve under Johnson, can be found in Opotowsky [31]. Some of the persons glowingly described departed from the administration during its first two years. An extremely favorable biography of President Johnson by a Pulitzer Prize winner is that of White [41]. A thoughtful assessment of presidential power is given by Theodore Sorensen [37].

1. Appleby, Paul: "The Role of the Budget Division," *Public Administration Review,* 17:156–158, Summer, 1957.
2. Binkley, Wilfred E.: *The Man in the White House,* The Johns Hopkins Press, Baltimore, 1958.
3. Binkley, Wilfred E.: *President and Congress,* 3d ed., Vintage Books, Random House, Inc., New York, 1962.
4. Brownlow, Louis: *The President and the Presidency,* Public Administration Service, Chicago, 1949.
5. Burns, James MacGregor: *Roosevelt: The Lion and the Fox,* Harcourt, Brace & World, Inc., New York, 1956.
6. Childs, Marquis: *Eisenhower, Captive Hero: A Critical Study of the General and the President,* Harcourt, Brace & World, Inc., New York, 1958.
7. Cornwell, Elmer E., Jr.: "The Presidential Press Conference: A Study in Institutionalization," *Midwest Journal of Political Science,* 4:370–389, November, 1960.
8. Corwin, Edward S.: *The President: Office and Powers, 1787–1957,* 4th ed., New York University Press, New York, 1957.
9. Corwin, Edward S., and Louis W. Koenig: *The Presidency Today,* New York University Press, New York, 1956.
10. Donovan, R. J.: *Eisenhower: The Inside Story,* Harper & Row, Publishers, New York, 1956.
11. Fenno, Richard F.: *The President's Cabinet,* Harvard University Press, Cambridge, Mass., 1959.
12. Finer, Herman: *The Presidency: Crisis and Regeneration,* The University of Chicago Press, Chicago, 1960.
13. Hart, James: *The American Presidency in Action, 1789,* The Macmillan Company, New York, 1948.
14. Heinlein, J. C.: *Presidential Staff and National Security Policy,* University of Cincinnati, Department of Political Science, Cincinnati, 1963.
15. Heller, Francis: *The Presidency,* Random House, Inc., New York, 1961.
16. Herring, Pendleton: *Presidential Leadership,* Holt, Rinehart and Winston, Inc., New York, 1940.
17. Horn, Stephen: *The Cabinet and Congress,* Columbia University Press, New York, 1960.
18. Hyman, Sidney: *The American President,* Harper & Row, Publishers, New York, 1954.
19. Hyman, Sidney (ed.): "The Office of the American Presidency," *Annals,* 307:1–216, September, 1956.
20. Jensen, Amy LaFollette: *The White House: And Its Thirty-three Families,* 2d ed., McGraw-Hill Book Company, New York, 1962.
21. Johnson, Walter: *1600 Pennsylvania Avenue,* Little, Brown and Company, Boston, 1960.
22. Kane, Joseph Nathan: *Facts about Presidents,* The H. W. Wilson Company, New York, 1959.
23. Koenig, Louis W.: *The Invisible Presidency,* Holt, Rinehart and Winston, Inc., New York, 1960.
24. Kraus, Sidney (ed.): *The Great Debates: Kennedy vs. Nixon,* Indiana University Press, Bloomington, Ind., 1962.
25. Laski, Harold J.: *The American Presidency,* The Universal Library, Grosset & Dunlap, Inc., New York, 1960.
26. Longaker, Richard P.: *The Presidency and Individual Liberties,* Cornell University Press, Ithaca, N.Y., 1961.
27. MacBride, Roger L.: *American Electoral College,* The Caxton Printers, Ltd., Caldwell, Idaho, 1960.

28. Manchester, William: *Portrait of a President: John F. Kennedy in Profile,* Little, Brown and Company, Boston, 1962.
29. May, Ernest R. (ed.): *The Ultimate Decision: The President as Commander-in-Chief,* George Braziller, Inc., New York, 1960.
30. Neustadt, Richard E.: *Presidential Power,* John Wiley & Sons, Inc., New York, 1960.
31. Opotowsky, Stan: *The Kennedy Government,* Popular Library, Inc., New York, 1961.
32. Rossiter, Clinton: *The American Presidency,* Harcourt Brace & World, Inc., New York, 1960.
33. Schubert, Glendon A., Jr.: *The Presidency in the Courts,* The University of Minnesota Press, Minneapolis, 1957.
34. Seligman, Lester G.: "Presidential Leadership: The Inner Circle and Institutionalization," *The Journal of Politics,* 18:410–426, 1956.
35. Sherwood, Robert: *Roosevelt and Hopkins,* Harper & Row, Publishers, New York, 1948.
36. Silva, Ruth C.: *Presidential Succession,* The University of Michigan Press, Ann Arbor, Mich., 1951.
37. Sorensen, Theodore C.: *Decision Making in the White House: The Olive Branch or the Arrows,* Columbia University Press, New York, 1963. Foreword by John F. Kennedy.
38. Truman, Harry S: *Memoirs,* vol. I, *Year of Decisions,* vol. II, *Years of Trial and Hope,* Doubleday & Company, Inc., Garden City, N.Y., 1955.
39. Truman, Harry S: *Truman Speaks,* Columbia University Press, New York, 1960.
40. Tugwell, Rexford G.: *The Enlargement of the Presidency,* Doubleday & Company, Inc., Garden City, N.Y., 1960.
41. White, William S.: *The Professional: Lyndon B. Johnson,* Houghton Mifflin Company, Boston, 1964.
42. Williams, Irving G.: *The American Vice Presidency: A New Look,* Random House, Inc., New York, 1954.
43. Williams, Irving G.: *The Rise of the Vice Presidency,* Public Affairs Press, Washington, D.C., 1956.

Case Study Materials

Koenig, Louis W.: "The Presidency: Foreign Aid to Spain and Yugoslavia," in Alan Westin (ed.), *The Uses of Power,* Harcourt, Brace & World, Inc., New York, 1961.

See cases listed in selected bibliography for Chapter 15, "Congress at Work and Play."

Law Case Cited:

Humphrey's Executor v. United States, 295 U.S. 602 (1935).

CHAPTER

17

ADMINISTRATION AND BUREAUCRACY

A modern bureaucracy* carries on activities that a politically effective portion of the public expects of government, or at least permits the popular assembly to enact into law. The bureaucracy performs its tasks in a specialized, largely impersonal manner and, in a democracy, is at least to some degree responsive to the demands of the popularly elected members of the executive and legislative branches of government. Its activities are, *in the ideal,* responsive to popular will. In practice, they must be *acceptable* to the effective groups in society.

***BUREAUCRACY. Any large organization that is characterized by specialization of the work assignments of personnel, essentially impersonal relationships both among persons in the agency and with those in external clientele groups, and a formal hierarchical structure.**

The bureaucracy serves many functions. In the social system, it provides the expertise that makes possible the provision of highly complex programs in a modern society. To the individual, it offers a chance for a job and status advancement (especially for socially deprived members of ethnic and racial groups) or provides wanted goods or services. The political party sees a portion of it as a source of placement possibilities for party workers, and hence, as a motivational resource and a basis of support for the President who is anxious to make a good record. To leaders of interest groups, members of the bureaucracy may represent either threats to their goals or important allies located in strategic positions. To all, the bureaucracy is too important to be ignored.

BUREAUCRACY AND BUREAUCRATS

"Bureaucracy" and "bureaucrat" are both words of opprobrium in the United States. Government has so recently grown large, and career civil servants are so far outside the main traditions of the nation that the symbols created in citizens' minds are far different from what the terms mean to social scientists.

In this book, a bureaucracy is any large organization that is characterized by (1) specialization of the work assignments of personnel, (2) essentially impersonal relationships with both persons in the agency and in external clientele groups, and (3) a formal hierarchical structure. Any member of a bureaucracy is a bureaucrat. In this sense, the Department of Health, Education, and Welfare is operated by a bureaucracy, so is the First Marine Division, the United States Steel Corporation, the Society of Jesus, the American Red Cross, and the American Bar Association. Not only are the postman, the internal revenue tax examiner, the Army colonel, and the Assistant Secretary of State bureaucrats, but so are the corporation accountant, the president of General Motors, the complaint clerk at the local department store, the secretary of the state Farm Bureau Federation, and the career "international representative" of a labor union.

There are differences between public and private bureaucracies, however, and differences in citizen attitudes toward them. In the American culture, the governmental manifestation of bureaucracy is especially objectionable, for we are deeply concerned with maintaining a sense of individual personality in respect to government.[1] We can tolerate the delays, red tape, errors, and impersonal character of bureaucracy in relation to private business: the hospital desk clerk who is impertinent or wants a sick person to answer the questions on three long forms before admission is granted; the huge mail order house that sends us shoes when we ordered gloves; the insurance company that issues us an incorrect premium notice; or the largest appliance dealer in town, whose repairman comes on Thursday when he was due on Monday. We know that, in most cases, even though inconvenience and annoyance are involved, we can take our trade elsewhere. But we do not feel the same sense of tolerance for governmental bureaucracy because we cannot find a substitute for it in most cases. The characteristics of bureaucracy are the same in each case, but there are greater pressures to humanize and constrain these characteristics under the pressure of economic competition.

We should hasten to add, however, that we are talking of differences in *attitudes* toward bureaucracy here. Differences between private and public bureaucracies may also exist to some degree in fact as well, but government civil servants are frequently anxious to serve courteously, promptly, and competently. The public librarian who patiently searches an hour for a bit of information some citizen badly wants compares favorably in the minds of many a citizen with the attendant in the private parking lot who puts a dent in a person's car bumper. The absence of the profit motive in government eliminates one factor by which the supervisor may evaluate a subordinate, and some practical differences may stem from this, but it seems likely that they are exaggerated in image as compared with fact.

[1] Robert E. Lane, *Political Ideology,* The Free Press of Glencoe, New York, 1962, pp. 18–20 and elsewhere; David Riesman, *The Lonely Crowd,* Yale University Press, New Haven, Conn., 1950.

The Problem of Bureaucracy. All large organizations are made up of people with definite sets of attitudes, all of them leading to a general atmosphere of conformity:[2]

> If the bureaucracy is to operate successfully, it must attain a high degree of reliability of behavior, an unusual degree of conformity with prescribed patterns of action. Hence, the fundamental importance of discipline, which may be as highly developed in a religious or economic bureaucracy as in the army.

If these assumptions about bureaucrats are correct—and evidence that they are universally valid is lacking—it follows that there is a danger that one's abilities and training become blind spots, that the individual becomes so accustomed to reacting in a well-inculcated manner under a given set of stimuli that he becomes inflexible under conditions requiring flexibility. The individual is thus unable to adjust to changes in the environment, and this situation, if applied to a large portion of the population, could result in disaster under certain conditions. The process is along these lines:

[2] Robert K. Merton, "Bureaucratic Structure and Personality," *Social Forces,* 18:560–568, May, 1940. Merton was drawing upon the earlier ideas of Max Weber, Thorstein Veblen, and John Dewey.

Figure 17-1

As in a Trade Union or Congress, Seniority Is Important to the Bureaucrat

"Move from Egypt? But I've just begun to accumulate some seniority!"

By permission of Burr Shafer.

(1) Devotion to rules is required in order to achieve efficiency in a large, impersonal bureaucracy; (2) this devotion ultimately causes rules originally created for practical reasons to become absolutes not to be questioned by anyone and not to be tempered by the application of "common-sense" modifications; (3) the uncritical acceptance of absolutes leads to inflexibility of bureaucratic policy and bureaucratic personality; and (4) finally, the elements originally established to create efficiency lead to inefficiency through inadaptability to changing social and economic environments.

Such, at least, is the theory. That it is to some degree true is scarcely to be questioned. But whether or not thinking human beings can really become almost complete automatons in spite of themselves and whether or not the theory applies more to America, with its organization man, than it does to such highly bureaucratic nations as France, England, Germany, or Denmark has not been demonstrated empirically. Some outstanding students of bureaucracy, including the German social scientist Max Weber, thought this general behavior pattern to be a universal characteristic, but this remains an unproved hypothesis.

Bureaucratic change. Change certainly does take place within a bureaucratic structure. The high level of technical skills possessed by members of government agencies almost necessarily involves them in policy innovation and change. Bureaucracies tend to be innovative under certain conditions:

1. When their members are seeking to bring agency programs closer to professional values and standards. Agencies, public or private, and local, state, national, and even international in scope, that perform similar functions tend to form professional associations. One of the functions of these groups is to establish and later to modify concepts of optimum professional standards, which members identify with the public interest; another is to give legitimacy to such standards. Since an individual member within the group gains status through the approval of other members, he wants his agency to secure legislation moving toward professional optimums. Thus, health departments seek expanded programs for tuberculosis and polio eradication; but they will not support national compulsory health insurance, public payment of cost of care in hospitals for the chronically ill, or other programs not approved of by public health physicians or members of the closely allied profession of private medical practitioners. Postal innovators will introduce a ZIP code; but they will not be leaders in a move to integrate the Birmingham post office.

2. When it is believed to be advantageous to gratify power holders in Congress or the White House. It may sometimes be well to increase one's social capital with these persons; in exchange, other favors may later be sought—for a favorite program, perhaps, or an increase in pay or rank for oneself or a valued colleague.

3. When defensive action is thought necessary to prevent gains in power or status by another competing agency.

4. When a civil servant is sympathetic with the social goals of a political leader. It is incorrect to view him as accepting only the values of his peer group. He may aid a political figure—quietly and unofficially if necessary—in order to help to secure changes they both believe in.

5. When a civil servant believes it is his *duty* to provide technical professional information and ideas in respect to a proposed policy change, even when he does not approve of the proposal. In such cases, the beliefs of the bureaucrat will probably condition his behavior and affect his degree of enthusiasm for the task, but he may accept the legitimacy of the demands of the would-be political innovator and act accordingly. On the other hand, he may believe the legitimacy of professional standards to be more important than the legitimate right of the officeholder to change policy. He may choose to become an obstructionist. A high-ranking member of the Armed Forces, for example, may testify before Congress in favor of policies he knows the President wants, and he may or may not hint that his own (professional) opinion is a different one.

Resistance to change. Bureaucracies tend to block or obstruct change, except when conditions such as the above are present. Whether or not Weber's rule of bureaucracy is a universal characteristic, within the American culture we have not solved the problem of providing for systematic change in large-scale, impersonal bureaucracies.

The economist W. W. Rostow has noted that "in dealing with this

Figure 17-2

Bureaucracy Is Intended Only as a Means to an End

"The grain didn't get through—but I brought you a new price administrator."

By permission of Burr Shafer.

problem, the nation is inhibited in both business and government" by certain characteristics of "national style:"[3]

1. Our empirical approach to problems in which we discount the future and all projections of trends that are not already clearly obvious.

2. The use of specialists who deal with segments of a problem, with few persons able or expected to develop an overall view of major problems.

3. The tendency to refuse to give major policy makers time for "coherent thought and reflection"—we load them down with responsibility for details.

4. A tendency to give all units within an administrative organization a voice in major decisions touching their areas of operation—giving bureaucrats a chance to protect the *status quo* if they choose to do so.

5. A tendency to view all major policy decisions as—properly—compromises among all interested parties, thus "strengthening the inertia innate to any large-scale unit."

Bureaucratic orientation. In a democracy, there is always a potential conflict between the bureaucrat, with his orientation toward the approval of peer groups (professionals in the same field), and the politician, with his orientation toward voter approval. The bureaucrat is likely to innovate whenever he believes doing so will move his agency closer to professional standards and goals. The politician is likely to do so whenever he believes innovation will move governmental activity in the direction of grass-roots demand.

Innovation is also a function of various interest-group leaders and specialists. They serve as important alternatives to the government bureaucracy whenever a political leader chooses to seek new ideas. Their advice may be based on professional values (e.g., that from highway builders' associations), a particular ideology (e.g., from the American Farm Bureau Federation), or a political-action group seeking adoption of a plan to provide for a social problem as perceived by ordinary citizens (e.g., from an *ad hoc* group supporting compulsory national health insurance). Innovation is perhaps somewhat more encouraged by lobbyists than by members of the government bureaucracy because the values and motives of the former are the more concerted. Some variety in values and motives within the bureaucracy comes, however, from the existence of "political" as well as "career" executives, that is, from persons who are appointed from outside the civil service and need not share fully in the values and goals of the particular agency.

Symbols of Legitimacy. The career civilian or military bureaucrat, like the President, congressman, judge, or anyone else who makes decisions in the name of government that importantly affect the lives of citizens must cloak himself in a mantle of legitimacy. Citizens must believe that the

[3] Adapted from W. W. Rostow, *The United States in the World Arena,* Harper & Row, Publishers, New York, 1960, pp. 498–499.

bureaucrat has a *right* to make the decisions he makes if they are to accept these decisions.

The symbols of legitimacy of a military man are obvious: the uniform, the shining bars and stars of rank, the multicolored ribbons (or "fruit salad") on his chest. The civilian bureaucrat usually wears a business suit to the office, although many agencies, such as the Post Office, the Bureau of Customs, the Forest Service, and the Park Service, have some uniformed personnel. But he, too, must have some symbols, or he will not be accepted in his role by the public. Some of his distinguishing marks include the following:

1. An appropriate college degree or degrees. This is the age of the expert, and one of the most common requirements for admission to a profession is a degree and perhaps also passing a qualifying examination, such as that for admission to the bar.

2. Quite commonly he has passed a civil service examination and has received a Civil Service Commission certification indicating a certain classification (e.g., GS-12, meaning that he is twelve steps up on the general schedule of classified civil servants). His colleagues, both higher and lower on the general schedule, will be keenly aware of another civil servant's status, and their attitude will be reflected in the manner in which they refer to him when dealing with persons outside the agency.

3. He has a title (e.g., Deputy Administrator, Special Projects Officer).

He also secures status and acceptability through demonstrated expertise. (The local sheriff assumes that the FBI agent is one of a homogeneous lot that has proved itself; he calls on the special agent for help with confidence.) His neutralist or nonpartisan posture also adds to recognition of him as an expert.

Status symbols within both private and public bureaucracies are important—perhaps an electric typewriter, a corner office, a private secretary, or a reserved automobile. As an example of the extremes to which battles over symbols can be carried, we might point to a much publicized struggle in 1949 between the chairman and the general counsel of the National Labor Relations Board. When the Board moved into new quarters, each claimed the principal suite (which contained a complete private bathroom). When the chairman won the first round, the general counsel went to the Public Building Administration and demanded equal facilities. Members of the Administration staff were not surprised; they said they "often receive such requests from executives."[4] His demand was acceded to.

The Federal bureaucrat is not fully accepted in our society (but then, neither is the President, senator, or even the Supreme Court justice). To the advocate of small-town individualism, he symbolizes, not legitimate governmental authority, but rather big government, red tape, gobbledygook, and a major force pressuring for higher expenditures and, hence,

[4] Associated Press dispatch, Feb. 17, 1949.

higher taxes. The bureaucrat as a member of a professional group often does support higher standards, of course. Because we are increasingly dependent on him, the bureaucrat's status has been gradually rising in the age of specialization that has accompanied the growth of urban society.[5]

Activities of the Bureaucracy. What does the government bureaucrat do? Almost everything. Government today performs a vast number of functions and requires almost all of the skills known to modern society. The civil service, although it has been subjected to a great many criticisms (many of them based on fact), includes a large number of persons dedicated to their jobs and often performing them without complaint, despite lack of public support and frequent congressional criticism, by no means all of it justified or well informed:[6]

> Washington visitors . . . see a heterogeneous mass of Government office workers; but they do not see a State Department courier standing guard over his diplomatic pouches at a rain-swept Belgrade airport or a Public Health nurse making her rounds by dogsled at Kotzebue, Alaska; a smoke-jumper from Missoula parachuting into a flaming Montana wilderness or an agricultural expert setting out high-yielding rubber trees in Ghana; a United States Information Agency film technician showing movies to a primitive tribe in Paraguay or an engineer providing water for camps on a Greenland icecap by extending a nuclear probe into a glacier and creating a subterranean lake.

Myths. There are many myths about the Federal civil servant. One is that he cannot lose his job, once hired. The procedures for dismissal are, indeed, more complicated than they are in private business (this is especially the case for Armed Forces personnel), but in fact more than 13,000 Federal employees are dismissed each year for inadequate performance. Government employees do claim sick leave when they merely want the day off—so do persons in private industry. In both cases, they are often caught, and there are resulting penalties. The notion that Federal employees have no incentive to do more than their routine jobs is similarly untrue. Innovators in the Department of Defense have been made eligible for bonuses of up to $25,000 per year—a plan similar to those commonly found in private industry.[7]

The Powers of Bureaucracy. How does the bureaucracy accomplish its tasks? It does so by marshaling a number of resources. These may be formal or informal. Many are dependent upon the job situation.

Formal power. The bureaucracy has its fundamental power base in the formal acts of Congress, which establish both the programs and the

[5] See Paul N. Ylvisaker, *Intergovernmental Relations at the Grass Roots,* The University of Minnesota Press, Minneapolis, 1955.

[6] John D. Weaver, "The Unglorified Civil Servant," *Holiday,* April, 1962, p. 86.

[7] Fletcher Knebel, "Bureaucrats Are People," *Look,* May 14, 1957. See also Franklin P. Kilpatrick and others, *The Image of the Federal Service,* The Brookings Institution, Washington, D.C., 1964.

procedures by which they are to be carried out. These formal rules, or laws, are not usually detailed, however. At least, they are not sufficiently detailed to cover the great bulk of the contingencies faced by agency decision makers in their daily tasks.

In the tradition of American government, the formal powers are also restricted by a variety of checks and balances. What Congress grants, it can, if it has sufficient motivation, also take away by repealing or amending the law. The President can alter bureaucratic relationships by use of his powers of reorganization, and he does do so—again, if the motivation is sufficiently strong. One governmental agency may compete with another, as the Department of the Navy sometimes competes with the Department of the Air Force, or as the Department of Defense competes with the Department of State over policy domination in some strategic area of the world. Even within a single agency, there may be considerable competition, as there has sometimes been within the Department of Agriculture between agencies interested primarily in the wants of the commercial farmers and those interested primarily in the problems of marginal farmers.

Skills as power. Every bureaucracy derives its power in part from the technical skills possessed by its members. It is always difficult for the amateur to offer effective criticism of the professional. In a complex society, members of any bureaucracy possess knowledge that is shared by few, if any, other persons, and this knowledge makes others dependent upon them, giving them power.

Divide and perhaps conquer. The American bureaucracy derives some of its strength from the separation-of-powers system to which many citizens of the nation are dedicated. Congressmen compete with the President for the domination of policy in various areas, and this very competition allows professional administrators in government agencies to play one off against the other. This strength is balanced by certain checks: administrators must be wary of both power centers, and they may at any time be the victims of the political activities of either. Senior bureaucrats must fear both Congress and the President. The latter is perhaps the greater threat, but both serve to keep him from total complacency.

Ideological support. A bureaucracy may receive its support from the beliefs of the typical citizen, beliefs that in some cultures (such as those of Great Britain or Germany) accord it great deference. In the United States, this type of power base has been generally absent, but in the years since World War II, the urban middle classes have increasingly deferred to the "expert"—the specialist—for they have come to accept the importance of such a person in private bureaucracies in an age of specialization. The middle-class organization man distrusts politicians, but has more confidence in the functional specialist than does the advocate of individualism or the working-class citizen. The latter believes that large numbers of persons who seek more benefits and privileges deserve what they can get by the very fact of their numbers. Any confidence in expertise increases the power of the bureaucracy.

PUBLIC SUPPORT OF BUREAUCRACY

What is the view of the public toward the bureaucracy that administers the functions of government? How has it changed through time? We have some empirical evidence on the subject.[8]

Party affiliation and attitudes. A study of attitudes toward the public service that was conducted in a metropolitan area (a similar study in a small town far from a metropolitan area may well have produced very different results) showed that public attitudes toward the bureaucracy were about the same, regardless of political party affiliation.

Acceptance of the social function of the bureaucracy. Metropolitanites generally accepted the present scope and function of governmental bureaucracy, and this was true of high-status citizens as well as of unskilled workers. "All the various strata, not just the lower social groups in the metropolitan community, have developed a stake in and a reliance on these new functions of government."[9]

Ambivalent attitudes toward bureaucracy. While the bureaucracy was generally accepted, citizens also had some doubts about the true worth of many governmental services and about whether bureaucrats were committed to principle. These doubts were found less among younger than older people, however, indicating that the generation raised under the ideology of the social service state accepted it more than did their parents, who witnessed its birth.

Consistency of attitude. Citizens tended, in general, either to accept or to reject the performance of government agencies and their bureaucrats. That is, there was a considerable degree of consistency in the evaluations made by the individual citizen.

Lack of knowledge. Most citizens had little knowledge of the functions or procedures of governmental agencies. "Public administrators," the researchers noted, "must face the reality of a relatively uninformed citizenry."[10] This is not, however, a matter of "lower class ignorance, for lack of knowledge penetrates deeply into the middle class."

Estimate of the economic worth of government. The typical citizen disapproved of red tape and the high cost of government. The researchers concluded that "the results of our probing of these topics are too convincing to dismiss the findings that a near majority feel hostile when these standards of administrative behavior are brought into question. These negative and hostile feelings were concentrated at the bottom of the social pyramid, where simultaneously the demands for more government administration predominate."

[8] This section borrows from Morris Janowitz, Deil Wright, and William Delany, *Public Administration and the Public,* University of Michigan, Institute of Public Administration, Ann Arbor, Mich., 1958. See chap. 8 for detailed data. See also, for generally similar findings, Kilpatrick and others, *op. cit.*

[9] Janowitz, Wright, and Delany, *op. cit.,* p. 102.

[10] *Ibid.,* p. 104.

Views on corruption and favoritism. There was no general belief that corruption exists in government, but most citizens "accepted without a sense of moral indignation the perceived importance of political pull in securing aid from administrative agencies."[11]

The prestige of public employment. The prestige of public employment, in terms of social reputation, respect, deference, esteem, and recognition accorded public employees, increased considerably between 1929, the last year before the Great Depression, and 1954, a quarter of a century later.[12] One study has indicated the following:

1. When Leonard D. White examined the prestige of public service just before the Great Depression began, the status of persons in various job categories in private business invariably rated higher than similar jobs in government. A quarter of a century later, a government stenographer rated higher in prestige than one in private business; accountants and watchmen rated about even; but physicians in private practice were given a significantly higher status rating than those employed by government.[13] (At the lower end of the salary scale, government tends to pay as well or better than private employers. As the pay scale in private business increases, the government pay scale usually increases more slowly.)

2. Metropolitanites, in 1929, rated private employees as being much more courteous to clients and customers than were public employees. By 1954, however, this difference had disappeared, and the two classes were rated equally (see Table 17-1).

3. Lower-income and lower-class persons, Negroes, and lesser-educated persons tended to rank government employment as having higher status than did other groups (see Table 17-2). These differences "underline the real as well as the symbolic attractiveness of a government career and job for those who find themselves at the bottom of the economic and social pyramid."[14]

The objective in a complex democratic society is, presumably, to develop a bureaucratic pattern of behavior that is based on democratic consent. In order to secure this, it seems reasonable to want a bureaucracy that does not have extremely low or extremely high prestige.[15] The former may imply the existence of a large number of persons who have so little confidence in the existing political system that they would rather sabotage it than support it. The latter may imply the existence of a large number of persons who are willing to accept in docile and uncritical fashion the activities of the governmental bureaucracy. Neither situation would seem to be healthy for democracy.

[11] *Ibid.*, p. 106.

[12] The comparison is with Leonard D. White, *The Prestige Value of Public Employment,* The University of Chicago Press, Chicago, 1929.

[13] Janowitz, Wright, and Delany, *op. cit.*, table XVI.

[14] *Ibid.*, p. 68.

[15] *Ibid.*, p. 57.

TABLE 17-1

ATTITUDES CONCERNING COURTESY OF PUBLIC AND PRIVATE EMPLOYEES (In per cent)

Reaction	1929*	1954†
Private employees more courteous	60	29
Both equal	22	29
City employees more courteous	18	27
Don't know; not ascertained		15
Total	100	100

* Figures obtained from a study reported by Leonard D. White, *The Prestige Value of Public Employment,* The University of Chicago Press, Chicago, 1929.

† Figures obtained from a study by Deil Wright reported in the source reference.

SOURCE: Adapted from Morris Janowitz, Deil Wright, and William Delany, *Public Administration and the Public,* University of Michigan, Institute of Public Administration, Ann Arbor, Mich., 1958, table XVII.

TABLE 17-2

GROUP DIFFERENCES IN THE PRESTIGE VALUE OF PUBLIC EMPLOYMENT (In per cent)

Social characteristics	Regard for public employment				
	High	Middle	Low	Unknown	Total
Income:					
Under $2,000	30	42	21	7	100
Over $8,000	15	33	44	8	100
Social class:					
Lower lower	37	38	21	4	100
Upper middle	14	34	43	9	100
Race:					
White	26	37	31	6	100
Negro	44	33	18	5	100
Education:					
Less than six grades	27	47	15	11	100
High school diploma	31	31	33	5	100
Beyond high school	14	34	47	5	100

SOURCE: Adapted from Morris Janowitz, Deil Wright, and William Delany *Public Administration and the Public,* University of Michigan, Institute of Public Administration, Ann Arbor, Mich., 1958, table XVIII.

THE HISTORY OF PERSONNEL POLICIES

In the early days of the Republic, it was assumed that the top nonelective administrators in government would come from the upper classes of society. Indeed, there was not much choice in the matter, for these were the only persons of education and sophistication. The ordinary job of clerk—the clerk-typist of today—was occupied by a man who had a family to support. He had no skill other than a legible hand, but he supported his family on it. The Massachusetts or Virginia aristocrat did not ask his political allegiance in giving him a job.

Party considerations early became a factor in making bureaucratic appointments, however. Neither Washington nor John Adams appointed anyone other than a Federalist to the judiciary. The two strongest men in the very first Cabinet, Secretary of State Thomas Jefferson and Secretary of the Treasury Alexander Hamilton, appointed to their departments persons sympathetic to their own philosophies. Jefferson, once he became President, was concerned about the fact that a bureaucracy drawn from a single class did not share the values that he thought important for the young Republic. He did not, however, find excuses for dismissing Federalists. Instead, he satisfied himself with replacing conservatives with members of his own party as vacancies appeared.

The Patronage-spoils System. The Jacksonian, with his heavy emphasis upon equality and representativeness and his hostility to a class-ordered society, gave strong support to the patronage system, sometimes called the spoils system, from the expression of Senator William L. Marcy (Democrat, New York): "To the victor belong the spoils."

The frontiersman believed that upper-class control of nonelective positions in the bureaucracy could be prevented by changing government employees each time the Chief Executive changed. The first manifestation of this point of view came before the Age of Jackson, probably as a result of the demands of members of Congress; the Tenure of Office Act of 1820 made the terms of many Federal employees coincide with that of the President, thus providing the Chief Executive with a simple, unembarrassing means for replacing persons beholden to his predecessor. (The act included in its provisions offices that are still important political plums: district attorneys and customs collectors.) The patronage concept reached maturity with Andrew Jackson's inauguration (1829). In his first message to Congress, that spokesman for egalitarianism declared that government jobs are so "simple that men of intelligence may readily qualify themselves for their performance."

This concept was probably valid in thirteenth-century England, when there was no clear distinction between the king's household and his government. In those days, the simplicity of government was revealed by the trivialities of the records that were kept. (King John took eight baths during one six-month period at a cost of from 2 to 5 pence each.) And perhaps the concept was still valid in the first part of the nineteenth century, but in any case, Jackson and his supporters really believed that it was more important for the bureaucracy to be representative of the common man rather than skilled and neutral.[16] As is often the case with

[16] Herbert Kaufman, "Emerging Conflicts in the Doctrines of Public Administration," *American Political Science Review,* 50:1057–1073, December, 1956.

governmental institutions, policies that begin for one purpose are continued for another: The party faithful saw the patronage system as a means for securing rewards, and the original purpose of the policy was lost in its attractiveness as a means for providing incentive to party workers.

The government-employee–party-active relationship is not a new one. In fourteenth-century India, which had an elaborate system of post offices and post roads, the Moslem rulers used the local postmaster as a political observer and reporter. He was the local eyes and ears of the caliph. In twentieth-century America, the local postmaster still must be cleared for appointment with the congressman of the district if the congressman is a member of the same party as the President (except in the smallest communities—those of less than the first three classes of post offices). After taking office, the postmaster can no longer overtly take part in political activities.

Patronage remains significant today to the party in power, particularly in connection with the offices of customs collector, United States marshal, district attorney, and "Schedule C," or nonclassified, policy-making positions. Another important area of patronage appointment that remains is that of part-time employees, such as substitute rural mail carriers and census takers. For the 1960 census, for example, the Republican party leaders were able to appoint about 400 census supervisors at $500 a month for about five months, 10,000 crew leaders, and 160,000 enumerators—in all, about $45 million in salaries to be paid to good party workers—an important consideration in a presidential election year (alternate Federal censuses coincide with presidential election years). The Democrats had a similar opportunity to award the faithful in 1940 and in 1950. (At the time of each census, leaders of the party out of power predictably "deplore" the "abuse" of the census-taking procedure by turning it into a "patronage plum." In fact, however, the census is taken in a competent fashion.)

The Quest for Neutral Experts. The surviving patronage positions in the Federal government are often coupled with a requirement of competence. Today governmental tasks are much too complex to be handled by the intelligent but unskilled workers Jackson eulogized, and patronage is severely limited.

The movement for a merit plan for selecting government employees began to reach meaningful proportions immediately after the Civil War. Scandals involving corruption and incompetence, together with the growing complexity of government, led to demands for civil service reform. These demands were accelerated by developments in the high-quality, high-status British civil service. It was from that country, indeed, that reformers borrowed the concept of *neutral competence,* and this was to replace representativeness as the principal consideration in personnel policy development.[17]

[17] *Ibid.,* p. 1060.

> The core value of this search was ability to do the work of government expertly, and to do it according to explicit, objective standards rather than to personal or party or other obligations and loyalties. The slogan of the neutral competence school became, "Take administration out of politics."

This reform movement was led by upper-middle-class persons who at the same time were campaigning to reform city government, put it on a businesslike, neutral-competence basis, and reduce the power of political leaders who did not accept middle-class values and relied on patronage to build political machines that were largely independent of the business leaders and high-status families of the community. Both movements had Hamiltonian overtones; both represented a reaction to the heavy doses of applied democracy of the first half of the nineteenth century.

The reformers could not effectively challenge unrestrained democracy even though some wanted to do so. The concept was now well established. But they did have a strong basis for arguing that the ordinary man could not necessarily handle any given government job. And events aided their campaign for a professional bureaucracy. Britain established a comprehensive merit plan of civil service in 1870; President Grant established the first executive merit plan for some positions the next year. Grant's early efforts were not successful, but reformers organized and redoubled their efforts. In 1881, the same year that the National Civil Service Reform League was established, President Garfield was assassinated by a psychologically unstable office seeker. Two years later, the Pendleton Act was passed. Although it has been amended many times, it remains the basis of the merit system to this day.[18]

> The objectives of the program were confined principally to controlling the selection of government workers by taking the power to hire staff from the hands of executive heads (who were politicians) and lodging it with experts who, if they did not actually appoint personnel, at least could screen out all but those who could pass tests of one sort or another. This aspect of the program spread rapidly in the federal government; despite the subsequent growth of the federal service, about nine out of ten government employees today are under some form of merit appointment. But the process did not stop with the removal of the appointing power from politics; over the years, the Civil Service Commission extended its surveillance to dismissal, promotion, and position classification; eventually, with the aid of new legislation [the Hatch Act of 1939], the political activities of civil servants were reduced to little more than voting. A wall was erected between the government bureaucracy and the politicians, a wall policed by the Civil Service Commission.

Unintended results. The reformers' plan for a professional civil service achieved some of the goals of reformers, but it created problems, most of them probably not envisioned by the reformers:

1. It created some powerful civil service positions that were, in practice, relatively independent of the department head or even of the President.

[18] *Ibid.*, p. 1061.

Experts filled the positions, but they were not subject to control or coordination by anyone. Key civil servants developed close working relationships with interest-group representatives and relevant congressional committee chairmen. To their reference groups they came to owe answers and explanations, but this was less true of their administrative superiors, who were obligated to many groups and not dependent on a single one.

2. Congress could not control the professional bureaucracy. Its supervision was intermittent. Most congressmen are amateurs in the fields in which the bureaucrats are experts. At best, they could give only general guidelines; occasionally, through resolution or statute, they could overrule a bureaucratic decision.

3. Similarly, the judges on the courts discovered that they could not guide or control a professional administrative bureaucracy. Under their own rules and ancient traditions, they are limited to refereeing bona fide disputes in specific cases. Their procedures are formal, deliberative, and slow. Many cases become moot before they are decided; only a tiny percentage of disputed administrative decisions can, in any case, be appealed to the courts.

4. The governmental decision-making process, as a result of a lack of a key locus of control, became highly dispersed, some of the power being located in Congress, some in the President, some in the political administrators who are appointed by the President but often quite independent of him (see Chapter 16), some in the court, and some in the administrative civil service. Although the parts were to a degree interdependent and served as a check upon one another, in large degree decision making was fragmented and the decision makers highly autonomous.

The Doctrine of Executive Leadership. As government became more complex, criticism of the splintered pattern of decision making mounted. A number of forceful, imaginative, and ambitious Chief Executives, beginning with Theodore Roosevelt (1901–1909), spurred on the critics who believed that further change in the administrative machinery was needed. These critics agreed that governmental activities were not coordinated; that one agency's policies conflicted with those of another; that conflict and bureaucratic rivalry (empire building) were rife; that some functions were more than adequately performed, while no one assumed responsibility for others; that the system encouraged neither "efficiency" nor "economy" (two vague, but frequently used, terms of the critics); and that no single person knew what was happening or was responsible for what happened.

What solution could be proposed to end this chaos? The reformers hit upon the traditional leader in policy formation and administrative supervision, the Chief Executive. He had performed this function from ancient times and was now to be restored to his former place of importance. They called for greater executive authority over administrators of all kinds. A major demand was for adequate staff in the Executive Office and for the executive budget. The latter was intended to give a central focus in the

Executive Office to the problem of balancing off the various claims to the funds of government. Earlier, appropriations were made piecemeal by Congress, agency by agency, with little attention to total expenditures or to any rational planning in balancing off one set of demands against another. The reformers also urged that the sprawling Federal civil establishment be telescoped from hundreds of agencies into a small enough number—perhaps no more than twenty or so major ones—for the President to give them his direct attention and oversight.

The doctrine of executive leadership was strongly expressed in the reports of the Commission on Efficiency and Economy (1912), which was appointed by President William Howard Taft. Incidentally, Taft was not nearly so committed to the view expressed as his predecessor, Theodore Roosevelt, had been. T.R. had called the President the "steward of the people" and insisted that he had a major responsibility for policy leadership and administration. The philosophy was reiterated and embellished in the *Report of the President's Committee on Administrative Management* (1937), written by a group led by Louis Brownlow, and in the report on *Organization of the Executive Branch of the Government* (1949), prepared by the Hoover Commission, which was headed by the former President. These reports, especially the former, urged strong presidential fiscal leadership and control, and both recommended that responsibility be made dependent on:[19]

> . . . pulling the administrative functions of the independent regulatory commissions back under the President, on drawing the government corporations back into the hierarchy, on bringing personnel management under close direction by the President, on strengthening the White House staff, on getting the General Accounting Office out of the pre-auditing field and returning this operation to the executive branch.

A Little of Everything. The present administrative pattern of the Federal government is a reflection of the American tendency to compromise, to take something from each school of thought, and to use whatever it is that seems to work at the moment. Neat, symmetrical administrative theory is not important or even meaningful to most Americans. And indeed, there is probably no one simple answer to the question of how the Federal administration "ought" to be organized. Its structure and responsibilities are too complex, too unstable, too unpredictable for a simple rule of organization. Thus, there are cycles and vogues in administrative theory, just as there are in women's dress. The Brownlow–Hoover concept of executive leadership, for example, has since been questioned by some political scientists.[20]

In practice, politicians have adopted some of the rhetoric of each of the three schools of representative bureaucracy, neutral competence, and

[19] *Ibid.*, p. 1065.

[20] See, for example, Charles S. Hyneman, *Bureaucracy in a Democracy*, Harper & Row, Publishers, New York, 1950.

executive leadership. After the organizational preferences of various political forces have been balanced off, it is possible to rationalize the result in terms of any of the theories or any combination of them. Postmasters, marshals, United States attorneys, collectors of customs, and some other officials are still chosen on a patronage basis. Until the early 1950s, collectors in internal revenue were too, but after some scandals, they were replaced by career civil servants known as district directors of internal revenue.

The independence of many agency experts was obvious in the 1960s in such phenomena as the Federal Reserve Board, which is to control banks, but is itself controlled by bankers, and the Interstate Commerce Commission, which is usually dominated by the corporations engaged in interstate commerce. Or it is seen in the National Guard Bureau of the Department of the Army, which is under the President as Commander in Chief, but which has often successfully defied both the Chief Executive and his political representative, the Secretary of Defense, by appealing directly to Congress. Or it is seen in the Army Corps of Engineers, which has close allies in Congress, for the annual Rivers and Harbors Act is a major "pork barrel" in that it allows congressmen to vote for "good" things (dams, deep-river channels, flood control plans) that are beneficial to their own districts. Other branches of the Department of Defense, an agency whose members are supposedly taught to obey uncritically the orders of superiors, have also developed congressional support so as to make themselves relatively independent of the Commander in Chief.

Some agencies and their staffs are relatively independent of both the President and Congress. The Federal Bureau of Investigation is a well-known case. In 1955, President Eisenhower appointed to the Federal Power Commission a member who immediately cut out for himself the role of champion of the consumer. This was not a generally expected role definition, for the Commission has generally been dominated by the power industries. The member ran into opposition, especially from natural gas interests, which viewed him as a proponent of stringent regulation. When he came up for reappointment in 1960, pressures on the President made it inexpedient to reappoint him.[21]

In similar fashion, the individual drug manufacturing firms and the Pharmaceutical Manufacturers' Association have great influence over the Food and Drug Administration (FDA), which must approve new ethical drugs before they can be sold. The FDA has generally been sympathetic to the interests of major manufacturers. In one instance, a specialist in that agency appealed for support from a superior in a case where a new drug might lead to addiction, only to be told: "I will not have my policy of friendliness with industry interfered with." In another case, the Federal Trade Commission conceded that advertisements of a drug company were misleading, but refused to censure the firm even though the agency was

[21] *The New York Times,* May 1, 1960.

created by Congress to protect the consumer against such things as misleading advertising and dangerous drugs.[22]

Structural Reorganization. Although demands for change in the administrative structure of the executive branch of government have been common during the last three or four generations, major changes have been slow in coming. This is in part because various interest groups have a stake in preserving the present organizational structure of the bureaucracy, in part because most of the members of each organization have a similar stake. The Association of American Railroads has established relationships with the Interstate Commerce Commission that are familiar and, for the most part, convenient to its members. A change in the status of the Commission by combining it with other regulatory agencies, by depriving it of its relatively independent status, or changing its formal powers might offer a threat to the railroads. Similarly, a bureaucrat whose power position or job security is well established in the existing structural pattern often cannot estimate confidently the effects of possible changes. Unless he stands clearly to gain in power or freedom from control by others, his safest course is normally to oppose change.

From the time of the Commission on Efficiency and Economy in the administration of President Taft to the present, reformers have tended to seek to concentrate additional power over the bureaucracy in the office of the President. Congress, under pressure to exert greater control over the bureaucracy and unable to find plans that would vest that control in itself, has accepted these demands. The reorganization acts of 1939 and 1949 have given the President power to make reorganization plans. These must be submitted to Congress, but they go into effect automatically in sixty days if they are not rejected by both the House and Senate. Most of the proposals submitted under the acts have been accepted by Congress, but both Congress and the President are under pressure from interest groups and the bureaucracy. As a result, most proposed changes have been relatively modest in scope, for they would otherwise involve the President in complicated quarrels with Congress and with groups upon which he is dependent for reelection, policy innovation, or effective administration of politically important programs.

WHO ARE THE BUREAUCRATS?

The bureaucracy grows in size, and it grows unsystematically. The demands of the moment and the concerns of a sizable public are reflected in Federal hiring practices. In one decade, a spurt of growth may be in the

[22] John Lear, "Drugmakers and the Government—Who Makes the Decisions?" *Saturday Review,* July 2, 1960, pp. 37ff. See also the introduction to chap. 8, above.

Navy; in another, in the public health field, in a depression, in public welfare; in yet another period, in the Air Force. But despite popular folklore to the effect that the bureaucracy is a Frankenstein that, once created, grows and grows whether needed or not and despite anything anyone can do, the bureaucracy grows because people want governmental services. The Post Office expands because each year there are more people mailing more items. The Bureau of Public Roads grows because people want excellent highways; the National Aeronautics and Space Administration (NASA) grows because people associate missiles with national prestige and security—and so it goes. More than one-half of Federal employees are members of the military or of civilian agencies that are concerned with defense (e.g., NASA) or with former servicemen (e.g., Veterans Administration).

The Size of the Bureaucracy. The United States had about 131,000 civilian employees in 1884, one year after the merit system went into effect. Ninety per cent of them were patronage appointees. By the time Theodore Roosevelt began to emphasize new Federal programs, this number had doubled, but in the year he became President (1901), the State Department had only about 100 employees stationed in Washington, and its routine operations were supervised by a man with the inglorious title of chief clerk. In 1964, it had over 10,000 employers operating under a number of assistant secretaries.

In times of stress and trouble, the Federal bureaucracy increased especially rapidly, more than doubling during the Great Depression, for example.[23] In 1963, some 2.4 million persons—or about 3.4 per cent of the total American civilian labor force—were in Federal civilian jobs. Of these persons, about 85 per cent held competitive merit-system appointments, and nearly 90 per cent were stationed outside of Washington. In the years since World War II, government employment has remained quite stable as a percentage of the total nonagricultural labor force (see Table 17-3). The figure has been about 14 per cent in the postwar years. (The 1960 percentage was higher because of a mild recession that affected private employment more than public.) Federal employment has declined slightly as a percentage of total government employment since 1950.

The Civil Service System. The United States Civil Service Commission consists of three members, no more than two of whom may belong to the same political party. It is not the only merit system of the Federal government. At least five agencies, the Atomic Energy Commission, the Central Intelligence Agency, the Federal Bureau of Investigation, the Foreign Service of the State Department, and the Tennessee Valley Authority, have their own merit systems. (Government bureaucracies seek to gain

[23] See Paul P. Van Riper, *A History of the United States Civil Service*, Harper & Row, Publishers, New York, 1958.

independence from the staff agencies controlling personnel and finance, each arguing that its tasks are unique and must therefore be handled separately. The neutral-competence supporters have often been sympathetic to these arguments.)

The general pattern over several generations has been to increase the number and kinds of positions subject to merit-system control. There is usually a reversal of this trend, however, when a change takes place in the party occupying the White House. For example, in 1953, after the Republicans had been out of power for twenty years, the Eisenhower administration asked that the Commission establish Schedule C. This is a list of exempt positions that includes confidential secretaries, administrative assistants, and persons in policy-making positions, that is, posts that require persons who will support and further administration policy in controversial partisan areas. The Eisenhower administration spokesman felt that, without such a group, it would sometimes have to depend on Democrats or determinedly neutral persons to carry out policy.

Congress has generally been willing to support presidential recommendations whenever the President agrees to give up patronage control in favor of the merit system. The principal exceptions have been when the patronage, although nominally the President's, is actually distributed by congressmen of the President's party. This explains why postmasters are still, in practice, patronage appointments and why the daily operations of an individual post office are under an anonymous career official, the superintendent of the mails, rather than the postmaster. (In 1952, President Truman recommended the elimination of nearly all remaining patronage positions in the Post Office. Congress rejected his proposal.)

TABLE 17-3

GOVERNMENT EMPLOYMENT TRENDS, 1929–1960 (In thousands)

Year	Employment				
	Total Wage and Salary	Total, government*	Government (% of total)	Total, Federal (civilian)	Federal (% of total government)
1929	31,041	3,066	9.9	534	17
1935	26,792	3,477	13.0	748	22
1940	32,058	4,202	13.1	1,128	25
1945†	40,037	5,944	14.8	3,375	51
1950	44,738	6,026	13.5	2,117	33
1955	50,056	6,914	13.8	2,378	32
1960	52,895	8,455	16.0	2,421	27

* Federal, state, and local.

† Figures for 1945 distorted by effects of World War II.

SOURCE: Adapted from Daniel H. Kruger, "Trends in Public Employment," *Proceedings of the Fourteenth Annual Meeting, Industrial Relations Research Association,* 1961, tables I and II.

Political Executives and Career Administrators. There is no value-free method by which to determine which administrative posts should or should not be subject to appointment by the President or his department heads, and which should be chosen by competitive examination. All bureaucrats make policy, to a degree. At some indefinite place in the hierarchy, not necessarily the same place from one agency to another, stability and technical competence become more important than loyalty to a particular President or party.

There are certain differences in perspective between the political executive and the career administrator, although they may not be as great as is popularly supposed. The public assumes many of the former to be incompetent hacks, though in practice few of them are. They are customarily drawn from successful political executives at other levels of government (mayors, governors, state elected officials), business executives, labor union officials, newsmen, and university administrators. Their orientation differs from that of career civil servants principally in that they are more easily subjected to pressure or the expectation that they consider the effects of a decision in terms of the next election. The career man is more heavily oriented toward the customs, practices, values, and goals of his particular profession (public health administration, say, or highway engineering) and to the values and behavior patterns of the career bureaucracy.

The political executive is less committed than the career man to the agency he heads. He is "an outsider" who may be regarded as an interloper and, perhaps, as a potential enemy rather than as a friend. And he is less concerned than the career agency head in the "institutional maintenance needs" of the agency, that is, in the protection of the agency from assaults from other agencies, from Congress, or from the President. Members of every government agency (or department of a private corporation) share a strong in-group feeling. They want autonomy from out-group nonmembers, who may want to influence agency administrative practices. Members want someone to fight to protect the agency's status, budget, and place in the administrative hierarchy. The career man in the top agency position has a greater motivation for sharing in the staff's desire that he do this task well, and he is almost certain to be an "old Washington hand" who may know his way around congressional committee rooms or the White House staff offices better than the political executive.

Acceptance of the career administrator. It is likely that future administrations will accept career executives in all but a few top positions.

1. Bureaucrats who have spent years in Washington agencies are usually middle-of-the-roaders, rarely very reactionary or radical in their views and hence willing and able to serve Presidents of both parties. Furthermore, they usually are devoted to the principle of neutrality and do not wish to sabotage the President, except perhaps where they regard his proposals as *professionally* unacceptable (e.g., a health insurance bill that is not in accord with the values of the medical profession or public health specialists).

2. The President cannot afford to fill important posts with hacks—he

has to make a good record for himself and the party—and qualified men are not easily attracted to Washington. They make a sacrifice in terms of their own major careers in private business or in whatever other bureaucracy they are members of. They also find themselves subject to more public criticism in Washington; they often take a sharp salary cut; they must learn a different administrative style and new power relationships; and they can do no more than hope that they can climb back on the career ladder back home after a few years away in a job for which they will not gain credit, even if well done. The career man, on the other hand, sees government administration as his permanent professional commitment. He generally knows the job and the environment within which it exists. He also generally commits his full talents to the task and does not have one eye on another career ladder.

Checks on the Civil Service. The civil servant does not fit the image of the Horatio Alger myth. He is a specialist whose expertise is difficult for the citizen and congressman to evaluate. His job security and assured income contrasts with the insecurity of the small-business man, of the assembly-line worker, or of many congressmen. His importance in a complex age of specialization make him suspect. Under all of these circumstances, he is a victim of suspicion, if not attack.

Item: Congressmen long ago discovered that assaults on the bureaucracy are often effective devices for securing support in their constituencies and

Figure 17-3

In Politics, Blame Is Sometimes Assessed According to Vulnerability Rather than Guilt

"Now that we're at peace again, let's hang the couriers we used for all those insulting notes."

By permission of Burr Shafer.

for gaining headlines. A common congressional complaint, for example, is that bureaucrats withhold information from them and the public—a charge that may often have validity, and a circumstance that is encouraged in part by the very hostility of congressmen. (Congressmen themselves withhold information from the public, of course. The general rule among both bureaucrats and politicians is to avoid releasing information that is to their disadvantage.)

Item: Lawyers, and especially judges, have long been suspicious of the trend toward administrative—as distinguished from judicial—decision making. As government has entered into new areas of activity, there has been a tendency to establish boards that act much as legislative or judicial bodies do. The Interstate Commerce Commission, which establishes rates for railroad and bus lines, is an example. So is the Federal Trade Commission, which, acting much like a court, decides when advertising is or is not ethical and, hence, when it is or is not legal.

In addition, individual government administrators may decide questions that have far-reaching effects on individuals. For example, a decision by an Internal Revenue Service official that a citizen owes a certain amount of income tax has the force and effect of a court decision unless the individual can prove that he does *not* owe the amount claimed. In none of these cases do the procedures necessarily follow those of the courts or fit the ancient traditions of the law. Whenever the issue of administrative decision making comes up, the legal profession, which is well represented in Congress, demands that only lawyers be appointed to commissions that act as deliberative bodies, that judicial procedures be used before such groups, and that appeals to the courts be automatically permitted.

Item: In the period of the early 1950s, when concern about Communist infiltration into American government was greatest, the loyalty of members of the bureaucracy was challenged. The vast bulk of bureaucrats were loyal, but the general suspicion in which the bureaucracy is held encouraged some to raise doubts. A few persons of doubtful loyalty or persons who might be security risks because of personality characteristics or susceptibility to blackmail (e.g., alcoholics, gamblers, homosexuals) were uncovered, but the willingness of the public to have the Federal bureaucracy combed for untrustworthy individuals greatly damaged its morale, and hence, its self-confidence in doing its assigned job. To a considerable degree, the professional bureaucracy is a "sitting duck" for political assaults because it is a relatively new institution and not fully trusted by the typical citizen.

THE CONCEPT OF ADEQUATE STANDARDS

The political process would be much simpler if we had objective criteria for measuring adequate standards of service and performance levels in government. But we do not. Such standards are culturally determined; as such they vary with time and geographic location. The people of a small rural county may not—probably do not—expect the civil servants in the courthouse to be selected by a merit system, and they probably do not expect them to have a great deal of training for their jobs. In most cases, public employees probably meet community expectations as to standards.

Professional Standards. Because of their vested interest, professional organizations set standards for their areas of government activity. These standards are often spoken of as being "optimum"—a word that somehow has come to be used in newspaper editorials and political speeches as if it meant "minimum acceptable" instead of "best." Psychiatrists prescribe standards both for service levels and for administrative organization of mental hospitals; educators, for public schools; social workers, for public welfare; and so on. The goal is usually set so high that few governmental units can claim to meet them. Thus in the postwar era, public health administrators established standards for a health unit that could operate effectively in furnishing basic services. Yet in 1948, a survey showed that only forty-seven counties (less than 2 per cent) and seventeen cities (less than .5 per cent of those over 5,000 population) in the entire United States met the standards.[24] The citizen might well wonder how realistic they were and what reasonable standards might be.

Politicians sometimes use the optimum goals of professional organizations for their own political propaganda. So do nonelective administrators, who are often themselves members of such groups. Congressmen frequently find it difficult to defend themselves if they do not provide a full program of services or if their programs are criticized as substandard. Their problem is further complicated because neither the politicians nor the public can fairly judge the criteria used or whether they provide for minimal or ultimate goals. Furthermore, of course, each professional organization deals only with goals in its own area of governmental service, while the beleaguered legislator must balance off one such demand against another, and all of them against what the public is willing to pay.

THE CONCEPT OF THE PUBLIC INTEREST

Theorists writing about administrative behavior have used a great many words in seeking to develop a notion of what would be accepted as the public interest in the decision-making process. This is understandable, since public administrators are supposed by citizens to be serving the public at large and not a minor portion of it. The typical citizen no doubt thinks that the duty of the government is to serve the public interest. He does not define it precisely. Certainly he is not likely to view government,

[24] National Health Assembly, *America's Health,* Harper & Row, Publishers, New York, 1949, p. 61.

as political scientists tend to, as serving a large number of clientele groups rather than a single public at large.

Administrators themselves probably are not much interested in or aware of what philosophers say about the public interest. To the extent that they consider the concept consciously or subconsciously, their implicit assumptions concerning its nature seem to include such items as the following:

1. The administrator tends to identify the public interest with the expectations of his professional peers. If he is a physician, a social work administrator, a military officer, or other professional person, he is likely to think that the standards established and the administrative methods approved by his profession are both right and in the public interest. A social work textbook, for example, argues that executive and legislative instructions to social workers are "unwarranted" and invasions of a field in which professional judgments should be the rule.[25]

2. He tends to accept the expectations of his administrative superiors and to view them as representative of the public interest. This is the road to both convenience and security. It is a simple and effective rationalization.

3. He identifies his personal value system with the public interest through the process psychologists call "projection." His own views quite surely are held by a large number of persons in the general public, but he has no way of knowing what proportion of the public. In any case, this approach minimizes personal psychological strain. Of course, an administrator is often called upon to do things that do not fit his personal values; in such cases, the more easily he can accept his superior's position as the public interest, the easier it is for him.

4. He tends to reach a decision—as do elective politicians—that will minimize interest-group or clientele-group pressures upon himself and his agency. He seeks to anticipate the demands of such groups. It is not difficult to identify the views of the most interested persons or groups in relation to a particular policy or program with the general good. The tendency is in this respect to identify the public interest with the wishes of the interested publics.[26]

RED TAPE, THE PICAYUNE, AND GOBBLEDYGOOK

Red tape—strict adherence to the forms and routine of office—is to be found in private and public bureaucracies everywhere. In part, it is a result of the desire of the members of a large, impersonal organization to protect themselves by making sure that their actions are in accord with established policy. If in doubt, the safest course is to apply as literal an

[25] H. H. Stroup, *Social Work: An Introduction to the Field,* American Book Company, New York, 1960, pp. 282–283.

[26] Avery Leiserson, *Administrative Regulation,* The University of Chicago Press, Chicago, 1942, p. 14.

interpretation of the rules as possible and to keep a written record of every move. One is less likely to get into trouble that way, and it also provides a framework within which to make decisions.

Certain other factors contribute to the existence of governmental red tape. One is the fact that in a democracy there is a need to account ultimately to the people for governmental actions. This accounting may be clumsy and at times obscure, but the requirement that bureaucrats follow the law as closely as possible stems from the notion that government cannot do what it is not authorized to do. Furthermore, Americans have never trusted their governments very far, and the statutes and administrative codes have long been filled with minute detail designed to limit the freedom of action of administrators. The result is an increase in the amount of red tape.

The seemingly ridiculous examples of red tape that are sometimes produced may be nothing more than by-products of the necessary work of carrying out the requirements of the law. The Interstate Commerce Commission once recommended that the ferry line between Weehawken, New Jersey, and Manhattan double the fare for uncrated elephants. Such examples can make bureaucrats appear absurd, but they may result from a request for an overall increase in rates. The ICC cannot fairly be criticized if a ferry line occasionally hauls elephants.[27]

Bureaucrats do sometimes seem to glorify the picayune. In 1942, an Army lieutenant was promoted because he devised a plan to save 250,000 envelopes for the public relations office at Fort Knox, Kentucky. He suggested that no envelopes be used for press releases, but that instead they should be folded, stapled, and addressed on the blank side.[28]

Bureaucrats are sometimes lax in their work, occasionally to the point of embarrassment. In 1962, the General Accounting Office reported that the United States Forest Service had in recent years permitted mining claims on public lands to be "used for purposes not related to mining"; in one case, for the operation of a house of prostitution; in another, for the operation of a nudist colony. A spokesman for the offending agency conceded that "in some cases Forest Service action to abate unauthorized uses of mining claims has not been sufficiently aggressive."[29]

Bureaucratic procedures are not always of standards adequate to encourage public confidence. In one controlled experiment that was conducted, to be sure, by a man with felonious rather than scholarly intent, identical income tax returns were sent to two different district directors of internal revenue. In each, a claim was made for a refund of $321.20. In one district, all but $4.70 of the claim was disallowed. In the other, the man was paid the full amount, with $10.37 added as an interest payment.[30]

[27] On the general subject, see A. W. Gouldner, "Red Tape as a Social Problem," in H. D. Stein and R. A. Cloward (eds.), *Social Perspectives on Behavior*, The Free Press of Glencoe, New York, 1957.

[28] *The New Yorker*, Jan. 11, 1951.

[29] United Press International dispatch, June 2, 1962.

[30] *Life*, Apr. 12, 1963.

Pressures on the bureaucracy to spend its funds on an annual basis—a phasing that may be unnatural and inappropriate to its operations—and the unpredictability of the legislative body in voting funds may also lead to behavior that citizens often regard as unsatisfactory and "unbusinesslike." Thus in 1950, the General Services Administration discovered that one Federal agency had on hand enough light bulbs to last for ninety-three years, given its current rate of use. It also had a two hundred and forty-seven-year supply of loose-leaf binders—but for some reason (or no reason), only a one hundred and sixty-eight-year supply of filler paper for them.

Gobbledygook—pompous verbosity and jargon—seems to be endemic to bureaucracies. The Office of Price Administration during World War II, concerned that ordinary businessmen often did not know what directives meant, hired a language specialist. In one case, he found the following alleged communication:

> Unless the Office of Price Administration or an authorized representative thereof shall, by letter mailed to the applicant in 21 days from the date of filing application, disapprove the maximum price as reported, such price shall be deemed to have been approved, subject to non-retroactive written disapproval or adjustment at any later time by the Office of Price Administration.

The specialist made the following translation:

> You must wait three weeks before you can change the ceiling price you applied for. O.P.A. can always change that price. If they do, they will write you a letter.

Someone in the Veterans Administration once replied to an applicant for a pension: "The non-compensable evaluation heretofore assigned to you for your service-connected disability is confirmed and continued."[31] If the veteran had enough education, he may have been able to understand that the VA had reviewed his case and was continuing to deny him a pension.

Perceptions of gobbledygook and red tape are culture-bound. They mean one thing to middle-class persons, who may ignore them or view them with annoyance or with amused tolerance. But they mean something else to the less-educated lower class:[32]

> To a person from the middle class, the fact that documents are required by a public [welfare] agency seems to be obvious and rational. Yet this judgment misses a basic fact about the poor generally, and the aged poor in particular: that they are precisely the ones least equipped to deal with the

[31] *Time,* May 7, 1947.

[32] Michael Harrington, *The Other America: Poverty in the United States,* Penguin Books, Inc., Baltimore, 1963, pp. 121–122.

bureaucracy of the welfare state. . . . There are those who develop their relations with welfare to a fine art, but there are many more who are literally terrified by the forms and the apparatus of a relief office.

Gobbledygook is probably a combination of inadequate ability in language usage, an effort to be legally precise in order to avoid court disputes, and a defense mechanism by which the bureaucrat protects himself from the citizen, for the latter feels confused and defeated by incomprehensible terms and expressions.

The bureaucrat is often ridiculed unfairly by critics, however, especially by critics who make appeals to conventional wisdom by making references to seemingly absurd activities—activities that may actually be scientifically or professionally sound. In 1962, Senator Paul Douglas of Illinois, although a highly educated man and a former university professor, complained that the National Institutes of Health had been wasting public money: It seemed the agency had spent funds to study the "social role of the aging wild ungulate," to make a "stereotactic atlas of the beagle brain," and to determine the information contained in echoes. Newspaper reporters had great fun with his report; the public scarcely had a chance to learn that each project had a purpose in scientific research.

Mediocrity exists in government agencies as in all organizations. We hear of the stupid and unimaginative more often than of the creative, more often of the stereotyped plodder than of the red-tape cutter. But a bureaucracy contains all types. During the attack on Pearl Harbor on December 7, 1941, a Navy chief petty officer refused to issue airplane parts without a requisition and a signed receipt; an Army colonel, trying to be helpful, told an Air Force colonel that he would send him a liaison officer; the Japanese commander of the task force never believed in the operation and ran from the scene without following up on his advantage, just as Union General George Meade had failed to pursue his advantage after Gettysburg. But it is also important that an admiral took over the supply depot mentioned above by commandeering some Marines with bayoneted rifles and that there were countless cases of heroism and quick thinking that saved lives and important military equipment.[33]

WHO IS IN CHARGE?

The Chief Executive. The President is important in the administrative process, not alone because he has the power to hire and fire department heads, but also because he is the popular leader, the coordinator of a variety of different programs and interests, the principal architect of policy, and the liaison between the agencies that provide services and the clientele groups who receive them (see Chapter 16).

[33] Illustrations from Gordon W. Prange, *Tora, Tora Tora!* McGraw-Hill Book Company, New York, 1963.

Figure 17-4

A BUREAUCRACY CONSISTS OF SEVERAL CATEGORIES

Category	Recruiting process	Characteristics	Major tasks	Educational level
Top management 	Appointed from political or civil service ranks; loyalty to administration in power often thought very important.	Relatively unrestricted by "red tape;" good education; much and varied experience.	Long-range planning; protection of values, methods, and personnel of agency from outside assault.	At least 4 years of college is common.
Middle management 	Administrative competence as tested by examination.	More devoted to rules of procedure than above; sometimes see both agency head and Congress as obstacles to good agency work.	Daily operations of agency.	At least 4 years of college almost prerequisite
Professional and technical staff	Formal examination or selection from list of licensed professionals.	Devoted to work; sometimes only dimly aware of political process and hostile to it; may be oriented more toward professional peers than to the agency.	Technical and professional tasks such as those of the lawyer, engineer, geologist, accountant.	Usually at least 4 years of college; often graduate or professional degrees.
Clerical, manual, and routine worker staff. 	Formal examination or straight hiring.	Some, but relatively low skills; often low aspirations; see government work as "a job."	Relatively routine, but essential to getting the agency's work done.	Most jobs, high school diploma or less.

The Department Head. Beneath the President, but above middle management and the clerical and minor employees, is the principal administrator—the agency head or head of a large division. He plays a vital role in policy formulation because he is likely to know his particular governmental activity better than the Chief Executive or the legislators. If he does not, he has easy access to those who do, but if this is the case, he is often at the mercy of the career civil servant specialist who may release information selectively in order to influence the positions of political administrators. He advises the Chief Executive, who wants ideas on a program; he testifies before congressional committees, telling them what he wants them to know and often skillfully withholding information that is unfavorable to his point of view.

The agency head as a symbol. The top executive, like the President and members of Congress, spends a great deal of time in symbolic activities. While matters requiring his decision pile up on his desk, he trudges from one meeting to another, often spending an afternoon in the White House, or in an interdepartmental meeting, or as an ex officio member of some board, or at a convention of a professional group with which his agency has important relations, making a comment here and there, or perhaps a platitudinous speech of welcome. In this way, his activities follow much the same pattern as those of executives in large private corporations.

From a rational or "efficiency" point of view, this activity may seem enormously wasteful, yet it is actually most important. At the top level, the administrator (often if he is a division or bureau head, he has worked his way up and knows the tasks of the lesser positions within his agency) leaves to trusted aides much of the actual work that goes out over his signature. He spends most of his own time in molding the agency members into an effective working unit, reassuring them of their importance by expressing their values in public speeches and by awarding a pin to the clerk-steno who has just completed thirty years of service; and seeking to maintain smooth relationships between the agency and its clientele groups, its pressure-group support, the Chief Executive, Congress, and potential friends and enemies of all kinds. His principal job is to understand and to communicate to others the values, loyalties, and goals of his organization.[34]

The informed citizen should also understand that, in the process of seeking to placate their various publics, the personnel in individual departments often come into conflict with one another. They compete over budgetary matters and in seeking status in the community. Some department heads feud publicly with other department heads—with resultant damage to all of government, since the citizen is likely to believe the worst that each official says about other officials.

[34] In this connection, see Philip Selznick, *Leadership in Administration,* Harper & Rowe, Publishers, New York, 1957. See also Norton E. Long, *The Polity,* Rand McNally & Company, Chicago, 1962.

Because the status and even the survival of a government agency may depend upon the way it is perceived by the public, large agencies maintain their own public-relations staffs. These may not often be large (Congress will generally see to that), and part of their activities may have to be disguised as other assignments, but they are vital.[35]

BUREAUCRACY AND DEMOCRATIC GOVERNMENT

The problem of bureaucracy in contemporary America is essentially this: Citizens want many services from their governments, but the values of the culture imply that there is a danger of losing democratic control over policy making if professional bureaucracies grow large.

Not all citizens are in favor of the expansion in the size and number of governmental services that has taken place since the beginning of the Great Depression (1929). Probably no citizen favors having his government furnish all of the services that it supplies. But many citizens support each service. At the same time, regardless of whether a bureaucracy is developed and selected through merit-system examinations or on the basis of patronage appointments, today's jobs are technical and complicated. By their nature, they indicate the necessity for the use of qualified specialists. And qualified specialists do not speak lay language. The result is a desire for service coupled with a popular suspicion of bureaucracy and no little fear of the implications for democracy in its growth. People like the product of government; they do not like the means that seem necessary in order to deliver the product.

Bureaucracy as the Antithesis. Keeping in mind the political ideologies that have guided Americans in evaluating politics, it is understandable that bureaucracy should come to be regarded as the antithesis of democracy. Several decades ago, when the proponents of a professional bureaucracy also gave support to the concept of integrated administrative control under the Chief Executive, they reinforced one popular fear with another. There has, further, been a tendency in both folk philosophy and in some academic writing to romanticize the representative character of legislative bodies—national, state, and local. Furthermore, this same combination of forces has been lined up at times in support of the idea that "whatever the people want is right, and they should have it." Hence, if the people want a chaotic pattern of government, it must be right; if they prefer amateur legislative opinion to that of professional bureaucratic opinion, the former must be better. This type of idea seems to stem from Rousseau's romantic notion of the "general will," and it is reflected in the Latin expression: *Vox populi, vox dei* (The voice of the people is the voice of God). The

[35] On the attitudes, role perceptions, and problems of high-level administrators, see C. H. Coates and R. J. Pellegrin, "Executives and Supervisors," *American Sociological Review,* 22:217–220, April, 1957.

difficulty with this self-congratulatory notion is that the *vox populi* can be interpreted in a great many ways by congressmen, bureaucrats, White House aides, and editors. And what seems to be the voice of the people today may be viewed by those same people as all a horrible mistake tomorrow (see Chapter 9). The congressman, who must perforce take the short view, and the bureaucrat, who is sometimes permitted the luxury of the long view, may both speak with the voice of the people—if the problem is viewed from the vantage point of the historian.

We may assume that it is difficult at times to turn the bureaucratic troops around or to divert their path; that red tape and literal interpretations of the rules are endemic to bureaucracy; that mature bureaucracies tend to resist innovation and lack initiative; and that trained specialists are sometimes impatient with unknowing laymen: We do not need to assume at the same time that bureaucrats wish to destroy the system in which, as citizens, they too live.

A Closing Note. The detailed application of policy on a day-to-day basis cannot be considered apart from other phases of policy making. For that reason, the topic of administration and the behavior patterns of the bureaucracy appears in other chapters of this book as well as here. Relations with Congress, the President, and the courts are discussed in Chapters 14, 15, 16, and 18. Issues involved in matters of internal security and the civil rights of civil servants are discussed in Chapter 19.

SELECTED BIBLIOGRAPHY

For this chapter, the reader will find two periodicals especially useful, the *Public Administration Review* and the *Administrative Science Quarterly.* Both contain many useful articles; the latter emphasizes the findings of empirical or behavioral research. Additional reference material and relevant information may be found in the textbooks on public administration such as that of Pfiffner and Presthus [16].

The public interest as it relates to the bureaucracy is discussed in Friedrich [9] and the references to the topic in Chapter 8. Bureaucracy as a problem in democratic society is a familiar and important topic. It is discussed by Appleby [2], Blau [5], Eisenstadt [7], and Merton [14]. Bureaucracy is satirized by Parkinson [15]; its history in America is told by White [24 to 27].

Ideological factors as they relate to the civil service are of concern to Kaufman [12] and Sorauf [20]. The two Hoover commissions sought to apply ideological considerations to bureaucratic practice (see Fesler [8]).

Simon [19] and Waldo [22] discuss bureaucratic behavior. The special function and problems of top management are discussed by Bendix [3], Bernstein [4], David and Pollock [6], and Selznick [18].

1. The American Assembly: *The Federal Government Service,* Columbia University, Graduate School of Business, New York, 1954.
2. Appleby, Paul: *Big Democracy,* Alfred A. Knopf, Inc., New York, 1945.
3. Bendix, Reinhard: *Higher Civil Servants in American Society,* University of Colorado Press, Boulder, Colo., 1949.

4. Bernstein, Marver H.: *The Job of the Federal Executive,* The Brookings Institution, Washington, D.C., 1958.
5. Blau, Peter M.: *The Dynamics of Bureaucracy,* The University of Chicago Press, Chicago, 1956. (Available in paperback.)
6. David, Paul T., and Ross Pollock: *Executives for Government,* The Brookings Institution, Washington, D.C., 1957.
7. Eisenstadt, S. N.: *The Political Systems of Empires: The Rise and Fall of the Historical Bureaucratic Societies,* The Free Press of Glencoe, New York, 1962.
8. Fesler, James W.: "Administrative Literature and the Second Hoover Report," *American Political Science Review,* 51:135–144, March, 1957.
9. Friedrich, Carl J. (ed.): *The Public Interest,* Nomos V, Atherton Press, New York, 1962.
10. Friendly, Henry J.: *The Federal Administrative Agencies: The Need for Better Definition of Standards,* Harvard University Press, Cambridge, Mass., 1962.
11. Kaplan, H. Eliot: *The Law of Civil Service,* Matthew Bender & Company, Inc., Albany, N.Y., 1958.
12. Kaufman, Herbert: "Emerging Conflicts in the Doctrines of Public Administration," *American Political Science Review,* 50:1057–1073, December, 1956.
13. Leiserson, Avery: *Administrative Regulation,* The University of Chicago Press, Chicago, 1942.
14. Merton, Robert K. (ed.): *Reader in Bureaucracy,* The Free Press of Glencoe, New York, 1952.
15. Parkinson, C. Northcote: *Parkinson's Law and Other Essays in Administration,* Houghton Mifflin Company, Boston, 1957.
16. Pfiffner, John M., and R. Vance Presthus: *Public Administration,* 4th ed., The Ronald Press Company, New York, 1958.
17. Rosenblum, Victor G.: *Regulatory Agencies: How to Get into TV,* Harcourt, Brace & World, Inc., New York, 1961.
18. Selznick, Philip: *Leadership in Administration,* Harper & Row, Publishers, New York, 1957.
19. Simon, Herbert A.: *Administrative Behavior,* 2d ed., The Macmillan Company, New York, 1957.
20. Sorauf, Frank J.: "Patronage and Party," *Midwest Journal of Political Science,* 3:115–126, May, 1959.
21. Van Riper, Paul P.: *A History of the United States Civil Service,* Harper & Row, Publishers, New York, 1958.
22. Waldo, Dwight: "Bureaucracy" in *Collier's Encyclopedia,* Crowell-Collier Publishing Co., New York, 1962, vol. 4, pp. 732–739.
23. Waldo, Dwight: *The Study of Public Administration,* Random House, Inc., New York, 1955.
24. White, Leonard D.: *The Federalists: 1789–1801,* The Macmillan Company, New York, 1948.
25. White, Leonard D.: *The Jeffersonians: 1801–1829,* The Macmillan Company, New York, 1951.
26. White, Leonard D.: *The Jacksonians: 1829–1861,* The Macmillan Company, New York, 1954.
27. White, Leonard D.: *The Republican Era: 1869–1901,* The Macmillan Company, New York, 1958.

CHAPTER

18

LAW AND THE JUDICIARY

The German social scientist Max Weber stated that governmental authority is justified by appeal to tradition, appeal to legality, or by charismatic leaders* whose actions of "psychic coercion" are widely accepted as proper. In America, the courts use all three bases in their major role as legitimizer of public policy. Americans have felt that something more than the legislative process is needed for making policy. They desire an independent body that will stand above the political battle and judge acts to determine whether they are in harmony with the Constitution.

***CHARISMA. Natural, inspirational leadership. Originally (in the New Testament), it referred to a "gift" stemming from God's grace, but since Weber's time, it has referred to secular leadership as well. See Carl J. Friedrich,** *Man and His Government,* **McGraw-Hill Book Company, New York, 1963, especially pp. 114–115.**

THE LAW

Its Application in Primitive and Complex Societies. Disputes in simple societies can generally be settled by appealing to the gods for a sign, by combat, or by ordeal. The Biblical story of Cain and Abel includes settlement by the first two of these techniques. As society grows more complicated through division of labor and multiplication of social roles, the need for a more predictable and equitable method of settlement becomes greater. In international affairs, we still sometimes try to settle disputes with bombs and armies, but within nations the function of peaceful conflict resolution has gradually become the responsibility of government officials. In primitive societies, decisions are made by chiefs or priests; in modern societies, decisions are made by persons with specialized occupations who are called judges. Personal justice tends to be arbitrary, however; and this fact, reinforced by custom and a desire for predictability, has gradually led to the establishment of some rules as precedents for other cases. Thus in England the king appointed circuit judges; through their decisions, a common law for the nation gradually developed.

The eminent legal scholar Roscoe Pound has said, "The real foe of absolutism is law." The web of precedents developed in law helped limit the arbitrary power of English kings, and this evolved into the form of government called "constitutional government," that is, government by rules that limit the actions of governors. Not only was there a uniform law under which all citizens were, ideally, treated equally, but the rulers themselves were limited in their actions by this law.

Over the bronze doors of the marble palace that is the home of the United States Supreme Court is engraved "Equal Justice under Law." No society has completely achieved this ideal, but the existence of one set of rules that are applied impartially in all disputes underlies our conception of the social function of the courts.

Types of Law. When cultures are young, law is generally thought of as "natural law," divinely inspired or revealed as were the Ten Commandments. Later, as we see in the history of Western Europe, law came to be considered a manifestation of the natural order of the universe; and since it was "natural," man could discover it without supernatural assistance. Finally, the conviction developed that law is an instrument invented by man to suit his own needs.

The legal scholar John Austin, an Englishman who wrote early in the nineteenth century, insisted that law was man-made through government. This concept is called "positive law." There is no law of ethics or morals, Austin argued, that stands above government-made law. According to this concept, what governments determine is the law, no matter how unjust it may seem to individuals.

American legal scholars have added yet another concept, that of "sociological law." While agreeing that law is made only by government, advocates of this viewpoint argue that law must be applied by courts according to current social and economic viewpoints. Thus, while the writers of the Constitution did not specifically define flogging as "cruel and unusual punishment," and perhaps the Founding Fathers themselves did not think that it was, we tend in our day to define it as just that. (Delaware still permits it, although the question of its constitutionality is before the courts.) This school of judicial thought emphasizes that law should be adjusted continually to social and economic realities in order to resolve conflicts within a society and hence to provide a stable social system. These adjustments reflect the dominant political ideology of the day.

Americans have made use of all three concepts of law, and a lively argument continues about the importance of each. Conscientious objectors to war claim that there is a higher law than the law that is government-made. The writers of the Declaration of Independence openly stated that they were discovering nature's law, and the authors of the Bill of Rights, which is part of the Constitution, seemed to follow their lead. The Constitution itself has come to be considered as the font of true law because, though man-made, it has served the nation so well that a myth has developed which places it psychologically, as well as legally, above man-made law. In the various interpretations of its clauses, however, there has been more than enough room for the introduction of sociology, for the phrases of the document are general. The President and Congress have participated in such interpretation, but legally the Court can nearly always make the final pronouncement. Did, for example, the Founding Fathers consider the transportation of stolen cars or the transmission of electricity across state lines to be "interstate commerce"? The Supreme Court does, and bases its decision on the Constitution. The Founding Fathers, however, antedated both Thomas Edison and Henry Ford and so had to leave such interpretations to others.

Symbols of Legitimacy: The Cult of the Robe. The symbolism of courts is calculated to awe the visitor and, in effect, tell him that the courts are impartial arbiters and legitimizers of the law. This is why judges alone among major civilian officials wear a uniform—a black robe. The emphasis on the role of chief legitimizers adds to the symbolism of the judicial role.

The atmosphere of the Supreme Court is especially calculated to subdue the visitor. The Supreme Court building, constructed in 1936, is so ornate that Louis D. Brandeis, a justice at the time of its completion, refused to use the suite set aside for him. Inside the door is an elegant sign. It reads, "Silence." Attorneys sitting in the front benches are warned by attendants to button their coats before the session begins. Newsmen receive the justices' opinions in a newsroom downstairs so that the decorum of the Court is not disturbed. As the justice begins speaking, the script is shot downstairs by a pneumatic-tube device. The Court has its own legal jargon—one observer has called it "professional pig Latin."

The justices themselves are impressive in their black silk robes. The solicitor general, the attorney for the government, wears a cutaway. This was formerly true of other lawyers as well. One has recalled that when he first appeared in court in 1892, he was refused admission because he was not properly dressed. Justice Horace Gray whispered to his colleagues, "Who is that beast who dares to come here with a gray coat?" The lawyer borrowed a morning coat and all was well. But as a reminder of ancient judicial traditions, quill pens are still placed at the lawyers' desks.

The justices are prisoners of formal procedures that have the psychological effect of enhancing the dignity of the Court. They courteously refer to each other as "brethren" and each day when the Court is in session, before taking their places, each shakes hands with every other, even though, as Justice James Byrnes remarked in his autobiography, they may have all seen each other previously. They file in, at a signal, from behind a red curtain. The Chief Justice of the United States (before 1929, merely "of the United States Supreme Court") takes the big leather chair in the center. The others sit on his left and right according to seniority.

Judges outwardly emphasize their impartiality by divesting themselves of securities in corporations that may have cases before courts. They may also disqualify themselves in cases in which one of the participants is a relative or friend or in which the judge has had some close association with the parties concerned. The justice himself makes this decision, and his interpretation of responsible action is sometimes challenged. There is also a contrary pressure to minimize disqualifications lest there be too few justices hearing a case. In the late 1940s, justices sniped at each other over the issue of proper disqualification. In the past, there have been a number of instances in which the justice has had an interest, but did not step aside. Thus, in the case of *Marbury v. Madison,* in which Chief Justice Marshall ruled that the Supreme Court had the power of judicial review, Marshall was a party at interest. As Secretary of State in the Adams administration, Marshall had neglected to send Marbury his appointment as justice of the peace, and the question involved was whether Marbury had to receive official notice in order to have a right to the commission. In most cases, though, the justices pride themselves on their strict impartiality and seek to avoid all suspicion of personal interest in cases they rule on.

FUNCTIONS OF THE JUDICIAL PROCESS

The judiciary in American government has a special position with special powers. The courts can declare acts of the President, statutes of Congress, and provisions of state constitutions null and void according to the Federal Constitution. In few other democracies do the courts decide such important policy questions and in few other nations are judges so revered. In America, we have tended to stress the negative side of judicial review—how it has blocked action of the President or Congress. As we shall see, however, in its positive aspect, judicial review has more often resulted in approval and, in fact, acceptance of many changes that earlier courts rejected as unconstitutional. The result has been to bestow added legitimacy to all public policy and stability to the democratic system of peaceful change. Most Southerners accepted the legitimacy of the school integration order, once the Court placed its stamp of approval on the policy. Others have accepted personally distasteful decisions because of court action.

In the time of Andrew Jackson, the French visitor Alexis de Tocqueville wrote, "The major issues of American life sooner or later appear as questions for decision by the courts." Although some observers have argued that the power of the Supreme Court has been weakened in recent decades, the criticism leveled against the contemporary Warren Court is as intense as criticism has been at any time in our history, indicating that the justices still make important and often highly controversial decisions about public policy. This chapter is intended, among other things, to place the policy-making aspects of the courts in perspective.

The courts have a second major function in democratic systems—to apply general rules to specific cases. Law cannot achieve legitimacy unless there is some assurance that it will be equitably applied. In democracies, as we shall see, special procedures have been elaborated by the courts to ensure equality before the law. The specific application of statutes to cases is the more routine aspect of judicial policy making, at least, as compared to the constitutional function. This, nevertheless, is the function that forms the bulk of the work load of courts.[1]

The Legal Myth. The Supreme Court has been enshrined in myth, and this myth has become one of the sharpest weapons available to the justices. The official doctrine has been that the judges place the disputed statute next to the Constitution, apply some ancient rules of jurisprudence, and it becomes obvious to them that the statute is either constitutional or unconstitutional. Because they are acting out this special ritual, they are presumably unaffected by their own personal prejudices and desires or by the pressures of public opinion. Their decision is claimed to be based on logic and the pure application of legal formula.

The folklore of justice has been sharply criticized by legal scholars and by the justices themselves. Justice Oliver Wendell Holmes, before World War I, admonished his brethren that the Fourteenth Amendment did not enact the rugged individualism of the English philosopher Herbert Spencer into the Constitution. Earlier, Holmes in his writings on the common law had concisely stated the position that judges make, rather than find, law:[2]

> The life of the law has not been logic: it has been experience. The felt necessities of the time, the prevalent moral and political theories, intuitions of public policy, avowed or unconscious, even the prejudices which judges share with their fellow-men, have had a good deal more to do than the syllogism in determining the rules by which men should be governed. . . . The very considerations which judges most rarely mention, and always with an apology, are the secret root from which the law draws all the juices of life. I mean, of course, considerations of what is expedient for the community concerned.

The doctrine that the justices attempt to resolve societal conflict—although a more realistic description than that which emphasizes textual interpretation—is also misleading; for if the judges make, rather than discover, law, the undemocratic nature of their life tenure makes them subject to attack. The nine Delphic oracles are replaced by nine very human men who are trying to legislate their own prejudices into law—prejudices that, in some cases, have been repudiated by the voters over several elections.

Modern social scientists, armed with measurement techniques, have

[1] See Robert A. Dahl, "Decision-making in a Democracy: The Supreme Court as a National Policy-maker," *Journal of Public Law,* 6:279–295, Fall, 1957.

[2] Oliver Wendell Holmes, *The Common Law,* Little, Brown and Company, Boston, 1881.

Figure 18-1

THE MYTH IS ONE OF OBJECTIVITY: THE PRACTICE IS ONE OF DIVISION ALONG IDEOLOGICAL LINES

Cases* / Scale score†	Douglas	Black	Warren	Brennan	Whit-taker	Frank-furter	Harlan	Stewart	Clark	Votes
Scale score†	29	27	25	23	6	4	3	3	1	
Marshall v. United States, 1171	+	—	+	+	+	+	+	+	+	8–1
Greene v. McElroy, 1400	+	+	+	+	+	+	+	+	—	8–1
Ladner v. United States, 209	+	+	+	+	+	+	+	+	—	8–1
Smith v. United States, 991	+	+	+	+	+	+	—	—	—	6–3
Lee v. Madigan, 276	+	+	+	+	+	—	—	+	—	6–3
Burns v. Ohio, 1164	+	+	+	+	+	—	—	NP	+	6–2
In re Sawyer, 1376	+	+	+	+	—	—	—	+	—	5–4
Farmer's Union v. WDAY, 1302	+	+	+	+	—	—	—	—	+	5–4
Barr v. Matteo, 1335	+	—	+	+	—	—	—	+	—	4–5
Howard v. Lyons, 1331	+	—	+	+	—	—	—	—	—	3–6
Brown v. United States, 539	+	+	+	+	—	—	—	—	—	4–5
Bartkus v. Illinois, 676	+	+	+	+	—	—	—	—	—	4–5
Frank v. Maryland, 804	+	+	+	+	—	—	—	—	—	4–5
Irvin v. Dowd, 825	+	+	+	+	—	—	—	+	—	5–4
Beacon Theatres v. Westover, 948	+	+	+	+	—	NP	—	—	+	5–3
Vitarelli v. Seaton, 968	+	+	+	+	—	—	+	—	—	5–4
Uphaus v. Wyman, 1040	+	+	+	+	—	—	—	—	—	4–5
Barenblatt v. United States, 1081	+	+	+	+	—	—	—	—	—	4–5
Harrison v. N.A.A.C.P., 1025	+	—	+	+	—	—	—	—	—	3–6
Raley v. Ohio, 1257	+	+	+	+	—	—	—	NP	—	4–4
Pittsburgh Glass v. U.S., 1237	+	+	+	+	—	—	—	—	—	4–5
Rosenberg v. United States, 1231	+	+	+	+	—	—	—	—	—	4–5
Anon. 6 & 7 v. Baker, 1157	+	+	+	+	—	—	—	—	—	4–5
Mills v. Louisiana, 980	+	+	+	—	—	—	—	—	—	3–6
Abbate v. United States, 666	+	+	+	—	—	—	—	—	—	3–6
New York v. O'Neill, 564	+	+	—	—	—	—	—	—	—	2–7
Harris v. United States, 560	+	+	—	—	—	—	—	—	—	2–7
Draper v. United States, 329	+	—	NP	—	—	NP	—	—	—	1–6
Williams v. Oklahoma, 421	+	—	—	—	—	—	—	—	—	1–8
Total participations:	29	29	28	29	29	27	29	27	29	256
Inconsistent votes:	0	4	0	0	0	0	1	4	3	12

Legend: + For the civil liberty claim
— Against the claim
NP Nonparticipation

Coefficient of reproducibility: .953‡

* The figures following case titles represent the beginning page of the case in the Supreme Court Reporter, volume 79.

† But for his nonparticipations Stewart could have been ranked 5th instead of 7th. This fact emphasizes the need for caution in interpreting the significance of the rank order within blocs when the S.S. differences are as narrow as in the 1958 term.

‡ Tests for chance occurrence indicate this scale pattern is highly significant.

The 1958 Warren Court was divided on civil liberties cases between dogmatic libertarians and cautious pragmatists. Charles Whittaker was the "swing man," (S. Sidney Ulmer, "The Analysis of Behavior Patterns on the United States Supreme Court," Journal of Politics, *22:629–653, November, 1960.)*

been able to scale the justices on such diverse issues as attitudes on civil liberties cases, the rights of criminals, or general liberalism and conservatism. In other words, the justices form blocs, so that a member's position can be predicted on some subjects with a fair degree of accuracy. Such findings destroy the myth that there is only one way in which the words of the Constitution can be interpreted. As Max Lerner has written, "Judicial decisions are not babies brought by constitutional storks."

The Twilight of the Supreme Court? Recent analysts of the judicial process (the legal realists) have seen modern justices at a disadvantage, for although there are still citizens who react in terms of the myth, the justices themselves no longer wholly believe in their freedom from the values they have been taught. But at the same time, the legal myth has had an effect on the behavior of the judges. The justices sit in an environment that makes them tense in their effort to be neutral.

One reaction has been for the justices to fashion a doctrine of judicial restraint; that is, they consciously attempt not to substitute personal values for those of legislative bodies and attempt to place the burden of proof on an act's unconstitutionality rather than on its constitutionality. The doctrine of judicial restraint requires that the Court will not declare a statute unconstitutional if it can avoid doing so by deciding the case on some other basis. In cases of doubt, the assumption is to be made in favor of constitutionality. If the case can be decided by state law without raising a Federal question, it is so decided. The application of this doctrine has, however, not been consistent.

The second reaction has been for the Supreme Court to retreat from an entire field of national cases. Since 1937, the Court has generally avoided attack from the Congress or President. It has recognized that in matters of foreign affairs or war it has little check on the President. Through judicial interpretation of the interstate commerce clause, it has also largely put aside its veto of actions in the economic field—though the ruling of President Truman's seizure of the steel mills as unconstitutional in 1952 was a reassertion of some power in this field. In effect, however, it has decided to follow the election returns as interpreted by the President and Congress in matters of regulation of the economy.

This does not mean, however, that the Court is like a toothless tiger with no role to play in modern policy making. Several facts help clarify the Court's position:

1. In the past, the Court has not been able to withstand the combined opposition of Congress and the President for long. It has only been able to delay action for a time; in the end, it has lost all its major battles either by reversing itself as new judges are appointed or by being reversed through constitutional amendment (see Chapter 4). It continues to have the power of throwing monkey wrenches into the machinery, though it pays a price in public prestige and will probably not be successful in the long run for, as Justice Felix Frankfurter has noted, "the Court's

authority—possessed neither of the purse nor the sword—ultimately rests on sustained public confidence in its moral sanction."

2. There is growing awareness that the Court is not always the final word on what the Constitution means. Congress, the President, and the voters who support them also interpret the document, and when they agree on an interpretation, the Court generally accepts it.

3. Congress and the President frequently disagree. In recent times, the Court has more frequently sided with Presidents against Congress, though the position could change at a future time. In any case, disagreement between Congress and the President offers the Court an opportunity for action as a referee and, hence, as the effective decision maker.

4. The Supreme Court may also rule on the constitutionality of state actions. This is the field of influence it has always had. Most statutes declared unconstitutional have been state acts. The role of arbiter of the federal system has become of even greater significance as the Court has retreated from the position of major policy maker on the national level. The decisions on racial segregation, on criminal procedures in state courts, on deprivations of civil liberties by state and local officers, and on apportionment of state legislatures are the major opinions the court has issued since the days in which it unsuccessfully battled the New Deal program of Franklin Roosevelt.

The Supreme Court is in its twilight only if one accepts the image of the Court as the exclusive custodian and interpreter of the Constitution. It is true that policy no longer depends so much on whether, as President Theodore Roosevelt once said, "a judge on the Supreme Court [comes] down head or tails." In national matters, justices have acquired the habit of generally coming down heads. But even so, they still perform an important function of legitimating the actions of the government in the eyes of the nation. Ordinarily, in dealing with Federal cases today, new ideas are justified by precedents (traditions); they are fitted into the Constitution; and the logic of the law is put behind the action of Congress or the executive branch. The legal jargon and ritual provides the important air of solemnity required to convince us that new law is as valid as old law. Finally, the Court has carved for itself a new role as arbiter of the federal system, which in many respects is uniting a highly diversified nation that is facing international crises.

Other Functions of the Courts. Judicial institutions perform several functions in American politics. Several observers have noted that the courts, with their prosecuting attorneys and judges, provide an excellent career ladder in politics and help in part to explain the affinity of law for a political career. Politicians may leave the bench or a prosecutor's post to run for governor, congressman, or even President. At the same time, the courts provide a haven for defeated candidates if they are lawyers. For political parties, Federal court posts provide plums that can be used to reward the party faithful. As we have seen, senators, who must approve Federal judicial appointments, have been especially skilled in using senatorial courtesy in respect to judicial posts to advance their own political fortunes.

THE LEGAL PYRAMID

The United States Constitution may be viewed as standing at the apex of a hierarchy of laws. As in any hierarchy, the highest-ranking position takes precedence over those below, and the courts are bound to recognize the established order. The Constitution parcels out law-making powers to Congress and the President, prohibits certain kinds of law making to every legislative body or administrative officer, and leaves all unassigned powers to the states. (The states parcel out their own law making powers in their own constitutions.)

Below the Constitution and next in order, according to the "supreme law of the land" clause, are treaties and statutes (written laws of Congress)—assuming, of course, that these are legally adopted and are within the meaning of the Constitution. (If they are not, they are not valid law and can be set aside by the courts.) Next come the administrative orders and directives (or in legal terms, ordinances) of Federal administrators. These must have been issued under authority of congressional statute or presidential order in areas where the President can act in the absence of legislation.

Independent of Federal powers are state powers. However, when the two conflict and the Federal action is constitutional, it is supreme. The state constitutions are legally superior to state statutes and gubernatorial directives. Below them comes the common, or judge-made, law.

The common law is made up of unwritten interpretations of judges in cases over the years, dating back to the time of Henry I of England (1100 to 1135). It is based on the principle of *stare decisis* ("Let the decision stand"), by which each case is decided, whenever possible, on the basis of an essentially similar earlier case. There is no Federal common law, although the courts apply the principle of *stare decisis* where they find it applicable. Federal courts apply United States or state statutes or common law, where applicable, or they rule that a case has no standing in Federal court.

A second type of law, tracing its history back to the Middle Ages, is "equity." It was devised by judges for special cases where common law would result in injustice. Injunctions, for example, are equity proceedings to *prevent* an injury or wrongful act; common law would only be applicable after injury occurred. Like common law, equity has also made use of precedents.

Below statutes are administrative rulings and the ordinances passed by local government bodies.

In all cases within the hierarchy, if a rule at one level conflicts with a rule at a higher level, it is null and void. In the event of conflict, an alternative always exists—to change the statute law or the constitution, whichever is necessary, but this is the uncommon solution.

THE SYSTEM OF COURTS

Most attention paid to the courts is in terms of its dramatic policy-making functions. The Supreme Court tells President Harry Truman that he cannot seize the steel mills, and headlines all over the nation blare out the fact. The rest of what the courts do is dismissed by the average citizen as dull routine.

What occurs in the lower courts defines public policy for the average citizen. The Supreme Court can generally only set broad policies; the lower courts fill in detail. If communication between lower courts and the Supreme Court were instantaneous, then only what the Supreme Court declared on broad policy would be important at any given moment. In fact, communication is not instantaneous. Appeal takes a long time and is often abandoned because of its expense. Only what the Supreme Court considers of great importance is reviewed; at other times, lower courts decide. Sometimes they must innovate policy.

Even when the Supreme Court has ruled, there may be delays in implementing its policy at lower levels, as was seen in the actions of lower Federal courts of the South on civil rights matters. What the Supreme Court ultimately decides generally prevails throughout the court system in due time, but during an interval that may be of short or long duration, citizens live with the decisions made by lower courts. And this is the level at which most decisions are made.

The interrelationships within the Federal system of courts and the relationships between state and Federal systems of courts need to be examined before one hastens to the dramatic arena of the Supreme Court and its policy pronouncements.

The American system of courts is not a single hierarchy; rather, there are parallel systems of courts with different constituencies. While the United States Supreme Court is the final interpreter of the Constitution, independent action by state and lower Federal courts exists.

Federal Courts. Each state and major territory has one or more Federal district courts. These are the work horses of the federal system, hearing "in the first instance" about 125,000 cases annually. About 4,000 of these cases are appealed to the Courts of Appeals (formerly called circuit courts). The Courts of Appeals also have the duty of reviewing and enforcing the orders and actions of many Federal administrative agencies and departments, including the Federal Trade Commission and the National Labor Relations Board. The Constitution makes no mention of specific lower Federal courts: The Courts of Appeals with eleven circuits and 75 judges, and the district courts, with ninety-one districts and 311 judges were established by congressional statute. (The figures are as of 1962.)

In the United States Courts of Appeals decisions are generally made by a panel of three, while in all but a few types of cases, the district judges sit individually, with or without jury, depending on the type of case and the wishes of the parties. Federal court procedures tend to be stricter than those in most states in protecting the civil rights of participants. The trend of the present Supreme Court has been to keep them that way.

Special Federal courts. There are also several specialized Federal courts, established to hear special kinds of cases. These include the Court of Claims, dating from 1855. It permits the national government to settle claims against itself. Before its existence, citizens could get such settlement only by special act of Congress; and many claims, particularly for small amounts, are still settled this way. The Court of Customs and Patent Appeals was established in 1910 to review decisions of the Customs Court,

Figure 18-2

THE FEDERAL COURT SYSTEM

COURT	NUMBER	NUMBER OF JUDGES (1962)	PRINCIPAL DUTIES
Supreme	1	9	Final appeal, major cases only
Courts of Appeals	11 circuits	75	Routine appeals from lower Federal courts and administrative tribunals
District	91 districts	311	Principal trial court in cases of Federal jurisdiction
Tax	1	16	Cases involving disputes on taxes owed the United States
Military Court of Appeals	1	3	Appeals from general courts martial
Territorial	4	4	Trial courts in American territories
Claims	1	5	Claims for damages against the United States
Customs and Patent Appeals	1	5	Appeals on customs and patents disputes
Customs	1	9	Cases involving customs duties

the Patent Office, and the Tariff Commission. These two courts were declared constitutional courts in 1953 and 1958, respectively; this means that their judges have the same life tenure and status as Federal judges who preside in the regular court hierarchy and that the courts are largely free of nonjudicial duties.

Congress has also created "legislative courts," in which it sets the terms of office and to which it sometimes delegates administrative as well as judicial duties. These include the Customs Court, the Court of Military Appeals, and territorial courts.

State Courts. Each state has established its own system of courts to hear cases involving its constitution, statutes, and ordinances. The hierarchical structure of such courts generally follows that of the Federal courts but varies widely in details.

There is no automatic right of appeal from state to Federal courts. The state courts are organized independently of the Federal courts and are only tied to them in that they too are bound by the Federal Constitution.

Administrative Integration. The Chief Justice of the United States is the head of the Federal judicial system. He has the power to shift judges temporarily from one Federal circuit or district to another when dockets are crowded. The Supreme Court sponsors judicial conferences at district and circuit levels to discuss court procedures, make studies, and recommend to Congress legislation concerning the courts. The Supreme Court also has attached to it the administrative office of the United States courts. Its director, who is appointed by the Supreme Court, gathers statistics and information about the operation of the Federal court system. His reports can be subtle prods to lower courts that fall behind in their work or are lax in their procedures. This administrative centralization of the Federal system has occurred mainly since 1922. There was additional legislation in 1939.

Some states give similar powers over the state court systems to their state chief justices or supreme courts. (In a few states, considerably more powers are granted.)

Jurisdiction. Not all disputes are heard in Federal courts. Most, in fact, cannot be, but are settled in courts at the state level, with no appeal to the Federal courts. Federal courts hear cases only if a constitutional question, Federal statute, or treaty is involved; if the matter is a dispute occurring on shipboard; and if certain parties are involved.

The latter include disputes in which the national government is a party, those involving foreign diplomats or citizens of foreign nations, and those between two or more states or citizens of different states. There is some overlapping, since it may not be immediately clear which aspect of a case will be emphasized. Also, some cases involving states or their citizens may be tried in state courts, for Congress has granted concurrent jurisdiction. A case involving a possible Federal question may begin in a state court, as did many civil rights cases, since they concerned state law; or, if it is clear that a Federal question is involved, the case may be introduced by the parties directly into the Federal courts. The Supreme Court's position that cases be settled by state law, if possible, discourages the invention of peripheral Federal questions.

Federal Courts in Action. Most cases enter the Federal courts at the district level. Only in a few matters do the Supreme Court and the Court of Appeals have original jurisdiction.

The district courts are trial courts. They hear the original controversy and determine the questions at issue, the relevant facts, and render a judgment. In the ordinary run of cases, appellate courts, such as the Court of Appeals and the Supreme Court, are supposed only to review points of law, not fact. There are a few exceptions.

A decision is reversed on appeal if the application of a law is judged to be wrong, if it does not follow from the evidence, or if faulty procedures were followed. Witnesses and juries are not used in appellate courts.

Cases can be classed as criminal or civil. In criminal cases, the government is the plaintiff, acting as protector of the peace, and the accused is the defendant. Civil cases are those in which no crime is involved—disputes over wills, for example. The government may be one of the parties in a civil case (collection of unpaid taxes), but it is always a party in criminal cases. Procedures differ for each type of action.

In the civil case, the first step is framing the point at issue through complaint by one party and answer by the other. Next follows the hearing stage. It may or may not be before a jury, as the parties wish or, in some cases, as the law provides. Attorneys present arguments, evidence, witnesses, and have the right to cross examine opposing witnesses. Then follows the decision stage. The judge charges the jury, summarizing the facts and relevant law. The jury must usually present a unanimous verdict for the plaintiff to win, although in state courts, there is something of a trend away from this rule. The judge may set aside the findings of the jury in certain cases, but this is uncommon.

In criminal cases, following an arrest, the accused has the right to appear at a preliminary hearing before a judge; he will determine whether there is sufficient evidence to warrant holding the prisoner for trial. If charges are not specified and if such a hearing is not held promptly, a representative of the prisoner can appear before a judge to demand a hearing through the writ of habeas corpus. The judge sets bail for less serious crimes. Formal charges are then made in one of two ways: by a grand jury indictment or, in many states, on information of the prosecutor. At the trial, the judge is a generally neutral presiding officer who applies the rules. As in civil cases, he charges the jury after the evidence has been heard. In specific situations, he may set aside the jury verdict in civil cases; in criminal cases, he may suspend the sentence.

These procedures are based on the notion—very roughly similar to that of the scientific method—that if "proper" procedures are used, the result will normally be just and that those concerned will feel they have had a fair hearing. The definition of "proper" is the result of a long tradition of justice. First, courts require that a genuine controversy exist, and that the accused is protected from unreasonable search, seizure, or interrogation. Further, the accused must be accorded a speedy and public trial, assistance of counsel, and reasonable bail. He has the right to an impartial jury; to subpoena witnesses; to know the charge and the specific law claimed violated; not to suffer cruel and unusual punishments or be placed on trial again, once acquitted (double jeopardy); and he has the right to acquittal in cases of doubt.

Somewhat over half the cases heard in Federal district courts are civil actions. In about 40 per cent of these, the United States is a party. They include cases to recover overpayments by the United States government, those arising out of labor disputes and Food, Drug and Cosmetics Act actions, and claims made against the government. About one-third of the civil cases involve citizens of two different states (e.g., in auto accidents). The rest involve admiralty disputes or special Federal questions (trademarks, copyrights, antitrust suits).

Criminal cases generally involve narcotics, auto theft, illegal immigration, liquor and internal revenue violations, national security, kidnapping, fraud, or theft.

Federal Court Trends. One cannot assume that the lower courts continually innovate policy, but they also are not without some opportunities. No one really knows the extent of lower court policy making. Cases are commonly routine, based on well-established facts. But novel cases continually arise. The result is Federal policy making by courts in both substantive and procedural matters. Important innovations need to be legitimized by the Supreme Court or by Congress and the President. But most lower court actions stand as the more or less routine application of Federal government control to the actions of citizens.

Changes are, however, occurring, particularly in procedural matters. An overview of the Federal court system since the beginning of the twentieth century reveals these distinct trends:

1. A clearer hierarchy of courts in terms of division of labor, with the Supreme Court handling the most important constitutional questions.

2. A strengthening of the Chief Justice as the administrative supervisor of the Federal court system to bring about uniformity in procedures, greater efficiency, and a balance of the work load among the judges at each level.

3. A greater professionalization of judicial positions, insulating judges from the more mundane pressures of the political arms of government (life terms, generous salaries and retirement benefits, and duties that are, for the most part, judicial).

4. An encouragement of interaction among the Federal judges at each

level and with the Federal judges at other levels (through judicial conferences).

Integration, professionalization, and independence from the other political arms of government have been the goals. Such reforms have generally been encouraged by the professional legal groups, university law school professors, and the organization of Federal judges themselves through the judicial conferences. The members of the Supreme Court and its Chief Justice have also often exercised crucial influence in getting Congress and the President to agree to this program.

CONSTITUTIONAL POLITICS

Some have said that Chief Justice John Marshall, who enunciated the doctrine of judicial review in *Marbury v. Madison* (1803), was making an unconstitutional grab for power. The argument is now irrelevant, for the Supreme Court's power to make interpretations on the constitutionality of statutes is clearly part of our unwritten Constitution—part of what a disinterested Martian would miss if he tried to understand our government just by reading that document.

The facts of the case were that the Adams administration had made some last-minute judicial appointments as it was leaving office. Among them were some minor ones for justice of the peace. Jefferson's Secretary of State, James Madison, refused to deliver the commissions. Marbury brought suit to force Madison to give him his J.P. commission. According to the Judiciary Act of 1789, the Court had power to hear such cases. But Marshall argued that that part of the act was an unconstitutional expansion of the Court's jurisdiction. But Marshall avoided an important issue: Should the Court's interpretation of the Constitution (judicial review) have greater authority than the combined interpretation of President and Congress?

In recent years, the less important duties of the Supreme Court have been limited so as to give members more time for cases involving constitutional questions. In the late nineteenth century, minor cases comprised about 40 per cent of the docket. In 1891, justices were relieved of circuit duties (although they technically remain assigned to circuits), and in 1925 they were given increased power to determine the selection of the cases they wish to hear.

The Supreme Court has additional powers. Interpreting what Federal statutes mean in a specific case can have important policy implications. For example, labor supporters of the Clayton Act of 1914 at first agreed with the head of the nation's major labor union, who called the act "labor's Magna Charta." Court interpretation, however, in their eyes, made the effect of the act practically meaningless. An additional power of courts is that of declaring individuals in contempt of court and imposing sentence upon them.

The most important source of power for all courts, but especially for the

United States Supreme Court, is derived from the great deference accorded it by the general public. The tradition of judicial independence, which is supported by public opinion, prevents Congress or the President from using to full effect some of the most important weapons they hold against the courts.

The Court and Congress. Legally, Congress can quickly bring the Supreme Court to its knees.

The number of justices is not determined by the Constitution, but is set by Congress. It has varied from five to ten, though for almost one hundred years, it has remained at nine. Both the Federalists in 1800 and the Radical Republicans in 1866 reduced the number to prevent Presidents of the opposition from filling vacancies as they occurred. Abraham Lincoln, on the other hand, persuaded Congress to increase the number in hopes of packing the court for favorable decisions on Civil War cases.

Congress also decides the jurisdiction of the Supreme Court, except for a small number of cases that arise from disputes between foreign nationals and American citizens and between states. Only these last two are mentioned in the Constitution. The Reconstruction Congress of 1866, mentioned earlier, took away from the Court the power to rule on certain policies; and a case then actually before the Court was withdrawn from its jurisdiction (*Ex parte McCardle*). In its ruling, the Court acquiesced, though it had agreed to hear the case.

Congress sets the salaries of all judges and the monetary details of their retirement. It also can make all rules of procedure for the courts, though it has delegated some of this power to the courts. Finally, only the Supreme Court is mentioned in the Constitution. Congress sets up the lower Federal courts and decides how many judges will serve on each.

The Senate has the additional function of confirming all judges. It rejected George Washington's nominee for Chief Justice and has refused confirmation to several Supreme Court nominees. It can delay through lengthy hearings, as it did in the appointment of Thurgood Marshall, legal counsel of the National Association for the Advancement of Colored People, to a judgeship. Through senatorial courtesy, it dictates the choice of lower court judges. The Congress also may impeach judges, and most impeachments in the nation's history have been of lower court judges. (Of twelve impeachments, nine were of judges; four of them were removed from office.) A number of lower court judges have resigned when threatened with impeachment.

Congress may also initiate constitutional amendments. If three-fourths of the states ratify their proposal, it is adopted as part of the Constitution. Three times Congress has used this method to reverse the courts—with the Eleventh, Fourteenth, and Sixteenth Amendments.

The President and the Courts. The President has fewer direct powers over the courts than does Congress, but his influence is, nevertheless, considerable.

The President nominates all Federal judges. In respect to the Supreme Court, his selections are ordinarily accepted. On the average, Presidents appoint a Supreme Court justice about once every twenty-two months, but not since 1930 has a nominee been rejected by the Senate.

The President is head of the bureaucracy that enforces the laws. Andrew Jackson is supposed to have said of a decision, "John Marshall has made his decision, now let him enforce it." Franklin Roosevelt once had a speech prepared to explain why he would not follow an expected decision of the Court on a gold standard case. The decision turned out to be favorable to his wants, and he was saved an act of defiance. A lesser issue is the battle that has persisted for at least thirty-five years between the Supreme Court and the Bureau of Patents. It indicates the limits of Court power over executive agencies. The Court has frequently demonstrated its disapproval of many patents issued—an estimate by one justice is that 10,000 less would be issued each year if the Supreme Court had the time to review every patent decision.

Presidents have occasionally used their personal powers with the electorate to fight the courts. President Theodore Roosevelt recommended recall of unpopular state decisions by a vote of the people, but he never had the courage to directly confront the courts. Franklin Roosevelt proposed, quite legally, an expansion of the Supreme Court up to fifteen members by the appointment of a justice for every member over seventy years of age. (His plan was rejected by Congress.) Jefferson encouraged his supporters in Congress to impeach Supreme Court justices whose decisions seemed to him unreasonable. (He too failed.) Despite these setbacks, the public pressure generated by Presidents seems to have had its effect, for the justices generally treat the threat of a presidential onslaught with considerable respect. Franklin Roosevelt, having lost the Court-packing battle of 1937, found that he had nevertheless won the war; the Court, with no change in membership but under pressure from the Chief Justice, began to uphold important New Deal legislation. Chief Justice Hughes above all wanted to save the dignity and powers of the Court, as President Roosevelt wanted to save his program. Each got much of what he wanted.

The Court and Democratic Values. One of the Court's constitutional strengths is, paradoxically, one of its greatest weaknesses in a democratic society; Presidents serve at most for two terms, congressmen stay in office as long as they can get reelected, even bureaucrats retire at sixty-five, but Supreme Court justices may serve as long as they live. They are thus constitutionally almost completely secure from the pressures of public opinion. This very security invites comparisons to a council of elders in a primitive society.

Justices in the past have occasionally continued to serve when they were blind or deaf. At least one member of the Court in the last century was judged to be senile by his colleagues; from time to time he was unable to recognize the Chief Justice. In 1869, Congress provided the first retirement system and, in 1937, established a more generous system, with full pay after a minimum of ten years of service at the age of seventy or fifteen years at the age of sixty-five. Yet on the average, justices have served 6½ years beyond the time they would be eligible for full retirement benefits. Of the eighty-seven vacancies on the bench between 1789 and 1962, 55 per cent resulted from the deaths of justices while serving. In recent years, a trend seems to be developing for voluntary retirements. Some of these men continue to hear occasional cases in the lower Federal courts at the assignment of the Chief Justice.

Questions of the capability of justices to serve has not been the major criticism of life tenure, however. Presidents from Thomas Jefferson on have argued that exponents of political doctrines repudiated at the polls have retreated to the Supreme Court. The political commentator Mr. Dooley (Peter Finley Dunne) once said, "The Supreme Court follows the election returns," suggesting that the Court did indeed respond to public pressure. One legal scholar has added, "Yes, the Supreme Court follows the election returns—but those of about a generation ago."

The drumbeat criticism that a body beyond the reach of the electorate is deciding some of the most crucial issues facing the nation is one to which the Court is especially sensitive. The justices, although secure in their tenure, are vulnerable to pressure. The Court has quite often retreated in the face of adverse criticism from a President, Congress, or the public.

The courts, perhaps more than either the Congress or the President, benefit from the fluid nature of the American governmental system. If Congress and the President could agree most of the time, the power of the courts would decline. However, in a system of shared powers, the courts have been able to carve out and maintain a role based on their power to declare laws and ordinances unconstitutional.

JUDICIAL PROCEDURES AS POLITICAL WEAPONS

The formal procedures of the Supreme Court are austerely simple. As a result of a change of rules lobbied through Congress by Chief Justice William Howard Taft in 1925 (an informal agreement had been made with Congress), the nine Supreme Court justices need hear only the cases that any four justices wish to hear. This change was designed to limit consideration to important cases involving policy questions. Justices review cases in which there is an automatic appeal because an action has been declared unconstitutional by lower courts, those in which one of the parties argues for an appeal, and any other case in state or Federal courts that the justices regard as involving an important Federal question. The Court, however, decides when an important question is ripe for hearing. Thus it has been criticized both for admitting trivial disputes and for shutting the door against important cases. Many questions are decided by summary decisions without a written opinion.

The Court sits from October until sometime in June. For two weeks, the justices hear oral arguments by attorneys. Each side in a case is given one hour to present its arguments, though sometimes this time period is shortened or, on rare occasions, lengthened. Time is precisely noted by a system of warning lights on the attorney's stand. It is said that Chief Justice Hughes, who was a strict timekeeper, once cut off a lawyer in the middle of the word "if." The justices interrupt the lawyers freely and informally with questions and comments. Lawyers for each side also submit detailed written briefs, which the justices may study before or after the oral arguments.

On Fridays, the justices meet in secret to discuss the week's cases. The Chief Justice begins by summarizing each case. The justices then give their views in order of seniority. A vote is then taken in order of reverse seniority. The Chief Justice assigns the writing of the opinion for the majority if he is on that side; if not, the senior justice of the majority makes the assignment. Any justice may, however, write a concurring or dissenting opinion. After the two weeks of hearings, another two weeks are set aside for study and the writing of opinions. Usually on the next Monday, opinions are briefly summarized by the justices who have written them, and the decision is announced.

This formal procedure, while simple, lends itself to considerable political maneuvering in the furtherance of policy goals. It can be used to defend the Court against Congress, the President, or private citizens. It is the internal part of protecting the Supreme Court as an institution. The weaving together of three strands, furtherance of policy preferences, and external and internal defense of the Court as an institution, is what is meant by the "politics of judicial procedures." Such procedures, like procedures in Congress or in the executive branch, are not neutral. They are weapons in the fight to achieve policy and institutional goals and are sometimes used by justices with rare skill. Some examples follow.

The Certiorari Game.* Agreement by any four justices makes it mandatory for the Court to hear a case. In the 1950s, the liberal wing of the Court, in the view of some critics, crowded the calendar with cases involving employee injuries under the special railway and marine acts. Unlike other cases of employee injuries that are settled by workmen's compensation, the employees in these cases must sue for damages. The cases brought up were generally those won by employers, and frequently they were re-

---

***CERTIORARI.** **A writ from a superior court ordering an inferior court to deliver up the records of a case.**

versed.[3] The Supreme Court majority thus indicated to Congress its disapproval of the Federal Employees Liability Act and the related Jones Act by turning the Court into a workmen's compensation bureau. The Court does the same for criminal procedures at the lower court levels by accepting any letter written in any fashion by any state or Federal prisoner who claims he did not receive a fair trial. Reviews of such cases are time-consuming, but they are also embarrassing enough to lower courts to encourage a more strict adherence to proper trial procedures.

The Court protects itself as an institution by selectively refusing certiorari in politically sensitive cases. In implementing its decision to outlaw segregation, the Court moved gradually, taking up one new aspect after another. Logically, it could have accepted all major questions at one time and dealt with them together. It is better politics to move ahead to the goal gradually—or at least, so the Court seemed to believe when it failed to grant certiorari in a case involving segregation in housing. The same process of gradual change is typical of Court action in the other two major questions in which it has been embroiled; apportionment of state legislatures and civil liberties.

Justice Felix Frankfurter and others have often pointed out that refusing certiorari does not mean that the Court agrees with the lower court verdict, but simply that the case does not raise a novel constitutional question in the view of four justices. Nevertheless, the effect of such a refusal is to support the lower court, and this is also the case when dealing with cases in summary fashion by merely affirming, without opinion, the lower court decision. What the failure to grant certiorari seems to mean is: "The lower court decision stands—at least for today. Tomorrow the Court may feel differently." Groups like the National Association for the Advancement of Colored People plan their appeal strategy carefully. They seem to feel that too many refusals to hear a particular type of case has an adverse effect on its prospects.

The Hearing. Justice Felix Frankfurter became notorious for his forceful and persistent questioning of attorneys presenting oral briefs; some lawyers called it the "Felix problem." On occasion, when an attorney becomes confused by such questioning from any of the justices, a sympathetic justice has fed him questions that give the answer he may be looking for, along the line of "Wouldn't it be true that . . . ?" This is a minor part of the skirmishing over policy questions and is a technique also commonly used in legislative debates, where one legislator will ask another a question that includes the answer.

More important is the service that the hearing serves for the Court. As one justice has said, the justices want to know what is the milk in the coconut. They want to know what policy questions are involved and the implications of particular actions. The procedure is similar to a congres-

[3] Glendon Schubert, "Policy without Law: An Extension of the Certiorari Game," *Stanford Law Review,* March, 1962, pp. 284–327.

sional investigation, with the difference that the witnesses (lawyers) are trained professionals who can be expected to communicate succinctly.

The Court in Conference. The heart of the Supreme Court's activities is the secret conference during which a case is discussed after the oral hearing, or earlier, when the decision is made as to whether or not to grant certiorari.

The Court is too small to set up committees and delegate to them types of cases in the fashion of Congress disposing of its work. Every justice must participate in every decision that is made; therefore, every justice must be apprised of all the facts and arguments. What occurs is an interaction among nine men, one of whom is formally designated as the leader. In such a situation, personal relations become important: they have an effect on both the satisfaction that justices derive from their jobs and the amount of work they are able to accomplish effectively.

The findings of small-group research can be useful in understanding Supreme Court deliberations. First, the Court has a set of norms, sanctions, and rewards that are designed to protect it as an institution. To the world, it must make a united front if it is to be fully effective. Justices bent on wasting time in conference must be restrained. Justices who too often dissent may feel silent social pressure to desist. Justices who handle difficult assignments well may bask in the pleasure of their colleague's obvious approval. Just as the Western Electric bank-wiring girls (in the Hawthorne experiments of Elton Mayo) or as college students in general have ways of defining and enforcing group standards for a reasonable term paper, so the justices have a norm of what is proper behavior—what constitutes pulling one's load and acting in socially acceptable ways.

The Court also has a system of norms based on seniority of its members. The justice with lowest seniority acts as messenger and doorman for the secret conference room. Thus, sixty-one-year-old Oliver Wendell Holmes trotted back and forth when he was appointed in 1902. In contrast, former all-American quarterback Byron (Whizzer) White, forty-four, almost escaped the roadwork altogether—Arthur Goldberg was appointed a few months after him (in 1962). Seating is in order of seniority, as is giving opinions in conference; but, as we have noted, voting is in reverse order. It is assumed that the senior justices should not influence the voting of junior members, but this arrangement also gives senior members an opportunity to shift when they see the drift of the formal vote. The judge with greatest seniority on the majority side assigns the writing of the opinion if the Chief Justice is in the minority. All of these are subtle aspects of an initiation process by which groups socialize their members to the significance of group membership and the requirements of group behavior.

Conference leadership. The Court in conference needs two kinds of leadership with two purposes: (1) to get its job done with as little waste of time as possible; and (2) to maintain a spirit of teamwork and high morale among members. The leadership pattern differs as personnel change. In the Hughes Court, both functions were performed by the Chief Justice himself. In the Stone Court, no one consistently filled either role. In the Taft Court, the Chief Justice handled the social leadership role, while Justice Van Devanter, who had his confidence, exercised task leadership by keeping discussion to the point. There is also the possible combination of reversing this type of leadership.

The effect of these configurations can be great in terms of the Court's status and its ability to counter criticism. In the Stone Court, there was open wrangling among the members (particularly Black and Jackson), with a decline in the Court's prestige, morale, and production. Conferences were long, tiring, and unsatisfying. On the other hand, under Hughes the Court operated as a smooth machine while facing one of the greatest crises in its history, the Court-packing plan of 1937. Justices who were in violent disagreement did not permit policy differences to spill over into personal antagonisms. There was some dissatisfaction, but production was high, with efficient use made of the justices' time. The Taft Court seems to have hit a balance between these two. The majority worked in close harmony, and morale was high. On the other hand, there were longer and more frequent conferences than under Hughes.[4]

When it operates in harmony in conferences, when its tasks are carried out with reasonable efficiency, and when personal relations of the justices are harmonious, the Court is strong in the face of criticism, even when there is disagreement among members. When leadership is missing, the Court flounders and gives ground to either the legislative or executive branch, or to both.

Strategies of Opinion Writing. Court opinion is argument designed to educate the public to the policy questions and interests involved in a given course of action. The educational process is perhaps as important when the Court is divided as when it is united. But the Court as an institution is stronger if dissents are kept at a minimum and if the justices speak in one voice, a fact recognized by all the participating justices. What results could be described in terms of game theory: The jockeying for position is very much like what occurs when a legislature seeks common ground—views are frequently compromised so that a majority can be formed.

The reason that this is particularly true of the Court relates to what we have called the folklore about the Court. Important questions are best decided with large majorities rather than by narrow 5 to 4 or 4 to 3 decisions. To be avoided if at all possible is a split decision—4 to 4. The reaction of the citizens to a split decision is thought to be: "If the Constitution is that muddy for the judges, it must be a fairly shaky decision." Reformers have suggested that on questions involving the declaration of

[4] David J. Danelski, "The Influence of the Chief Justice in the Decision Process," in Walter F. Murphy and C. Herman Pritchett (eds.), *Courts, Judges and Politics,* Random House, Inc., New York, 1961, pp. 497–508.

unconstitutionality, the Court be required to have an extraordinary majority as, for example, 6 to 3 or 7 to 2. These comments imply that it is to the institutional advantage of the Court to prevent splits and dissents. Generally, one of the aims of the Chief Justice is to "mass the court." One of the most successful of such efforts was that of Chief Justice Warren, who guided the Court to a 9 to 0 decision outlawing segregation in the schools. He succeeded in keeping the Court unanimous for a number of years over a number of other cases that grew out of that decision.

The Chief Justice has been less successful on other issues. Frequently, the majority opinion is watered down somewhat to persuade some dissenters to join the majority. On occasion, opinion writers have included verbiage that made little sense to them because it would draw over one vote. Chief Justice Hughes, who guided the Court through the difficult period of attack from President Franklin Roosevelt, is said to have voted several times against his convictions in order to make what was a bare majority into a larger one.

The function of dissent. There are occasions when compromise is impossible because opinions are held too firmly. Dissent then becomes a means for educating the public concerning an alternative policy. Dissenting justices may hope that their views will later be read with approval by students of law and other judges. Several justices have become famous because their dissenting views in one generation became public policy in the next. Oliver Wendell Holmes was perhaps the most noted dissenting judge.

A dissent also can serve as a warning or an encouragement to interest groups that, given new appointments to the Court, the majority position might change. A dissent may also simply be the last cry on behalf of a discarded doctrine. Justice James McReynolds, after the change in position in the Court in 1937 toward New Deal measures, forcefully restated the arguments of the old majority on several occasions. The advantages possessed by the writer of the dissent are these: His disagreement always to some degree embarrasses the majority; and, while the majority opinion may be stated in equivocal language, his dissent can be forceful and ringing since it need compromise with no one.

The assignment of opinions. In massing the court, Chief Justices can appeal to reason or even use their own prestige to influence colleagues. Some students have claimed than an occasional justice has an affinity for agreeing with Chief Justices: when a new Chief Justice comes on the scene, he changes his views to coincide with the new leader. But justices have virtually permanent tenure and can afford to be independent. Therefore, the greatest power the Chief Justice has in encouraging unity in the Court is in the assigning of opinions. This is a weapon that can be used to discipline as well as to reward. Justices are human beings. They like to write what are considered to be precedent-making opinions. They like to think that their words will be carefully studied by constitutional lawyers for centuries and that they will become staple reading for students in public-law classes. The Chief Justice holds in his hands this gift on most occasions. He may seek to gain greater consensus by using the strategy of assigning the opinion to the justice whose opinion is closest to the minority.

The writing of opinions may also be used to throw off balance potential critics of the Court. Generally, to lend prestige to an important opinion that changes precedent, the Chief Justice himself writes it. Another technique used is to assign the opinion to a conservative if it is likely to be viewed as a liberal pronouncement, and vice versa. Probably the most openly calculated choice of opinion writing for public-relations purposes occurred when the Chief Justice was persuaded by another justice to switch the writing of the opinion outlawing the white primary, a decision that would be unpopular in the South. It had been given to Felix Frankfurter, a Jew, a liberal, a political independent, a former professor who had been born in Europe and was appointed from abolitionist New England. It was reassigned to Stanley Reed, a Kentucky-born moderate who had spent much of his nonjudicial career in Democratic party politics.

The final reading of opinions also is a weapon of the Court. The staging of the announcement has a formality that is impressive to all but the most cynical. The opinions are often printed in full in the Monday *New York Times,* as are the messages of Presidents to Congress or the text of important legislation.

POLITICAL PRESSURES FROM OUTSIDE THE COURT

Individuals and groups cannot directly lobby the justices. The myth of the Court and the cult of the robe prevent such open attempts at shaping the policy decisions of this highly select elite. This does not mean that the Court is not sensitized to certain pressures, however. It operates in an environment that is somewhat special—in some respects, it is similar to that of the other two branches, but it is also quite different. A review of those groups and individuals to which the Court is most sensitive and the way they can bring pressure to bear is instructive in understanding why decisions are more than simply the personal opinions of justices or solely the result of pure legal logic.

The President and Congress View the Court. The legal powers of the Chief Executive and Congress in respect to the Supreme Court have already been discussed. They are sufficient to crush the Court if they are fully applied. The principal informal power rests in the fact that the President is often viewed as the embodiment of public opinion. Congress likewise can claim to have a democratic mandate. When both agree in viewing the Supreme Court with disfavor, the latter is badly pressed. It is pushed into the unwelcome position of seeming to be an undemocratic, aristocratic elite dictating to a democratic nation. Its only defense then is in the myth of the Court as an impartial arbiter.

As one observer has noted, however, the Supreme Court seldom overestimates its political power potential. Generally, it pursues the same policies aimed at by at least one of the other branches, as well as by private groups in society.

In the past, the Court was the favorite of the business and conservative interests that frequently were able to dominate Congress and the Presidency. With the rise of strong Presidents in the twentieth century, and especially since 1937, the Court's alliance has shifted. Its more recent decisions have tended to be supported most strongly by those who are crucial in the election of our Presidents—civil rights groups, urbanites, organized labor, and those pressing for the strengthening of civil liberties. Most of these groups have also preferred Federal action to state action, just as Presidents commonly have.

The Solicitor General Views the Court. In about one-half of the cases heard in the Supreme Court, the government is a "party at interest." The Solicitor General, who argues almost all of the government's cases, thus has close ties to the Court. A number of men who have held this office, such as Stanley Reed, who served during the Presidency of Franklin Roosevelt, have themselves become justices. A greater number have become judges in the lower Federal courts.

The Solicitor General is, in theory, a subordinate of the Attorney General. In practice, he is so important to the President, his program, and his potential position in the history books that the Chief Executive personally makes the selection. Ordinarily, he is chosen with great care and a special concern for his competence in the exacting role.

The tactic of most men holding this office has been to gain the confidence of the justices. Each wishes to encourage the justices in the notion that, when he does appeal a case, there is good reason to grant certiorari and perhaps to overrule a lower court decision. Thus a Solicitor General may issue a "confession of error" that shows his clear disagreement with the handling of the case in the lower courts by lawyers representing governmental agencies, and he will refuse to appeal the case, even when the government has lost, because he regards the government argument as flimsy. Such actions do not win the love and respect of the lawyers of governmental agencies affected, but they do preserve the image of the Solicitor General as a sophisticated and able attorney. The criticism has been made by government lawyers that the Solicitor General's staff is more loyal to the Supreme Court than to the executive branch. If this is so, it is because on him rests the administration's case. Presidents select with an eye to the prestige of the appointee. President Kennedy's choice was Archibald Cox, a respected professor of the Harvard Law School, whose writing on legal subjects has received the careful attention of many legal scholars.

But this relationship between Solicitor General and Court is a two-way street, just as are all personal interactions that occur with regularity over time. As the Solicitor General is successful in building up his reputation for careful pleading and a thorough mastery of cases, so the justices feel some compunction to live up to his expectations of their behavior. This is a subtle influence relationship that cannot be easily documented. But justices are human and have egos. They do not like to feel that their actions are viewed with disapproval by one whom they meet almost daily and whose legal acumen they have come to respect.

State and Lower Federal Courts View the Court. The action of the Supreme Court is often only a review of how a lower court decided a case. If the Supreme Court justices disagree with the decision, their action is frequently to order the lower court to rehear the case. Thus in the 1962 case of *Baker v. Carr,* the Supreme Court merely told the Federal district court that it had been incorrect in assuming that it did not have the power to decide whether the apportionment of the Tennessee Legislature was fair. The Supreme Court directed the lower court to hear the case, but gave no criteria by which to judge it or suggestions as to how to implement an order it would issue, if any, based on its review of the case.

What happens to cases remanded to the lower courts? In roughly one-half of them, the parties winning a retrial lose the case again, but on other grounds. Lower Federal court justices do not always comply completely with the spirit of a Supreme Court decision in cases where it is cited as a clear precedent. Compliance in state courts is even less common. This does not mean that the Supreme Court is openly defied, though it sometimes has been; in such circumstances, costly delays usually result. (Justice, especially in the marginal cases where the high court is trying to drag a reluctant lower judiciary with it, is extremely expensive. Victory in such cases depends upon generous financing as well as able lawyers. It costs about $20,000 to appeal a case to the Supreme Court, and such an appeal, even if victorious, may not end the litigation necessary to win a case.) A common tactic is for the lower court judge to accept a lawyer's argument that a case may present a special feature that places it outside the principle enunciated by the Supreme Court in another case. The slow implementation of the school segregation decision by state courts in the South, following the lead of local attorneys general, is an example.[5]

The lower Federal courts. The Supreme Court irritates the sensibilities of lower court justices by overruling their decisions, sometimes in stinging language, and by finding fault with procedures in their trials. But both Federal and state court judges have weapons for retaliation. They may express themselves publicly in speeches to professional associations, in their opinions, in law journals, and in the public press. Some of the lower court justices have considerable local political influence. Some have great professional prestige—occasionally more than some Supreme Court justices.

[5] Samuel Krislov, "Constituency vs. Constitutionalism: The Desegregation Issue and Tensions and Aspiration of Southern Attorneys General," *Midwest Journal of Politics,* 3: 75–92, February, 1959.

The Federal lower court judges also have occasional personal contact with Supreme Court justices through the regularly scheduled district and circuit judicial conferences. Such confrontations, or even the prospect of them, may at least serve to temper the phrasing of an opinion. The conferences work both ways, of course: The Supreme Court justices use the same conferences to influence the beliefs and procedures of the lower court bureaucracy. (Friction with the lower courts has also been reduced through the justices' influence on judicial appointments, an influence regularly used by Chief Justice Taft.[6]) But the conferences have also sometimes endorsed legislation designed to reverse a position taken by the Supreme Court. Such endorsements are given publicity in congressional committee hearings by those displeased with the Court ruling.

Federal district and circuit judges serve for "good behavior" or, in effect, life. They are nominated by the President and confirmed by the Senate, and they are overwhelmingly of the party of the President making the nomination. Senatorial courtesy requires that the nominee be approved by the senator or senators of the state involved, providing they are of the President's party. During the Eisenhower period, the Senate majority leader, Lyndon Johnson of Texas, though a Democrat, succeeded in persuading the Republican President to nominate his choice to a post as a Texas district judge by blocking action on other matters. In effect, what generally happens is that the senator selects the judges in his area from among the lawyer-politicians who have supported him.

The state judiciary. State judges have even more independence of the Supreme Court. The doctrine of judicial restraint requires that the Supreme Court rule only if a Federal question is clearly involved. If the case can be settled in another way so that only state law is involved, it will not be reviewed. Some state judges have framed their opinions skillfully so that their arguments discourage Federal review. They also evade the intent of Federal decisions by technicalities more often than lower Federal court judges do.

State judges also may influence public opinion by speeches and writing: The most dramatic recent instance of this came in 1958, when the Conference of State Chief Justices, a group formed with the encouragement of the American Bar Association, publicly criticized the Supreme Court for centralizing power in Washington by unnecessarily deciding against the states.[7] The major public criticism concerned decisions in the civil liberties, subversion, and criminal-procedure areas, and some Southern justices probably were also critical of the trend in civil rights cases. The Supreme Court's *Nelson* decision offers an example of what the group attacked. This decision held that, since Congress had taken action in the field of

[6] Walter F. Murphy, "Chief Justice Taft and the Lower Court Bureaucracy," *Journal of Politics,* 24:453–476, August, 1962.

[7] Conference of Chief Justices, *Report of the Committee on Federal-State Relationships as Affected by Judicial Decisions,* Virginia Commission on Constitutional Government, Richmond, 1959.

sedition by passing the Smith Act, Congress had indicated a desire to preempt this field: As a result, state legislation on sedition was invalid. The Supreme Court retreated somewhat from this position in *Uphaus v. Wyman* by holding that states could still legislate on matters involving sedition against state governments.

Criticism of state judicial decisions is often politically explosive in effect. A rebuke by the Supreme Court is sometimes viewed as an affront, not just to the judge or the local court, but to the entire state.

Law-enforcement Officers View the Court. Recent decisions of the Court have insisted that law-enforcement officers, especially on the Federal level (the FBI, an arm of the Department of Justice, in particular), but also on state and local levels, follow more strictly procedures protecting the civil liberties of suspected criminals. These procedures concern search, seizure of evidence, evidence gained by wiretapping, third-degree methods, etc. Enforcement officials have claimed in some cases that these rulings have placed heavy handicaps on their efforts and that the Court is unnecessarily concerned about the civil rights of criminals. These officials are well organized at the state level. The prestige of the FBI with congressional committees and the general importance of the Attorney General, who heads the Department of Justice, make the law-enforcement fraternity formidable as an opponent. On the other hand, the trend toward professional police personnel and standards is tending to accommodate procedures to the views of the Court.

Lawyers View the Court. Fewer than one-half of the members of the legal profession belong to the American Bar Association. This is partly because lawyers are individualistic and partly because the association has generally reflected the views of its more conservative members since its inception. The association has been critical of the Warren Court and has kept up a steady criticism of its more liberal rulings. Such criticism has its effect on public opinion and touches the sensibilities of the justices, as was indicated when the Chief Justice publicly announced his resignation from the association. Through its meetings and publications, the association also has an effect on the opinions held by many lawyers.

A different kind of influence is that of the university law schools and the law journals published by some of them. Since 1930, articles in journals, especially those of the most prestigeful schools, have been cited occasionally in opinions. Justices respect these schools for their standards of scholarship, as is indicated by the fact that they often choose their law clerks from them. They are sensitive to opinions coming from this source, although such opinions tend to be liberal rather than conservative. Congressman Wright Patman claimed, however, that corporations were paying legal scholars to plant articles against strict antitrust enforcement in such journals. Most observers regard this, if accurate, as an infrequent occurrence that is discouraged by the professional standards of the scholars themselves. The charge has also been made in the conservative *U.S. News and World Report* that the young law clerks chosen each year by the justices (two for each justice and three for the Chief Justice) influence their employers toward liberal doctrines. The charge is generally denied by both justices and former law clerks who have written on the subject.

Interest Groups View the Court. The most direct way an interest group can lobby before the Supreme Court is by carefully shepherding along the route cases that will raise questions that the Court will rule on in their interest. Part of the problem is getting the proper cases; another is making sure that the Federal question is raised in the most effective way possible in the lower courts; another is getting the case into a sympathetic lower court so that favorable decisions may be achieved there. Economic interest groups, such as organized labor and corporations, have engaged in such strategies. Two small groups, the Jehovah's Witnesses religious sect and the National Association for the Advancement of Colored People, have also been especially successful in this area.

Another type of lobbying takes place through writing an *amicus curiae* (friend of the Court) brief in a case before the Court. This is a brief in support of one of the parties. It is supposed to state new ideas; it may also offer a parade of prestigeful individuals or groups who are indicating in this way their position on the case. In the late 1940s, the court decided that this method was being abused; now it only permits such briefs if both parties in the case agree to their admission.

Social Scientists View the Court. The Supreme Court has not paid much attention to what social scientists think of it, aside from showing some interest in the scholarship of behavioralists who have mapped voting blocs of the Court or have used other such methods to explain judicial actions. However, most justices have come to accept the views of the sociological school of jurisprudence, which holds that law stems from experience and that its purpose is resolving conflicts in society. As a lawyer, Justice Louis D. Brandeis began to use briefs that cited social statistics and to state the effect of a decision in social and economic terms. The "Brandeis brief" has become increasingly common in recent years. In the segregation cases, the testimony of social scientists on the effect of school segregation on Negro children was admitted in a brief before the Court, although the data used have since been subjected to serious criticism both by legal traditionalists and by other social scientists on technical grounds. Such is the rather modest influence thus far of the social scientists on judicial decisions.

The Public Views the Court. Justice Robert Jackson, in a series of lectures delivered at Harvard shortly before his death, concluded that public opinion is the final protector of the Court. This is the view that has been presented here. The Court may defy public opinion in matters of secondary importance when one of the elective branches sides with it. When criticism mounts, however, the Court has always beaten a retreat. At the same time, the public has preserved the Court from the kinds of direct attacks that the President and Congress could constitutionally make upon it: reduction in the Court's jurisdiction over some cases arising from the Constitution, as was proposed by Senator William Jenner in the 1950s; impeachment of justices for political reasons, as was proposed by the founder of the John Birch Society and others; or packing the court by adding additional judges, as was proposed by President Franklin Roosevelt.

The public still seems to feel that there is wisdom in having three policy-making branches in government, one of which can play the role of independent arbiter and place or withhold the stamp of legitimacy on the actions of government.

The Court and Its Critics. The Warren Court has been severely criticized by congressional groups that have been able to form a coalition in Congress and thus thwart presidential action on many issues—economic conservatives, who are frequently Republicans, and conservative Southern Democrats. Southerners have been critical of the Court's civil rights decisions, and conservatives generally have disapproved of the civil liberties decisions and those limiting the powers of state governments.

It is not difficult to see why the Court's action has invited such attack. On the national level, Congress and the President have been able to develop bold policies in the international field, but few new programs affecting the domestic social arrangements have been passed since 1937, despite the campaign promises of Presidents and the platforms of both major parties. From the stalemate have come only minor improvements or changes in existing legislation, such as the extension of social security benefits, the reorganization of welfare policy, or the increased Federal highway program. The Supreme Court, on the other hand, has encouraged what promises to be two social revolutions on the domestic scene: ending segregation in public schools and public facilities, and breaking the hold of conservative rural and small-town residents on state legislatures. (Since state legislatures establish congressional districts, the resulting increase of urban pressures will also be felt in the national House of Representatives.) A more quiet reform, but one with widespread effect, is the insistence on higher standards in the judicial procedures in state courts and stricter protection of civil liberties in state and Federal police work.

Any such program of social reform invites criticism and bitter enmity, and it will as long as the Supreme Court pursues it. It also invites support. The discerning student will note that the Court's allies are members of the contemporary majority that forms the constituency of presidential nominees. They subscribe to big-city and suburban ideologies, for the most part. The Court has thus chosen to ally itself mainly with the politically potent forces of the future rather than those of the past, as it once did.

THE UNITED STATES DISTRICT ATTORNEYS

The United States Supreme Court is a highly visible institution. It can gain headlines on any "decision Monday." Yet, with rare exceptions, the high court "does not render either the initial or the final decision in a case. The justices typically formulate general policy, leaving specific application to judges of inferior state and Federal courts. Lower court judges have different backgrounds, ambitions, loyalties, and perspectives than do Supreme Court Justices."[8] The same might be said of the men who represent the government in lower court cases, the United States district attorneys. They do not necessarily share the goals, values, or loyalties of the Attorney General or the Solicitor General, who performs the counterpart to their role before the Supreme Court.

District Attorneys as Political Appointees. Although formally nominated by the President, in practice they are chosen by the senator (or senior senator) from the state involved, if he is of the President's party. (If he is not, the selection is made by the state party organization.) Others may be consulted, but the senator has the final word. This does not often result in the job going to a political hack, however, for it is a high-prestige position, much sought after by attorneys who are active in the party. A district attorney often has a strong desire to please his colleagues in the state party organization and to make a favorable impression upon the state's voters, for by doing so he furthers the cause of his party and the prospects of his own career. But district attorneys also seek to please the judges before whom they appear; with their professional reputations at stake, they do not enjoy being criticized in opinions from the appeals court or Supreme Court benches. An impressive performance in the role can have a large pay off: Many United States district and appeals court judges are selected from among the district attorneys.

Discretionary Powers. The powers of the district attorneys are great; with rare exceptions (when the Attorney General personally intercedes), they decide the agenda for the district court in matters involving the Federal criminal code and in civil cases in which the United States is a party. Should a charge of mail fraud be entered against a subject, or should it be a lesser charge? Should a person who interferes with a United States marshal (a representative of the district court) in a school integration conflict be charged with a serious crime, such as insurrection against the United States? Or should the matter be left to the judge, who could find him in contempt of court and, if sympathetic to local pressures against desegregation, assess a minor penalty? Or should the man not be charged with a Federal crime at all, but be turned over to local authorities with a recommendation that he be charged with the common-law offense of disturbing the peace—in which case he might likely go free altogether?

[8] Murphy, *op. cit.*, p. 453.

These decisions are made by the local district attorney, and he is rarely overruled from Washington. (If he is totally uncooperative with presidential policies, he can be publicly censured or even dismissed. Such action, however, might embroil the President in a conflict with the senator who originally sponsored the district attorney, and the President might badly need that senator's help and support for important administration measures.)

Sometimes the decision in setting the agenda for the court is made initially by someone other than the district attorney or a member of his staff. Dozens of Federal agencies have their own attorneys, civil servants whose primary loyalty often is to the agency, not to the party or district attorney. These men commonly decide whether or not the law has been violated. For example, an Internal Revenue Service review officer decides whether to ask for a criminal charge or to merely assess civil penalties in a case of underpayment of income tax. But regardless of his decision, the case is tried in the home state of the defendant; therefore, the district attorney decides whether there is enough evidence to bring a case before the grand jury and whether the trial jury is likely to convict or to feel sympathetic toward the defendant. Perhaps he also decides whether it would be politically wise to enter a criminal charge in the case. It is normally the district attorney who decides whether to ignore law violations, to go easy on the violator, or to throw the book at him. Public attitudes, newspaper coverage, pressure from Washington or the state party organization or a bar association, the degree of alacrity of his own staff, and other factors limit the scope of his discretion, but it is nearly always broad.

The district attorney not only sets the agenda by which cases are begun or not begun, he is also responsible for handling cases that are remanded, or returned, to the district court from a higher court. A remanded case is accompanied by instructions from the higher court on some controversial point of law. If the instructions are counter to the wants of the district attorney, a number of techniques by which he can still win the case are available to him. He may, for example, emphasize some other point of law or fact as a basis for his case, avoiding the roadblock placed before him by the higher court. The final disposition of the case is ordinarily made in the trial court. While the district attorney cannot control the disposition, he may strongly influence it, and he may well pursue a policy that is disapproved of by the Attorney General, the United States Supreme Court, and even the President who appointed him. Through his diligence or indolence, his beliefs and commitments, he is a central figure in shaping what we call Federal justice.

POLICY MAKING BY THE COURTS

Like chairmen of congressional committees, Federal judges are at the center of conflicts between ideologies. As Jefferson said of the Federalists, life tenure invites defeated minorities to retreat into the Court system.

Ideological lags are dramatic when justices, reflecting the viewpoints of one political generation, rule on the politics of another.

Justices, unlike other officials, can only be approached by interest groups indirectly. Nevertheless, a myriad of influences shape their decision making. A number of such factors have been reviewed in this chapter without any attempt to order them in terms of importance.

Internal factors include first, and probably foremost, judicial procedures. Actions taken from the lower courts to the Supreme Court follow well-established steps. Procedures occasionally provide handles for those skillful enough to use them to further their preferred policy choices.

A related internal factor is the personality and ability of the judges themselves. Most study has been concentrated on the Supreme Court and its Chief Justices. A court may, like the Presidency, be a pulpit from which men can wield a moral influence on their fellows and on citizens at large. (The study of interactions of judicial personalities, especially in the Supreme Court, reveals much about this process.) Judges hold the weapon of high prestige along with procedural weapons. Judges are viewed as legitimizers of social action. When they are attacked politically, even those who stand to gain by the attack are uneasy. The judges' knowledge of their role and of the expectations citizens have of that role profoundly affect judicial decision making. The various levels of a court system also influence one another.

Outside factors are the general opinions of Congress, the President, and the public, as well as the more specialized opinions of agents of the court, the law schools, professional colleagues of the bar, state judicial and police officers, and interest groups involved in litigation. Such influences vary in accordance with their source and the times. When a large body of outsiders unite in criticism, however, the Supreme Court is likely ultimately to retreat. It may do so gracefully, but still it will retreat.

The list of minor influences on decision making could be extended indefinitely to include what judges eat for breakfast and sporadic street noises. This is not a description of a specific decision, but of major influences that are frequently present. Within the framework of ideology, supplemented by the major internal and external influences noted, court cases are decided and policy is made by the judiciary.

SELECTED BIBLIOGRAPHY

Charles Warren [44] wrote the standard history of the Supreme Court in 1937. He was a political conservative who defended the Court's use of judicial review. The Court's chronological history is extended through 1958 by Mason [17], who carefully details the events occurring under the Chief Justices from Taft through the beginning of Warren's service. A complementary approach is that of describing section by section the constitutional interpretations made by the Court. From a number of such books available, Pritchett [28] is especially clear and thorough.

Two discussions of the organizational and procedural aspects of the United States court system are useful. Abraham [1] has written a readable description with comparisons to British, French, and Soviet systems of law. Mayers [21] is more detailed and now slightly out of date in minor details, but still excellent for reference on terms, organization, and procedures.

The Supreme Court is a small group. Every member has great potential for influencing the outcome of deliberations. A number of excellent biographical studies demonstrate this. Such works on Chief Justices are to be expected given the importance for policy making of the Chief Justice's formal role. For recent works, see Pusey [32] and Mason [20]. A selection of nine biographies, including the major justices of the nineteenth century, is found in Dunham and Kurland [10]. Associate justices have also left their stamp on the Court's decisions because of the force of their logic and character; for example, Holmes, Brandeis, Black, and Frankfurter [12, 13, 16, 19, and 23].

The oldest controversy involving the Supreme Court is that over the exercise of judicial review. Beard [2] argues that this power was intended by the Founding Fathers. Commager [8] offers a forceful dissent to the appropriateness of the practice in a democracy, stating concisely the Holmes-Frankfurter position. A defense is made by Black [5], based on the need for legitimation of governmental action in every political system. Relations of the Supreme Court with President and Congress, but going beyond the question of judicial review, are found in Murphy [24], Pritchett [30], and Schubert [39].

Students of the courts have been among the first to apply behavioral methods of research. An early work by Pritchett [31] used bloc analysis to classify justices by agreement and disagreement on a series of decisions. A recent discussion of this and other social science techniques applied to judicial behavior is found in Schubert [40].

Several works discuss the Supreme Court as a political body. Peltason [26] and Schmidhauser [37] emphasize the group approach to policy making. Rosenblum [35] illustrates his points with a detailed analysis of two sets of cases. Frank [11] is among the most insightful writers about the Court as a policy-making institution. In addition, several collections of essays discuss the myriad aspects of the Supreme Court and the Federal court system. These have been edited by scholars who emphasize the policy-making approach rather than a legalistic casebook analysis. Murphy and Pritchett [25] are perhaps the most helpful to the neophyte, but works by Schmidhauser [36], Schubert [38] and Scigliano [42] are also first rate.

1. Abraham, Henry J.: *The Judicial Process,* Oxford University Press, Fair Lawn, N.J., 1962 (paperback).
2. Beard, Charles: *The Supreme Court and the Constitution,* Prentice-Hall, Inc., Englewood Cliffs, N.J., 1938, reissued 1962.
3. Bickel, Alexander M.: *The Least Dangerous Branch: The Supreme Court at the Bar of Politics,* The Bobbs-Merrill Company, Inc., Indianapolis, 1962.
4. Black, Charles L.: *Perspectives in Constitutional Law,* Prentice-Hall, Inc., Englewood Cliffs, N.J., 1963.
5. Black, Charles L.: *The People and the Court,* The Macmillan Company, New York, 1960.
6. Cahill, Fred V., Jr.: *Judicial Legislation,* The Ronald Press Company, New York, 1952.
7. Cardozo, Benjamin: *The Nature of the Judicial Process,* Yale University Press, New Haven, Conn., 1921.
8. Commager, Henry Steele: *Majority Rule and Minority Rights,* Oxford University Press, Fair Lawn, N.J., 1943.
9. Curtiss, Charles P., Jr.: *Lions under the Throne,* Houghton Mifflin Company, Boston, 1947.

10. Dunham, Allison, and Philip B. Kurland (eds.): *Mr. Justice,* The University of Chicago Press, Chicago, 1956.
11. Frank, John P.: *Marble Palace,* Alfred A. Knopf, Inc., New York, 1958.
12. Frank, John P.: *Mr. Justice Black: The Man and His Opinions,* Alfred A. Knopf, Inc., New York, 1949.
13. Freund, Paul A.: *On Understanding the Supreme Court,* Little, Brown and Company, Boston, 1951.
14. Friedrich, Carl J. (ed.): *Justice,* Nomos VI, Atherton Press, New York, 1963.
15. Jackson, Robert H.: *The Supreme Court in the American System of Government,* Harper & Row, Publishers, New York, 1955, reissued 1963.
16. Lerner, Max: *The Mind and Faith of Mr. Justice Holmes,* Little, Brown and Company, Boston, 1943.
17. Mason, Alpheus Thomas: *The Supreme Court, from Taft to Warren,* Louisiana State University Press, Baton Rouge, La., 1958.
18. Mason, Alpheus Thomas, and William M. Beaney: *The Supreme Court in a Free Society,* Prentice-Hall, Inc., Englewood Cliffs, N.J., 1959.
19. Mason, Alpheus Thomas: *Brandeis: A Free Man's Life,* The Viking Press, Inc., New York, 1946.
20. Mason, Alpheus Thomas: *Harlan Fiske Stone,* The Viking Press, Inc., New York, 1956.
21. Mayers, Lewis: *The American Legal System,* Harper & Row, Publishers, New York, 1955.
22. McCloskey, Robert G.: *The American Supreme Court,* The University of Chicago Press, Chicago, 1960.
23. Mendelson, Wallace: *Justices Black and Frankfurter,* The University of Chicago Press, Chicago, 1961.
24. Murphy, Walter F.: *Congress and the Court,* The University of Chicago Press, Chicago, 1962.
25. Murphy, Walter F., and C. Herman Pritchett (eds.): *Courts, Judges and Politics,* Random House, Inc., New York, 1961.
26. Peltason, Jack W.: *The Federal Courts in the Political Process,* Random House, Inc., New York, 1955.
27. Peltason, Jack: *Fifty-eight Lonely Men: Southern Federal Judges and School Desegregation,* Harcourt, Brace & World, Inc., New York, 1961.
28. Pritchett, C. Herman: *The American Constitution,* McGraw-Hill Book Company, New York, 1959.
29. Pritchett, C. Herman: *The American Constitutional System,* McGraw-Hill Book Company, New York, 1963.
30. Pritchett, C. Herman: *Congress versus the Supreme Court, 1957–60,* The University of Minnesota Press, Minneapolis, 1961.
31. Pritchett, C. Herman: *The Roosevelt Court: A Study in Judicial Politics and Values,* The Macmillan Company, New York, 1943.
32. Pusey, Merlo: *Charles Evans Hughes,* The Macmillan Company, New York, 1951.
33. Roche, John P.: *Courts and Rights: The American Judiciary in Action,* Random House, Inc., New York, 1961.
34. Rodell, Fred: *Nine Men,* Random House, Inc., New York, 1955.
35. Rosenblum, Victor G.: *Law as a Political Instrument,* Random House, Inc., New York, 1955.
36. Schmidhauser, John R. (ed.): *Constitutional Law in the Political Process,* Rand McNally & Company, Chicago, 1963.
37. Schmidhauser, John R.: *The Supreme Court: Its Politics, Personalities and Procedures,* Holt, Rinehart and Winston, Inc., New York, 1960.

38. Schubert, Glendon A. (ed.): *Constitutional Politics,* Holt, Rinehart and Winston, Inc., New York, 1960.
39. Schubert, Glendon A.: *The Presidency and the Courts,* The University of Minnesota Press, Minneapolis, 1957.
40. Schubert, Glendon A.: *Quantitative Analysis of Judicial Behavior,* The Free Press of Glencoe, New York, and Michigan State University, Bureau of Social and Political Research, East Lansing, Mich., 1959.
41. Schwartz, Bernard: *The Supreme Court: Constitutional Revolution in Retrospect,* The Ronald Press Company, New York, 1957.
42. Scigliano, Robert (ed.): *The Courts: A Reader in the Judicial Process,* Little, Brown and Company, Boston, 1962.
43. Swisher, Carl Brent: *The Supreme Court in Modern Role,* New York University Press, New York, 1958.
44. Warren, Charles: *The Supreme Court in United States History,* rev. ed., Little, Brown and Company, Boston, 2 vols., 1937.
45. Westin, Alan F. (ed.): *The Supreme Court: Views from the Inside,* W. W. Norton & Company, Inc., New York, 1961.

Cases Cited in Chapter 18

Baker v. Carr, 369 U.S. 186 (1962).
Ex parte McCardle, 7 Wallace 506 (1869).
Marbury v. Madison, 1 Cranch 137 (1803).
Pennsylvania v. Nelson, 350 U.S. 497 (1956).
Uphaus v. Wyman, 360 U.S. 72 (1959).

Case Study Materials

1. Alsop, Joseph, and T. Catledge: *The 168 Days,* Doubleday & Company, Inc., Garden City, N.Y., 1938.
2. Pritchett, C. Herman, and Alan F. Westin (eds.): *The Third Branch of Government: Eight Cases in Constitutional Politics,* Harcourt, Brace & World, Inc., New York, 1963.
3. Vose, Clement E.: *Caucasians Only: The Supreme Court, the NAACP and the Covenant Cases,* University of California Press, Berkeley, Calif., 1959.
4. Westin, Alan F.: *The Anatomy of a Constitutional Law Case,* The Macmillan Company, New York, 1958.

PART III

PUBLIC POLICY

What is the general character of the policies that emerge from the American political process?

Support for specific civil liberties is not as widespread in fact as in popular ideal, but it is greater among opinion leaders than others. An ideology of tolerance has been a significant influence in American historical experience. Principal issues in recent decades have centered around freedom of expression, equality of opportunity, and the necessary elements of a fair trial, or procedural due process, and naturalization policy. *(Chapter 19, Society and Individual Rights.)*

The seemingly chaotic and sometimes contradictory domestic policies of government can be given some degree of order through an ideological analysis. The ideas of the emerging suburban-centered political majority stress the goal of creating a well-adjusted society, economy and government, while treating the unadjusted minorities in terms of professional criteria. *(Chapter 20, Federal Domestic Policy.)*

American foreign policy since World War II has emphasized containment, regional alliances, economic aid to uncommitted nations, effective military deterrents of Communism and support of the UN as means for dealing with a world in transition. The President, Congress, and parts of the executive bureaucracy, particularly the State Department and Department of Defense share legal powers. A policy consensus emerges from the interaction of informed groups of officials as occasionally influenced by specialized publics. (*Chapter 21, American Foreign Policy.*)

CHAPTER

19

SOCIETY AND INDIVIDUAL RIGHTS

Do most Americans feel free to speak their minds? The answer is "Yes," according to an intensive study of civil liberties made during the cold war. This nationwide public-opinion survey revealed that only 13 per cent said "No," so far as they were themselves concerned, although 41 per cent thought some other Americans were no longer as free to say what they thought as formerly. Less than 2 per cent were personally "much bothered" about the infringement on their own right to speak their minds.

Are most Americans very concerned about other problems of civil liberties in the abstract? The answer is "No." Although the survey was conducted at the time of the televised Army-McCarthy hearings in 1954, 30 per cent of the national sample could not even name a congressman or senator who was investigating subversion. While the nation was being accused by many writers as succumbing to a wave of hysteria, less than 1 per cent named Communist subversion as a problem they personally ever worried about—the figure rose to 6 per cent when respondents were asked specifically to name governmental problems.[1]

Were most Americans, therefore, generally tolerant of nonconformists? The answer is again, "No." Thirty per cent said they felt individuals should not be allowed to speak in favor of government ownership of railroads or big industries, 60 per cent would not allow a speech against churches or religion, and 45 per cent would not permit Socialists to publish their own newspapers. These are, of course, opinions given off the cuff, perhaps with little reflection, to an interviewer. All of the acts that are objected to do occur in America with little hindrance, despite the disapproval of substantial numbers of American citizens.

Who then upholds American standards of tolerance for nonconformists? One answer emerged from another sample taken in the same survey of leaders in a number of middle-sized cities. Communication research has tended to confirm that a rather wide gap exists between asserted belief and actual behavior. Filling this gap are leaders at all levels who, in the political process of decision making, supply a structuring of events that can result in a rapid

[1] Samuel A. Stouffer, *Communism, Conformity and Civil Liberties,* Doubleday & Company, Inc., Garden City, N.Y., 1955.

shift of opinion. Community leaders surveyed were less likely than the average American to treat problems of civil liberty as if a quick and simple decision disposed of the problem. Consistently they took what the author describes as "sober second thoughts." They were also more tolerant by far of nonconformity. Even the leaders of highly conservative organizations such as the American Legion or the Daughters of the American Revolution were consistently more tolerant of free expression than the population as a whole. Tolerance appears to be a function of social and probably political participation.

Second, tolerance for nonconformity was greater among individuals in the whole population who had had a variety of experiences than it was with others (a finding that harmonizes with greater tolerance among leaders). Those with life-styles that resulted in maintaining a large measure of social distance from others were less tolerant of deviants. The same fact has been documented in many studies of racial discrimination.[2] A scaling showed 66 per cent of college graduates in the "more tolerant" group. Other types showing higher tolerance were those twenty-one to twenty-nine years of age, those living in metropolitan areas, and those living in the West. Concentrations of "less tolerant" were found among the elderly, the poorly educated, Southerners, small-town dwellers, and farmers.

The most important factor associated with tolerance of nonconformists was education, for example, when Southern college graduates were compared with college graduates in other sections, 62 per cent of the Southerners were in the "more tolerant" group, 64 per cent in the Middle West, 78 per cent of the East, and 73 per cent in the Far West.

This points to a significant group within society in which intolerance of difference is what can be described as a "social problem." Persons in this group have limited experience and often live in poverty and in relative isolation from modern society. They are sometimes characterized by a sense of alienation. Students of mass movements have found such frustrated persons willing to become "true believers" in totalitarian political groups. They tend to regard strangers with suspicion and sometimes lump together as Communist conspirators all who are part of a new industrial society that they do not understand—members of some ethnic and racial minorities, labor leaders and big-business men, residents of large cities and their suburbs, college professors, and even those desiring fluoridation of water systems. Students of the nature of racial prejudice have isolated similar groups that seem ready to vent their frustrations upon the nearest scapegoat available. In terms of the political ideologies described in Chapters 6 and 7, frustration might also perhaps develop from an outmoded ideology. To those who still view the small-town ideology as the most

[2] Samuel A. Stouffer and others, *The American Soldier,* Princeton University Press, Princeton, N.J., 1949, vol. I, chap. 19. Morton Deutsch and Mary Evans Collins, *Inter-racial Housing: A Psychological Study of a Social Experiment,* The University of Minnesota Press, Minneapolis, 1951.

liberalizing set of ideas created in America, the movement to an urban society with its new definitions of freedom may be viewed as a mammoth conspiracy engaged in by many persons, even including the President and the heads of the Army, Navy, and Air Force.[3]

What do these findings mean for civil liberties in America today? They suggest that perhaps a degree of broader tolerance is possible. Intolerant types of individuals will become fewer in number as the trends of modern society continue. The spread of education, the continuing urbanization and the accompanying impersonality of society, the breaking down of regional, ethnic, and racial isolation, the mobility of Americans, army service, high school or college education for almost all, and even the sympathetic portrayal of different types of people in the mass media of radio, television, motion pictures, newspapers, magazines, and paperback books—all work to some degree to this end. In the same way, the increasing activity of the national government in this field reduces the suppression of nonconformity by vigilantes composed of local isolates. After reviewing the history of civil liberties in America, one scholar concludes that most Americans are more free in the impersonal society of today than they were 150 years ago in communities whose citizens behaved very much as do the less tolerant in contemporary society.[4]

But not all of the problems of civil liberties are caused by those whose intolerance is a reaction to social or psychological frustration. Tolerance may also be defined as giving the individual the benefit of the doubt. It need not mean closing one's eyes to the possible harm that may result to others if an individual is permitted to express himself as he wishes at any time, in any manner. The fine line, which is not easy to find, between the rights of the individual and those of society must still be drawn, even in a world inclined toward tolerance. That line is drawn by means of the political process after the goals and values of the individual have been weighed against possible harm to society.

THE AMERICAN DEMOCRATIC HERITAGE

Gunnar Myrdal, a Swedish sociologist, a generation ago made a classic study of the position of the Negro in American society. He concluded that the cement of American government and society is a common ideology or belief system. Its ideals are the traditional democratic goals of freedom

[3] Eric Hoffer, *The True Believer,* Harper & Row, Publishers, New York, 1951; Gordon W. Allport, *The Nature of Prejudice,* Anchor Books, Doubleday & Company, Inc., Garden City, N.Y., 1954; and Daniel Bell (ed.), *The Radical Right,* rev. ed., Anchor Books, Doubleday & Company, Inc., Garden City, N.Y., 1963.

[4] John Roche, "American Liberty: An Examination of the 'Tradition of Freedom,'" in Milton R. Konvitz and Clinton Rossiter (eds.), *Aspects of Liberty,* Cornell University Press, Ithaca, N.Y., 1958, pp. 129–162.

and equality. Its roots are found in the religious teachings of some of the early American settlers; in the English common law, which was taken over with little change by American courts; and in the philosophy of the Era of Enlightenment, which was the faith of many of the Founding Fathers. The ideals are stated in the Declaration of Independence, the Preamble to the Constitution, and the Bill of Rights. Almost every President since Washington has exercised leadership through appeals to this common creed.[5]

This widespread agreement on generalities was empirically documented in a study comparing opinions in Ann Arbor, Michigan, and Tallahassee, Florida. More than 90 per cent of the respondents agreed that majorities should rule and minorities should have the right to persuade others. They also believed in democracy as the best form of government.[6]

Americans sometimes shrug off talk of these ideals as Fourth of July oratory or flag-waving because they have frequently been disregarded in practice. The leaders who added them to the nation's basic documents included slaveholders, for example. The country was hardly ten years old before critics of the government were imprisoned through the Alien and Sedition Acts. During the eras of the Know-Nothing party before the Civil War, the Red scare of the 1920s, the relocation of the Japanese from the West Coast during World War II, and McCarthyism in the early 1950s, it seemed that Americans had forgotten this creed.

Myrdal argues, however, that these ideals are primary data for a social scientist who is trying to understand American government and society. Our liberal tradition is so important that it usually has an ultimate effect on the important choices to be made. No matter how far Americans stray, in practice, from their ideals, these beliefs have always been at hand to be effectively appealed to by any disadvantaged group. The leaders in each of the movements noted above were finally discredited in terms of dominant opinion. This belief system, emphasizing liberty and equality, acts as a national conscience, Myrdal argues; for this reason, he titled his study of the American Negro, *The American Dilemma.*

The poet Robert Frost has summarized the nagging quality of this belief:[7]

> That's a hard mystery of Jefferson's.
> What did he mean? Of course the easy way
> Is to decide it simply isn't true.

[5] Gunnar Myrdal, *The American Dilemma,* Harper & Row, Publishers, New York, 1944.

[6] James W. Prothro and Charles M. Grigg, "Fundamental Principles of Democracy: Bases of Agreement and Disagreement," *Journal of Politics,* 22:276–294, June, 1960.

[7] Robert Frost, "The Black Cottage," from *Complete Poems of Robert Frost,* Holt, Rinehart and Winston, Inc., New York, 1959, pp. 75–76.

It may not be. I heard a fellow say so.
But never mind, the Welshman got it planted
Where it will trouble us a thousand years.
Each age will have to reconsider it.

Putting Content into a Creed. As Robert Frost suggests, ideal principles about freedom and justice for all, however inspiring, are not self-executing.[8] Content must be given to glittering generalities. Rights and liberties held by Americans must be defined in terms that are meaningful to most members of society. Thomas Jefferson argued that each generation must create its own definition, and he calculated that a political revolution should occur every eighteen years and eight months. Americans have always refashioned definitions for achieving their ideals as the conditions under which they live have changed. When the dominant life-style of Americans has changed so as to evince new experiences, a revision of the method for achieving basic ideals has tended to follow. Each environment has its own ideals, which are expressed as political ideologies (see Chapters 6 and 7). But each also retains something from earlier ideologies, and so a common thread runs through our belief systems, stretching back to colonial times.

The Bill of Rights states many of the ideals of the American creed in vague absolutes. Goals such as the following are to be secured for every American under all conditions: freedom of belief and expression, freedom of religion and assembly, equality of opportunity, and due process in legal procedures. But the principles are easier to accept than specific applications of them. Every attempt to make more precise definitions leads to political disputes and problems. Under some conditions, complete freedom of expression—irresponsible use of it—may endanger society and the government itself. Justice Oliver Wendell Holmes used the illustration of shouting "Fire" in a crowded theater. Freedom of assembly does not permit a parade on a downtown street on a Saturday afternoon without a permit. Equality of opportunity cannot be achieved over a weekend in a society led by men whose ancestors owned slaves. Defining due process in legal procedures in such a manner that no innocent person will ever be convicted would probably hopelessly handicap the police.

Precisely where the line between conflicting goals should be drawn is based, in a sense, on an approximation of the statistical probabilities of what will occur. Americans have generally sought to give a special preference to the ideals of individual freedom. We have been willing to take a calculated risk on freedom of expression for deviant social and political doctrines, have attempted to encourage the spread of equality of opportunity at the risk of racial disorders, have been willing to take a chance that the guilty will sometimes escape punishment to ensure that most innocent persons will not be penalized.

[8] Widespread disagreement existed in Tallahassee and Ann Arbor over specific methods of implementing general beliefs. Prothro and Grigg, *op. cit.*

Political Ideologies and the American Creed. Each of the major political ideologies of America has been an attempt to give content to the vague American creed, with the goal of further liberating the individual. Each belief system sought to strike off chains that would permit citizens to pursue more fully their own ideas of happiness.

During the Presidency of Andrew Jackson, the ideology of frontier individualism was designed to smash the political powers of an incipient aristocracy. The ideology of industrial individualism, conceived in small-town America, moved from a philosophy of mercantilism to one emphasizing that government interference would negate free expression, to the detriment of the individual and society as well. Only as America moved to the big city did some Americans argue that private groups as well as government might suppress the individual. Government was conceived of as a referee, since it was argued by those subscribing to the social service ideology that freedom depended on a measure of *equality*. The worker in the sweatshop, the child at work in the factory, the poor and aged could not be really equal or free.

Robert Hutchins, when president of The Fund for the Republic, argued that these ideas of what he calls "underdogism," dominant while he was a youth, are no longer relevant. The issue for most Americans, he says, no longer is scarcity or exploitation of man by man. Americans are living in a new kind of society—one in which the typical American fills a white-collar job in a large organization and lives in relatively comfortable surroundings.[9]

Liberties and Rights in Modern America. The trends in present-day society all encourage more governmental activity in defining the rights and liberties of citizens. As in most fields, the Federal government has been given much of this increased responsibility.

Urbanization of society inevitably creates some new problems for individual freedom. Beyond the repressions attacked by the social service ideology are those created by a society of large-scale organizations in which the individual is a relatively helpless unit. The phrase "You can't fight City Hall" applies to the bureaucracies of corporations, unions, universities, as well as to governments. Telephone company executives wishing to change to a complete number system and to abandon letter prefixes, or union leadership wishing to add $5 a year to dues, may be as irresistible as a government agency set on purchasing one's land for a special use—possibly more so. An individual blacklisted by large organizations has few employment alternatives in his special area of competence. Under such conditions, procedures for making decisions about individuals become crucial and are of importance to almost all. Such trends can generally be resisted only through group action—action generally directed toward the political arenas.

[9] Robert Hutchins, "Ideas, Institutions, and American Liberty," in Konvitz and Rossiter, *op. cit.,* pp. 3–14.

There is also in modern society an increased tendency to recognize personal status in a large-scale bureaucracy on merit (competence plus effort). Given this goal, ethnic and racial minorities seek the positions they feel they deserve in a white-collar society and ask for government enforcement of such rights. Those whose status is based on climbing up through a bureaucracy tend to be less sure of themselves than were yester-

Figure 19-1

Segregation Is Not Unique to the South

Some Northerners who denounce segregation do not send their own children to integrated schools. To many upper-middle-class citizens, the problem is academic. (By permission of Jules Feiffer.)

day's elites, whose status was derived from wealth or family position. The latter could more readily defy opinion; the former are in positions that encourage caution, lest status be lost. The ambivalence of the typical suburbanite when a white-collar Negro family moves into his neighborhood is demonstrated in a report about such an incident, *But Not Next Door*. None of the subjects wants to admit to an outright bias; they speak instead in terms of property values. The resulting problem typically involves government.[10]

A further cause for government interest in civil liberties and rights stems from the cold war with the Soviet Union and the possibility of Communist espionage as a threat to American interests. Some observers, such as Harold Lasswell, have argued that a society faced with a continuing outside threat steadily restricts liberty in favor of security until finally a garrison state results, one similar to that portrayed in *1984*.[11] The cold war has caused a tightening of American security procedures, and the almost inevitable consequence has been increased caution in the expression of opinion. Another result has been to encourage a hastening of the spread of equality of opportunity. One-third of the world, mostly nonwhite, is uncommitted to East or West. These nations hold the balance of power for the world of the future.

A change in political ideology in response to new conditions is in the process of formation. One of the major premises about civil rights and liberties of the individual is discernible; that is, a preference for experts over politicians in handling questions of policy, including those in the area of rights and liberties. For example, the high prestige of the Federal Bureau of Investigation under J. Edgar Hoover is, in part, the result of an early use of scientific methods of criminal investigation. The mammoth fingerprint files, the chemical analyses of evidence, the willingness to cooperate with and train personnel of state, city, and county police agencies, the recruitment of agents from the ranks of lawyers and certified public accountants—all have enhanced the organization's image as a scientific and professional investigative agency that most Americans feel is appropriate for investigating the delicate questions of subversion and disloyalty.

In the same way, the almost unanimous conclusions of professional anthropologists, sociologists, psychologists, and biologists on race issues have by now largely undermined a traditional contrary position.

Other results of modern trends appear to be a nostalgic yearning for decentralization within large-scale organizations (the suburb in the metropolis, the state in the Union) and a tendency to view political problems in psychological terms. The deviant, as was noted earlier, is viewed as primarily neurotic or psychotic.

[10] Harry Rosen and David Rosen, *But Not Next Door,* Obolensky, Inc., New York, 1962.

[11] George Orwell, *1984,* Harcourt, Brace & World, Inc., New York, 1949. See Harold Lasswell, *National Security and Individual Freedom,* McGraw-Hill Book Company, New York, 1950.

Robert Hutchins, in the essay noted previously, saw the central problem of the new society as the powerlessness of the individual in the face of uncontrollable oligarchies. The tendency of the emerging ideology is to depend on the procedures prescribed by experts. An older method of pitting power base against power base in a political struggle is shunned.

POLICY MAKING FOR CIVIL LIBERTIES AND RIGHTS

The legal basis for most citizen rights is found in the ten amendments added to the Constitution at the insistence of the Antifederalists. Although not a single article, they are known as the Bill of Rights. The First Amendment contains those guarantees generally referred to as the rights of individual expression. The guarantees of equality of opportunity are found in the Thirteenth and Fourteenth Amendments, added during the Civil War. These are collectively the basic *substantive* rights,* since democratic government is inconceivable without them. Rights of due process in legal matters are mainly found in the Fifth and Fourteenth Amendments. These are the basic *procedural* rights.* They seek to guarantee whatever society at a given time regards as a "fair" trial and "fair" treatment by administrative officers and bodies.

***SUBSTANTIVE RIGHTS. These provide for personal liberty as against government. They include freedom of expression, religion, and assembly. PROCEDURAL RIGHTS guarantee the elements of a fair trial in terms of contemporary interpretation of Anglo-American legal and cultural traditions.**

Prior to the growth of an urban, industrial society and the political ideologies accompanying it, there were two separate systems of rights and liberties for citizens in America. National protection extended only to a limited number of cases in the area of treason, sedition, and citizenship. State constitutions and statutes permitted a great variety of both procedures for criminal cases and regulations affecting expression and opportunity for individuals. In the period following World War I, the process of combining these provisions into one national system of rights and liberties was begun. The process is still continuing.

Rights and Liberties Are Nationalized. The Bill of Rights, which contains most of the constitutional provisions protecting civil liberties, was directed exclusively against the national Congress and administration. The state governments were not affected. The legal basis for changing this pattern was found in the Fourteenth Amendment, which was adopted after the Civil War (1867). It says that *no state* shall deprive any person of life, liberty, or property without due process of law. The Court has gradually applied most of the Bill of Rights to the states, using these words as the technical legal basis. Nationalization of these rights was begun in 1925, when the United States Supreme Court (in *Gitlow v. New York*) announced that it would use the definition found in the First Amendment (1791) as a guide in defining "liberty" in the Fourteenth Amendment. It reads, "Congress shall make no law respecting the establishment of religion, or prohibiting the free exercise thereof; or abridging the freedom of speech, or of the press; or the right of the people peaceably to assemble, and to petition the Government for a redress of grievances."

What followed was a series of cases overturning state acts; for example, acts to censor a "scandal sheet" newspaper before publication, to force children of a religious group to salute the flag each morning or be expelled from school, or to prohibit parochial grade schools. In 1937 (*Palko v. Connecticut*),[12] Justice Cardozo, speaking for the Supreme Court, defined Federally protected rights as including other parts of the Bill of Rights that are "of the very essence of a scheme of ordered liberty."

A less significant but potentially important act of nationalization by the Court came when the principle of *national preemption* was borrowed from interstate commerce cases and applied to civil liberties cases. This principle holds that when the Federal government acts in certain fields, state statutes are no longer valid. In 1941, the Supreme Court applied it to state acts regulating aliens. In 1956 (*Commonwealth of Pennsylvania v. Nelson*), all state laws relating to national sedition were terminated by a single Supreme Court decision. (States can still act against sedition of the state.)

The same process has occurred with respect to police and court procedures. For example, the United States Supreme Court has ruled that juries cannot be made up so as deliberately to exclude workingmen or Negroes and that evidence obtained by third-degree methods or by illegal search and seizure cannot be used in either state or Federal courts. In addition to precedent-making cases, the Supreme Court has given greater attention to appeals from inmates of state and Federal prisons for a review of their convictions. Following a tendency of the Court to reverse convictions on the basis of faulty technical procedures, the number of such appeals swelled to several hundred annually. By 1947, a special miscellaneous docket for such cases had become necessary. Some critics have claimed this has turned the highest court in the land into a common police court, since few precedents emerge from these rulings. (That is, they are *ad hoc* decisions, dealing only with the procedures that were used in a particular case. General principles of law for use in future cases ordinarily do not result.) The majority of the justices seem to feel, however, that setting prisoners free is an excellent way to remind state judges of the importance of the nuances of legal procedure.

[12] Complete citations to cases will be found in the Selected Bibliography at the end of this chapter.

The Fourteenth Amendment was written to enforce national standards of equality of opportunity, and it is perhaps ironic that civil rights in this area were among the last to be nationalized. In 1896 the Court (in *Plessy v. Ferguson*) announced that separate but equal treatment of racial groups was permissible. This decision largely vitiated the early effect of this amendment. The first ruling challenging the separate but equal doctrine occurred in 1938 (*Gaines v. Canada*) over admittance of a Negro to a professional school at the University of Missouri. The Court modified the rule to insist that alternative facilities must *in fact* be equal. In 1954, in the school segregation case (*Brown v. Board of Education of Topeka*), the Court overturned the doctrine in respect to education by holding that facilities separated on the basis of race could not by definition ever be made equal. The Court relied heavily on the *psychological* fact that separation by race created in itself feelings of superiority or inferiority in pupils. The justices unanimously held that legal equality or even actual equality of physical facilities and staff was not enough. They expected all states to proceed with all "deliberate speed" toward compliance with the new interpretation of the Constitution.

Figure 19-2

The Ideal in Civil Liberties Is Urged by the Few: The Typical Citizen Will Settle for What Is Good Enough

"About this 'Liberty or Death' business, Mr. Henry. Isn't there some reasonable position in between?"

By permission of Burr Shafer.

Politics and Civil Liberties. In matters of liberty and rights, the Supreme Court has held the center of the stage because of the politics of the situation and the special legitimacy accorded its pronouncements. The Court has the advantage of being, in the eyes of most citizens, the interpreter of the Constitution and the protector of the liberties it guarantees. Its pronouncements are regarded as coming from above the political battle. Many who disagree with it on specific decisions feel constrained to obey its orders.

Congress has taken the role of protector of the national security. Frequently it and the executive branch tie each other's hands on civil liberties questions. Because of the committee system, the rule of seniority, and the filibuster, the groups dominating Congress are by nature those generally unsympathetic to the further extension of civil liberties and rights in an urban society. Representatives from small towns of the Midwest and South dominate in legislative decisions. Acts designed to further equality of opportunity (in 1957, 1960, 1964) were compromises reluctantly granted. Measures aimed at repressing the Communist party were passed in 1940, 1950, and 1954. To some degree, these acts have been interpreted by both the executive and the courts contrary to original congressional intentions. The most effective political weapon of Congress has been its educational or propagandistic use of committee investigations, which frequently reflect the premises of the small-town ideology of industrial individualism in a world that has somehow, to its advocates, gotten out of joint.

The Presidency, on the other hand, is somewhat handicapped in this field. Executive actions favoring extension of civil liberties are likely to be misinterpreted by many voters. The public support given Senator Joseph McCarthy against the State Department indicates the high level of distrust of many citizens. In addition, Presidents must somehow get along with Congress, and they never hold many trump cards. John F. Kennedy, when campaigning in 1960, criticized the Eisenhower administration for not desegregating all Federally supported housing by executive order. Kennedy, as President, hesitated through his first two years to take this action, although he had earlier said it required nothing more than "a stroke of the presidential pen." He did not want to antagonize supporters of administration programs in Congress. (He finally acted a few days after the 1962 midterm election.)

The President rules over a house divided in respect to many civil liberty questions. He is head of the executive police agencies within the Department of Justice and elsewhere, and their responsibility is to protect society; on the other hand, the politics of getting elected generally produces a President who is sympathetic to extending individual freedoms and advisers who favor such action. Problems of international affairs also encourage this position. But the President frequently must content himself with setting up study commissions or endorsing the positions of groups that are willing to act, such as the Civil Rights Commission (established by a 1957 act). He can also claim to be carrying out court orders. But congressional politics and internal bureaucratic politicking sometimes reduce him to a state of political ambivalence on civil rights questions.

Thus, to a large degree, the Supreme Court has had a policy vacuum to step into. As the politically weakest of the three major branches, it has generally moved with caution. Its decisions have been vague in defining the content of most rights and liberties, being explicit mainly about what is *not* constitutional. It has moved toward new positions gradually, sometimes at a slow pace. It has occasionally backtracked, as it did from the libertarian position that sound trucks could not be forbidden because this would be a deprivation of free speech.

The Supreme Court has, however, capitalized on its position as referee of a federal system. It more frequently overrules state than Federal actions and has generally sought clear-cut cases before overruling the President or Congress. It sometimes avoids showdowns where the public is not likely to believe in the legitimacy of its rulings and sometimes retreats from what appears to be its preferred ruling. For example, in the Watkins case of 1957, the Court dismissed a contempt of Congress citation on the grounds that the mission of the House Un-American Activities Committee was too vague. Two years later, in the Barenblatt case, the Court backtracked and upheld a contempt conviction on the grounds that the purpose of the investigation and the questions had been made sufficiently clear to Barenblatt.

Few interest groups act in support of the Supreme Court on behalf of civil liberties, aside from racially or ethnically based organizations such as the National Association for the Advancement of Colored People (NAACP), or the American Jewish Congress. The American Civil Liberties Union is a very active small group of libertarians who are supported by private donations. They have acted in the defense of civil liberties for Nazis and Communists as well as for religious and antireligious minorities. The funds of all these groups are severely limited. Their chosen mission is not to right all wrongs. Rather, with some political astuteness, they attempt to select test cases that, when brought to the Supreme Court, will set new precedents. Through such actions and in their literature, they hope to influence the leaders in society who are willing to give "sober second thought" to the problem of individual freedoms.

The Court's willingness to take action to expand areas of individual freedom at some risk to society has subjected it more often to intense political criticisms rather than praise. Among its most forceful critics have been the American Bar Association; law-enforcement officials; the heads of the state supreme courts; "patriotic" societies, including some self-proclaimed patriotic groups whose major aim it is to impeach the Chief Justice; and Southern groups that are critical of civil rights decisions. The Court has responded to such criticism by symbolically drawing more tightly about itself the traditional judicial robes that signify impartiality.

Figure 19-3

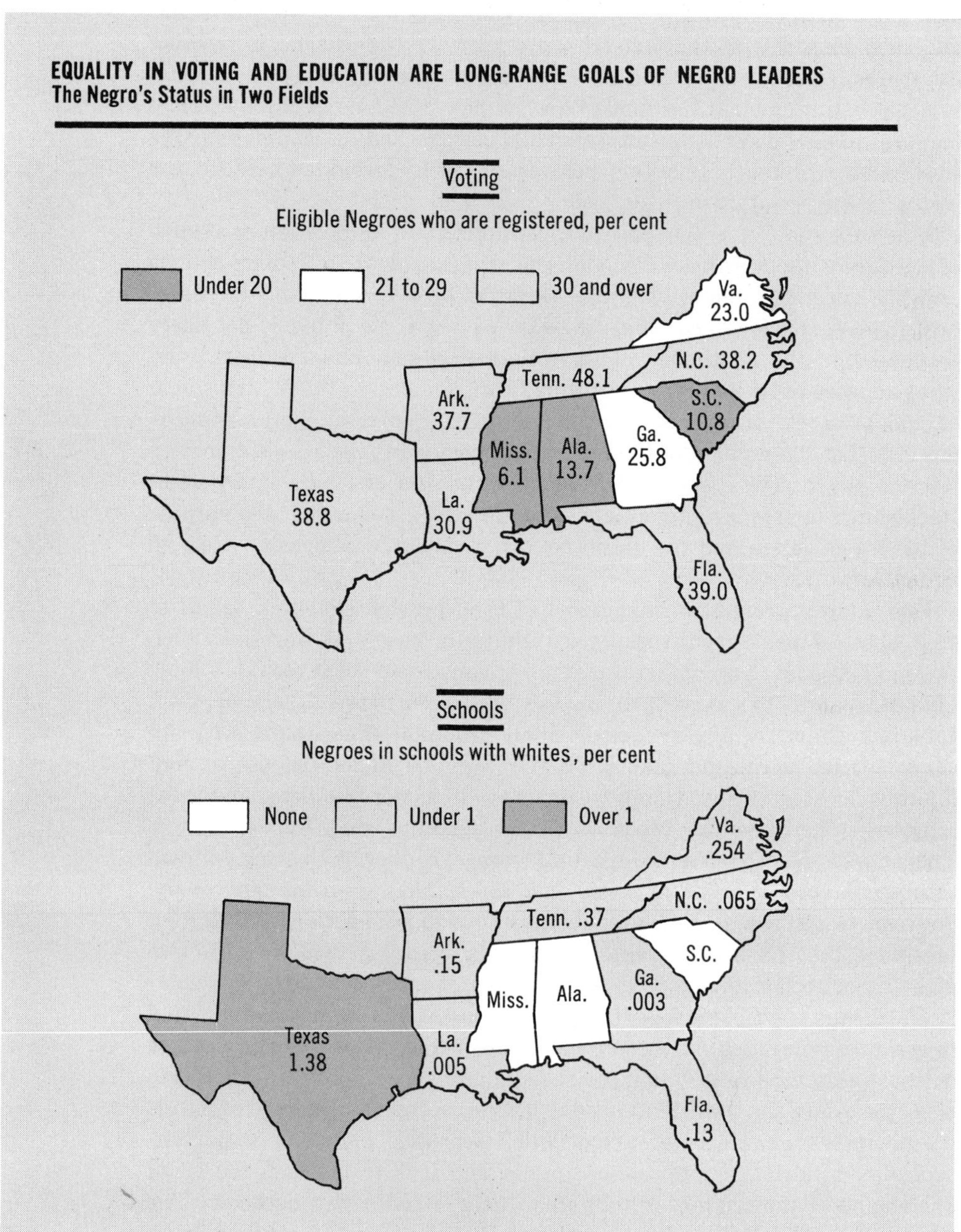

The New York Times, *Sept. 24, 1961.*

The Impact of a Judicial Decision on Enforcement. The meaning of civil liberties and rights is often determined in the first instance by the bureaucrat or police officer who deals with the citizen. The Indian who is refused admittance to a restaurant, the distributor of religious tracts who is told he must desist, the out-of-state driver who is tried by a local justice of the peace without the barest essentials of reasonable judicial procedures often cannot afford the luxury of appeal through the hierarchy of courts.

Judicial decisions are not self-enforcing. The theory of the legal system assumes that lawyers will counsel their clients in terms of the latest decisions and that acts declared illegal will thus, through a "multiplier effect," gradually disappear. This may take many years, however. For example, the Supreme Court first declared segregation on interstate buses unconstitutional in 1946. A decision of 1950 was more sweeping and clear in its intent. In 1955, the Interstate Commerce Commission issued a regulation implementing the decision. In 1964, groups of "freedom riders" were still boarding buses for Mississippi in an attempt to force desegregation of transportation facilities.

A study of the decision concerning released time for religious teaching in public schools also showed a considerable degree of noncompliance. The Supreme Court had first ruled that no classes be held on public school property. A second ruling upheld released-time programs during school hours if instruction took place off public school premises. In religiously homogeneous communities where there were no dissident elements strong enough to protest or bring court action, the rulings were evaded or ignored. The second ruling was interpreted by interest groups, school administrators, and state officials to mean that nonsectarian study of religion in public schools, injection of "moral and spiritual" values into state school curriculums, Bible reading and prayers in the public schools, wearing of religious dress by public school teachers, and singing hymns were all permissible. Administrators and citizens thus are likely to second guess or anticipate the Court on the basis of its latest decisions.[13]

The difficulty exists with procedural as well as substantive questions. Two generations ago, Gaetano Mosca described the essence of civilized government as a system of "juridical defense" that was characterized by "a prevalence of law and public decrees over the appetites of particular men."[14] This is a good statement of the goals of the American legal system. Enforcement procedures are, however, frequently keyed to social and political realities, despite rules that demand equal treatment before the law. Except for traffic violations, few middle-class Americans have contact with the police or the courts. The persons typically involved in civil liberties or rights cases, except for those involving racial minorities, are

[13] The above examples are from Frank J. Sorauf, "Zorach v. Clauson: The Impact of a Supreme Court Decision," *American Political Science Review*, 53:777–791, September, 1959.

[14] Gaetano Mosca, *The Ruling Class*, McGraw-Hill Book Company, 1939, p. 130. (Also available in McGraw-Hill paperback.)

frequently on the fringes of society: the out-of-work drifter, the professional radical, the religious enthusiast. Such persons often are not viewed sympathetically by most middle-class Americans, who tend to class them somewhere along a continuum from bores to social menaces. It is relatively easy, therefore, for law-enforcement and administrative agencies to be tempted to adopt a double standard, not paying close attention to the individual rights of such persons. Where standards of professionalism are found, the double standard tends to disappear. Frequently, however, those who need the protections of civil rights most are the least likely to receive them.

FREEDOM OF EXPRESSION

The astronomer Karl Frederick Gauss discovered that many phenomena in nature tend to form a bell-shaped curve when their frequency of variation is plotted. Social phenomena offer many examples. Even in a "well-adjusted" society, some 4 or 5 per cent of the population will not fit the generally accepted pattern. There will always be some deviants, whether the society be dominated by "squares" or "beatniks."

The Expression of Deviant Viewpoints. The theory of democracy assumes that nonconformists can never be wholly eradicated. It assumes that deviants, in fact, serve a useful self-correcting function. Social critics, even when their views do not prevail, provide the feedback that every organized activity requires. Thus expression by individuals is a necessary condition for democratic government (a substantive right).

A basic problem of such feedback from deviants is that the individual at the mean (the typical citizen or conformist) is apt to regard such expression as heresy. Democratic theory holds that unorthodoxy should not, however, be a reason for suppression. The classic statement is that of Voltaire, "I disapprove of what you say but I will defend to the death your right to say it."

The justification for control is on a more mundane level of order and security. The basic political fact is that national survival or self-preservation is paramount. In a crisis, the most treasured constitutional guarantees may be overridden. Even in times of no crisis, threats to safety, order, and security cannot be lightly dismissed.

At one extreme of a continuum of political activity is thought. At the other is action to carry out thought. In between is the expression of opinion about an action that might be carried out. Thought is unregulated. Action is commonly regulated in the interests of safety and order. Neither is generally a political question. The political difficulties lie in the regulation of expression. For example, what a man thinks about his senator is his own business. If he says, "Someone should punch Senator Zilch in the nose," he is on the doubtful and dangerous ground of expression. If he actually punches Senator Zilch in the nose, he will be headed for jail.

The Clear and Present Danger Doctrine. The United States Supreme Court has devised a rough guide for judging which expressions can be permitted. The "clear and present danger" doctrine first appeared in the opinion of Justice Oliver Wendell Holmes in the Schenck case in 1919. It states that expression may be restricted only when there is a clear and present danger of evils that the government has a right to prevent. Justice Brandeis in *Whitney v. California* in 1927 expanded the doctrine to require that "no danger flowing from speech can be deemed clear and present unless the incidence of evil is so imminent that it may befall before there is an opportunity for full discussion." The application of this doctrine presents many political difficulties. Holmes, for example, remembering vividly the draft riots that plagued the North at a crucial point in the Civil War, regarded those who supported the position of conscientious objectors during World War I as serious threats to the nation.

The Dangerous Tendency Doctrine. A second doctrine, called "dangerous tendency" or "gravity of the evil," has been especially fashioned to deal with political problems presented by the American Communist party. Some Americans have regarded members of this group primarily as deviants espousing economic and political heresy. Others have been impressed by the record of Communist parties elsewhere, the forceful overthrow of a democracy such as Czechoslovakia, and the revelations of Communist espionage in America. These persons have regarded the Communist party as a conspiracy similar to that of a gang organized to plan a crime, but with a different purpose. They have argued that, while the danger from such conspiratorial activity is not immediately clear or immediately present, forming an organization to advocate overthrow of the government by force with the clear encouragement of a foreign power represents a tendency dangerous enough to justify control. To such persons, this kind of organization involves a serious potential or probable danger, one that can be repressed in the interest of national self-preservation.

This doctrine was applied in the Dennis case in 1951, when the conviction of Communist party leaders was upheld, and it has been given uneven application since. The Supreme Court has not formally abandoned the clear and present danger doctrine; its inconsistent decisions on membership in subversive organizations have been, in part, the result of changes in Court membership.

Communist Party Members: Peaceful Citizens or Conspirators? Congress has passed three acts aimed at controlling the activities of the Communist party. In each, the party is clearly regarded as a seditious conspiracy. The Smith Act of 1940, the Alien Registration Act, makes it unlawful to teach, advocate, or distribute information that advocates violent overthrow of government. The Internal Security Act of 1950, also known as the McCarran Act, establishes the Subversive Activities Control Board; after hearings, this board indicates those organizations it deems to be part of a conspiracy to set up a dictatorship controlled by a foreign power. Such organizations must then register with the Attorney General, providing him with much information about their membership, finances, and officers. Privileges of travel, officeholding in organizations such as unions, and employment in defense plants are denied members of such organizations. Other provisions permit deportation of aliens and detention of domestic Communists in time of emergency. The Communist Control Act of 1954 specifically names the Communist party as an organization denied the ordinary rights and privileges of other organizations and falling within the class or organizations covered by the Internal Security Act of 1950.

Presidents have also acted: The preparation of a list of subversive organizations by the Attorney General was authorized by President Truman in 1947; A loyalty security program to remove from public service persons of doubtful loyalty was also established in 1947. President Eisenhower extended the latter to cover "security risks," including alcoholics and homosexuals and some people who had relatives behind the iron curtain. This somewhat reduced the stigma of dismissal. It also relaxed the demands for evidence, since implicit or explicit charges of treason were not involved. The agency head was placed in charge of clearance procedures. The program also covers government-related activities in the defense effort, such as "sensitive" positions with private firms working on government contracts.

In the Dennis case (1951), the conviction of eleven leaders of the Communist party under the Smith Act was upheld. In its decision, the Court argued that the Communist party was conspiring to teach and advocate violent overthrow of the government. In the 1957 Yates case, the Dennis decision was modified by noting that there was a difference between preaching an abstract doctrine and actually teaching unlawful conduct. Later, in the Scales case (1957), the Court said that "active" membership as opposed to "mere" membership in an organization advocating overthrow of the government by force constituted a crime. Thus it appears that only Communist leaders who are actively conspiring are guilty of criminal activity in peacetime.

Both the composition of the Court and the pressures on it were different in 1951 (the beginning of the McCarthy investigations) from what they were a decade later. The small-town viewpoint, exemplified by Chief Justice Fred Vinson, had been replaced by the viewpoint of Chief Justice Earl Warren, who came from the governorship of an urban-industrial state, and a Court whose composition reflected an urban rather than a small-town background.

The registration provisions of the Internal Security Act of 1950 were upheld in 1961 (*Communist Party v. Subversive Activities Control Board*) after the Communist party had refused to register as required. The Court also upheld the loyalty and security clearance programs of the government, noting that government employment has always been a privilege and not a right. The use of unidentified informers—the part of the subversive control program most at odds with customary judicial procedures and most criticized—has not been approved in all cases. The right to a hearing in all nonsensitive positions has been affirmed (*Cole v. Young,* 1956), as has the necessity of following in every case whatever clearance procedures the agency head has established (*Service v. Dulles,* 1957). On technical grounds, the court set aside the right of the State Department to deny on security grounds a passport to a citizen wanting to visit abroad (*Kent v. Dulles,* 1958).

In 1954, Congress passed the Immunity Act, permitting congressional committees and Federal district courts to grant witnesses immunity from prosecution. The act was an attempt to gain information from witnesses who had refused to testify on grounds of self-incrimination under the Fifth Amendment. In 1956, in the Ullman case, the act was upheld. Subsequently, however, the Court decided that granting immunity on the Federal level did not protect one from prosecution by a state court, or vice versa (*Knapp v. Schweitzer,* 1958).

Other actions relating to subversion have been the institution of state and Federal loyalty oaths, and Federal censorship of the mails. Loyalty

Figure 19-4

Under Any Form of Government, Dissent Is Risky and May Be Heavily Penalized

"I STILL think that retort I gave Oliver Cromwell was rather clever."

Here, J. Wesley Smith shows more courage than usual, but at heavy short-run costs. (By permission of Burr Shafer.)

oath programs have been upheld, though the disclaimer requirements* attached to the National Defense Education Act and National Science Foundation loans and scholarships were subsequently removed because a number of the nation's major universities refused to participate in the program. In the words of A. Whitney Griswold, former president of Yale: "It removes a provision not only futile as a safeguard against genuine subversion but which discriminated against college students by placing them in a class apart from other Americans and telling them in effect that they could not be trusted."[15] In 1961, the Kennedy administration ended the screening of publications from foreign countries, but Congress re-instituted the practice in the same year.

***DISCLAIMER REQUIREMENT. A loyalty oath declaring the signer will defend the United States Constitution against its enemies, foreign and domestic. Once required of recipients of National Defense Education Act and National Science Foundation loans and scholarships.**

Speech and Press. The authors of any commercial book are subject to suit for libel if they are guilty of untruthful defamation of character. They must also take care in quoting others, since the Supreme Court has ruled that a suit against a newspaper, rather than its nationally syndicated columnist, is permissible. Likewise a classroom instructor in his lectures is subject to suit for slander. In general, courts are more lenient in dealing with slander than with libel, for written words become a permanent record. Greater than average freedom is granted to those reporting public events, teachers in classrooms, and public officials acting in official capacity, but the line is not easy to draw. Congressmen, however, are immune from all suits for statements made on the floor of Congress. There are abuses of this freedom from time to time, but conducting public business under constant threat of suit would be difficult and perhaps impossible.

Libel and slander rulings (except for the fairly unusual charge of *criminal* libel) are not, strictly speaking, limits on civil liberties, for they deal with torts—damages to a person by another person rather than a government. Written or spoken expression may be subject to criminal action, however, in such cases as incitement to crime, contempt of court, obscenity, and seditious utterance. Obscenity in recent years has caused problems for the Supreme Court, since many works of art from the times of Chaucer and Shakespeare have been subject to such charges. The works of such men as D. H. Lawrence, James Joyce, and Henry Miller have inspired many local attempts at censorship. In the Roth case (1957), the Supreme Court held that works of obscenity are outside the protection of the First Amendment. An obscene work was defined as one having as its central purpose and dominant theme an appeal to the prurient interest of the average citizen without "any redeeming social importance." One of the dissenting justices commented somewhat acidly that obscenity could not

[15] *The New York Times,* Oct. 20, 1962.

as easily be recognized in literature as could poison ivy among other plants. The psychologist Frederic Wertham has argued that action should also be taken against the glorification of brutality and sadism found in comics, television programs, and many paperback books. His argument, which is not accepted by all psychologists, is that such portrayals have a direct relationship to juvenile crime and thus are, in fact, an incitement to crime.

Censorship prior to publication and the prohibition against distribution of published materials, while occasionally encountered on college campuses in respect to student publications, is not permitted for privately published newspapers and books (*Near v. Minnesota,* 1931). Voluntary precensorship occurred, however, during World War II. Precensorship of motion pictures was permitted in the period from 1915 to 1952, however, on the ground that movies are entertainment, not information media. Film officials strongly objected to this ruling, arguing that films often contain a social message and thus should be subject to prior restraint. In *Joseph Burstyn, Inc., v. Wilson* (1952), the Court brought movies under the protection of the Constitution. Then, in *Times Film Corp. v. Chicago,* the Court ruled that states and local government might require licenses for films before showing. The film involved in the case was *Don Juan,* which had been produced in Austria. The decision was 5 to 4.[16] Later the Court held in the Kingsley Film Corporation case concerning the motion picture, *Lady Chatterley's Lover* that censorship could not take place because of advocacy of ideas in the movie. The movie had been attacked on the ground that it discussed adultery with approval.

Newspapermen have in the postwar years mounted a campaign for greater access to governmental news and public records. They argue, on the basis of evidence uncovered by a House committee headed by Representative Frank Moss (Democrat, California), that government agencies sometimes suppress information for reasons other than national security. Yet editors are sometimes more interested in news than in national safety. At the beginning of World War II, one newspaper revealed the fact that the United States Navy had broken the code of the Japanese Navy—a serious breach of security in wartime. On the other hand, "security" claims can be an easy crutch by which to classify information that could be embarrassing to an official. Some scientists have likewise argued that governmental restrictions on scientific information are too severe.

Governmental control is exercised in some cases by decisions of the Postmaster General on what will be carried in the mails. The magazine *Esquire* for a period lost its second-class mailing permit on grounds of obscenity. It carried its suit to the Supreme Court and won. The Federal government also exercises control over radio and television through the granting of licenses by the Federal Communications Commission.

A concluding note: One group in the Supreme Court holds that there

[16] Frederic Wertham, *The Seduction of the Innocent,* Holt, Rinehart and Winston, Inc., New York, 1954.

should be no restrictions on expression, not even for slander or libel. Justice Hugo L. Black has stated: "I believe with Jefferson that it is time enough for government to step in to regulate people when they do something, not when they say something."[17]

Assembly, Petition, and Association. Governments may issue permits to regulate meetings in public buildings or in such public places as the streets or parks. Restraints must, however, be "reasonable." Discrimination among groups is not permitted, but regulation that prevents serious disruption of public use of public facilities is. Mayor Frank Hague of Jersey City once refused permits for any meetings of Labor union organizers and other groups he considered to be left-wing. The Supreme Court (in *Hague v. C.I.O.,* 1939) ruled his action unconstitutional. A religious group, the Jehovah's Witnesses, tried to parade down a New Hampshire street on a Saturday afternoon without previous permission from the local government. The Court (in *Cox v. New Hampshire,* 1941) ruled that permits could be required, providing the local ordinance applied to all groups.

The right of the people or their representatives to petition government causes few problems beyond those concerned with regulation of lobbying. Between 1840 and 1845, Congress refused to receive abolitionist petitions, but the arguments of John Quincy Adams, a former President, and then a congressman, resulted in repeal of the rule against doing so.

Freedom of association is implied from the Bill of Rights. It is not specifically mentioned. The principle of "reasonable" regulation again holds. A case of this type not involving Communists was *National Association for the Advancement of Colored People v. Alabama,* which was decided in 1958. The state required the filing of membership lists. The Supreme Court ruled that this was not a reasonable regulation of an otherwise lawful group, since such publication would be likely to cause members to be subject to reprisals. Except for organizations regarded as subversive to the community, as the NAACP perhaps is by some Southerners, regulations are not often severe. And organized groups generally can exercise some political power in their own defense.

Religious Practices. The Founding Fathers were convinced that an official state church was an evil and therefore prohibited it explicitly in the First Amendment. On this basis, the Supreme Court has set aside religious qualifications for holding office, including a Maryland requirement that public officials believe in God (*Torcaso v. Watkins,* 1961). But making a precise definition of separation of church and state has not been easy. The coins of the nation feature the motto "In God We Trust." Congress added to the pledge of allegiance to the flag after World War II the words "under God." Official government ceremonies, including the opening of Supreme Court and congressional sessions, begin with a prayer. The armed services

[17] Edmond Cahn, "Justice Black and First Amendment Absolutes," *New York University Law Review,* 37:549–563, June, 1962.

have chaplains and chapels, and public officials from the President on down commonly are sworn into office with their hand on a Bible.

The most perplexing problems of separation have concerned education. Many religious groups desire religious instruction for their children, arguing on a basis that psychologists generally consider valid: "As the twig is bent so grows the tree." An attempt by the state of Oregon to prohibit private schools was invalidated by the Court (in *Pierce v. Society of Sisters of the Holy Name,* 1925). The Supreme Court has held consistently that government cannot favor one religious group over others or coerce individuals into religious observance. In *Zorach v. Clauson* (1952), upholding released-time classes off public school property, it approved of cooperation to aid religious observance. Justice William Douglas in the majority opinion said:

> When the state encourages religious instruction or cooperates with religious authorities by adjusting the schedule of public events for sectarian needs, it follows the best of our traditions. . . . To hold that it may not would be to find in the Constitution a requirement that the government show a callous indifference to religious groups. That would be preferring those who believe in no religion over those who do believe.

A good deal of such cooperation already exists. The right to use public funds to transport children attending private schools has been upheld (*Everson v. Board of Education of Ewing Township,* 1947). Parochial schools participate in the school-lunch program. Church-sponsored schools of higher education have received dormitory loans under the Housing Act of 1950, were approved for students using the GI Bill or other governmental scholarships, and have cooperated in training and research programs for government officials and employees.

A companion problem is: How much religion may legally be presented in public schools? There are few rulings on the subject, although the decision of 1962, which outlawed a prayer approved by the state regents for the New York public schools, was widely and perhaps erroneously interpreted as outlawing all religious teaching. The ruling was based, however, on the theory that a prayer was composed by a public body and thus recommended as a specific form of religious worship, thereby giving it special status. Further litigation in this area is to be expected. Meanwhile, many elementary and secondary schools often do include religious practices. These vary from Bible study to prayers, and children in almost all public schools sing carols at Christmas.

EQUALITY OF OPPORTUNITY

Legal guarantees for a rough measure of equality of opportunity in democratic societies are based on the notion that where there is discrimination, it should be "reasonable" discrimination. The mentally ill and children (under twenty-one, in most states) are thus not allowed to vote. Democratic belief also stresses that potentiality must be taken into account. Mental illness, given the proper treatment, often may be cured. In a modern society, a sufficient number of young people may attain the characteristics of adulthood more quickly than was the case when twenty-one was first declared the age of adulthood. Minimum basic norms of equality are thus defended because of the potential inherent in individuals.

Racial and Ethnic Discrimination. In 1960, in upper-middle-class Grosse Pointe, a suburb of Detroit, realtors were revealed by the state attorney general to have devised a scale of discrimination that read like a social scientist's research proposal. Residents were given point ratings on such social attributes as type of job, neatness in dress, grammar, and twenty-eight other characteristics. To be eligible to purchase Grosse Pointe real estate, a person needed 50 points. However, those of Polish descent needed 55 points; South Europeans, including those of Italian, Greek, Spanish or Lebanese origin, 65 points; and those identified as Jews, 85 points. Negroes and Orientals were excluded entirely.[18]

Discrimination in America has never been directed at Negroes alone. Puerto Ricans who settled early in New York, Indians in states with reservations, Orientals along the West Coast, and Latin-Americans in the Southwest have all suffered from such intolerance. More recent immigrants have suffered also. Until 1960, no Catholic had been elected President. No Negro or Oriental and, until recently, no Jew ever has been seriously considered for nomination by a major party, though members of all these groups have been elected to Congress, and Jews and Catholics have been appointed to the Supreme Court.

Most action by government is in response to discrimination against Negroes. One in nine Americans is of that minority group. Such discrimination is more than a Southern phenomenon. In Northern areas, discrimination is perhaps more subtle and is based in large measure on non-governmental actions, such as employment and residential policies. In the Southern states, discrimination has been incorporated into the formal legal system until recently.

The evidence of anthropologists and psychologists overwhelmingly indicates that discrimination on the basis of race or ethnic group membership is unreasonable because it lacks a scientific basis. The evidence presented in the school segregation cases of 1954 shows that, while Southern whites score higher on a number of tests than do Southern Negroes on the average, there is (1) an overlap in intelligence levels that would lead to considerable integration of Southern schools if schools were established only on the basis of ability to learn; (2) Negroes who move North strikingly improve their intellectual performance—in fact, those who have

[18] Statement of Commissioner Lawrence Gubow, Michigan Corporation and Securities Commission, before the U.S. Commission on Civil Rights, Dec. 14, 1960, Detroit, Mich.

been away from the South longest have improved most; (3) the average of Negroes on intelligence tests in some Northern states surpasses the average of whites in some Southern states.[19]

The effects of discrimination indicate that treatment accorded Negroes falls far below the minimum norms required for a democratic society, a fact frequently noted in Soviet propaganda to the uncommitted colored nations of the world. Economically, most Negroes are at the lower end of the wage scale—the last to be hired, the first to be fired. Their average wage for a family in 1960 was $3,075 as compared to $5,137 for whites. The report of the President's Commission on Goals for Americans states that in

[19] For a critical evaluation of evidence presented by social scientists in these cases, see Herbert Garfinkel, "Social Science Evidence and the School Segregation Cases," *Journal of Politics,* 21:37–59, February, 1959.

Figure 19-5

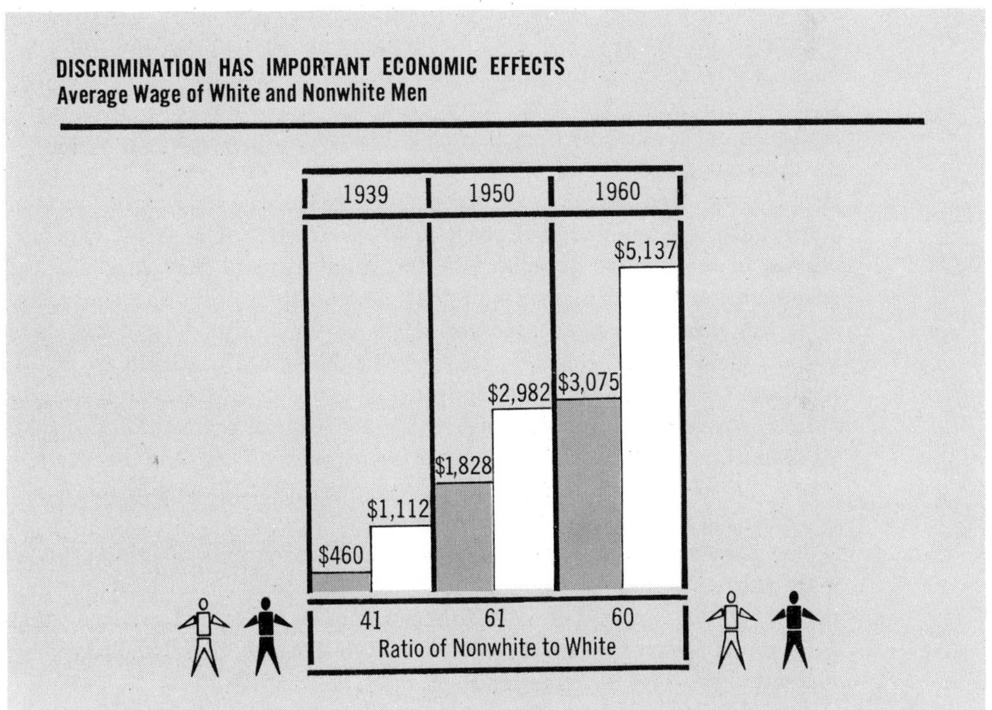

In 1939, the average nonwhite man's wage was only 41 per cent of the average white man's. By 1950, this had risen to 61. But the improvement stopped there; after another decade, the figure was only 60.
(The New York Times Magazine, *Nov. 11, 1962.*)

1960 the Negro's life expectancy at birth was 7.5 years less than that of a white person. The differences were not the result solely of infant mortality rates; at age twenty-five, the Negro's life expectancy still stood at 5.8 years less than for the average white. The highest rates of crime and juvenile delinquency are also found among Negroes, a fact that many sociologists and psychologists attribute in part to discrimination patterns. A legislative hearing in New York State heard evidence that the death penalty was "inherently a penalty that discriminated against the poor and the ignorant of minority groups." Of 50 persons sentenced to death between November 27, 1957, and November 26, 1962, 29 were Negro and 11 Puerto Rican. Of 18 then in the deathhouse, 7 were Negroes and 5 were Puerto Ricans.[20] Of the 11 actually executed, 10 were Negro and 1 was Puerto Rican.

Other evidence also suggests that patterns of discrimination probably affect adversely the psyches of those who discriminate as well as those who are discriminated against. In 1962, the President's Council of Economic Advisers issued a statement that said racial discrimination costs the American economy $13 billion a year in wasted resources.

"Stateways Do Not Make Folkways"? William Graham Sumner, a sociologist writing at the beginning of this century, argued that mores and folkways could not be changed by governmental action. Events have proven otherwise. Social scientists have discovered the important role played by leadership elites at all levels of society. Southern opinions have changed, for example. In 1942, only 21 per cent of Southerners interviewed believed that Negroes were equal to whites in intelligence. By 1956, only fourteen years later, the number had risen to 58 per cent.[21] The trend can also change in the reverse direction. A 1962 study by two Southern political scientists found that members of the eighteen to twenty-nine age group were the most convinced segregationists in the South. The researchers gave as the probable reason for this the fact that white youths in the South had been subjected to a more concentrated exposure of the case for segregation because of the furor caused by the 1954 school segregation decision. At that time, members of this group were between ten and twenty-one years of age.[22] However, even the most segregationist groups in the South expected the segregation pattern to change.

The survey also indicated that acceptance of patterns of integration is more prevalent among the well-educated, those who have lived in other parts of the nation, and those with experience in the armed services—that is, as noted earlier in respect to belief in civil liberties, those who have had a greater variety of life experiences.

An additional finding was that, contrary to the beliefs of Southern

[20] "Death Law Seen Aimed at Negroes," *The New York Times*, Dec. 8, 1962.

[21] Herbert H. Hyman and P. B. Sheatsley, "Attitudes toward Desegregation," *Scientific American*, 195:35–39, December, 1956.

[22] This study by Donald R. Matthews and James W. Prothro was reported in *The New York Times*, Sept. 23, 1962.

whites, a majority of Southern Negroes favor integration. Their willingness to support legal rulings (stateways) for desegregation (changing folkways) through "freedom rides," sit-ins, the mammoth 1963 march of over 200,000 people on Washington, and economic boycotts substantiates this finding.

Governmental Actions against Racial Discrimination. Equality demands the end of slavery as its first goal. This issue was decided by the Civil War. The Court (in *Pollock v. Williams,* 1944) decided that requiring persons to work off a debt or go to jail for debt was a form of slavery and peonage and therefore unconstitutional under the Thirteenth Amendment.

The most decisive actions taken by the Supreme Court against discrimination have been in the areas of desegregating primary elections in the South, interstate travel, and education, and in the 1963 overturning of the conviction in a sit-in case. In 1948, the Court also declared restrictive covenants* unenforceable in the courts. Two points to note: First, the Supreme Court has dealt with questions on a case-by-case basis. It has not as yet declared segregation on the basis of race illegal in every aspect of society. Second, the Supreme Court has not demanded overnight compliance. Its orders in the school segregation cases were to proceed "with all deliberate speed." Eight years after the decision, there were still three Southern states in which almost no change had taken place.

***RESTRICTIVE COVENANT. An agreement among property owners not to sell to members of specified minority groups, generally, Negroes, Mexicans, or Orientals.**

Nevertheless, the Supreme Court decisions from 1938 on have placed segregationists on the defensive. The key has been the increase in Negro voting in both North and South, coupled with the shift of such votes from the Republicans to the Democrats in New Deal days. This shift, decisive in elections in several large industrial states, has made it necessary for both parties to continue to bid for Negro support. Voting in the South was encouraged by the Civil Rights Act of 1957, the first such act in eighty years. It empowered the Justice Department to bring civil suits to help Negroes secure voting rights. The Civil Rights Acts of 1960 and 1964 further broadened this power.

In the 1957 act, Congress also established the Civil Rights Commission, which has acted in large measure like a congressional investigating committee, except that its products tend more to reflect values held within the executive department. Its studies of Negro voting led to the changes of the 1960 act, and its series of reports is the most definitive study of Negro discrimination of the postwar period.

The executive department has shown more favor to civil rights measures than has Congress, partly because of differences in political constituency. President Roosevelt in 1941 established the wartime Fair Employment

Practices Committee. In 1947, the President's Commission on Civil Rights, appointed by President Truman issued a report, *To Secure These Rights.* On the basis of this report, President Truman sent a strongly worded message to Congress, pointing out what government could do to protect minority groups. The presidential position led to a defection from his party by the Southern States' rights party, commonly called the Dixiecrats. President Truman's unexpected reelection made civil rights reform one of the issues to be respected by all subsequent politicians running for the Presidency.

Executive action has contributed to reducing segregation in the Armed Forces, the appointment of Negroes to judgeships and executive posts, and the prohibition of discrimination in public contracts. A 1962 Civil Service Commission study of Federal government employment showed that Negroes had made strong gains in movement up the scale to middle- and upper-rank positions during the Kennedy administration.[23] The Federal government, through the Attorney General's office, also makes decisions on civil rights enforcement. The 1962 case against Prince George County, Virginia, to force integration in schools receiving Federal aid (they receive such aid because the dependents of military personnel at Fort Lee attend schools in the county), seemed to be based on the argument that a county must provide public education and that this system must be desegregated. The prompt use of Federal troops and marshals in schools to carry out court orders, as in Little Rock, Arkansas, and Oxford, Mississippi, are further examples. However, in 1962 Martin Luther King criticized the FBI for assigning agents to the South who were almost exclusively white Southerners.[24]

The National Science Foundation and the Office of Education both adopted policies in 1962 for sponsorship of programs on a nondiscriminatory basis. In April, 1963, the President's Civil Rights Commission called for an ending of all Federal aid for the state of Mississippi because of its policies of discrimination.

Federal action has been copied in some states. In 1962, twenty-two had some form of fair employment practices legislation. School administrators in some cities with large Negro populations, such as Detroit and New York, have decided that future texts should show an integrated nation and give full recognition to the important contributions made by Negroes to American history.

The prevailing ideology of middle-class, white-collar suburbanites, which calls for respect of the opinion of experts and avoidance of racial clashes, has sometimes favored and sometimes hindered achievement of Negro demands in the civil rights area.

[23] "Negroes Improve Federal Job Rank," *The New York Times,* Oct. 16, 1962.

[24] "Dr. King Critical of F.B.I. in South," *The New York Times,* Nov. 19, 1962.

PROCEDURAL DUE PROCESS

Erle Stanley Gardner, author of the Perry Mason mystery stories, for a number of years conducted a "court of last resort" for persons in prison charged with crimes they claimed they had not committed. Aiding him were specialists in fields of scientific crime detection retained by a national magazine. The summary of his experience indicates that his group uncovered a number of striking instances of slipshod police investigatory methods and court procedures. He concludes that injustice of this sort is one of the greatest factors for "perpetuating crime and molding the habitual criminal." But he also pays tribute to the efforts of professionals in police work and the law who are attempting to rectify these conditions.

Two points are particularly relevant: (1) Crime detection in a modern society is complex, and some old-style procedures, often based on small-town values, are no longer appropriate; and (2) professional standards in police work are emerging and are gradually being adopted. The United States Supreme Court seems to have reached roughly similar conclusions.[25]

Police Methods. Courts guide the police by indicating what they will permit to be submitted as evidence at a trial.

Almost every American has watched the scene: Police take shifts in questioning a suspect under white-hot lights. After a considerable period, he confesses to a crime. Is this familiar movie routine legally permissible? The United States Supreme Court (in *Ashcraft v. Tennessee,* 1944) set aside a conviction and ruled that evidence obtained by such psychological third-degree methods was inadmissible. It had earlier found against evidence obtained by brutality and threats (*Brown v. Mississippi,* 1936). In addition, all confessions, it declared, must be corroborated by other evidence. In 1961, the Court (in *Mapp v. Ohio*) ruled that evidence obtained by "unreasonable" search and seizures could no longer be admitted in state courts. (It was already prohibited in Federal courts.) In most cases, this meant that the police must obtain a search warrant after showing cause to a judge; exceptions depended on proving that circumstances did not permit securing a warrant. Evidence obtained by wiretapping of phones is not permitted in Federal courts, but can be admitted in state courts. In recent Congresses, legislation has been introduced to permit such evidence in Federal cases involving subversion, but by 1965 had not been adopted. The rule does not, however, prevent wiretaps from being used to obtain leads to other evidence that is admissible in a Federal court. The Supreme Court has also insisted on prompt arraignment of an arrested person before a judge, to whom the arresting officer must show cause for the arrest. The basic right of habeas corpus is to prevent arbitrary

[25] Erle Stanley Gardner, *The Court of Last Resort,* Pocket Books, Inc., New York, 1954.

arrest and detention *incommunicado*. In the McNabb case (1943), the Court ruled invalid a confession obtained while the prisoner was illegally detained. The Court has also applied to Federal courts the ancient common-law rule against entrapment (*Sherman v. United States,* 1958), that is, against tempting a person into committing a crime. The case involved a narcotics purchase from an informer who met the addict in a physician's office where both were supposedly under treatment.

All of these requirements to some degree handicap police work, and have occasionally resulted in known criminals being freed on what are described by editors and reporters as "technicalities." At the same time, they are in harmony, for the most part, with an increased emphasis on professionalism in police work and dependence on scientific police detection.

Trial Methods. The basic procedures of criminal trials require that the accused be brought before a judge to determine if there is sufficient evidence to hold him. The routine is to seek a writ of habeas corpus. The accused must be charged with breaking a specific law. If he is held, in most cases aside from murder, bail is set. At his trial, the accused has the right of counsel and the right to cross examine witnesses against him. He may waive jury trial and need not testify against himself. In the Malloy and Murphy cases, the Court held that if he does testify in state court, the testimony cannot be used against him in Federal court and vice versa. He may not be tried more than once for the same alleged crime. (This does not prevent trial in both state and Federal courts for the same act, or a second trial in case of a hung jury or declaration of mistrial.) If found guilty, cruel and unusual punishments (as decided by the cultural values of the moment) may not be administered. He has statutory rights of appeal.

Special procedures are required to convict a person of treason (specifically defined in the Constitution as levying war against the United States or adhering to or giving aid and comfort to its enemies). Unless the suspect confesses in open court, two witnesses must testify to having seen him commit the crime.

The tightening of state trial procedures began in modern times when the Supreme Court (in *Moore v. Dempsey,* 1923) held that a state trial conducted under threat of mob action was invalid. In 1935 (*Norris v. Alabama*), the Supreme Court began to insist that juries, when used, must be broadly representative of the populace. Conviction was set aside in one case because no Negro had ever served on a jury in the county of trial where there was a large Negro population.

Father C. Dismas Clark, a Jesuit referred to in the press as the "hoodlum priest" because of his work with criminals, once said his great concern was with "the mighty power of the state in its interminable facilities to investigate as opposed to the minute abilities of the poor to produce witnesses, obtain competent lawyers or be bonded."

In 1963, in *Gideon v. Wainwright,* the Court ruled that all persons involved in criminal prosecutions in state courts have the right of assistance by counsel for their defense. This was already the rule in Federal courts. In other respects, state procedures are generally less strict than are the Federal, but the differences are becoming less.

Dropping of the grand jury* procedure of indictment in state cases has been permitted. In many states, it has been replaced in whole or in part by the simpler method of filing an "information"* with the judge by the prosecuting attorney. Under this method, the prosecutor states that he is holding a person for trial upon a specified charge for which he believes he has ample evidence to justify trial.

***A GRAND JURY inquires into crimes committed within its area of jurisdiction, decides on the probability of guilt, and whether or not to hold a suspect for trial. (A PETIT JURY decides questions of fact at a trial.) If a person is held for trial at the request of the prosecutor (the United States attorney in Federal cases), the grand jury returns an INDICTMENT. If the person is held on accusation of the grand jury itself, the formal action is termed a PRESENTMENT. An INFORMATION does not require grand jury action. It is a sworn statement of accusation filed with the appropriate trial court by the prosecutor. Use of the information procedure in Federal felony cases is not possible because of provisions in the Fifth Amendment.**

Military jurisdiction. The Supreme Court has ruled that military courts (courts-martial) do not have jurisdiction over a person once he has been discharged from the Armed Forces. Similarly, civilians abroad cannot be tried in peacetime by courts-martial. The Uniform Code of Military Justice of 1950 spells out military procedures and in some cases permits appeals to civil courts.

Eminent domain. Governments may take private property for public use if just compensation, as legally determined, is given. This right of eminent domain provides for special procedures. The affected citizen or corporation may appeal the administrative decision on compensation to the courts. In general, the Supreme Court has interpreted the right to condemn property in broad terms, permitting it to be exercised in cases "affected with a public interest," even though the property is not taken by a government. Thus, a railroad or a privately owned utility may use the government's right of eminent domain if needed in order to secure a necessary right of way.

Quasi-judicial Procedures. Some governmental activities lie in a twilight zone between the procedures of the executive and those of the judiciary. The Court has had to rule on many cases involving such "neither fish nor fowl" agencies as the Federal Communications Commission, the Federal Power Commission, and the Federal Trade Commission. It has, for example, declared (in *Hannah v. Larche,* 1961) that the Civil Rights Commission is not a judicial body and therefore can obtain evidence through secret informers and need not permit cross examination of these sources by counsel for the defense, as would be required in a court of law.

Similar leeway has been granted to legislative investigating committees, though the Court has attempted to apply a rule against "fishing expeditions"—the search for evidence without a specific charge (*Watkins v. United States,* 1957). Legislative bodies are, however, specifically prohibited by the Constitution from using two procedures: They may not try, convict, and sentence a specific individual through legislative action (called a "bill of attainder"); and they may not declare to be crimes, acts of persons that have taken place before the law against the act was passed (called retroactive legislation). They may not even increase the penalty for a crime already committed. All of these are classed as ex post facto laws.

Administrative procedures. The Court has tended to place heavier restrictions upon the procedures of administrators than upon either quasi-judicial or congressional groups. The trend has been toward the imposition of procedures imitative of the courts. Thus in various cases, administrators have been required to give due notice of hearings, to separate the investigating function from that of the decision maker who imposes penalties, and to grant the right of cross examination of witnesses in certain circumstances. In addition, the Court has often sustained a right of appeal from administrative decisions to the regular courts.

CITIZENS AND ALIENS

American citizenship has come to be considered a civil right. The precise method of attaining citizenship was for a long time vague, since the United States Constitution recognized both state and national citizenship. The issue was first confronted in the Dred Scott case (1857). The Supreme Court ruled that Wisconsin could not grant national citizenship to a Negro. America was committed to remaining all white. But the decision was short-lived. It was overturned by the Civil War. In 1868, the Fourteenth Amendment made national citizenship primary and forbade discrimination in granting citizenship on the basis of race, creed, and religion, and that is the policy today.

The two principles by which natural-born citizenship is awarded are *jus soli* (the law of the soil, or birth on American territory) and *jus sanguinis* (the law of the blood, or citizenship by American parentage). Our history is one of expanding both interpretations in harmony with the tenets of the American creed. Soil has been interpreted as any American territory, including American warships at sea. (Vietnamese born on American warships while parents were evacuated from North Vietnam are technically American citizens.) And in 1898, the Supreme Court ruled that children born on American soil, even of alien parents who themselves were not eligible for citizenship, were American citizens (in the Wong Kim Ark case). Children of diplomats representing a foreign nation are, however, excepted.

Citizenship may also be acquired through naturalization. But from our earliest history, naturalized citizens have held a somewhat "second-class" status in comparison to citizenship of the natural-born. The naturalized person is not eligible to become President or Vice President and must be a citizen for nine years to be eligible for election to the House of Representatives. More importantly, Federal law since 1907 has held that a naturalized citizen would lose citizenship if he returned to his former home country and lived there over an extended period. But the Supreme Court in *Schneider v. Rusk* (1964) rejected this proviso and thus took a large step in the direction of making naturalized and natural-born citizens equal in status.

The Immigration and Nationality Act of 1952, the McCarran-Walter Act, provided that a naturalized citizen loses citizenship if he or his parents entered the United States illegally, gave false information in applying for citizenship, or subsequently joined the Communist party. These provisions were applied retroactively. The Supreme Court has insisted that the act of joining of the Communist party be in full recognition of its implications, but it has not abrogated the other restrictive provisions not applicable to the natural-born. Earlier controversy raged over the status of pacifists, since those swearing allegiance to the United States were required to affirm that they would defend it against its enemies, foreign and domestic. In 1929 pacifists were denied citizenship by naturalization, but the Supreme Court in 1946 decided they were eligible if willing to serve as noncombatants. Congress affirmed this in a 1950 act, though it insisted that pacifism must be based on religious rather than solely on moral principles.

Naturalization procedures were at first handled exclusively by state and Federal courts, but serious abuses of the law resulted, including preelection ceremonies sponsored by political organizations that were interested primarily in swelling their turnout and very little in legal requirements. In 1906, the Immigration and Naturalization Service was given primary responsibility for examining applicants. The swearing-in ceremony in court is now mainly a matter of form, though its symbolic significance is great. Aliens desiring citizenship must, in addition to qualifications already noted, show good moral character, be able to read, write, speak, and understand English, have a knowledge of the history and principles of American government, and declare an attachment to the United States. They must also have resided in the United States for five years of uninterrupted residence before applying. The schoolroom classes on citizenship, portrayed in the sketches by Leonard Q. Ross in *The Education of H*Y*M*A*N K*A*P*L*A*N,* are now a familiar part of Americana.

Simplified procedures for naturalization have been devised for foreigners who marry American servicemen. Congress may also grant citizenship to individuals by special act. Winston Churchill was granted citizenship as an honor, but citizenship has also been granted to informers or others who have rendered special service to the nation. In the past, large groups have also been granted citizenship by special act; most recently the residents of Guam in 1950. But "nationals," who are neither aliens of citizens, still exist. These people, residents of American Pacific trusteeship territory, for example, are noncitizens subject to United States jurisdiction. In effect, they have a kind of ward status between that of citizen and alien.

As citizenship procedures have become more liberal, so too have attitudes in respect to renunciation of citizenship. The law has been that deserters, Americans who serve in a foreign army or vote in a foreign election, as well as those who formally renounce American citizenship lose that citizenship. But the trend in judicial cases has been to require the definite formal renunciation. Desertion or voting abroad is not enough, according to recent judicial decisions. Nor is marriage to a foreigner. As early as 1922, in the Cable Act, Congress decided that American women did not automatically lose citizenship by marrying foreigners.

Immigration Policy. Related to the question of citizenship is that of immigration of foreigners who plan to reside in America for long periods of time without becoming citizens. Aliens may sue and be sued, cannot be prohibited from owning property, and have many of the common rights and immunities of citizens. They also must pay taxes and are subject to military duty in certain circumstances. But they also are liable to restrictions, some of which are severe. They may not vote or serve on juries and are often prohibited from entering certain professions or militarily sensitive employment and may be denied such benefits as pensions, welfare payments, or workmen's compensation. Their property may be confiscated, and they may be interned if America goes to war with their homeland. Since 1940, by the provisions of the Smith Act, they must register and be fingerprinted. The McCarran-Walter Act added that they must keep the Attorney General's office notified of their employment. And they may be deported in summary fashion for a growing list of reasons, including membership in the Communist or other totalitarian party, conviction of certain crimes, or by order of the President. The act of 1952 specifically permitted procedures that would be contrary to due process of law in other circumstances.

Administration of immigration procedures has been improved to lessen unnecessary suffering. Since 1927, admission visas have been granted by American consuls abroad, a procedure that almost guarantees permanent residence to those permitted to come. But final determination is still made by officers of the Immigration and Naturalization Service. This has resulted in shared administration by the State Department and the Attorney General's department.

As early as the 1830s, there were political movements whose purpose was to restrict immigration of the Irish. Movements aimed at other ethnic groups have existed since. President Franklin Roosevelt once reminded the Daughters of the American Revolution that both he and they were descended from immigrants and revolutionaries. But the knowledge that all but the Indians are emigrés or their descendants has not slowed down the movement to restrict entry, for those who are already citizens often see themselves as having a right to decide who should join them.

The first restrictive immigration law was adopted in 1882. It was sponsored by labor unions desiring to reduce the competition of immigrant labor. The Chinese (who were originally welcomed so they could help build the transcontinental railroads) were specifically excluded; so were the feebleminded, paupers, convicts, and "lunatics." In 1885, contract labor was declared illegal. Congress added anarchists and the immoral (a provision aimed at prostitutes) to the list in 1903. Illiterates and all Orientals from an Asian-Pacific zone were excluded, despite Woodrow Wilson's veto, in 1917. In 1921, the first severe restriction on immigration was passed as a temporary measure. The flood tide of a million Europeans a year was cut by the formula to a trickle of about 150,000. In 1924 the formula was changed, but the restriction was made permanent. Minor changes, such as a repeal of Chinese exclusion during World War II, were made over the next twenty-five years(see Chapter 15). In 1952, a major codification, the Immigration and Nationality Act, commonly called the McCarran-Walter Act, passed over President Truman's veto. It raised the total quota to 154,467.

The basic policy between 1917 and 1952 eliminated Orientals on a racial basis. The provision was then changed to give all nations a quota of at least 100. Racial discrimination was no longer explicit. But the requirement that anyone with one-half ancestry of those races commonly found in the Asian-Pacific zone be counted as of an Asian nation, even though he might have been born elsewhere, indicated that the rationale was based on racial discrimination. A presidential commission in 1953, in its report *Whom We Shall Welcome* particularly criticized this feature of the act. The quotas for each nation were based in the act on their percentage of 1920 population. It was a national-origins formula. Southern Europeans, such as Greeks and Turks, continued to have minute quotas compared to the demand, while Northern European immigrants often totaled less than their national quotas. Immigrants from the Western Hemisphere were permitted quota-free entry, though other requirements, including those of self-support and national security, have kept the number small, except for the influx from Cuba after the Castro revolution.

Following World War II, special provisions were made to admit 205,000 displaced persons. The original act of 1948 was renewed in 1950 for 341,000; in 1953, for 209,000. After the Hungarian revolt of 1956, unused 1953 quotas totaling 38,000 were renewed. But until a change in 1957, these entries were charged against the nation, using up quotas through the next 200 years. Special provisions have also permitted admittance of such diverse groups as sheepherders, informers, and families of United States servicemen.

Visiting aliens, granted visas for a specific period, have also been subject to strict regulation by the requirements of the 1952 act. But protests from agencies in the United States wishing to entertain distinguished foreigners, the promoters of the tourist trade, and counteractions in retaliation by foreign nations have led to some relaxation of procedures. Fingerprinting may be waived by the Secretary of State's office if the Attorney General agrees, and visitors need no longer identify themselves by race.

Thus far, the history of American policy to noncitizens shows a steady drift away from the principles of the original American ideal. Part of that drift is accounted for by the openness of American policy at the nation's inception. Any formal control, even the most reasonable, would of necessity have been in the direction of a lessening of opportunity. A second reason for the trend is the trade unions' fear of cheap immigrant labor. Finally, the problems of the cold war, espionage, and sabotage have led many Americans to feel that a greater emphasis on security at the expense of individual freedoms is required. Nevertheless, unlike most other great powers, America has continued a policy of admitting large numbers of immigrants.

But in two ways the current trend in respect to noncitizens is out of harmony with early American principles. Discrimination is still covertly based on race, ethnic background, and religion, rather than—as the President's Commission of 1953 suggested—on grounds that could more reasonably be justified (need of certain skills in America, asylum from tyranny, reunion of families, or population pressure abroad). Second, arbitrary procedures seem less the result of a reasonable judgment of the probable dangers involved than of a hysterical reaction following the revelations of Communist conspiracy and successful revolutions in Czechoslovakia and China and Communist duplicity in the invasion of South Korea.

RIGHTS, LIBERTIES, AND POLITICS

Because the meaningful content of civil rights and liberties is important to everyone who lives in the United States, the authors have concentrated in this chapter upon the actual contemporary interpretations of the courts, the bodies that, for the most part, give content to the general terms used in the Constitution. But the major theme of this book should not be forgotten: Civil liberties, despite the legal fiction that they are areas of discretion which lie *beyond* government, are essentially the product of social experience and governmental policy. Civil rights and liberties have meaning only as they are expressed by governmental agencies. Both, therefore, are determined and periodically modified by values and pressures in much the same fashion as are policies regarding, say, agriculture or urban renewal.

The courts, in shaping policy, are influenced by many things, but particularly by the social experience of the nation. These are translated into policy through the belief systems of the individual justices of the Supreme Court and the lesser judges; the "mood" of the times, that is, the prevailing dominant value system as modified by recent events; the kinds of pressures asserted upon the courts by active groups; the level of interest and activity directed into some particular area by Congress or the President; the expectations regarding America held by citizens of other nations; the traditions, ideals, customs, judicial precedents, and other influences flowing from the past. All of these have been discussed in earlier chapters. They are briefly mentioned here so that we do not fall into the easy trap of assuming that rulings on rights and liberties are self-enforcing. Civil liberties are surely hothouse flowers that could not survive in today's severe climate without the protection of government. The politics of rights and liberties is as complex as any of the many difficult areas of public policy making. And it is today one of the most conflict-ridden and "visible" issues confronting the nation.

SELECTED BIBLIOGRAPHY

The philosophers of the Era of Enlightenment, who influenced so greatly the thinking of the writers of the Constitution and the Bill of Rights, assumed a rational political citizenry with a strong commitment to the values of civil liberties and rights. Modern-day social scientists, armed with the tools of the opinion survey and depth interviewing, have had a corrosive effect on their more optimistic assumptions. From such analysis, a more realistic image is emerging of political man in democratic society and the degree of his commitment to civil rights and liberties. The most thorough study to date is that of Stouffer [38], but many others have also dealt with aspects of the subject [1, 16, 19, and 27].

The traditional problem of civil liberties has been that of protecting the rights of expression for the individual while preserving the institutions of society. The classic statement is that of John Stuart Mill [28]. See also Chafee [5]. Attempts to realign the balance in terms of an American society faced with a cold war are found in Hook [21] and Cook [8]. Among the most pessimistic notions is that of the garrison state as described by Lasswell [26] and Orwell [31]. Especially noteworthy collections of essays have recently appeared, reviewing the history and problems of liberty in a society of large-scale organization and technology [6, 15, 20].

A continuing series of books and monographs on specialized topics of civil liberties have been published by the Cornell University Press of Ithaca, New York, under the advisory editorship of Robert E. Cushman. For a current review of cases and events, see the monthly newsletters and annual reports of the American Civil Liberties Union. The Freedom of Information Center of the School of Journalism at the University of Missouri issues reports of speeches or public statements relating to freedom in mass media. The professional commitment of the center makes it particularly sensitive to problems of *government* censorship and access to governmental information.

The 1954 school desegregation decision was given after much of the basic sociological and psychological study of problems of equality in America had occurred. Summaries are found in Allport [2] and Myrdal [29]. The five reports of the United States Commission on Civil Rights [40] outline recent developments. Key [24] describes the political relevance of discrimination patterns in the South. For current reports of race relations events, see the

Southern School News, and the *Race Relations Law Reporter*, published by the Vanderbilt University School of Law.

The position of the Supreme Court as self-designated protector of liberties is discussed critically by Commager [7], who states the Holmes-Frankfurter position. Detailed behavioral analysis of Court handling of civil liberties cases is found in Pritchett [33, 34] and Ulmer [39].

Less study has been made of the political relevance of judicial procedures for democratic society aside from occasional exposés by journalists. Studies meriting attention are by Fellman [11] and Frank [13]. Karlen [23] provides a short description of state and Federal procedures.

1. Adorno, T. W., E. Frenkel-Brunswick, D. J. Levinson, and R. N. Sanford: *The Authoritarian Personality*, Harper & Row, Publishers, New York, 1950.
2. Allport, Gordon W.: *The Nature of Prejudice*, Beacon Press, Boston, 1954.
3. Bell, Daniel (ed.): *The Radical Right*, rev. ed., Anchor Books, Doubleday & Company, Inc., Garden City, N.Y., 1963.
4. Boles, Donald E.: *The Bible, Religion and the Public Schools*, The Iowa State University Press, Ames, Iowa, 1961.
5. Chafee, Zechariah, Jr.: *Free Speech in the United States*, Harvard University Press, Cambridge, Mass., 1941.
6. Commager, Henry Steele, and others: *Civil Liberties under Attack*, University of Pennsylvania Press, Philadelphia, 1951.
7. Commager, Henry Steele: *Majority Rule and Minority Rights*, Oxford University Press, Fair Lawn, N.J., 1943.
8. Cook, Thomas I.: *Democratic Rights versus Communist Activity*, Random House, Inc., New York, 1955.
9. Cushman, Robert E.: *Civil Liberties in the United States*, Cornell University Press, Ithaca, N.Y., 1956.
10. Davis, Elmer: *But We Were Born Free*, The Bobbs-Merrill Company, Inc., Indianapolis, 1954.
11. Fellman, David: *The Defendant's Rights*, Holt, Rinehart and Winston, Inc., New York, 1958.
12. Fraenkel, Osmond K.: *The Supreme Court and Civil Liberties*, Oceana Publications, New York, 1961.
13. Frank, Jerome: *Courts on Trial: Myth and Reality in American Justice*, Princeton University Press, Princeton, N.J., 1949.
14. Frazier, E. Franklin: *Black Bourgeoisie*, The Free Press of Glencoe, New York, 1957.
15. Friedrich, Carl J. (ed.): *Liberty*, Nomos IV, Atherton Press, New York, 1962.
16. Fromm, Erich: *Escape from Freedom*, Holt, Rinehart and Winston, Inc., New York, 1941.
17. Harris, Robert J.: *The Quest for Equality*, Louisiana State University Press, Baton Rouge, La., 1960.
18. Hartz, Louis: *The Liberal Tradition in America*, Harcourt, Brace & World, Inc., New York, 1955.
19. Hoffer, Eric: *The True Believer*, Harper & Row, Publishers, New York, 1951.
20. Hofstadter, Richard, and Walter P. Metzger: *The Development of Academic Freedom in the United States*, Columbia University Press, New York, 1955.
21. Hook, Sidney: *Heresy Yes—Conspiracy No!* The John Day Company, Inc., New York, 1953.
22. Hyman, Herbert H., and P. B. Sheatsley: "Attitudes toward Desegregation," *Scientific American*, 195:35–39, December, 1956.

23. Karlen, Delmar: *The Citizen in Court: Litigant, Witness, Juror, Judge,* Holt, Rinehart and Winston, Inc., New York, 1964.
24. Key, V. O., Jr.: *Southern Politics in State and Nation,* Alfred A. Knopf, Inc., New York, 1950.
25. Konvitz, Milton R., and Clinton Rossiter (eds.): *Aspects of Liberty: Essays Presented to Robert E. Cushman,* Cornell University Press, Ithaca, N.Y., 1958.
26. Lasswell, Harold: *National Security and Individual Freedom,* McGraw-Hill Book Company, New York, 1950.
27. Lipset, Seymour Martin: *Political Man,* Doubleday & Company, Inc., Garden City, N.Y., 1960.
28. Mill, John Stuart: "Essay on Liberty," in *Utilitarianism, Liberty, and Representative Government,* E. P. Dutton & Co., Inc., New York, 1950.
29. Myrdal, Gunnar: *The American Dilemma,* Harper & Row, Publishers, New York, 1944. (Also available in McGraw-Hill paperback.)
30. Newman, Edwin S.: *The Law of Civil Rights and Civil Liberties,* Oceana Publications, New York, 1960.
31. Orwell, George: *1984,* Harcourt, Brace & World, Inc., New York, 1949.
32. Paul, James C. N., and Murray L. Schwartz: *Federal Censorship,* The Free Press of Glencoe, New York, 1961.
33. Pritchett, C. Herman: *Civil Liberties and the Vinson Court,* The University of Chicago Press, Chicago, 1954.
34. Pritchett, C. Herman: *The Political Offender and the Warren Court,* Boston University Press, Boston, 1958.
35. Rourke, Francis E.: *Secrecy and Publicity: Dilemmas of Democracy,* The Johns Hopkins Press, Baltimore, 1961.
36. Schwartzman, Ruth, and Joseph Stein: *The Law of Personal Liberties,* Oceana Publications, New York, 1960.
37. Spicer, George W.: *The Supreme Court and Fundamental Freedom,* Appleton-Century-Crofts, Inc., New York, 1961.
38. Stouffer, Samuel A.: *Communism, Conformity, and Civil Liberties: A Cross-section of the Nation Speaks Its Mind,* Doubleday & Company, Inc., Garden City, N.Y., 1955.
39. Ulmer, S. Sidney: "Supreme Court Behavior and Civil Rights," *The Western Political Quarterly,* 13:288–311, June, 1960.
40. United States Commission on Civil Rights, *Voting, Education, Employment, Housing,* and *Justice,* 1961. A report in five volumes.

Law Cases

Ashcraft v. Tennessee, 322 U.S. 143 (1944).
Barenblatt v. United States, 360 U.S. 109 (1959).
Brown v. Board of Education of Topeka, 347 U.S. 483 (1954).
Brown v. Mississippi, 297 U.S. 278 (1936).
Cole v. Young, 351 U.S. 536 (1956).
Communist Party v. Subversive Activities Control Board, 351 U.S. 115 (1956).
Cox v. New Hampshire, 312 U.S. 569 (1941).
Dennis v. United States, 341 U.S. 494 (1951).
Dred Scott v. Sandford, 19 Howard 393 (1857).
Engel v. Vitale, 370 U.S. 421 (1962).
Everson v. Board of Education of Ewing Township, 330 U.S. 1 (1947).
Gideon v. Wainwright, 372 U.S. 335 (1963).
Girouard v. United States, 328 U.S. 61 (1946).
Gitlow v. New York, 268 U.S. 652 (1925).
Hague v. C.I.O., 307 U.S. 496 (1939).
Hannah v. Larche, 363 U.S. 420 (1961).
Hannegan v. Esquire, 327 U.S. 146 (1946).

Kent v. Dulles, 357 U.S. 116 (1958).
Knapp v. Schweitzer, 357 U.S. 371 (1958).
Malloy v. Hogan, 12 L. Ed. 2d 653 (1964).
Mapp v. Ohio, 367 U.S. 643 (1961).
McNabb v. United States, 318 U.S. 332 (1943).
Minersville School District v. Gobitis, 310 U.S. 586 (1940).
Missouri ex. rel. Gaines v. Canada, 305 U.S. 337 (1938).
Moore v. Dempsey, 261 U.S. 86 (1923).
Murphy v. Waterfront Commission of N.Y., 12 L. Ed. 2d 678 (1964).
NAACP v. Alabama, 357 U.S. 449 (1958).
Near v. Minnesota, 283 U.S. 697 (1931).
Norris v. Alabama, 294 U.S. 587 (1935).
Palko v. Connecticut, 302 U.S. 319 (1937).
Pennsylvania v. Nelson, 350 U.S. 497 (1956).
Pierce v. Society of Sisters of the Holy Name, 268 U.S. 510 (1925).
Plessy v. Ferguson, 163 U.S. 537 (1896).
Pollock v. Williams, 322 U.S. 4 (1944).
Roth v. United States, 354 U.S. 476 (1957).
Scales v. United States, 355 U.S. 1 (1957).
Schenck v. United States, 249 U.S. 47 (1919).
Schneider v. Rusk, 12 L. Ed. 2d 218 (1964).
Service v. Dulles, 354 U.S. 363 (1957).
Sherman v. United States, 356 U.S. 369 (1958).
Times Film Corp. v. Chicago, 244 F. 2d 423 (1957).
Torcaso v. Watkins, 367 U.S. 488 (1961).
Ullman v. United States, 350 U.S. 422 (1956).
United States v. Wong Kim Ark, 169 U.S. 649 (1898).
Watkins v. United States, 354 U.S. 178 (1957).
West Virginia State Board of Education v. Barnette, 319 U.S. 624 (1943).
Whitney v. California, 247 U.S. 357 (1927).
Yates v. United States, 355, U.S. 66 (1957).
Zorach v. Clauson, 343 U.S. 306 (1952).

Case Studies

1. Lewis, Anthony, *Gideon's Trumpet,* Random House, Inc., New York, 1964.
2. Muse, Benjamin: *Virginia's Massive Resistance,* Indiana University Press, Bloomington, Ind., 1961.
3. Pritchett, C. Herman, and Alan F. Westin (eds.): *The Third Branch of Government: Eight Cases in Constitutional Politics,* Harcourt, Brace & World, Inc., 1963. Cases 1, 3, 4, 5, 6, and 8.
4. Record, Wilson, and Jane Cassels (eds.): *Little Rock, U.S.A.,* Chandler Publishing Company, San Francisco, Calif., 1960.
5. Taper, Bernard: *Gomillion versus Lightfoot,* McGraw-Hill Book Company, New York, 1962.
6. Thurber, James, and Elliott Nugent: *The Male Animal,* in John Gassner (ed.), *Best Plays of the Modern American Theatre,* Crown Publishers, Inc., New York, 1947.
7. Vose, Clement E.: *Caucasians Only,* University of California Press, Berkeley, Calif., 1959.
8. Westin, Alan F. (ed.): "The Supreme Court: Bookies and 'Bugs' in California," in *The Uses of Power,* Harcourt, Brace & World, Inc., New York, 1961.

CHAPTER

20

FEDERAL DOMESTIC POLICY

At first glance, the Federal government's domestic policies look chaotic. A county agricultural agent, paid with Federal as well as state and local funds, visits farmers and advises them on how to grow larger crops. Sometimes he can pass along to them a revolutionary technique developed by the state experiment station, which is also in part supported by Federal funds. But other agencies of the Federal government in effect buy up surplus crops at prices pegged to the artificially high level current between 1909 and 1914 and store them at high cost. The government also pays the farmer to raise less. The United States Department of Agriculture simultaneously encourages the expansion of commercial farming and the preservation of the family farm.

There are other examples. In 1948, the Supreme Court, in *Shelley v. Kraemer,* announced it would henceforth refuse to enforce agreements made among property owners not to sell their real estate to members of religious or racial minority groups (restrictive covenants); it was not until after the 1962 midterm elections, two years after taking office, that President Kennedy found it politically possible to announce plans for integration of all Federal public housing and prohibition of discrimination in the granting of Federal Housing Agency or Veterans Administration (GI) guaranteed mortgages or the sale of homes carrying such guarantees.

Labor is guaranteed the right to organize, but business can claim tax write-offs for the costs of moving plants to areas where labor is unorganized. Labor can bargain for working conditions that include featherbedding (extra make-work) and may insist on following inefficient methods of work, but industry is granted some tax write-offs for automation that may result in workers losing their jobs. (The Federal government does have a retraining program for such displaced workers.)

THE PRAGMATIC AMERICAN APPROACH

A list of what might appear to be logical inconsistencies in Federal policy could be continued almost indefinitely. For almost every policy, another can be found that partially contradicts or sometimes undermines it. These inconsistencies are not, however, inconsistencies from a political standpoint. The political institutions do not assume that there is only one self-evident value to be recognized. For every policy concession to one value, another concession can usually be found to some other value that partially compensates for it. Acting on the political premise that most value claims are legitimate, there is no inconsistency.

Interest-group Pressures. Federal programs thus are designed to give a little to almost everyone: laborer, businessman, and farmer; Negro and Southern white, urbanite and rural resident; young and old; immigrant and those whose ancestors traveled the Mayflower; the handicapped and the flourishing. The detail of domestic public policy is not the result of a carefully devised plan; it is a response to many pressures.

Ideological Claims. The rewards that different interests within society receive are frequently economic, but almost every policy also grants ideological rewards. The representatives who fight to prevent the building of a Federal dam or for aid to depressed areas are generally not concerned with economic interest alone. They are usually also guided by ideological belief, just as are Supreme Court justices when ruling to uphold the rights of minority religious, racial, or radical political groups. Ideology, as noted earlier, forms a picture or image of what reality is as well as what it should be. It is shorthand for what individuals and groups believe society should be like. A simple economic analysis of who gets what, when, and how will not alone unravel the policy tangle.

Important political ideologies in different periods of history have been identified with majority political parties (see Chapter 10). These ideological commitments provide both participants and analysts with a pattern for what might appear to be merely a scuffling of group interests for economic advantage.

The process of making domestic policy is a process of trying to satisfy as many varied claims for protection and aid as possible, providing they fall within the boundaries of a broad prevailing ideological consensus. The substance of domestic policies changes over time as the boundaries of ideological consensus change. Since the days of the New Deal, there has been a gradual victory for the social service ideology over that of industrial individualism, which was centered in the small town. Battles have been over the *status quo* and extension of the logic of the social service ideology, rather than a choice between that ideology and a return to the small-town viewpoint of industrial individualism. Thus, even in conservative administrations, social security is expanded, an urban renewal program is begun, and massive Federal expenditures are made on highways. But the older viewpoints are not dead, even though nearly all presidential candidates for the major parties since 1936 have supported the social service viewpoint rather than that of industrial individualism. With the movement of population to the suburbs, there is evidence that a new ideology modifying that of the social service state is coming into being.

Ideology is often the basis for pragmatic political alliances on specific issues. Every economic interest looks for allies on an ideological basis. Executives of natural gas companies wanted state rather than Federal legislation: (1) They thought state legislation would be weaker; and (2) they were aided by many individuals and groups who have no personal stake in natural gas, but believe that, in terms of the small-town ideology, the less government regulation there is, the better for the economy and the country. Likewise, an organization wanting to assist migrant workers expects sympathy and some support from those who, while they receive no direct benefit themselves, subscribe to the social service state ideology.

Thus the ideology often serves to recruit a political majority for what may be a minority interest. It blends private economic interests into a larger framework. In the process, a pattern of consistency in domestic politics emerges, one that rather unevenly conforms to the majority ideology of the period.

The Open Society and Open Government. Our society is called an "open" one, that is, competition among groups based on economic, social, racial, and political interests is encouraged. It also encourages competition among viewpoints. Few interests or potential interests are so suppressed that they cannot organize a political power base of some importance.

Paralleling the open society is what can be described as an open government. Access in fact, if not always in psychological perception, is available at some point, in some area of government, for any group having some slight measure of political power. The openness of government encourages such ready access as well as a variety of policy responses, as different arenas of government, each with some power to act independently, respond in different ways. A President sends troops to Little Rock to force school integration, while Congress stymies a Federal aid-to-education bill in part because it may force such integration. The Supreme Court refuses to permit evidence obtained by wiretapping into Federal courts, while police agencies of the Federal bureaucracy use such devices daily. Even within each major branch of government, access by opposing interests and variety in policy responses is common. Committees of Congress battle each other, as do agencies within the executive branch. Some lower courts try to hamper the implementation of some Supreme Court decisions, and the Supreme Court itself has bitterly divided in 5 to 4 decisions.

Changes in Personnel and Changes in Views. American government, being democratic, also encourages flexibilty and change in the viewpoints of its personnel. Candidates, including those already in office, tend to anticipate the wants of whomever they regard as their clientele groups. The variety in constituencies is great, differing for the presidential candidate, the congressman, and the potential Supreme Court nominee. Most of these attitudes do not completely change on taking office; the clientele group is still favored, although the office itself tends to bring competing considerations into clearer focus.

New viewpoints are also introduced by frequent personnel changes—the election of a new President, the shift in congressional leadership when the congressional majority changes, the appointment of new justices to the Supreme Court and of new personnel to the higher bureaucracy. The impact of particular individuals in important positions of power can be great. The retirement of a Justice Felix Frankfurter, a Lyndon Johnson as Senate majority leader, or a J. Edgar Hoover as Director of the Federal Bureau of Investigation opens the position to some interest groups and closes it off for others.

In Summary. With a governmental system in such flux, with a system of divided responsibility that invites pressures from different interest groups at different points, domestic policy tends to be made on a piecemeal basis that attempts to satisfy diverse, politically potent minorities. The *status quo,* generally an expression of an older ideology, is difficult to change; while a minority can preserve present policy, it generally takes an unusual majority to change it. Officials must usually be content to chip away with changes that are compromise responses to the specific and immediate problems of some minority interest. Small adjustments take the place of wholesale reorganization. Policy inconsistencies abound. Only over a long view can a pattern be discerned as there is a gradual shift from an older political majority and its political ideology to the ideological expectations of a new political majority.

DOMESTIC POLICY FOR AN EMERGING SOCIETY

The typical American constituency has changed drastically since World War II. The experience of the average American, the new political majority, is different from that of the average American in prewar New Deal days.

In receiving the 1962 Nobel Prize for literature, author John Steinbeck, who had written such reformist literature as *The Grapes of Wrath,* said: "Thirty years ago you could tell an underdog. Today it's a little harder to recognize one." Part of the reason was that the Depression had been left behind. From 1947 to 1960 the fastest-growing consumer products were air conditioners, TV sets, clothes dryers, and boats. All had increased production by more than 400 per cent.

The Breaking up of the Old Society. There has also been a reshuffling of population that is blurring old geographic ethnic and social distinctions. The old South is gradually breaking up, as is aristocratic and ethnic New

England. The ethnic minorities that gave the New Deal its votes are no longer stacked in the ramshackle apartments of great cities. Negroes are entering a new life, and Roman Catholics are no longer social isolates. American subcultures, with their once distinctive social experiences and ideologies, are being blurred by a vast shift in population.

The pattern resulting from this population reshuffling is one of supercity or metropolitan areas. Even such sparsely populated states as Utah, Arizona, and Colorado have more citizens living in cities than in small towns or rural areas. America is a nation of metropolitans. But within the supercities, another great shuffling has been occurring—a move to suburbia. The suburban way of life is radically different from any that the majority of Americans have ever had. From it springs a new outlook and style that the ads in magazines hold up as the American ideal (cookouts, casual sportswear, and station wagons). From it also is emerging a different political viewpoint that will shape domestic policy by singling out a distinctive set of issues. This is not to say that the suburban viewpoint is correct and that previous American political ideologies are false—truth or falseness in relation to ideologies cannot be demonstrated empirically. The importance of the ideology of the suburbs is its timeliness—it is the way the emerging American majority looks at politics in light of its experiences.

The Political Ideology of the Emerging Society. The emerging society idealizes a technological world. Its members prefer that problems be decided by applied technology rather than through political struggle. They prefer the expert (the city manager, the government scientist) to the politician. In their practices (nonpartisan elections, "coolness"), they strive to avoid controversy.

The typical member of the new society is an organization man. His experience entails an acceptance of large organization in government, business, and society. Most of these new organization men are cogs in some large governmental or industrial corporation. The entrepreneur idealized by the small-town ideology of individualism is not the hero of the man in the gray flannel suit. The organization man is ready to accept bigness as here to stay.

Yet if bigness is to be accepted for efficiency's sake, a degree of decentralization is also preferred to preserve some semblance of democratic procedure and the importance of the individual. The preference for small suburban governments for oligopoly rather than monopoly, and for mixed state-Federal rather than exclusively Federal programs are examples of such inclinations.

The new man is also unlike the blue-collar ideal of trade unionism, but he does share some values with organized labor. He is a white-collar worker who reveres education and rise in status, but he also wants security. He is the result predicted by James Burnham in *The Managerial Revolution*. However, where Burnham saw the new man as acting in the tradition of the old entrepreneur, he is more likely to act "cool" and low pressure and to give a good deal of thought to public relations; as David Riesman noted, he is "other-directed."

The kind of a society the new man wants to create is, as William Whyte, Jr., suggests in *The Organization Man,* a rather antiseptic, technological organization, to be administered as a well-adjusted system, populated by harmonious, well-adjusted individuals.

Whether the blandness of suburbia can provide the same moral impetus for action as did the small-town and large-city ideologies is unknown. Some see this middle-class mildness as bound to be thrust aside as those less well adjusted and more anxiety-ridden strive for dominance. For the present, the outward calm of suburbia reigns.

Public Policy and the Emerging Society. Two distinct sets of policy are emerging as the result of this American political viewpoint. One encourages the purposeful building of the well-adjusted society, a land of technology. The other broad policy is to take care of the marginal members of society either by "retooling" them or by building a floor of minimum living standards under those who cannot be retooled. The maladjusted include the marginal farmer who does not adapt his small holdings to modern technology; instead, he operates inefficiently at a substandard level. Others are the poorly educated or those whose education or skills are of little value in a technological age; some of them are the unskilled unemployed who have been replaced by automation. Also, at least for the moment, the unadjusted include members of unaccepted minority and racial groups, such as Negroes and Puerto Ricans, who present a problem to those holding the suburban ideology. On the one hand, suburban ideology encourages the members of such minority groups to join the emerging society; on the other hand, because of his concern about status, the suburbanite discourages full integration.

The Changing Style of Politics. The transition between one way of political thinking to another is never smooth or consistent. It is particularly difficult when, as is generally the case, the politicians managing the governmental system adhere to the older ideologies. Such is the case today. Many congressmen still respond in terms of local small-town interests and ideology. The new suburbia is more grossly underrepresented in that body than were the large cities in the New Deal days.

The President also has difficulty adjusting to the suburban mood. He cannot easily champion substantive domestic policy for, to supporters of the emerging ideology, his image is more important than the issues he espouses. He must preserve the stance of impartial arbiter. At all costs, he must not appear as a political scrapper and in-fighter. Harry Truman and Richard Nixon, for example, were thought by some to have lost status in suburbia because they were regarded as old-fashioned in-fighters. It is difficult for a President to grasp a domestic policy issue and be dramatic about it. (According to the new ideology, members of the opposition are not villains but "misguided.") Favoring a program of Federal aid to local sewage systems or even schools lacks the excitement that the old New Deal issues had. His problem in the domestic area is that all policies are viewed as self-evidently right (because all the experts take that view) or they are "dirty politics" and should not have been raised. It is difficult to dramatize a real issue, such as providing water for growing cities; it is easier to project a political image. Leaders increasingly adopt the technique of winning token or partial victories against the "politicians" who are arrayed against them. Only in the field of foreign affairs can the President enunciate bold new policies with some assurance of enthusiastic suburban support.

The result is frustration and uncertainty in many domestic policy fields. Issues can no longer be precisely stated in the old liberal-versus-conservative terms. There is rather an "above-politics" blandness about the political process that is forcing a gradual change in harmony with the new ideology. The kind of mood can be perhaps best visualized by comparing the bases of the three most recent political ideologies of Americans (1) The small-town viewpoint, the product of industrial individualism, largely emphasized moral issues—the heavy drinker was the town drunk; (2) the social service ideology of the large cities emphasized a class-oriented sociology—the heavy drinker was a victim of society; (3) the modern organization man in suburbia emphasizes a psychological approach—the heavy drinker is emotionally ill; he is an alcoholic. While one ideology prescribed cure through copybook maxims and another be rebuilding society, the new view prescribes cure through expert treatment.

The kind of politics that results is the conventional struggle among economic interests for advantage, coupled with a rather uneasy appeal by many politicians for support in terms of the old ideologies. Within government, such views are still in the ascendancy, but politicians sense they are out of harmony with the growing segment of society. Increasingly, the important political victories are those of the bureaucracy, giving control to administrators rather than shaping policy in Congress. The holding of the Presidency becomes crucial for domestic politics. The viewpoint of those appointed to regulatory commissions is of growing importance. Finally, the court order is becoming an increasingly important means of making domestic policy for the new society.

Approaches to decision making. In broad overview, the supporters of the emerging ideology have two approaches to governmental action. One is that of cooperative federalism. The Federal government, through its superior financial resources, encourages state action and higher professional standards; the states administer the program. The mammoth interstate highway program of 1956, in which the Federal government assumed 90 per cent of the cost, is an excellent example in terms of the goals of the new society. If such action is impractical and issues must be handled nationally, they would favor their being settled by presidential or court action or day-to-day professional administration of the regulatory commissions and the bureaucracy in a kind of political bargaining with private interests.

In a technological society, the professionally neutral civil servant replaces the politically oriented administrator and the vote-seeking congressman as the public defender. The ideal is policy administered rationally, according to the pronouncements of experts in the field, rather than policy shaped by political pressure.

THE ISSUES AT STAKE

The major domestic issues can most conveniently be classified in accordance with the views of those dedicated to the contemporary social service myth. This is, of course, not the only way of viewing them and it is decidedly not the way those who hold to earlier ideologies view them. But the emerging viewpoint will increasingly be the style of American domestic politicking until another viewpoint emerges in response to new experiences and changed purposes. The broad division is between issues concerned with building the new well-adjusted America and caring for those who do not fit into the new scheme. Sometimes, of course, issues overlap, and these will be noted.

In classifying the issues that involve building the new America, it is helpful to further classify them as building (1) an environment for the well-adjusted society, (2) the well-adjusted economy, and (3) the well-adjusted government. The issues that concern those who do not quite fit into the new technological society will then be dealt with, followed by a note concerning issues that are largely slighted or avoided.

The division used is not the traditional one, and while the authors feel it adds to the clarity of ideological analysis, it separates topics commonly considered together. For example, the park and recreational aspects of conservation are dealt with as an environment for the well-adjusted society; the development of resources, under the economy; and agriculture, under the unadjusted minorities.

AN ENVIRONMENT FOR THE WELL-ADJUSTED SOCIETY

The new society is dominated by not merely an urban world, but by suburbia. It is helpful to deal with the physical and social world as if it were one, for the physical world of suburbia makes it possible to raise a new generation of Americans in what many would regard as being socially and psychologically desirable circumstances, away from the dirt, traffic, danger, crime, and racial and social antagonisms of the aging core city. Suburbia is a well-adjusted haven of security—at least, such is the ideal.

Thus, matters of physical arrangements have a clear relationship to social arrangements, and the two are treated together here.

Urban Renewal. Under the social service ideology, urban renewal and redevelopment were conceived of as a means to eliminate socially inefficient and high cost slums and were thus tied to public housing legislation. The renovating aspect of the program has been one reason for contemporary urbanite support, for it is a way of dealing with the greatest problems of the new society.

Another aspect is, in practice, however, given more stress today. It is, in fact, the major result of most urban renewal programs. While urban renewal may result in some cases only in a reshuffling of the large-city slums, it leaves behind a new central city with gleaming downtown civic, cultural, and business centers flanked by luxury apartments. For the new suburban society, this is the ideal for a downtown. Gone are the untidy brick buildings. In their place is a shining center, perhaps with a mall, that pleases the visiting suburbanite. He can be whisked from suburbia to this antiseptic center without much consideration for what lies in between; metropolitan man has developed tunnel vision.

The program. In 1962, the Urban Renewal Administration reported that there were 971 urban renewal projects in 533 cities, including a range from cities as small as Lawrenceville, Georgia (population 3,804) to those in the entire state of New Jersey. Only four states had no enabling legislation for such aid, and an additional four states had no projects at that time. Six of the eight were sparsely populated Mountain and Great Plains states. The other two were South Carolina and Louisiana.

The urban renewal program is designed to encourage cities to redevelop areas that are blighted and to make a master plan of conservation and development for the whole city. The Urban Renewal Administration of the Housing and Home Finance Agency makes loans and grants for the acquisition, clearing, and preparation of blighted areas for the construction of new buildings. The cleared land may be used for public buildings, for public or private housing projects, or it may be sold to private developers. The urban renewal grants also specify an intensification of building- and zoning-code enforcement, a program of relocation for displaced persons, and financial participation by the city.

The first urban redevelopment program was included in the 1949 Housing Act. It was followed by a more comprehensive program in 1954, during the Eisenhower administration. A later act in 1959 included encouragement of clearance projects in college communities. The 1961 act, under the Kennedy administration, made provisions for loans for improving public transportation facilities, for acquiring "open spaces" adjacent to cities for recreational purposes and for regional metropolitan planning. All of these later expansions of the program harmonize exceptionally well with the aims of building the society of the suburban ideology.

The interest groups most active on behalf of such programs have been large-city chambers of commerce, mayors, and downtown businessmen. The United States Chamber of Commerce has taken a stand against such "governmental handouts," but local chambers, anxious to see their communities renewed, have generally supported the program. A Congress still oriented to the individualistic ideology has reluctantly expanded the program financially. There has also been a certain amount of foot dragging among core-city spokesmen because of the displacement of urban minorities primarily to benefit the businessman. Here, as in many cases, the typical blurring of the simple conservative-liberal dichotomy occurs. The urban renewal program has steadily been expanded toward the goal of encouraging a rationally planned (well-adjusted) metropolis and is likely to remain a continuing Federal policy commitment.

Federal Housing Legislation. The urban renewal program is an outgrowth of the public housing efforts of the New Deal under the early social service state ideology.

These projects have always faced the opposition of the National Association of Real Estate Boards because of supposed competition and their conflict with the ideology of individualism. Support has generally come from large-city officials and labor group leaders. Recent criticism has been that the projects do not adequately serve the needs of an emerging society in which the encouragement of home ownership is to be preferred over any kind of welfare subsidy in housing. The failure of the program to "reform" the persons taken from the slums and the general bleakness of the institution-like high-rise apartment projects have been severely criticized. In addition, the clearing of land has generally displaced a disproportionate share of Negroes. Unable to relocate in the less crowded projects, they have been moved from one intolerable environment to another. Thus, the result has been, in some cases, the further intensification of racial clashes throughout a city.[1] Nevertheless, for many of the nation's largest cities, public housing has become a necessity to care for the marginal members of society. The projects may be uninspiring, but many regard them as a step toward ensuring minimum standards.

The first public housing act was that of 1937. It was extended in 1949, but subsequently opponents in Congress were able to reduce annual appropriations to considerably below the amounts authorized in that act. The 1954 provisions broadened the objectives of the program to include neighborhood conservation. The 1959 act included loans to private developers for the construction of low-cost housing, especially for the elderly. The 1961 act extended loans to include rural housing and provided funds for the more than 100,000 units that had been authorized by the 1949 act but for which Congress had not previously appropriated funds.

[1] See Editors of Fortune, *The Exploding Metropolis,* Anchor Books, Doubleday & Company, Inc., Garden City, N.Y., 1957.

Public housing, which began as the central feature of a social service state program of reform, has now become a feature secondary to broad metropolitan planning and renewal. It is continued because of its value as a stopgap in the greatest urban communities, providing at least minimum standards. In the 1960s, however, increasing emphasis has been placed on preventing the conditions leading to deterioration.

Insured loans. A program of the social service ideology that has been most readily accepted by middle-class suburbanites is that of Federal insurance of bank-financed mortgages for purchase of homes. This is handled by the Veterans Administration (GI loans) and the Federal Housing Administration (FHA) programs. Most bankers and real estate men have favored the extension of the program since its inception in 1932. The early act permitted direct loans; later activity has been limited chiefly to insuring loans made by others. The loans may be made to purchase homes, generally only new homes or recently built homes that meet FHA standards, or to renovate older homes.

It is because of the generous loan provisions guaranteed by this Federal program that many suburbanites have been able to purchase their homes. The program has also led to the granting of bank-administered loans without the traditional guarantees required of an earlier generation.

Housing remains a critical issue for the inhabitants of the emerging society. In the decade following 1950, Americans demolished about 1½ million substandard housing units. Experts estimated there were about 10 million such units still left, with more being added each year. Some of these were jerrybuilt homes that had been erected in the outer suburbs under lax building and zoning provisions. To stop such deterioration as well as to remove what has already deteriorated is a major goal for the contemporary technology-oriented society. The suburbanites tend to prefer to leave the solution to the experts rather than the politicians.

Transportation. The limited-access highways between cities, the expressway to the downtown area, and the blocked access of the curving or dead-end side street in the neighborhood are the ideal of suburbia. Traffic is separated from the pedestrian in what the engineer considers a rational, planned fashion for the greater safety and benefit of both.

The issue again cuts across the traditional conservative-liberal alignment. Commercial interests battle the limited-access features or the monopoly restaurants and service stations on the throughway, and railroads have opposed this boost to faster trucking. But the advantages for industry are many, including cheaper transportation and greater choice of sites for plant location. There are also advantages to the individual in terms of greater highway safety. About 38,000 persons are killed on our highways annually—a social waste by almost any standard. Under these circumstances, few directly oppose the program, but old-time reformers complain that if so much money is available for a consumer benefit such as elaborate freeways, we should also be able to find more money for social services such as hospitals, mental health casework, and the eradication of slums.

The earliest Federal highway aid began in 1916. In 1956, it was greatly expanded through the inauguration of a program for an interstate highway system to be completed in about 1970, linking nearly all cities of over 50,000 population with limited-access four- to six-lane freeways. The Federal government provides 90 per cent of the financing. Authorizations for expressways within major urban centers are included in the program. They accounted for almost three-fourths of the Federal aid for highways in the early 1960s.

Transit systems. Increasingly, there has been pressure on the Federal government to provide aid for ailing transit systems in urban areas. In 1962, Congress turned down President Kennedy's proposed program. The bill's sponsor, Senator Harrison Williams (Democrat, New Jersey) pointed out that many railroads have discontinued commuter service and that at least 300 small cities had lost bus service. In the large cities, bus service was retained, he argued, by paring costs for needed improvements in equipment, dropping unprofitable runs, cutting service, and raising prices for fares.[2]

The program is valuable for downtown businessmen as well as for shut-ins and low-income groups—a typical cutting across of traditional conservative-liberal alignments. It also is potentially attractive to suburbanites, intent on finding a cheap and easy way to visit the core city crowded with unparked cars. The opposition of the small-town-economy bloc, which views this as another unnecessary government subsidy was overcome by passage of the Urban Mass Transportation Act of 1964, which authorized $375 million in Federal grants to states and localities to assist public and private transport systems in cities.

Public carriers. The government has traditionally given aid to such carriers as the railroads and airlines, in part through liberal mail contracts. Both industries are regulated by Federal agencies; the railroads since 1887, and the airlines since 1926. The Interstate Commerce Commission, however, is regarded by many observers as being dominated by the railroads. Federal policy recently has tended to shift from viewing railroad mergers with suspicion to accepting more of them, in the hope that improvements may at least be made in freight handling operations.

The increasing use of air travel, combined with passenger anxieties concerning safety while flying, have encouraged expanded Federal services to pilots and supervision of the airways and airline equipment. Administrative organization for regulation has been modified from time to time, most recently in the establishment of the Federal Aviation Agency. The dominant pressures are for still stricter and more extensive Federal controls. Perhaps the greatest impact of the Federal government on air travel

[2] "Transit Hearings—Opening Statement by Senator Harrison Williams," Mar. 20, 1961.

has been through appropriations made since 1946 for airports and air terminal construction. Again, the pattern of government policy is in harmony with planning a technological society along the lines that specialists suggest.

Federal programs for water transportation mainly concern industry and local chambers of commerce that desire local dredging of harbors and channels. In 1940, a system of regulation of rates and services was established for the internal waterways under the review of the Interstate Commerce Commission.

Parks and Recreation. Yogi Bear in Jellystone Park and Smokey Bear, another television character who advises children not to set forest fires, symbolize a basic conflict in the national recreation field—a bureaucratic struggle over who should operate the national recreation program.

The United States Forest Service. The Forest Service is in the Department of Agriculture where Theodore Roosevelt put it because of scandals then affecting the Department of Interior. It is a high-morale, tightly knit, ingrown bureaucracy of forestry school graduates who have been oriented principally toward lumbering rather than recreation. (Hikers + picnickers = forest fires.) Its domain totals approximately the area of Texas, and it has charge of forests in most states, spread over a great many congressional districts.

The National Park Service. The National Park Service is in the Department of the Interior. Since 1872, when Yellowstone Park was established, it has supervised national parks, monuments, battlefields and other historic sites, memorials, parkways, cemeteries, and seashore and other recreation areas. The Department also includes the Fish and Wildlife Service, which watches over the annual migration of the nation's last forty whooping cranes and oversees a grant-in-aid program to the states for acquiring recreation lands, among other duties.

The Army Engineers. This group builds recreation areas as part of its rivers and harbors projects. The Army Engineers have long enjoyed support in Congress because of the pork barrel* possibilities in their projects.

***PORK BARREL. The source of this term is uncertain. It refers to public works projects undertaken by the government mainly because of their political value to local incumbent congressman. They are not authorized primarily for engineering or economic reasons. Each year, Congress passes a bill containing a long list of such projects—often they are to deepen river channels or harbors.**

A bureaucratic struggle. Very few large land tracts have been added to the national park system since the years before World War I, despite great national population growth and vastly increased park use. Park service demographers foresee a recreation "crisis" by 1975 and propose three measures to correct it: merging all recreation functions within one department—logically, they argue, it should be the Interior; acquiring more park lands quickly, before the last available sites disappear forever; and turning over immediately selected Forest Service land to the Park Service.

President Kennedy supported this program in a special message to Congress on natural resources, but the proposal met strong opposition. The Forest Service can generally depend upon lumbering and mining interests, which work the national forests on a lease basis, to fight their battles. They enjoy considerable congressional support even without this pressure. The creation of a genuine Department of Natural Resources by transferring the Forest Service to Interior, was the goal of former Secretary of Interior Harold Ickes, as expressed in his diaries. It was also recommended by a Hoover Commission task force on administration in 1949. (The commission sought to reorganize agencies on its version of a logical basis.)

Even the attempt to set up a council to oversee the wilderness areas of public lands and to ensure that no vehicles would be permitted in them has met stiff opposition. The Wilderness Preservation Act of 1964 established a plan for wilderness preservation, placing 9.1 million acres of Federal land in the system and authorizing future additional acreage.

Conflicts over land use. The issues are not as exciting as when the fight was between the "good" conservationists and the "bad" exploiters. Though fighting the exploiter is still occasionally an issue, the recreation conservationists now have strong support in all industries that manufacture vacation equipment or benefit from tourism—there is general agreement on the desirability of a national recreation program. Furthermore, land is less valuable today for grazing or lumbering (in an age of plastics) than it was at the beginning of the century. And today lumber companies do not devastate the land. Instead, they place advertisements in national magazines pointing out that they plant a tree for every one they cut down. The two major emphases of the recreation groups fit almost perfectly into the suburban ideology: park areas to visit on summer vacations and park lands and beaches near the supercities to visit on weekends. The latter has only received great attention since the 1958 report of the Outdoor Recreation Resources Commission recommended such acquisitions.

Typical of the recent controversies was that over the Indiana Dunes: one group wished to use this Lake Michigan site to expand the steel industry at Gary; the other wanted a beach park for a crowded supercity. A variation concerned the recent park land acquisition for the Cape Cod National Seashore Park. The opposition was from those who owned summer cottages and feared dispossession or inundation by tourists.

Education: A Central Concern. Three statements summarize the main Federal issues in education:

> Federal Aid to Higher Education has become imperative. I see no other way than for the Federal government, working with the state, to step in. —President Harlan Hatcher, University of Michigan, September 29, 1962.

It is unthinkable that any American child be denied the Federal funds allotted to other children because his parents choose for him a God-centered education.—Francis Cardinal Spellman, January, 1961.

It makes no sense that we should ask military personnel to make sacrifices and serve away from home and at the same time see their children treated as inferiors by local requirements that they attend segregated schools.—Attorney General Robert Kennedy, September 17, 1962. (The Justice Department filed suit against Prince George County, Virginia, to recover $2,556,548 the county had received in Federal "impacted area" aid because it is the site of Fort Lee, a military base).

Federal aid? Although most professional educators favor it, as do an increasing number of local school board members and community leaders, Federal aid to education had, in the early 1960s, come a cropper. By 1962, it had passed the Senate in eight sessions, only to flounder each time in the House. Sometimes, as in that year, it was not even reported out of the House Rules Committee for debate. Preventing its passage were the problems of aid to private and parochial schools and the fear of Southerners that desegregation strings would be tied to the program. The small-town economy bloc also opposed Federal aid and idealized the independent "little red schoolhouse."

In terms of the suburban ideology, Federal assistance for local education should be provided, just as it is in many other fields that were once viewed as exclusively local functions. Such assistance is not a break in tradition, either. Federal assistance to education has for some time been exceeded only by grants for highways and welfare. The Ordinance of 1787, which predated the Constitution, gave the proceeds from the sale of specific public lands to the states to be used for school construction. Other Federal programs include the Morrill Act of 1862 (establishing land-grant colleges), school-lunch programs, vocational agricultural training, aid for defense-impacted areas (having an unusual influx of children due to Federal projects, such as Army bases), National Science scholarship loans, and numerous grants to college and university faculty members for research.

Given these precedents, existing pressures, and the great demands for higher standards of education (Khrushchev once boasted that the Soviet Union graduates three times as many engineers as does the United States), it is likely that a general Federal-aid program will eventually be established. Both the Rockefeller Report and that of the Educational Policies Commission (1958) stressed the need to virtually double expenditures in order to raise teachers' salaries to a level commensurate with their importance to society, to build the schools and classrooms needed, and to lessen the burden in poorer states and poorer districts.

Lesser issues. Other peripheral issues concerning the Federal government relate to setting up a separate Department of Education at Cabinet level, the giving of prayers or religious instruction within public schools, and, if Federal aid is granted, raising educational standards. Mark Van Doren and Richard Heffron have criticized schools for lack of a serious, definite purpose and failure to maintain standards of excellence. Robert Hutchins, once president of The Fund for the Republic and before that of the University of Chicago, has said: "A good way to start finding the money that is needed for education would be to kick out of it the subjects, and activities, and the people that make no contribution to the development of intellectual power. Such an operation would produce vast sums."[3]

Health: What Is the Public Sector? Federal participation in this area is more important and extensive than most citizens realize. The familiar grant-in-aid program in this case is particularly for the building of hospitals. In addition, the Federal government underwrites much of the basic research into the causes of various diseases and mental illness. Finally, the Federal government defends the interests of the consumer—two illustrations are the 1962 legislation on the manufacture and sale of drugs or the 1964 report of the United States Public Health Service on cigarette smoking. A general health insurance program similar to the social legislation in the welfare field was consistently blocked in the 1950s and 1960s, though the need for care of those over sixty-five has become a major issue. In general, the issues fit the familiar pattern of suburban politics—a search for security, a heavy reliance on technology, and, generally, a lack of drama.

An issue still to be faced is that of compulsory immunization or control. (Public health specialists argue for a program requiring immunization against communicable diseases unless the person objects in writing.) Despite adequate technological knowledge, polio epidemics still occur, persons still die of tetanus, diphtheria, and rabies. All of these could be virtually eliminated through control programs. The United States Public Health Service has been generally timid, contenting itself with recommendations, as it did in the case of fluoridation of water, rather than serving as an advocate of legislation. Five years after the Salk vaccine was approved, nearly 30 million children and young adults still had received no polio shots, and over 10 million more had less than the three shots recommended as a minimum. A program of control would require the expansion of public health facilities, including the grants-in-aid to the states, with strings attached.[4]

THE WELL-ADJUSTED ECONOMY

The social service ideology has demanded regulation of the economy to meet the dominant demands of society. The development of economic insight has given to this process a technological aspect that has a particu-

[3] Mark Van Doren, "Education," in Huston Smith (ed.), *The Search for America,* Prentice-Hall, Inc., Englewood Cliffs, N.J., 1959, pp. 90–104; Robert M. Hutchins, *Fund for the Republic Bulletin,* February, 1959.

[4] Leonard Engel, "Why We Don't Wipe Out Polio," *Harper's Magazine,* September, 1961, pp. 77–80.

lar appeal to the middle-class suburbanite viewpoint. The vision is of a well-tooled and well-behaved economy that, through expert management, gives the blessings of prosperity to all citizens.

Recession, Inflation, and Rate of Economic Growth. Presidential aides had persuaded organized labor to settle the 1961 steel strike for what they regarded as a modest wage increase. Immediately after negotiations ended, the largest steel company announced a sharp price increase. In a nationwide address, President Kennedy promised to combat this inflationary action (which he incidentally regarded as a breach of faith) with every weapon at his disposal, including presumably, antitrust action and cancellation of purchase contracts with reassignment to any company holding the line, including perhaps foreign competitors. Inland Steel, a company with 10 per cent of steel production, announced it would not raise its price, and the price-rise movement collapsed, with even the largest producer giving up. In this case, the administration had succeeded in controlling economic forces, but not without political costs. It was roundly criticized by the political opposition and by many newspaper editors. The Federal government has about the same relation to the economy as a father has to an eighteen-year-old son with a convertible. Economic forces often vigorously resist governmental interference, but sometimes cry out for it. In the end, society—particularly its political components—holds the government mainly responsible for what happens.

Fighting inflation and recession. The Federal government has an array of monetary and fiscal tools to choose from in order to combat inflation or recession and to encourage economic growth at a reasonable rate. But, as with fathers and sons, difficulties are common. One problem stems from the fact that economists disagree about the health and future development of the economy. They base their thinking on a number of indicators that serve as a temperature chart, such as auto sales, freight-car loadings, housing starts, the wholesale-price index, and others. Like physicians, however, economists frequently disagree on the diagnosis as well as the prescription.

A Bureaucratic Struggle. This situation is aggravated within government because the tools for regulating the economy are held by a number of separate agencies within the executive branch. Occasionally, since World War II and particularly during the Truman administration, actions sponsored independently by the two have been contradictory.

"The Fed": One contestant. The Federal Reserve System, banker-dominated and largely independent of the President, was created in 1912 as a kind of national superbank that could control the national credit. At its head is a seven-man board whose members are appointed for fourteen-year staggered terms by the President or, rather, Presidents, since even a Chief Executive serving two full terms will appoint his fourth member just as he himself is leaving office. The Federal Reserve System comprises twelve district banks that deal directly with the member banks.

The Federal Reserve Board controls policy by its monetary decisions, which, in effect, expand or contract the amount of money in circulation. This it does by the requirement it places on the reserves that a bank must have on deposit in the System. These vary in proportion to total deposits. The interest rate the System sets for member banks wishing to borrow to replenish their reserves (called the rediscount rate) and the amount of buying or selling of government securities the System does on the open market are its two major economic controls. The Board's regulations also affect such matters as the amount of margin a person must have to buy stocks, that is, the amount of the actual cost of the stocks he must pay in cash: The higher the margin requirement, the greater the discouragement of speculative stock trading. In 1958, to combat a recession, the Board required only 50 per cent down payment, as opposed to 70 per cent during the rising market of 1961. The heart of the board's power is in actions that effectively determine the interest rate all banks charge. Through these actions, it directly encourages inflation or deflation.

The Comptroller of the Currency. The chartering, mergers, and liquidations

Figure 20-1

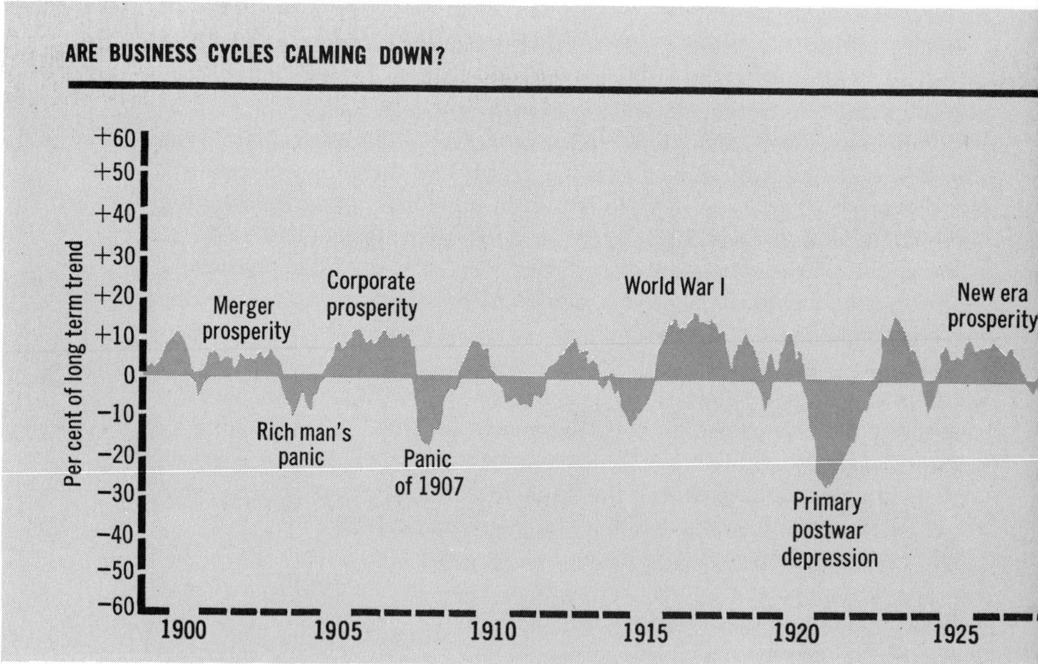

New government programs are most likely in recession times. (Cleveland Trust Company.)

of national banks, as well as regulation of branch banking are under the direction of the Comptroller of the Currency, who is appointed by the President. In the Kennedy and Johnson administrations, the Comptroller—often at odds with the Federal Reserve Board and the American Bankers Association—followed policies that state banking officials sometimes regarded as centralizing and leading toward a national system.

Others in the act. There are two major agencies within the executive department that aid the President in fiscal matters. They are the Treasury and the Bureau of the Budget. In addition to these, the three-man Council of Economic Advisers provides him and Congress with analyses of trends and makes recommendations concerning economic policy.

Many of the President's powers are also shared with Congress. These include policies relative to the tariff and tax programs. President Kennedy's tariff program of 1962 was designed to stimulate international trade, but it also contained provisions to subsidize industries affected adversely. His 1962 tax program contained special tax write-offs for equipment. This was designed to encourage industrial expansion. Both programs

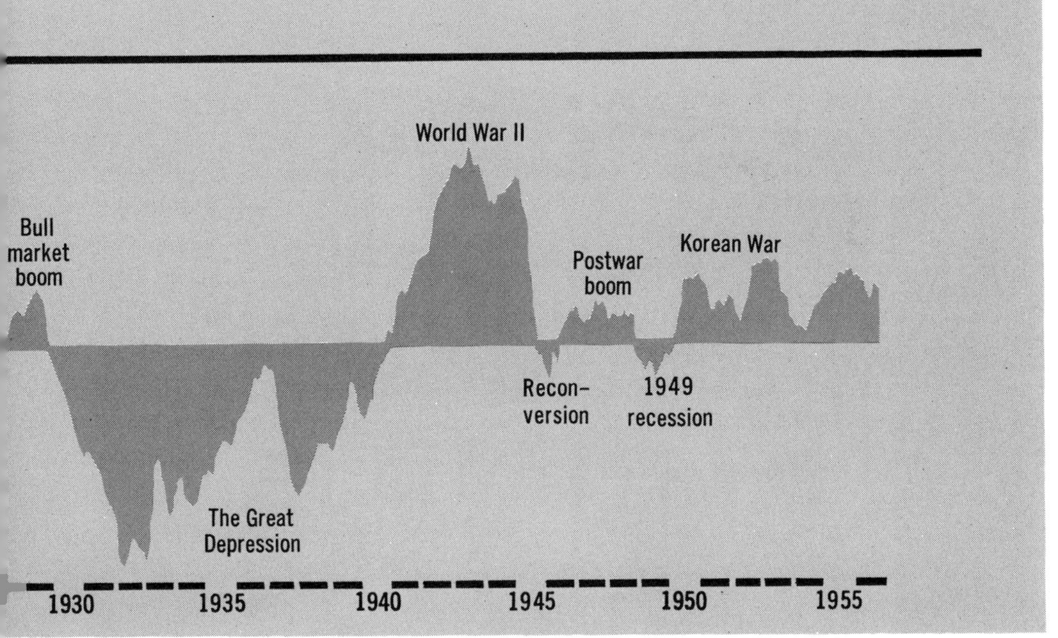

were scaled back somewhat by Congress. In 1964, President Johnson secured a tax cut to "boost the economy." The President's budget also directly affects the economy. Following the theories of Keynesian economics,* the national administration during the Great Depression engaged in large public works projects, with the resultant deficit financing serving as a stimulant to the economy. War spending has always been an inflationary pump primer. Defense spending, defense and the "peaceful purposes" missile program, and the interstate highway program all helped the nation recover from the 1958 recession.

***KEYNESIAN ECONOMIC THEORY. The whole theory is complex. Its most important implication for public policy is that governments can partly level out the swings in the business cycle by spending more than they receive in taxes during the downswing and less during the upswing. On this type of fiscal policy, see Paul A. Samuelson,** *Economics,* **6th ed., McGraw-Hill Book Company, New York, 1964.**

The President acting alone. The President can direct a speedup of Federal procurement of material during an economic lag. The requirements for

Figure 20-2

A New Tax Comes as a Shock

"Good heavens! This is terrible! It comes to three percent of my salary."

The income tax became a permanent American institution in 1915 after the tariff—traditional source of Federal revenue—began to decline. (By permission of Burr Shafer.)

down payments and the interest rate for government-guaranteed FHA and VA housing loans are also under presidential control. There are a number of additional stabilizers that can be somewhat expanded or contracted. These include the premiums for veterans' insurance, which have been occasionally distributed earlier than originally planned. Others are farm price-support payments, social security, and extensions of unemployment-compensation payments. The government, in extreme cases, may move to a regulated economy, in which prices and wages are frozen. It has done so during wartime crises. Some industrialists have argued that President Kennedy approached this point during peacetime when he succeeded in forcing the abandonment of announced steel-price increases.

A principal and unofficial weapon the President holds is his ability to inspire confidence in the administration's ability to cope with the problems of the economy. Franklin Roosevelt in his 1932 Inauguration Address transmitted an attitude by his words "We have nothing to fear but fear itself." President Kennedy was claimed by some to have lost the confidence of the business community because of his victory over the steel industry, which, it was argued, led to later stock market reverses. The economic viewpoint of citizens is a nebulous thing, resting on a kind of unreasoning trust; it is illustrated by the words of a Highland Park, Illinois, advertising man who had lost heavily in the May, 1962, stock market drop: "I haven't lost confidence," he said, "just money."[5] President Lyndon Johnson deliberately appealed to business leaders in an attempt to expand the national economic growth rate while simultaneously seeking political support.

Regulation for Whom? A Political Question. Gus Tyler, educational director of the International Ladies Garment Workers Union, has argued that unions must enter politics to protect their interests:[6]

> A worker's real income and real standard of living are immediately and directly affected by the cost of living, by monopoly price-fixing, by publicly controlled utility rates; by public policy on rents, housing, building subsidies; by tariffs on competing manufacturers or on consumer items; by the tax law; by the unemployment insurance and social security payments; by the vast complex of legislative and administrative activity that may flow from the full employment act; by the minimum wage law; by price supports on farm products; by the award of government contracts and the determinations about prevailing wages in those contracts; by regulations and laws concerning discrimination in employment.

The question of who benefits from governmental involvement in economic actions will always be a political issue. Several governmental tools that have a controlling effect on the economy may, when plotted on a neat

[5] *Time,* June 8, 1962, p. 19.

[6] Gus Tyler, *A New Philosophy for Labor,* The Fund for the Republic, New York, 1959, p. 11.

scientific looking economic graph, look similar. They, however, have widely different political effects. Deflation can be achieved by raising the interest rate. But this tends to cause hardship for small-business men and farmers, who lack financial reserves. Deflation can also be accomplished by raising taxes on corporate profits or by sharply reducing government-expenditure programs, among other methods.

Two Ideologies. Traditionally, there have been two ideological approaches to governmental involvement in the economy. The industrial individualism

Figure 20-3

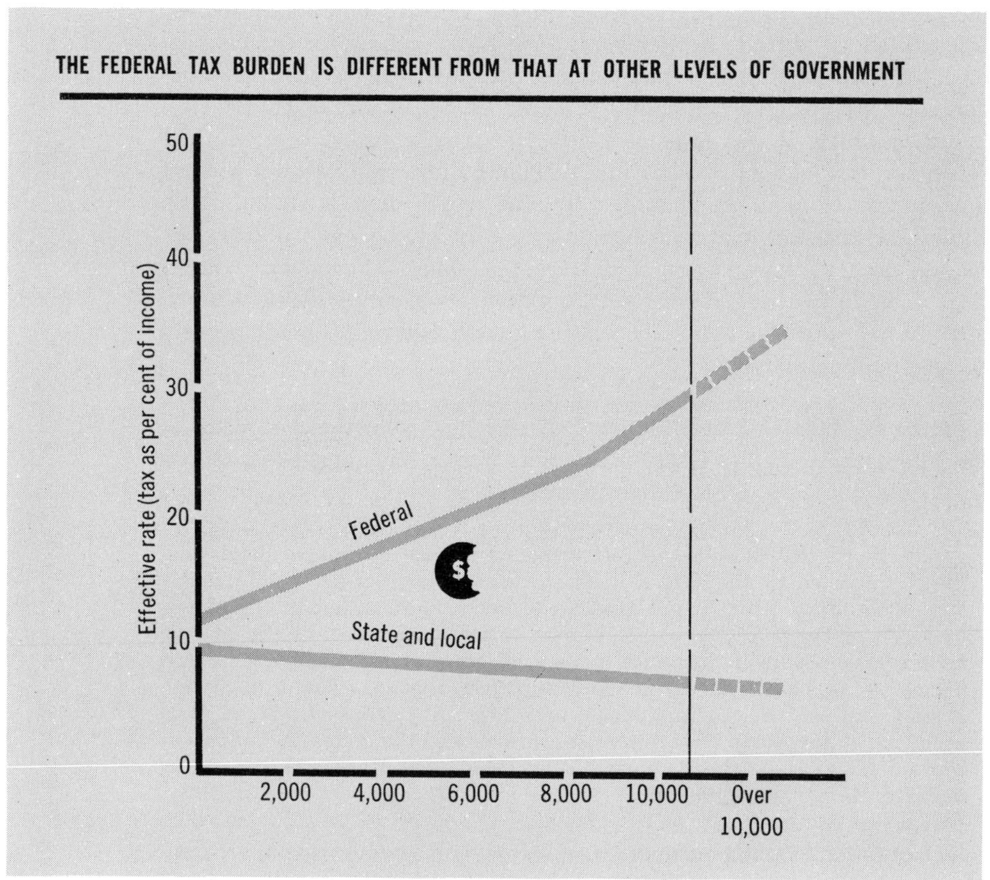

Federal taxes increase as ability to pay increases—they are "progressive." State and local taxes do the opposite and are "regressive." (R. A. Musgrave and others, Compendium of the Joint Committee on the Economic Report, *1957, p. 98.)*

viewpoint advocates a minimum of regulation, coupled with subsidies to business (high tariffs, tax write-offs, loans). It is argued that, if business is unregulated but encouraged, business activity will increase and create prosperity, which will filter down through society. The social service state ideology favors stricter business regulation (antitrust actions, price setting in monopoly industries, stock market regulation through the Securities Exchange Commission, fair-trade enforcement, wages and hours regulation, etc.) and a building up of consumer purchasing power by subsidization (public works programs, low-interest housing loans, unemployment insurance, etc., what Hubert Humphrey has described as the "percolate up" theory).

The postwar approach compromises by borrowing from both ideologies. It appears to support encouragement of major industries that can afford to act in what the organization man regards as a responsible manner toward employees and consumers. Effectiveness requires bigness. At the same time, Clark Kerr suggests in his essay for the President's Commission on National Goals, there should be a multiplicity of power centers to ensure a "workable competition."[7] The semimonopoly or oligopoly, as in the automotive field, is the white-collar model. While permitting such industrial organization, government regulation is used to encourage a broad distribution of benefits. The result is a typical blurring of traditional liberal-conservative distinctions. The Kennedy administration typified this blend in a number of ways: low tariffs; deficit spending and public works; a raise in the minimum wage; stepped-up fair-trade regulation; combating a steel price rise, on the one hand, and giving a tax deduction to expanding business rather than low-income consumers on the other, a corporation in which private industry shares space exploration benefits with government; the Republican head of a major Wall Street brokerage house appointed Secretary of the Treasury; a corporation executive who probably voted Republican in 1960 named to head the nation's biggest spending agency—the Department of Defense. The Johnson administration continued this middle-of-the-road policy blend.

Big labor and big industry. One attitude that sharply differentiates the postwar ideology from the older ones is a recognition that bigness is here to stay. Coupled with this is a view that both big labor and big industry must be regulated by government in what is popularly viewed as the public interest.

Labor-Management relations. The Taft-Hartley Act of 1948 attempted, in the eyes of businessmen, to redress some of the balance in listing unfair practices found in the earlier Wagner Act, which was written under the influence of the early social service ideology. The Taft-Hartley Act brought about several major changes in the government's handling of labor dis-

[7] Clark Kerr, "An Effective and Democratic Organization of the Economy," *Goals for Americans,* Prentice-Hall, Inc., Englewood Cliffs, N.J., 1960, pp. 149–161.

putes by several requirements: the Federal Mediation and Conciliation Service was made independent from the Labor Department; a sixty-day-notice period was required for any change of contract by management or labor; the President was permitted to appoint a fact-finding board, and management was permitted to make one final offer on which workers must vote. The latter requirement makes mandatory an eighty-day "cooling-off" period in which there can be no strikes or lockouts.

The government's role in national strikes has remained unchanged since. Compulsory arbitration, as through a labor court, has not been favored by any of the major parties at interest. The government's role has been to encourage voluntary arbitration and to offer its services as an independent third party.

Figure 20-4

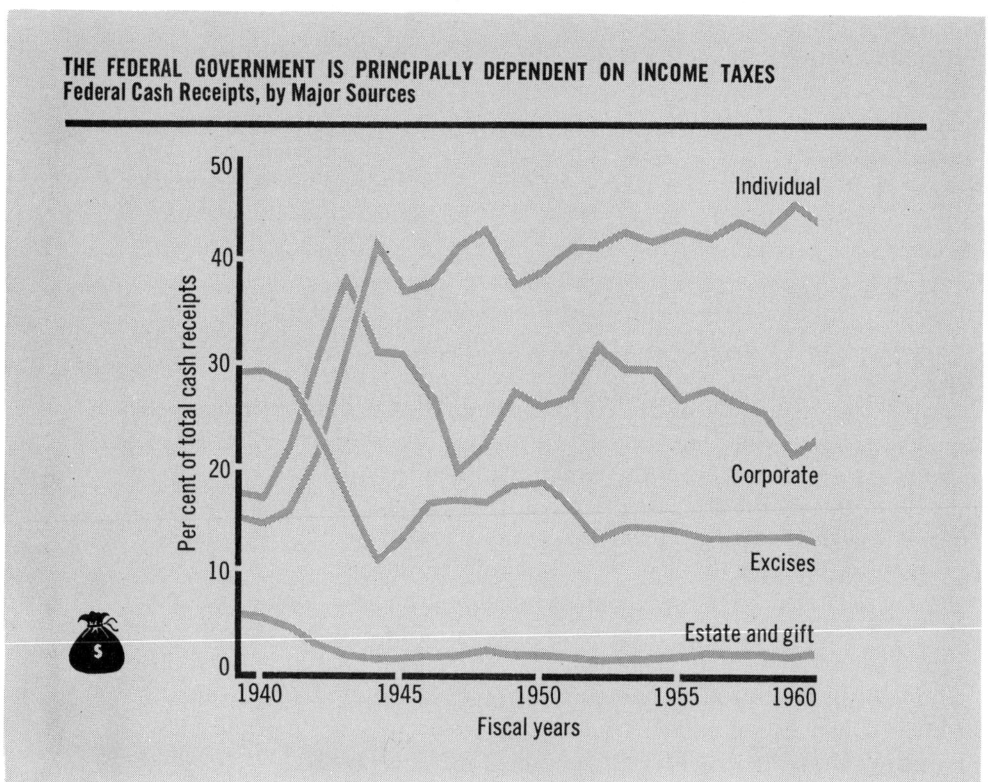

Growth and Taxes, *Committee for Economic Development, New York, 1961, p. 5. Based on data from the U.S. Department of the Treasury and the U.S. Bureau of the Budget.*

The Labor-Management Reporting and Disclosure Act of 1958 (the Landrum-Griffin Act) represents a different approach to labor-management relations; it conforms generally to current middle-class viewpoints. The goals are to ensure that union affairs will be conducted democratically; that union financial affairs will be conducted honestly and efficiently; and that union disciplinary actions against union members will be "fair." The law also requires employers and labor-relations consultants to report the following: payments for restraining employees from engaging in union activity; obtaining inside union information; and bribing union officials. These acts are illegal, but there is some doubt about the constitutionality of such reporting, since it could involve self-incrimination. The act is clearly designed to stop racketeering in unions and to encourage what its promoters regard as responsible and honest procedures.

Business regulation. The regulation of business has been achieved through the stepped-up activities of such Federal administrative agencies as the Federal Trade Commission, the Federal Communications Commission, and suits brought by the Attorney General. The successful suit against the major electric equipment manufacturing companies, resulting in fines and jail terms for some executives and numerous damage suits from governmental and private groups, is an example of such action.

An example of regulation for an emerging society is the Humane Slaughter Act of 1958, lobbied through almost alone by Mrs. Christine Stevens against opposition from meat packing (the American Meat Institute) and farmers' groups. The act states that the Federal government will buy only from packers who kill all their animals humanely. (About $250 million worth of meat products is bought by the Federal government each year.) "Humane killing" involves such devices as electric stunners and the CO_2 tunnel. Both are technological inventions that add to the costs of the small operator.[8]

Consumer protection. Along with regulation of industry and labor has been a growing trend toward increasing protection of the consumer. The Drug Regulation Act of 1962 contains a provision stating that a manufacturer must show that his product aids the user as is claimed. Previously, manufacturers needed only to show that their product was harmless, not that it had any positive qualities. Other parts of the Drug Act contain provisions for stricter testing and labeling of drugs, including a provision that the drug's generic name be printed in type at least half the size of its trade name.

Mainly through executive agency regulation and sometimes as the result of congressional investigations, there has been stricter enforcement of requirements for advertising claims, packaging practices, and television commercials. While the statement by the head of the Federal Communications Commission early in the Kennedy administration that television was

[8] Faubion Bowers, "That Mrs. Stevens, the Animals' Best Friend," *Harper's Magazine,* July, 1962, pp. 77–81.

a "great wasteland" had no direct legal effect on the content of commercials, it stimulated increased attention by stations to consumer interests in general. The book *Silent Spring* by the biologist Rachel Carson (1962) is another example of the trend; it caused a widespread reassessment of the effect on food products of the indiscriminate uses she claimed were being made of DDT and other insecticides. (The title refers to future springs when all birds will have died as the result of ingesting insecticides.)

President Kennedy established a Consumers' Advisory Council. It encouraged use of government documents by consumers (post office displays resulted) and maintenance of standards in the quality, safety, and performance of products (including a grading and labeling law); represented consumer viewpoints in government agencies; and announced procedures in the consumer-credit field, Federal-state cooperation for consumer protection, and consumer views on economic policies. Members of the council include prominent home economists and economists. Its activities are likely to result in proposals for further legislation and changes in administrative procedures.

This trend toward consumer protection is in harmony with the contemporary social service state ideology. Sometimes it fits the pattern of traditional liberal-conservative battles (with the unscrupulous operator suppressed), but often, as in the case of limiting violence on television, it cuts across previously held ideological lines. Just as medical men fight to eliminate quacks, so legitimate businessmen often have supported raising standards in their fields.

Present-day regulation is designed to enforce middle-class standards of honesty and decency without impairing efficiency. Action is as likely to be against labor as against business.

Conservation of Resources. The traditional issue of conservation was the preservation of resources for the public against reckless commercial exploitation. Typical of an emerging trend is the attempt to regulate so that both commercial development and other ends can be served. The most notable exception to the trend is in petroleum and natural gas production, where a large tax credit (a 27.5 per cent depletion allowance) frequently permits large profits and provides the financial strength and inclination to resist Federal regulation. In general, the battle has been fought in terms of Federal against state control. The petroleum industry prefers the latter, for it believes regulation would be weaker and more amenable to manipulation at the state level.

A more recent conservation emphasis is found in an attempt to implement programs limiting air and water pollution. Thus far, Congress has not attempted to limit auto exhaust fumes. The Department of the Interior has, however, experimented with economical means for controlling air pollution by industry and for developing new water supplies from salt water. In 1956, a matching program of grants to communities was initiated for programs to control water pollution.

Traditional conservation programs continue: the work of the Bureau of Reclamation to conserve water resources, the Tennessee Valley Authority, the regulation of power production by the Federal Power Commission and the development of power in a number of Federal projects, such as Bonneville and the TVA, as well as the forest and wildlife conservation practices already noted. Some of these, such as those involving wood products, have been partly outmoded by the use of plastics and other materials for industrial purposes.

The major issues of conservation concern an urban and technological economy: natural gas regulation, air and water pollution, the attempt to expand water-supply resources, and the rational development of minerals used in industry.

THE WELL-ADJUSTED GOVERNMENT

The political interests advantaged under present governmental arrangements do not always respond favorably to groups interested in reorganization in terms of an ideal model. The prevailing ideological goal is more efficiency in Congress, the courts, and the bureaucracy. This is to be achieved by a rational centralizing of bureaucratic responsibility (following the recommendations of administrative experts) rather than by reacting to political pressure (following the Hoover commission studies and recommendations of 1949 and 1950); an extension of civil service procedures and attitudes; a focusing of administrative responsibility in the Presidency, and an increased emphasis on congressional staff work and centralization. The Congressional Reorganization Act of 1946 reduced and rationalized the number of congressional committees and greatly increased staff, plus recurrent efforts to eliminate the filibuster and clip the arbitrary powers of the House Rules Committee, are examples. In this ideal model, the preferred congressional role is that of a dignified reviewer of broad policy; the preferred presidential role seems to be that of chief administrator rather than chief politician. The key concepts are increased professionalization and "Take the politics out of politics."

THE UNADJUSTED MINORITIES

In a technological society three groupings have been at a sharp disadvantage: the poorly educated, those wedded to small marginal enterprises, and those who are not accepted for reasons of race. The three categories are not mutually exclusive, but overlap to a great degree.[9]

[9] See especially Michael Harrington, *The Other America,* The Macmillan Company, New York, 1962. Available in paperback, Penguin Books, Inc., Baltimore, 1963.

Civil Rights and the Southerner. The issues involved in civil rights are discussed in Chapter 19. Here two points need be noted. First, members of the middle class have ambivalent attitudes toward the acceptance of minority groups. Ideologically (because all the experts have told them it is so), the educated middle-class citizen recognizes the unscientific character of the older notions of race. In modest ways, the aspirations of Negroes to achieve education and white-collar status are encouraged. At the same time, integration threatens the status and self-esteem of such whites. A Negro neighbor, a Negro supervisor, a Negro playmate causes status anxiety. In balance, however, change is gradually toward full legal acceptance of Negroes.

Second, many white Southerners are likewise marginal in a technological society since they operate in a one- or two-crop economy. This condition is changing and with it typically come changes in attitudes on civil rights. In Southern cities, Negroes have made continuing gains in the face of ambivalence on the part of the new Southern white-collar white as the Southern rural areas lose population and political power at the expense of Southern and Northern cities.

Agriculture and the Farmer. The "farm problem" is in reality at least two major problems. One is that about 70 per cent of the farmers operate at a bare subsistence level. Most of these are on farms in the South; others live in marginal pockets of land throughout the nation. Most such farmers are too poor to profit from farm loan provisions or agricultural extension aid, and they sell too little on the commercial market to be affected by the price-support programs. Second, most have little education; many in the South are Negroes. They cannot easily be moved from farms into industrial jobs because they lack skills, and many face racial discrimination. Still, every year many are leaving farms, as the conditions in the slums of many Northern cities testify. In the thirty-year period between 1930 and 1960, roughly 40 per cent of all farmers left farming.

The major agricultural program affecting such farmers is the experimental Area Rural Development program, started in 1958 to improve the total facilities in any given community. It has been tried in about one hundred counties scattered around the nation. It is, in effect, an "operation bootstrap." Part of the program is to encourage industry to enter such communities. Since 1961, the government has also offered direct aid to such depressed areas and aid for retraining for other jobs. The Economic Opportunity Act of 1964 (the "war on poverty") expanded this program. It provided for a job corps, adult education program, a work-training program, and a "domestic peace corps," called Volunteers in Service to America (VISTA).

Farm surpluses. The agricultural problem most persons are familiar with concerns the remainder of the agricultural community—the commercial farmers, the creators of farm surpluses. These surpluses have been caused by a technological revolution that has greatly increased production in the face of an essentially inelastic demand in an industry that has millions of small competitors. Since 1938, the Federal government has attempted to attack this surplus problem by several methods. One has been through price-support loans: the farmer obtains a government loan, giving produce as collateral. He may redeem the produce or he may choose to let the government take the collateral in payment for the loan. In return for such loans, the farmer gets an acreage allotment based on his past production of the crop. Thus, price supports limit acreage and therefore, it was originally assumed, production. Technology has frustrated this approach: Production per acre has increased remarkably (in 1937–1941, the farmer produced an average of 14.5 bushels of wheat per acre, 19.8 in 1955, and 27.0 in 1958). Farmers had been required to participate in this program for wheat, but in 1963 rejected quotas in a referendum which proposed stiffer restrictions for wheat. Cotton and tobacco production are still controlled. For the other eighteen crops under supports, the farmer himself may choose whether he wants to participate or take his chances on the open market and grow as much as possible.

The Soil Bank program, inaugurated in 1956, permits farmers to take land out of production and be paid to do so. In legal terms, the government leases the land on the condition it be placed in grass for grazing or legumes. Yet this will result in higher fertility, and thus higher production, when the land is put back into crops.

Price supports and Soil Bank are the basic programs. The government also attempts to reduce surpluses in other ways— through the school-lunch program and through a 1954 act permitting gifts or sales to foreign nations under certain conditions. A 1962 act permits foreign sales for dollars as well as foreign currency.

Surpluses are mainly in wheat, corn, and cotton. The most efficient farmers receive the largest payments because every move to limit the amount any farmer can receive has always been omitted from the bill. The ten largest farmers in 1957 received $3.5 million in supports and $500,000 in Soil Bank payments.

Proposed solutions: The maximizing of interests. Three approaches to the problem have been proposed.

1. Supports gradually should be reduced and the return made to a free market economy (the "flexible support" program). The Farm Bureau Federation, supported by many Midwest corn-hog farmers, favors this method. It would eliminate a great many marginal farmers and encourage further the merging of farms into large holdings. It is in harmony with individualistic ideology.

2. Price supports should be kept high, but acreage allotments made mandatory for all crops, at the same time encouraging a reduction in the number of farms. This would put the government in the position of planning farm production. The Kennedy and Johnson administrations sought and gained some of these goals.

3. Farm prices should be allowed to drop to whatever level the market decides and the government, through direct payments, should make up the difference between that price and a pegged price decided in advance. This, it is argued, would give consumers the benefit of lower prices while aiding the farmer. This is the Brannan plan of the late 1940s, which is favored by the National Farmers Union, whose strength is in the wheat states.

The suburban ideology would presumably favor the reduction of nonprofitable subsistence farming with humane efforts to "retool" the dispossessed farmers. The 1962 flexible-support program and the Kennedy farm program both were aimed toward that end. The latter provided for a pilot program of payments to help farmers put their land into recreation, wildlife, and other conservation uses and included clauses extending mandatory controls by issuing certificates permitting production. Observers have compared the certificates to negotiable public utility franchises, a

Figure 20-5

AGRICULTURAL SURPLUSES ARE A NATIONAL PROBLEM—AND EXPENSE
Your Family's Share of U.S. Surplus Commodities

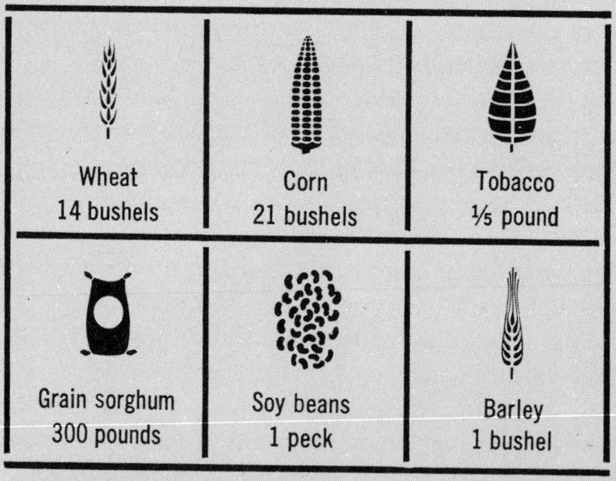

Wheat 14 bushels	Corn 21 bushels	Tobacco ⅕ pound
Grain sorghum 300 pounds	Soy beans 1 peck	Barley 1 bushel

At the end of 1958, Federal government surplus commodity stocks in inventory amounted, on a per family basis, to the amounts shown in the chart above. Investment in surplus commodities and crop loans now represents $131.89 per U.S. family.

Tax Foundation, Inc.

familiar regulation device used by government. Whichever program is finally adopted, it seems likely that the number of farming units will continue to be reduced until some method is found that enables some measure of control over production so that it will not exceed demand. As one observer has written, "Anyone inviting U.S. Steel or General Motors to produce at capacity and take pot luck on prices would rightly be judged a crank."[10]

The Poorly Educated and the Handicapped. The major goal of the emerging ideology is rehabilitation— it forswears punishment and is opposed to subsidies that can be avoided. The small-town ideology of individualism stressed the moral: "God helps him who helps himself." The social service ideology amended this to stress welfare: "God (or the government) helps him who cannot help himself." The contemporary suburban ideology amends further to: "God (or the government) helps people to help themselves," which introduces concepts from modern psychology.

In line with an ideology that regards deviants as ill, there is an increasing emphasis on administrative procedures rather than either police action or aid without effective supervision. Traditional methods used by the Bureau of Narcotics have been criticized recently by both the American Medical Association and the American Bar Association, which jointly published *Drug Addiction, Crime or Disease?* in 1961. The Boggs Act of 1952 and the Narcotics Control Act of 1956 (both strongly supported by the Bureau) sharply increased the prison terms of addicts and illegal narcotics retailers ("drug pushers"). Critics argue that it is precisely such a small-town moralistic and punitive approach to the problem that makes addicts criminals. A President's Conference on Narcotics and Drug Abuse in 1962, attended by 400 medical and social scientists and law-enforcement and public officials condemned sending addicts to prison for long periods and strongly supported "civil commitment" in hospitals, followed by parole.

A tightening of administrative procedures is evident in the major welfare reform act of 1962, which was adopted with little controversy. The act emphasized rehabilitation programs (Federal matching grants were upped to 75 per cent of costs). Where in the past assistance was denied if both parents were in the home, the new law emphasizes holding the family together, and assists where both parents are unemployed. A professional social worker approach is substituted for either a "get tough" moralistic or a "market-baskets-for-the-poor" attitude.

In line with this clinical rehabilitative attitude, aid to depressed areas (where unemployment is high and living standards low) emphasizes both retraining programs for people who have been replaced by automation and public works programs for improvement of parks and mental hospitals.

[10] Hans Landsberg, "A New Approach to the Farm Problem," *The Reporter*, Apr. 12, 1962, pp. 34–37.

The Medicare bill for those over sixty-five, a governmental insurance program fiercely debated in the early 1960s, bases such government aid on social security; it was a semi-insurance program requiring contributions from those aided. Medical care remains the area of greatest insecurity for the average citizen, despite private programs of insurance. A prolonged illness in most middle-class families would wipe out savings, put the family in heavy debt, and perhaps permanently incapacitate the major wage earner.

The permanently handicapped, either physically or because they are too old to be retrained for an industrial society, present the greatest problems. There has been a gradual expansion of direct aid programs to bring this group up to minimum levels of decent subsistence. Major emphasis, however, is on preventive and rehabilitative programs. These receive the top priority.

Figure 20-6

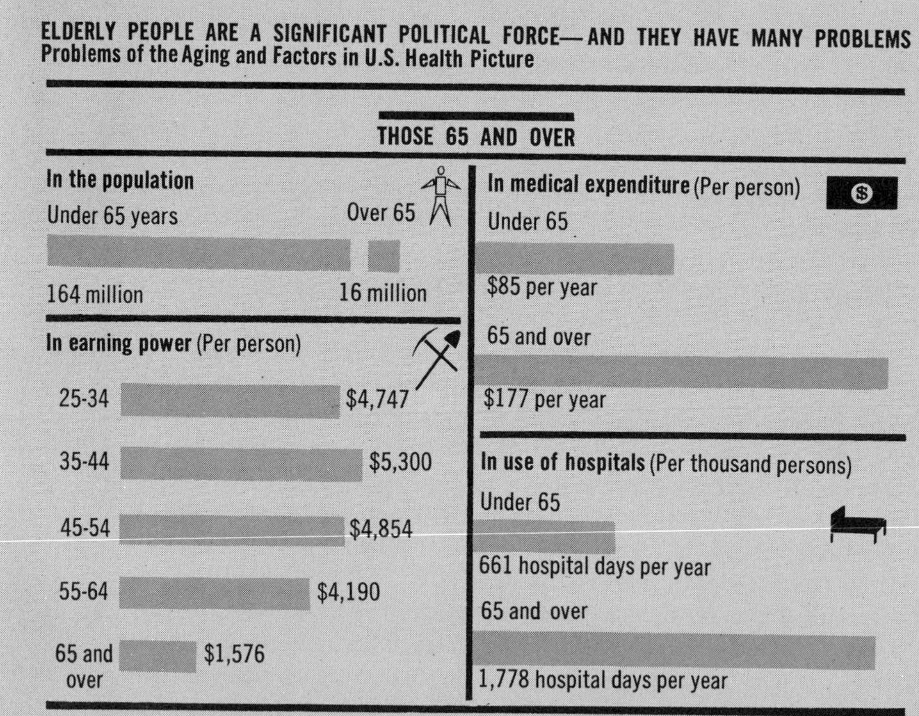

The New York Times, *Feb. 12, 1961.*

POLICIES FOR THE SIXTIES: AN OVERVIEW

This chapter has stressed the fact that domestic policy has taken on a new cast with the growing importance of the middle-class suburbanite ideology (stressing adjustment) over either small-town (moralistic) or working-class (class-oriented) viewpoints. This does not imply that interest groups striving for their own ends and insisting that these ends are in the public interest will not continue as an important part of the political process. Nor do the authors argue that this ideology is "right." Many "experts" who recognize the limits of knowledge in their own fields are themselves concerned about the readiness with which some treat them as all-knowing. We do argue that the general middle-class viewpoint of the suburbs is gaining acceptance in government because the politically effective majority has experiences that harmonize with this viewpoint.

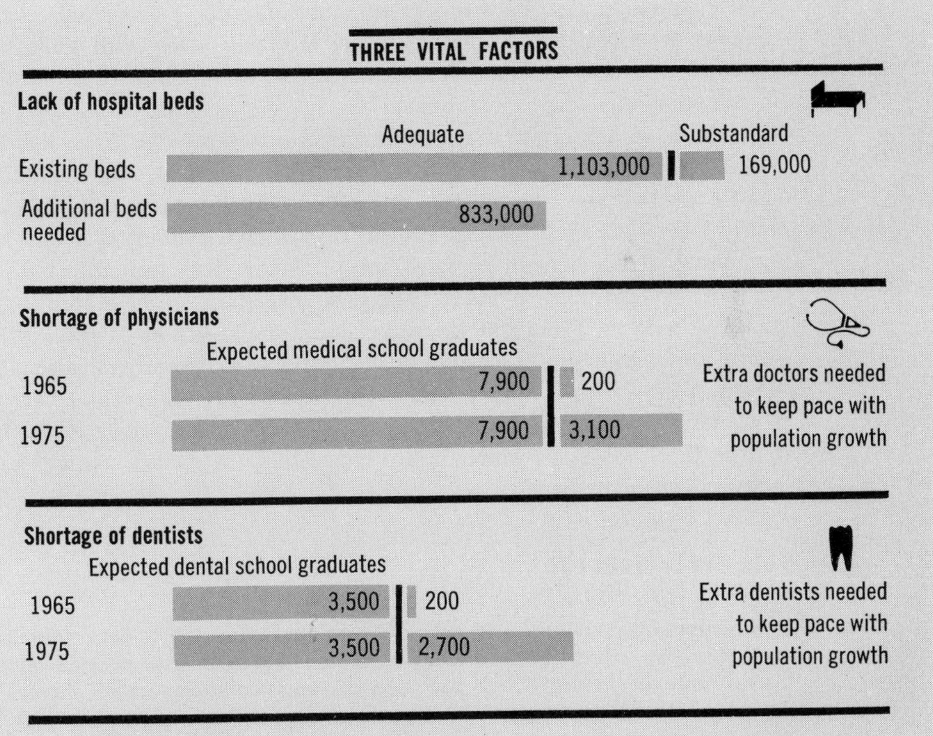

Imperceptibly and somewhat haphazardly, this view is pushing national domestic policy in a given direction. That direction is toward the attempt to create a technological society based on a "mixed economy," with decisions shared by government and business. The major tasks in both the public and private sectors are to be handled by large white-collar organizations, decentralized where practical to encourage democratic procedures. The aim will be to gain security for all consumers, and there will be an attempt to deal with marginal persons humanely, building a minimum floor under those who are permanently maladjusted and rehabilitating those who can be attuned to contemporary society.

At least one issue is not adequately met by the suburban political ideology—that of civil and economic liberties. An adjusted society stresses conventionality and the avoidance of conflict. Innovation, however, depends largely upon the maladjusted, sometimes upon the heretic. Can such individualists be tolerated in a society that is becoming increasingly standardized and in which change is expected to be gradual and the result of group (often committee) action? The same question is relevant for individualists in the economic sector of society. How will the individual entrepreneur fare in contrast with the organization man? The Federal government's Small Business Administration grants loans, tries to see that small business gets a share of government contracts, teaches better management practices, and provides advice. However, even with these aids, can small business prosper? Americans might also ponder the question: Should small business be encouraged?

We have earlier noted that political energy often stems from the frustrated, from those who are dissatisfied with the *status quo*. In Chapter 22, we will ask (but not answer) questions about whether the bland social and political style of suburbia can prevail over the discontented in our contemporary technological society and whether the well-adjusted can produce the imaginative ideas needed to maintain social stability in a changing society. From the viewpoint of the believers in democracy, the central problem facing the well-adjusted society of large organizations and suburban life-styles is that of preserving individual liberty and both the right and the utility of dissent. The way in which this problem is met may well be the basis upon which future generations of Americans will judge today's decision makers.

SELECTED BIBLIOGRAPHY

The bibliography on domestic policies is almost infinite. The selections listed emphasize two aspects. Some listings are included because they provide valuable insights into particular policy problems or are good introductory surveys for one unacquainted with a particular functional field. Other readings are included because they stress the political setting of a particular governmental service.

This chapter has argued that the liberal-conservative alignments of New Deal days are no longer appropriate in determining the positions of groups and individuals in the suburban society of the 1960s. A key word characterizing that society is "affluent," as is argued by Galbraith [14], a Harvard economist and adviser to the Kennedy administration. While there is general agreement that his description catches the prevailing mood of the times, a series of detailed studies have shown that many Americans do not participate in this affluent society. For an incisive comment on "Our Invisible Poor," see the book-review article by MacDonald [23], who assesses the works of Harrington [18], Kolko [21], Morgan [25], and others, all of whom are concerned with those we have described as the "unadjusted minority" in a metropolitan society.

The mood and problems of suburbia are well reflected in three books. Whyte's study of the Park Forest development near Chicago [38] is a detailed description of the social and political aspects of what he feels will be a pattern of living for most Americans in the future. College graduates will recognize themselves in this work. Wood's book [41] is an analysis of the ideology of suburbia, with emphasis on its political implications. The essays by the editors of *Fortune* review the problems faced by a metropolis, from the downtown slums to the commuting pattern [10]. The book focuses on the problem of building a new kind of society designed to satisfy the needs of residents. It argues that the theories guiding "reformers" are nostalgic rather than visionary or realistic. This view is echoed in Jacobs [19].

Rachel Carson's *Silent Spring* [8] is similarly typical of the reform approach to policy making found in a suburbanite society. While such literature would once have moralized on the trusts, this work treats the question of the commercial uses of chemical insecticides from the consumer viewpoint. Her claims have been challenged by others, and the book has produced considerable controversy.

Politics in a number of areas that many Americans regard as routine governmental operations have been examined by a number of social scientists and historians. Some of these are older works, now somewhat outdated in terms of factual materials, but they are still relevant to contemporary politics. Among the best are Hardin on agriculture [17], Hamilton on industry [16], and Calkins on labor [7]. Maas [22] has done a classic study of the "pork barrel" aspects of policy making for the nation's water resources. Garceau [15] shows how one organized interest group, the American Medical Association, is organized for political action.

A review of the most important policy questions facing Americans in the 1960s is found in the report of the President's Commission on National Goals [31]. For an issue likely to become even more significant in the future than it has been in the past—medical care—see the work by Somers and Somers [35]. Also consult current issues of the *Congressional Quarterly*.

1. Babbidge, Homer D., Jr., and Robert M. Rosenzweig: *The Federal Interest in Higher Education,* McGraw-Hill Book Company, New York, 1962.
2. Bach, George L.: *Federal Reserve Policy Making,* Alfred A. Knopf, Inc., New York, 1950.
3. Banfield, Edward C., and Morton Grodzins: *Government and Housing in Metropolitan Areas,* McGraw-Hill Book Company, New York, 1958.
4. Bernstein, Marver H.: *Regulating Business by Independent Commission,* Princeton University Press, Princeton, N.J., 1955.
5. Bornet, Vaughn Davis: *Welfare in America,* University of Oklahoma Press, Norman, Okla., 1960.
6. Burns, Eveline M.: *Social Security and Public Policy,* McGraw-Hill Book Company, New York, 1956.
7. Calkins, Fay: *The CIO and the Democratic Party,* The University of Chicago Press, Chicago, 1952.
8. Carson, Rachel L.: *Silent Spring,* Houghton Mifflin Company, Boston, 1962.

9. Christenson, Reo M.: *The Brannan Plan: Farm Politics and Policy,* The University of Michigan Press, Ann Arbor, Mich., 1959.
10. Editors of *Fortune: The Exploding Metropolis,* Doubleday & Company, Inc., Garden City, N.Y., 1957.
11. Fainsod, Merle, Lincoln Gordon, and Joseph C. Palamountain, Jr.: *Government and the American Economy,* W. W. Norton & Company, Inc., New York, 1959.
12. Ferguson, E. James: *The Power of the Purse,* The University of North Carolina Press, Chapel Hill, N.C., 1961.
13. Foss, Phillip O.: *Politics and Grass: The Administration of Grazing on the Public Domain,* University of Washington Press, Seattle, Wash., 1960.
14. Galbraith, John K.: *The Affluent Society,* Houghton Mifflin Company, Boston, 1958.
15. Garceau, Oliver: *The Political Life of the AMA,* Harvard University Press, Cambridge, Mass., 1941.
16. Hamilton, Walton H.: *The Politics of Industry,* Alfred A. Knopf, Inc., New York, 1957.
17. Hardin, Charles M.: *The Politics of Agriculture,* The Free Press of Glencoe, New York, 1952.
18. Harrington, Michael: *The Other America: Poverty in the United States,* The Macmillan Company, New York, 1962; Penguin Books, Inc., Baltimore, 1963.
19. Jacobs, Jane: *The Death and Life of Great American Cities,* Random House, Inc., New York, 1961.
20. Knight, Douglas (ed.): *The Federal Government and Higher Education,* Spectrum Books, Prentice-Hall, Inc., Englewood Cliffs, N.J., 1960.
21. Kolko, Gabriel: *Wealth and Power in America: An Analysis of Social Class and Income Distribution,* Frederick A. Praeger, Inc., New York, 1962.
22. Maas, Arthur A.: *Muddy Waters: The Army Engineers and the Nation's Rivers,* Harvard University Press, Cambridge, Mass., 1951.
23. MacDonald Dwight: "Our Invisible Poor," *The New Yorker,* 82:132, Jan. 19, 1963.
24. McCune, Wesley: *Who's Behind Our Farm Policy?* Frederick A. Praeger, Inc., New York, 1956.
25. Morgan, James N., and others: *Income and Welfare in the United States,* McGraw-Hill Book Company, New York, 1962.
26. Ostrom, Vincent: *Water and Politics,* The Haynes Foundation, Los Angeles, Calif., 1953.
27. U.S. Outdoor Recreation Resources Review Commission: *Outdoor Recreation for America,* 1962.
28. Owen, Wilfred: *Cities in the Motor Age,* The Viking Press, Inc., New York, 1959.
29. Patton, James G.: *The Case for Farmers,* Public Affairs Press, Washington, D.C., 1960.
30. Peltason, Jack W., and James MacGregor Burns (eds.): *Functions and Policies of American Government,* 2d ed., Prentice-Hall, Inc., Englewood Cliffs, N.J., 1962.
31. President's Commission on National Goals: *Goals for Americans,* Spectrum Books, Prentice-Hall, Inc., Englewood Cliffs, N.J., 1960.
32. Reagan, Michael D.: "The Political Structure of the Federal Reserve System," *The American Political Science Review,* 55:64–76, March, 1961.
33. Rossi, Peter H., and Robert A. Dentler: *The Politics of Urban Renewal: The Chicago Findings,* The Free Press of Glencoe, New York, 1962.
34. Selznick, Philip: *TVA at the Grassroots,* University of California Press, Berkeley, Calif., 1949.

35. Somers, Herman M., and Anne R. Somers, *Doctors, Patients, and Health Insurance,* The Brookings Institution, Washington, D.C., 1961.
36. Strayer, Paul J.: *Fiscal Policy and Politics,* Harper & Row, Publishers, New York, 1958.
37. Wengert, Norman: *Natural Resources and the Political Struggle,* Random House, Inc., New York, 1955.
38. Whyte, William H.: *The Organization Man,* Anchor Books, Doubleday & Company, Inc., Garden City, N.Y., 1957.
39. Wilcox, Clair: *Public Policies toward Business,* rev. ed., Richard D. Irwin, Inc., Homewood, Ill., 1960.
40. Willmore, Jerold N. (ed.): *Critical Issues and Decisions,* U.S. Department of Agriculture, Graduate School, 1962.
41. Wood, Robert C.: *Suburbia: Its People and Their Politics,* Houghton Mifflin Company, Boston, 1958.

Law Cases

Griffin v. County School Board of Prince Edward County, L. Ed. 2d 409 (1964).
Hurd v. Hodge, 334 U.S. 24 (1948).
Shelley v. Kraemer, 334 U.S. 1 (1948).

Case Study Materials

1. Banfield, Edward C.: *The Case of the Growing Problem (Agricultural Policy),* American Foundation for Continuing Education, Chicago (undated).
2. Meyerson, Martin, and Edward C. Banfield: *Politics, Planning and the Public Interest: The Case of Public Housing in Chicago,* The Free Press of Glencoe, New York, 1955.
3. Pinner, Frank A., and others: *Old Age and Political Behavior,* University of California Press, Berkeley, Calif., 1959.
4. Ridgeway, M. E.: *The Missouri Basin's Pick-Sloan Plan: A Case Study in Congressional Policy Determination,* The University of Illinois Press, Urbana, Ill., 1955.
5. Silverman, Corrine: *The President's Economic Advisers,* University of Alabama Press, University, Ala., 1959.

CHAPTER 21

AMERICAN FOREIGN POLICY

Alexis de Tocqueville, the French observer of American customs, argued that democracies are the least suited of all types of government for the direction of foreign policy. The national interest, he believed, is often placed second to the demands of local politics, the pressures generated by interest groups, the ambitions of politicians trying to "look good" at home, and emotional impulses and demands by the electorate for quick and simple solutions to all problems. In recent times, the writer and commentator Walter Lippmann has made similar points. Unlike domestic politics, they argue, there may be no second chance to correct mistakes in foreign policy making, and therefore the risk involved in popular participation in policy making in foreign affairs is too great.

FOREIGN POLICY MAKING IN A DEMOCRACY

The Budget Bureau, in 1953 proposals, eliminated an appropriation request for work on Oahe Dam in South Dakota because the administration wanted to economize. Rapid negotiations took place between the state's senior senator and the Director of the Budget. The $8.25 million for the dam was restored. The senator explained to his constituents what had happened:

> With Budget approval, it now appears we'll get our eight and a quarter million, and last week I fulfilled my part of the promise. On motions made by me in the Senate Appropriations Committee, $8,000,000 was cut from the funds approved for State Department personnel.[1]

America, like all nations, has made blunders in foreign policy and these have been exploited in political campaigns, sometimes in badly distorted versions. The Central Intelligence Agency (CIA) invasion fiasco in Cuba (1961), the trivial, but impolitic, comments of a Peace Corps volunteer on a postcard mailed from a new African nation (the same year), the China "tangle," the

[1] Holbert N. Carroll, *The House of Representatives and Foreign Affairs,* The University of Pittsburgh Press, Pittsburgh, Pa., 1958, p. 184.

tariff on Danish blue cheese, the missile lag relative to the Soviet Union, the Korean conflict, the loss of a U-2 spy plane over the Soviet Union, and other major and minor incidents and policies have been vigorously criticized by Americans themselves—sometimes, it is argued, to the detriment of the conduct of foreign policy.

But many Americans will not concede that foreign policy should be made differently from domestic policy. To do so would be to suggest that there is consensus on the goals and methods that American foreign policy should pursue. In the example of the Oahe Dam, the senator concerned had been generally critical of the State Department and its policies since World War II. His action, while of benefit to South Dakota constituents desiring a dam, was also consistent with the foreign policy stands he had taken and the kinds of action he appeared to believe would best serve American interests abroad.

American foreign policy making has been open to all interests and individuals who have the desire and political resources to participate. Disagreement based on differences in political ideologies have been common, despite efforts to end debate "at the water's edge." Though some serious errors can be pointed to, the United States has had many foreign policy successes. Within a short period of time between 1940 and 1950, the nation accomplished a direct about-face in foreign policy—a revision of basic principles that had dated back 150 years to Washington's Farewell Address and his warnings about "entangling alliances." Our nation moved with considerable boldness, taking a new tack that required unusual sacrifices in money, materials, and men. A nation whose foreign policy can so readily respond to the requirements of the moment perhaps deserves more credit than some of its critics have been willing to give it. The conduct of American foreign policy has had its brilliant successes as well as its dismal failures.

But in the past there has been a major difference between foreign and domestic policy making. The broad electorate or the broad spectrum of interest groups is less frequently concerned with day-to-day operations in the foreign policy field. Thus, more than in the domestic policy field, pressures shaping policy arise from the diverse viewpoints and interests within government itself; for example, congressional committees, the State Department, the Executive Office of the President, the military, and, depending upon the issue, specialized units of the bureaucracy such as the

Departments of Commerce, Labor, Agriculture, and the Post Office. These reflect special viewpoints, including the application of political ideologies to the conduct of foreign policy.

Thus far, Americans have been successful on the whole. In the past, they had the advantage of isolation and more opportunity for correcting failure before it was too late than they have now. The world has become more perilous for America. Yet Americans continue the experiment of shaping an effective foreign policy within the framework of democratic institutions.

A WORLD IN TRANSITION

Since World War II it has been recognized by all but a few nostalgic romanticists that a new world is in the process of coming into being—its precise character uncertain. The decline of Europe as a world center had begun by the time of World War I. The breaking up of the great European overseas empires followed World War II. When the fighting ended, the greatest powers of the world were, for the first time since the Middle Ages, non-European. The homes, factories, and economies of such great nations as Great Britain, France, Germany, and Italy were in a shambles. Europe was in eclipse, and it was unlikely, even with a determined effort to recover, that the world positions European nations once held would ever be attained by them again.

A central question has been: What kind of world will emerge? But there is no answer on which all Americans can agree. The question in part concerns material standards of living and the survival of particular nation-states, but even more it is a matter of ideology and values. Will the Western heritage of freedom or the Communist bloc go the way of Greek and Roman civilizations? Will it be a world in which warfare with atomic weapons may occur? It is with the question of what kind of world is emerging that American foreign policy is intimately concerned. The function of a foreign policy is to help shape new conditions in ways that will protect America's very existence and the values it, as a nation, has defended.

If Americans were agreed on the most important questions to be dealt with and how to deal with them, policy making would be only a question of technical expertise. But there is conflict over ends and means, or the desire to achieve inconsistent ends (e.g., "Preserve peace," but also "Drive the Communists out of the satellite nations"). Thus, defining the kind of world Americans want and how to achieve this are at the heart of the democratic controversy over the conduct of foreign policy.

The International Political Scene. But the major characteristics of the transitional world we have lived in since World War II can be discerned. These conditions, whether we approve of them or not, are real. Any realistic American foreign policy must take them into account.

The impact of technology. In the postwar period, technology has come of age. The flying Jennies of World War I and the B-29s of World War II, are obsolete. So is the type of atomic bomb exploded over Hiroshima. It killed 78,150 Japanese and injured 37,425, but is now as outmoded as the Model T.

It is easy to recognize the effect of modern technology on weapons such as the hydrogen bomb or the latest missile to carry it. The peacetime technological revolution is less frequently noted. The prewar assembly lines seem as primitive as medical practice in a world without antibiotics.

Figure 21-1

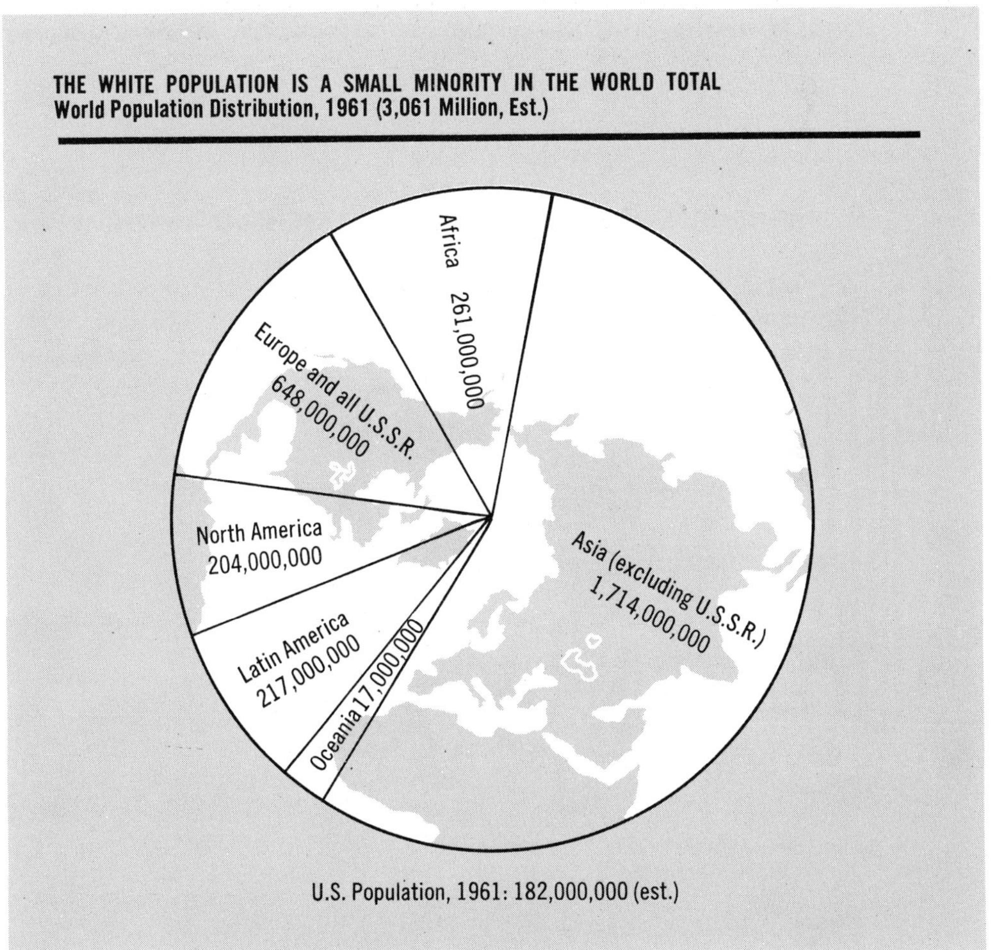

This revolution holds the promise that it may be possible to eliminate poverty and most illness for all of the citizens of the world. Scientific knowledge now doubles every eight years, on the average. There is no nation, however poor, that does not have an educated class that sees technology as the hope for changing what has long been regarded as unchangeable, for making commonplace what has always been regarded as luxury. Technological advance can no longer be the monopoly of a few; all desire it. The once exotic concept of "progress" is now a world dream.

Two major world powers. Since World War II, two major military powers exist in the world: the United States and the Soviet Union. Each heads an alliance. The Soviet alliance expects that the governments of the Western world will inevitably suffer an economic and political collapse that will be followed by the establishment of Communist systems by citizens. "We will bury you," Nikita Khrushchev once said, and he seemed to expect this to happen in his lifetime. As is common with persons who believe in a form of predestination, the Communist bloc has demonstrated a willingness to act to speed up what its leaders regard as inevitable. Believing that they

Figure 21-2

Technology Changes So Rapidly That It Is Difficult to Know What Is Really Obsolescent

"Why don't you rewrite that part about the 'rocket's red glare,' Francis? Rockets are practically obsolete."

By permission of Burr Shafer.

are acting in terms of a higher morality, Communist leaders have often condoned and encouraged practices that most Americans regard as ethically questionable. Their efforts are not only military. They seek to undermine the Western powers, using the ideological, diplomatic, or economic weapons at hand. But the Soviet Union, like America, is limited in the weapons it can use; by Western strength and skills on the one hand, by the Russian ideology and by the Russian allies on the other. The two blocs thus face each other in a state of imperfect, competitive coexistence. While it seems the Western world will not immediately crumble, neither will the world of the Communists.

The emerging nations. A bipolar analysis of world politics is, however, an oversimplification. Allies have proved restive, as was signified by the China-Russia split in the Soviet bloc and by France's independent course under De Gaulle, which led to recognition of Communist China and a weakening of NATO ties.

But equally important, Western and Communist power blocs face one another over a no man's land that contains 1½ of the 3½ billion human beings who inhabit the world. For the most part, this neutral ground is made up of the former colonial empires of the European nations, plus the nations of South America. Their preference is to be committed to neither East nor West. Their style is intensely nationalistic. Their first impulse is to acquire freedom and then to root out the last vestiges of colonialism. Next on their agenda is technological advancement. A locally owned and operated steel or electric plant donated by a foreign power may be run in a pathetically incompetent fashion for the moment, but it stands as a symbolic promise of what the future will hold.

These uncommitted nations hold the balance of power for the future and promise a shifting in power allocations. The way they develop and what kinds of actions they will favor will, to a great degree, shape the answer to the question: What kind of world will emerge?

Another nation is also thought by some to be gradually emerging—a United Europe. Its most promising enterprise has been the Common Market, even without Britain. If political unity can occur on the European continent in a form that promises strength and stability, most observers expect the balance between the two major powers to shift markedly because of the industrial skills and resources of the European Continent.

The Limits of Foreign Policy. "We exercise only influence, not the sovereign right to dispose." So wrote a former member of the State Department's policy-planning staff about the ability of a foreign policy staff to affect conditions and events.[2] The same is, of course, true of the strategists of the Communist bloc.

[2] Charles B. Marshall, *The Limits of Foreign Policy,* Holt, Rinehart and Winston, Inc., New York, 1954, p. 15.

Americans sometimes act as if only the decisions we make count, as if, when world politics do not operate according to plan, the failure stems from blundering or even treason by our leaders. Yet there are some conditions we could not change, no matter how much we wished—for example, the nationalist aspirations of Asians and Africans. At best, we can only attempt to channel such forces in directions that seem to us desirable. We can only live with other conditions and shape our policy to minimize their effect—for example, the Soviet lead in booster rockets. The difficulty in conducting foreign policy, then, is less frequently in selecting overall goals, although even these sometimes are in conflict. Rather, it is in selecting the means by which to achieve what we intend.

Morality and Foreign Policy: The American Style. Americans have sometimes embraced a perfectionist morality in foreign policy. ("There is no substitute for victory," or "There must be unconditional surrender of the Axis powers," or "All agreements should be open covenants openly arrived at.") These simplistic approaches had particular appeal to the isolationist spirit and to utopianism. They are at variance with the pragmatic conduct of domestic political affairs, where the viewpoint of "half a loaf is better than none" is the common one.

The charge of overmoralizing cannot be completely substantiated in recent times, however. Americans have accepted such choices as giving aid to the dictatorships of Poland, Yugoslavia, Spain, and Portugal—decisions that many Americans regard as unpalatable choices. Many Americans have come to recognize that a realistic morality in foreign affairs takes the best choice perceived to be available under the prevailing conditions, knowing that sometimes, to attain one goal, a nation must sacrifice part of another.

One school of international students, repelled by the perfectionist morality typical of the isolationist period, has been charged with embracing a "get-tough" or *realpolitik* approach to foreign policy. Such a viewpoint ostensibly disregards moral values in policy making and argues that its major aim should be survival and that survival can best be ensured through superiority in weapons.

Most Americans have believed, however, that our national purpose was something other than survival for its own sake. We have waged war under Washington, Lincoln, Wilson, Franklin Roosevelt, and Truman to achieve other aims; in particular, we have fought for the ideals of Jefferson as they were stated in the Declaration of Independence and for what Lincoln called "the last, best hope of the world." Rightly or wrongly, we are likely to continue to consider that our national purpose is more than simple survival, that the American nation has something to offer to the practice of governing men and nations that is too valuable to lose. This idealistic element of our foreign policy is never wholly absent, and it has been institutionalized in Lincoln's Second Inaugural Address, Wilson's dream of a League of Nations, Roosevelt's Good Neighbor policy and the Four Freedoms, Truman's Point Four program, Eisenhower's Atoms for Peace program, and Kennedy's Peace Corps. This stand of morality is so ingrained as to be a permanent part of our nation's foreign policy style, and, in the opinion of many Americans, it gives that policy strength rather than weakness.[3]

POLICIES FOR A WORLD IN TRANSITION

"Gibraltar-America," "Go it alone," and other slogans of isolationism were, it was thought by most Americans, put out on the curb for the trashman following World War II. The nation moved from the old neighborhood to one of the big houses on the hill and joined the country club. The forming of the United Nations under American leadership seemed to symbolize the end of one era of our nation's history and the beginning of another. America would henceforth take an important place in the community of nations and would work out its destiny in that role.

The change did not immediately bring the hoped-for results. Instead, America found itself in a cold war, and a mood of utopian romanticism gave way to a realistic reassessment of our position in world affairs. At times, some Americans have wanted to try to return to comfortable isolation. At times, some have wanted to make the cold war a hot one and bring the wearying competition to an end, one way or another. Isolationism, which was an aspect of the ideology of the small town, has been revived in news forms. Unilateralism has become a popular approach for segments of America and for important members of congressional committees. While not a majority, the proponents of this viewpoint have been articulate in demanding a return to the kind of world that existed at the beginning of the century when, singlehandedly, "we whipped the Spaniards, freed Cuba and added to our territorial possessions." Nostalgia has called for a return of the conditions under which small-town America flourished. But for most Americans, most of the time, the only palatable policy choice has been that of peaceful coexistence under cold war conditions.

As is the case in domestic policy, foreign policy has somewhat erratically tended to follow programs that harmonize with the dominant political ideology of the metropolis. The welfare orientation of the social service state, as well as a desire to let technical specialists solve problems, is present; the concept of helping persons to help themselves is, as in domestic policy, replacing an approach of pure aid. The reliance on technology for creating a safe world is predominant. We tend to assume that nations that learn modern means of production and distribution from us will support us politically.

[3] For a discussion of the problems of moral choice in foreign policy making see Arnold Wolfers, "Statesmanship and Moral Choice," in Harold K. Jacobson (ed.), *America's Foreign Policy,* Random House, Inc., New York, 1960, pp. 67–85.

The alternatives chosen, given the policy commitment of peaceful coexistence, have been those of most conflicts: stop enemy advances; win the uncommitted; subvert enemy strength; build military power. Filling in the details of these broad policy choices has raised the major policy problems in the period following World War II. Controversy has been continuous, but, as has been the case in the domestic area, the general trend has been in harmony with prevailing political ideology.

Support of the United Nations. The United Nations was formed at the end of World War II by the victors as a form of collective security against future aggression. Its permanent headquarters are in New York. Its major organs are the General Assembly, in which each nation has one vote; the Security Council of eleven members, always including the United States, the Soviet Union, Great Britain, France, and China, which allows a veto by the permanent members of proposed actions; the Economic and Social Council; the Trusteeship Council; the International Court of Justice; and a permanent Secretariat.

When the United Nations was created, the United States and her allies clearly dominated voting within the Security Council and the General Assembly. With the admission of large numbers of new Asian and African nations, Western domination of the organization became less certain, but it remained clear that the Communist nations were in a distinct minority, a fact that helped to account for Communist hostility toward the UN. Most American professional diplomats believe that the UN continues to be of great value to the United States as a medium for propaganda designed to influence the neutral states, a clearinghouse for technical information, an arena for settling conflicts between smaller powers, and a place in which the United States and the U.S.S.R. can meet without the elaborate formalities and the problems of who is to lose face that are involved in formal meetings of the heads of state or their foreign affairs representatives.

The Economic and Social Council supervises organizations that contribute to improving social and economic standards in member nations; these are the International Labor Organization, the Food and Agriculture Organization, the International Monetary Fund, the International Bank for Reconstruction and Development, the Educational, Scientific, and Cultural Organization (UNESCO), and the International Civil Aviation Organization. The work of these units is aimed at eliminating what some specialists have regarded as "causes of war." United States support for the United Nations is symbolized by giving its ambassador to the organization Cabinet status.

The Policy of Containment. The followers of Karl Marx know that he foretold the inevitable collapse of capitalist nations. Americans, with no equivalent prophet but with an optimistic belief in their destiny, have held out a similar hope for Communist countries. In part, United States policy is based on the premise that the Communist nations are following the familiar imperialist designs of Alexander, Napoleon, Hitler, and others who have learned that the glory road may end on a cliff of doom. It is argued that if an empire-building nation is contained, its citizens, no longer groggy from the heady wine of expansion, will take a more realistic look at their domestic arrangements. Such a look by the Communist nations would, it is assumed, have encouraging results for the nations of the West. Presidents have generally accepted this analysis and thus concluded that the first step in the cold war policy was to stop the Communist parade. Our first efforts were in Europe, and these methods were transferred less successfully to Asia.

The major method was making treaties with the principal nations that form a ring around the Soviet Union in the West and establishing with them, in 1949, a military organization called the North Atlantic Treaty Organization (NATO). The premise of the organization is that an attack on any one nation will be regarded as an attack on all. Unlike most treaties, the treaty on which NATO was based brought into being a unified defense force, with its own command directed by an American. Basic military decisions have been worked out within the NATO framework (e.g., rearming West Germany and setting up missile bases in Europe), and strategy is coordinated, as are weapons. Fifteen nations, including Greece and Turkey, are members.

The Southeast Asia Treaty Organization (SEATO), the pact with Australia and New Zealand (some of its activities were later included under SEATO), and the short-lived Bagdad Pact were similar military alliances, all designed to ensure friendly nations that we would go to their support if they were attacked. We also gave direct military and economic aid to such nations. Aid for Greece and Turkey when they were threatened with a Communist take-over and, later, the Marshall Plan for European Recovery were designed to strengthen our allies economically and militarily. Direct aid was part of this policy; it was also bolstered by the lowering of United States tariff barriers and the encouragement of European economic unity through the Iron and Coal Community, the Benelux Agreement, and the European Common Market. These were economic agreements among European nations to eliminate tariff barriers. Part of our policy has also been to draw West Germany, our former enemy and a nation of great economic potential, into this community.

A long-standing American alliance has been the Organization of American States (OAS), which includes twenty-one nations of North, Central, and South America. The organization was established under another name in 1890. It seeks, through cooperative efforts, to meet common problems. Actions against the Castro government of Cuba formed a principal part of its agenda in the early 1960s. The OAS is more commonly recognized by the name of its secretariat, the Pan American Union. The Alliance for Progress, which stems from the Punta del Este, Uruguay, Charter of 1962, has complemented the OAS activities. Its goal is to raise the average annual cumulative growth in per capita income in Latin America by 2.5 per cent over a ten-year period and to substantially improve levels of education, health, and housing.

The containment of communism has entailed more than the building up of allies; we have also had to show our willingness to fight small wars with conventional weapons for the limited end of preserving the *status quo* of boundaries. In Korea, we provided the greatest share of United Nations forces and suffered more than 157,000 casualties in a three-year period (1950–1953). America has also shown its willingness to halt further Communist expansion in West Berlin, Southeast Asia, Latin America, and the Congo.

The most notable successes of this policy have been in Europe. The most notable failure has been in China. After China fell to the Communists, we have refused to recognize the new regime, even though it rules nearly 700 million people. The most galling failure has been in Cuba, on our own doorstep, although, by prompt and firm action, we succeeded in causing the removal of Soviet IRBM missiles that had been installed there in 1962.

Winning the Uncommitted. Keeping the uncommitted nations out of the Communist orbit has not been enough. We have also sought to win them to our side. We have extended military and economic aid, but an important weapon has been a nebulous and intangible one—prestige. We hope to influence the political development of these independent nations by showing them the advantages of our system as we help them meet their problems.

We have attempted to present the humanitarian side of America through such economic-aid programs as Point Four (assistance for industrial development) and the Peace Corps. We have supplemented these programs by assistance through the agencies of the United Nations and such private associations as the Red Cross and CARE. We have, through the Voice of America, good-will missions of dignitaries, including the President, and other propaganda devices, presented our case.

Our greatest postwar setback in this battle for prestige was in space exploration. By permitting the Soviet Union to outdistance us in rocket boosters, we enabled its leaders to claim that their type of economic and political system was superior to ours. To nations wanting desperately to advance technologically, the Soviet progress, under totalitarian methods, from underdeveloped nation to a world power in only thirty years is impressive.

America has also had to be on the defensive in the ideological battle because of discrimination against nonwhite citizens and visitors. Refusals to give service at roadside hamburger joints along U.S. Highway 40 (near Washington), as well as the more explosive events that have occurred in Little Rock, New Orleans, Albany, Georgia, and Oxford, Mississippi, steadily sap such prestige as we have built up in neutral nations through other means.

American policy in winning over the uncommitted nations has been neither wholly a success nor wholly a failure. Perhaps a recognition of what the Communist system entails is now more widespread than it was at the end of World War II, when even many Americans seemed to regard communism as a brand of reform, a little to the left of such movements as the nineteenth-century barn burners of rural New York. The massacres in East Germany and Hungary, the need to wall in East Germans at Berlin, the Chinese invasion of Tibet, and subsequent incidents on the Indian border were perhaps more helpful than our own achievements in destroying somewhat the world's image of communism.

Subverting Communist Nations. Short of going to war, subverting the regime of a totalitarian nation is difficult and, at most times, probably impossible. At one point in history, it was hoped that a chain reaction of revolutions might be set off that would liberate the Communist satellite nations and

Figure 21-3

A Leader Is Everyone's Target

"Act friendly and display an appreciative interest in Earthly accomplishments. As a rule, avoid political discussions, although some criticism of the United States is always considered good form."

Drawing by Dedini; © 1962, The New Yorker, Inc.

perhaps sweep through China without requiring outside military help. The revolts in East Germany in 1953 and in Hungary in 1956 were followed by brutal Soviet repression, which showed the limitations of a "liberation-without-aid" policy. The revolts were put down, and the United States did not intervene militarily to change the outcome. Instead, by means of a stepped-up propaganda drive through Radio Free Europe (nongovernmental) and the Voice of America of the State Department, Americans have attempted to build a foundation for some future time of liberation, but not to encourage precipitate action.

We aided two attempts to overthrow regimes which were associated with the Communist orbit. The attempt in Guatemala was successful; the attempted invasion of Cuba was an embarrassing and tragic failure.

The other hope of subversion was to encourage division within the Communist system of nations. This we attempted by granting aid to Yugoslavia and Poland. The encouraging signs of friction between China and Russia over such matters as Albania were watched hopefully. This was the ultimate split hoped for by some. Some Americans argued that admitting Communist China to the United Nations might encourage such a development.

Military Security. "I believe that military power is but the negative aspect of a dynamic foreign policy. It buys us time. It gives us the opportunity and what we do with that time . . . on the economic, social and political fronts in the long pull will be decisive as to whether we will succeed in winning over the forces of tyranny," said Walter Reuther, president of one of America's most powerful unions, to the AFL-CIO Conference on World Affairs in 1960.[4]

To some critics, the problem of the 1950s was that American foreign policy concentrated too much on military competition with the Communist nations, overlooking the ideological and economic conflicts. Major emphasis in defense effort and spending was placed for a time on the atomic weapons of "massive retaliation." At the same time, we faced military problems that required the conventional weapons suitable for fighting the kind of brush-fire wars we faced in Korea and Southeast Asia. In terms of continental defense, high priority was given antimissile missiles and detection systems. Little was done for civil defense, aside from the private building of fallout shelters by some citizens.

Coupled with the build-up of military might has been an attempt to limit the use of certain weapons and, if possible, to reach some agreement on disarmament. The Test Ban Treaty of 1963, in which most nations joined, was such a step. Under its terms, the testing of nuclear weapons is to be conducted underground.

[4] *Proceedings of the AFL-CIO Conference on World Affairs*, AFL-CIO, New York, 1960, p. 124.

PRESIDENT, CONGRESS, AND AMERICAN FOREIGN POLICY

Foreign policy making presents a great challenge to a democracy because the issues are complex; there is often a felt need for secrecy and dispatch; and the stakes are too high to permit fumbling. In its broad outlines, the process of foreign policy making is similar to domestic policy making: a policy proposal is shaped in the executive branch and runs the gamut of criticism by Congress and interested publics.

The major differences between foreign and domestic policy relate to the characteristics of foreign policy noted above. The executive, constitutionally and practically, has more power to shape such policy, while Congress and the public have less opportunity for review. The attentive foreign policy publics within the total population are generally fewer in number than they are in most domestic policy areas, but the attentive publics within the government itself are often more numerous.

The process of decision making is based on grants of constitutional power and organizational structure. These define who the major decision makers will be.

The Constitution and Foreign Policy. Nowhere is the tendency to make a political struggle out of what in other countries is generally an administrative question more evident than in the constitutional provisions for making American foreign policy. A few important grants of power to specific agencies are spelled out, but about many of the most important powers, the Constitution says not a word. The major participants are the President, numerous executive agencies, the Senate, and the House of Representatives.

The Constitution specifies that foreign policy matters are the responsibility of the national government alone. No state can make a treaty with a foreign nation or set up special tariffs or declare war. States can, however, impinge on foreign policy making by their actions. President Theodore Roosevelt was embarrassed by Californians who legally discriminated against Orientals, just as later Presidents have had to attempt to explain to the uncommitted nations why the national government permits certain racial policies in Southern states.

The major constitutional grants of power can be briefly summarized: The President is the Commander in Chief of the Armed Forces, but the Congress must declare war. The President may make treaties, but the Senate must ratify them by a two-thirds vote. The President may accept the credentials of foreign emissaries and appoint our diplomatic representatives, but the Senate must confirm the major appointments. In addition, the Constitution grants to Congress the power to make laws (over which the President has a veto) that affect such foreign policy matters as tariffs, foreign-aid appropriations and policy, and the organization of executive agencies for the carrying out of foreign policy.

Expansion of the Formal Powers. The conditions under which foreign policy is made tend to favor the President since, as has been noted, decisions must often be made secretly and executed with dispatch. A President could react immediately to the invasion of South Korea by North Koreans, but Congress would have been inclined to debate action proposals at length. Before the Constitution was adopted, Alexander Hamilton observed that the President would tend to gather to himself all powers in foreign affairs "which the Constitution does not vest elsewhere in clear terms."

Presidential actions create precedents. To the formal grants of power, a series of customs has been added that have the force of constitutional law. Many of the President's powers are based on interpretations made in the past by Presidents faced with foreign policy problems. The President, as Commander in Chief, may send the Armed Forces to foreign nations and involve them in conflict and undeclared war, as Jefferson did when he sent the Marines to engage the Barbary pirates who were menacing American shipping from the African coast ("the shores of Tripoli"). The President can also skirt the Senate's treaty-ratifying powers by making executive agreements without Senate consent, as Jefferson did when he agreed with the agents of Napoleon for the purchase of the Louisiana Territory. Texas was annexed by executive agreement. Such agreements have become quite common in the years since the Franklin Roosevelt administration. For example, President Roosevelt agreed to send fifty destroyers to Great Britain in return for bases in the Caribbean during the period of America's official neutrality in the early days of World War II, and he reached wartime agreements at international conferences at Moscow and Yalta. So did Truman at Potsdam. The NATO treaty of 1949 resulted in over 10,000 executive agreements to secure greater uniformity in military equipment and procedures among the NATO nations. The President's power to accept the credentials of foreign diplomats has meant that he alone has the power to grant United States recognition to a new foreign nation or regime and also to break off such recognition. Thus Franklin Roosevelt decided to recognize the Soviet Union after it had been in existence for over fifteen years without any official notice from the United States. And Dwight Eisenhower decided, without action by Congress, to break off diplomatic relations with Cuba.

Presidents have announced policy objectives. Presidents have always utilized their power to address Congress or the people in order to enunciate foreign policy principles. Washington's Farewell Address contained his warning against "entangling alliances." James Monroe, in a message to Congress, staked out the United States sphere of influence in the Western Hemisphere in what is now known as the Monroe Doctrine. Woodrow Wilson enunciated the Fourteen Points and Franklin Roosevelt the Four Freedoms statement as well as the Atlantic Charter (which was also an executive agreement). Many presidential statements have become guiding policies, sometimes because they were supported by Congress and the nation, but sometimes because they occurred at critical periods when

Congress could not act to consider the President's action and citizens had little choice but to accept an accomplished fact or to repudiate their principal spokesman in the international arena.

The limits of expanded powers. While the President has gained great powers, a word of caution must be inserted. In a democracy, power is never absolute. In a continuing political process, actors are likely to meet each other more than once. Franklin Roosevelt created deep congressional enmities by the destroyer-base executive agreement, enmities that were permanent and showed up in other connections over the years. Some of President Truman's advisers may have concluded in the late 1940s that he could and perhaps should intervene in the Chinese civil war by sending United States troops, but that neither Congress nor the people were ready to support the full-scale military effort required. President Eisenhower perhaps reached the same conclusion in respect to Indochina in 1954. Presidents before Franklin Roosevelt may have seriously considered recognizing the Soviet Union, but they must have concluded that the political costs would be too great.

In situations where the exercise of great powers is contingent on political support, as in a democracy, such powers may be effectively limited by the political process, even though the formal powers seem unchecked.

The Foreign Policy Functions of Congress. The powers of the two houses are not equal. The special function of the Senate in foreign affairs adds to the status of its members and they jealously protect this special function.

The foreign policy functions of the Senate. The treaty power of the Senate is less important today than it was during the nation's isolationist period, when it seemed to be of towering significance because one-third plus one member of the Senate could veto presidential proposals for new policies through treaties. This change has resulted in some shift of power from the Senate to the House of Representatives, since the important foreign policy issues now are the trade policy acts and the appropriations measures.

Yet senators have not surrendered their high status in foreign policy affairs. They like to emphasize their role as statesmen. They are aided in this by the privilege of unlimited debate, a Senate history of prominence in foreign policy areas, and the advantage each member has in being 1 man in 100 rather than 1 in 435. Senators are also more likely than House members to reflect the viewpoints of the dominant political ideology (see Chapter 14).

The Senate confirmation requirement for ambassadors, ministers, consuls, and high-ranking State Department nominees also gives the senators a special opportunity to dramatize opinions and thereby sometimes influence presidential policy direction (a point exploited as the theme of a novel).[5] Senator Joseph R. McCarthy, at the height of his Communist-

[5] Allen Drury, *Advise and Consent,* Doubleday & Company, Inc., Garden City, N.Y., 1959.

hunting days, succeeded in having at least one presidential nominee rejected. While he later failed in respect to President Eisenhower's nomination of Charles Bohlen as Ambassador to the Soviet Union, it was reported after the battle that the Senate majority leader, Robert A. Taft, told the President, "No more Bohlens." Democrats, in control of the Senate during most of the Eisenhower administration, succeeded in embarrassing the President by showing that in one case, the businessman he had nominated to represent us in an Asian nation did not know the name of its Prime Minister; in another case, the nominee could not explain what NATO was. The old Senate weapons still have some effectiveness.

The Senate and House compared. The continuing high status of the Senate in foreign affairs is reflected in a number of ways. Senators are more frequently chosen by the President to represent the nation at foreign conferences. (The precedent was established in 1946, when Republican and Democratic members of the Senate Foreign Relations Committee played leading roles in the Paris Peace Conference and the subsequent organization of the United Nations in San Francisco.) House members have been occasionally appointed to important posts. (One appointment to the United Nations delegation seems to have changed the congressman's subsequent voting pattern to one more friendly toward that body. The appointment thus had a highly practical purpose.)

Senate debates and votes are watched by the nation; only rarely does a House foreign policy speech attract attention. Senate investigations of foreign policy questions have generally been given wide press coverage. In the Senate, among the most prestigeful committees is the Foreign Relations Committee. In the House, a competent observer has noted how the Foreign Affairs Committee must fight for control over bills with other committees and is frequently overruled by the Appropriations Committee; hence, the committee ranks "far down the line in prestige and popularity" with House members.[6]

The Senate is often friendly to foreign-aid proposals; in the House, the meat ax is more frequently applied. House members also more frequently bottle up administration proposals and seek to bargain with the White House or State Department for changes. Riders to appropriation bills, that is, amendments not connected with the substance but which the President must accept with the bill, often originate in the House. Important House-devised qualifications—the requirement that 50 per cent of all goods shipped under the Marshall Plan be carried in United States vessels, the tariff on Danish blue cheese, the proposal that no aid be given to Communist nations, the provision for reduction in aid to Britain unless she consented to the unification of Ireland (subsequently deleted from the bill)—all brought screams of anguish from allies and the administration. Most show the ideological preferences or parochial orientation of the House members who, through an amendment, are attempting to bolster a sick industry

[6] Carroll, *op. cit.,* p. 274.

back home or to appeal to a local ethnic voting bloc. Senators who have statewide constituencies frequently prefer to be viewed as statesmen; House members often act like county courthouse politicians.

The contemporary importance of appropriations for foreign policy. The relatively greater unfriendliness of the House to foreign spending is in part caused by the position of its Appropriations Committee. In its battle to influence policy, Congress places a double hurdle on money bills. The authorization for a spending program is passed separately from the appropriation. The first is handled by the substantive committee, in this case the Senate Foreign Relations Committee and the House Foreign Affairs Committee. The appropriation bill is reported out by the respective Appropriation Committees. Thus, the amount actually appropriated may be considerably less than that authorized; frequently, this is the case in respect to foreign aid. The Senate Foreign Relations Committee has such high status that its recommendations for authorized expenditures are frequently followed at the appropriations stage. Several of its members serve on the Appropriations Committee, which is not true of their counterparts in the House. In the House, a bipartisan coalition frequently cuts deeply into the foreign-aid bill. The strength of the House Appropriations Committee derives from two factors: (1) It has almost complete power over appropriations for projects desired in individual congressional districts, and congressmen do not antagonize its members lightly; and (2) the Senate representatives in any conference committee usually increase the House figure somewhat. Thus, House members who are favorable to greater spending can argue that the House figure will be increased in conference committee.

An additional check on the Chief Executive's handling of foreign policy is the generally adhered to requirement that foreign-aid appropriations be for only one fiscal year, thus necessitating an annual review.

Congress and the foreign policy bureaucracy. Congress has sometimes used its power to set up or revise executive agencies in order to influence foreign policy direction. To get a bill out of the Ways and Means Committee in 1953, the Eisenhower administration had to agree to raising the number of members of the bipartisan Tariff Commission from six to seven members. Committee members reasoned that the extra member, giving a majority to their party, would be likely to reflect their protectionist views.[7] The power to revise and eliminate agencies is a standby power that Congress may use in order to bargain or to cripple a program.

Congress as a policy initiator. In general, Congress sits as a critic of administration policy. Its questions of administrative leaders during hearings do not generally probe to determine alternative policies, but rather seek to make the administrator justify the policy he is proposing. The process has much in common with a father who is critically quizzing a daughter on the merits of a new boy friend without having an alternative swain to suggest or sponsor.

[7] *Ibid.*, pp. 52–53.

On a few occasions and about a few matters, Congress does express a policy preference. This is most frequently done by resolution in one house or by concurrent resolution. Such resolutions do not have the force or effect of law; on the other hand, they have the advantage of not being subject to veto. They are a means of attracting attention and giving prestige to a policy position. Thus Congressman (and shortly after, Senator) William Fulbright's resolution made during World War II that the United States join an international organization in the postwar period attracted widespread attention and served notice that Congress was not inclined once more to follow the path of isolationism charted after Woodrow Wilson's League of Nations plan was rejected in 1919.

The principal area in which Congress has succeeded in setting policy over the objection of all Presidents is citizenship requirements and immigration. The McCarran-Walter Act was passed over President Truman's veto and survived President Eisenhower's suggestion that it be revised. Presidents have been partially successful in urging a "borrowing" against future immigration quotas after such events as the Hungarian revolt or in order to ease the problems of displaced persons, but not in changing the basic principle of immigration quotas based on ethnic and racial origins. As indicated in a case study of the repeal of the Chinese Exclusion Act (Chapter 15), such a standard has been a constant source of embarrassment to executive officials dealing with representatives of the nonwhite nations of the world.

The frustrating role of Congress. When the record on foreign policy making is reviewed, the role of congressmen stands out as a frustrating one. The President and the executive departments are the major source of congressional information. (The story is often retold of the isolationist member of the Senate Foreign Relations Committee who in 1939 publicly announced to President Roosevelt that his private overseas sources of information had assured him that a European war would not break out that year.) If the President refuses to give information or indicates he must withhold it for security reasons, congressmen have little recourse but to accept his decision.

The position of congressmen is even more frustrating because of their suspicion, often correct, that the United States is already committed to a course of action before their aid is sought. As Abraham Lincoln learned when, as a congressman, he opposed President Polk's war with Mexico, a congressman cannot repudiate the President's policy without repudiating the nation in the eyes of the world.

Congress, also, is never sure how the money it appropriates for foreign policy matters is being spent. Otto Passman, chairman of a House appropriations subcommittee during the early years of the Kennedy administration, openly lamented that he could not get an itemized account from the State Department in the same way he could from the managers of his business enterprises back home in Monroe, Louisiana. Firsthand knowledge is harder to come by than it is in domestic program areas, and somehow the suggestion that waste and scandals are being engineered by "ugly

Americans" overseas is much more easily believed. Added to this is a distrust of the President, even when he is of the same party. The fear is ever present that he is trying to bypass Congress, to co-opt it to support his views without giving any real consultation or consideration to its views and that, through his prestige, party position and patronage, he is manipulating enough members to buy support for his position rather than winning converts through reasoning.

Finally, the congressman must be concerned about the impingement of foreign policy decisions upon specific interests in his home district and potential opponents who will charge him with "squandering money abroad while he does nothing for us back home." In 1952, the Democratic chairman of the Senate Foreign Relations Committee, who generally gave strong support to the President, repudiated Truman's foreign-aid proposals in part, it was said, because of the anticipated tactics of the strong opponent who was preparing to run against him in his home state at the next election.

A mood of negativism often pervades Congress as it joins the President in fashioning foreign policy. The Constitution outlines its role and gives it some powers that can be used to ensure its position of influence. Yet Congress cannot, except in rare instances, make policy. The situational requirements and the powers held by the President give him the central position, and he may, if he wishes to suffer the political costs, almost go it alone without Congress.[8] Thus Congress is like the wealthy woman with a young suitor. She constantly fears that he loves her for her money rather than for herself alone; but at the same time, she is afraid he may be thinking of leaving her.

A Word about the Courts. The Supreme Court, through its power of judicial review, can restrain, at least temporarily, both Congress and the President. In practice, the Court has generally taken the position that those who conduct foreign policy must have the power to do what must be done to preserve the nation—the first law is the survival of the state. Thus some of the activities of Abraham Lincoln in the early days of the Civil War were upheld or overruled on technical grounds only after the conflict. In the same way, the Court upheld President Roosevelt's order to remove Japanese citizens from their West Coast homes during World War II and place them in detention camps. (Two justices, a liberal and a conservative, vigorously dissented.) A most significant explanation of the Court's position was given in the Curtiss-Wright case.[9] The justices held that in foreign affairs the President has "a degree of discretion and freedom from statutory restriction which would not be admissible were domestic affairs alone involved."

The Court in a 1920 case, *Missouri v. Holland,* overruled a Missouri law

[8] This section is based partly on Richard C. Snyder and Edgar S. Furniss, Jr., *American Foreign Policy,* Holt, Rinehart and Winston, Inc., New York, 1954, pp. 439–456.

[9] *United States v. Curtiss-Wright Export Corporation,* 299 U.S. 304 (1936).

on duck hunting because the nation had agreed to a different set of regulations in a treaty with Canada. There has been considerable speculation over the possibility of actually applying the provisions of some of the postwar treaties accepted or proposed (such as the United Nations Declaration of Human Rights). They might overrule some state actions, particularly laws enforcing racial discrimination. Many of these acts are now being overruled on constitutional grounds, and so the flurry of excitement has now subsided concerning the treaty-making power and the power to make executive agreements that came to a head in the proposed Bricker amendment during the early days of the Eisenhower administration. The proposal would have required treaties to be implemented by legislation. Another provision, requiring that all treaties be consistent with the Constitution, was subsequently affirmed by the Supreme Court in *Reid v. Covert.*

Potentially the Court can affect foreign policy in important ways. The justices, however, seem reluctant to do so lest they tie the President's, and hence the nation's, hands in the complicated and dangerous road we must travel in the future.

ORGANIZATION FOR POLICY ADMINISTRATION

The executive departments help the President administer policy but, as students of bureaucracy are aware, these agencies also come to have points of view and purposes of their own independent of the President or Congress. Each of the major agencies on which the President depends for advice and aid in formulating foreign policy has its distinctive style of thinking and action. Foreign policy is, to a great degree, the blending of the viewpoints of the State Department, the Defense Department, the American delegation and staff at the United Nations, and such specialists as the presidential advisers on science and space technology. In addition, as many as fifteen other agencies, Departments of the Treasury, Commerce, and Agriculture, for example, have staffs permanently located abroad and so have an interest in some aspects of our nation's international policies. Still other agencies may become involved, since at any moment, what has generally been considered a domestic matter may become a foreign policy matter. The treaty mentioned previously that abridged the rights of the states to have open duck season on birds that migrated from Canada to the United States is a case in point.

To blend the viewpoints of the Presidency and Congress and to take into account the many agencies that from time to time are interested in particular policies requires additional aid for the President. The White House staff has at times served to coordinate activities and produce new policy innovations. A President may turn for help to someone officially unconnected with government, as President Wilson did in the case of Colonel House. The major coordinating agency is the National Security Council, on which sit representatives of the military, the State Department, and other agencies, including the Budget Bureau. The latter organization can particularly help achieve a degree of policy consistency through its handling of budgetary requests of individual agencies. (See Chapter 16.)

All government agencies are important in the devising and carrying out of foreign policy. The organizational framework of the national government tells a great deal about the kinds of help the President will be offered and the ways decisions will be shaped.

The Department of State. The department responsible for most foreign policy matters has a rather nondescript title. In most nations, it is known as a ministry of foreign affairs, or something on that order. The term Department of State was adopted in the United States a few years after the Constitution went into effect when the Department was given the task of keeping all official records, foreign and domestic. The Department no longer keeps all such records, but it still has some duties relative to domestic affairs.

Selection of the Secretary. In 1912, President Woodrow Wilson shocked some political observers by appointing an old Democratic wheel horse, William Jennings Bryan, as Secretary of State. Bryan, however, was in a position to claim some high reward, and the post was the most prestigeful one in the Cabinet. He had ensured the President's nomination at the Democratic National Convention in Baltimore by switching his considerable party following into the Wilson column. The result was that foreign policy was conducted by one who considered himself, with some justification, the real leader of the Democratic party, while the President was a Johnny-come-lately. The appointment also meant that the President's principal adviser was a man whose personal inclinations were strongly pacifist and isolationist. Wilson was never able to meet the delicate political task of reconciling the differences in viewpoint between Bryan and himself, and in time the Secretary resigned.

Often the requirements of domestic politics require such arrangements, sometimes for long periods, during times of great foreign policy decisions. In Wilson's case, however, Bryan resigned within three years. Franklin Roosevelt seems to have selected Cordell Hull as his Secretary of State because of his high prestige in Congress, where he had served for many years. Roosevelt was later unwilling to pay the political price of replacing the Secretary and equally unwilling to trust his judgment, except on reciprocal-trade policy. Thus, the President developed a number of techniques for bypassing his Secretary, such as working through his undersecretary, Sumner Welles (Hull finally insisted that he be dismissed), working through special presidential aides such as Harry Hopkins, or dealing directly with the heads of foreign nations himself. The Secretary did not even attend all of the wartime conferences with leaders of the Allies. The pretext was that the subjects discussed concerned exclusively military matters.

There are several alternative relationships possible. A President may dismiss a Secretary he considers to be acting without sufficient consultation as Harry Truman did in the case of James Byrnes. A President may also, in effect, abdicate his responsibilities and permit the Secretary to make foreign policy. This was largely the case when Charles Evans Hughes served Warren Harding and when John Foster Dulles served Dwight Eisenhower.

The theoretically ideal arrangement, of course, is when the Secretary has the President's complete confidence. He then, in effect, becomes an extension of the President himself, exercising powers in harmony with the President's wishes. Such relationships have occurred, but a decentralized political system such as ours does not guarantee them.

The Secretary and the Department. The Secretary of State has duties other than advising the President on high policy. He must also supervise the day-to-day transactions handled by a department of approximately 13,000 American citizens and 10,000 hired foreign nationals. Secretaries are almost always at a disadvantage in facing this task. Their average tenure is only about two to three years. In some respects, the Department is more bureaucratically rigid than most. It has set procedures, and the viewpoints of its personnel do not easily change. It also conducts a mammoth amount of business. Every day, the Department's cable traffic alone exceeds the output of the Washington bureaus of the major news services. Every day, it is concerned with American representation in an average of fifteen international meetings and with its membership in over 400 official international organizations. Every day, dozens of incidents, major and minor, are reported from its 300 offices abroad and at home. To many of these, the State Department must make some official response: It may be to a foreign nation wishing to have one of its dignitaries officially invited to the United States. It may be in answer to a church group demanding more protection for its missionaries abroad. It may be in response to a new Soviet threat in Berlin.

Departmental personnel frequently make direct requests for action. For example, in 1950, our Ambassador to Chile dispatched a cable to Washington; it was passed on by the State Department to the House Ways and Means Committee and later found its way into a printed report: "Chile is very interested in copper tax. Please impress on Congress that this is not the time to slap a friendly democratic country and intensify its economic crises, especially when we have to look to that country for copper in the event of a major war."

Mastering an organization of such complexity is not an easy task for a beginner. Perhaps that is why Presidents in the years since World War II have increasingly selected men who have had some experience in the lower echelons of the State Department. Men such as Acheson, Dulles, Herter, and Rusk were a departure from the policy of appointment to pay off political debts. They suggest the postwar tendency to develop a professional cadre to head the Department.

Internal organization and policy making. Like all bureaucracies, the State Department is designed so that some matters will be handled in routine fashion at the lower levels, while others are handled at higher levels of the hierarchy. The subject matter with which the Department deals, however, encourages two conflicts within its internal organization. One is the conflict between those stationed in Washington and those stationed abroad; the other is between national and functional specialists.

Until quite recently, the division between foreign- and domestic-based personnel was encouraged. There were two types of employees with separate pay scales, qualifications, and benefit systems. Most American overseas were Foreign Service officers, while most of those in Washington were under civil service. Following the implementation of the Wriston committee study in 1954, there has been a gradual merger of these two groups into one service and a greater rotation of personnel between service at home and abroad.

Foreign policy lends itself to specialization in the affairs of a particular nation. This provides for some advantages, but its disadvantages are to be found in a restricted outlook. For this reason, functional agencies that cut across the affairs of many nations have been established: Economic Affairs, Cultural Affairs, Intelligence and Research, and others. The Hoover Commission in 1949 investigated the conflicts between functional and geographic entities within the department and concluded that action decisions should be made by the "national desk" (which usually refers to many rooms of desks devoted to a particular nation). Functional agencies, it said, should provide information and advice. This division of responsibility was formally accepted, but is not always strictly followed.

The State Department and the public. The Department has a great handicap in its public relations because it has no clientele group that it can depend upon for domestic political support, as do the Departments of Commerce, Agriculture, and Labor. It has the added handicap of having to deal with foreigners, often with exaggerated respect. The Department's necessary emphasis on protocol annoys those committed to the ideology of small-town America, where isolationism has had its strongest support.

Henry Wriston, a university president and State Department consultant, describes an experience that occurred as he was leaning out of his office window on a hot summer day in 1920:[10]

> A "rubberneck wagon" was passing and the guide was addressing his captives through a megaphone: "On your right is the State, War, and Navy Building. It has eight miles of marble corridors. Here Uncle Sam supports thousands of people in ease, idleness, and luxury. On your left—" I have never since heard so graphic a description of the popular image of the Department.

The importance of the Department's public relations was most dramatically illustrated by the widespread public acceptance of many of the most

[10] Don K. Price (ed.), *The Secretary of State,* Prentice-Hall, Inc., Englewood Cliffs, N.J., 1961, p. 76.

unrealistic of Senator Joseph McCarthy's attacks against the Department in the early 1950s, a period that its personnel refer to as "the terror."

Some positive steps have been taken to change the departmental image. After World War II, it moved to a new building located in what was once a swamp known as Foggy Bottom. The Department has stepped up its recruitment program for the Foreign Service so that the 250 new officers it recruits annually from the nation's colleges and universities are among the most intelligent graduates. Presidents have also tried to build up the Department from its decline under Franklin Roosevelt, who often confided to his intimates that the Foreign Service was too rigid in its outlook to be trusted with a truly imaginative program. The foreign-aid program, which was once independent of the Department, is now executed by one of its agencies, though it continues to enjoy semiautonomous status.

Presidents have also shown an inclination in the postwar period to recruit Foreign Service career officers for ambassadorial posts (Charles Bohlen and George Kennan, Ambassadors to the Soviet Union, are recent examples). The most important posts are generally beyond their means, however, since Congress has set expense accounts and salaries so low that only the wealthy can afford to represent the United States in the nations of Western Europe, where an embassy is expected to be a social as well as a diplomatic center. These posts are still generally given as rewards to large contributors in presidential campaigns. Many such "civilian" appointments have had the effect of "shaking up" Department personnel (as was demonstrated in the Irving Berlin musical *Call Me Madam*, based on the career of Washington socialite Perle Mesta), but a few have bordered on becoming minor disasters.

While the importance of the State Department appears to be rising, its influence in foreign affairs, both in formulation and execution of policy, will probably never again be as great as it was during the period of isolationism when issues of foreign policy were not usually central. While the principal representative from the Department in each nation is designated as the chief of all United States personnel within that nation, he must more often negotiate than issue orders in dealing with representatives of other United States agencies.

The Defense Department and Foreign Policy. As generals and admirals are fond of saying, their role in United States policy has afforded either feast or famine. At present, it provides a feast, both in terms of material property and status. A college seeking to enhance its reputation selects a career general for its head. Industry combs through the services for officers it can lure away. The President selects high officers for important nonmilitary assignments. Voters elect them to Congress and to the Presidency itself. While in the past, the nation has starved the military and put it in cold storage between wars, military expenditures in recent years have accounted for the greatest share of a huge national budget.

The "military mind." Some Americans have viewed the current prominence of the military as an ominous sign for a democracy. They argue that civilians should always dominate the military. Their objection to military influence is that the military is dedicated to procedure and form more than most bureaucracies are. There is a special uniform, a strict division of duties and privileges between a leadership elite and a nonofficer mass, and a code that discourages internal criticism. Added to this is a dedication to the values of security and order over other values, a tendency that makes its response to social change rigid and authoritarian. While some military personnel quite readily fit this stereotype, many do not—at least, not when they enter into civilian roles.

Countervailing forces. For most of our history, American foreign policy seemed to include an assumption that military implications were irrelevant. Today, policy makers believe that a military point of view must be considered if rational policy is to be formed, even though military values may ultimately be partly sacrificed to achieve other ends. The danger signal for a democracy is heard, they believe, not when military men have influence, but rather when all matters of foreign policy are decided purely in terms of military values. Then the "garrison state," of which the political scientist Harold Lasswell has warned, is at hand. To assume that a specialist in one area is a specialist in all fields is the fallacy upon which military oligarchy is based. In times of war, or perhaps even more during the nerve-racking years of cold war, the temptation has been to think only in military terms.

One of the countervailing forces limiting military influence is the rivalry between bureaucracies that is built into the military organizational structure; despite the integration of the separate services into one Department of Defense following World War II, there is still a considerable amount of interservice competition. Disagreements exist over the value of different types of weapons, and jurisdictional disputes accompany the development of almost every new aircraft, rocket, gun, or missile. Each service is represented on the Joint Chiefs of Staff, a staff agency designed to plan broad strategy. The position of chairman of the Joint Chiefs of Staff is rotated among the services. The very method by which the chairman is selected is indicative of the fact that the services are not fully integrated. Another indication lies in the fact that, while the Department has a Secretary, the civilian heads of the Air Force, Army, and Navy are also Secretaries.

Ambassador to the United Nations. This post was given Cabinet status in order to emphasize its importance. The President personally selects the head of our delegation and meets with him frequently in order to discuss United States policy in that body. Like the Secretary of State, he is an emissary rather than a free agent, and thus must work in close harmony with the President. The increased status of the position encourages a degree of independence from the Secretary of State.

Coordination of Foreign Policy: The National Security Council. The State Department is often poorly equipped politically to coordinate foreign policy when basic interests of other government agencies are at stake. Its officers are not always successful in persuading the President and Congress to accept their viewpoint. The Maritime Commission once successfully defied a State Department order to transfer certain vessels to foreign nations. Congress backed the Maritime Commission and criticized the Department for "interfering" in the operation of an "independent" commission.

In the past, matters of dispute have been negotiated between the State Department and other agencies through a network of interdepartmental committees. The Kennedy administration scrapped many such bodies as a waste of time, though a few that had demonstrated their usefulness were retained. These have generally been bodies having the confidence of Congress, well-established policies, and an experienced secretariat.

The principal overall coordinating body for foreign policy is the National Security Council, formed in 1947. Its members are the President and Vice President and the Secretaries of Defense and State. The President may invite other persons to attend on a regular basis. The Central Intelligence Agency reports to this body.

The National Security Council, under our system of government, cannot be a decision-making body similar to the British War Cabinet. It can be only advisory to the President, who by himself makes the final decision. On the other hand, it has proven useful in two respects. It provides the President with a regularly scheduled meeting of his principal foreign policy advisers, and it has led to some degree of coordination in administration, as well as to a regular exchange of viewpoints among the principal foreign policy agencies. But the National Security Council, like the Cabinet, is only as useful as the President wishes to make it. In recent years, Presidents have added members or invited them to specific meetings on an informal basis, thus adding to the Council's flexibility.

THE SYSTEM OF POLICY CONSENSUS

The American People and Foreign Policy. Citizen opinion about foreign policy matters is generally vague and uninformed. Interest of most citizens is low, except when they are directly affected, as in losses of friends or relatives in combat. Gabriel Almond has called public opinion on foreign policy a "mood—a superficial and fluctuating response." Public-opinion surveys have indicated great lack of knowledge; 30 per cent of the population is totally unaware of most foreign policy issues. A *New York Times* survey published in 1959 found that at the height of the Berlin crisis, 40 per cent of a representative sample of citizens did not know that West Berlin was an enclave surrounded by Communist territory.

Despite this vagueness, the opinions of ordinary citizens do provide foreign policy guidelines on the basis of expectations, rather than specific instructions to the national leadership. Public attitudes and values tend to rule out some alternatives, serve as a general direction setter, and finally, as a court of last resort. President Franklin Roosevelt recognized this when he retreated quickly from the position of his 1937 Chicago speech to "quarantine the aggressor nations." Like many presidential leaders, he assumed that he must shape public opinion, but could not get too far ahead of it. New directions are shaped by events such as the Pearl Harbor bombing or the Soviet subversion of Czechoslovakia.

The Informal Minority. Perhaps 10 per cent of the public follows foreign policy closely. These are the opinion leaders or attentive publics—either self-selected or leaders because of position. The latter group includes people in the news media and the heads of some organized interest groups. The conclusions and, perhaps more precisely, the attitudes of these leaders are transmitted in simplified form to the ordinary citizens whose confidence they hold.

There are a very few organized interest groups that follow changes in foreign policy making. They include civic groups such as the Foreign Policy Association and the League of Women Voters, other organizations interested in broad economy and lower taxes, and such specialized economic interest groups as the petroleum industry, manufacturers affected by tariffs, and agricultural producers. Even the latter are more likely to be interested in foreign policy intermittently than on a day-to-day basis. Occasionally, religious and ethnic groups exert pressures on particular decisions. Many American Jews have been concerned about policy toward Israel and its neighbors. Polish-American groups have sought to influence policy relative to Communist Poland.

Governmental Decision Makers. In general, the major interest groupings concerned with shaping foreign policy are within the government itself, and these tend to be interests based on ideological viewpoints and considerations related to agency power and status. The average congressman or senator is generally free to vote according to his conscience on foreign policy matters, except where a local industry or nationality group is involved. Government agencies also seek to protect their clientele industries, but the major executive agencies that follow foreign policy making are interested in terms of preservation of agency influence and buttressing a particular point of view.

The picture is not one, furthermore, of a monolithic executive department, united within itself and facing an equally united Congress. Alliances cut across both branches of government. Some congressmen support the military as strongly as does the civilian head of the Defense Department, while other congressmen are committed to an emphasis upon foreign economic aid. In the same way, executive agencies sometimes "leak" information to Congress or the press in hopes of stirring up opposition to other agencies in the executive branch that seem to be winning a particular policy struggle. Neither the agencies and personnel making up the State Department nor those of the Defense Department are united internally on all issues.

Consensus Building. Under these confused conditions, foreign policy on a particular subject is discussed by those who feel they have a direct interest and want to act. From the discussion swirling back and forth across Congress and the bureaucracy, a foreign policy consensus sometimes results. In the final showdown on any issue, the decision is influenced most by the agency having the necessary political power to bear in the right place at the right time, but often the two major institutions having such power, the Presidency and the congressional leadership, agree.

Sometimes a lesser official holds the power. After the German dirigible *Hindenburg* exploded in 1937, the Secretary of the Interior, Harold Ickes, acting unilaterally, continued to refuse to permit nonexplosive helium to be shipped to Germany. Under existing law, he had exclusive control over export permits. (Ickes claimed the Nazi leaders of Germany would divert the use of the helium to military purposes—although he could easily have restricted the export permits to the amount of helium needed by commercial dirigibles.) The political costs of dismissing the Secretary were greater in the eyes of the President than were those of permitting him to make this decision. Congress, likewise, was unwilling or unable to take this power from him.

Thus, it is not always possible to determine upon what political power a minor decision will hinge if the process of consensus building fails to persuade all the participants. It is safe to assume that the President will in most major cases prevail or that he will be able to at least prevent anyone else from taking positive action. Congress will usually be unable to withstand the President's pressure if he is backed by an aroused public, but in many matters where citizen opinion is not clearly formed, it will be able to stalemate presidential policy or at least cripple it, should it choose to do so.

Foreign policy making differs from domestic policy making principally in the lack of continuing interest and necessary information on the part of ordinary citizens and many of the most highly organized interests. This tends to limit participants to those within the government—to leaders who are concerned to a much greater degree than the citizen is. The value of the system is that foreign policy is generally the result of a consensus from among many informed viewpoints. Its danger exists in potential stalemate at a critical juncture; more precisely, at a critical period when the international situation is superficially and deceptively calm.[11]

[11] The analysis in this section is based in part on Roger Hilsman, Jr., "Congressional-Executive Relations and Foreign Policy Consensus," *American Political Science Review*, 52:725–744, September, 1958.

SELECTED BIBLIOGRAPHY

The discussion of grand strategies of foreign policy has occupied many political scientists who, in their own youth, lived through the period of isolationism and the approach of war with Germany and Japan. A book revealing the illusions of isolationism and signaling a new American realism is that of Kennan [23]. The same realistic appraisal of American interest in shaping foreign policy is found in Morgenthau, one of whose several important works is listed here [32]. Lasswell [25], in his formulation of the garrison state resulting from a period of prolonged crisis, also takes this approach, as does the study of foreign and military policy in the world of nuclear powers by Kissinger [24]. Each of these books has had an impact on the shaping of American policy. Another work featuring the idealism common to American foreign policy thinking is that of Rostow [37], who argues that an American definition of the national interest must be based on humanistic values as well as considerations of security.

A number of scholars have concentrated on studies of how American foreign policy is in fact made and administered. A general framework is proposed by Snyder, Bruck, and Sapin [41]. The authors of this text found Almond [1] and Hilsman [18] especially useful. A work that is supplementary to Almond's on the role of the public in democratic policy making is by Rosenau [36]. Among the studies of the congressional role in foreign policy making, that of Carroll [4] is thorough in examining each standing committee involved, and that of Dahl [5] is particularly insightful as to the pressures that converge on a legislator and affect the way he views the facts and theories of foreign policy making. Other useful studies on the congressional role are by Farnsworth [7], Grassmuck [15], and Robinson [34].

The role of the State Department and the Secretary of State has received greater attention as the department has attempted to recapture its preeminent role. Macmahon [27] and McCamy [29] are standard works, although somewhat outdated. Elder [6] offers a more recent study. Price [33] has edited a series of incisive essays on the subject. Graebner [14] provides a selection of historical studies of the Secretaries of State in the twentieth century through John Foster Dulles.

Perhaps because of the concept of the garrison state, increasing emphasis has been given in recent years to the military and to the effect of the military mind on democratic policy making. See the materials in Furniss [10], Huntington [19, 20], Janowitz [22], and Sapin and Snyder [38]. The last listed is paperbound and, while older, is still an excellent introduction to the subject. There is also a collection of essays by political scientists whose viewpoints range from emphasis on preparedness to pacifism [11].

The collection of essays by Rosenau [35] emphasizes decision-making studies using the empirical approach. Those of Goldwin and Stourzh [12] and Jacobson [21] are concerned with the kinds of policy being made. The University of Tennessee collection [43] is a reassessment by academics and practitioners. For collections on specific problems, see Goldwin [11, 13]. On the role of the new nations of the world, see Silvert [40].

World Politics, published quarterly by the Institute of International Affairs, emphasizes empirical studies of decision making and the theory of decision making. *Foreign Affairs,* published quarterly by the Council of Foreign Affairs, places emphasis on policy content. Other useful publications are *Foreign Policy Reports,* also published by the Foreign Policy Association on a biweekly basis, the weekly *Department of State Bulletin,* and the *United Nations Bulletin,* published every two weeks by the United Nations Department of Public Information.

Public Policy

1. Almond, Gabriel A.: *The American People and Foreign Policy,* Frederick A. Praeger, Inc., New York, 1961. Originally published in 1950.
2. Bloomfield, Lincoln P.: *The United Nations and U.S. Foreign Policy,* Little, Brown and Company, Boston, 1960.
3. Carleton, William G.: *Revolution in American Foreign Policy,* Random House, Inc., New York, 1961.
4. Carroll, Holbert N.: *The House of Representatives and Foreign Affairs,* The University of Pittsburgh Press, Pittsburgh, Pa., 1958.
5. Dahl, Robert A.: *Congress and Foreign Policy,* Harcourt, Brace & World, Inc., New York, 1950. (Also available in paperback, W. W. Norton & Company, Inc., New York, 1964.)
6. Elder, Robert E.: *The Policy Machine: The Department of State and American Foreign Policy,* Syracuse University Press, Syracuse, N.Y., 1960.
7. Farnsworth, David N.: *The Senate Committee on Foreign Relations,* The University of Illinois Press, Urbana, Ill., 1961.
8. Finletter, Thomas E.: *Foreign Policy: The Next Phase,* Harper & Row, Publishers, New York, 1958.
9. Fosdick, Dorothy: *Common Sense and World Affairs,* Harcourt, Brace & World, Inc., New York, 1955.
10. Furniss, Edgar S., Jr. (ed.): *American Military Policy,* Holt, Rinehart and Winston, Inc., New York, 1957.
11. Goldwin, Robert A. (ed.): *America Armed: Essays on United States Military Policy,* Rand McNally & Company, Chicago, 1961.
12. Goldwin, Robert A., and Gerald Stourzh (eds.): *Readings in American Foreign Policy,* Oxford University Press, Fair Lawn, N.J., 1959.
13. Goldwin, Robert A. (ed.): *Why Foreign Aid? Two Messages by President Kennedy and Essays,* Rand McNally & Company, Chicago, 1962.
14. Graebner, Norman A. (ed.): *An Uncertain Tradition,* McGraw-Hill Book Company, New York, 1961.
15. Grassmuck, George L.: *Sectional Biases in Congress on Foreign Policy,* The Johns Hopkins Press, Baltimore, 1952.
16. Griswold, A. Whitney: *The Far Eastern Policy of the United States,* Yale University Press, New Haven, Conn., 1963 (paperback).
17. Hauser, Philip M. (ed.): *Population and World Politics,* The Free Press of Glencoe, New York, 1958.
18. Hilsman, Roger, Jr.: "Congressional-Executive Relations and the Foreign Policy Consensus," *American Political Science Review,* 52:725–744, September, 1958.
19. Huntington, Samuel P.: *The Soldier and the State,* Harvard University Press, Cambridge, Mass., 1957.
20. Huntington, Samuel P. (ed.): *Changing Patterns of Military Politics,* vol. III, The International Yearbook of Political Behavior Research, The Free Press of Glencoe, New York, 1962.
21. Jacobson, Harold K. (ed.): *America's Foreign Policy,* Random House, Inc., New York, 1960.
22. Janowitz, Morris: *The Professional Soldier: A Social and Political Portrait,* The Free Press of Glencoe, New York, 1960.
23. Kennan, George F.: *American Diplomacy: 1900–1950,* The University of Chicago Press, Chicago, 1951.
24. Kissinger, Henry: *Nuclear Weapons and Foreign Policy,* Anchor Books and Anchor Science Study Series, Doubleday & Company, Garden City, N.Y., 1960.
25. Lasswell, Harold D.: *National Security and Individual Freedom,* McGraw-Hill Book Company, New York, 1950.
26. Lerche, Charles O., Jr.: *America in World Affairs,* McGraw-Hill Book Company, New York, 1963.

27. Macmahon, Arthur W.: *Administration in Foreign Affairs,* University of Alabama Press, University, Ala., 1953.
28. Marshall, Charles B.: *The Limits of Foreign Policy,* Holt, Rinehart and Winston, Inc., New York, 1954.
29. McCamy, James L.: *The Administration of American Foreign Affairs,* Alfred A. Knopf, Inc., New York, 1950.
30. McClelland, Charles A.: *Nuclear Weapons, Missiles and Future War: A Problem for the Sixties,* Chandler Publishing Company, San Francisco, Calif., 1960.
31. Morgenstern, Oskar: *The Question of National Defense,* 2d ed., Vintage Books, Random House, Inc., New York, 1961.
32. Morgenthau, Hans J.: *Politics among Nations: The Struggle for Power and Peace,* 3d ed., Alfred A. Knopf, Inc., New York, 1960.
33. Price, Don K. (ed.): *The Secretary of State,* Prentice-Hall, Inc., Englewood Cliffs, N.J., 1961.
34. Robinson, James A.: *Congress and Foreign Policy,* The Dorsey Press, Homewood, Ill., 1962.
35. Rosenau, James N. (ed.): *International Politics and Foreign Policy,* The Free Press of Glencoe, New York, 1961.
36. Rosenau, James N.: *Public Opinion and Foreign Policy,* Random House, Inc., New York, 1961.
37. Rostow, W. W.: *The United States in the World Arena,* Harper & Row, Publishers, New York, 1960.
38. Sapin, Burton M., and Richard C. Snyder: *The Role of the Military in American Foreign Policy,* Doubleday & Company, Inc., Garden City, N.Y., 1954.
39. Schelling, Thomas C.: *The Strategy of Conflict,* Harvard University Press, Cambridge, Mass., 1960.
40. Silvert, K. H. (ed.): *Expectant Peoples, Nationalism and Development,* Random House, Inc., New York, 1963.
41. Snyder, Richard C., H. W. Bruck, and Burton Sapin (eds.): *Foreign Policy Decision Making: An Approach to the Study of International Politics,* The Free Press of Glencoe, New York, 1962.
42. Spanier, John W.: *American Foreign Policy since World War II,* Frederick A. Praeger, Inc., New York, 1961.
43. University of Tennessee, Department of Political Science: *Government and World Crisis: A Symposium,* Knoxville, 1962.
44. Vandenbosch, Amry, and Willard N. Hogan: *Toward World Order,* McGraw-Hill Book Company, New York, 1963.
45. Westerfield, Bradford W.: *Foreign Policy and Party Politics,* Yale University Press, New Haven, Conn., 1955.

Law Cases

Hirabayashi v. United States, 320 U.S. 81 (1943).
Korematsu v. United States, 323 U.S. 214 (1944).
Missouri v. Holland, 252 U.S. 416 (1920).
Reid v. Covert, 354 U.S. 1 (1957).
United States v. Curtiss-Wright Export Corporation, 299 U.S. 304 (1936).

Case Study Materials

1. Cohen, Bernard C.: *The Political Process and Foreign Policy: The Making of the Japanese Peace Settlement,* Princeton University Press, Princeton, N.J., 1957.
2. Rovere, Richard H., and Arthur M. Schlesinger, Jr.: *The General and the President,* Farrar, Straus & Cudahy, New York, 1951.

PART

IV

CONCLUSION

What trends can be expected to influence the general character of future American public policies?

The best predictor for the future is the past. Established trends—increasing population, wealth, automation, urbanization, and leisure, for example—can be expected to continue. If they do, policy patterns of the past will probably also continue. But these patterns will fail to remove the sources of dissatisfaction of certain groups, particularly those who are unable to earn an adequate living, racial minorities, marginal farmers, and those committed to ideologies of the past. The imponderable is: How effectively will the discontented react in the political arena? *(Chapter 22, Ideology, Life-styles, and the Future.)*

CHAPTER

22

IDEOLOGY, LIFE-STYLES, AND THE FUTURE

This book has attempted to analyze the American political process by looking at the four I's of politics: ideas, institutions, interests, and individuals. In particular, the authors have used an analytical device through which ideologies have been interpreted as being related to (but also interacting with) life-styles and life experiences. Institutions, interests, and individual motivation have been seen as related to ideology and changing with it, although not necessarily at the same pace. Because changes in life-styles and life experiences are reflected in changes in governmental institutions, processes, and policies, it is appropriate for this last chapter to consider possible changes that can be anticipated for the future.

How will populations and living patterns change in the coming years? How will changes in the techniques of production affect life-styles? Who will be the politically discontented? Will they organize effective protest movements? Will they be responsible for a new and dominant political ideology? How will external pressures from Communist and uncommitted nations affect our domestic politics? Answers for some, but not all, of these questions can be approximated.

DIVERSITY AND POLITICS

The diversity that is America produces great differences in political patterns from one state to another and even within a given state. Diversity contributes to political conflict. Yet our shared values commit us to the preservation and advancement of our nation and its economy. We have learned how to compromise our differences and have become somewhat tolerant of those whose values and life-styles are different from our own. But we still have much to learn. We still have serious conflicts resulting from conflicting goals such as the one between those of the small-business man and those of organized labor. And there is still a broad discrepancy between some of our ideals and some of our practices, as in the case of the status of the Negro.

How can we think in terms of *the* American "political system" when there is almost no consistent national party structure in the United States? How can we fit into a single mold the vigorous two-party competition of Minnesota and the usual one-partyism of Georgia? Or the machine politics of Chicago and the bland nonpolitics of suburbia? Or the strategies of the United Automobile Workers in Michigan, which has not endorsed anyone other than a Democrat in years, and the International Longshoremen and Warehousemen's Union of Hawaii, which may endorse a candidate in any party? Or the segregationists in the Democratic party and the civil rights liberals in the same party? Or the Goldwater Republicans and the Rockefeller Republicans? Yet we must do so. For that is the way Americans have structured their political system, and that is what we are accustomed to. The future will depend upon our ability to build on the basis of such a polyglot system. Movement toward the goals that a general, dominant culture defines will be gradual. There are no simple techniques by which we may suddenly find ourselves where we wish to be. The real world is rarely the world of our dreams. The ideal is established more to be striven for than to be achieved. Easy solutions almost never are available for difficult and complex problems. The issues that plague us, the continuing areas of conflict, can be battled and nibbled away at; they cannot be eliminated overnight. This fact, well known to professional administrators, diplomats, and technicians, is a major item in distinguishing their attitudes from those of the uninformed citizen, who often wishes idly for a grand solution.

AMERICA'S ASSETS

What is it that Americans have to work with in the future? Is ours a decadent nation, unduly concerned with material comforts and no longer willing to protect the ideals that made us what we are? Possibly. It seems unlikely, but the social sciences are not yet exact enough to give a scientifically meaningful answer.

We might recall, however, that in World War I many Europeans doubted the fighting ability of the American soldier, yet our men, in the short time they were committed to battle, proved that they had as much determination to win as did any group of soldiers. In the late 1930s, the Nazi Germans believed America had become too complacent and "soft" to fight, or, at least, to fight effectively. But they were proved wrong. In Korea, the results were not as decisive, but those who would raise the old criticism would do well if they reserved their judgment. In World War I, Americans were naïve, confident, and determined to prove their abilities. In World War II, they had no doubt that their way of life was at stake. In Korea, the meaning and purpose of the fighting was never clear to the ordinary citizen, and it was not apparent that the American way of life was at stake. The few defectors in that war, however much publicized, do not necessarily demonstrate anything of importance for the future.

There is no reason to believe that Americans are not as determined as ever to defend their nation and what it stands for. Indeed, during World War II, America's allegedly "soft" citizen-soldiers fought, among other reasons, in order to preserve and return to the material luxuries that the world associates with our nation. American advertisers, fearful that the returning GI would doff his uniform and reveal new and radical wants and ideas, spent many of their wartime advertising dollars telling the members of the Armed Forces that they were fighting to come back safely to exactly what they had left. And indeed, these advertisements were well received. The young fighting man really did want to come back to apple pie and bathtubs and air conditioning and the established American way of life. All he wanted was more of what he truly believed to be its benefits.

Some critics of America, here and abroad, have warned that the fall of Rome was preceded by complacency, free handouts to the plebeians, a long history of good luck and victories over foes, and a concern for material comforts. But there is no *scientific* evidence that history does, indeed, repeat itself. As a matter of fact, historical circumstances probably never do repeat themselves in anything approximating identical terms. It is easy to argue, for example, that there are many more factors that distinguish contemporary America from mature Rome than there are factors that are analogous. Whatever the eventual fate of America, there is no convincing evidence that she has reached the top of her possibilities. The American Dream is modified from time to time, but it has never been shattered, and there is no reason to assume other than that we will continue to strive to make it a reality.[1]

Some of Our Assets. Despite hundreds of differing subcultures, despite periodic changes to adjust to a changing world, there are some characteristics of America and her citizens that endure and have endured from colonial days. These include, in particular, the concepts of fair play, generosity, and progress.

Item: The concept of fair play In 1801, Alexander Hamilton had a once-in-a-lifetime chance for revenge against his long-time enemy, Thomas Jefferson. Because of a flaw in the system provided in the original Constitution for the election of President, Jefferson, who had been selected for the White House by members of his Democratic-Republican party, finished the race with no more electoral votes than Aaron Burr, who had been intended for the vice presidency (see Chapter 4). Under provisions in the Constitution, such a deadlock is to be resolved by the House of Representatives. Hamilton, of modest beginnings, had achieved great success in the world and, like many another self-made man, tended toward the conservative views of the well-to-do: Jefferson, born an aristocrat, could afford to concern himself with the problems of the common man. Hamilton greatly disapproved of Jefferson's views ("His politics are tinctured with fanaticism"), but as the recognized head of the Federalist party, he urged his followers in the House of Representatives to vote for Jefferson instead of Burr. Hamilton apparently did not base his position on the intent of the electorate. Had

[1] The question of whether Americans can make the hard choices "wisely and maturely" is discussed in Leland Hazard, "Our National Goals: The Hard Choices," *Harvard Business Review,* 41:22ff., May-June, 1963.

he done so, he would have ensured himself a hero's role in the history books. But such a view was not consistent with his skepticism concerning the ordinary voter. However, he did resist the personal temptation for revenge and argue that it was more important to do what he regarded as the right thing by selecting the person he believed to be the more honest, more reliable man:[2]

> If there is a man in the world I ought to hate, it is Jefferson. With Burr I have always been personally well. But the public good must be paramount to every private consideration.

Jefferson was elected President, and Hamilton, who was killed in a duel with Aaron Burr a few years later, is remembered in American history, among other reasons, for having put his convictions about the welfare of the Republic above his desire for personal satisfaction.

Not all Americans, even in high places, have always behaved so nobly, of course. Some of Hamilton's political colleagues had sought to curb criticism of the Federalist Adams administration by the Alien and Sedition Acts of 1798. They showed no respect for the principle of freedom of communication, which Jefferson understood to be central to the existence of representative government. There have been many other cases of disregard for our heritage: In 1865, Secretary of War Edwin M. Stanton showed a contempt for fair play as embodied in civil rights in his relentless pursuit of those who assassinated President Lincoln. A. Mitchell Palmer, Wilson's Attorney General, took the same approach in his attack upon real and fancied enemies of the United States during and just after World War I. In 1917, a great crowd gathered in the town square of Dyersburg, Tennessee, to watch a mob burn at the stake a Negro who had been accused (but not convicted) of raping a white woman—only one of nearly two thousand lynchings* that have taken place in America during this century (90 per cent of them involving Negro victims). Yet these are the exceptions. In all of the history of the Republic, Americans have again and again demonstrated their belief in the importance of fair play and of "doing right." It is a cornerstone of our value structure. And we may well be moving toward rather than away from our goal. To use one possible measure, in the 1950s, there were six lynchings—far fewer than in previous decades.

***LYNCH.** **To kill as punishment for an alleged crime without due process of law, usually committed by a mob.**

Item: The concept of generosity. Americans are generous, charitable, and sentimental. They have doubts about the resourcefulness of those on public

[2] See Broadus Mitchell, *Alexander Hamilton,* The Macmillan Company, New York, 1962, vol. 2, chap. 25. Quotation from p. 491. Also, Frank van der Linden, *The Turning Point: Jefferson's Battle for the Presidency,* Luce Publishing Co., New York, 1962.

welfare, but they support large welfare budgets. They support protective tariffs, which aid the manufacturer rather than the consumer and are regarded as hostile behavior abroad; but they have also permitted scores of billions of dollars to be spent in foreign aid, partly in the belief that it is the "right thing to do," with only the vaguest idea as to how they or their nation may benefit. And when brother fought brother in the tragic Civil War, the man in the White House stated the ideal of his people:[3]

> With malice toward none, with charity for all, with firmness in the right as God gives us to see the right, let us strive to finish the work we are in, to bind up the nation's wounds, . . . to do all which may achieve and cherish a just and lasting peace among ourselves and with all nations.

A few weeks later Lincoln was dead, almost as if he had acted out the part of the hero in a Greek tragedy, and congressmen, with their sights aimed lower than the ideal, were to make a mockery of his word. But there can be little doubt that his words reflected an image of America and of right behavior that was then and remains today what we, in the ultimate, want.

Item: The belief in progress. Progress is a concept in which Americans have so much confidence that they find it difficult to believe that the future may not hold still more of the same. The whole history of the nation is one of a movement toward "progress." This kind of confidence is likely to help generate further effort to achieve the goals we can agree upon. It is also likely, however, to create some problems for Americans in international relations, for many Americans find it nearly impossible to believe that there are intelligent people in the world who, given the chance, might not choose democracy, single-family homes, hot dogs, private ownership of business, electric or gas clothes dryers, competitive elections, the English language, a television set in every home, and the idea of progress itself.

The belief in progress gives Americans a goal, a purpose in life, even though individuals may not define the term in the same way. Even in an age of military stalemate, revolutionary political aspirations in new nations, and rampant collectivism in most of the world, Americans continue to see progress in terms that are, to be sure, different from what they were fifty or a hundred years ago, but still in terms that are traditional and, to most people, not uncomfortably different from what "they have always been."

THE NATION LEAVES THE TWENTIETH CENTURY

The social scientist cannot predict exactly. He can, however, project statistical trends. He can say that, if the measured past movements of social phenomena continue on their present paths into the future, or that, given certain assumptions about changes in trends, certain resulting conditions

[3] Abraham Lincoln, Second Inaugural Address, Mar. 4, 1865.

will exist at a specific point in time. The trends we describe today may well be the actual issues of public policy tomorrow. It would seem worthwhile at this point, therefore, to take a look at the America we may find around the year 1980.[4]

More People and More Problems. There may well be more than 245 million people in the United States in 1980; at least, there will be if a projection of the Bureau of the Census proves to be accurate. The figure for the year 2000 may be around 331 million (see Table 22-1). In percentage terms, there will be more children under seventeen than there were at the time of the census of 1960; these additional children will be living in cities, and governments will be faced with greater problems of juvenile delinquency. In the decade preceding the 1960 census, the number of persons under eighteen increased by 37 per cent; those over sixty-five, by 35 per cent, while the age group in between increased by only 7 per cent.

By 1980, there may be 5.5 million more persons past the present conventional age of retirement than there were in 1960; with a continuation of current inadequate provisions for the retirement years, there will be increasing demand for governmental financial assistance to the aged—to furnish recreational services and to provide subsidies for housing, medical care, and other expensive services. Issues relative to these services that

[4] This section borrows from Hans H. Lansberg and others, *Resources in America's Future*, The John Hopkins Press, Baltimore, 1963. See also the Selected Bibliography.

TABLE 22-1

PROJECTED FUTURE TRENDS, UNITED STATES*

	1960	1980	2000
Population	180 million	245 million	331 million
Labor force	73 million	102 million	142 million
Gross national product (GNP)	$504 billion	$1060 billion	$2200 billion
Automobiles in use	59 million	120 million	244 million
Automobile production, annual	6.7 million	12.6 million	25.9 million
Agricultural production, value	$21 billion	$29 billion	$38 billion
Industrial production (Index: 1957 = 100)	108	249	564
Government expenditures	$100 billion	$242 billion	$551 billion
Net exports	$3.0 billion	$3.1 billion	$17.8 billion
New dwelling units	1.5 million	2.6 million	4.2 million

* 1960 value of the dollar used in all cases.

SOURCE: Hans H. Lansberg and others, *Resources in America's Future,* The Johns Hopkins University Press, Baltimore, 1963, various tables.

Figure 22-1

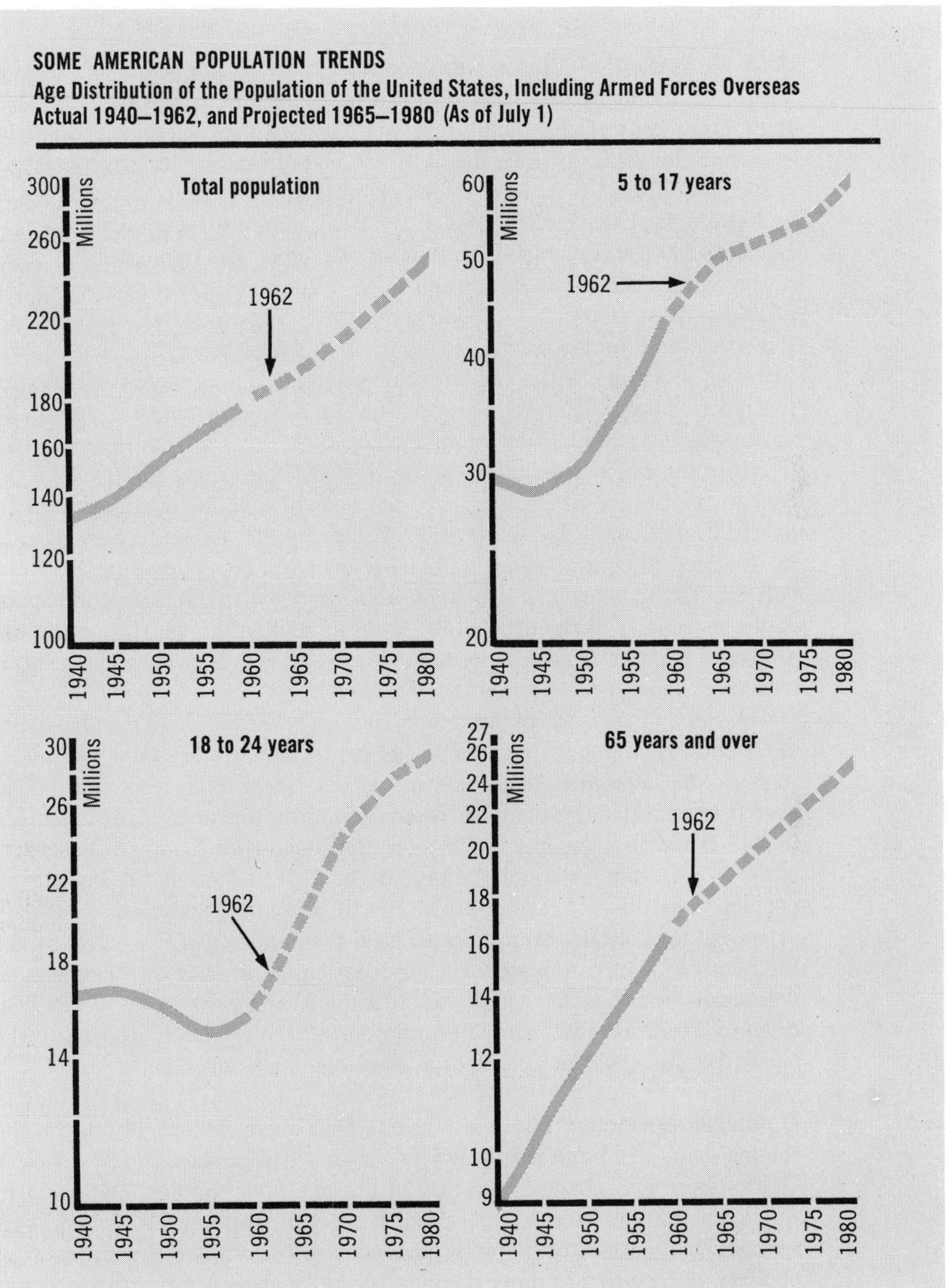

U.S. Bureau of the Census

were acute in the early 1960s can be expected to intensify, for despite corporate and other retirement plans, most members of the working force do not make adequate plans for their retirement or the support of their widows.

Where Will People Live? There were about 20 million Americans on farms in 1960, but this figure will have dropped to 17 million or less by 1980—less than 7 per cent of the population will have to provide food enough for everyone. Incidentally, this feat will not be approached by any nondemocratic nation, and it will be an important basis for the continued wealth and strength of the United States. By 2000, agricultural productivity will be 50 to 100 per cent higher than it was in 1960. The population of small towns will increase from 34 million to 48 million (in urban places of 2,500 people or less) between 1960 and 1980. Core cities of standard metropolitan areas will increase from 58 million to 72 million. The truly great increase, of course, will come in suburban areas. Los Angeles will become the nation's second largest metropolitan area. California will remain the most populous state in the Union.

While the white population of the United States increased by 17.5 per cent in the decade preceding 1960, the nonwhite population increased by nearly 27 per cent. The faster rate of increase for nonwhite persons may be expected to continue in the next few decades. Nonwhites, furthermore, will become increasingly urbanites and residents of Northern industrial states, especially of the core cities. Even in 1960, although the percentage of nonwhites was highest in some Southern states and in Hawaii, the state with the largest Negro population was New York.

The rates of increase of American Indians (46.5 per cent) and persons of Oriental background (around 44 per cent) were greater than the rate of increase of Caucasians in the decade of the 1950s. This trend can be expected to continue; both the increasing numbers and increasing urbanization of nonwhites, together with migration out of the South, will tend to increase demands for equal rights and equal protection of the law for all persons, regardless of race or color. It will, similarly, become increasingly expedient for political candidates to heed the demands of these groups, for the nonwhite population will not only participate in elections, but in such politically crucial states as Illinois, Michigan, and New York, it will continue to constitute the "swing" group upon whose votes the election in the particular state and in presidential elections may depend.

A Metropolitan America. The most spectacular development of all in the coming years will be in the growth of urban areas, particularly of suburbs. Unless there is a change in values of a scope and rapidity unequaled in American history, we can expect that the urbanizing trend in general and the suburban pattern of living in particular will continue. This means that by 2000, 331 million or more people may be creating a serious land shortage problem. There will be a sharp increase in conflict over the uses and reuses of land for residential living, agriculture, industrial production, transportation, and recreation. Water will become a scarce commodity. Conflicts will rage over its use for irrigation as against industrial use, and there will be increasing demands for "tastier" (actually, less tasty) water, for treatment will be intensified as pollution increases. Government will increasingly be called upon to referee disputes and to finance urban service programs.

Because it is easier to raise additional revenues at the Federal level than at the state and local levels, the urbanizing trend will increase pressures

Figure 22-2

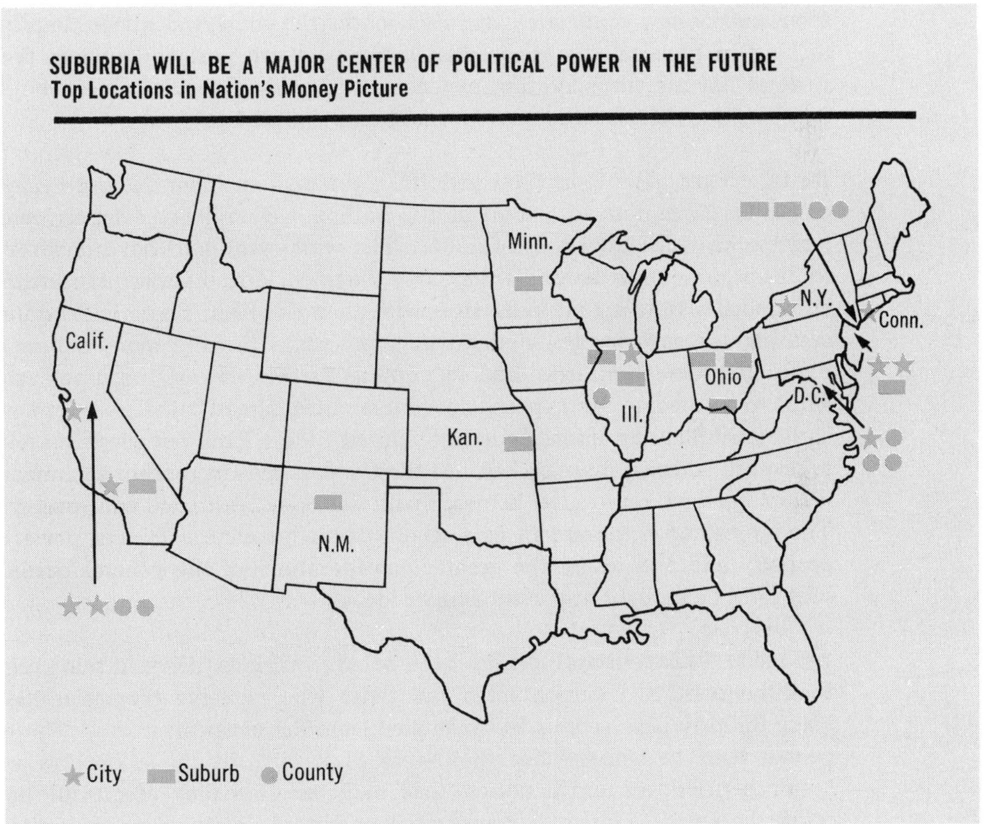

Suburbs are not only growing rapidly; they also are becoming centers of wealth, an important resource in political campaigns. The richest counties, cities, and suburbs in the United States are shown here. (U.S. Bureau of the Census.)

for Federal aid in meeting the high cost of providing wanted services in metropolitan areas. In the 1960s, there were strong demands for the creation of a Department of Urban Affairs at Cabinet rank. Although the proposal was stopped on the first few tries, principally by members of the House of Representatives from rural and small-city areas, it seems likely that such an agency will be created in the future. There are demands for Federal aid in many areas: public health, urban planning, urban renewal, planning for water-supply and sewage-disposal plants, expressways, parking facilities, and others. Some grants are already available.

The strong pressures for a program of Federal aid to education is in part a reflection of the urbanizing trend, for the urban way of life produces demands for greater skills, more specialization in instruction, higher teacher salaries, and larger physical plants. The high birth rate since the beginning of World War II, encouraged by almost uninterrupted prosperity and complicated by the suburban movement which has sometimes placed thousands of new youngsters into a school district which was almost totally lacking in physical facilities adds to the pressure. (Most demands for Federal aid are for operating expenses; such aid, if forthcoming, would free local tax dollars to be used for plant and equipment.)

The Labor Force. Between 1960 and 1980, the civilian labor force may increase by 29 million to a total of 102 million. (By 2000, the labor force may be nearly double that of 1964.) The work week will have declined from forty hours to around thirty-five, thus providing breadwinners with an opportunity to spend more time with their families. There will be increasing pressure for the Federal government to provide more national parks and recreation areas and to improve further the existing ones. An effort to save some open spaces near large cities, already underway in the early 1960s, will be intensified; The United States Park Service will seek to acquire additional areas; because these areas already contain a number of summer and year-round homes, there will be considerable controversy. The long-standing argument over where the rights of privacy and private property end and where the greater considerations of the general public begin will be brought into even sharper focus.

Who Will be the Discontented? It has been noted in various places in this book that the politically discontented are those who perceive themselves as being unfairly deprived, or feel alienated from the political process. These people tend to believe that they were "left out" in the allocation of society's privileges and bounties, they may feel that they are unable to affect the political forces that make the important decisions, or they may have both reactions. In the former case, they may become intensely active in political movements. In the latter, they will not be very active unless some political leader first convinces them that, through organization and action, they can actually affect political decisions concerning the allocation of society's resources.

The discontented of the next generation are most likely to be found in four groups: (1) Negroes and other nonwhites; (2) the technologically unemployed, principally the losers to automation; (3) marginal farmers and farm workers; and (4) the physically, mentally, and educationally handicapped. These groups are not mutually exclusive. All of them share a relative deprivation in earning power when compared with society in general. None of these groups is without resources under the present ideology and political pattern. Negroes began to show effective political action in the 1950s. Organized labor has sought to aid Negroes, those affected by automation, the elderly, and others. Middle-class do-gooders seek to help the socially maladjusted through support of programs for welfare, mental health, school dropout prevention, retraining, and others. Marginal farmers are not well organized, although groups such as the Farmers' Union do help them, and congressmen are aware of their voting power. But even with political support, under the present system these groups will continue to be and often also to feel deprived.

In 1936, President Franklin Roosevelt said that one-third of the nation was "ill-housed, ill-clad, ill-nourished." In the mid-1960s, although the concept of minimum standards had been raised somewhat, the ratio had not changed much. One estimate, using United States Bureau of Labor Statistics criteria, found that about 25 per cent of the American population—40 to 50 million people—still live in "poverty."[5] By the Bureau's standard, poverty is defined as an annual income of less than $4,000 for a family of four, or less than $2,000 for an individual living alone. To the middle class, the poor are less visible today than in the past. Because of "tunnel vision," suburbanites move from the suburbs to their places of business or to shopping centers, their eyes on the freeway ahead. The poor still live in the central city, but they no longer are a few blocks away from the middle class, on "the other side of the tracks"—the middle class has gone to the suburbs. Many among the poor are over sixty-five or under eighteen (the aged and the school dropouts). Clothing has also tended to make the poor invisible, in contrast to the situation common in societies of the past. It is difficult to distinguish the dress of Americans by class and income today (this is especially true of women), for "it is much easier in the United States to be decently dressed than it is to be decently housed, fed, or doctored."[6]

Twenty-five per cent of our poor are Negroes and Puerto Ricans. (In 1958, the average nonwhite income was 58 per cent of that of the average white.) Nearly one-half of the persons sixty-five years of age and over are

[5] Michael Harrington, *The Other America: Poverty in the United States,* The Macmillan Company, New York, 1962. Reprinted in paperback by Penguin Books, Inc., Baltimore. Citations given here are taken from the latter. Harrington has served in editorial capacities for socialist and Roman Catholic publications, and so might be suspected of writing an emotion-based polemic, but his data are largely from United States government publications.

[6] *Ibid.,* p. 13.

in the "poor" category. So are most persons who are farm workers or have unskilled jobs in office buildings, hotels, restaurants, hospitals, laundries, and carwashes. The poverty-stricken have higher rates of mental illness[7] and poorer health (they cannot afford adequate medical care) than others.

The percentage of poor families as compared with the total number of families declined from 68 per cent in 1936 to 23 per cent in 1960. But this figure is derived only by ignoring the changing value of the dollar. During the same period, families with less than $4,000 income saw their share of the national income drop from 35 per cent to 7 per cent.[8]

The social service state has been of little, if any, help to the chronically poor. Migrant and other farm workers and many of the elderly are not helped at all, except by direct relief (which has been available to them since the seventeenth century). The social service ideology "had been stimulated by mass impoverishment and misery, yet it helped the poor least of all. Laws like unemployment compensation, the Wagner Act, the various farm programs, all these were designed for the middle third in the cities, for the organized workers and for the . . . big market farmers."[9]

The economically deprived are thus still a very large proportion of our population. But they are less concern to the middle class today than they once were. There is still a widespread belief that they do not exist or that, if a few do, it is because "They are lazy." And they are less powerful politically today than they were in the 1930s when better-educated persons, more whites, and more persons with values oriented toward those of the middle class were among the low-income people of society. Thus:[10]

> In the past, when poverty was general in the unskilled and semi-skilled work force, the poor were all mixed together. The bright and the dull, those who were going to escape into the great society and those who were to stay behind, all of them lived on the same street. When the middle third rose, this community was destroyed. And the entire invisible land of the other Americans became a ghetto, a modern poor farm for the rejects of society and of the economy.

Furthermore:[11]

> The problems of the future are the very ones that are with us today; a relatively large population exposed to the risk of dependency because of

[7] Thomas S. Langner and others, *Life Stress and Mental Health,* New York University Press, New York, 1963; and Oscar Lewis, "The Culture of Poverty," *Trans-action,* 1:17–21, November, 1963.

[8] Leon H. Keyserling and others, *Poverty and Deprivation in the United States,* Conference on Economic Progress, Washington, D.C., 1963.

[9] Harrington, *op. cit.,* p. 17.

[10] *Ibid.,* p. 18.

[11] Margaret Greenfield, *Social Dependency in the San Francisco Bay Area: Today and Tomorrow,* University of California, Institute of Governmental Studies, Berkeley, Calif., 1963, p. 5.

underemployment and low income, ill health, and intergroup tensions due to widespread discrimination against ethnic minorities. Continued dependency arises out of economic and social conditions as well as the physical or mental incapacity of the individual. Unless some modifications occur in the socio-economic patterns . . . the next two decades will see little change in the burden of public assistance.

One other group, partly overlapping with the four named above but fundamentally very different from them, deserves mention: the adherents of older ideologies, especially advocates of individualism and of isolationism. These people find the politics of the current era frustrating, confusing, and sometimes meaningless. Governmental programs are dysfunctional in terms of their goals; political rhetoric is couched in unacceptable language; the direction of social movement seems "all wrong."

Will the above groups, or most of them, join for political action? Or will some of them become totally alienated and withdraw from politics? Or will all have to settle for crumbs from the political table otherwise groaning with the material goodness of a suburban, middle-class society of organization men and prosperous union-led semiskilled workers in automated factories? Or will the suburbanites and their bland, genteel social service state be a "pushover" for the determined, anxiety-ridden discontented? Political

Figure 22-3

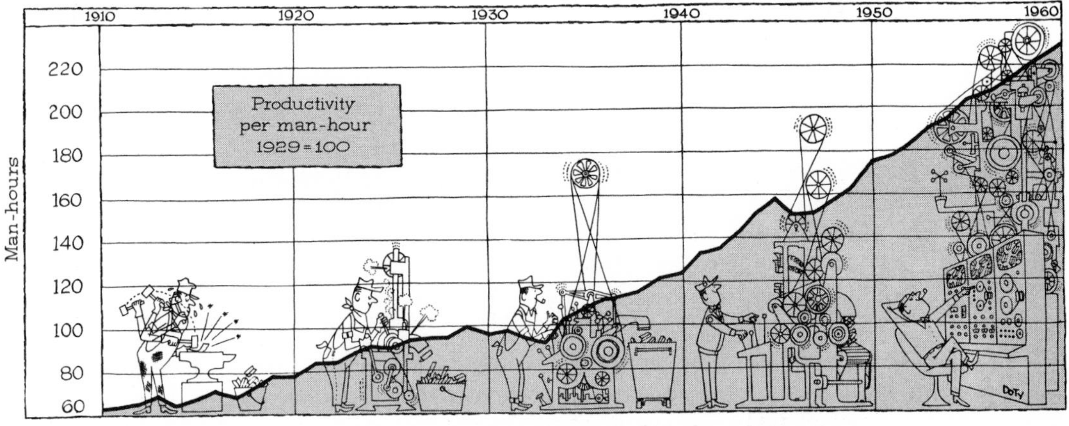

The New York Times, *Feb. 4, 1962.*

scientists do not know the answers. If the discontented do reject existing ideologies and develop another one that will share the political scene with that of the social service state, what will it be like? Will it lead to a type of fascism under a demagogic leader? Or an anti-intellectualism and denial and rejection of the actual conditions of the modern world (in terms of methods of transportation, communication, industrialization, and metropolitanization), as is found in Birchism? Or a new era centering around the wants of the marginal workers of both urban and rural America under a democratic system? Or will the result be some political system as yet undreamed of? We do not know.

The nation is also faced with strong external threats. It is possible that the outside pressures on America, with their resulting anxieties, may ultimately have a greater effect than any other consideration on domestic programs, American life, and political styles. The major threat to democracy may come from the outside rather than from differences over domestic matters. Will America cease to be a first-rate world power between now and 2000? Not likely, but will we cease to *believe* that we can remain a world power? Will we cease to perceive ourselves as a world power? And if we do, could we as a nation accept this psychological blow without losing our poise and our confidence in our ability to cope with domestic problems? These are major questions that, for now, cannot be answered.

The Age of Automation. One of the great problems will be in putting to work 29 million additional persons by 1980 and more than 69 million more by 2000 in the face of a strong trend toward the automation of industry. The use of continuous automatic production mechanisms, of feedback control devices, of electronic computers, and of self-regulating machines will vastly increase production, but will require far fewer men for each operation. In other words, American productivity per worker, already the highest in the world, will soar far higher. Gross national product may quadruple in the less than two generations between 1960 and 2000.

It will be possible in the coming years to scatter plants all over the nation, with less concern given to location of labor force. Workers will be more isolated from one another in lonely jobs, watching soulless machines; thus, the company will have greater potential control over them; and they may possibly be subject to greater mental strain as a result of the increased speed of production, the constant attention required, and the high cost of mistakes.

Unemployment is not a result of automation alone. It also stems from a general lack of skills and education. For a considerable period in American history, industry needed large numbers of unskilled workers, but increasingly the tasks these persons once performed are the ones being automated. In 1962, as a result, unskilled workers constituted the largest category of unemployed—one out of eight unskilled workers had no job. In general, the higher the skills, the less problem in finding employment.

In 1962, unemployment was also concentrated among younger people, particularly among those who had dropped out of high school before receiving a diploma. Among those aged fourteen to nineteen in the labor market, 13.4 per cent could not find a job. Of all unemployed, 75 per cent of the men and 65 per cent of the women had not completed high school; of part-time workers, 75 per cent had not completed high school. Race was also a factor. Negroes have always been the last to be hired, first to be fired in industrial America. In 1963, unemployment was nearly three times as high among nonwhites as among whites. Negroes, on the average, have less education and lower skills than whites and so are doubly penalized.

Automation and government policy. Automation will leave a trail of social wants that will affect government at all levels, national, state, and local. The national government will probably have to cope with such problems as may arise if consumer purchasing power does not rise rapidly enough

Figure 22-4

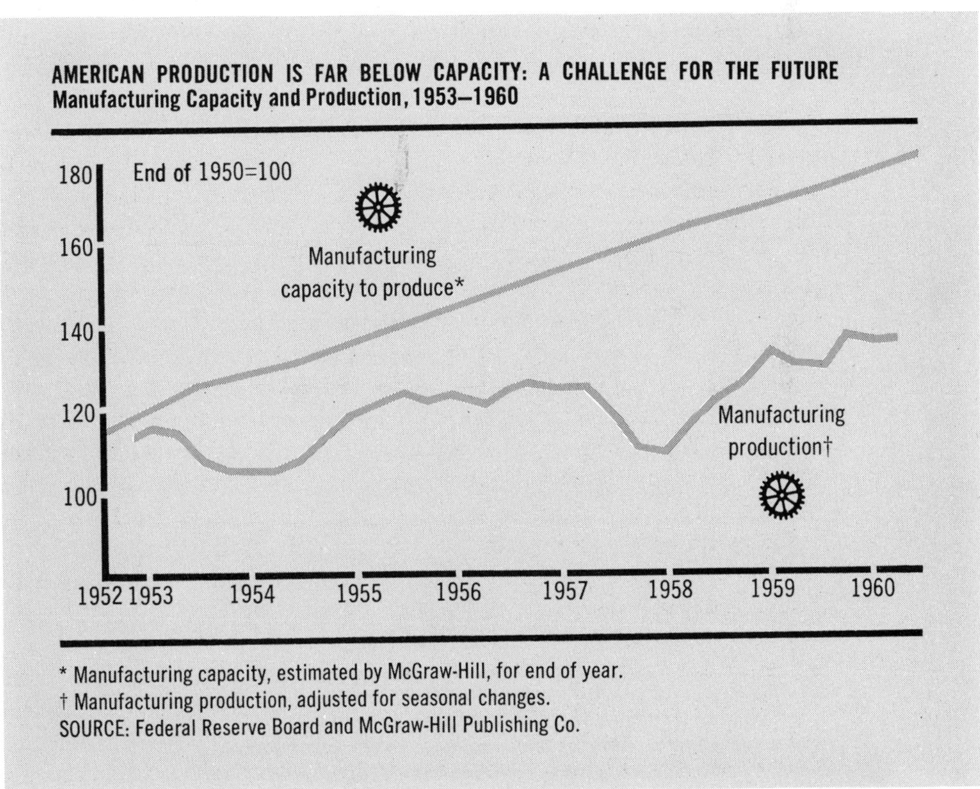

Economic Programs and Policies for the 60s, *AFL–CIO, Washington, D.C., 1960.*

to equal automation's increased productivity and if automation further stimulates the tendency toward concentrated control of industry and industrial mergers. (It is possible, however, that automation will give small business competitive advantages not existing under conventional factory methods.)

Figure 22-5

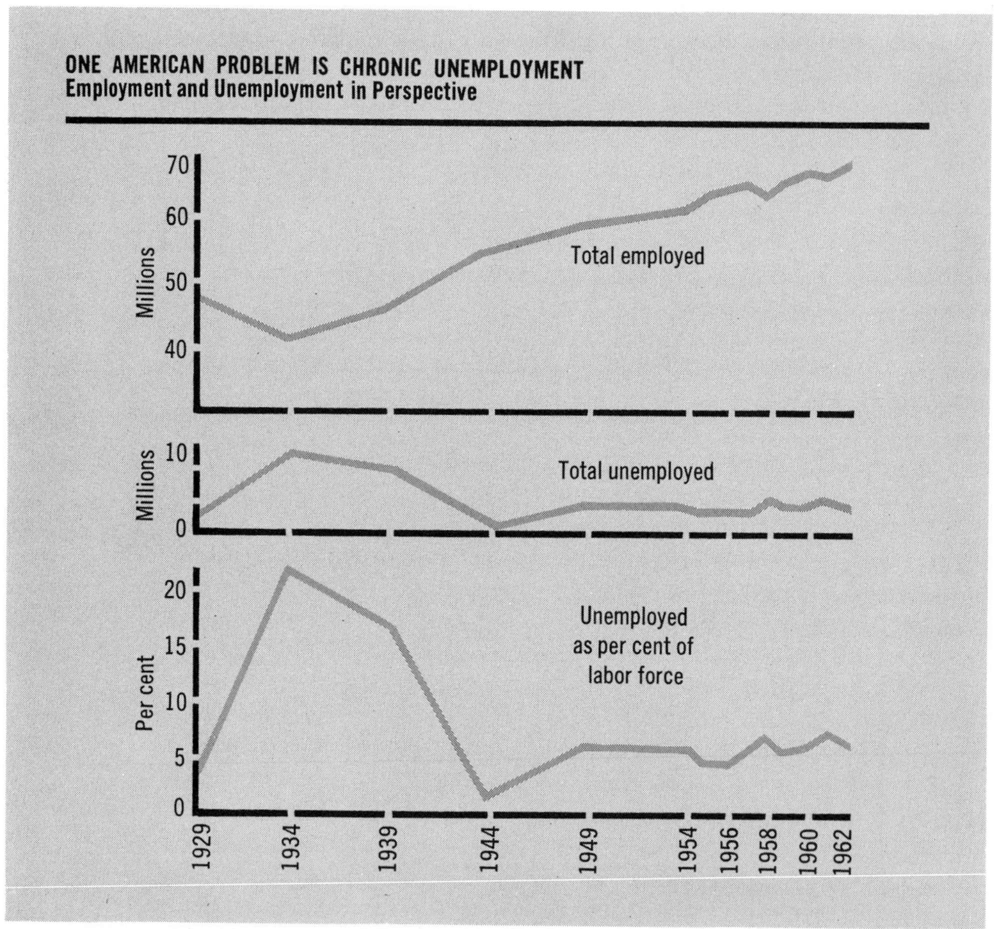

Employment and unemployment in perspective. Employment trends in the United States show an ever-expanding number of jobs available to the labor force despite periodic disruptions by depression (1930s) and recession (1958). Although unemployment is a problem (and always has been one) current discussions of the subject often obscure the fact that 68 million people are now at work—more than ever before in United States history. (Better Living, *Du Pont Company, 17:3, July–August, 1963.)*

Figure 22-6

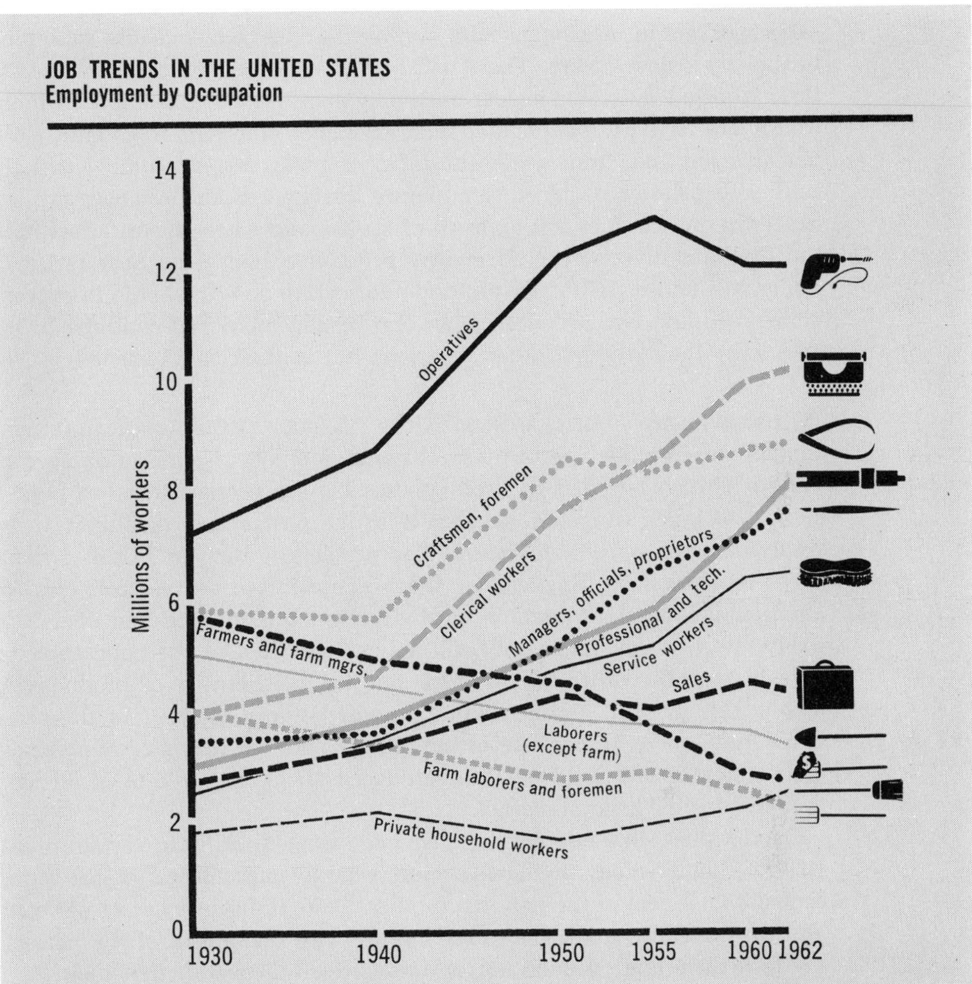

*The shift in job patterns over the last 30 years is shown above. A sharp spurt in industrial jobs (operators, craftsmen, and foremen) between 1940 and 1955 has ended, and employment is now leveling out. The same period saw an even faster rise in clerical, managerial, and professional employment. Clerical jobs are now beginning to level off, but the other two fields show no letup. The most dramatic decrease comes in farming, through improvement in farm equipment. More jobs have been displaced by improved farm technology than by improved technology and "automation" in all of United States industry combined. (*Better Living, *Du Pont Company, 17:3, July–August, 1963.)*

Bitter battles will be fought as Congress considers reducing the work week, which has been established at forty hours since the days of the Great Depression. Organized labor, anxious to "spread the work around," will campaign for a shorter week and will ask for Federal programs to assist workers in making socially approved and psychologically satisfying uses of their new leisure. There will be demands for Federal assistance to those affected by technological unemployment, for the retraining of those whose jobs have been automated, and for higher minimum wage laws. Both management and, from a slightly different angle, organized labor will encourage legislation designed to minimize the chances for prolonged strikes. Since the public does not approve of strikes and since strikes affect both the firm and the worker adversely, Presidents and their Secretaries of Labor will find it politically profitable to seek to do all possible to prevent serious work stoppages. Both labor and management will continue to try to modify the National Labor Relations Act to their own benefit .

The Yeoman Farmer: Vanishing American? The efficiency of the American farmer, unapproached elsewhere in the world and an object of admiration even of Nikita Khrushchev, has in itself produced a grave crisis that has been a subject of much congressional debate in the past and is not likely to be resolved in the immediate future. The problem is that, as in the agricultural revolution in England in the seventeenth century, technological changes have made it possible to produce much more food and fiber with many fewer farmers. Not only will about 7 per cent of the population be able to feed the other 93 per cent, but the distribution of productivity among this handful of the population will be very uneven. In the early 1960s, only about 10 per cent of the farm population consisted of commercial farmers, but this 10 per cent produced about 90 per cent of all food and fiber for the general market.

Land values, like population, have been concentrating in certain areas. In 1922, land values in the five most wealthy agricultural states represented 33 per cent of the national total; in 1956, the figure was 41 per cent, and the states were not the same.[12] Iowa, with one-fourth of the nation's grade A farm land, was no longer among them. The shift that took place was largely from rural and general farming states to industrial states, where truck and dairy farming were emphasized.

A major problem in social policy has arisen in the years since about 1919: the number of persons needed to operate the nation's farms is far less than the number who wish to be farmers. The problem is complicated by the fact that farming is not just an occupation but, despite a diminishing distinction between rural and urban society, a way of life. The yeoman farmer is an American folk hero who is believed to lead the truly good life. Given this image, it is difficult for the marginal farmer, using outmoded

[12] Ernest Kurnow, "Land Value Trends in the United States," *Land Economics,* 36:341–348, November, 1960.

equipment on inadequate acreage, to convince himself and his family to leave the farm and become an unskilled factory worker in the city. He would earn more money, it is true, and his family could have more material things, but he would lose status and would have to become accustomed to a very different life-style and to associate with different people, some of whose ways he would view with hostility.

Because of these political factors, congressmen have been reluctant to adopt policies that would encourage the movement of unneeded persons from farms into the cities. Instead, a great variety of subsidy plans have been proposed, and some adopted. Because the subsistence farmers greatly outnumber the commercial farmers, it has been politically advantageous to provide for farm supports, even though they have resulted in great surpluses that the Federal government has purchased and stored with no plan for disposition.

Continuing economic pressures will make it increasingly difficult for the noncommercial farmer to continue to occupy the land, even with subsidies, and the question of national agricultural policy will continue to be a difficult one for Congress. Advocates of agricultural efficiency will continue to call for an end to ever-increasing amounts of stored surpluses and "the subsidization of inefficiency," with its accompanying costs—but surpluses are expected to continue throughout the twentieth century despite large population increases.[13] The spokesmen for the small farmer will plead for the preservation of the family farm and an honored way of life, but their comments will be rejected by others who view this as romantic, sentimental nonsense and believe that farming should be considered a business, not a unique way of life. Congress, which has demonstrated little willingness to come to grips with this touchy political problem, will eventually have to decide on a meaningful policy which will have important social as well as economic overtones. In the meanwhile, it remains inexpedient for Congress to authorize the disposition of unused surpluses in foreign countries where they are badly needed, for farm organizations view such proposals as threats to the international markets they hope to see established. A national agricultural policy, like virtually all policies formulated by Congress, represents a compromise among conflicting pressures; therefore, it will probably never be a policy that economists would regard as systematic and rational, but in the future some of the anomalies within it will probably, under strong pressures, be reduced in scope.

FISCAL POLICY AND FULL EMPLOYMENT: KEEPING AN EVEN KEEL

During the Great Depression years, many economic advisers to the Federal government, under the influence of the ideas of the Englishman John Maynard Keynes, urged that the government assume responsibility for

[13] Lansberg and others, *op. cit.*

maintaining stability of prices and a high employment level. The theories of Keynes are too complicated to be described even in elementary terms here.[14] In essence, they call for the government to spend more than it receives during deflations and recessions, when prices and employment levels are falling, and to recoup its losses by spending less than it receives during inflationary periods of price increases and hyperemployment.

There have been many difficulties in the application of this theory, the most serious of which has been that it has been politically easier to engage in deficit spending than to pay off debts during prosperity. Not only is there great popular pressure to reduce the income tax with the first hint of a surplus, but inflation, though denounced by almost everyone, is in fact popular, provided it is not too rapid. After all, many investors in the stock market count on a certain amount of inflation as a basis for profit; businessmen often borrow money for inventory or for capital expansion, and inflation permits them to pay off their debts with cheaper dollars; and a belief that money saved will be eroded by inflation encourages consumer spending "while the money is still worth something," which is welcomed by retailers and manufacturers alike.

There are a large number of built-in stabilizers in the economy today—built in by congressional action over a period of years. These are designed to offset trends toward either inflation or deflation and to prevent such catastrophes as the ruinous inflation that took place in Germany in the 1920s or the tragic Great Depression in this country a few years later. Thus tax receipts increase automatically when inflation is threatened and decrease when the opposite is the case. Unemployment compensation and welfare grants are pumped into the economy when employment declines. More in the area of discretion, the Federal Reserve Board makes technical changes in banking and borrowing procedures and in margin requirements on stock market transactions as economic conditions change. Both Congress and the President can make additional changes, particularly in taxation and spending policies if they seem indicated.

All of these factors have brought the United States close to a "managed economy" in which the Federal government seeks to keep the economic boat on an even keel. Despite the horrors of the Great Depression, quite a few economists and businessmen doubt the wisdom of entrusting this power to government, a social institution that businessmen and almost all Americans have long distrusted. Yet the principal question today and in the future is likely to be not whether the Federal government should be involved in efforts to balance the economy and keep people at work, but rather, how it is to do this. The question is certain to create great conflict because the stakes are high in the decisions to be made, and because conventional wisdom relative to such policies is everywhere to be found. Indeed, economists have not themselves achieved consensus. Conservative

[14] See Paul A. Samuelson, *Economics,* 6th ed., McGraw-Hill Book Company, New York, 1964, chap. 18.

economists tend to see major problems as being the maintenance of price level and a favorable balance of international trade. Liberal economists see the economic growth rate and full employment as the greatest problems. Each group offers sophisticated arguments in support of its position. As a leading member of the profession has said, however, a government "in which fiscal and monetary policies work automatically, untouched by any human intelligence, is not now anywhere in sight. But social innovations to reduce lags in diagnosis and therapy hold forth promise."[15]

Future conflicts will center around a number of problems: managing an almost constantly increasing debt; the powers to be enjoyed by the Federal Reserve Board as supervisor of the nation's credit system, tax policy, and expenditures (especially for "pump priming" or employment-creating purposes); and the emergency powers to be given the President.

NUCLEAR DIPLOMACY

Americans have never sought a world leadership role, as did the leaders of imperial Rome, Nazi Germany, or the Soviet Union. But they find themselves in such a position, nevertheless. The naïveté of World War I is past; so is the bewilderment following World War II, the awesome realization in the early 1950s that man had finally achieved one form of the ultimate in learning—how to destroy not merely individuals and cities, but all of mankind; and the shock a few years later in discovering that the Soviet Union was actually ahead of the United States in at least some aspects of rocketry.

All of these attitudes and events added to the stew of American politics, a politics in which the ordinary citizen has traditionally expected simple solutions to problems, in which America is expected to win over all adversaries because she stands for what is right, in which righteousness, prodded sometimes by the use of force, is seen as the answer to sticky international situations. As the 1952 elections, protesting the cold war and Korea, and public-opinion polls have shown, Americans have found their new world role not only perplexing, but anxiety-producing and frightening as well. We have not yet come to understand the distinction between the political solution to international issues ("If they don't listen to reason, send in the Marines to show them") and the diplomatic one (learning to live patiently with problems that cannot be solved by earnest belief in what is considered right, by rifle fire, or by any simple remedy). Political maturity is expected of America, whether she likes it or not. Her policies in this age cannot be based upon political panaceas, but must reflect mature diplomacy and a realization that nations, like individuals, may need to see the achievement of goals in long-range rather than simple and immediate terms.

[15] *Ibid.*, p. 361.

Prospect: Annihilation. Perhaps no issue that confronts the American people, Congress, and the President in the coming decades can compare in importance with the problem of finding an effective policy in relation to the Communist nations of the world. Communism cannot be wished away, and it cannot be destroyed by a preventive war as might have been possible in the period immediately after World War II. This is so if for no other reason than that the Communist nations, like America, possess "nuclear fusion devices," as the Department of Defense euphemistically terms hydrogen bombs. In 1964, Communist China became the fifth nation possessing nuclear weapons. By 1980, as many as a dozen nations may possess these world destroyers, making the chance of their use much more than six times as great as it was when only the United States and the Soviet Union possessed them. Given the fact that even the most momentous decisions are not necessarily made by calm, rational men, these weapons in the hands of unpredictable persons present great and vast dangers to the world that cannot easily be dissipated, but may be controlled if a realistic evaluation of the problem is shared by all concerned.

Congress, the President, and the specialists in the State Department will need to tread a tightrope, and the survival of both the nation and mankind may well rest on their ability to do so. The problem will involve finding a national policy that (1) will prevent nuclear warfare, (2) will preserve the honor of America and the self-respect of Americans, and (3) will be accepted by the typical American, who has always tended to want to relieve his anxieties by finding the quick, simple solution that the irresponsible or unknowing are often willing to hold out before him.

Congress and the President will also be faced with the problem of considering the demands not only of those who favor a show of force in times of crisis ("saber rattlers"), but also of those who demand unilateral disarmament, if necessary, in order to end the arms race. Both extreme views are regarded by specialists in the Departments of State and Defense as unrealistic and dangerous beyond justified risk. It is probable that neither will be adopted, but both will receive much attention. As politicians, congressmen will continue to talk about and hope for a final solution to international tensions and threats. But they will probably accept, with reluctance and hesitation, the views of the diplomats: Decisions about international relations are vastly complex and highly interrelated, so that one decision influences other decisions and relationships; and international relations are a complex series of problems to which we make periodic adjustments in seeking national goals, but for which there is no ultimate and permanent solution.

The Military in a Threatened Nation. The hydrogen bomb has been called the "ultimate weapon." It is not, however. We can expect many more "improvements" in the techniques of destruction. The neutron bomb, which will kill people but not destroy buildings, is already technologically feasible. Prospects for gas and germ warfare have scarcely been touched, and the use of artificial satellites for the launching of weapons is being studied in the Pentagon. Many techniques not yet dreamed of by the common man will probably be well known by 1980 or the years immediately following. Keeping pace with potential enemies in technological developments will result in powerful demands upon Congress, and granting funds to produce even a small fraction will be fantastically expensive.

Because defense policy is largely the result of congressional balancing off of the demands of various professional military groups (few civilian interest groups have the technical competence to get involved in a significant way), bureaucratic rivalries constantly face Congress and will continue to do so in future years. The Navy, fundamentally based on weapons operating on and beneath the sea, will resist proposals for an all-nuclear rocket defense. The Air Force insists that missiles, because they travel through the air, should be under its direction and command. Some of its high officers argue that, despite the vastly greater speed and increasing accuracy of ballistic missiles, manned aircraft still have an important place in our defense program. The traditional American elite corps, the United States Marines, and the Army infantry are committed largely to the use of conventional weapons; they feel that their type of fighting is of great importance in brush-fire skirmishes, which they consider a possible means of preventing nuclear warfare. Leading military specialists, indeed, vacillate between demands for total nuclear preparedness and emphasis upon the continued importance of conventional weapons and military units. Some specialists have argued for huge thermonuclear weapons of 50 megatons of power or more, others for a greater number of much smaller devices, others for primary deployment of nuclear weapons through the use of nuclear-powered submarines. Congress, in the absence of any degree of certainty as to what kind of defense pattern is optimum and under pressure from citizens who fear that the nation may not be safe from attack no matter how much money is spent, is likely to choose something from the recommendations of all the specialists. A diversified but large defense budget is likely to be the answer for many years to come. Many specialists, themselves uncertain, believe this to be the policy that involves the least risk. In game theory, this is called a mixed strategy.

A problem that presents itself to Americans, as it has to others throughout history when they resort to massive armaments for their own defense, is maintaining a qualified body of military specialists without losing policy control to them. Even with the election of the war hero Dwight D. Eisenhower to the Presidency in 1952, Americans continued their traditional insistence upon the subordination of the military to the civilian components of government. There have been warnings that a garrison state, even one based upon missiles rather than vast armies, threatens democratic values. This threat has so far remained largely academic, even though the increased importance of and reliance upon military leadership makes the possibility of military domination a future possibility. In the coming years, there will probably be some members of Congress who will insist that we defer to the desires and expertise of military leaders, but their influence will in most cases probably be offset by the traditional rejection of this approach in America.

Alliances for National Survival. In the period after World War II, the United States entered into a number of agreements with other nations that were designed to provide mutual security in various parts of the world (see Chapter 21). All of them have been viewed as threats by the Communist nations and opposed by them as such. These agreements have been viewed by American diplomats not only as giving us alliances to oppose the Communist bloc, but also as a means of giving our allies a sense of participation in decision making beyond that of merely saying, "I agree." The significance in making these groups work successfully is testified to by the seriousness with which the Communist nations attack them and seek to discredit or destroy them. These alliances are likely to be continued into the future, and they are relatively noncontroversial in the eyes of congressmen.

A more important issue of conflict involves American aid abroad. It is likely that many Americans and their congressional representatives will continue to feel that funds appropriated for foreign nations is equivalent to pouring money down a rat hole. Arguments will be made that "you can't buy friendship." But it is not friendship that America seeks as much as it is the prevention of commitments to communism. Presidents and Secretaries of State, keenly aware of the success—or at least qualified success—of military and economic aid abroad, will in all likelihood continue to support such programs on an extensive scale. These recommendations will be criticized and investigated in Congress, but it seems likely that present policies will, in essence, be continued into the indefinite future.

The United Nations as Symbol of Conflict. America's membership in the United Nations will continue to be a matter of some controversy. It serves as a symbol of America's complex international responsibilities and involvements to those who would preserve the traditions of the ideology of isolationism. But all future Presidents and their Secretaries of State will probably continue to support the United Nations because it will be viewed as a convenient and effective arena for presenting the American point of view to an international audience that includes both the uncommitted nations, which we want to court, and the Communist nations, with which we must negotiate. Despite the continuing increase in the number of uncommitted nations that are being carved out of Africa and Asia, the United States and her allies will probably continue to dominate the Security Council and have an adequately strong voice in the General Assembly and the Secretariat.

SOME GENERAL PROSPECTS

We have some techniques for measuring the general direction in which the United States is traveling. They permit us to gain some idea of what the future may be like, for the course of American history will not likely suffer abrupt changes in direction. New inventions, discoveries, and technologies build on the old. New governmental policies, despite the fulminations of campaign oratory and the wishful thinking of some citizens, are usually marginal modifications of existing policies. Even so, estimates of the future are always danger-filled, and the seer often looks foolish when later generations read what he has written.

Changing technology and social values, not to mention wars or unexpected changes in the international balance of power, among other things, may drastically change the path we see ahead of us. These changes can take place with great suddenness and can have enormous effects upon social institutions. Public policies developed in the 1930s and based upon declining population trends of that day (such as the social security program) made less sense when applied under the conditions of the post-1942 birth and death rates. New discoveries that might greatly reduce the incidence of cancer and heart disease or delay their effects would result in a suddenly increased life span, which would influence dozens of governmental policies—adding sharply to an already seriously inadequate financial retirement plan for the elderly, complicating the administration of the social security agency, adding to the strain on the Federal program of aid to the elderly, complicating programs in housing, recreation, mental health, and dozens of other areas. Wars, large and small, could bring great changes and, very possibly, disastrous changes to our life-styles and, in the event of total war, to our very institutions of democratic government. A serious depression might lead to monumental revamping of Federal programs of money and credit controls, economic production controls, and welfare, and it might produce further major changes in the relationship between government and business, as happened once before during the Great Depression.

Given present trends, the pattern of Federal government policy can be expected to develop generally along the following lines:

The Social Service State. The social service ideology will probably remain dominant for an indefinite period of time. There is no indication that it may be fundamentally altered in the near future. If this is correct, heavy service demands at all levels of government will continue, and as new problems arise, government will be one of the first, rather than one of the last, social institutions that people will turn to for help. The frontier tradition of individualism will continue to be influential, and political propaganda will be verbalized in the language of this tradition, but it will serve only as a brake on the general trend.

Elections. Presidential elections will continue to turn on the impression that a majority of voters have concerning the ability of a particular candidate to protect the nation from communism without resort to full-scale warfare, as they have since 1952. Congressional seats in both houses, on the other hand, will be decided principally on the basis of domestic policy matters, personality considerations, and traditional voting alignments. Most citizens will look to the White House and not to Congress in their hopes for peace in the world and preservation from communism. The suburbanite feeling for a bland politics will continue to reinforce the traditional American belief in voting for the man. The result will be an increase in split-ticket voting. This will encourage two-party politics in more constituencies, but will further weaken party responsibility and discipline.

The Presidency. Despite 1964, presidential candidates will nearly always be middle-of-the-roaders, men who avoid the extremes. But Presidents will be more liberal than the leaders of their party in Congress and they will, by the reluctance of Congress to break new ground (among other reasons), continue to be the principal innovators of policy. Presidents will also tend to reflect urban views and concerns more than Congress will—particularly more than the House of Representatives. This will tend to reinforce the tendency of Congress to be more conservative than the White House and the trend toward executive leadership in policy making.

Federal Domestic Policy. Federal domestic programs will gradually expand in scope as population increases and the cultural concept of a "decent" standard of living rises. Because less effort is required at the Federal than at the state level to secure expanded programs, there will be a continuing trend toward more and larger grants-in-aid by the Federal government for programs that will be administered primarily by state or local officials. These trends have not been rapid in the postwar years, though nearly every Congress since 1947 has added at least one new Federal grant program. If, however, there should be a substantial decrease in defense expenditures in the future, the pressures on Congress will be such that Federal domestic expenditures should increase very considerably.

Cooperative Federalism. Federal-state-local relationships will become more elaborate as many kinds of services are provided increasingly on an intergovernmental basis. Cooperative federalism will be central to much domestic policy development. This tendency away from a separation of functions by governmental level will not necessarily mean a decline in the policy-making importance of state or local governments. As the bureaucracy continues to become professionalized at all levels, objectives and values also tend to become standardized. This, in turn, encourages a sense of cooperation rather than exploitation among officials and employees at the lower levels. Furthermore, as mass communication, more years of education, and other factors diminish regional and subcultural differences in American society, the feeling that policy is being imposed from the state or national capitals will tend to decline, thus reinforcing the trend among public employees toward a common set of objectives.

Interest Groups. Interest groups will increase in number, for Americans will increasingly join with others who share their goals in an attempt to overcome the anonymity of urbanism. They will tend more and more to seek to influence elections as well as legislation and administrative decisions, for elections will increasingly depend upon the use of costly media of mass communication rather than upon elaborate organizations designed for local party workers to meet the voter face to face.

The Bureaucracy. The myriad of specialists in the Federal bureaucracy, already of considerable influence in policy making, will become even more specialized and will increase their influence and importance. In defense and foreign policy decisions, their influence will be especially felt, but they will affect all types of decisions, particularly those in which they possess something approximating a monopoly of skills or knowledge. This tendency will be sharply criticized by many, but both Congress and the presidential staff are increasingly dependent upon them, and their prestige will continue to climb.

Parties. Political parties will become generally of greater importance as government expands in a society that will become increasingly impersonal and in which social roles will become increasingly specialized. The individual will have much at stake in governmental decisions, and his best way to influence those decisions will normally be through membership and activity in a party and in interest groups. Whether the parties will move toward bipolarization, that is, toward having conservatives in one and liberals in the other, is not clear. There has been much discussion of the possible emergence of a two-party South, but this is likely to develop quite slowly, except perhaps in the case of presidential contests. In contrast, urbanization in New England is tending to weaken traditional Republican dominance there. But the parties are likely to continue to reflect parochial and regional idiosyncrasies and to represent grand coalitions, no matter how deeply we gaze into the crystal ball.

The Judiciary. The Federal courts, and particularly the United States Supreme Court, will continue to be involved in controversy as a result of the policy-making powers of this branch of government—particularly as they affect civil rights matters. Not only will segregationists continue to argue that the courts have improperly made policy decisions that could and should be made by local governments or by the legislative branches of governments at all levels, but conservatives will bemoan the failure of the courts to set aside legislation that is incompatible with the doctrine of *laissez faire*. They will also criticize the Court for its greater concern for social rights than for property or economic rights.

The courts will very likely continue, however, to serve as an alternative policy-making locus, taking action in areas where the legislative and executive branches have hesitated to move. In particular, they are likely to lead the way in setting national policies relative to civil rights, particularly in desegregation and in the reapportionment of state legislatures. What new areas of battle the Supreme Court may enter in future years cannot easily be seen.

Paying the Piper. Taxation, as always, will be a matter of conflict. Griping about taxes is as traditional for civilians as griping about food is for soldiers. Because Americans have not been taught to associate taxes with services and because the relationship is, in any case, not obvious, all citizens hope for tax decreases. And because most citizens feel incompetent to evaluate defense programs and do not want to jeopardize national security, the tendency is, and so it will remain, to urge tax cuts by cutting down on "unnecessary" expenditures in the domestic policy area. But as has been noted, all tax-supported domestic programs are considered very important and necessary by various groups. In times of high government income, some will argue for a tax cut; others will argue that the national debt should be reduced. The former alternative is much the more popular, however. In the event of a recession or even a decline in the rate of growth of national wealth, there will also be demands for tax reduction in order to divert consumer funds to stimulate the economy. There apparently will be numerous fiscal years in which the Federal government will continue to have deficits, for no fiscal plan appears yet to have been worked out that will simultaneously (1) maintain governmental services and defense programs at levels demanded by the balance of forces upon Congress, and (2) not act as a deflationary brake upon the economy. If taxes are cut without a cut in programs, the national debt will probably rise. It is politically inexpedient to cut domestic services. It is unlikely that significant cuts can be made in the defense budget in the foreseeable future. To collect substantially more taxes than are used for governmental operations in order to retire the national debt would be deflationary and would threaten a business recession. Hence the dilemma of fiscal planners and the continuing political hassles over budgets, taxes, and spending. The future offers more of the same.

A Closing Note. We can safely assume that, despite occasional lapses and inconsistencies, Americans will remain firmly committed to democracy as a way of government in the future. Whether we can preserve democracy effectively in a world in which most peoples of the earth do not live in democracies and whether we can understand why they do not, remains to be seen. And it remains to be seen whether the nation that became great under one set of conditions can remain so under quite another.

As to the numerical dominance of nondemocratic nations, two points should perhaps be made: First, the Communist nations are well established and, as far as we know, enjoy strong support from their citizenry. Our policy will probably be to weaken them whenever possible, but the prospects for the toppling of Communist governments anywhere in the immediate future are poor. It can be our hope, but success in dealing with communism may depend in part upon learning to live with it. Some version of the "competitive coexistence" Communist line may have to be our basic policy too, for a long time to come. The problem will be in finding techniques for effective competition.

Second, the nations that are neither democratic nor Communist are probably a greater puzzle to Americans. Yet we will have to learn to accept the fact that many of the states formed since the end of World War II will not become democracies in the foreseeable future. In many of them, a politics of personalism, of following a single leader (Touré of Guinea, Nkrumah of Ghana), is the prevailing pattern and one that suits the particular culture. Furthermore, to the peoples of many of the newly created nations, democracy does not symbolize freedom, but rather carries with it the image of the colonial power that long dominated their land. What, they ask, did democracy ever do for us? Why should we adopt it? These attitudes are strange to Americans, but successful coping with world problems in the future may depend upon our learning to understand them.

While no confident answers can be given, it is at least interesting to ask whether our nation can be as great in the future in an age of mass communication and modern technology, as it was in the past. Some bemoan the fact that the economic system of individualism that was appropriate for making America a great industrial power in the nineteenth century is no longer adhered to and that in recent years a "mixed economy" has developed. Is this a handicap to America in future competition for world leadership? Most economists do not think so, but some have doubts. Perhaps a more important puzzle results from the fact our political style today is totally different from the one we had in the years when the nation was developing.

Item: The press today would never permit a constitutional convention to meet in secret sessions as did the one that produced the United States Constitution in 1787. Editors would complain that such a procedure would be "undemocratic" and would represent a violation of freedom of the press. Yet the glare of publicity that would be focused upon such a meeting today almost certainly would produce a less enduring and effective document than the one actually written. Publicity would bring every powerful interest group into the act, all of them with legitimate concerns, but most of them seeking palliatives for short-range problems rather than offering help in writing a document for the ages. There were, to be sure, built-in interest groups at the Constitutional Convention, but the environment permitted something of a long view to those who were willing to take it.

Perhaps of even greater importance is the fact that conventional knowledge is brought into the decision-making process when publicity permits the uninformed to hear of the issues and to bring their views to bear. The Founding Fathers, for example, provided a method by which the Constitution could be adopted, the only one they thought could be effective. It called for no direct vote of the people on the Constitution and allowed the new document to go into effect even though only three-quarters of the states approved it. One can imagine the fate of such proposals if they had been exposed to publicity before their adoption.

Item: Could scme of our most able Presidents and congressional leaders of the past have been elected, given contemporary public-relations techniques? Men such as Jefferson, Madison, and Lincoln had unimpressive speaking voices. Most of the people who voted for them had never seen them or heard them speak. Lincoln's famed arguments against Stephen A. Douglas in the Illinois senatorial race of 1858 made more of an impression upon historians than upon the voters—he lost the election. What would have been the effect on the public and on history if the ceremonies dedicating a military cemetery at Gettysburg, Pennsylvania, had been tele-

Figure 22-7

J. Wesley Smith Has Learned Nothing During the Course of This Book

"Dogs and monkeys will fly through the sky in machines that will strike terror into the hearts of men. Horseless carriages will grow bigger and bigger, then smaller and smaller. Women will paint their nails the color of blood, and the paint sellers will have a scandal that will rock the nation..."

We hope we have communicated with the reader, even though we have not reached J. Wesley. (By permission of Burr Shafer.)

vised? At the time, the small audience directly reached had been impressed by the lengthy oratory of the flamboyant Edward Everett, but had scarcely noticed the brief remarks, delivered in a weak voice by the sad-faced, ever-brooding President of the United States. Yet his short address was to become one of the classic pieces of prose in the entire history of the English language. Could Lincoln (who won in 1860 only because his opposition was splintered) have been reelected in 1864 against a dramatic crowd-pleaser, had there been television or even radio in those days? Could Jefferson have won in 1800, or Madison eight years later? We cannot answer these questions, but the implicitly related question of whether we can secure tomorrow's most able men for the critical decision-making posts in government may be of the utmost importance to the future of democracy.

Will Americans, with their continuing apathy about world problems and the problems of people who live differently from themselves, be able to meet a truly serious world crisis? There is no obvious answer, but it has been noted that world leaders in the recent past have given the wrong answer to the question. While Americans are still vigorous and competent, continued ability to cope with future problems may depend upon our becoming less parochial than we have been in the past and upon our more complete understanding of the forces at play in the modern world. Understanding or, at least, support for those who do understand is necessary. Refusal to face issues and flag-waving are poor substitutes for rational planning and a calm, determined approach to issues that must be adequately met if we are to preserve our most important values. Americans have successfully met most of their problems in the past. It is reasonable to assume that they can do so in the future.

SELECTED BIBLIOGRAPHY

This is the chapter for which appropriate readings will most quickly change. Perhaps a librarian can help the reader more than the authors can, for many scholars, congressional committees, government agencies, and private foundations are involved in the search for likely patterns for life tomorrow. Many worthwhile publications appear each year.

Economic factors that will shape the future are considered by such men as Bogue and Beale [2], Brown [3], Drucker [5], Stieber [8], and a congressional joint committee [7]. Historians write of the future as well as the past, although they are, for the most part, doubtful as to whether the latter is a guide to the future or whether man can ever control events [Heilbroner, 6].

Future changes in political patterns and styles are less easily predicted than are economic and social changes. But the question as to whether Americans have lost their vigor, zest for life, and willingness to win against any odds is at least partially answered by Biderman [1], who finds that, contrary to the opinions of many journalists of the day, Americans in the Korean conflict were soldiers equal to any in our other wars.

The future of the Republic lies today, as it always has, with the next generation. The authors find nothing in the evidence so far produced to indicate that that generation is not equal to the challenge.

Conclusion

1. Biderman, Albert D.: *March to Calumny,* The Macmillan Company, New York, 1962.
2. Bogue, Donald J., and Calvin L. Beale: *Economic Areas of the United States,* The Free Press of Glencoe, New York, 1961.
3. Brown, Harrison: *The Next Hundred Years: Man's Natural and Technological Resources,* The Viking Press, Inc., New York, 1957.
4. Denison, Edward F.: *The Sources of Economic Growth in the United States and the Alternatives before Us,* Supplementary Paper 13, Committee for Economic Development, New York, 1962.
5. Drucker, Peter F.: *America's Next Twenty Years,* Harper & Row, Publishers, New York, 1957.
6. Heilbroner, Robert L.: *The Future as History,* Harper & Row, Publishers, New York, 1960.
7. Joint Committee on the Economic Report, 84th Cong.: *Automation and Technological Change,* 1955.
8. Stieber, Jack (ed.): *United States Industrial Relations: The Next Twenty Years,* Michigan State University, Labor and Industrial Relations Center, East Lansing, Mich., 1958.
9. Whyte, William H., Jr., *The Organization Man,* Doubleday & Company, Inc., Garden City, N.Y., 1957. (Paperback.)

THE CONSTITUTION OF THE UNITED STATES OF AMERICA

Preamble. We, the people of the United States, in order to form a more perfect union, establish justice, insure domestic tranquility, provide for the common defence, promote the general welfare, and secure the blessings of liberty to ourselves and our posterity, do ordain and establish this Constitution for the United States of America.

Article I

Section 1. All legislative powers herein granted shall be vested in a Congress of the United States, which shall consist of a Senate and House of Representatives.

Section 2. 1. The House of Representatives shall be composed of members chosen every second year by the people of the several States, and the electors in each State shall have the qualifications requisite for electors of the most numerous branch of the State legislature.

2. No person shall be a Representative who shall not have attained to the age of twenty-five years, and been seven years a citizen of the United States, and who shall not, when elected, be an inhabitant of that State in which he shall be chosen.

3. Representatives and direct taxes shall be apportioned among the several States which may be included within this Union, according to their respective numbers, [which shall be determined by adding to the whole number of free persons,][1] including those bound to service for a term of years, and excluding Indians not taxed, [three fifths for all other persons].[2] The actual enumeration shall be made within three years after the first meeting of the Congress of the United States, and within every subsequent term of ten years, in such manner as they shall by law direct. The number of Representatives shall not exceed one for every thirty thousand, but each State shall have at least one Representative; [and until such enumeration shall be made, the State of New Hampshire shall be entitled to choose three, Massachusetts eight, Rhode Island and Providence Plantations one, Connecticut five, New York six, New Jersey four, Pennsylvania eight, Delaware one, Maryland six, Virginia ten, North Carolina five, South Carolina five, and Georgia three].[3]

[1] Modified by the Fourteenth Amendment.
[2] Superseded by the Fourteenth Amendment.
[3] Temporary provision.

4. When vacancies happen in the representation from any State, the executive authority thereof shall issue writs of election to fill such vacancies.

5. The House of Representatives shall choose their Speaker and other officers; and shall have the sole power of impeachment.

Section 3. [1. The Senate of the United States shall be composed of two Senators from each State, chosen by the legislature thereof, for six years; and each Senator shall have one vote.][4]

2. Immediately after they shall be assembled in consequence of the first election, they shall be divided as equally as may be into three classes. The seats of the Senators of the first class shall be vacated at the expiration of the second year, of the second class at the expiration of the fourth year, and of the third class at the expiration of the sixth year, so that one third may be chosen every second year; [and if vacancies happen by resignation, or otherwise, during the recess of the legislature of any State, the executive thereof may make temporary appointment until the next meeting of the legislature, which shall then fill such vacancies].[5]

3. No person shall be a Senator who shall not have attained to the age of thirty years, and been nine years a citizen of the United States, and who shall not, when elected, be an inhabitant of that State for which he shall be chosen.

4. The Vice President of the United States shall be president of the Senate, but shall have no vote, unless they be equally divided.

5. The Senate shall choose their other officers, and also a president pro tempore, in the absence of the Vice President, or when he shall exercise the office of President of the United States.

6. The Senate shall have the sole power to try all impeachments. When sitting for that purpose, they shall be on oath or affirmation. When the President of the United States is tried, the Chief Justice shall preside: and no person shall be convicted without the concurrence of two thirds of the members present.

7. Judgment in cases of impeachment shall not extend further than to removal from office, and disqualification to hold and enjoy any office of honor, trust, or profit under the United States: but the party convicted shall nevertheless be liable and subject to indictment, trial, judgment, and punishment, according to law.

Section 4. 1. The times, places, and manner of holding elections for Senators and Representatives shall be prescribed in each State by the legislature thereof; but the Congress may at any time by law make or alter such regulations, except as to the places of choosing Senators.

[2. The Congress shall assemble at least once in every year, and such meeting shall be on the first Monday in December, unless they shall by law appoint a different day.][6]

[4] Superseded by the Seventeenth Amendment.

[5] Modified by the Seventeenth Amendment.

[6] Superseded by the Twentieth Amendment.

Section 5. 1. Each House shall be the judge of the elections, returns, and qualifications of its own members, and a majority of each shall constitute a quorum to do business; but a smaller number may adjourn from day to day, and may be authorized to compel the attendance of absent members, in such manner, and under such penalties, as each House may provide.

2. Each House may determine the rules of its proceedings, punish its members for disorderly behavior, and, with the concurrence of two thirds, expel a member.

3. Each House shall keep a journal of its proceedings, and from time to time publish the same, excepting such parts as may in their judgment require secrecy; and the yeas and nays of the members of either House on any question shall, at the desire of one fifth of those present, be entered on the journal.

4. Neither House, during the session of Congress, shall, without the consent of the other, adjourn for more than three days, nor to any other place than that in which the two Houses shall be sitting.

Section 6. 1. The Senators and Representatives shall receive a compensation for their services, to be ascertained by law, and paid out of the Treasury of the United States. They shall in all cases, except treason, felony, and breach of the peace, be privileged from arrest during their attendance at the session of their respective Houses, and in going to and returning from the same; and for any speech or debate in either House, they shall not be questioned in any other place.

2. No Senator or Representative shall, during the time for which he was elected, be appointed to any civil office under the authority of the United States, which shall have been created, or the emoluments whereof shall have been increased, during such time; and no person holding any office under the United States shall be a member of either House during his continuance in office.

Section 7. 1. All bills for raising revenue shall originate in the House of Representatives; but the Senate may propose or concur with amendments as on other bills.

2. Every bill which shall have passed the House of Representatives and the Senate, shall, before it becomes a law, be presented to the President of the United States; if he approve he shall sign it, but if not he shall return it, with his objections, to that House in which it shall have originated, who shall enter the objections at large on their journal, and proceed to reconsider it. If after such reconsideration two thirds of that House shall agree to pass the bill, it shall be sent, together with the objections to the other House, by which it shall likewise be reconsidered, and if approved by two thirds of that House, it shall become a law. But in all such cases the votes of both Houses shall be determined by yeas and nays, and the names of the persons voting for and against the bill shall be entered on the journal of each House respectively. If any bill shall not be returned by the President within ten days (Sundays excepted) after it shall have

been presented to him, the same shall be a law, in like manner as if he had signed it, unless the Congress by their adjournment prevent its return, in which case it shall not be a law.

3. Every order, resolution, or vote to which the concurrence of the Senate and House of Representatives may be necessary (except on a question of adjournment) shall be presented to the President of the United States; and before the same shall take effect, shall be approved by him, or being disapproved by him, shall be repassed by two thirds of the Senate and House of Representatives, according to the rules and limitations prescribed in the case of a bill.

Section 8. 1. The Congress shall have power to lay and collect taxes, duties, imposts, and excises, to pay the debts and provide for the common defense and general welfare of the United States; but all duties, imposts, and excises shall be uniform throughout the United States;

2. To borrow money on the credit of the United States;

3. To regulate commerce with foreign nations, and among the several States, and with the Indian tribes;

4. To establish a uniform rule of naturalization and uniform laws on the subject of bankruptcies throughout the United States;

5. To coin money, regulate the value thereof, and of foreign coin, and fix the standard of weights and measures;

6. To provide for the punishment of counterfeiting the securities and current coin of the United States;

7. To establish post offices and post roads;

8. To promote the progress of science and useful arts, by securing for limited times to authors and inventors the exclusive right to their respective writings and discoveries;

9. To constitute tribunals inferior to the Supreme Court;

10. To define and punish piracies and felonies committed on the high seas, and offenses against the law of nations;

11. To declare war, grant letters of marque and reprisal, and make rules concerning captures on land and water;

12. To raise and support armies, but no appropriation of money to that use shall be for a longer term than two years;

13. To provide and maintain a navy;

14. To make rules for the government and regulation of the land and naval forces;

15. To provide for calling forth the militia to execute the laws of the Union, suppress insurrections, and repel invasions;

16. To provide for organizing, arming, and disciplining the militia, and for governing such part of them as may be employed in the service of the United States, reserving to the States respectively the appointment of the officers, and the authority of training the militia according to the discipline prescribed by Congress;

17. To exercise exclusive legislation in all cases whatsoever, over such district (not exceeding ten miles square) as may, by cession of particular

States, and the acceptance of Congress, become the seat of the government of the United States, and to exercise like authority over all places purchased by the consent of the legislature of the State in which the same shall be, for the erection of forts, magazines, arsenals, dock-yards, and other needful buildings; and

18. To make all laws which shall be necessary and proper for carrying into execution the foregoing powers, and all other powers vested by this Constitution in the government of the United States, or in any department or officer thereof.

Section 9. [1. The migration or importation of such persons as any of the States now existing shall think proper to admit, shall not be prohibited by the Congress prior to the year one thousand eight hundred and eight, but a tax or duty may be imposed on such importation, not exceeding ten dollars for each person.][7]

2. The privilege of the writ of habeas corpus shall not be suspended, unless when in cases of rebellion or invasion the public safety may require it.

3. No bill of attainder or ex post facto law shall be passed.

[4. No capitation, or other direct, tax shall be laid, unless in proportion to the census or enumeration hereinbefore directed to be taken.][8]

5. No tax or duty shall be laid on articles exported from any State.

6. No preference shall be given by any regulation of commerce or revenue to the ports of one State over those of another: nor shall vessels bound to, or from, one State, be obligated to enter, clear, or pay duties in another.

7. No money shall be drawn from the Treasury, but in consequence of appropriations made by law; and a regular statement and account of the receipts and expenditures of all public money shall be published from time to time.

8. No title of nobility shall be granted by the United States: and no person holding any office of profit or trust under them, shall, without the consent of the Congress, accept any present, emolument, office, or title, of any kind whatever, from any king, prince, or foreign State.

Section 10. 1. No State shall enter into any treaty, alliance, or confederation; grant letters of marque and reprisal; coin money; emit bills of credit; make anything but gold and silver coin a tender in payment of debts; pass any bill of attainder, ex post facto law, or law impairing the obligation of contracts, or grant any title of nobility.

2. No State shall, without the consent of the Congress, lay any imposts or duties on imports or exports, except what may be absolutely necessary for executing its inspection laws: and the net produce of all duties and imposts, laid by any State on imports or exports, shall be for the use of the Treasury of the United States; and all such laws shall be subject to the revision and control of the Congress.

[7] Temporary provision.

[8] Modified by the Sixteenth Amendment.

3. No State shall, without the consent of Congress, lay any duty on tonnage, keep troops, or ships of war in time of peace, enter into any agreement or compact with another State, or with a foreign power, or engage in war, unless actually invaded, or in such imminent danger as will not admit of delay.

Article II

Section 1. 1. The executive power shall be vested in a President of the United States of America. He shall hold his office during the term of four years, and, together with the Vice President, chosen for the same term, be elected, as follows:

2. Each State shall appoint, in such manner as the legislature thereof may direct, a number of electors, equal to the whole number of Senators and Representatives to which the State may be entitled in the Congress: but no Senator or Representative, or person holding an office of trust or profit under the United States, shall be appointed an elector.[9]

[The electors shall meet in their respective States, and vote by ballot for two persons, of whom one at least shall not be an inhabitant of the same State with themselves. And they shall make a list of all the persons voted for, and of the number of votes for each; which list they shall sign and certify, and transmit sealed to the seat of the government of the United States, directed to the president of the Senate. The president of the Senate shall, in the presence of the Senate and House of Representatives, open all the certificates, and the votes shall then be counted. The person having the greatest number of votes shall be the President, if such number be a majority of the whole number of electors appointed; and if there be more than one who have such majority, and have an equal number of votes, then the House of Representatives shall immediately choose by ballot one of them for President; and if no person have a majority, then from the five highest on the list the said House shall in like manner choose the President. But in choosing the President, the votes shall be taken by States, the representation from each State having one vote; a quorum for this purpose shall consist of a member or members from two thirds of the States, and a majority of all the States shall be necessary to a choice. In every case, after the choice of the President, the person having the greatest number of votes of the electors shall be the Vice President. But if there should remain two or more who have equal votes, the Senate shall choose from them by ballot the Vice President.][10]

3. The Congress may determine the time of choosing the electors, and the day on which they shall give their votes; which day shall be the same throughout the United States.

[9] Modified by the Twenty-third Amendment.
[10] This paragraph superseded by the Twelfth Amendment, which, in turn, is modified by the Twentieth Amendment.

4. No person except a natural-born citizen, or a citizen of the United States, at the time of the adoption of this Constitution, shall be eligible to the office of President; neither shall any person be eligible to that office who shall not have attained to the age of thirty-five years, and been fourteen years a resident within the United States.

5. In case of the removal of the President from office, or of his death, resignation, or inability to discharge the powers and duties of the said office, the same shall devolve on the Vice President, and the Congress may by law provide for the case of removal, death, resignation, or inability, both of the President and Vice President, declaring what officer shall then act as President, and such officer shall act accordingly, until the disability be removed, or a President shall be elected.

6. The President shall, at stated times, receive for his services a compensation, which shall neither be increased nor diminished during the period for which he shall have been elected, and he shall not receive within that period any other emolument from the United States, or any of them.

7. Before he enter on the execution of his office, he shall take the following oath or affirmation: "I do solemnly swear (or affirm) that I will faithfully execute the office of President of the United States, and will, to the best of my ability, preserve, protect, and defend the Constitution of the United States."

Section 2. 1. The President shall be commander in chief of the army and navy of the United States, and of the militia of the several States, when called into the actual service of the United States; he may require the opinion, in writing, of the principal officer in each of the executive departments, upon any subject relating to the duties of their respective offices, and he shall have power to grant reprieves and pardons for offenses against the United States, except in cases of impeachment.

2. He shall have power, by and with the advice and consent of the Senate, to make treaties, provided two thirds of the Senators present concur; and he shall nominate, and by and with the advice and consent of the Senate, shall appoint ambassadors, other public ministers and consuls, judges of the Supreme Court, and all other officers of the United States, whose appointments are not herein otherwise provided for, and which shall be established by law: but the Congress may by law vest the appointment of such inferior officers, as they think proper, in the President alone, in the courts of law, or in the heads of departments.

3. The President shall have power to fill up all vacancies that may happen during the recess of the Senate, by granting commissions which shall expire at the end of their next session.

Section 3. He shall from time to time give to the Congress information of the state of the Union, and recommend to their consideration such measures as he shall judge necessary and expedient; he may, on extraordinary occasions, convene both Houses, or either of them, and in case of disagreement between them, with respect to the time of adjournment, he may adjourn them to such time as he shall think proper; he shall receive ambassadors and other public ministers; he shall take care that the laws be faithfully executed, and shall commission all the officers of the United States.

Section 4. The President, Vice President, and all civil officers of the United States, shall be removed from office on impeachment for, and conviction of, treason, bribery, or other high crimes and misdemeanors.

Article III

Section 1. The judicial power of the United States shall be vested in one Supreme Court, and in such inferior courts as the Congress may from time to time ordain and establish. The judges, both of the Supreme and inferior courts, shall hold their offices during good behavior, and shall, at stated times, receive for their services a compensation, which shall not be diminished during their continuance in office.

Section 2. 1. The judicial power shall extend to all cases, in law and equity, arising under this Constitution, the laws of the United States, and treaties made, or which shall be made, under their authority;—to all cases affecting ambassadors, other public ministers, and consuls;—to all cases of admiralty and maritime jurisdiction;—to controversies to which the United States shall be a party;—to controversies between two or more States; [—between a State and citizens of another State;][11]—between citizens of different States;—between citizens of the same State claiming lands under grants of different States, and between a State, or the citizens thereof, and foreign States, citizens, or subjects.

2. In all cases affecting ambassadors, other public ministers, and consuls, and those in which a State shall be party, the Supreme Court shall have original jurisdiction. In all the other cases before mentioned, the Supreme Court shall have appellate jurisdiction, both as to law and fact, with such exceptions, and under such regulations, as the Congress shall make.

3. The trial of all crimes, except in cases of impeachment, shall be by jury; and such trial shall be held in the State where the said crimes shall have been committed; but when not committed within any State, the trial shall be at such place or places as the Congress may by law have directed.

Section 3. 1. Treason against the United States shall consist only in levying war against them, or in adhering to their enemies, giving them aid and comfort. No person shall be convicted of treason unless on the testimony of two witnesses to the same overt act, or on confession in open court.

2. The Congress shall have power to declare the punishment of treason, but no attainder of treason shall work corruption of blood, or forfeiture except during the life of the person attained.

[11] Limited by the Eleventh Amendment.

Article IV

Section 1. Full faith and credit shall be given in each State to the public acts, records, and judicial proceedings of every other State. And the Congress may by general laws prescribe the manner in which such acts, records, and proceedings shall be proved, and the effect thereof.

Section 2. 1. The citizens of each State shall be entitled to all privileges and immunities of citizens in the several States.

2. A person charged in any State with treason, felony, or other crime, who shall flee from justice, and be found in another State, shall, on demand of the executive authority of the State from which he fled, be delivered up, to be removed to the State having jurisdiction of the crime.

[3. No person held to service or labor in one State, under the laws thereof, escaping into another, shall, in consequence of any law or regulation therein, be discharged from such service or labor, but shall be delivered up on claim of the party to whom such service or labor may be due.][12]

Section 3. 1. New States may be admitted by the Congress into this Union; but no new State shall be formed or erected within the jurisdiction of any other State; nor any State be formed by the junction of two or more States, or parts of States, without the consent of the legislatures of the States concerned as well as of the Congress.

2. The Congress shall have power to dispose of and make all needful rules and regulations respecting the territory or other property belonging to the United States; and nothing in this Constitution shall be so construed as to prejudice any claims of the United States, or of any particular State.

Section 4. The United States shall guarantee to every State in this Union a republican form of government, and shall protect each of them against invasion; and, on application of the legislature, or of the executive (when the legislature cannot be convened), against domestic violence.

Article V

The Congress, whenever two thirds of both Houses shall deem it necessary, shall propose amendments to this Constitution, or, on the application of the legislatures of two thirds of the several States, shall call a convention for proposing amendments which, in either case, shall be valid to all intents and purposes, as part of this Constitution, when ratified by the legislatures of three fourths of the several States, or by conventions in three fourths thereof, as the one or the other mode of ratification may be proposed by the Congress; provided [that no amendment which may be made prior to the year one thousand eight hundred and eight shall in any manner affect the first and fourth clauses in the ninth section of the first article; and][13] that no State, without its consent, shall be deprived of its equal suffrage in the Senate.

[12] Superseded by the Thirteenth Amendment, so far as it relates to slaves.
[13] Temporary provision.

United States by citizens of another State, or by citizens or subjects of any foreign State.

Amendment XII [September 25, 1804]

The electors shall meet in their respective States, and vote by ballot for President and Vice President, one of whom, at least, shall not be an inhabitant of the same State with themselves; they shall name in their ballots the persons voted for as President, and in distinct ballots the persons voted for as Vice President, and they shall make distinct lists of all persons voted for as President, and of all persons voted for as Vice President, and of the number of votes for each, which lists they shall sign and certify, and transmit sealed to the seat of the government of the United States, directed to the president of the Senate;—the president of the Senate shall, in the presence of the Senate and House of Representatives, open all the certificates, and the votes shall then be counted;—the person having the greatest number of votes for President, shall be the President, if such number be a majority of the whole number of electors appointed; and if no persons have such majority, then from the persons having the highest numbers not exceeding three on the list of those voted for as President, the House of Representatives shall choose immediately, by ballot, the President. But in choosing the President, the votes shall be taken by States, the representation from each State having one vote; a quorum for this purpose shall consist of a member or members from two thirds of the States, and a majority of all the States shall be necessary to a choice. And if the House of Representatives shall not choose a President whenever the right of choice shall devolve upon them, before the fourth day of March next following, then the Vice President shall act as President, as in the case of the death or other constitutional disability of the President.—the Person having the greatest number of votes as Vice President, shall be the Vice President, if such number be a majority of the whole number of electors appointed, and if no person have a majority, then from the two highest numbers on the list, the Senate shall choose the Vice President; a quorum for the purpose shall consist of two thirds of the whole number of Senators, and a majority of the whole number shall be necessary to a choice. But no person constitutionally ineligible to the office of President shall be eligible to that of Vice President of the United States.[14]

Amendment XIII [December 18, 1865]

Section 1. Neither slavery nor involuntary servitude, except as a punishment for crime whereof the party shall have been duly convicted, shall exist within the United States, or any place subject to their jurisdiction.

Section 2. Congress shall have power to enforce this article by appropriate legislation.

[14] Modified by the Twentieth Amendment.

Amendment XIV [July 28, 1868]

Section 1. All persons born or naturalized in the United States, and subject to the jurisdiction thereof, are citizens of the United States and of the State wherein they reside. No State shall make or enforce any law which shall abridge the privileges or immunities of citizens of the United States; nor shall any State deprive any person of life, liberty, or property, without due process of law; nor deny to any person within its jurisdiction the equal protection of the laws.

Section 2. Representatives shall be apportioned among the several States according to their respective numbers, counting the whole number of persons in each state, excluding Indians not taxed. But when the right to vote at any election for the choice of electors for President and Vice President of the United States, Representatives in Congress, the executive and judicial officers of a State, or the members of the legislature thereof, is denied to any of the male inhabitants of such State, being twenty-one years of age, and citizens of the United States, or in any way abridged, except for participation in rebellion, or other crime, the basis of representation therein shall be reduced in the proportion which the number of such male citizens shall bear to the whole number of male citizens twenty-one years of age in such State.

Section 3. No person shall be a Senator or Representative in Congress, or elector of President and Vice President, or hold any office, civil or military, under the United States, or under any State, who, having previously taken an oath, as a member of Congress, or as an officer of the United States, or as a member of any State legislature, or as an executive or judicial officer of any State, to support the Constitution of the United States, shall have engaged in insurrection or rebellion against the same, or given aid or comfort to the enemies thereof. But Congress may by a vote of two thirds of each House, remove such disability.

Section 4. The validity of the public debt of the United States; authorized by law, including debts incurred for payment of pensions and bounties for services in suppressing insurrection or rebellion, shall not be questioned. But neither the United States nor any State shall assume or pay any debt or obligation incurred in aid of insurrection or rebellion against the United States, or any claim for the loss or emancipation of any slave; but all such debts, obligations, and claims shall be held illegal and void.

Section 5. The Congress shall have power to enforce, by appropriate legislation, the provisions of this article.

Amendment XV [March 30, 1870]

Section 1. The right of citizens of the United States to vote shall not be denied or abridged by the United States or by any State on account of race, color, or previous condition of servitude.

Section 2. The Congress shall have power to enforce this article by appropriate legislation.

Amendment XVI [February 25, 1913]

The Congress shall have power to lay and collect taxes on incomes, from whatever source derived, without apportionment among the several States, and without regard to any census or enumeration.

Amendment XVII [May 31, 1913]

The Senate of the United States shall be composed of two Senators from each State, elected by the people thereof, for six years; and each Senator shall have one vote. The electors in each State shall have the qualifications requisite for electors of the most numerous branch of the State legislature.

When vacancies happen in the representation of any State in the Senate, the executive authority of such State shall issue writs of election to fill such vacancies.

Provided, That the legislature of any State may empower the executive thereof to make temporary appointments until the people fill the vacancies by election as the legislature may direct.

This amendment shall not be so construed as to affect the election or term of any Senator chosen before it becomes valid as part of the Constitution.

Amendment XVIII [January 29, 1919]

Section 1. After one year from the ratification of this article the manufacture, sale, or transportation of intoxicating liquors within, the importation thereof into, or the exportation thereof from the United States and all territory subject to the jurisdiction thereof for beverage purposes is hereby prohibited.

Section 2. The Congress and the several States shall have concurrent power to enforce this article by appropriate legislation.

Section 3. This article shall be inoperative unless it shall have been ratified as an amendment to the Constitution by the legislatures of the several States, as provided in the Constitution, within seven years from the date of the submission hereof to the States by the Congress.[15]

Amendment XIX [August 26, 1920]

1. The right of citizens of the United States to vote shall not be denied or abridged by the United States or by any State on account of sex.

2. Congress shall have power, by appropriate legislation, to enforce the provisions of this article.

Amendment XX [February 6, 1933]

Section 1. The terms of the President and Vice President shall end at noon on the 20th day of January, and the terms of Senators and Representatives at noon on the 3rd day of January, of the years in which such

[15] Repealed by the Twenty-first Amendment.

terms would have ended if this article had not been ratified; and the terms of their successors shall then begin.

Section 2. The Congress shall assemble at least once in every year, and such meeting shall begin at noon on the 3rd day of January, unless they shall by law appoint a different day.

Section 3. If, at the time fixed for the beginning of the term of the President, the President elect shall have died, the Vice President elect shall become President. If a President shall not have been chosen before the time fixed for the beginning of his term, or if the President elect shall have failed to qualify, then the Vice President elect shall act as President until a President shall have qualified; and the Congress may by law provide for the case wherein neither a President elect nor a Vice President elect shall have qualified, declaring who shall then act as President, or the manner in which one who is to act shall be selected, and such person shall act accordingly until a President or Vice President shall have qualified.

Section 4. The Congress may by law provide for the case of the death of any of the persons from whom the House of Representatives may choose a President whenever the right of choice shall have devolved upon them, and for the case of the death of any of the persons from whom the Senate may choose a Vice President whenever the right of choice shall have devolved upon them.

Section 5. Sections 1 and 2 shall take effect on the 15th day of October following the ratification of this article.

Section 6. This article shall be inoperative unless it shall have been ratified as an amendment to the Constitution by the legislatures of three fourths of the several States within seven years from the date of its submission.

Amendment XXI [December 5, 1933]

Section 1. The eighteenth article of amendment to the Constitution of the United States is hereby repealed.

Section 2. The transportation or importation into any State, Territory, or possession of the United States for delivery or use therein of intoxicating liquors, in violation of the laws thereof, is hereby prohibited.

Section 3. This article shall be inoperative unless it shall have been ratified as an amendment to the Constitution by conventions in the several States, as provided in the Constitution, within seven years from the date of submission hereof to the States by the Congress.

Amendment XXII [February 27, 1951]

Section 1. No person shall be elected to the office of the President more than twice, and no person who has held the office of President, or acted as President, for more than two years of a term to which some other person was elected President shall be elected to the office of the President more than once. But this Article shall not apply to any person holding the office of President when this Article was proposed by the Congress, and shall not prevent any person who may be holding the office of President, or acting as President, during the term within which this Article becomes operative from holding the office of President, or acting as President during the remainder of such term.

Section 2. This Article shall be inoperative unless it shall have been ratified as an amendment to the Constitution by the legislatures of three fourths of the several States within seven years from the date of its submission to the States by the Congress.

Amendment XXIII [March 29, 1961]

Section 1. The District constituting the seat of Government of the United States shall appoint in such manner as the Congress may direct:

A number of electors of President and Vice President equal to the whole number of Senators and Representatives in Congress to which the District would be entitled if it were a State, but in no event more than the least populous State; they shall be in addition to those appointed by the States, but they shall be considered, for the purposes of the election of President and Vice President, to be electors appointed by a State; and they shall meet in the District and perform such duties as provided by the twelfth article of amendment.

Section 2. The Congress shall have power to enforce this article by appropriate legislation.

Amendment XXIV [January 23, 1964]

Section 1. The right of citizens of the United States to vote in any primary or other election for President or Vice President, for electors for President or Vice President, or for Senator or Representative in Congress, shall not be denied or abridged by the United States or any state by reason of failure to pay any poll tax or other tax.

Section 2. The Congress shall have power to enforce this article by appropriate legislation.

This glossary includes all definitions displayed in the text, or found in the body of the text, plus additional terms. Where possible, terms from other social sciences are borrowed from accepted textbook definitions. Terms from the other social sciences included in this section are taken from the following books, unless other references are given.

Arnold W. Green, *Sociology,* 4th ed., McGraw-Hill Book Company, New York, 1964.

Paul B. Horton and Chester L. Hunt, *Sociology,* McGraw-Hill Book Company, New York, 1964.

David Krech, Richard S. Crutchfield, and Egerton L. Ballachey, *Individual in Society,* McGraw-Hill Book Company, New York, 1962.

Paul A. Samuelson, *Economics,* 6th ed., McGraw-Hill Book Company, New York, 1964.

For terms not listed in this glossary, check the above references or the dictionaries listed below:

Joseph Dunner, *Dictionary of Political Science,* Philosophical Library, Inc., New York, 1964.

Jack Plano and Milton Greenberg, *The American Political Dictionary,* Holt, Rinehart and Winston, Inc., New York, 1963.

Alien. A resident noncitizen.

Alienation. A psychological state in which the individual feels estranged from society. He believes that he is not performing a role at a status level for which he is qualified or to which he is entitled. In politics, the alienated person tends to feel that he is unable to influence the selection of public officials or the determination of public policy.

Amicus curiae. A Latin phrase meaning "friend of the courts"; in Anglo-American jurisprudence, a judge usually has discretionary power to permit persons who are not actual parties in a legal proceeding to present briefs in which they argue a position relative to a pending case and seek to influence the decision. In this manner, the judicial system recognizes that a specific case may have social implications extending beyond the parties directly involved. Briefs are often filed as *amicus curiae* by civil rights and other groups interested in social action when the case seems relevant to their cause.

Anomie. As first used by the sociologist Emile Durkheim, the term referred to a state of relative normlessness in a social system. Today it has come to refer to psychological as well as sociological elements, to a state of mind involving a sense of separation from the group. The individual tends to believe that society lacks meaningful values; he, at least, does not understand prevailing values.

Anxiety. A vague, unfocused, and highly persistent fear. It produces a compulsion toward some type of behavior to relieve the tension. The behavior may have political implications.

Apportionment. The allocation of legislative seats to constituencies. Apportionment may be done using a more or less permanent formula or an *ad hoc* basis. The United States Senate is permanently apportioned, using a simple formula. The formula now used for apportioning the House dates from 1930. It leaves districting, or the setting of specific boundaries for the seats allocated, to the state legislatures. Legislative action is, however, subject to court review.

Attainder, bill of. A legislative action declaring the guilt of and punishment for an individual. Attainder involves the assumption by the legislature of a judicial function.

Attitude. An enduring system of positive or negative evaluations, emotional feelings, and pro or con action tendencies with respect to a social (or political) object. (Krech.)

Authority. Legitimate power. Generally, power is legitimatized by an ideology justifying the reasons for selection of power wielders (e.g., the divine right of kings or constitutional government), but more subtly by the dominant image of the particular public role (e.g., the President is seen as having authority to send troops to quell a riot, but not to seize the steel industry in peacetime).

Availability. Possessed by an actual or potential political candidate whenever his public image, social background, institutional memberships, job experience, and other characteristics are viewed by a large segment of the membership of society as being appropriate for the office sought.

Behavioralism. Essentially a point of view and an approach toward the study of politics. The principal unit of analysis is not the *institution,* but the *individual* as he behaves in groups and in relation to other individuals. It stresses empirical and statistical methods, the objective being to build theory.

Bureaucracy. Any large organization that is characterized by specialization of the work assignments of personnel; essentially impersonal relationships both among persons in the agency and with those in external clientele groups; and a formal hierarchical structure.

Caste system. A stratified society in which social position is entirely determined by parentage, with no provision for achieved status. (Horton and Hunt.)

Caucus. The nominating caucus is a preliminary and private meeting of certain self-appointed members of a political party for the purpose of selecting candidates. It is to be distinguished from the meetings or conferences of party members in a legislature for the purpose of deciding committee assignments and the party's position on public issues; the latter caucuses are referred to as the Senate Republican conference, the House Democratic caucus, etc. (Hugh A. Bone, *American Politics and the Party System,* 2d ed. McGraw-Hill Book Company, New York, 1953.)

Charisma. Natural, inspirational leadership. Originally (in the New Testament), it referred to a gift stemming from God's grace, but since Weber's time, the term has been used to refer to secular leadership as well. (Carl J. Friedrich, *Man and His Government,* McGraw-Hill Book Company, New York, 1963, especially pp. 114–115.)

Checks and balances. Separate branches of American government are given legal powers by which they can check each other and thereby maintain a balance in which no branch can consistently override the others.

Citizen. A full member of the state, who owes the state his allegiance and is entitled to the privileges, rights, and benefits of his membership.

Class (social). In some social models, a self-conscious group whose members occupy similar social positions, and who share a similar life-style, set of values, and behavior pattern. In practical terms, members of a class have little internal communication and the class is commonly identified by certain quantitative indicators—in particular, wealth, income, education, and occupation.

Cloture. A rule to close off debate in the Senate. A favorable vote of two-thirds of the senators voting is required. One-sixth of the membership (seventeen senators) can force a vote through petition.

Coalition. An alliance of individuals, factions, or parties for political-action purposes. It is usually temporary and may be for some particular purpose rather than for all types of political activity.

Committee of the whole. Technically, the whole legislative chamber sitting as a committee of itself. It is used by the House to permit relaxation of formal procedures and nonrecord votes. Bills passed in committee of the whole are formally voted on officially and for the record later; at this time, legislators may, if they wish, change their position since they know on which side of the question the majority is likely to be.

Communism. A political system in which legitimate rule rests exclusively with the working class (proletariat). It is characterized by a small leadership elite, a single political party, and complete control by the elite over economic and social institutions. Also a political ideology that incorporates the above and is based on the ideas of Karl Marx and his intellectual successors.

Confederacy. A political association of independent states brought together for certain purposes, usually foreign diplomacy and mutual defense.

Power relationships between levels are determined by agreements among the states, and the central unit possesses only delegated powers.

Conference committee. A committee consisting of members of both houses in a legislature. Its task is to iron out differences in bills that have passed each house in a different form. Members are appointed by the Speaker of the House and President of the Senate.

Conscientious objector. A person who declines to render military service because of his moral or religious beliefs.

Conservatism: Belief that change in social and economic systems should be cautious and relatively slow, and that the burden of proof should be carried by advocates of change.

Constitution. The fundamental law; the rules about rule making. It describes the basic structure of government and allocates political powers. This allocation is made among levels of government, among branches of government, and between government and the individual.

Containment. A general principle of American foreign policy first enunciated by President Truman in 1947. It states that a primary aim of American policy is to contain communism within existing boundaries, with the hope that prevention of expansion would encourage collapse of Communist systems.

Cross pressure. Social and psychological forces upon the individual that tend to conflict and hence partially cancel one another out. They result from overlapping organizational memberships or conflicting psychological identifications. Cross-pressured persons tend to withdraw from political participation.

Culture. The pattern of all those arrangements, material or behavioral, which have been adopted by a society as the traditional ways of solving the problems of its members. (Krech.)

Cultural values. Beliefs shared by the members of a society, or by the typical occupants of various positions (roles) in the society, of what is desirable or undesirable. Values are widely shared by the members of a society.

Democracy (liberal). Democracy in a complex society is a political system that affords frequent opportunities for changing the governing officials and a social mechanism that permits nearly all of the adult population to influence major public-policy decisions by choosing from among genuine competitors for public office and through other procedures viewed by most citizens as legitimate.

Democracy (totalitarian). A political system that begins by defining a goal (or a theory of the good life) that is often seen in idealistic terms and attempts to mold society to a pattern designed to lead to the goal. Totalitarian democracies, as distinguished from liberal democracies, are more interested in the ends than in the means (the procedures by which rules are made).

Discharge of bills. A majority of the elected members of either the House or Senate may require a bill to be reported out of a committee by signing a discharge petition.

Dual federalism. The legal theory that the two levels of government in a federal system are coequal sovereignties, each supreme in its own sphere and each performing functions separate and distinct from the other. It was first expressed as a theory by the Supreme Court during the Chief Justiceship of Roger B. Taney (1836–1864), reached its peak around the time of World War I, and was discarded by the Court in *United States v. Darby,* 312 U.S. 100 (1941).

Elite. The principal power holders in a social or political system. A system may have a monolithic elite or a number of competing or cooperating elites. Members of the elites in any political system are likely to include the principal elective and party officeholders, high-ranking civil and military administrative officers, interest-group leaders, and communications-system leaders.

Eminent domain. The right of the government to take private property for public use. Just compensation, as determined by the judicial process, must be given.

Ethnocentrism. The practice of judging other cultures and subcultures by the values and standards of the culture of the person doing the judging. It almost necessarily results in the conclusion that one's own community, nation, or way of life is superior to all others. Studies of the authoritarian personality have concluded that such individuals are highly ethnocentric.

Ex post facto ("after the fact"). A criminal law applied retroactively. Such a law is prohibited by the Constitution. The prohibition does not extend to tax or other noncriminal law.

Fascism. A political system that is based on the absolute authority of the state, a dictatorial leader, a single political party, and complete government control over economic and social institutions.

Father figure. A person who provides for another a psychological substitute in the role of the father. In politics, such a figure may be perceived in the role of protector and provider for the people of a community, political organization, or nation generally, or specifically for the *individual.* (Krech.)

Favorite son. A candidate for President who is presented by his home state to the national convention, even though his chances for nomination are poor. Votes for a favorite son are most common on the first ballot. The practice is supported for a variety of motives: It serves to hold a delegation uncommitted so as to permit bargaining, to permit stalling until trends become clear, to honor a distinguished local politician, to help gain publicity and support for a candidate seeking election to office within the state, or to offer a candidate who may, in the case of a stalemate, be nominated.

Federal system. A system in which power is divided between a central government and regional governments, each legally supreme in its own area of jurisdiction. Relationships between central and regional governments may be either competitive, cooperative, or a mixture of both.

Filibuster. A technique of continuous speaking to prevent a vote from being taken. In Congress, the technique is applicable only in the Senate, not in the House of Representatives.

Folkways. Behavior patterns or acts of relatively minor importance to the society. Persons who violate them are viewed by conventional persons as odd, but they are not severely punished.

Frontier individualism. An American ideology that was dominant from the beginning of the nineteenth century until the Civil War. It emphasized the values of the frontier yeoman farmer. In general, it held that government should perform functions that could benefit the common man. It was, hence, intensely empirical. The ideology was individualistic, not for doctrinaire reasons, but because most of the problems of the frontier farmer or merchant could be met only by himself, sometimes working in concert with his neighbors.

Full faith and credit. A clause of the Federal Constitution requiring that the legal acts and records and judicial proceedings of one state be recognized as valid in the courts of every other state in respect to civil matters (such as divorces, wills, and contracts).

Game theory. An attempt to predict actions based on strategies used in games of strategy. The theory is conservative in that the tactics chosen will always be those guaranteeing minimal losses. It is based on the model of economic man.

Government (as an institution). The machinery that administers the state.

Grant-in-aid. Funds granted by one governmental unit to another. Stipulations are generally made on procedure to be followed in spending the funds. Some grants-in-aid require contributions by the recipient unit.

Gross national product. As calculated by the United States Department of Commerce, this is a figure equal to the total amount paid for the production of goods and services, plus indirect business taxes paid, plus allowances for depreciation of capital investments. (Samuelson.)

Habeas corpus. A writ or order directing a jailer to produce a prisoner in his custody in court so the judge may determine if the person is legally detained. The basic purpose of habeas corpus is to prevent arbitrary arrests and detention in secret.

Hypothesis. A tentative, unverified statement of the relationship of known facts; reasonable proposition worthy of scientific testing. (Horton and Hunt.)

Ideology. Ideology may be described as "folk philosophy" concerning the good life. It is not as systematic or as sophisticated as philosophy; it evolves gradually, not as the product of any single thinker. In this sense, it resembles folk songs more than works of serious composers. Ideology consists of a network of interrelated normative values that emerge from a particular life-style and environment. It serves a double role: it helps to direct action toward the satisfaction of existing wants and to establish new goals for an individual or group.

Image. The way in which an event, institution, group, or person is perceived. The image does not necessarily reflect reality and is not perceived in the same way by all persons.

Independent regulatory commission. An administrative agency regulating a specific segment of the society or economy, but independent in that the agency is not part of the President's administrative hierarchy. Its members normally cannot be removed summarily by the President or Congress. Such commissions normally use procedures that are similar to those of legislative or judicial bodies.

Industrial individualism. An American ideology dominant between the Civil War and the Great Depression. It was characterized by the belief that business was the most important component in the social system and that government should perform only traditional services—services that politically significant businessmen desired.

Influence. Control over the actions of others. An attribute of leadership. The control is usually imperfect.

Institution. A component part of a system. In politics, it is a part of the mechanism through which government carries out its tasks. It is established on a formal legal basis in most cases and is usually intended by its builders to be permanent, though not necessarily unchanging. Congress, the Presidency, and the Department of Health, Education, and Welfare are political institutions, for example.

Institutionalized power. A regularly established set of relationships among participants in the policy-making process that is consciously understood by the participants.

Interest group. A collection of individuals who, on the basis of one or more shared attitudes or common habits of response, make certain claims upon other groups in the society for the establishment, maintenance, or enhancement of forms of behavior that are implied in the shared attitudes. Groups become *political* interest groups by making their claims directly upon government or indirectly upon other groups through government. *Interests* exist independently of *interest groups*. Interest groups differ from political parties chiefly in that they do not seek to capture public offices for members, but rather attempt to influence public policy. (Pressure group has the same meaning.)

Keynesian economic theory. The economic theory of John Maynard Keynes, an Englishman who wrote in the 1920s and 1930s. Its most important implication for public policy is the idea that governments can partly level out the swings in business cycles by spending more than they receive in taxes during the downswing and less during the upswing. (Samuelson.)

Kitchen Cabinet. An informal group of advisers to the President. The members may hold positions on the White House staff, other positions in government, or no formal office at all. The term has been common since Andrew Jackson's time.

Law of diminishing marginal utility. As the amount of a good that is used increases, the marginal utility of the good—the additional usefulness or satisfaction added by its last unit—decreases.

Leadership. Uniting people in pursuit of a goal.

Left (political). The portion of the political continuum that includes liberal or radical positions. An individual's position on the continuum may differ by issue.

Legitimacy. A condition that exists when people believe in their government's (or ruler's) right to rule and in the rightness or propriety of the principal institutions, procedures, and policies of the political system of which they are a part.

Liberalism. Advocacy of gradual change toward policies that better provide the good life (as defined by the advocate) for the individual, with such change taking place within the legitimately established political system. Liberalism includes a dissatisfaction with the *status quo* and a belief in progress through change.

Life-style. A concept (with impressionistic connotations) that refers to the kind of life lived by people in different situations. It covers the ways of living that accompany life cycles, statuses, career stages, changes through time resulting from technological developments, and other stages of development of individuals or groups of individuals.

Lobbyist. The agent or representative of an interest group, who seeks to influence public policy. Lobbying consists of seeking to influence legislative and administrative officials in a variety of ways so that their actions will be favorable to the group doing the lobbying. Lobbyists may also be in charge of the dissemination of propaganda to the general public.

Logrolling. A basic strategy in legislative bodies in which support on one bill is traded for support on another.

Lynch. Killing—usually by a mob—in punishment for an alleged crime without due process of law.

Mores. Behavior patterns or acts of vital importance to the members of a society. Violation of mores is drastically punished, often through legal action.

Name candidate. Any candidate who gains or hopes to gain political support because his name is similar to or identical with that of a well-known, popular person.

Nazism. A form of fascism practiced by Adolf Hitler and his followers. The legitimacy of power was based on a doctrine of "Aryan" racial superiority.

Norms. Standards of behavior or shared common understandings that define common expectations in a culture or society.

Oligarchy. Government by the few, as distinguished from government by one or by the many.

One Great Cause theory. It holds that all important social events can be traced to a single event or phenomenon that is the exclusive or overwhelmingly dominant cause of other events or phenomena. Most social scientists are now convinced that there are usually many causal factors in social events, no one of which is ordinarily predominant.

Opinion leaders. Individuals who act as agents for conveying political information and sentiments to less informed or passive audiences.

Paranoia. Systematic delusions that involve feelings of persecution. The individual often suffers great mental anguish because of his belief that "everyone's against me."

Parliamentary system. A system of government in which power is concentrated in the leadership group of the main legislative body. Instead of a separation of powers, there is a fusion of powers among the branches of government. Under this system, the Prime Minister is leader of the majority party or dominant faction in the parliament.

Personalism. A form of politics in which support or opposition is directed toward a specific individual rather than toward policies, ideologies, or parties.

Pluralistic society. A community composed of groups holding a variety of ideological positions, each possessing political power through being able to share in decisions regarding public policy.

Pocket veto. Disapproval of a bill passed in the last ten days of a session. No veto message is required. The President simply does not sign it.

Political party. A group of people banded together for the purpose of seeking to win elective public offices. As such, a political party differs from an interest group, which is a collection of people banded together for the purpose of promoting or protecting social, economic, or ideological interests. American parties are loose confederations of persons who may hold conflicting ideologies.

Political science. The study of the allocation through government of benefits, rewards, deprivations, and punishments for members of a society.

Political system. The interrelated institutions and processes by which the decisions of government are made. More specifically, it involves the *actions* of persons in many patterned, interrelated *roles.* Thus the study of politics involves the analysis of what, why, and how persons do things in carrying out their political activities and how their actions affect other persons. By *patterned roles,* we mean that actions can, to a considerable extent, be anticipated in advance, and that both the political actor and his observers share to a considerable degree an understanding of what the particular role should be.

Poll tax. A tax used for political purposes around the beginning of this century as one of a number of disfranchising devices aimed mainly at the Negro in the South. The poll tax must be paid in order for one to vote in elections. A poll or head tax had earlier been common as a means of revenue and was not associated with voter eligibility. The Twenty-fourth Amendment prohibits the use of the poll tax in connection with elections to Federal offices.

Pork barrel. Public works projects undertaken by the government mainly because of their political value to local congressmen and not primarily for engineering or economic reasons. Each year Congress passes a bill containing a long list of such projects—often they are to deepen river channels or harbors. The source of the term is uncertain.

Power. Ability to share in decision making, that is, in the determination of the allocation of benefits, rewards, deprivations, and punishments.

Presidential system. A system of government that is characterized by a separation of powers among the legislative, executive, and judicial branches and a chief executive who is independently elected.

Pressure group. See definition for an interest group.

Propaganda. A technique of social control. "As a technique, it is the manipulation of collective attitudes by the use of significant symbols (words, pictures and tunes), rather than violence, bribery, or boycott." (Harold Lasswell, *Propaganda and Promotional Activities: An Annotated Bibliography,* The University of Minnesota Press, Minneapolis, 1935, p. 3.)

Prestigeful. Possessing high status, or being highly regarded. The term is not standard English, but is in common use in the social sciences.

Projection. The process of ascribing to other persons one's own values and beliefs. Thus, by projection, the voter may assume that a politician whom he admires shares his views on public policy.

Proportional representation. A device for electing the members of a legislative body in such a way as to reflect all groups or factions in proportion to their strength. It is used in multimember districts rather than single-member districts and is an alternative to geographic representation. Proportional representation is less common in America than in Europe.

Public interest. A working hypothesis, not an analytical concept, that is used by elected officials and public administrators in their decision making, and that operates to remind them that the survival of the groups they represent hinges on their consideration of the legitimate interests of others. To politicians, editors, and many lay persons, the "public interest" is often to be found in policies they personally prefer; it is a propaganda term. Its great value to a political system lies in its mystical importance: it is a goal that every citizen and official of good will should strive for.

Radical. An advocate of rapid and extensive change toward new social and economic policies, even if such change would destroy or greatly alter existing legitimatized institutions.

Radical right. A popular term for the extreme right portion of the political continuum. Technically, a person who fits in this portion of the continuum is a *reactionary.* As terms are used in this book, this one is self-contradictory.

Rationality. Quality of being consistent with reason, that is, having deductions logically inferred from known data.

Rationalization. The process of justifying one's wants, beliefs, and behavior when they are challenged by oneself or others. The justification takes the form of inventing reasons which the individual believes are the real reasons. (Krech.)

Reactionary. An advocate of return to a real, romanticized, or imaginary earlier ideology, political process, or set of social, economic, or political institutions.

Red tape. Strict adherence to the rules and routine of office and to the resulting forms, procedures, and delays.

Reference group. Individuals or groups (real or imagined) whose values or standards an individual takes into consideration in making his self-evaluation and in forming his attitudes.

Restrictive covenant. An agreement among property owners not to sell to members of specified racial, ethnic, or religious minority groups; generally Negroes, Mexicans, or Orientals.

Right (political). The portion of the political continuum that includes conservative or reactionary attitudes. An individual's position on the continuum may differ by issue.

Role. The manner in which a status position is supposed to be filled; it is the group's expectation of conduct in a status. (Green.)

Rules Committee. One of the most powerful committees of the House of Representatives. Its stated purpose is to prepare the agenda for House action. But it may delay or even block consideration of bills that are reported out of subject-matter committees.

Sanction. That which induces compliance, including rewards and punishments.

Senatorial courtesy. A practice in which the senators of the majority party automatically reject any presidential nomination if it is opposed by the senior majority-party senator from the state in which the Federal office concerned is located. This tradition does not apply to offices that have jurisdiction in more than one state (e.g., Cabinet officers, Supreme Court justices).

Seniority rule. A practice in which posts are awarded on the basis of length of time served. It is used in Congress for selecting committee chairmen from among the majority-party members.

Sentiment. A disposition to act in a particular way that results from an individual attitude.

Single-member district. A single representative from a geographic area. For other methods see *proportional representation.*

Social capital. Good-will credits earned by one individual in relation to another. A President, for example, who has given patronage to a state politician has earned social capital. He may hesitate to expend it for a trivial purpose because he may later need the politician's support on an important matter. The folkways of politicians demand that claims against accumulated social capital be honored.

Social distance. The degree of intimacy acceptable to an individual between himself and a typical member of a social group.

Socialism. A type of economic system. The term is variously used to describe an economic system in which the principal means of production and distribution are owned and controlled by the government; in Marxist-Leninist theory, the transitional stage between capitalism and communism; or the program of any Social Democratic or other party that seeks a greater sharing of wealth and security through the activities of democratic government. In the last case, the term refers to both an economic and a political system.

Social science. The systematic study of human beings and human behavior as people interact with one another. Social science includes social anthropology, economics, political science, social psychology, sociology, and some fields of geography.

Social service state. An elaborate set of Federal-state-local relationships that have developed to meet heavy demands for governmental service. In the social service state, government is one of the first, rather than one of the last, social institutions people turn to for help with personal and social problems (as they define them individually).

Society. A group of people who share a common culture.

Sovereignty. The supreme power of the state; the locus of ultimate decision making, from which there is no appeal. It is a legal concept introduced by Jean Bodin, a Frenchman, in 1576. In modern political science, the term is generally not used except in international relations theory. When used in connection with political relationships within a nation, the concept is often vague and ambiguous.

Stare decisis ("Let the decision stand."). The principle on which the common law, or judge-made law of the Anglo-American nations, is based. The decision in each case is based upon the rule established in an earlier case that involved essentially the same question.

State. An organized political community possessing sovereignty, independence, and territory. The term "state" does not have the same meaning as the term "government." The latter is the machinery that manipulates the power of the state.

Status. An individual's position in relation to other positions held by other individuals in a social group or grouping. The essence of status is a defined superior-inferior relationship, that is, dominance and subordination—always within a set of rules. (Green.)

Stereotype. A simple, generalized concept or image, especially of a social group. Stereotypes tend to be widely shared by members of a given society. The term comes from a mold used in newspaper production.

Stewardship theory. This theory holds that the President has something akin to inherent powers of office, which permits or even requires him to do anything necessary to protect the nation—so long as his acts are not unconstitutional. The theory is also closely associated with the idea that the President has an obligation to provide leadership in policy development. The Whig theory, in contrast, holds that the President can do only those things clearly authorized by the Constitution or Congress and should leave policy development to Congress.

Subculture. A part of the total culture that is a distinctive segment of society (e.g., an ethnic, racial, or regional group).

Substantive rights. Provision for personal liberty; these rights include freedom of expression, religion, and assembly. *Procedural rights* guarantee the elements of a fair trial in terms of contemporary interpretations of Anglo-American legal and cultural traditions.

Symbol. Any term or concept that is intentionally used to stand for or represent something else. (Krech.)

Theory. Throughout this book, the term refers not to models of an ideal as seen by some individual, but to an explanation for the functions performed by the various parts of an interrelated system and to the way in which these parts relate to one another. In this sense, "theory" does not differ from "practice"; rather, the former explains the latter.

Treason. Giving aid and comfort to an enemy state.

Unitary system. A system in which all power, formally, rests with the central government; other governments possess only delegated powers, and the system of power relationships is determined by the central government alone.

Values. Beliefs about what is desirable, or a "good," and what is undesirable, or a "bad." Values reflect the culture of a society and are widely shared by the members of the culture. If the individual accepts a value for himself, it may become a goal for him. (Krech.) A group of loosely clustered values and beliefs constitute an *ideology*.

Voluntary group. An association of people organized to pursue a particular activity or objective. The purpose of the voluntary group is often limited to a particular interest that is not necessarily valued by society as a whole. Voluntary groups are formed without government coercion and gain their membership from persons who join of their own volition.

NAME INDEX

SUBJECT INDEX

Subject Index